THE LIVES OF THE POPES

VOL. XV.

THE
LIVES OF THE POPES
IN THE MIDDLE AGES

BY THE

RT. REV. MONSIGNOR HORACE K. MANN, D.D.

"De gente Anglorum, qui maxime familiares Apostolicæ Sedis semper
existunt" (*Gesta Abb. Fontanel.*, A.D. 747–752, ap. M.G. SS. II. 289).

RECTOR OF THE COLLEGIO BEDA, ROME ; CORRESPONDING MEMBER OF THE ROYAL ACADEMY OF
HISTORY OF SPAIN ; MEMBER OF THE ACCADEMIA D'ARCADIA AND OF THE R. SOCIETÀ ROMANA
DI STORIA PATRIA.

THE POPES AT THE HEIGHT OF THEIR
TEMPORAL INFLUENCE

INNOCENT II. TO BLESSED BENEDICT XI.
1130–1305

(A) THE POPES AND THE HOHENSTAUFEN, 1130–1271

VOL. XV
ALEXANDER IV. TO GREGORY X., 1254–1276

LONDON :
KEGAN PAUL, TRENCH, TRUBNER & CO., LTD.
ST. LOUIS, MO.: B. HERDER BOOK CO.
1929

1888

PRINTED IN GREAT BRITAIN BY
STEPHEN AUSTIN AND SONS LTD., HERTFORD

A LIST OF THE PRINCIPAL ABBREVIATIONS
USED IN THIS VOLUME.

Potthast . . . = *Regesta Pontificum Romanorum*, ed.
A. Potthast, 2 vols., Berlin, 1874.

Reg. . . . . = One of the volumes of the *Registres des Papes* in course of publication by the French Schools of Athens and of Rome, ed. Fontemoing, Paris.

L. P. . . . . = *Liber Pontificalis*, 2 vols., ed. L. Duchesne, Paris, 1886.

M. G. H. or Pertz . . = *Monumenta Germaniæ Historica*, either *Scriptores* (M. G. SS.), *or Epistolæ* (M. G. Epp.) or *Poetæ* (M. G. PP.).

P. G. . . . . = *Patrologia Græca*, ed. Migne, Paris.

P. L. . . . . = *Patrologia Latina*, ed. Migne, Paris.

R. I. SS. . . . = *Rerum Italicarum Scriptores*, ed. Muratori, Milan, 1723 ff., or the new ed. in course of publication.

R. F. SS. . . . = *Recueil des Historiens des Gaules*, ed. Bouquet and others, Paris, 1738 ff.

R. S., following an edition of a book. = The edition of the Chronicles, etc., of Great Britain and Ireland, published under the direction of the Master of the Rolls.

Rymer or Foedera . . = *Foedera, Literæ, etc., ab anno* 1101 *ad nostra usque tempora*, accurante T. Rymer. Unless the contrary is stated, we quote from the original ed., London, 1704 ff.

v

Other abbreviations will be readily understood by reference to the *Sources* prefixed to each biography.

The sign † placed before a date indicates that the date in question is the year of the death of the person after whose name the sign and date are placed. The sign * placed before the title of a book indicates that the author of these volumes has seen the book in question favourably mentioned, but has not examined it himself.

TABLE OF CONTENTS

ALEXANDER IV.

A.D. 1254–1261.

Sources.—Unfortunately no contemporary biography of Alexander IV. has come down to us, and equally unfortunately the greater part of his Register is not yet in print, though C. Bourel de la Roncière published the letters of the first two years (1254–6) as far back as 1902 (Paris).[1] This latter misfortune is, however, to a considerable extent minimized by the publications of Rodenberg (*Epp. e regestis Rom. Pont.*, vol. iii), Bliss (*Calendar of Papal Registers*), Theiner, etc.—publications which have been noticed in previous volumes.

L. Delisle, moreover, found in the *Bibliothèque nationale* at Paris, a fragment of the Register of the last year of Alexander's pontificate, Dec. 12, 1260–May 25, 1261, the day of his death. It is a fragment of the seventh book of his Register, which corresponded with the seventh year of his reign, and is an original copy of the beginning of that book. It contains some forty-six bulls or letters of which Delisle printed a brief analysis. Till this was published, most of them were inedited, only five of them having been analysed by Potthast.[2]

In connexion with the documents issued by the papal chancellary in the days of Alexander, we may note that a very large proportion of them is concerned with privileges of every kind for different religious Orders, with the Teutonic Knights and crusades against the pagan Prussians and Livonians, with the Inquisition and the treatment of heretics, and with the granting of indulgences. The indulgences granted are generally for forty or a hundred days. Once at least an indulgence of a year was granted, and this was in connexion with a home for the blind (Potthast, 17934).

[1] J. de Loye and P. de Cenival published in one volume (vol. ii) the letters of the third year of Alexander's reign in 1917. As in the first volume, most of the letters are of no general historical importance.

[2] L. Delisle, " Fragment du dernier registre d'Alexandre IV.," ap. *Biblio. de l'école des Chartes*, vol. xxxviii (1877), p. 103 ff.

In the review known as *Bibliothèque de l'école des Chartes,*[1] Mons. H. F. Delaborde has published a brief set of instructions given by St. Louis IX. to his envoy at the court of Alexander IV. in connexion with the treaty of Paris (1258) between France and England.

Some account of the principal chroniclers who will be quoted in this biography has already been given ; but a word or two may be added about the continuations of Matthew Paris.   The year 1259 saw the finish of the *Chronica Majora* of that lively historian.   With all his faults Paris was intelligent, keenly interested in the great events which were taking place around him, and industrious.   These qualities helped him to collect a large mass of most useful material, and the close of his chronicle meant a distinct loss to future ages.   His work was continued by men who were in nearly every way his inferiors.   One of them is often described as *Matthew of Westminster*.   There was in reality no such person ; but a chronicle was drawn up at Westminster which was founded on the *Great Chronicle* of Matthew Paris, and was continued by an anonymous monk down to the year 1307.   This Westminster Chronicle, along with some other continuations of Paris,[2] has been published by H. R. Luard in his *Flores Historiarum*, 3 vols., London, 1890, *R. S.*   The official continuator, as it were, of Paris at St. Albans was William Rishanger, who, we know, was 62 years of age in 1312, and became a monk of that monastery in 1271.   His chronicle from 1259–1306, ed. H. T. Riley, London, 1865, *R. S.*, is sparse and dry.   Liébermann (ap. *M. G. SS.*, xxviii, p. 512 f.) and others have called in question Rishanger's authorship of this chronicle.   They would set it down as one of the anonymous continuations of Matthew Paris, and would assign its composition to a period later than 1323.

Modern Works.—The latest and fullest biography of Alexander IV. is the reliable German work (*Papst Alexander IV.*) of Dr. F. Tenckhoff, Paderborn, 1907.   Another German writer, Dr. F. Schillmann, has published a brief notice, with a number of the original documents, concerning Alexander's relations with the

[1] Vol. xlix (1888), p. 630 ff.   "Instructions d'un ambassadeur envoyé . . . à Alex. IV."

[2] E.g., " Passages from the Eton and other MSS. (from 1245–1323) not contained in the text of the *Flores Historiarum*," ap. vol. iii. *Flor. H.*, pp. 239–349.   C. D. Yonge published a translation of the *Flowers of History*, London, 1853, for Bohn's series.

Greeks :   " Zur byzantinischen Politik Alexanders IV.", ap.
Römische Quartalscrift, vol. xxii (1908), nos. 2, 3, and 4, p. 108 ff.

CONTEMPORARY SOVEREIGNS.

WESTERN EMPERORS.

The great Interregnum,1254–73.

Rivals :

Richard,   earl of Cornwall,
  Alfonso X., King of Castile,
  1257–72.

LATIN EMPERORS OF THE EAST.

Baldwin II., 1228–61.

EMPERORS OF NICÆA.

John III., Vatatzes, 1222–55.

Theodore II., Lascaris, 1255–8.

Michael   VIII.,   Palaologus,
  1259–82. He recovered Constantinople in 1261.

ENGLAND.

Henry III., 1916–72.

FRANCE.

St. Louis IX., 1226–70.

CHAPTER I.

THE EARLY LIFE OF RINALDO CONTI. HE IS ELECTED
POPE, AND ANNOUNCES HIS ELECTION TO THE
WORLD.

The birth-
place of
Alexander.

THERE can be seen from the Sacro Speco at Subiaco,
in a wild gorge near the source of the rushing Anio,
the village of Genna or Jenne. Here lived that branch
of the family of the Conti of Segni from which
Alexander IV. was descended. The castle of Genna
belonged to the great abbey of Subiaco, and had been
given as a fief by abbot Simon to Philip de Marano,
the great grandfather (proavus) of the Pope, and to his
sons in 1176. This is known to us by a bull of Alexander
himself in which he decided that the said castle belonged
to his nephews John and Rainaldus.[1] And a document
preserved by Muratori shows that the latter was still
holding it in 1291 ; for it sets forth that " Dominus
Raynaldus Masimi de Genna paid a golden obol on the
feast of All Saints to the Church of Rome for lands and
property held " in Castro de Trebis ", the castle of
Trevi, the next village to Genna at the head of the
Anio.[2] At Genna there was born Rinaldo (Raynaldus,

---

[1] Delisle, n. 28, p. 110, September 9, 1260. Concerning Rainaldus
and other relations of Alexander, see his *Reg.*, vol. ii, nn. 2351-2,
2398, and 2411. On account of various acts of violence perpetrated
by Rainaldus (per nobilem virum Raynaldum Rubeum, nepotem . . .
Alexandri P. predecessoris nostri), Urban IV. had to threaten to deprive
him of all rights over Genna—" ipsum omni jure quod in . . . Vallis-
prete nec non Genne castris . . . perpetuo studeat auctoritate nostra
privare." Ep. May 11, 1262 ap., *Reg.*, vol. iv, n. 2904, p. 42.

[2] Ap. Gell, *The Topography of Rome*, pp. 278-9. *Cf.* Theiner,
Cod. Dip., i, n. 258, p. 136, for Raynald's investiture with this fief by a
silver cup ; November 21, 1257.

4

or Reginald) Conti, afterwards Alexander IV., and if he is sometimes called " of Anagni " it is because Genna is in that diocese.[1] Once when he was Pope, Alexander paid a visit to his birthplace after a stay at Subiaco ; and the little hamlet can now boast that at least one papal bull bears its name.[2]

Rinaldo was the son of Count Philip of Segni, one of the brothers of Gregory IX. He was educated at Anagni, and was for " many years " a canon of its cathedral.[3] At some period before the year 1227, he became *camerarius* or treasurer of the Roman Church, and in the year named was one of the " six honourable men " whom Gregory made cardinals.[4] From 1227 then till 1234 or 1235, he was cardinal deacon of St. Eustachio [5] ; but in the year 1231 he was nominated to the see of Ostia and Velletri.[6] At length, perhaps in August, 1234, and certainly in March, 1235, he succeeded to the diocese of Ostia, and in the May of that year we have documents signed by him as bishop.[7] According to Ptolemy of Lucca,[8] he was an exemplary bishop, and ruled his diocese well, both spiritually and temporally.

Rinaldo becomes a cardinal.

The fact that Rinaldo Conti was Gregory's nephew did not, doubtless, stand in the way of his promotion ;

His learning and piety, and his attachment to the Franciscans.

[1] Saba Malaspina describes him (L. i, c. 5) as " natione Campanum, oriundum de quodam castro quod Genna dicitur ".

[2] Potthast, 17944.

[3] *Cf.* Mat. Par., *Abbrev. Chron.*, ed. Madden, iii, 341 *R. S.*, and Tenckhoff, quoting vol. xxv of the *Vatican Registers*, f. 108, c. 779, and f. 155, c. 234.

[4] Alberic Trium Font., *Chron.*, ap. *M. G. SS.*, xxiii, p. 920 f.

[5] *Cf.* Potthast, vol. i, p. 939.

[6] Alberic, *l.c.*, p. 929 " Rome tres episcopi cardinales a papa electi sunt, videlicet d. Renaldus camerarius in Hostiensem, etc." Hence in 1232, Oct. 21, Gregory IX. spoke of him as " the elect of Ostia ". Potthast, n. 9022.

[7] Potthast, n. 9919. *Cf. ib.*, ii, p. 1286, and Eubel, *Hierarchia Cathol.*, p. 6.

[8] *Hist. Eccles.*, lib. xxii, c. 17, ap. *R. I. SS.*, xi.

but we have reason to believe that his learning and piety had the greatest share in his advancement. For we have it on the authority of Salimbene that " he was a literary man much given to the study of theology, and that he took pleasure in performing the duties of his state, in preaching, saying Mass, and consecrating Churches ".[1] Hence when he was Pope we find him sending for certain books which had been left by his predecessor in the sacristy of the Church of St. Francis at Assisi.[2] He gave one proof of his literary tendencies when he wrote collects and hymns[3] in honour of St. Clare whom he himself canonized.[4] Like Grosseteste and many of the greatest men of his age, he was devoted to the new Orders, and especially to the Franciscans and Poor Clares. He followed cardinal Ugolino (Gregory IX.) as " the governor, protector and corrector " of the Franciscan Order (1227–61), and insisted on remaining its " cardinal protector " till his death.[5] As, in addition to all this, he loved to have Franciscans about him,[6] it came to be said that he had been a Franciscan himself. That, however, is a mistake ; for, as the Franciscan Salimbene himself noted, he was only " a cardinal of the Order of Friars Minor " inasmuch as he was its protector.[7]

His devotion to St. Clare. He was particularly attached to St. Clare ; and Thomas of Celano,[8] or whoever was her first biographer, says

[1] *Chron.*, p. 453. *Cf.* Ptolemy of Lucca, *Hist. Eccles.*, lib. xxii, c. 17, ap. *R. I. SS.*, xi.

[2] Potthast, n. 16021.   [3] Salimbene, pp. 383 and 453.

[4] Sept. 26, 1255. Potthast, n. 16025.

[5] Pp. 162, 302, and the ep. of Philip of Perugia " de cardinalibus protectoribus ", ap. *M. G. SS.*, xxxii, p. 681.

[6] *Cronica minor Erphesfurt.*, an. 1255, ed. Holder-Egger, p. 663.

[7] *L.c.*, p. 383.

[8] Robinson, in his Introduction to *The Life of St. Clare*, p. xxv ff., shows that he was almost certainly the author of the contemporary *Life* of the Saint, and that he was probably commissioned by Alexander IV. to write it.

that "having heard that Clare was becoming worse in health, the lord of Ostia (Rinaldo) hastened from Perugia to visit the spouse of Christ to whom he had been a father by reason of his office, a protector by reason of his solicitude, and ever a devoted friend by reason of his most pure affection (September, 1252). He nourished the invalid with the Sacrament of the Lord's Body, and fed the other Sisters with words of salutary exhortation. Clare with tears besought so great a father that, for the name of Christ, he would ever be mindful of her soul, and the souls of the other Ladies. But, above all else, she begged that he would ask the lord Pope (Innocent IV.) and the Cardinals to confirm the privilege of Poverty.[1] This the faithful supporter of religion not only promised in word, but fulfilled in deed ".[2]

After the death of the Saint (August 11, 1253), the same contemporary biographer tells us that " the Vicar of Christ with the cardinals " went to St, Damiano where she had breathed her last. " When the time came to commence the divine service, and the Friars were beginning the Office of the Dead, the Lord Pope (Innocent IV.) interrupting said that the Office of Virgins and not the Office of the Dead ought to be recited, so that it seemed as if he would fain canonize Clare before her body had been given burial. But that most eminent man the lord of Ostia replying that they ought to do what was more customary in such cases, Mass for the dead was celebrated. Then, at the instance of the Sovereign Pontiff, in the presence of the cardinals and of the prelates, the bishop of Ostia, taking the subject

---

[1] *Cf. supra*, vol. xiv, 189 f.

[2] *Vita Claræ*, Robinson's Eng. trans., p. 63 f. Cardinal Rinaldo drew up on Sept. 16, 1252, for the " Poor Ladies " a new and truly Franciscan rule which Innocent IV. solemnly approved on Aug. 9, 1253. *Cf.* Robinson, *ib.*, p. 96.

matter of his discourse from the Vanity of Vanities
(*Eccles*, i, 2), eulogized in a splendid sermon her who
had despised vanity so nobly ".[1] Though the process
of Clare's canonization was begun immediately, it was
reserved, as we have said, for that " most clement
Prince, the lord Alexander IV., a man who was the
friend of everything holy, the protector of Religious,
and the firm support of Religious Orders " [2] to complete
the work. " Two years having elapsed since her death,
and the day of her passing to the Lord being at hand,
the happy Alexander, to whom this grace had been
reserved by the Lord, having convoked a multitude of
prelates and clergy, reverently and with the utmost
pomp inscribed Clare in the catalogue of the Saints,
and ordained that her feast be solemnly kept throughout
the Church, he himself, with his whole court, having
first celebrated it with the greatest solemnity. These
things took place in the principal church at Anagni
in the year of our Lord's Incarnation, 1255." [3]

Further close connexions with the Franciscans. Rinaldo's love for the Franciscans stood out also
very clearly in his affection for the Minorite Rainaldo
da Tocca. Salimbene avers that his friendship for
him exceeded that of Jonathan for David, and that,
if the whole world had spoken ill of the friar, the Pope
would not have hearkened to it. He would even open
the door of his room for him barefooted. " This,"
continues the gossiping brother, " was seen by another
Friar Minor, to wit, Brother Mansuetus de Castellione
Aretino, who was alone with the Pope at the time.
Mansuetus was a friend of mine, and told me what
I am now relating." [4] Rinaldo's partiality for the
Franciscans was shared by his family. He had a sister
who was a Poor Clare, and a nephew who was a Friar
Minor. And yet, points out Salimbene, he did not make

---

[1] *Ib.*, pp. 72–3.　　　　[2] *Ib.*, p. 90.
[3] *Ib.*, p. 91.　　　　[4] *Chron.*, p. 453 f.

the one an abbess, nor the other a cardinal. In fact, he did not, continues the brother, make a single cardinal, though there were only eight in his time.[1] The friendship of Rinaldo for the Franciscans was reciprocated by them, and, if we can believe Salimbene always eager to enhance the importance of his Order, it was they who induced Gregory IX. to make him a cardinal.[2]

With this close friendship between cardinal Rinaldo and the Franciscans before our eyes, we are prepared to see Pope Alexander legislating in their favour. The striking virtues of the early Franciscans and Dominicans and the good which they everywhere accomplished caused the people to flock to their churches, and in many instances, no doubt, to the real detriment of ecclesiastical law and order. But the opposition which they aroused had its origin in too many instances, not in a well-regulated wish to preserve order, and to prevent injustice, but in sheer jealousy. By unduly dwelling on difficulties and occasional abuses [3] certain of the secular clergy induced Innocent IV. not long before he died to rescind certain privileges which had been granted to the various Orders, especially the Franciscans and Dominicans. On November 21, 1254, he issued a bull in which he forbade religious to receive people from other parishes into their churches on Sundays and Holidays, to hear their confessions without the permission of their own parish priest, to preach at certain times, to admit unreservedly the dead from other parishes to be buried in their grounds, etc.[4]

Rinaldo annuls legislation against the Friars.

---

[1] *Ib.*   [2] *Ib.*, p. 383.

[3] " Sane gravis et clamosa querela nostris assidue auribus inculcatur, quod nonnulli vestrum suis juribus et finibus non contenti parrochianos alienos præsumant temere ad divina recipere contra canonicas sanctiones, etc., etc." Bull of Innocent, Nov. 21, 1254, printed in full ap. Eubel, *Bullar. Francisc.*, p. 259 f.

[4] *Ib.*

Though there was no doubt need of legislation to regulate the relations between the newly arisen popular Orders and the old established parochial clergy, the bull of Innocent was too uncompromising. Accordingly one of the first acts of Alexander IV. was to annul the decree of his predecessor on the ground that what is done in haste or in the midst of pre-occupations must be reconsidered at leisure ; and it was his intention, he declared, to submit the questions which had been hurriedly decided upon by Innocent to mature reflection.[1] As we have already remarked, the prolonged considerations of Alexander on the subject of the religious Orders led him rather to extend than to curtail their privileges. Especially was he friendly to St. Bonaventure and the Franciscans.[2]

Character of Alexander.

Religious historians, therefore, like Matthew Paris and Salimbene, show themselves very ready at seeing faults in Innocent IV. and virtues in Alexander IV.

We need not here recall the unfounded stories circulated by Paris and other religious in connexion with the death of Innocent IV.,[3] but we may state here what Salimbene says of Alexander IV. Like Eglon, he tells us, he " was exceeding fat " (Judges, iii, 17), and was, moreover, kind, merciful, pious, just, and God-fearing.[4] This description of him is no doubt just, inasmuch as it squares

---

[1] Ep. to all the clergy, Dec. 22, 1254, ap. *ib.*, p. 261 f. *Cf.* Salimbene, pp. 418–20, 453.

[2] Writing to " Bro. Bonaventure, minister-general of the Order of Friars Minor, he said (*Reg.*, ii, n. 2263, Oct. 21, 1257) : " Nos enim, qui ejusdem profectum et augmentum ordinis toto cordis zelamur affectu, tibi in omnibus que tuum contingunt officium, firmiter apostolico favore adesse proponimus, ac, ut idem, ordo sub tuo regimine titulis refulgescat insignibus, omnen quam poterimus, intendimus opem et operam adhibere."

[3] *Cf. supra*, vol. xiv, p. 147 n.

[4] *L.c.*, p. 454.

with what other sources tell us regarding his personality.[1]
When, however, the friar goes on to state that he did
not engage in wars, but lived peaceably like Honorius III.
before him, and Clement IV. after him,[2] the talkative
friar must be understood to speak relatively to such
a Pope as Innocent IV. He had, indeed, " no interest
in the affairs of Princes and Kingdoms," [3] but he had
no Frederick II. to struggle against. If he was peaceful,
avoided war, and as far as possible followed the line of
least resistance, it was because he was naturally of a
rather weak character.

Whilst he was a cardinal, Rinaldo was often employed Legations.
on important legations. With Thomas, cardinal-priest
of S. Sabina, he had to deal with the struggle between
the Romans and Viterbese (1231–3), and helped in its
settlement.[4] We next find him working for peace in
Lombardy along with the same cardinal,[5] striving to
reconcile the Lombards with Frederick II., 1236–7.
Much has been stated by modern writers as to the personal
relations between Innocent IV. and Cardinal Rinaldo.
But as these statements rest more on the point of view
of their authors than on actual historical evidence,

[1] *Cf.* Herman of Altaich, *Ann.*, 1253, ap. Böhmer, *Fontes*, ii, p. 510 ;
and Mat. Par., v, 472, who, however, adds that he was disposed to be
led astray by flatterers, and by the suggestions of the avaricious. See
also the later authority of abbot John Long de Ypra (Johannes
Iperius) † 1383, *Chron. S. Bertini*, ap. *M. G. SS.*, xxv, p. 848. The
Chronicler adds that he was fond of a joke (jocundus, risibilis), and
that their Abbot Gilbert, known from his munificence as the " golden
abbot ", was one of the Pope's special friends.

[2] *L.c.*, pp. 454, 36.

[3] Herman, *l.c.* " Non tantum curans de negociis principum et
regnorum."

[4] *Cf. supra*, vol. xiii, pp. 282–3, and Tenckhoff, p. 6. We are assured
that documents in the public archives of Viterbo prove the many
benefits conferred by Cardinal Rinaldo " upon this our province ".
Cristofori, *Le tombe dei Papi in Viterbo*, pp. 287. *Cf.* pp. 288–9.

[5] *Cf. supra*, vol. xiii, p. 233 ff., and Salimbene, *Chron.*, p. 383.

they may here be passed over, and we may just note
the fact that he was frequently employed by Innocent
as he had been by Gregory. When Innocent fled to
Lyons, the cardinal of Ostia, was one of the four cardinals,
who, in accordance with the will of the Pope, remained
for a time in Italy (1244).[1] Then, with his three companions, he was duly summoned to the council of Lyons
(1245) [2] ; and, after its celebration, he returned with them
to Italy to carry out the duties assigned to him.
Accordingly, in obedience to the Pope's injunctions,
Rinaldo had to punish the people of Alatri for their
barbarous treatment of the citizens of Ferentino.[3] About
a year later, he was commissioned to restore " to the
consuls and commune of Ferentino " a pledge of 300
pounds of the denarii of the Senate for having, according
to promise, destroyed the walls of the castle of Teclene.[4]

The Pope was in regular communication with these
four officials, now informing them of the progress of
his negotiations with Frederick,[5] and now giving them
various instructions as to their relations with different
communes,[6] or bidding them grant some favours to
certain Friars Minor.[7] Some of Innocent's letters were
directed to Rinaldo alone,[8] and in some of Rinaldo's
own letters after he had become Alexander IV., we
find him referring to what he did as vicar in Campania
and the Maritima in conjunction with cardinals Stephen

---

[1] Carbio, *vita Inn.*, c. 13. The other three were Stephen, card.-p.
of Sta. Maria in Trastevere, vicar of the city ; Rainer, card.-d. of Sta.
Maria in Cosmedin, legate in Tuscany, the Duchy of Spoleto, the March
of Ancona, and the Patrimony of Blessed Peter ; and Richard (Riccardo
Annibaldi), card.-d. of S. Angelo, count of the Campania and the
Maritima.

[2] Potthast, 11523.   [3] *Ib.*, 11765, July 31, 1245.
[4] *Ib.*, 1/2231, July 18, 1246.   [5] *Ib.*, July 1247, n. 12592.
[6] *Ib.*, Oct. 22, 1248, n. 13060.
[7] *Ib.*, 13747, July 12, 1249 ; 14002, June 26, 1250.
[8] *Ib.*, 14467, Jan. 7, 1252, in connexion with the protection of
certain nuns ; 14483, 14725, 14873.

and Richard, who were also vicars in those parts (1245).[1]
It may then safely be concluded that whether Innocent's
intercourse with Rinaldo was cordial or not, it was
not strained.[2]

Immediately after the death of Innocent (December 7, Election of Rinaldo as Pope, 1254.
1254), to whom Rinaldo had administered the last
sacraments, word of the event was sent to cardinal
William Fieschi, the late Pope's nephew, who was in
command of his army, and he was urged to hasten to
Naples for the election of a successor to his uncle.[3]
Meanwhile, terrified at the defeat of the papal forces by
Manfred, the cardinals were contemplating flying from
Naples. Fortunately, however, there was a strong man
in the city who prevented their dispersion and consequent
delay in the election of a Pope. This man was Bertholinus
Tavernerius of Parma, who had married Innocent's
niece Helen. He had been made Podestà of Naples
by his uncle,[4] and as soon as he discovered the fear of
the cardinals, he promptly enclosed them in the house
in which Innocent had died, and gave them to understand that there they would remain until they had elected
a Pope.[5]

Whilst awaiting the arrival of cardinal William,
the other cardinals of course, discussed the likely
candidates, and from the words of the author of the
Golden Legend, we may conclude that one of these was
a great friend of the late Pope, Walter of Vezano, archbishop of Genoa.[6] At length cardinal William arrived

[1] Ep. Jan. 28, 1255, ap. Rod. iii, p. 331.
[2] Tenckhoff, p. 23. Cf. his chap. i, where more details of Rinaldo's
early career are given.
[3] Carbio, c. 42. Cf. supra, vol. xiv, p. 147.
[4] Saba M., Hist., i, c. 5 ; Salimbene, pp. 453 and 603-4.
[5] Salimbene, p. 604, says of Bertholinus : " Curialis homo fuit et
valens et potens et intimus meus amicus." Cf. Carbio, l.c., and
Jamsilla, ap. R. I. SS., viii, p. 541.
[6] Jac. de Voragine, Chron. Jan., Pars. xii, c. 6, ap. R. I. SS., ix,
p. 48-9.

in Naples, and after he had prayed for a time by the grave
of his uncle, he was escorted " with sorrow and tears ",
to the house where the other cardinals, twelve in number,
were enclosed.[1] The work of election began on Friday,
December 11, after the Mass of the Holy Ghost had been
sung ; but no conclusion was reached on that day.
Early on the following day, the cardinals resumed their
labours, and about nine o'clock in the morning, the cardinal
of Ostia was elected *by compromise*. Thereupon the
cardinal-deacon Octavian placed the papal mantle on
the best man amongst them as he said, and Rinaldo
Conti was acclaimed Alexander IV.[2] This was on
December 12, and Salimbene says that he heard about
it at Ferrara on the feast of St. Thomas of Canterbury
(December 29).

Immediately the choice of the cardinals was made,
the *Te Deum* was intoned, and the new Pope was solemnly
escorted to the episcopal palace.   Here he was met by the
clergy and people ; and then, after giving them the solemn
papal benediction, he was taken back to the house or
palace of Peter della Vigna where he had been elected.[3]

Alexander
announces
his election
to the
Catholic
world.

Two days after his enthronization, Alexander announced
his election to the Catholic world.[4] Among the others
he wrote to our King, Henry III. He told him of the
death of Innocent IV. on December 7, in the midst
of a career of the greatest utility to the Church ; then
of his funeral obsequies and of his own election after
a brief delay. He assured Henry that the thought of

[1] Carbio, *l.c.*

[2] *Ib., cf.* Salimbene, p. 453 : " Oct . . . imposuit mantum meliori
homini de curia, ut dixit . . . et dictus est P. Alexander quartus,"
and Saba, *l.c.* : " Et ut nova de more nominis impositio sequeretur
beatitudinis tantae fastigia, ipsum nomen ad literam æquaret sua
interpretatione præcellentiæ tantæ omen vocari meruit Alexander."

[3] Carbio, c. 42.

[4] Potthast, nn. 15596–601.

all the qualities necessary for the exalted position to which his brethren wished to raise him, had caused him, conscious of his shortcomings, to shrink from it and with tears to implore them to place the burden on stronger shoulders.[1] Overcome, however, by the importunities of his brethren, he had to take up the cross trusting that God would help him to carry it.

The letter to Henry concluded with exhortations to him to be true to God and His church and to love justice ; while similar letters sent to others closed with earnest requests for prayers.[2]

[1] " Propterea exoravimus cum lacrimis, et usque ad contristationis et indignationis offensam, eisdem fratribus importabilem nobis ingerentibus Apostalatus sarcinam, duximus resistendum orantes eos . . . ut a nobis calicem hunc transferrent, et traderent alteri fortiori." Ep. Dec. 22, 1254, ap. Rymer, i, 536 ff.

[2] E.g., to the Master General of the Dominicans, ap. Raynald, *Annales*, an. 1254, n. 76. The inscription is wanting in Raynaldus. *Cf.* Potthast, n. 15600. See also the letter to the Commune of Parma, ap. Rod., iii, p. 315 ff.

CHAPTER II.

THE AFFAIRS OF THE KINGDOM OF SICILY AND OF THE EMPIRE.

Manfred's rebellion.

THE first matter that called for Alexander's attention was the rebellion of Manfred. Just before his accession, Manfred, the natural but subsequently legitimized son of Frederick II., had thrown off the feudal subjection which he owed to Innocent IV., and had defeated the papal army sent against him under Berthold of Hohenburg and the legate, cardinal William Fieschi.[1] But the Sicilian question did not stand by itself. Manfred professed to be acting as regent for the infant Conradin,[2] whom Conrad had left as the heir of his pretensions in Germany, and whose party was still holding out against William of Holland. Moreover, in North Italy the savage tyrant Ezzelino da Romano,[3] as the principal leader of the Ghibellines, was still upholding the imperial interests, or his own, against a hopelessly divided number of free cities.

Measures taken by Alexander against it, 1255.

Accordingly, to cope with the situation, Alexander began by endeavouring to secure the loyalty of the friends of the Church. Before a month after his election had passed, he had written a number of letters to Berthold of Hohenburg, who willingly or unwillingly had resigned to Manfred the regency of the Kingdom of the Two

---

[1] *Supra*, vol. xiv, p. 147.

[2] " Gerens se pro pædagogo Corradini." *Mem. Potestat. Reg.*, ap. *R. I. SS.*, viii, p. 1120.

[3] Benvenuto da Imola, *Inf.*, c. xii, p. 410 ed. Lacaita, quotes Mussatus of Padua, " the friend of the Muses," and says that in a tragedy which he composed he made E. da R. the offspring of the devil.

16

Sicilies to which he was entitled by the will of Conrad.[1] By these he confirmed him in his office of Seneschal of the Kingdom of Sicily, and in the possessions which Conrad or Innocent had bestowed upon him. Similar letters were addressed to the Seneschal's brothers.[2] The object of all of them was alike. It was to assure them of his support, immediately against Manfred or remotely against Conradin. What he did for the Hohenburgs in the Kingdom, he did also for various of its cities. He confirmed the privileges of Palermo and Brindisi which, he declared, had shaken off the vile subjection in which they had been kept, and had returned to the sweet yoke of the Roman Church.[3]

To lessen the power of Ezzelino da Romano and the Ghibelline faction in Lombardy, Alexander encouraged Alberic da Romano in his resistance to his tyrannical brother [4]; appealed to the loyalty of Guelf cities like Genoa and Bergamo [5]; and strove to keep the peace within well-disposed cities like Milan.[6]

In Germany, Alexander naturally supported the claims of William of Holland to the imperial crown, and soon began to enter into negotiations with him about bestowing it upon him.[7] In due course, however, without having the slightest intention of recognizing the baby Conradin as King of the Romans, he assured the envoys of the

---

[1] Rod., iii, nn. 356–9, p. 324 ff., Jar. 11, 1255.

[2] Ib., nn. 360–1, Jan. 18, 1255. Cf. nn. 371, 373–5, p. 330 ff.

[3] Ib., n. 410, p. 369. Sept. 5, 1255, to Palermo : " Quia civitas vestra prima inter alias Sicilie de vili subjectione . . . exurrexit, conceptum jamdudum subjiciendi se dulci et suavi Ecclesie Romane dominio laudabile propositum in partum habita opportunitate producens, nos, etc." N. 414, p. 371, Sept. 30, 1255, to Brindisi.

[4] Ib., n. 348, p. 317, Dec. 22, 1254. Cf. Pott., n. 15757, March 20, 1255.

[5] Ib., nn. 350, 352, Jan. 5 and 8, 1255. Cf. Pott., n. 16244.

[6] Rod., l.c., n. 397, May 1, 1255.

[7] Cf. epp. of Aug. 28, 1255. ap. Potthast, nn. 16003–4 ; and Regesta Imp., n. 5260a. For details see Tenchkoff, pp. 139–49 ; and see his chap. 6 for the Pope's relations with Germany generally.

child's guardians that he would respect his rights.
Addressing Agnes, countess Palatine of the Rhine
and Duchess of Bavaria, and Conrad's wife Elizabeth,[1]
the Queen of Jerusalem and Duchess of Suabia, he
assured them that it was his desire not merely to preserve
intact the rights of Conradin, King of Jerusalem, and
Duke of Suabia, but to increase them by special favours.
Moreover, he urged them to send a solemn embassy
to him to further the child's interests.[2]

Alexander's careful refraining from any mention of
the title of King of the Romans in connexion with
Conradin, must by itself have convinced his party that
he was not likely to support his candidature for that
honour. They had assuredly no need to wait to be
certain of this till letters arrived from Alexander to all
the spiritual and temporal lords of the Empire, reminding
them that William of Holland was King of the Romans
and the destined Emperor, and denouncing all opposition
to him.[3]

The interests, however, of Conradin in Sicily which,
like Innocent, Alexander was prepared to favour, were
his interests. As the father of that Prince had left his
child in charge of the Church,[4] Alexander would seemingly
have been willing to recognize him as his royal vassal
in that country, if circumstances had permitted.

---

[1] Conradin's mother was the daughter of Otho II., the Illustrious,
Duke of Bavaria, who became Count Palatine of the Rhine by his
marriage with Agnes.

[2] Potthast, n. 15649, Jan. 23, 1255.

[3] Ib., nn. 16003-4, Aug. 28, 1255. Cf. Rod., iii, n. 413, Sept. 20, 1255.

[4] Conradin was left " ex testamento regis Conradi sub baliatu
Romanæ Ecclesiæ", says the fourteenth century author of the Chron.
Siciliæ, c. 29, ap. R. I. SS., x, p. 821. Though this is a late authority
it is a good one, as it largely relies on contemporary documents. It runs
from 820–1328. Cf. a brief Chronicle which goes to 1359 in the Sicilian
dialect : " Re Corrao morsi, e remasi Corradino suo figlio per lo suo
testamento bajulato de la Santa Ecclesia." Chronichi di Sichilia, ed. V.
di Giovanni, Cronache Siciliane, p. 177, Bologna, 1865.

But, between the rights of both Conradin and Alexander The designs of Manfred. himself, stood the formidable figure of Manfred Lancia, who from his mother Bianca had inherited beauty of person,[1] and from his father, Frederick II., ability and an unbridled ambition. Of gracious form, affable and learned, he was, says Saba Malaspina, also virtuous until the desire of ruling perverted him.[2] His lust of power had been realized by Conrad who, as we have seen, left the regency of the Kingdom in the hands of Berthold. But Manfred soon brushed aside the Regent, and now attempted to brush aside his overlord, Alexander. At first he professed to be acting in Conradin's name, and he would appear to have imposed upon the child's guardians, seeing that, without any reference to the rights of Alexander as overlord, they named Manfred regent of the Kingdom in their ward's behalf (April 20, 1255).[3]

Meanwhile, after his defeat of Berthold and cardinal Negotiates with the Pope. William Fieschi, Manfred with his Germans and cruel Saracens proceeded to extend his power over the main-land of the Kingdom of Sicily, both by diplomacy and by force.[4] In his efforts he was ably supported by his uncles, the Lancias, especially by Galvano Lancia, who had been secretly working for him in the papal court itself.[5] Negotiations were, however, opened between him and the new Pope. But the Prince (of Taranto), as *Jamsilla* always calls Manfred, declared

[1] A chronicler (Jac. Aquensis, *Chron. imag. mundi*, ap. *Mon. hist. pat. SS.*, iii, p. 1573) says that Branca, one of the many concubines of Frederick, was " ultra modum pulcra (*sic*) ".

[2] *Hist.*, i, c. 5, p. 795. " Nam moribus et scientia decorare studuit animum antequam eum regni cupido perverteret."

[3] Balan, *Storia d'Italia*, vol. iv, p. 24, quoting *Liber pactorum*, MS. della Marciana di Venez., vol. ii, p. 61 f., and Böhmer-Ficker, *Regesta Imp.*, v., n. 4771. *Cf. ib.*, * 4772, p. 884. *Cf. Jamsilla*, p. 571.

[4] *Jamsilla*, p. 541 ff.

[5] *Ib.*, p. 542.

that the basis of them would have to be the acknowledgment of himself as Regent for Conradin, though he spoke of increasing the tribute paid to the Holy See if that were done.[1] This bait was not attractive enough to win papal recognition of the rebel's position, and Alexander cited Manfred to appear before him to answer for the murder of Borello.[2] This citation involved further negotiations; but, while the Prince's envoys were talking about peace, their master was continuing the extension of his power, or, as his panegyrist expresses it, was devoting his attention to subduing part of his own Principality of Taranto which had revolted from him.[3]

Alexander takes action against Manfred, 1255. Perceiving that he was being played with, Alexander took action. He replaced such unreliable Sicilian officials as he could with his own people from the Campagna, urged the Milanese and Florentines to prevent Manfred's uncle, the Marquis Lancia, from marching to the aid of his nephew[4]; and called his vassals to arms.[5] He then excommunicated Manfred for the murder of Borello (March 25, 1255)[6] and, in the month of June retired from Naples to Anagni, after appointing the distinguished cardinal-deacon of Sta. Maria in Via-Lata, Octaviano de Ubaldinis, his legate in the Kingdom, and giving him

---

[1] *Ib.*, p. 543. " Compositio autem super eo tantum esset, ut census pro ipso regno Romanæ ecclesiæ augeretur."

[2] *Cf. supra*, vol. xiv, p. 146.

[3] *Jams.*, p. 544. " Licet autem Princeps nuntios ad Romanam Curiam pro tractanda pace misisset, nihilominus ipse ad conquirendam terram ad suum specialiter Principatum pertinentem . . . intendebat."

[4] Potthast, nn. 15709–10.

[5] Saba, *l.c.*, p. 794. For the calling up of the feudal levies, *cf.* *Cronache di Fermo*, n. 240., p. 412, and *ib.*, n. 234, p. 411, ep. of Alex., Jan. 27, 1255, " pro petendo nobilium et aliorum Ecclesiæ devotorum auxilio . . . ex causa liberationis regni Siciliæ de manibus violentorum." Ed. G. de Minicis, Florence, 1870.

[6] Potthast, 15765.

full power to preach a Crusade against Manfred and his Saracens.[1]

Moreover, as Conradin's guardians showed no dis- Renewed offer of the crown of Sicily to Prince Edmund. position to make any move against Manfred, but were on the contrary coming to an understanding with him, Alexander turned to "the royal race of England ",[2] and renewed the offer of Sicily to Prince Edmund already made by his predecessor. In a long and important bull addressed to the young Prince on April 9, 1255, he said that in response to his request, he confirmed to him the Kingdom of Sicily on certain conditions— conditions which we have set forth elsewhere. Among these was that Edmund's father, Henry III., should pay all the expenses which the Roman Church had already incurred in connexion with the Sicilian affair, and which amounted to 135,541 marks " of good new and legal sterling money ".[3] He was also to be responsible for any interest, etc., which might accrue in connexion with that sum.[4] After paying certain instalments, Henry was to come in person or was to send a *Captain* with a suitable force to take possession of the Kingdom. Failing to do this, he was to lose the sums he had already advanced for the undertaking, to be excommunicated, and to have the whole of his Kingdom put under an interdict. In conclusion, he assured Edmund that all the conditions had the full approval of his envoy, the Bishop of Hereford. Neither the King nor the Prince could plead that they did not know the obligations they were taking upon themselves.

This important document was soon followed by others in which Alexander commuted Henry's vow of leading

---

[1] Saba, *l.c.*, p. 794 ; *Jams.*, pp. 545-6.

[2] Ep. to Henry ap. *Ann. de Burton*, p. 339 ; " Regale genus Angliæ."

[3] Rymer, i, 897. The Pope adds that the large sum named included 20,000 marks freely granted by the King to the Pope and the cardinals.

[4] " Ac insuper de dampnis, expensis et interesse, ac aliis . . . plenam satisfactionem impendet." *Ib.*

an expedition against the Saracens in the Holy Land
into a vow to lead one against the Saracens of Manfred
in Sicily[1]; and in which he directed that all moneys
raised in England for the Palestine Crusade should be
made over to Henry for the Sicilian Crusade.[2] In due
course (c. October 18) the young Edmund was, to the
great joy of his parents, formally invested with the
Kingdom by the bishop of Bologna, by means of a ring.[3]

Defeat of
cardinal
Octaviano,
September,
1255.

Having thus, as he had hoped, secured the intervention
of the English in the affairs of the Kingdom of the
Silicies, Alexander retired, as we have said, to the strong
hill town of Anagni, and left cardinal Octaviano to
face the growing power of Manfred. With a large army
of Tuscans and Campanians, the Cardinal took up his
position at Foggia with a view to the siege of the Saracen
stronghold of Lucera,[4] the key of Apulia, the fortress
which with Andria to the south sufficed to keep in check
the plain of Apulia with its populous cities, disposed
at all times to change and to the cause of the Popes.[5]
The papal army, which appears to have been larger than
that of Manfred, remained completely on the defensive,
and was soon rather besieged than besieging.[6] On the

---

[1] Ep. May 7, 1255, ap. Rymer, i, p. 548. The letter tells how Manfred
made common cause with the Saracens of Lucera, and with them
especially attacked the friends of the Church and liberty. Manfred
"cum infidelibus . . . sarracenis Luceriæ detestabiliter . . . adhæsit,
eisque nefando foedere copulatus ipsorum præcipue contra Christianos
assumpsit . . . auxilium, etc." Cf. ib., pp. 547 and 552, to the archbishop and Rostand on this commutation. These two were also
commissioned to make a like commutation for the King of Norway
and his people. Ib., epp. of May 11 and 12, p. 549 f.

[2] Ib., p. 552 f., and Potthast, nn. 15863–7, May 15–17, 1255.

[3] Mat. Par., v, 515 ; Ann. Burton, i, 349.

[4] Saba, p. 794 ; Jams., 561–2.

[5] Lenormant, A travers l'Apulie, i, p. 78 f. According to Jamsilla,
who gives copious details of this campaign, Foggia and its neighbourhood was well supplied with everything necessary for men and horses.
P. 572.

[6] Jams., p. 574 ; Saba, p. 794.

other hand, the activity of Manfred in cutting off supply
columns brought such a state of famine on the Legate's
army that, despite the natural fertility of the neighbourhood of Foggia, "a chicken could scarcely be bought for
a horse." [1] Disheartened by Manfred's success, the
cardinal, after failing, according to *Jamsilla*, to defeat
his enemy by an act of treachery, asked for terms of
peace.[2] It was finally agreed between them that the
Prince, "in his own interest and in that of his nephew
Conradin, should hold the Kingdom with the exception
of the Terra di Lavoro which was to be granted to the
Church. If, however, the Pope would not accept these
terms, it was to be left open to the Prince to recover
the Terra di Lavoro also." [3] After this the Legate
"with the whole of his innumerable army" withdrew
into the Terra,[4] seemingly in August or the very beginning
of September, 1255.[5]

As to the fact of the Cardinal's retreat, there is
unanimity among the authorities ; but as to the cause
of it different reasons are given. Saba Malaspina says
that, according to some, the Tuscan and Campanian
leaders were anxious to fight, but that Octavian would
not allow them, because he was a Ghibelline at heart,
and was devoted to the House of Hohenstaufen in general
and to Manfred in particular.[6] Others again believed

The cause of the Cardinal's discomfiture.

---

[1] *Jams., ib.*

[2] Pp. 572 for the treachery, and 576 for the request for peace.

[3] *Jams.*, p. 577.

[4] *Ib.*

[5] A letter of Alexander to Henry III. dated Sept. 18, 1255. The
letter, which is a call for Henry's prompt help, speaks of the retirement of the cardinal as of a recent fact.

[6] *L.c.*, pp. 794–5. "Asseritur quod illius amoris instantia quem
in eo (Manfred) conceperat, et dilectionis etiam instigatus quam Domus
cardinalis prædicti ad Fredericum habuerat, cui sub Gebellinitatis
nomine quantum poterat adhærebat, idem cardinalis . . . fines regni
Manfredo spontanea liberalitate dimisit, rediitque in Campanian
quasi victus." Octavian was a man, certainly of great influence, but

that, as a cleric, " on whose shoulders arms rest not well," he was averse to fighting, and unfitted to be a commander. But the same thoughtful author observes that it is more rational to suppose that the Cardinal retreated because he found that while his army steadily diminished, that of Manfred steadily increased.[1] This is no doubt the correct reason, for Alexander assured our King Henry that the Cardinal's failure was caused by treachery [2]— a statement well borne out by what *Jamsilla* relates of the low cunning of Berthold of Hohenburg, whose great aim was so to serve both Manfred and the Pope that he might be benefited by the victor.[3]

The Pope will not accept the Cardinal's peace.

However all this may be, Alexander refused to accept the conditions of peace to which Octavian had agreed,[4] and called upon Henry of England to hasten to his help, for the danger was pressing, but could be met by prompt action, " as that part of the Kingdom which had first adhered to the Church, and the Isle of Sicily, too, were still loyal to it." [5]

we have to wait for later writers, Dante and his commentators, to learn that he was a confirmed Ghibelline. Dante (*Infer.*, c. x) puts him in Hell beside Frederick II. as an impious epicurean ; and his great commentator Bevenuta da Imola, says (*Coment. in Inf. X.*, vol. i, p. 357, ed. Lacaita) " fuit magnus protector et fautor Ghibelinorum ", and that he once declared : " If I have a soul, I have already lost it a thousand times for the Ghibellines."

[1] P. 795.

[2] Ep. just cited, p. 564. He tells Henry that all was going well with the Cardinal, but " tandem quorundam proditorum faciente nequitia, de quibus quod fideliter agerent præcipue sperabatur, tot fuere fabricata contraria . . . quod propter hæc (cum liquido appareret dolus, proditio atque fraus) coactus est idem Legatus in Terram Laboris . . . redire ".

[3] P. 574. Hence our King Henry attributed the collapse of the Cardinal's campaign to the treachery of Berthold : " contigit per proditionem marchionis de Herebroke." Ep. March 27, 1256, ap. Rymer, i, 584. *Cf.* a letter of his to the cardinal of St. Angelo where he speaks of the treachery of all the Hohenburgs. *Ib.*, i, p. 587. *Cf.* *Flores Hist.*, iii, p. 246.

[4] *Jams.*, p. 580.   [5] Ep. cit.

The success of Manfred was at once felt in all the parts A Crusade proclaimed against Ezzelino, 1255. where the House of Hohenstaufen or their supporters were struggling for supremacy. In North Italy it gave fresh courage to Ezzelino da Romano, against whom Alexander found it necessary to proclaim a crusade. Addressing the clerical and lay nobility and the communes of Lombardy, Romagna, and the March of Treviso, as well as the Doge of Venice, he reminded them of the excesses of Ezzelino. Especially, he said, in the March of Treviso was the Catholic faith and the Christian religion perverted by that man of blood, Ezzelino, who was stained with the cruel slaughter of noble and plebian alike. He told them that he had named Philip, the archbishop-elect of Ravenna, as his legate, and had bidden him rouse the faithful against the tyrant, and give them the Cross, granting them the same indulgences as were granted to those who went to the Holy Land.[1]

It was necessary also for Alexander to act against He forbids the election of Conradin as King of the Romans, 1256. the Hohenstaufen in Germany. William of Holland, the second of the rivals of Frederick II., and of Conrad IV., had perished in an expedition against the Frisians (January 28, 1256) who had revolted just as he was preparing to march to Rome for the imperial crown. The adherents of the Hohenstaufen thereupon only naturally began to work for the general acceptance of the claims of the child Conradin. Alexander, however, could not think of recognizing them. If Conradin were elected King of the Romans, and Manfred was to remain true to his profession of loyalty to him, it would mean that the imperial crown and that of Sicily would continue to remain on the same head. Accordingly, in order to make it perfectly plain that he refused any kind of recognition to Conradin's claims, he even took upon himself, as if the Empire was absolutely vacant,

---

[1] Ep. Dec. 20, 1255, ap. Rod., iii, p. 378.

to confer, in the place of the King of the Romans, the
regalia upon the bishop of Verdun.[1] Then somewhat
later he forbade Gerard, archbishop of Maintz, under
pain of excommunication, to elect Conradin as King of
the Romans, and instructed him to forbid his co-electors
to do likewise under the same penalty. Conradin was
a scion of a race that had grievously persecuted the
Church, and moreover, as a child, was quite incapable
of fulfilling the imperial function of being " the advocate
or defender of the Church ".[2]

Continual
progress of
Manfred,
1256.

Meanwhile, whilst Germany was without a ruler,
and almost without a claimant to its headship, Manfred
continued to consolidate his power. At a General
Assembly (Curia Generalis) of his party held at Barletta
on February 13, 1256, he deposed a number of the officials
of the Kingdom, and replaced them by Galvano Lancia
and other members of his family. Then, as the Pope
persisted in refusing his offer of a compromise, he invaded
the Terra di Lavoro, and soon became master of practically
the whole of it.[3] With success, according to Saba, at
any rate, came deterioration of character. He gave
way to the two vices of lust and cruelty that had so
disgraced his father,[4] and proceeded, now with the utmost
severity, not only against such of the nobility as were

---

[1] Ep. March 28, 1256, ap. *ib.*, p. 390. He granted them on the
condition that he should take the customary oath of fidelity to the
future King of the Romans, " when his election had been confirmed
by the Apostolic See."

[2] Ep. July 28, 1256, ap. *ib.*, p. 397 ff.

[3] *Jams.*, p. 580 f.

[4] " Namque invalescente sævitia, sanguinis atrocitas et libidinis
incentivum jam eidem adimere cœperant quicquid studiosus virtutibus
compararat, et a se ipso priore vita et moribus dissidens, virum mutatus
in alterum, etc." Saba, p. 796. *Cf. Chron. Aquense* in Moriondo,
Mon. Aquens., ii, 157, ap. Balan, *Storia d'Italia*, iv, 39 ; and Villani,
Cron., vi, 46, ap. *R. I. SS.*, xiii, who says he was more dissolute than
his father, and believed only in bodily pleasures.

disposed to favour the Church, but also against those who were devoted to Conradin.[1]

Convinced at last that without external aid there was no hope of resisting Manfred, Alexander again turned his thoughts to Henry, and with renewed energy urged him to come without delay to secure the Kingdom for his son. Henry was, indeed, meanwhile occupying himself with remote preliminaries in connexion with the Sicilian affair, and raising money for it,[2] but he was making no real preparation for actively engaging in it, nor even for repaying the Pope for the money which he had expended over it, and which had completely drained his resources, and even exhausted his credit.[3] About these two points, Alexander complained bitterly to the King. He was doing nothing either in a military or in a financial direction; and meanwhile the Pope was suffering from the importunities of the Roman bankers who were threatening to lay hands on the possessions of the churches of Rome which had been pledged to them.[4] Moreover, the operations of cardinal

Appeals to Henry to resist Manfred, 1256-7.

---

[1] " Sed nec pepercit illis qui erga factum infantis (Conradin) zelo pietatis accensi." He then proceeds to give specific examples. Saba, *l.c.*

[2] *Cf.* Rymer, i, p. 572-3, 7, 9.

[3] So he had told Henry in his letter of Sept. 18, 1255, ap. Rymer, i, 564. "Cum pro ipsius promotione negotii exhauriverimus omnino Cameram nostram, innumera contraxerimus debita, etc." *Cf.* ep. Nov. 9, 1256, ap. *ib.*, p. 613; and a letter of Alexander printed by Langlois in his paper, " Nova Curie," ap. *Rev. Historique*, Jan., 1905, p. 62: " Ita quod non poteramus de cetero mutuum invenire."

[4] Ep. to the bishop of Hereford, Feb. 5, 1256, Rymer, i, 581. "Ab eisdem mercatoribus jugiter stimulemur, et mercatores Romani parati sunt, nisi satisfaciat eis in termino ad possessiones Ecclesiarum urbis quæ obligatæ sunt eis avidas manus extendere." A number of magnates of the Kingdom, nearly all ecclesiastical, in writing to Henry to say how glad they were that his son had been named their King, add that their joy is dependent upon " his wished for coming not being longer put off !" Ep. of March 18, 1256, ap. *Annal. Burton*, p. 397 f. In his replies to this and similar letters Henry assured his correspondents that, though the preparation of the necessary armament was delaying him at present, they might absolutely rely on his help in the following summer. Epp. ap. *ib.*, pp. 398-401.

Octavian against Manfred were, for lack of funds, quite suspended, and the portions of the Kingdom which were faithful to the Church were constantly diminishing. If the King does not send money and troops, he will have to annul the grant of Sicily which he had made to him (February 5, 1256).

Henry asks
for delay.

Henry was disturbed at this threat, as he professed to have the Sicilian affair very much at heart. His agents were accordingly instructed to work for the election of a King of Germany who will be " devoted to the Roman Church and favourable to him ", lest, if the French get their way in this matter, his Sicilian scheme will be gravely injured. The Pope must be asked to send a suitable cardinal to manage the German election, and to grant him more time in which to pay his debts, and to send an expedition to Sicily. For the reverses which the cardinal legate has suffered in the Kingdom render it impossible for him to fulfil his obligations within the agreed time. However, by the Feast of St. John the Baptist (June 24), nearly 24,000 marks will be paid off.[1] But no Prince could pay 135,540 marks between February and September (the feast of St. Michael).[2]

It is granted.

On the matter of delay, Alexander showed himself disposed to yield (June 11),[3] and meanwhile pushed forward the payment of moneys from the tenths, etc., to the King with all the vigour he could.[4] At length,

[1] Epp. to William Bonquer, and to the Pope himself. March 27, 1256, ap. ib., i, 583–5. Cf. epp. ib., p. 586, where Prince Edward agrees to take up his father's obligations in the matter of Sicily should he die (quod absit) before they are fulfilled.

[2] Ib., pp. 584 and 587 in a letter of Henry to the cardinal of St. Angelo.

[3] Ib., p. 593. Cf. p. 608 for ep. of Sept. 27.

[4] Epp. of August and Sept., 1256, ib., pp. 598–605. Cf. ep. of Sept. 27, 1256, to Rostand bidding him compel the Scotch bishops to help to pay off the debts which the Holy See has contracted : " pro tuicione ecclesiasticæ libertatis potissime autem pro negocio Regni Siciliæ." Ib., p. 608.

on October 6, after consultation with the cardinals, he granted Henry an extension of six months, to count from December 1, 1256, within which time the money and men necessary for the Sicilian expedition were to be forthcoming.[1] But he did not fail to point out to him that his dilatoriness had caused the loss of the favourable position held by cardinal Octavian, and that he would be disgraced in the eyes of the world and of posterity if he were to fail in carrying out his design.[2]

Not long after this an event occurred which, had there been any genius and character in either Henry or his brother, Richard of Cornwall, might easily have secured Sicily for Edmund, and opened up a period of paramount English influence on the continent of Europe. But of Richard of Cornwall the French are reported to have said that he was "unwarlike, without brains (imbecillis), and without any experience in military affairs".[3] If this criticism was partially true of Richard, it was still more true of Henry. The event in question was the election of Richard of Cornwall as King of the Romans.

Election of Richard of Cornwall to the Empire, 1257.

From what has been already said [4] it will have been gathered that both the English and the French had been using all the influence they could to ensure the election of a King of Germany who would be a support to their particular nationality. But the only thing that the diplomats succeeded in doing was to bring about a divided election. Either because they had already received some of Richard's great riches,[5] or

---

[1] *Ib.*, p. 611, or ap. Rod., iii, p. 404 ; Bliss, p. 338.

[2] Ep. Nov. 9 or 10, Venerabilis frater noster, Rymer, i, 612.

[3] Mat. Par., v, 605.

[4] *Supra*, p. 28.

[5] The *Annals of Colmar*, an. 1257, ap. Böhmer, *Fontes*, ii, p. 3, say that Richard " by his presents obtained the Kingdom of the Romans". *Cf.* Wykes, *Chron.*, p. 112, *R. S.*, and *Ann. Hamburg.*, ap. *M. G. SS.*, xvi, p. 384.

because they hoped to do so, the archbishop of Cologne and some other of the seven electors chose Richard of Cornwall as King of the Romans on the Octave of the Epiphany in 1257.[1] Somewhat later (April 1), the French, according to Matthew Paris, succeeded in inducing some of the electors to choose Alfonso X., el Sabio, King of Leon and Castile as King of the Romans.[2] Richard was, however, duly crowned at Aix-la-Chappelle on May 17, 1257. But as the only idea of those German Princes who had elected him was to finger his money, so his only idea of making himself respected was by scattering money.[3] " And whilst his money lasted," record the Annals of Strasburg with grim humour,[4] " he was escorted by the Princes of Germany to the different imperial cities and towns on the Rhine, and was by them received with honour owing to their respect for the Princes who were with him. But when he reached Basle his money was exhausted, and the Princes left him ; giving him a bill of divorce, saying that it was not his person they loved but his money. He returned to his own country by another route, and his memory perished with a noise."

---

[1] Mat. P., v, 601 ff. Paris says that Richard was chosen because he was of tried fidelity, firmness, and wisdom ; spoke a language like that of the Germans, and was wealthy. *Cf.* the full statement of the election of Richard and Alfonso by Urban IV., Aug. 31, 1263, ap. Rymer, i, p. 762 ff. ; Wykes, *Chron.*, p. 111, *R. S.*, Herman of Altaich, *Annales*, ap. B., *Font.*, ii, p. 512. As far as England was concerned, the election of Richard was a misfortune. It diverted from it his wealth, and his moderating influence in the struggle between King Henry and the barons.

[2] v, 624. *Cf. ib.*, pp. 622, 657. Alfonso, the Learned, never set foot in Germany.

[3] *The Annals* of the free city of Hamburg (ap. *M. G. SS.*, xvi, 384) hit off the situation well : " Stulta Anglia, quæ tot denariis sponte est privata, stulti principes Alimanniæ qui nobile jus suum pro pecunia vendiderunt."

[4] Ap. B., *Fontes*, ii, p. 110.

No doubt for the future peace of England, it was Henry again not ready for the Sicilian expedition, 1257. just as well that Richard, " by the grace of God, King of the Romans, ever Augustus," [1] was a simple-minded open-handed English gentleman instead of being a bold, clever, needy adventurer. For, had he been the latter, the English position in France would have been re-established, and an English Prince would have been seated on the throne of the two Sicilies. As it was, Richard was incapable of doing anything for Henry or England, for he was unable to help himself. Meanwhile, his still weaker brother continued to talk about the Sicilian expedition. He assured the Pope that he had fixed upon an upright and energetic leader for it,[2] and that, because he had it very much at heart, he was ready to follow the advice of the Roman Church and make peace with France.[3]

But though Alexander continued to do what he could for Henry, and " on his behalf " solemnly ex-com-municated Manfred on Holy Thursday (1257), still, " owing to the King's negligence and inertia," as he complained, the only result was that he was even yet being harassed by the wearisome complaints of the bankers.[4]

The complaint just alluded to was penned on June 3. A further delay is granted to Henry, 1257. The six months grace granted to Henry during which he was to have paid the *Sicilian* debts of the Holy See, and to have taken action in the Kingdom had passed by, and he was still the Pope's debtor, and had still to send a single soldier to Sicily. Alexander was naturally

[1] See some of his diplomas, *ib.*, p. 231 ff.

[2] Ep. May 10, 1257, ap. Rymer, i, 620.

[3] Ep. *ib.*, p. 621 : " Quia negotium Regni Siciliæ plurimum residet cordi nostro volentes ut felicem sortiretur eventum, etc."

[4] Ep. to Rostand, June 3, 1257, ap. *ib.*, p. 624 : " Estne ista grata et debita nobis vicissitudo favoris, ut permittat nos vexari a merca-toribus, et eorum querimoniis affici tædiosis."

annoyed, and there was talk of Henry's renouncing
all claims to Sicily on his son's behalf. Fresh envoys
and letters passed between the two,[1] and while Edmund
sent a golden bull to the Pope asking for a modification
of the terms on which Sicily had been granted to him,[2]
Henry sent him a letter of excuse and explanation a
day or two later. He thanked the Pope for the favour
he had done him in granting Sicily to his son, and
acknowledged the obligations arising therefrom. It
was true that, with regard to the payment of the debts
contracted in his behalf by the Holy See, he had not
done what he desired, but the clergy of the realm had
given and were still giving him trouble about the payment
of the tenth and the other dues conceded to him by the
Pope.[3] Moreover, just when he had arranged to send
Henry de Castella, the brother of the King of Castile,
as his General (Capitaneus) with a large sum of money
to Apulia, an eruption of the Welsh had prevented
him from carrying out his intention. Henry therefore
begged the Pope, under the circumstances, to arrange
matters so that " we, our heirs and the whole realm of
England may with its wonted devotion, be ever obedient
to the Roman Church, and that we may not incur any

[1] Cf. ap. Rymer, i, pp. 628–35.

[2] " In cujus rei testimonium bullam nostram auream præsentibus
duximus apponendam." Ib., p. 629, June 26.

[3] This was true enough. Not unnaturally the majority of the English
clergy and nobility regarded the Sicilian undertaking as " an impossible
venture ". Accordingly when, " at a great parliament," in the Mid-Lent
of 1257, Henry made a dramatic appeal to them for aid by presenting
Edmund to them attired in the native dress of Apulia, he succeeded
indeed in making " the ears of all tingle " when he told them that he
was bound for the sum of 140,000 marks, but not in winning their
goodwill.   And when he claimed a tenth " according to the new
valuation without the deduction of any but necessary expenses ", they
would only consent to give him 50,000 marks on condition of his
observing the Magna Carta. Mat. Par., v, 623 : On the English barons'
view as to the " impossible negotium " of Sicily, see their protest to
the Pope, ap. Rymer, i, p. 660 ff.

loss from an affair from which no advantage will accrue to us ". He knew, he went on to say, that he had bound himself by various penalties, but he was acting from love to his mother the Roman Church, who had ever stood by him in adversity.[1]

Henry at the same time commissioned his agents to strive for a modification of the terms of the grant. They were to try to get the penalty clauses struck out. If they could not get them all struck out, they were rather to keep the interdict clause than the one which threatened the withdrawal of the grant of Sicily altogether. And if they could not effect the alteration of any of the conditions of the grant they were to strive for a prolongation of the time limit. With the Pope's consent they were to treat with Manfred. It should be suggested that Manfred should retain his Principality of Taranto, and restore the Kingdom to Edmund, who should marry Manfred's daughter. Among the many other alternatives set before the royal envoys on which they might treat, were a number only to be broached on the supposition that neither the Pope nor Manfred would agree to any of the proposals of the King already mentioned. One of these set forth that, if the Church were to bestow the Kingdom on another from whom it should obtain the reimbursement of the sums already spent by it on the affair, then Henry should receive back what he had paid, and should renounce all claims to the Kingdom possessed by him or by his son.[2]

Of the many propositions made by Henry, the one to which the Pope agreed was a further delay. On December 12, Alexander granted the King till June,

---

[1] Ep. June 28, 1257, ap. Rymer, i, 630.

[2] Cf. the diplomatic minutes ("Instructiones de variis tractandi modis circa negotium Siciliæ "), drawn up for the instruction of Henry's envoys to the Pope, ap. Rymer, i, p. 632. Cf. others, ib., pp. 633-4, June-July, 1257.

1258, to fulfil his obligations, and while he declared that he had not actually fallen under any of the spiritual penalties to which he had bound himself, he laid down that they would nevertheless bind him in the future.[1]

Manfred openly opposes Conradin, and is crowned, 1258.
Any chances, however, that Henry ever had against Manfred were brought to an end by the coronation of that astute prince in the middle of the following year. Feeling that he had sufficiently established his power, Manfred issued a general proclamation throughout the whole Kingdom to the effect that no one was in future to speak of Conradin as the heir to the throne of Sicily, but that all were to regard him as Frederick's successor.[2] He also caused letters to be forged purporting to come from nobles in Germany, and stating that Conradin was dead.[3] It was to no purpose that the guardians of Conradin turned to the Pope, and by the hands of two envoys sent him a number of open letters from various nobles, "with their seals affixed to them," proving that the Prince was alive. Manfred procured their assassination by a distinguished but bankrupt noble, "Raulus of the house of the Surdi." [4]

Unaided, Alexander was wholly unable to resist the

---

[1] Ep. Dec. 12, 1257, *ib.*, p. 646. *Cf.* ep. Jan. 19, 1258, *ib.*, p. 652.

[2] Saba, p. 796. *Cf.* the brief phrase of Bartholomew of Neocast. "Quo (Conradin) negato." *Hist. Sic.*, c. 5.

[3] This is affirmed by most of the other contemporary authors as well as by Saba. "Fici dire come Corradino era morto." *Chronichi di Sichilia*, p. 177. " Asserens Corradinum fuisse mortuum." *Chron. Sic.*, c. 30 ap. *R. I. SS.*, x, p. 822. *Cf. Chron. Pont. Mant.* ap. *M. G. SS.*, xxiv, 216, and *Chron. Pont. et imp. S. Barthol.* Ap. *ib.*, xxxi, p. 225. " Postmodum conficta ejusdem Conradi morte se fecit coronari in regem " ; *Chron. de rebus in Italia*, p. 242. On this Ghibelline chronicle, see *supra*, vol. ix, p. 308 n. *Cf.* also *Mem. Potestat. Reg.*, ap. *R. I. SS.*, viii, 1120.

[4] Saba, p. 797 ; *Chron. P. M., l.c.* He was also credited in the Roman court and in that of Richard of Germany with the desire of bringing about the assassination of Henry III. and his two sons Edward and Edmund, and of Richard himself and of Conradin. *Annal. Burton.*, p. 395.

progress of Manfred. His one hope, Henry of England, was doing nothing but asking for further delays,[1] while acknowledging the endless favours he had received from Rome.[2] It is true that the Barons of England, " most devoted " to the Holy Father, promised him their aid, but it was offered on conditions.[3] The conditions were that the King should agree to reforms and that the Pope should remove the objectionable foreigner Aylmer from the See of Winchester. The Barons say that the King engaged in the Sicilian affair against their advice, but that, if the King will accede to their request, they will nevertheless so take the matter up that he may be able to bring it to a successful termination. They beg him to hearken to their request in the name of " the unity and peace of the Kingdom of England which has ever been and is devoted to you ". But Alexander could not grant their petition without breaking with the King, and this he naturally did not feel disposed to do.[4]

Manfred was accordingly crowned with no little pomp at Palermo [5] (August 10, 1258), though as many of the bishops of the Kingdom as dared kept away from the ceremony on one pretext or another.[6]

But the restless ambition of Manfred was not satisfied with the rich and noble Kingdom of the Two Sicilies.

Manfred agitates all Italy.

[1] Epp. of July 7 and 28, ap. Rymer, i, p. 664 f.

[2] Ep. Aug. 1, 1258, *ib.*, p. 666

[3] "SS. Patri in Christo Alexandro . . . S. Universalis ecclesiæ summo Pontifici, Communitas Comitum, procerum . . . aliorumque Regni Angliæ, cum subjectione debita " . . . " Nos vestri devotissimi." Ep. ap. Rymer, i, p. 660 ff., *c.* June, 1258.

[4] See his answer to the barons, ap. Mat. Pat., *Addit.*, vi, 410 ff.

[5] For the progress of Manfred's power in the island of Sicily itself see the *Annales Siculi* of the Dominican Conrad, ap. *R. I. SS.*, i, pt. ii, pp. 278–9, and the *Continuation* of Malaterra, ap. *R. I. SS.*, v, p. 605.

[6] Saba, p. 798 ; *Chron. Sic., l.c.*, Mat. Par., v, 722 ; *Jamsilla*, p. 584. Even the last-named author says that previous to his coronation Manfred had consulted the interests of Conradin " and his own ".

He would extend his sway as widely as that of his father. Accordingly he began to intrigue everywhere with the friends of his house or with the enemies of the Church.[1] " Would that he had not harassed the States of the Church," is the reflection of the sage, Saba Malaspina.[2] As it was, however, he had soon all Italy in a turmoil. He brought about disturbances in his own interest in Liguria, Tuscany, and the March of Ancona. In Liguria and Central Italy, he supported the Marquis Oberto Pallavicini, "a prudent and noble man, though a Ghibelline and a persecutor of the Church."[3] He roused the remnant of the Ghibelline party in Tuscany, and especially the city of Siena " which was devoted " to the imperial House " and on the contrary hostile to the Church ".[4] Furthermore he took advantage of party strife in the March of Ancona to make friends with one side, and sent help to it. For a time, too, his party in north Italy acted in co-operation with the unspeakable tyrant Ezzelino da Romano, the ruler of the Trevisan March.[5] In Rome he promised aid to the Senator Brancaleone who, independently of the Pope, was ruling the city with a strong hand.[6] The natural result of all this energetic and unscrupulous intrigue was that " the reputation of the King continued to grow, while the losses of the Church increased, and the depression of the Guelfs became deeper ".[7]

---

[1] Villani, *Chron.*, vi, 45, ap. *R. I. SS.*, xiii, p. 187, tells us with what care he came to an understanding with all the cities of Italy which were Ghibelline, and faithful to the Empire, and how he aided them with his German knights, " making with them a league and alliance (taglia e compagnia) in Tuscany and in Lombardy."

[2] *Hist.*, ii, c. 2, p. 800.   [3] *Ib.*

[4] *Ib. Cf.* Potthast, 17879, 17946, 18055.

[5] *Chron. de rebus*, 1258, p. 243. *Cf.* p. 244 : " Eodem tempore Ubertinus de Andito—habuit soldum a rege Manfredo pro Placentinis extrinsecis."

[6] Mat. Par., v, 664, 699.   [7] Saba, ii, c. 2.

Alexander on his side was not idle. As early as the Action of Alexander against Manfred and his supporters. year 1256, he had named Philip Fontana, archbishop of Ravenna, his legate in Lombardy to oppose Ezzelino.[1] If some of Philip's doings were not such as are to be looked for from archbishops,[2] he was at any rate an able and energetic man. Soon after his appointment, he came to Ferrara, and was listened to by Salimbene and a Jewish friend (March, 1256). In a loud voice he informed the people that the Pope had sent him to oppose Ezzelino, and that he wished to raise a Crusade against him for the restitution of the exiles from Padua. Those who joined the Crusade could gain a plenary indulgence. "Let no one say that it is impossible to fight against a fiendish man whom the very devils fear, for nothing is impossible to God who will fight for us."

An army was raised,[3] and, inspired by a lay Franciscan brother, another friend of Salimbene, the crusaders stormed Padua, a place which Ezzelino no more feared to lose than God, says the friar, fears to fall from heaven.[4] Ezzelino, however, did not lose heart, but two years later (c. September, 1258) defeated and captured the legate, and thereby "saddened the whole March, terrified a great part of Lombardy, frightened Romagna, and what is worse, brought grief to the Holy Apostolic See".[5] Next year, however, (c. spring, 1259), envoys were sent to

[1] This he did at the request of the Marquis of Este and other magnates of the March. *Cf. Mon. Patav*, l. ii, p. 691 ; and Rolandini, *Chron. March. Trivix.*, viii, c. 1 ; and *Lib. regim. Padue*, p. 323, ap. *R. I. SS.*, viii, pl. i, new ed. Alexander had already taken action against Ezzelino in 1255. *Cf.* Potthast, 15897, June 17.

[2] He had a great desire to be Pope. Salimbene, *Chron.*, pp. 401, 433.

[3] Potthast, n. 17249, Apr., 1258. On the ground that " all men are by nature equal ", the Pope declared all Ezzelino's slaves free. *Cf.* Epp. July 3 and 4, 1258, ap. Potthast, 17331-2, or Rod., iii, n. 481, p. 445.

[4] Salimbene, *ib.*, p. 394 ff.

[5] Rolandini, *Chron. Trix.*, xi, c. 9, *cf. Mon. Pat. Chron.*, p. 700, and *Ann. Cremon*, ap. *M. G. SS.*, xxxi, p. 19.

Alexander from Venice, Padua, Mantua, Ferrara, and
other cities begging him to send them as legate, Henry,
archbishop of Embrun.[1] A league was formed of all
the friends of the Church, and the tyrant was defeated,
and died of his wounds (October, 1259).[2]

He seeks
help from
Perugia, etc.

Alexander, however, knew well that success against
Ezzelino did not mean that he had scored at all heavily
against Manfred, as Ezzelino was fighting much more
for himself than for any King, and dominant influence
in north Italy was in the hands of the Ghibelline
Pelavicini. Accordingly, he did not cease to strive
to obtain help against Manfred himself. To put all
possible pressure on our King to make him act in behalf
of his son, he informed him that he must rescind the grant
of Sicily to Edmund unless he fulfilled all its conditions
in full (December 18, 1258).[3] A month or so later, he
tried to induce Perugia which had remained true to
the Church, to lend him its support (January 11, 1259).
He begged the authorities of the city to do this by aiding
Orlando de Ferentino and Anibaldi, relatives of the
Pope and rectors of the March of Ancona, which Manfred
was reported to have already invaded.[4]

Henry asks
for further
time.

Whatever success Alexander may have had with
Perugia, he had none with Henry. He only got more
letters pleading for more time.[5] The King was able,

---

[1] *Ib.* c. 11. It was to no purpose that Alexander begged Pelavicini,
and the other Ghibelline leaders to release the captured legate. Philip,
however, managed at length to escape from his prison. *Mon. Pat.
Chron.*, ap. *R. I. SS.*, viii, p. 710.

[2] *Ib.*, xii, cc. 8–9 ; Saba, ii, c. 3 ; *Mon. Pat., Chron.*, ap. *R. I. SS.*,
viii, pp. 702–5. By Ezzelino's admission of Frederick II. into Italy
by Verona when that emperor wished to seize Lombardy, " there
arose," says this author, " an inexorable discord between the Roman
Church and the Empire, through which many thousands of men in
different parts of the world perished. The perfidious Ezzelino was the
beginning, middle, and end of all these evils."

[3] Rymer, i, 379, Rec. ed.   [4] Potthast (17448).

[5] Ep., March 12, 1259, Rymer, i, 672.

however, to point out that he had taken an important step forward by making peace with France.[1] A few months later, he begged the Pope to send him a legate with whom he might treat at length regarding the Sicilian affair.[2]

Not only then did Alexander not receive any assistance from England, but the Guelfs were very badly defeated in central Italy. Rendered careless, perhaps, by the death of Ezzelino and, somewhat later, by that of his equally cruel brother, Alberic (August, 1260),[3] or over-confident in their numbers, or, as the Florentines, Villani and Dante, say, overwhelmed by treachery, the Guelf Florentines suffered a terrible defeat at the hands of the Sienese, helped by Manfred's cavalry, on the banks of the Arbia near the hill of Montaperti (September, 1260).[4]

The Ghibelline victory of Montaperti, 1260.

The slaughter of so many thousands of citizens at Montaperti, so bitterly bewailed by the Guelf bard Guitone d'Arezzo,[5] supplied the torch to fire a great penitential movement which suddenly sprang up in Perugia and the golden vale of Spoleto. A year of famine in many parts of Italy (1258) had been followed by a year of great pestilence, so that, says Salimbene, who was in the midst of it, "at the hour of vespers we had two dead in our Church at once,"[6] The famine and the

The Flagellants.

---

[1] Ep. May 20, 1259, *ib.*, p. 681.   [2] *Ib.*, p. 687.

[3] *Cf. Mon. Pat., Chron.*, p. 697, for the defection of Alberic from the Church party.

[4] *Chron. de rebus*, p. 249 ; *Mon. Pat.*, p. 714 ; Rolandini ; *Lib. reg. Pad.*, ap. *R. I. SS.*, viii, pt. i, p. 325, new ed.'; Dante, *Inferno*, x, 80 ff. ; G. Villani, *Cron.*, vi, 79, ap. *R. I. SS.*, xiii ; Saba, ii, l. 4. He speaks of Florence as : "cum parte Guelforum non minus vitiis quam delitiis affluens." *Cf. Chronique de la Bataille de M.-A.*, ap. *Chroniques Siennoises*, ed. de Dino, Paris, 1846.

[5] See his poem against the Florentine Ghibellines, who to gain the upper hand subjected themselves to the Germans and to the enemies of their commune—"unto a seigniory both cruel and base, and takes his bitterest enemy for his lord." See also his 14th letter.

[6] *Chron.*, p. 465. Thousands, he says, died in Florence and Milan.

plague were followed by the slaughter of Montaperti.
Men felt that the hand of God was heavy upon them.
Penance must lessen its weight. " At a time," says
the monk of Padua, " when all Italy was defiled with
vice and crime, a sudden manifestation of grief, never
heard of in the world before, displayed itself first among
the Perugians,[1] then among the Romans, and then among
almost all the peoples of Italy (Lombardy). So great
a fear of God fell upon men that nobles and commoners,
old men and young, children even of five years of age,
all with bare backs, walked two and two through the cities
in procession bearing leather thongs in their hands with
which, mid sighs and tears, they lashed their shoulders
till they ran with blood. Weeping as though they actually
beheld the Passion of Christ, they begged the mercy of
God, and the help of His Mother, and implored Him
who is appeased by penance to deign to spare them,
humbly acknowledging their sins. This they did during
a most severe winter, not only during the day, but by
the light of candles at night. In hundreds and thousands
and tens of thousands, preceded by priests with crosses
and banners, they went from church to church in the
different cities, and humbly prostrated themselves
before the altars. Through the small towns, too, and
the villages went the great processions, so that the very
fields and mountains seemed to re-echo with the voices
of those who cried on the Lord. For the time the strains
of secular music were hushed, and the lays of love were
heard not. Alone in city and village alike resounded
the mournful lamentation of the penitents, moving
hearts of stone and drawing tears from the eyes of the
most hardened. Women too, as well, noble matrons
and delicate maids as the women of the people practised

---

[1] Cf. Ann. Scheftlar. min., ap. M. G. SS., xvii, 344 ; Ann. Mellicenses,
ap. ib., ix, an. 1260 ; Mem. Potestat. Reg., ap. R. I. SS., viii, 1121. Cf.
I. Herford, " The Confraternities of Penitence," ap. Eng. Hist. Rev.,
vol. vi, Oct., 1891, p. 646 ff.

this penance in private." At first, at any rate, the most gratifying moral results followed this extraordinary outburst of mortification. " Those at enmity with each other were almost all reconciled,[1] usurers and robbers returned their ill-gotten gains. Men sunk in sin humbly confessed their iniquities,[2] and amended their lives. The prisons were opened, captives released, and exiles allowed to return to their own homes."

This sudden display of penance, which spread beyond the borders of Italy, set all men wondering, says our worthy chronicler, whence it arose. It derived not its origin, he continues, from the authority of the Supreme Pontiff, nor from the eloquence of a Preacher. It took its origin from some simple man who was inspired by the Holy Ghost who breatheth where He will.[3]

Oberto Pallavicini, however, says Salimbene,[4] " who was then lord of Cremona, avoided this blessing and devotion along with his fellow citizens of Cremona . . . And He set up a gallows by the bank of the Po, in order that if any were to bring across this custom of scourging they might die on the gibbet."[5] Manfred also kept the Flagellants out of his dominions, and both the monk of Padua and he of Parma (Salimbene) assure us that they did so for fear of losing their tyrannical authority. For, says the former, " the joy and security of tyrants spring from the discord of citizens. As the fish delights in the whirlpool, so they revel in the dissensions of their people."[6]

Pallavicini and Manfred discourage the Flagellants.

---

[1] *Cf.* Jacob. de Varag., *Chron. Jan.*, ap. *R. I. SS.*, ix, pp. 49–50.

[2] Salimbene, *Chron.*, p. 465, notes that the priests had barely time to eat as so many wished to confess their sins.

[3] *Mon. Pat., Chron.*, ap. *R. I. SS.*, viii, pp. 712–13.   [4] *L.c.*

[5] *Cf. Chron. Parm.*, ap. *R. I. SS.*, ix, pt. ix new ed., p. 22 ; and the Ghibelline *Chron. de rebus*, p. 250.

[6] *Mon. Pat. Chron., l.c.*, p. 714 : " Suspecta sunt quippe Tyrannis opera pietatis ; tam male agentibus omnino sunt lucis opera odiosa." This practice of flagellation soon degenerated and had to be stopped by ecclesiastical authority.

Manfred was now at the height of his power and influence in Italy, and he had, moreover, recently strengthened his position by marrying Helen, the daughter of Michael II., despot of Epirus (June 2, 1259). With the dowry which she brought him, he secured a hold over a portion of the eastern side of the Adriatic, i.e., over a strip of coast opposite Corcyra, including at least the cities of Belgrado and Valona (Aulon).[1] Furthermore, strong at home in the support of the Saracens of Lucera and their *gossips* (compatres) the German mercenaries,[2] Manfred did not scruple to come to an understanding with a Moslem who was to prove himself one of the most formidable enemies of the Christian name—with Bibars Bondochar (or Beibars Bandukdary, 1260–77), the once one-eyed slave who founded the dynasty of the Mameluke Sultans of Egypt. This able founder of a line which lasted 250 years, set himself to complete the destruction of the Christians in the Holy Land, and to arrest the progress of the dreaded Tartars. To accomplish his former purpose he strove to make alliances with Christians in the West in order that he might be able to act through them against their brethren. Owing to Manfred's attachment to his Saracen troops and his enmity to the Pope, he was regarded by the wily Sultan as a likely friend. Bibars, accordingly, sent him an embassy of which the chief was the historian

---

[1] *Cf.* Saba, ii, c. 4, etc. ; Barth. de Neo., c. 6, ap. *R. I. SS.*, xiii, p. 1019 ; Sanudo, *Istorie del Regno di Romania*, p. 107 ed. Hopf. *Cf.* Miller, *The Latins in the Levant*, pp. 109, 514 ; Gardner, *The Lascarids*, pp. 242–4. Unfortunately Huillard-Bréholles, *Recherches sur l'hist. des Normands*, cannot safely be followed as a guide to the career of Manfred because he relies too much on *authorities* which have since been proved to be forgeries, such as the *Anonymous of Trani*, and especially Matteo di Giovenazzo.

[2] *Jamsilla*, p. 562. To-day also (Jan., 1917) the Germans are *gossips* with equal enemies of civilization and Christianity—the unspeakable Turk.

Gemal-eddin. The historian's account of his visit to Manfred has been preserved by his pupil Abulfeda († 1331). "Manfred," says Gemal-eddin, "received me with kindness, and premitted me to remain with him in Apulia. I observed that he possessed many accomplishments, and a natural taste for the intellectual sciences . . . Not far from Barletta, the city in which I lived, was Lucera, a city wholly peopled by Moslems whom Frederick had brought from Sicily. Islamism was there openly practised, and the Friday was duly observed. The greater part of Manfred's officials were Moslems . . . When I left him, the brother of the King of France and the Pope, who is, as it were, the caliph of the Franks, were leagued against him. The Pope had excommunicated him on the charge of being favourable to the Moslems, and it was for the same reason that his father, Frederick II., and his brother Conrad, had been excommunicated." [1] Outside the Kingdom, however, and outside such places in Italy as he had in his actual possession, Manfred's power in the peninsula was not really great; for at this period, more than ever before, was Italy splitting up into small states that had no real concern for any interests other than their own. If therefore either Guelfs or Ghibellines in any locality found it convenient, neither party scrupled to ask the aid of the other,[2] or to do anything rather than have a powerful overlord.

[1] Ap. Michaud, *Bib. des Croisades*, iv, p. 482. The words of Djamal-ad-Din-ibn-Wasil, as our envoy's name is there spelt, are better given in Blochet's translation of Makrizi's *Hist. d'Égypte*, p. 374 f., note. On Bibars see S. L. Poole, *A hist. of Egypt*, p. 262 ff., and Muir, *The Mameluke Dynasty of Egypt*, p. 13 ff.

[2] Gregorovius, *Rome*, v, pt. ii, p. 339, in speaking of all patriotic Italians fixing their hopes on Manfred as a national king is reading nineteenth century history into thirteenth. It would be almost as reasonable to say now that all patriotic Africans are pining for Africa for the Africans.

Though this is true, it is equally true that the battle of Montaperti,

"The slaughter and the great havoc . . .

That coloured Arbia's flood with crimson stain," [1] was felt by the Guelfs generally to be a disaster to their cause ; and that by the Ghibellines, it was hailed with profound satisfaction. The Guelf refugees from Florence and the other Tuscan cities, quite driven to despair by their defeat, thought of obtaining help even from Conradin. They sent envoys to Germany, and offered to support the boy against his false uncle, Manfred, in return for aid given to them (1261). His mother, however, declared that the boy was not yet old enough to leave her, but that, as she was greatly incensed against the rebel Manfred, he should march to their help in due course. Meanwhile, as an earnest of his coming, they received his mantle lined with miniver, which on their return was displayed by the envoys to the people in the Church of St. Friano at Lucca.[2]

Alexander had, meanwhile, renewed the excommunication already pronounced against Manfred, and formerly excommunicated the Sienese and his other open supporters in Tuscany.[3] He moreover excommunicated all the bishops who had taken part in Manfred's coronation,[4] and, somewhat later (c. February, 1261), severely called to task the Pisans for entering into friendly negotiations with Manfred after the Guelf defeat.[5]

---

[1] Dante, *Inf.*, x.

[2] G. Villani, *Cron.*, viii, c. 84. ap. *R. I. SS.*, xiii ; Ptolemy of Lucca, *Annales*, an. 1262, ap. *ib.*, xi ; and especially the letter of the Florentines to Conradin and his answer, ap. C. de Cherrier, *Hist. de la lutte des Papes et des Empereurs*, ii, p. 508 ff. In the former letter mention is made of Manfred's Saracen, German, and *Greek* troops. In Conradin's answer he speaks of proceeding " especially against Manfred, formerly Prince of Taranto ". His letter is dated May 8, 1261.

[3] *Cf. supra*, p. 34 ; Potthast, 17969, Nov. 18, 1260.

[4] Pipinus, *Chron.*, iii, c. 5, ap. *R. I. SS.*, ix, p. 678.

[5] Potthast, 18055, Feb.-March, 1261.

But neither his actions nor his words produced any effect
on Siena or Pisa. On March 28, 1261, these two cities,
along with the now Ghibelline Florence, formed a league
with Volterra, S. Gemignano and other towns against
Lucca and the Florentine Guelf exiles.[1]

However, the defeat at Montaperti would appear
to have aroused for a moment the English claimant
to the Sicilian throne. " Edmund, by God's grace,
King of Sicily," sent his greetings to the people " of our
Kingdom ", informed them of his concern for their good,
and bade them receive him readily into the Kingdom.[2]
Further letters informed the world at large that he had
appointed certain proctors to receive the Kingdom in
his name,[3] and begged the Pope to continue his favour
to him as he would ever be obedient to him and to " our
mother the Church ".[4]

But more was needed than words against Manfred, Death of
and even these now failed Alexander. Further Alexander.
measures against the usurper were left to be taken by
Alexander's successor; for one of the consequences of
the defeat of Montaperti seems to have been a weakening
of the vital powers of the Pope. At any rate, on May 25,
1261, Alexander died at Viterbo, whither he had gone
a week or two before to avoid the summer heat of Rome.[5]
He was buried in the Cathedral of St. Lawrence in that
quaint old city of fountains, Viterbo,[6] but hitherto
all attempts to find any remains of his tomb have failed.[7]

---

[1] Archiv. di Siena, n. 739, cited by Gregorovius and Balan.

[2] Ep. of March 20, 1261, ap. Rymer, i, 720.

[3] Ep. of March 21, 1261, ib., p. 721.   [4] Ep., date, ib.

[5] Cf. the letter of Urban IV. to the archbishop of Rheims, etc.,
Sept., 1261, Potthast, n. 18133.

[6] Ricobald. Ferr., Hist. P.P., ap. R. I. SS., ix, p. 180. Cf. Regist.
d.Urbain IV., t. ii, n. 1, p. 2 ed. Guiraud.

[7] Cf. Acta SS., Propyl. Maii, p. 50**, and Cristofori, Le tombe dei Papi
in Viterbo, Siena, 1887, p. 277 ff., for the vain efforts that have been
made from time to time to find the tomb of Alexander IV.

CHAPTER III.

THE CITY OF ROME AND ITS SENATOR, BRANCALEONE.

The Senator Brancaleone. Of the six and a half years during which Alexander's pontificate lasted, he only passed about one and a half years altogether in Rome. He spent three winters there, those of 1255–6, 1256–7, and 1260–1. This was due to the unsatisfactory nature of his relations with the Senator, Brancaleone degli Andalò. In 1252, this able and energetic citizen of Bologna had, as we have seen,[1] been chosen Senator for three years by the Romans, in the hope that a stranger might bring them peace. In many ways, Brancaleone made just the kind of Senator that the turbulent Romans required. He curbed the insolence of the nobles, who in their lofty towers set the law at defiance ; and, during the reign of Innocent IV., he strove hard to keep that pontiff in residence in Rome, as he found that the presence of the Pope meant prosperity to the city. While, however, he wanted the Popes to reside in Rome, he did not desire that they should have any power therein, and he moreover favoured their enemies, Conrad and Manfred.

Of his behaviour towards Alexander, we can form an idea from the letter which that Pope wrote to him from Anagni (July 7, 1255). The Pontiff pointed out that it was illegal for him to seize papal servants and messengers when they went to the city on the Pope's business, and then to force them to serve in the army

---

[1] *Supra*, vol. xiv, p. 139 f. " Item quello anno (1252) misser Branchaliom dei Andaluò fu ellecto senatore de Roma." *Corpus. chron. Bonon.*, ap. *R. I. SS.*, t. xviii, pt. i, p. 131 new ed. He was chosen by the Romans " ad eorum voluntatem pro suo salario vi m. (arks) pro mense." *Ib.*, p. 132. *Cf.* Mat. Par., v, 358.

or in some civil capacity. He accordingly impresses " on his nobility " that he must not, from respect to him (pro reverentia nostra) cause certain of his servants whom he names to be interfered with in the manner mentioned.[1]

Whether Brancaleone gave heed to the Pope and discontinued the illegal practices alleged against him, does not appear to be known, and, in any case, the Senator was soon after this deposed from his office.

The Popes were therefore, under the circumstances, not too eager to live in the city. Alexander did not visit it till towards the close of November, 1255, when the three years rule of the foreign Senator had come to a violent end. According to William of Nangis, in consequence of an agreement between the cardinals and the nobility, the Senator was attacked in the Capitol. Compelled to surrender, he apparently gave himself up to the people, who at first imprisoned him in the Septizonium. Later on, however, they handed him over to the nobility, who shut him up in the historic Tower of Passerano, a castle of the Roman Campagna, which, resting on a very ancient foundation, and springing from an isolated rock, dominates the country on the Via Labicana some eighteen miles from Rome.[2] Here he was badly treated, and we are assured that he would have been killed but for the action of his brave wife, Galliana de' Savioli. She made her way to Bologna, and told its people how their fellow-citizen was being

He is imprisoned, 1255.

---

[1] Ep. ap. Rod., iii, n. 403, p. 361.

[2] Will. of Nangis, *Gesta Ludovic. IX.*, ap. *M. G. SS.*, xxvi, p. 638. " Populus posuit eum in custodia apud Septemsoles. Tandem traditus nobilibus in quodam castro S. Pauli quod dicitur Passavant (i.e., no doubt Passerano) fuit incaceratus et male tractatus." *Cf.* Mat. Par., v, 547 ; 563–4. It is unfortunate that with regard to the career of Brancaleone we are so dependent on the narratives of writers at a distance from Rome, especially on the confused narrative of Matthew Paris. On Passerano see Tomasetti, *La Campagna Romana*, iii, 506 ff.

treated. They, accordingly, put under stricter guard
the hostages whom they had received from Rome as
pledges of the security of Brancaleone. Nor was it
to any purpose that Bologna was laid under an interdict
for refusing to give up the hostages. The Bolognese
declared that they would endure it till their countryman
was delivered to them safe and sound.[1]

A new Senator. Brancaleone is released, 1256. The imprisonment of the Senator did not bring peace
to the city. The people were constantly fighting with
the nobility on his behalf, and at length procured his
release [2] (c. August, 1256). Meanwhile, however, a
new Senator had been elected. A Milanese, one Martin
della Torre, who was first chosen, declined the risky
honour, and it was bestowed on Manuello (Emmanuel)
de' Maggi or de Madiis of Brescia who had once been
podestà of Genoa. [3] This, seemingly, was in the spring
of 1256, and as we have seen Brancaleone was liberated
a few months later.

The new Senator is slain, and Brancaleone is recalled, 1257. The new Senator seems to have been quite unable
to preserve the peace of the city. According to Paris,
he was at the beck of the nobles, and devoted himself
to please them, especially the Annibaldi, and to oppressing
and impoverishing the people at their instigation. This
led to risings of the people; and as they were now
organized in guilds, and were well led by an Englishman,
one Matthew of Belvoir, a master-baker, their revolt was
successful. Manuello was slain, the Pope forced to leave
the city, and Brancaleone was re-elected Senator (c. May,
1257).[4]

[1] Ib.

[2] Mat. P., v, p. 573. A description of the fighting in 1256 is given by
some Sienese merchants to their Podestà, Rufino de Mandello. They
tell of the taking of the Poli (Torre dei Conti) and other towers.
Ap. Gregorovius, Rome, v, p. 321 n.

[3] Galvanus Flamma, Manipulus Florum, c. 290, ap. R. I. SS., xi,
p. 685 ; Ann. Genuen., l. vi, an. 1243, ap. R. I. SS., vi, p. 501.

[4] P. Cantinelli, Chron., " Eo anno (1257) reelectus fuit d.
Branchaleo de Andalo senator urbis Romæ." Cf. W. de Nangis,

It was not, however, very easy for him to re-enter the city, as ambushes were laid for him by the Church party. Nevertheless, he succeeded in his object (May 30, 1257), and then proceeded to take vengeance on his enemies.[1] He began systematically to destroy their towers and the strongholds into which they had converted many of the monuments of antiquity.[2] He is credited with destroying a hundred and forty of the towers of the nobles who were opposed to him.[3] But, as he spared a tower belonging to the Orsini,[4] we may conclude that not all the nobles were arrayed against him. Nor was the Senator content with levelling towers. He imprisoned some of their owners, exiled others, and even killed or mutilated others. Among those whom he killed, were two of the Annibaldi, nephews of cardinal Richard Annibaldi of Molaria, cardinal-deacon of St. Angelo.[5] Excommunicated with his adherents by Alexander, the Senator merely sent back word that, by an ancient privilege, the Senator could not be excommunicated. He even went so far, if we can trust Matthew Paris in all this, as to say that he would persecute the Pope himself and his cardinals even unto death.[6] The same

Gesta Ludov. IX., ap. *M. G. SS.*, xxvi, 644 ; and *Annales Ubervetani*, ap. *R. I. SS.*, t. xv, p. 129 new ed. The account in Mat. Par., v, 662, of these proceedings is inaccurate.

[1] W. de N., *ib.*

[2] Mat. P., v, 699, 709 ; W. de N., *l.c.* By the fourteenth century writer, Johannes Cabbalini de Cerronibus, he is credited with having destroyed the temple of Quirinus on the Quirinal. See his *Polistoria* ap. Urlichs, *Codex Urb. Rom. Topog.*, p. 144. And in harmony with this, we read that in 1348 the grand staircase leading to the Church of S. Maria Aracœli was built of marble taken from this temple. *Cf.* Rodocanachi, *Les Monuments de Rome*, p. 25.

[3] Mat. P., v, 699 and 709.

[4] W. de N., *l.c.*

[5] Mat. Par., v, 662, 664, and 699. The Colosseum was for a time in the hands of the Annibaldi.

[6] *Ib.*, pp. 662 and 664.

none too trustworthy authority goes on to assert that Brancaleone called upon the people to take up arms for the destruction of Anagni, " the birthplace of the Pope." Hearing of this, the people of the threatened city sent word to Alexander of what the Senator was going to do to his birthplace, and urged him to have pity upon his friends and relations. Thus adjured, Alexander felt compelled to humble himself, and to beg Brancaleone to spare Anagni " the city of his nativity ", lest he should incur the reproach of all mankind.[1] Considering, however, that Anagni was not the Pope's birthplace, it would seem that this story is another morsel of that large amount of unfounded gossip with which Paris has encumbered the pages of his " Greater Chronicle ".

Whether this is so or not, there is no reason to doubt the statement of Paris that Brancaleone restored " peace and tranquillity to Rome, and that the robbers whom they call ' bedeweri ' were dispersed as well as the malefactors both in Rome and in its vicinity." [2]   It seems also certain that, during the time that Brancaleone held office, Alexander had as much power in Rome as he had representation of any kind on the Senator's coins. These show, on the obverse, the Senator's name with S.P.Q.R. round the edge, with a lion *statant gardant* in the centre, and on the reverse the words Roma caput Mundi round the edge, and in the centre *Rome* seated wearing the senatorial crown and mantle, and holding the globe in her right hand and a palm in her left.

The death of Brancaleone: a new Senator, 1258. Not very much appears to be known about the second senatorial rule of Brancaleone. He was taken ill at the siege of Corneto, and was carried back to Rome where he died not long after, perhaps in April, 1258.[3] The Romans, says Paris, placed his head in a costly vase, and solemnly

---

[1] *Ib.*, p. 664.   [2] *Ib.*, p. 709.

[3] W. de N., *l.c. Cf. Chron. Bonon.*, ap. *R. I. SS.*, t. xviii, pt. i, p. 146 new ed.

placed it as a relic on a marble pillar "in memory of his valour and probity" [1] and then proceeded to the election of a new Senator. Disregarding a message from the Pope not to elect anyone as Senator without his consent, they followed the last instructions of Brancaleone, and elected his uncle, Castellano di Andalò. [2]

As in the case of his nephew, Castellano was elected Senator for three years. But he was either not so strong a man as his nephew or not so popular. At any rate, a party was formed against him, and two new Senators were elected, Napoleone di Matteo Rosso, an Orsini, the one seemingly whose tower was spared by Brancaleone, and Riccardo di Pietro, one of the Annibaldi. [3] Raising a force from among the lower orders in Rome (de mediocribus Romanis), the two Senators attacked Castellano, who fled to the castle of Sant Angelo (April, 1259). There, relying on the hostages which he had in Bologna, Castellano offered a stout resistance, while the Romans seized his family. [4] One result of the Flagellant movement in Rome was that the Romans set the late Senator's family at liberty (autumn, 1260). With them Castellano secretly fled to his native city of Bologna. [5]

When he returned home, Castellano did not let bygones be bygones; but, unmindful of the release of his own family by the Romans, succeeded in persuading the authorities of Bologna to refuse to send back the Roman hostages. Pope Alexander himself then took the matter up; and, on the continued refusal of the Bolognese to release the hostages, laid an interdict on their city,

The deposition of the new Senator, 1259.

Castellano causes trouble about the hostages, 1259–61.

---

[1] *Chron.*, v, 723.

[2] *Ib. Cf. Chron. Bon., l.c.* " E in quelo anno morì messere Branchalione d'Andalò . . . e alora li Romani tolseno mesere Castelano d'Andalò per 3 anni." He had been Podestà of Fermo, *ib.*, p. 147.

[3] With Mat. Par., v, 743. *Cf.* Potthast, n. 17579.

[4] *Cf.* Mat. P., *l.c.*, with the *Chron. Bonon., l.c.*, pp. 148 and 151.

[5] *Chron. Bonon., ib.*

and either directly forbade its Professors to continue
their lectures or deprived them of their right to teach.[1]
It was this last blow that broke the obstinacy of the civic
authorities, as it put an end to University life. The
students left the city, and the professors complained that
they could not continue their work.[2]

The Bolognese gave way at last, and in 1261 cardinal
Octavian was sent to their city solemnly to remove
the interdict.[3]

.The suc-
cessors of
the Andalòs.

Although Alexander was now free from the oppression
of the Andalòs, his difficulties with the Roman people
or their Senators had not come to an end. However
anxious the Romans might be about freedom for themselves,
they had no concern for the freedom of others, and were
as desirous as ever of forcing their less powerful neighbours
to acknowledge their suzerainty. Even the new Senators,
Napoleon Orsini and Annibaldi (1259–60), pursued
the same aggressive policy as their predecessors. Tivoli
was compelled by them to pay tribute to Rome as a
vassal city, and to receive its chief magistrate from it.[4]
They also endeavoured to force similar conditions upon
Terracina, but Alexander impressed upon its people that
they must be true to their oath of fidelity to the Roman
Church, and that they must not obey the Senators in
anything which appertained to the Government of their
city. At the same time, he gave them power to choose

[1] " La citade de Bologna era stata intradita delle messe e
privata del Studio e partito gli chierici e così stete piu d'uno anno."
Ib., pp. 157–8. *Cf.* p. 148.

[2] See the complaint of the famous legist Odofredus, *Ad fin. Comment.
in II. Cod. Part.*, cited by Tiraboschi, *Storia della lett. Ital.*, iv, p. 50.
He says he was late in beginning his book " propter interdictum hujus
civitatis, quæ erat interdicta occasione obsidum quos habebat d.
Castellanus de Andalò ".

[3] " In quelo anno mesere Ottaviano cardinale vene in Bologna per
li ostadexi di Romany . . . ed elo tolse via lo'ntradito." *Ib.*, p. 157.

[4] Gregorovius, *Rome*, v, 329.

as their magistrates any who were devoted to the
Roman Church, even if they did not belong to their
own city.[1]

But the Senators did not abandon their determination
to subject Terracina to their authority ; and this determination was upheld by the successors of Orsini and
Annibaldi, by John Savelli and Annibaldo Annibaldi
(1260–1), even though the latter was a nephew of
Alexander himself. This we learn from a letter addressed
to them from Anagni by the Pope (April, 1260) in which
he urged them to cease to molest Terracina and its
inhabitants.[2]

Savelli and Annibaldi, 1260–1.

Alexander would appear to have come to an understanding with these two Senators. At any rate he
returned to Rome during their year of office, and did
not leave it till he had quietened a serious disturbance
which followed their retirement from their position.
This was according, as it seems, to the custom at this
period, about Easter, April 24, 1261. The disturbance
was caused by the ambition of two Kings, of Richard
of Cornwall, King of the Romans, and Manfred, King
of Sicily. The former felt that his title as King of
Germany and future Emperor would be greatly helped
if he could become Senator of Rome, and that, with such
a position, he would be able to help his nephew, Edmund,
to make good his claim to the crown of Sicily. Manfred,
naturally also perceived that he would be in a still stronger
position against his English rival if he could secure the
Senatorship for himself. Richard relied as usual on
his money, and in this case, also on such influence as
he had in Rome through the presence of the English
cardinal John *Tolet* or *of Toledo* (cardinal 1244–† 1275).

Disputed election for the Senator-ship, 1261.

---

[1] Ep. May 18, 1259, ap. Potthast, n. 17579. The full names of the
Senators were Napoleon " Matthæi Rubei " and Richard " Petri de
Anninbaldo ".

[2] Potthast, n. 17826.

The *White* cardinal[1] spared no pains and money to
advance Richard's cause.   He declared that he not only
gave away or sold the silver vessels that were necessary
for his household, but had even borrowed money at
ruinous interest on the security of a convent which he
had built in the city.[2]   Richard's candidature was
nominally at least successful.   He was duly informed
that he had been elected Senator.[3]   But another party
favoured Manfred, and such disturbances arose in the
city that " no one was safe even in his own house ".[4]
Alexander intervened through the instrumentality of
James Pantaleon, Patriarch of Jerusalem, who was
destined to be his immediate successor, and who found
some means of putting an end to the disorders.   What
those means were our authorities do not tell us.[5]   It
would seem, however, that some compromise was effected ;
at any rate, neither Richard nor Manfred ever exercised
any Senatorial power, though Manfred continued to
press his candidature.

Alexander attends to local needs.   If Alexander never had much peace in Rome, he
contrived during his comparatively brief residence
therein, to attend to some local matters.   A mutilated
document in the *Liber Censuum*,[6] shows us that the roof
of the Lateran palace in general, and of the treasury
department of it in particular stood in need of repair.

---

[1] So called from his white Cistercian habit.

[2] See his letter to Henry III., an. 1261, ap. Rymer, i, 728–9. " Con-
trahendo mutuum non modicum sub maxima voragine usurarum."

[3] See the letter of the Commune of Rome to Richard. *Regesta Imp.*,
v, n. 14155.

[4] *Cf.* the poetical life of Urban IV by the contemporary, Thierry of
Vaucouleurs (Theodericus Vallicoloris), ap. *R. I. SS.*, iii, pt. ii, p. 408.

[5] " Compatiens (the patriarch of Jerusalem) igitur tamquam pastor
pius Urbi,
Invenit varias pacificacando vias.
Urbis majores mandat, pacique priori
Urbem restituit Pax venit, ira tacet." *Ib.*

[6] i, p. 592 ed. Fabre.

It appears that a Roman citizen, one Lawrence, known as " Cardinalis ", undertook the repairs. But although the document mentions the cleaning of spouts, and of some return to be made by the treasurer for the work, nothing more, unfortunately, can be gathered from it.[1]

The same *Liber Censuum* has preserved another document issued by this Pope at Anagni in the month of August, 1259.[2] It set forth that, as the souls of the faithful departed cannot themselves advance their salvation, it is natural that they should be helped by our prayers ; and accordingly laid it down that Masses should be said every year on September 5 by the Pope and the cardinals for the souls of the Popes and cardinals who had gone before them. Moreover, the Pope was on the same day to provide food for 200 poor people, and each cardinal for twenty-five. Further, on the death of a Pope, the cardinals were to sing a solemn requiem Mass, and were each of them to provide food for fifty poor, " for the soul of the deceased pontiff." The Pope and the surviving cardinals were to do much the same for the repose of the soul of a cardinal.

Masses and alms for deceased Popes and cardinals.

This last obligation cannot have weighed very heavily either on Alexander himself or on the cardinals, for during his reign there were not ten cardinals altogether. Moreover, " for fear of scandal," as he is reported to have said,[3] he would not, " though he had the plenitude of

Alexander does not create any cardinals.

---

[1] " Quia camerarius promisit propter hoc servitium dare unam vidandam (?) . . ." *Ib.* This document has escaped the notice of Lauer, *Le Palais de Latran.* The repairs were continued by Urban IV. " Hinc Lateranensem reparari fecit in Urbe
Aulam, cujus erat tecta ruina minans." Theodoric, *Vita,* p. 38, ed. Assier.

[2] Not 1265 as in Fabre's note 1, p. 585. *Cf.* Mat. Par., v, 491, who makes Alexander do in this matter for the *wicked* Innocent IV. what he really did for Popes in general.

[3] *Mon. Patav. Chron.,* p. 715. It is to be hoped, however, that he did not say such a foolish thing.

power," create any new cardinals. This was because
one party among the cardinals favoured government by
strong measures (" ædificare Sion in sanguinibus "),
and the other was averse to the shedding of blood.
Accordingly, not wishing to favour either party, says
the monastic chronicler of Padua, Alexander refused
to name any cardinals at all.[1] This policy of Alexander,
the outcome of some weakness of mind, or of will, or of
both, helped to bring about not imaginary scandal as
he feared but real scandal. When the important power
of electing a Pope fell into the hands of a few, the possibility of corruption prevailing among them was naturally
greatly increased. It is easier for designing people
unduly to influence a few, either by direct or indirect
bribery or by working on party or family or national
feelings, than it is for them to so affect a comparatively
large number. And the history of the elections of the
Popes serves clearly to illustrate the great evils arising
from elections of paramount importance being left in
the hands of a few.

Nor will he
decide be-
tween the
rival candi-
dates for the
Empire.

Alexander's timidity of character caused almost
as much mischief to the Empire as to the Papacy.
Although each of the candidates for the Empire, Richard,
duke of Cornwall, and Alfonso, King of Castile,
endeavoured by his ambassadors to obtain the verdict
of the Pope in his favour,[2] Alexander would not act.
" Unwilling to favour either candidate lest perchance
the peace of the Church should be troubled," he pretended
to deliberate on the matter, but would not give a decision.[3]

---

[1] *Ib.*

[2] *Cf. Chron. rythm. Golon. fragmenta,* p. 313 ed. Holder Egger, ap.
Chron. reg. Colon. Chron.; Pont. et imp., ap. *M. G. SS.,* xxiv, p. 216 ;
Mon. Pat. Chron., ap. *R. I. SS.,* viii, p. 697. However, Alexander went
so far as to express his preference for Richard as Emperor to all other
Princes. *Cf.* ep. March 14, 1259, ap. Potthast, 17512 ; and epp. of
Apr. 30, *ib.* 17549-50.

[3] *Mon. Pat., l.c.*

Not merely did he lose influence by this weakness, but
the Empire became weaker by its resources being
plundered [1] and, pending the confirmation by the Pope
of the more powerful prince, anarchy spread apace
in Germany.

[1] " Post mortem imperatoris Friderici (II.), imperii res quas quilibet
dominorum poterat confiscavit." *Chron. Colmar.*, p. 46, ap. Böhmer,
Fontes, ii. This seizing of the imperial property went on still more after
the departure of Conrad IV. from Germany. Towns too seized imperial
rights. The *Annals of Worms*, an. 1257, ap. *ib.*, p. 190, tell of such a
seizure by Oppenheim which Richard had to sanction, and which had
to hold good: " si potior rex a d. Papa confirmatus superveniret medio
tempore." *Cf. ib.*, an. 1258, p. 191, for a confederation of Worms and
Spires against any King except on certain conditions.

CHAPTER IV.

THE BRITISH ISLES.

Sources.—Before the pontificate of Alexander IV. terminated, the *Chronica Majora* of Matthew Paris unfortunately came to a close (1259). Despite his deep prejudices and his inaccuracy when dealing with foreign affairs, Matthew Paris was one of the best historians of the thirteenth century, if only because of the width of his interests. His *Chronicle* is full, and keeps us in touch with what was going on abroad. He was followed by a number of authors whose horizon was in every way more limited than that of the monk whose work they more or less directly continued. The most direct continuations of Paris were the *Flores Historiarum* of a supposed *Matthew of Westminster*, and the *Chronicle* generally assigned to Rishanger. The former was the work, first of " a certain brother " of the abbey of St. Albans, who tells us at the end of the *Chronicle* of Paris that he continued his work (to 1265), though he was not worthy to loose the latchet of his shoe [1] ; secondly (to 1307) of an equally anonymous monk of Westminster [2] ; and then (to 1325) of another monk of the same abbey (Robert of Reading). The *Flores Hist.*, a comparatively scanty record of facts, at first (to 1265) in sympathy with the barons, and then royalist in the hands of the Westminster monks, has been edited by H. R. Luard in 3 vols., R. S.[3] Robert of Reading is pompous and obscure, and is, moreover, a strong partisan, showing no little anti-papal and anti-Dominican bias.

William Rishanger, the other supposed continuator of the *Chronicle* of Matthew Paris, became himself a monk of St. Albans

---

[1] " Quod autem amodo appositum est (after the conclusion of the work of Paris in 1259) . . . cuidam alteri fratri sit ascribendum, qui tanti prædecessoris opera præsumens aggredi, indigne prosecuturus, eum non sit dignus ejusdem corrigiam solvere calciamenti." Mat. Par. *Chron.*, v, 748 n.

[2] This continuation at Westminster caused it to ascribed to be an imaginary *Matthew of W.*

[3] C. D. Yonge has translated the *Flowers of Hist.* to 1307 in 2 vols., London, 1853, Bohn's series.

in 1271, and was sixty-two years of age in 1312. It is certain that he was an historian, but it is not quite certain what histories should be placed to his credit. In the edition of Rishanger there are printed under his name a *Chronicle* from 1259–1306 ; *Annals of the Kingdom of Scotland* (1291–2) ; *Annals of England and Scotland* (1292–1300) ; and a number of fragments dealing with Edward I. The *Chronicle* assigned to him in the edition of J. O. Halliwell (Camden Society)[1] is now generally quoted as the *Narratio (or Chronicon) de bellis apud Lewes et Evesham*. It is a wordy production in the interest of the barons, and is generally acknowledged to be Rishanger's work, as also is the first of the unimportant fragments on Edward I. It is, however, more than probable that the *Chronicle* (1259–1306) is not from the pen of Rishanger, but was compiled after the year 1323, and hence is not of first-rate importance. Nor is there sufficient reason for ascribing the *Annals* to him. At one time, also, equally without good reason, a *Chronica S. Albani* (1259–96), edited by Riley as *Opus Chronicorum*,[2] was ascribed to Rishanger. It is a useful work and was drawn up by a monk of St. Albans at the command of Abbot John (1301–8). It was one of the links in that long chain of works, written at St. Albans, which recorded the history of our country from the twelfth to the fifteenth century.

John de Tayster or Taxter, a monk of Bury St. Edmunds and, like the monks of St. Albans, well disposed to Simon de Montfort, may also be regarded as a continuator of Matthew Paris, inasmuch as his chronicle seems to be original from about 1258 till the year when it ceases (1265). His work has not yet been published in its entirety ; but its brief original portion was first published by Thorpe as a continuation of Florence of Worcester (Eng. Hist. Soc.), and, as Bartholomew of Cotton incorporated that portion of Tayster's work, it may be read in Luard's edition of that author, London, 1859, *R. S.*, pp. 137–40.

With regard to the Barons' Wars, we may note a brief account by a monk of Battle Abbey first printed by C. Bémont, *Simon de Montfort*, p. 373 ff., Paris, 1884. For the same events the London chronicles are useful. The *Annals of St. Paul's at London*, ap. *M. G. SS.*, xxviii, present to us the work of a contemporary, often of an eyewitness, from 1250–74. Under the name of

---

[1] It has also been edited by H. T. Riley in Walsingham's (?) *Upodigma Neustriæ*, London, 1876, *R. S.*

[2] Ap. J. de Trokelowe, *R. S.*, pp. 3–59.

De antiquis legibus liber, Stapleton edited for the Camden Society a *Chronicle of the Mayors and Sheriffs of London (Cronica majorum et vicecomitum Londoniarum)* from 1188–1274. It was compiled by Arnold of Fitz-Thedmar, an alderman of the city († 1275), who favoured the King against the Barons. There is a translation of it by H. T. Riley, London, 1863. Of much less value is the *Chroniques de London,* 1259–1343 (Camden Soc., 1844), translated in three little volumes by Ed. Goldsmid, Edinburgh, 1885 f. It is the same as *The French Chronicle of London* printed by H. T. Riley at the end of his *Chronicles of the Mayors of London.* The *Chronicles* of John of Wallingford of St. Albans (446–1026, to which he added some continuations reaching to the year of his death, † 1258, ap. *M. G. SS.,* xxviii [1]) and of Henry of Silgrave (–1274), London, 1849, Caxton Soc., are of no great value, especially the latter. Of the *Political Songs,* published by Mr. Wright for the Camden Society, many are of historical importance for this period, especially *The Song of Lewes* (Carmen de bello Lewensi) which has been well published separately with a translation by C. L. Kingsford, Oxford, 1890.

In a rather curious book, *The manufacture of historical materiai,* London, 1916, Mr. J. W. Jeudwine justly denounces [2] " the exaggerated language of evil speaking which they (the chroniclers of the thirteenth century) were in the habit of using of all persons in authority ", and he adds with equal justice and discernment : " The abuse of the King or of the Church, the two great agencies for human advance in the Middle Ages, on the authority of unknown men making or repeating statements without proof and without first-hand knowledge, draws away the mind from the study of the causes underlying historical events, and deadens in the student any good instincts or high ideals." [3] The head and front of offending in this matter was Matthew Paris who so greatly intensified, if he did not create, this habit of hurling ill-founded abuse on those in authority, that it almost became a tradition in St. Albans. And, as St. Albans was for many, many years the historical centre of England, the false position in the eyes of many, both in his own times and since, in which Paris' abuse of them has placed the Popes, cannot easily be estimated.

---

[1] J. Stevenson in the " Church hists. of England " series, vol. iii, only translated the first part of this *Chronicle.*

[2] P. 154.   [3] P. 166.

Modern Works.—To those already cited add W. H. Blaauw's *The Barons' War*, London, 1844, or better, London, 1871, " with additions and corrections." The additions, for the most part, are, however, only concerned with heraldry and family history. We have used the edition of 1844.

ALTHOUGH in Alexander's *Register*, perhaps the greatest number of its documents relating to these Isles are concerned with dispensations for *pluralities*, i.e., for the holding by one individual of more than one ecclesiastical living,[1] the most important of his dealings with them turned directly or indirectly on the Sicilian affair. It was the chief cause of the pecuniary relations between England and Rome, and one of the causes of pecuniary difficulties in England itself. These in their turn bred discontent in the country against both the Pope and the King, and finally brought about the rising of the Barons against Henry III., and the interference of Alexander on his behalf.

The Sicilian affair was the source of the most important relations of Alexander with England.

The Pope's Register also shows that, besides an increase in the abuse of pluralities, the abuse of Provisions had not been killed by the adverse decree of Innocent IV. However, it also appears from it that privileges were not unfrequently granted to individuals to lessen the evil of the arbitrary disposal of benefices by the Popes themselves or their agents. Walter, bishop of Durham, for instance, obtained an indult " not to be compelled by any papal legate, not *de latere*, or other nuncio to make

Other relations between the Pope and England.

---

[1] Very often these dispensations were granted because the benefice held did not yield " a living wage ", and not unfrequently to enable the holder to devote time to study. Still it is clear that many were granted merely to gratify friends of the King or of the Pope. Raynald de Sarmineto, described as " papal subdeacon and chaplain ", Alexander's nephew, was rector of SS. Peter and Paul, Trayques, in the diocese of Lincoln. *Cf. Cal. of Papal Registers*, i, 493 ; and on July 28, 1257, Simon, abbot of Langley in the diocese of Norwich, grants an annual pension of 18 marks to Landulph, a kinsman of Alexander. *Cf. ib.*, p. 575.

provision to any one of benefices in his gift without special mandate making mention of this indult ".[1] But, from time to time, not at all often as it seems, Alexander would sweep aside all these and similar privileges by the "notwithstanding" clause. Accordingly, we see him deciding that "notwithstanding" even "the indult by which it is forbidden that an Italian should immediately succeed an Italian in England in prebends or benefices", Master Gregory of Naples, papal subdeacon and chaplain was to succeed to the benefice attached to the church of Wishire held by the late Matthew Vulcan, canon of Naples.[2]

Privileges granted by Alexander. Attention may here be called to one or two of the privileges granted by Alexander, on account of some interesting circumstance connected with them. For instance, on condition of the Cluniac monastery of Pontefract's setting aside a competent portion for a vicar, the Pope granted it the Church of Silkeston to help its revenues, because it was on the high road between England and Scotland, and took care of the numerous travellers and poor that passed by.[3] Then, because Aylmer, bishop-elect of Winchester, is a personage whose name is sometimes met with in these pages, we will record the indult by which, during the Pope's pleasure, he was not to be bound to be consecrated, "inasmuch as he is not thirty years old."[4]

Quarrel between Franciscans and the Benedictines of Bury St. Edmunds, 1257. Finally before entering on the disagreeable question of the money troubles in England caused by the Pope and the King, we will relate an incident which shows

[1] Bliss, *Calendar*, i, p. 310. *Cf.* other such privileges *ib.*, pp. 336, 345; and Alexander's general decrees on the subject of Provisions, ap. Rod., iii, nn. 391–2, p. 349 ff.

[2] *Ib.*, p. 346.

[3] *Ib.*, p. 314. *Cf. ib.*, p. 316, for his confirmation of the grant of a church in Wales to the monastery of St. Mary's in his beloved city of Anagni.

[4] *Ib.*, p. 321.

how the zeal of the friars was not always in accordance
with discretion or even with justice, and had at times
to be curbed by the Popes. Though, from having been
their Protector,[1] Alexander was well disposed towards
the Franciscans, he found it necessary at times to blame
them for imposing upon his goodwill towards them.
A fragment published in the *Monumenta Franciscana* [2]
from the *Registrum Werketone* gives us an instance of
the way in which occasionally they enroached on parochial
or manorial rights.[3] It appears that they had for some
time desired in vain to get a foothold in Bury
St. Edmunds, and, at last (1257), through a privilege [4]
of Alexander IV., were enabled to do so. No sooner
were they in possession than they hastily erected an
altar and " presumed to say mass thereon ", and, despite
the warnings of the monks, continued to do so. The
monks, accordingly, commissioned their agents to drive
out the friars and pull down their buildings. The outraged friars appealed to Rome, and the Pope denouncing
the monks as " sons of disobedience, heretics and
apostates ", ordered that they should be reinstalled.[5]
No sooner, however, was this mandate obeyed, than the
monks again forcibly expelled the friars, and would
appear to have convinced the Pope that the friars were
outraging their privileges. At any rate, on November 9,
Alexander wrote to the Minister and Franciscans of
England bidding them respect the rights of the monastery

---

[1] *Cf.* ep. of Nov., 1257, at Viterbo ap. *Mon. Francisc.*, ii, p. 274, *R. S.*
" Licet . . . ordinem vestram, ex eo potissime quod olim, dum in
minori essemus officio constituti, curæ nostræ fuit ab Apostolica sede
commissus, caritate præcipua diligamus, etc."

[2] Vol. ii, pp. 267–74, *R. S.* Also ap. *Memorials of St. Edmund's
Abbey*, ii, p. 263 ff., *R. S.*

[3] *Cf.* Mat. Par., *Chron.*, an. 1235, iii, 332, *R. S.*

[4] The fragment, p. 268. Alexander alludes to the privilege in the
letter just cited.

[5] *Ib.*, p. 270.

which was under the special protection of the Holy See
so that all scandal might cease.[1] However much he
knew when he wrote this letter, he did not order the
Franciscans to leave the place, and they were again
reinstated. As this restoration was effected by King
Henry III., the monks left the friars in peace for the
moment. But, on the death of Pope Alexander IV.,
whom they called the friars' charioteer,[2] they appealed
to Pope Urban IV. After careful examination of the
affair, Urban gave judgment in favour of the monks.
The friars were ordered to pull down what buildings
they had erected and to depart. Then, says the
Benedictine author of the *Registrum*, the friars came
humbly to the monks, and, confessing the wrong they
had committed, submitted. On this the monks received
them to the kiss of peace, refused to take any compensation, except that of the friars' prayers, for the expenses
to which they had been put, and gave them a piece of land
outside the boundary of the monastery's jurisdiction.
And so, concludes the writer, " where once pastured
brute beasts, faithful souls are now refreshed by the
word of God." [3]

Money
troubles in
England.

Though, therefore, naturally enough, the greater
number of documents that issued from Alexander's
chancery in connexion with the British Isles were
concerned with the granting of privileges and dispensations and with the routine matters of Church government,
such as the election of bishops,[4] and the delimitation
of their dioceses, still a number of them have reference
to matters mainly political. We have seen Pope

---

[1] Ep. cited above.

[2] " Qui fratrum extiterat currus et auriga." *Frag.*, p. 272.

[3] *Ib.*, pp. 273–4. The monk says that he wrote his account in 1263.

[4] The efforts of the King to override canonical elections were often
overcome by the candidates going to the Pope and being consecrated
by him. *Cf. Chron. of Abingdon*, pp. 47 and 48, ed. J. O. Halliwell,
for examples.

Alexander, year after year throughout the whole of his pontificate, calling upon Henry to fulfil the obligations which he took upon himself when he accepted the Kingdom of the two Sicilies for Edmund, and especially to pay the money he had agreed to pay for the prosecution of his son's claims.

But Henry's childish use of money involved him in such pecuniary difficulties that he never had enough to enable him to pay his just debts. He was personally extravagant, and squandered money on Poitevins, Provençals, and Savoyards.[1] Just before Alexander became Pope, a visit which, in most ostentatious style, he paid to St. Louis of France plunged him into still deeper debt. Matthew Paris represents him a month or two after Alexander's election to the papacy as complaining that his debts amounted to " two hundred thousand marks, nay, were I to say three, I should not exceed the bounds of truth . . . I am deceived on all sides . . . The yearly revenue of my son Edward amounts to more than fifteen thousand marks. I have, therefore, to live on money obtained in all quarters, from whomsoever and in what way soever I can acquire it ".[2]

The King's debts.

In the year 1254, then, Henry had much less than no money, and Alexander had soon to complain of an exhausted and insolvent treasury.[3] Money, therefore, was an urgent necessity to both Pope and King, if they were to perform even the ordinary functions of their position ; and so, with a mutual understanding, they proceeded to try to raise it.

---

[1] Cf. Mat. Par., v, 515.

[2] Mat. Par., an. 1255, v, 487–8. Just before this (p. 485) Paris declared that it was reported that his debts amounted " to more than 300,000 marks ".

[3] Cf. epp. of Sept. 18, 1255, and of Feb. 5, 1256, ap. Rymer, i, pp. 564 and 581.

Both the Pope's and Henry's difficulty in obtaining
grants of money arose to a large extent because it was
generally believed that their pecuniary embarrassments
arose from expenditure over the unpopular Sicilian
expedition. The proportion of Henry's debts arising
from this cause would seem to be not far from half of
his entire liabilities. At any rate, Alexander in his
bull of April 9, 1255, in which he enumerates the
conditions upon which Edmund was to have Sicily,
sets down Henry's liabilities in this matter as amounting
to 135,541 marks.[1]

Alexander's
efforts to
raise money
in England.

As most of this money at least had been expended
by Innocent and Alexander in their efforts to recover
the Kingdom of Sicily, relying on reimbursements
from England, Alexander was naturally anxious to
recover it. He accordingly sent officials over to this
country with instructions to collect it, either directly
for the King himself or indirectly by pushing on the
payment of the tithes which had been granted to Henry.[2]
These efforts to raise money resulted in the gravest
discontent against both the Pope and the King, which,
as far as the latter was concerned, ended in the *Provisions
of Oxford*, and civil war.

About the time that he dispatched James, bishop of
Bologna, vice-chancellor of the Roman Church,[3] to

---

[1] Rymer, i, 893 ff. *Cf. ib.*, 584, 587, epp. of Henry of March and Apr.,
1256. *Cf. Ann. de Burton*, p. 349, which speak of 200,000 marks ; and
Mat. Par., v, 623.

[2] A tenth of all the ecclesiastical property of England had been
granted Henry for three years in 1254. *Cf. Ann. de Burton*, p. 325,
ap. *Annal. Monastici*, i, *R. S.* And " by papal decision " ecclesiastical
property was held to apply to " manors and baronies held by
ecclesiastical persons ". *Cf.* ep. of Master Rostand "executor negotii
crucis ", ap. *ib.*, p. 354.

[3] Luard's suggestion (note to the *Chronica Maj.* of Paris, v, 499,
repeated in a note to the *Annals of Burton*, i, 349) that the bishop of
Bologna who invested Edmund was " cardinal Ottaviano Ubaldino,
tit. S. Maria *nova* " (it should have been S. Maria *in via Lata*) has caused

England, to invest the young Edmund with the Kingdom of Sicily by a ring (c. October 18, 1255),[1] Alexander also appears to have sent thither Rostand (or Rustand), " our sub-deacon and chaplain," and the diplomatist, Peter of Aigueblanche, bishop of Hereford, to arrange for the collecting of money. According to the *Annals of Burton*, at any rate, the three reached this country together.[2] Paris, who says that the chaplain was a Gascon by birth,[3] and is very unsparing in his denunciation both of him and of bishop Peter, tells us that they had been sent to collect tithes in England, Scotland, and Ireland for the Pope and for the King, and to absolve Henry from his vow of undertaking an expedition for the Holy Land, provided that he waged war against Manfred.[4] They had, moreover, received power from the Pope to divert to the Sicilian expedition moneys which had been allocated to the Crusade for the Holy Land.[5] " The business of the Kingdom of Sicily," as Alexander declared, was very dear to his heart, and he wished to uproot that noxious weed Manfred " from that so dear and fair garden of the Roman Church ".[6]

---

no little confusion. The bishop in question was Octavian's successor in the see, James, vice-chancellor of the Roman Church. *Cf.* Rymer, i, 573, ep. of Henry, who actually gives the bishop's name. *Cf. ib.*, p. 547, where the comma should be put after " Bononiensis ", and not after " olim ".

[1] *Cf.* Mat. Par., v, 499, 515, 520, 681, 722—a striking instance of the repetitions of Paris. *Cf. Ann. de B.*, p. 349.

[2] Pp. 348–50, and according to the *Annals* of Dunstable, p. 196, that was about Sept. 29.

[3] v, 519.

[4] *Ib. Cf. Ann. de Burton*, pp. 388–9, and epp. of Alex., May 3 and 7, ap. Rymer, i, p. 547 f.

[5] Rymer, i, 551, ep. Alex., May 15, addressed to the archbp. of Canterbury and Rostand. *Cf. Ann. de Burton*, i, 350, for similar papal letters in connexion with Rostand's mission.

[6] *Ib.*, p. 548, ep. May 7. " Pia matris Ecclesiæ studia circa prosecutionem negotii Regni Siciliæ (quod tamquam speciale ac præcipuum

It was dear to his heart, for it was a matter of life and death to the Papacy. Sicily in imperial hands meant the loss to the Popes of their temporal authority, and, with that, great hampering at least of their spiritual authority.[1]

Papal agents begin to collect money. Clerical opposition.

Master Rostand did not waste time before beginning the task allotted to him. He at once began to preach a Crusade against Manfred, and called upon all lovers of Holy Church to do the same ; [2] and he summoned the bishops to meet him in a council of which we shall speak presently. He then named deputies (October 23),[3] who as promptly ordered payment by the clergy of the tithes " in virtue of the obedience which they owed to the Holy See, and under pain of excommunication ".[4] But the clergy, indignant that money should be wasted on what they regarded as " the foolish, ill-considered Sicilian business ",[5] drew up a list of their objections to the taxation and sent it to the Pope. They contended that the grant of the tenth had been made to the King without their consent, and, " when there is question of putting an obligation on anyone, his express consent is necessary." [6] And, even if the tenth had been originally granted with their consent, that consent should be

residet cordi nostro) Manfredi quondam Principis Tarentin . . . superba rebellio impie impedire conatur . . . Henry's help is asked : " ut . . . tam venenosam pestem . . . auferre possimus . . . de tam caro et amœno Ecclesiæ Romanæ pomerio funditus extirpare."

[1] In the days of the emperor Henry VI. " the papacy saw itself forced to fight for its life. The death of Henry VI. removed the immediate danger; but the Papacy never forgot it." Rhodes. *Edmund, Earl of Lancaster*, p. 21.

[2] Mat. Par., v, 521.

[3] Ep. ap. *Ann. de B.*, pp. 353–4.

[4] Ep. of the deputies ap. *ib.*, p. 355.

[5] " Ad negotium stulte et incircumspecte pro regno incohatum Ciciliæ prosequendum." *Ann. de B.*, p. 360.

[6] " Cum agitur de aliquo obligando necessarius est ejus expressas consensus." *Ib.*, p. 360.

obtained again, if the purpose for which it was granted
was changed. They further professed not to be sure
that Master Rostand had the powers which he professed
to have ; and they protested against the action of the
bishop of Hereford who, pretending to be the procurator
of certain religious houses in the Roman curia, bound
them over to be responsible for large sums of money.[1]
Moreover, while protesting that they wished to pay
canonical obedience to Rome,[2] they objected to new

---

[1] " Propter hoc (the grant of Sicily to Edmund) episcopus Here-
fordiensis obligavit religiosos Angliæ mercatoribus in xxxviii millibus
marcarum Papæ persolvendas." Rob. de Graystanes, *Hist. de statu
eccles. Dunelm.*, c. 6, p. 42, ed. Surtees, 1839. Paris, v, 510 f., says
that he succeeded in doing this by fraudulently obtaining through the
aid of the King " three or four seals of important English prelates ",
and by showing certain letters to the Pope which " with foxlike cunning
he had extracted from certain prelates. He is further stated to have
secured the interests of certain cardinals whose business it was to draw
up the bulls on the subject. Paris proceeds, moreover, to give (v, 523)
what he professes to be one of these implicating bulls. I need not pause
to point out that it is without date or place of issue. It will be enough
to note that, " written with a style " at the bottom of the page in
Paris' own MS., are words practically calling attention to its forgery :
" Suspicio falsitatis in bulla." This tale about the fraudulent bulls
does not lose by want of repetition (v, 512, 523, 527, 559). It would
seem that, if such a crude " plot " as this succeeded, the prelates of
those times must have been much simpler men than their acts and
characters would lead one to suppose. The fact seems to have been
that various monasteries were simply ordered to pay various sums
without their being consulted. (See in illustration a letter of Alexander,
June 22, 1256, ap. Mat. P., v, 581 ff.). Through the agency of the
bishop of Hereford, " omnes ecclesias nigri vestis Angliæ usque ad xxx
millia marcarum sine omni procuratorio obligante." *Gervase of Cant.
Contin.*, ii, p. 205, *R. S. Cf.* Graystanes cited above, and Paris himself,
v, 533. Probably the bishop told the Pope that the clergy were not
paying taxes upon their " lay fiefs " (the manors, baronies, etc., of
which mention has already been made several times) and such a tax
was then called for as those fiefs might be supposed to yield.

[2] " Item protestamur nos ecclesiæ Romanæ, in casibus a jure concessis
propter bonum obedientiæ pro viribus facultatum nostrarum velle
subvenire." *Ib.*, p. 361.

valuations after the Norwich one,[1] and to " the royal simplicity " being seduced into binding the nation to agreements about which it had not been consulted. It was also pointed out that the levying of these taxes gave great opportunities for the oppression of the clergy by the laity.[2]

Except that Master Rostand ordered the Norwich valuation to be adhered to as far as possible,[3] nothing further seems to have come at the time of the protests of the English clergy, and " the whole English Church was decimated this year as in the preceding year by the bishop of Norwich ".[4] Yes, and even more so, because the manors and baronies held by the clergy which had been exempted from taxation under the Norwich assessment were now to be included. Such, Rostand had declared, was the decision of the Apostolic See [5] ; and such, as his assertion on this point had been called in question, was the decision formally repeated to him and to the bishops of England by Alexander himself (1256). In virtue of the obedience they owed him, the Pope called upon them to assess their property themselves, including therein their manors ; to send these valuations in writing to Rostand, and to pay the full tax for the three years.[6]

A council at London, c. Oct. 13, 1255.

About the same time that the King summoned a number of the nobility to London (October 13), in the vain hope of inducing them to grant him supplies for the Sicilian expedition,[7] Rostand " by papal authority convoked all

---

[1] Cf. supra, vol. xiv, p. 269 f.   [2] Ib., p. 362.
[3] Ep. of Jan. 29, 1255, ap. ib., p. 364.   [4] Ib.
[5] Ep. of Oct. 23, 1255, ap. Ann. de B., p. 354.
[6] Cf. his two letters of Sept. 2, 1256, ap. Rymer, i, 602. In the second letter, addressed to the bishops, he writes : " In virtute obedientiæ mandamus quatinus taxationes hujusmodi eidem Capellano (Rostand) in scriptis assignare . . . curetis ; præfatam decimam etiam de maneriis vestris tam pro biennio præterito quam pro anno præsenti secundum taxationes easdem, integre persolvendo."
[7] Mat. Par., v, 519.

the prelates of England to meet " at the same place, in
order that they might " obediently listen to the Pope's
behest (præceptum) ", and " as sons of obedience ", give
a favourable reply to it.[1] The bishops, however, were
anything but pleased at having henceforth to pay taxes on
their lay fiefs also,[2] and at having to pay arrears on them,
and that, too, in a limited period of time. According to
Paris, some declared that they would rather have their
heads cut off or be hanged than see the English Church
so grievously oppressed.[3] They talked of an appeal to the
Pope, " who is bound to open his breast as a harbour of
refuge to all that are oppressed,"[4] and because the
archbishop of Canterbury, Boniface of Savoy, was abroad,
and the See of York was vacant by the death of its archbishop, Walter Gray, they separated without coming to
any conclusion. Fulk Basset, bishop of London, however,
who is credited with being the soul of the opposition,
affecting to doubt Rostand's credentials, forbade any
proceedings to be taken under their authority.[5] And when
the King threatened him with the Pope's censure, he is
reported to have retorted that if the King and the Pope
took away his mitre, he would find a helmet.[6]

---

[1] *Ib.*, p. 524 f. It is very hard to follow Paris, our only full authority
at this period. One is distracted by his repetitions ; bothered by his
perpetually mixing gossip with solid fact ; perplexed by his chronological order or disorder ; and sickened by his whining. " If this money
had been collected, not only the English Church but the whole country
would have been reduced to the vilest slavery and *to irremediable
poverty.*" *Ib.*, p. 525.

[2] The King also " petebat a clero de laicis feodis sibi suffragium
exhiberi". *Ann. de Burton*, p. 360.

[3] v, 525.

[4] *Ib.*, 526. We say " talked of appealing to the Pope " because,
though in this place, Paris says the bishops did appeal to the Pope, he
says a little later on that, " if by common consent they had dispatched
a syndic or proctor to the Roman curia to plead for all of them, they
would all have enjoyed a happy peace." v, 532.

[5] Paris, v, 526.   [6] *Ib.*

Other councils in Dec., 1255, and Jan. and April, 1256.

Meanwhile Rostand and the King laboured hard to bring about a division among the bishops [1]; and so, when they again met in December they could come to no agreement but to put off giving an answer till the feast of St. Hilary (January 13, 1256).[2] The Pope and the King, twice repeats Paris, "like the shepherd and the wolf, were in alliance for the destruction of the sheep."[3] Accordingly, on the said feast, the bishops and archdeacons of England met once more in London, "to give a reply to Master Rostand," whom Paris describes as at once "the Pope's nuncio and the King's proctor".[4] In the course of the debate which arose, Rostand, in answer to the bishops' assertion of their rights, declared that all the churches belonged to the Pope. That is so, was the response ; they are his in so far as he is guardian and protector of them, but not as though he were their owner— just as all things belong to the King to defend, but not to dissipate at will.[5] The council ended by an appeal to Rome.

Alexander decides that the bishops must pay on their baronies.

Apparently before the appeal had been heard, Rostand met the bishops once again on the fourteenth day after Easter, which that year fell on April 16. Stiffened on this occasion by promise of support from the nobility, the bishops stood firm on the vexed question of the lay fiefs, and refused to pay a tax on their baronies.[6] But the case was decided against them in the papal court, and a mandate, dated Anagni, June 13, 1256, was addressed to Rostand bidding him compel the bishops to pay the tax from their manors or baronies.[7]

---

[1] *Ib.*, p. 527, and p. 532, n. 3, for the words: "Rex omnia perturbavit et perterruit."

[2] M. P., v, 532.   [3] v, 532, 540.

[4] v, 539.   [5] *Ib.*

[6] *Ib.*, v, 553. " Episcopi . . . animati per barones contradixerunt ne regi de baroniis suis aliquid contribuerent."

[7] Rymer, i, 595 : "Mandamus quatinus universos Prælatos . . . ut de proventibus Maneriorum suorum quæ largitione regali habere

Through all the exaggerations, omissions, and con- fusions of Matthew Paris, it is plain to see that the raising of money for the Sicilian expedition, and especially the broadening of the basis of taxation by the inclusion of the lay fiefs held by the clergy were very unpopular among that section of the English people that paid taxes either to Pope or King,[1] and must have caused no little irritation in England against the ways of the papal court.[2] It may even be that this irritation made itself so manifest at the January council that it even shook the firmness of Master Rostand to the extent that he declared that he

noscuntur, hujusmodi decimam solvant, monitione præmissa, auctoritate nostra per te vel . . . per alios, appellatione remota, compellas." *Cf.* letters of Sept. 2, 1256, ap. *ib.*, p. 602, to the same effect. The Cistercians were more successful in their appeal to Rome than the bishops. By letters addressed to the King (Rymer, i, 554) and to the Cistercian abbots (ap. Mat. Par., v, 555), May 25, *1255*, Alexander exempted them from payment of the tenth. As another instance of the confusion of Paris, we may note that he brings Rostand in collision with the Cistercians on May 14, *1256*, and states that, on appeal to Rome against him, they got a letter which he himself dates May 25, *1255*. A little further on (p. 558) he says that, as a result of the bishops' appeal in Jan., *1256*, they obtained some redress, and in proof of his assertion offers a letter of May 15, *1255*, which he describes as addressed " to the prelates of England ", but which is evidently addressed to some agents of an abbot about *their* monastery. There is question of money (" non pro vestris et *monasterii* vestri negotiis . . . mutuata " for which some bishop has pledged the property of a monastery. Truly it *is* a task working with Matthew Paris.

[1] Rostand in writing to Henry from Tours, June 24, 1257, tells him that he has informed the Pope how anxious he is to push forward the Sicilian affair, but that " the hearts of the prelates and of all the others are opposed to it on account of the exacting nature of the conditions set forth in the privilege bestowing the crown." Ep. ap. Langlois in an article entitled " Nova Curie " ap. *Rev. Historique*, Jan., 1905, p. 63. It was found in our Record Office.

[2] What is said by Mat. Par., v, 535, 559, on this matter of loss of devotion by the people " towards the Pope our father, and the Roman Church our mother " is set forth with the exaggeration of language which he generally employs when he has anything to say in opposition to the policy of the Popes.

would have to interview the Pope with regard to the bishops' contentions.[1] But, at any rate, he did not put this declaration into effect by leaving England for the papal court at the beginning of June, 1256, as Paris pretends.[2] When he did leave England in June, 1257, it was, as we shall see, on the King's business.

As a matter of fact, then, he remained in England all during the year 1256, as the trusted adviser of the King, and as one in whom Alexander had full confidence,[3] and to whom he declared that " the business of the Cross and all that concerned it " had been entrusted.[4] Throughout this year and the first half of the next, Alexander was constantly writing to the King or to the bishop of Hereford or to Rostand[5] to urge the prosecution of the Sicilian cam-

---

[1] Mat. Par., v, 540.

[2] *Ib.*, p. 560. He himself, v, 581, quotes a letter from Alexander to Rostand (dated June 22, 1256). *Cf. Ann. de Dunstap.*, p. 199, *R. S.* James, bishop of Bologna, had in any case, it seems, already left England. The story of this man as given by Paris affords another example of the ways of that writer. No less than three times (v, 515, 521, 532) does he tell us that he went away after getting rich on presents. This he does to keep before his readers the greediness of Roman officials. But the giving of presents to ambassadors was the order of the day. This is clear from Sir John Fortescue's (b. *c.* 1400 † *c.* 1476) *The Governance of England*, ed. C. Plummer, Oxford, 1885. Speaking with regard to the necessary expenses of the King : " Ffirst the kyny shall often tymes sende owt off this lande his ambassatours, as well to the pope, as to diuerse kynges." These men must be well furnished with money, etc. for the honour (worshippe) of the realm, and for the furthering of the business on which they are sent.

" Then the kynge shall beyre yerely charges unknowen in receyvinge off ligates and messengers sende ffrom the Pope, and off ambassatours sende ffrom kynges . . . wich will put the kyng to grete expenses while thai bith here, and at thair departynge thai most nedis haue grete giftes and rewardes, ffor that it is necessarie ffor the worship off his reaume." P. 124.

[3] Ep. ap. Rymer, i, 612, Oct. 7, 1256.

[4] Ep., Dec. 15, 1256, ap. *ib.*, i, 614.

[5] E.g., ep. Feb. 5, 1256, to the bp. of Hereford, ap. Rymer, i, 581; to the King, *ib.*, p. 593; to Rostand, ap. Mat. Par., v, 581, June 22 ; Rymer, i, 601, Aug. 25, etc.

paign, and particularly the repayment to him of the large sums he had expended over it, which had exhausted his treasury and the goodwill of his friends from whom he had borrowed money.[1]

All during this period also, Master Rostand worked hard in the interests of the Pope and the King to raise money for the Sicilian undertaking. There would seem to be no doubt that the latter was in his way really anxious about the success of the venture, and for fear lest the Pope should get to know the extent of the opposition to it in England, he ordered the Wardens of the Cinque Ports not to allow any cleric to leave England for the papal curia until he had taken an oath not to attempt anything there against the King's designs on Sicily.[2] But many of the bishops, as Henry, complained to cardinal Richard de Annibaldi, were very averse to paying taxes for the prosecution of the scheme; though, after canonical admonition by "that discreet man Master Rostand, a diligent and loyal performer of the task entrusted to him", they had promised to do so.[3] No one, however, had any confidence in the King, for he had no confidence in himself. Hence, though Alexander made more and more grants to him of ecclesiastical property,[4] both in England and Scotland,[5] and sent to Rostand's help another nuncio, John de Dia (or Diva),

---

[1] Ep. to Henry, June 11, 1256, ap. Rymer, i, 594 : " Cum pro ipsius promotione negotii exhauriverimus cameram nostram . . . omnium quasi mercatorum apud prædictam sedem morantium et multorum officialium et familiarium nostrorum ac aliorum etiam pro hujusmodi necessitate pecuniis jam receptis (ita quod non poteramus mutuum invenire) festinatum præparares succursum."

[2] Ep. Feb. 15, 1256, ap. R., i, p. 582.

[3] Ep. of April, 1256, ap. R., i, 587.

[4] Ep. Aug. 21, 1256, grant of the fruits of vacant benefices the collation of which belonged to the Pope, R., i, 597 (properly 599) ; then for a year of all vacant benefices Aug. 23, 1256, R., i, 598 (properly 600) ; of non-residents, Aug. 21, 1256, R., i, 597 (599) ; of the intestate, Aug. 25, 1256, R., i, 601, etc., R., i, 597 (599)–605 ; 607.

[5] Epp. Sept. 27, 1256, ap. R., i, 608 f.

a Franciscan, who is praised even by Matthew Paris,[1] the year 1256 passed by without any substantial aid in money, and without any military assistance whatsoever being forthcoming for Sicily.

The archbishop of Messina comes to England, 1257.Matters were no further expedited by the dispatch to Henry of another special nuncio, John Colonna, archbishop of Messina, who reached England in the early part of the year 1257.[2] He addressed the prelates, clergy, and people of the country in the chapter house of Westminster (April 2). But they gave him conclusive reasons against the prosecution of the Sicilian scheme. The expense of the expedition was too great, the distance was too great, and the King had to deal with too many powerful foes.[3] It is true, on the other hand, that on May 10 the King thanked Alexander for sending to him so splendid a man as the archbishop (talem et tantum virum), a man anxious for the honour both of the Pope and King. He assured the Pope that he had arranged with him to send for the Sicilian affair both an energetic captain and " a very large sum of money ". The archbishop would explain his intentions to the Pope, who is earnestly implored to uphold Edmund's claims.[4]

Disagreement between Henry and the Pope.As time, however, went on, Henry again failed to keep his engagements, and, doubtful as to how the Sicilian scheme would end, he forbade Rostand to continue repaying the merchant-bankers out of the proceeds coming in from the tenths and other sources. On the contrary, he bade him deposit the money in the new Temple, and leave

[1] v, 568, 681, 722. *Cf.* epp. of Alexander, June 11 and 13, ap. Rymer, i, 593, 595.

[2] See the credentials addressed to Henry in his behalf, Nov. 9 or 10, 1256, ap. Rymer, i, 612, and of Nov. 11, ap. *Ann. de Burton*, p. 385 ; Mat. Par., v, 614.

[3] See these reasons at length in the *Ann. de Burton*, p. 387 f., and 390 f. There would not, it was said, be money enough for the expedition if it could be coined from the mud.

[4] Rymer, i, 620.

it there. This brought a strong letter from the Pope and an order to Rostand to go on paying the bankers as before.[1]

Before this letter could have reached England, Master Rostand had left it. A report that reached Henry from the papal court to the effect that assassins had been sent to England to kill him and his sons seems to have only made him more obstinate than ever in his resolve to persevere with the Sicilian scheme, especially when this report was confirmed by a letter from his brother, the King of Germany.[2] He accordingly arranged for a very special mission to go to the Pope on the matter (June, 1257). It was to consist of Rudolf, archbishop of Tarantaise, Simon de Montfort, Earl of Leicester, Peter of Savoy, and John Mansel, and they were to strive for a modification of the terms on which the grant of Sicily had been made.[3] Master Rustand was commissioned to take documents to Simon and Peter, who were abroad.[4] This we are not told by Paris ; but in *three* places he takes occasion to inform us that Rostand was accused to the Pope, and even blamed by him, for amassing possessions " without regard to justice ".[5] The fact is that, on November 22, 1257, the Pope granted him permission to enjoy the fruits of his benefices for five years while engaged in the King's service, and on December 13 made him archdeacon of Agen.[6]

Rostand leaves England, June, 1257.

[1] Ep. of Alex. to Rostand, June 3, 1256, ap. *R.*, i, 624.

[2] *Ann. de Burton*, p. 395. *Cf. Royal Letters*, ii, pp. 116–17.

[3] *Cf.* letters of Prince Edmund, the King, etc., June 26 and 28, ap. *R.*, i, 629–34. Henry acted : " quia negotium Regni Siciliæ plurimum residet cordi nostro, volentes ut felicem sortiretur eventum." Ep., p. 630.

[4] Epp. ap. *ib.*, p. 634.

[5] v, 647, 666, 672. It is true that he had been granted a prebend in the Church of York, and presents.

[6] Bliss, *Calendar*, i, p. 354. Alexander had already shown his confidence in Rostand's " learning, virtue, and judgment " by naming him his legate in Gascony, and desiring to send him thither as " an angel (of peace) " but giving him permission to exercise his legatine commission even when residing in other parts of Henry's dominions.

Before he left England, Rostand, perceiving the disturbed state of public feeling, decided (voluit et decrevit) that proceedings in connexion with the taxes were to be suspended till the return of the King's envoys from the Roman court.[1] Then, on his way to Rome, he wrote to the King from Tours (June 24) telling him that a cardinal had suggested to him that the Sicilian difficulty might be met by a marriage between Edmund and the daughter of Manfred.[2]

Master Arlot, 1258. From Tours the nuncio made his way to Lyons, and thence to the Pope's court at Viterbo, where, as "counsellor (consiliarius)" of the King, he worked hard in the interests of Henry and his country. He reached Viterbo about November,[3] and, no doubt in conjunction with King's envoys,[4] arranged with the Pope for the dispatch of Master Arlot (or Herlot), papal subdeacon and notary, to replace him in England.[5] At any rate, we know that, "by the advice of our beloved son,

Epp. of Sept. 30 and Oct. 5, ap. *Reg.*, i, nn. 1538–9. Rostand showed how little he cared for the goods of this world by becoming a monk. He died in 1262.

[1] See a document in connexion with the Convocation of the Southern province in London, Aug. 22, 1257. "M. Rostandus in recessu suo . . . decrevit quod ab executionibus gravaminum inchoandis omnino supersedeatur donec nuncii d. regis a curia revertantur Romana." Ap. *Ann. de Burton*, p. 405.

[2] Ep. ap. Langlois, "Nova Curie," ap. *l.c.*, p. 63.

[3] On Oct. 13, 1257, it would appear that Alexander was not quite sure whether Rostand had left England, as he bids him, "in person or through another," execute a provision in favour of Stephen de Ponte. Rymer, i, 642. A document (*ib.*, p. 644) shows he was in Viterbo on Nov. 5.

[4] They were the archbishop of Tarantaise, and, instead of Simon de Montfort and Peter of Savoy, the bishops of Bath and Wells, and Rochester and Master Nicholas de Plympton.

[5] *Cf.* a mutilated letter ap. Rymer, i, 628, which Potthast refers to July–August, 1257, but which should be dated Dec. 12. *Cf.* Bliss, *Calendar*, i, p. 354, and a letter of Alexander, ap. *Ann. de Burton*, p. 410, and epp. ap. Rymer, i, 646, 652.

Master Rostand our chaplain and your counsellor," as Alexander wrote to Henry, arrangements were made for the discharging of the King's debts,[1] and for an extension of the time within which he had to fulfil his obligations relative to Sicily.[2]

When Masters Rostand and Arlot arrived in England about the beginning of March,[3] they found the country still more disturbed than when Rostand had left it. The King's arbitrary conduct, his incompetence, his extravagance, and his favouring of foreigners were becoming unbearable to the great barons and to the clergy. The people, too, were restive under the famine caused by the bad harvest of the previous year (1257). Arlot, accordingly, proceeded with tact. He expressed his regret that his daily needs forced him to apply for procurations, especially as everything was more than twice as dear as usual.[4]

Arlot and Rostand come to England, 1258.

But whilst Arlot and Rostand were proceeding with their business of urging the King to push forward the Sicilian enterprise and of raising the money for it, the Clergy and Barons were taking strong measures against the King. At the summons of archbishop Boniface, the clergy met at Merton on the Thursday before the feast of St. Barnabas (June 11).[5] The barons, with their retainers in force, met the King at Oxford on the feast itself (June 11). The clergy complained of the violation of their rights by the King. They were brought before secular tribunals regarding ecclesiastical matters, and were

The Provisions of Oxford, 1258.

---

[1] Ep. Jan. 1, 1258, ap. R. I. 650, and *ib.*, p. 656, for ep. May 30.

[2] Ep. of Jan. 19, 1258, of Alexander to Arlot, ap. Rymer, i, 652. The extension was " usque ad tres menses, in proximo futuris Kal. Junii inchoandos ".

[3] Mat. Par., v, 672 f. ; *Ann. de Burton*, p. 409, *R. S.*, and *Annals of Tewkesbury*, pp. 162-3.

[4] See his letter ap. *Ann. de B.*, p. 409.

[5] *Cf.* the summons of Boniface, ap. *Ann. de B.*, p. 412.

unjustly imprisoned ; their property was destroyed and their chartered liberties were infringed, etc.[1]

The Barons, under Richard de Clare, earl of Gloucester, Simon de Montfort, and others, complained of the arbitrary conduct of the King, of his violation of Magna Charta, of his favouring the foreigner, etc., and insisted that the chief officers of state and the fortresses should be put into the hands only of Englishmen, and that twenty-four persons, twelve from each side, should see to the observance of these conditions.[2] They then took strong measures against the foreign nobles, most of whom fled at once. They also decided to strive for the deposition of bishop Aylmer of Winchester. " The Barons," says the writer of a letter from whom these items are taken, " carried out their proceedings very roughly. It is to be hoped that all will turn out well." [3]

The barons ask the Pope to act against the bishop of Winchester ; and all ask for a legate, 1258.

It is to be observed that neither the Clergy nor the Barons make any complaint about the papal taxes nor about the Sicilian expedition. On the contrary, the Barons, offering their homage to the Pope, assure him that, if the King will, on their advice, reform abuses, they will help him in the Sicilian expedition, though he undertook it without their consent. At the same time they say that the Pope must modify the conditions on which Sicily was granted, as the King cannot perform them ; and they beg him to remove Aylmer from the See of Winchester, as he is the ruin of a country which is devoted to the Pope.[4]

---

[1] *A. de B.*, p. 412 ff. Already in May, 1257, when the prelates offered the King 42,000 marks for the Sicilian expedition, they had presented him with a list of some fifty grievances which the King promised to ameliorate. *Cf.* Mat. Par., v, 637 f., and vi, 353 ff., and *Ann. de B.*, p. 402.

[2] *Ib.*, p. 439 ff.

[3] Ap. *ib.*, p. 445. Aylmer was one of the twelve chosen by the King.

[4] " Sanctitati vestræ omni affectione qua possumus, supplicamus, quatenus sicut unitatem et pacem regni Angliæ, quod semper devotum vobis extitit et existet, diligitis, sæpedictum electum ab administratione

It appears, too, that they were anxious that a papal legate should be sent to England in order that, seeing the state of things with his own eyes, and armed with full powers, he might be able to provide a suitable remedy. Their request was put before the Pope in a long memorandum sent to him by his nuncio. This was, seemingly, the work of Arlot, and not of Rostand,[1] and does the very greatest credit to the nuncio's intelligent grasp of the situation, and to his real desire to benefit the country.

The memorandum is divided into two parts. The first treats of the Pope's successful efforts to bring about peace between England and France,[2] and declares that it will never be forgotten that " it was in the days of Alexander IV. that peace was made between the Kings. Lo ! the three Kings (of England, France, and Germany) have come together, and have agreed to serve thee in fear and obey thee in love. Confirm then what you have wrought in them by sending the cardinal we ask for " to confirm the peace.[3]

Arlot's memorandum to the Pope, 1258.

The second part of the memorandum is concerned with England in particular. It begins by asserting that " the

Wintoniensis ecclesiæ . . . . amoveatis omnino." The letter of the Barons to the Pope. Ap. *Ann. de B.*, p. 457, or Mat. Par., *Addit.*, vi, p. 400 ff. *Cf. supra,* p. 35, where the same letter is cited from Rymer, i, 660. *Cf.* two other letters of the Barons against Aylmer, ap. *Mat. Par.*, vi, pp. 406–10. They beg his paternal consideration " ut sub tegimine alarum vestrarum, Apostolico præsidio, in patrimoniis nostris optata gaudeamus tranquilitate." *Ib.*, p. 408. With the first of the Barons' letters to the Pope compare the King's letter to him of Aug. 1, 1258, ap. Rymer, i, 666.

[1] Unfortunately the document does not bear any name, date, or place of issue. It is ascribed to Arlot rather than to Rostand, because the latter appears to side with the King rather than with the Barons. As many of the important documents that belong to this period are undated, one cannot always be sure of the exact order of events.

[2] The treaty between the two countries was sworn to at Paris, May 28, 1258, and ratified by both parties in December, 1259. Langlois, *Hist. de France*, iii, 92.

[3] The memorandum, ap. *Ann. de Burton*, p. 463. " Cardinalem siquidem tres reges petunt pro communi pace firmanda."

King of England begs for a legate to be sent to him for the
reformation of the land " [1] ; and goes on to assert that the
relatives of the King, looking after their own interests,
have drawn him away from his duty to the country.
Hence " justice itself has been exiled from his kingdom ".
There is, however, hope for the future. The King has
sworn to govern by the advice of a council of the great
and wise men of the land. But as it is impossible for the
Pope fully to comprehend all that is happening in all the
countries subject to him, these men beg you to send a
legate by whose prudence these good beginnings may be
consolidated to the honour of God and to the glory of
the Roman Church and of you yourself. In making this
demand, they are aware that the coming of a legate
means expense, and that it will press especially hard on
many owing to the prevailing scarcity of food and the
existing taxes. Nevertheless, they earnestly beg for a
legate. To speak frankly, continues the author of the
memorandum, if you do not send a legate men will say
that the cause was " malice, avarice, or envy ". Malice—
because the evil-minded will say that you are not anxious
for the establishment of peace between Princes, for it is
easier to fish in troubled waters. Avarice—because it will
be conjectured that the legate was not sent because he
will receive a share of the revenues which would otherwise
go to the Pope, and the Roman Court will not have so
many cases sent to it ; and it is always sweeter to say it
is *mine* rather than it is *ours*. Envy—because if a legate be
not sent men without judgment will blame the cardinals

---

[1] *Ib.* *Cf.* the King's letter to the Pope, Aug. 2, 1259, ap. Rymer, i,
687. He says that he is sending the archbishop of Embrun (Henry of
Susa, afterwards bishop of Ostia, the great canonist, always cited as
" Hostiensis ". *Cf.* Tiraboschi, *Storia della Lett. Ital.*, l. 2, c. 5, p. 272 f.),
and Tarantaise, Master Rostand and Sir William Bonquer to ask for a
legate to settle the Sicilian affair, and internal affairs of England. It
must be remembered that the *King's* letters at this period were
dictated by his Council of Barons.

for being under the sway of this vice ; for they will say
that, because a particular person was asked for, the others
grew jealous and considered that they had been slighted.
Nor will it avail to say that the number of cardinals is
but few. This will only make men more annoyed, for they
will retort that that Holy Father is your fault, as you can
create new ones. This fine outspoken document concludes
with a request that its author's plain speaking may be
forgiven.[1]

Accordingly, in connexion with these documents setting
forth the grievances of the Barons against the King and his
foreign favourites, especially against Aylmer of Winchester,
a number of embassies passed backwards and forwards
between England and the Papal court.[2] Nor were there
wanting agents to put before the Pope the private views
of Henry regarding the action of his Barons.

Intrigues at the papal court, 1258-9.

Whether in consequence of these representations of his
vassal Henry, or because he did not grasp the seriousness
of the situation which Arlot had so well put before him,
Alexander decided not to send the desired legate. In a
letter which reached England seemingly some time after
August 2, 1259, he declared that he was ever anxious
to promote the cause of peace, and was naturally most
desirous of promoting the welfare of England. " For from

---

[1] *Ann. de B.*, pp. 463–6. Both Arlot and Rostand would appear
to have returned to Rome in the course of this year, 1258. Safe-
conducts were signed for them " returning to the court of Rome ",
Aug. 9, 1258. *Patent Rolls, Henry III.*, vol. iv, p. 650.

[2] *Cf.* e.g., Mat. Par., *Addit.*, vi, 405. *Cf.* epp. of the King of July 28,
1259 (Rymer, i, 664, about the setting out to the Pope of the archbishops of Tarantaise and Embrun, soon after Aug. 15 ; and of
March 16, 1259, whence it appears that Rostand who seems to have been
still in England towards the close of 1258 (*cf.* a papal letter addressed
to him Dec. 28, 1258, ap. Bliss, i, p. 362), was in Rome in the early
part of 1259. *Cf.* also ep. of Henry to him at the Roman court of
May 24, 1259. Rostand, though a bearer of the King's or Barons' letters
asking for a legate (Rymer, i, 687. *Cf.* Mat. Par., vi, 410), would be
probably acting in Henry's private interests.

that kingdom have ever come Catholic kings who, adorned
with faith and devotion, have ever striven to render themselves pleasing to God by a good life and to the Church by
obedience and humility. From that kingdom has the
Church received and is receiving sons of blessing and joy,
sons illustrious by their good deeds and good reputation,
sons who render opportune help and favour. It is a
gracious, beauteous and precious realm, which God has
blessed in everything." But the Sicilian affair has been
badly managed by the King, and before he can send one
of his few cardinals as a legate to deal with the condition
of affairs in England, he must be better informed about it.
Finally, with regard to Aylmer, he cannot yet proceed
against him, as no one has yet appeared in Rome to act
in his behalf.[1]

Complaints about Provisions, etc., 1259-60. Perhaps because they were irritated at Alexander's
refusal to comply with their requests, the King's
Counsellors complained to him about the abuse of
Provisions ; and, through the King, about encroachments on the royal authority in the matter of presenta-
tion to benefices during the vacancies of sees. The
Barons' letter is not extant, and the Pope's reply to it
is undated. But the former letter is no doubt connected
with the King's letter on the question of benefices, and

[1] Ep. to the King's counsellors ap. Mat. Par., vi, 410 ff. It is undated,
but is assigned by Luard to 1258. It would seem, however, that it
must have reached England after Aug. 2, 1259, when the King (i.e., his
counsellors) asked for a legate. Already, in May 20, 1259, a notice to
the Pope was drawn up to the effect "that the King has appointed the
archbishops of Embrun and Tarentaise and Master Rostand, etc., as his
proctors to sue for a legate to be sent to England for the affairs of
Sicily, and other affairs in England." *Calendar of Patent Rolls*, Henry
III., vol. v, p. 52. Probably soon after this Alexander made an effort to
secure the reinstatement of Aylmer. But the Barons would not listen
to his envoy brother Velascus. *Cf.* ep. of Henry to the Pope, Sept. 23,
1259, ap. *Royal Letters*, ii, p. 138 ff. It was written in the name of the
King but, of course, " by the barons and nobles our counsellors." *Cf.*
ib., p. 150 ff., for ep. of Jan. 18, 1260.

that is dated (January 16, 1260).[1] Alexander's answer, therefore, to these complaints may be taken to have been issued some six weeks later. He says that the Barons declared that they wrote to him because the bishops had told them that the correction of the grievances of which they complained belong to him. After observing that, in their letters, they had written things which they ought not to have written, " to the Vicar of Christ and to the successor of the Prince of the Apostles," the Pope proceeded to reply to the Barons' points in detail. They had declared that one result of Provisions was a dearth of learned Englishmen. To this Alexander, full of the admiration of England, which he had already shown himself possessed, gave a direct denial. " By the grace of God there is scarcely to be found in the wide world a kingdom or province which has so great a number of learned men as the realm of England. To-day in this country are to be found the beauteous fountains of Helicon itself, and from their sweet waters not only the people of England but strangers also draw the life-giving draughts which abundantly fructify the dry soil of their hearts, and refresh their minds athirst for knowledge. Here Philosophy, that liberal art which informs the uncultured minds of men, has taken up her abode. Here is the cradle of many men both learned and saintly, in whose company the army of the realms above rejoices, and from whom the ranks of the blessed are recruited. By the men of your land are Christians instructed. By them is the Catholic faith strengthened, and from their minds have such springs of learning burst forth that they have flooded the neighbouring countries with streams of science." [2]

He then made answer to the complaint that he had sanctioned the appropriation of churches by religious

---

[1] Ap. *Royal Let.*, ii, p. 145 ff.   [2] Ep. ap. *Ann. de B.*, p. 489 f.

houses to the great loss of religion. If that had occurred it was not in accordance with the intention of the Holy See.[1] On the contrary, it had always hoped that these concessions would cause the poor to be better cared for, and the divine service to be conducted more becomingly, for to these things were religions more especially vowed.

The Barons had hinted that the Pope had granted some of their parish churches to foreign monasteries, and had been very free in the matter of the granting of Provisions. Alexander, however, declared that a careful scrutiny of the register of his memory had failed to detect a single case of such a grant; and he maintained that he had not made frequent Provisions, and that those few which he had made had certainly not merited ill treatment for those who had received them.[2] Therefore, as the Barons had acknowledged that the remedying of these matters lay with him, it was not for them, " laymen and ignorant of the words of wisdom," to interfere with them. Nevertheless, as he is anxious to remove causes of scandal, he will put into execution whatever remedies the bishops to whom he will write may suggest.

Alexander absolves Henry from his oath to the Barons.

Altogether, it cannot be said that the great Barons made a good start in their attempt to govern the King and the country. They had offended the Pope, discontented the lesser tenants, the " communitas bacheleriæ

---

[1] Hence he ordered the bishops of Worcester, Lincoln, Salisbury, Coventry, and Llandaff to examine into " the reported cupidity of religious in getting churches appropriated to them, to the extinction in such churches of divine worship, the loss of episcopal rights, and the closing of the doors of promotion against poor and proficient clerks ". The bishops must remedy abuses where found. Ep. of March 1, 1261, ap. Bliss, i, 375. Alexander sent a similar mandate to the Provincial of the Dominicans and the Minister of the Franciscans bidding them see that vicars with fit portions are appointed to those churches held by religious. *Ib.*

[2] " Neque recolimus nos adeo crebras provisiones fecisse in regno prædicto, quod deberent et possent juste de hoc aliqui murmurare." *Ib.*, p. 490.

Angliæ ", and irritated the clergy. The effect of these mistakes was soon apparent. The " esquirehood " were not slow to manifest their discontent to Prince Edward and the Barons whom they accused of looking only after themselves. The Prince was only too glad to assure them that he had taken the oath at Oxford against his will, and declared that, if the Barons did not fulfil their engagements, he was ready to die for the country.[1] The irritation of the clergy showed itself somewhat later when, on May 13, 1261, in obedience to the command of the Pope,[2] they held a council and affirmed their liberties not only against the King but also against the Barons.

The failure of the Barons to propitiate Alexander showed itself a few weeks before his death. He hearkened to the prayers of the King, and on April 13, 1261, declared Henry absolved from the oath he had taken at Oxford. It was an unlawful oath, so the King contended, and so the Pope affirmed, because, as the King was the vassal of the Roman Church, he had no right to take an oath of such importance without the consent of the Pope and the cardinals, and because he had been forced to take it.[3] The Pope declared that the ordinances of the Barons

---

[1] *Ann. de B.*, p. 471.

[2] " De mandato P. Alexandri." *Gervas. Contin.*, ii, p. 212. The statutes of the legate Otho were reaffirmed. *Cf.* Hefele, *Conciles*, vi, p. 97 f., ed. Leclercq ; and Wilkins, *Concilia*, i, 746 ff. The decrees of the council were directed against the King as well as against the Barons. *Cf. Royal Letters*, ii, p. 191, whence we see that the royal agents succeeded in inducing Urban IV. not to confirm them : " nec unquam confirmabuntur constitutiones illius concilii contra vos." *Cf.* Urban's own letter, Jan. 30, 1263, ap. Rymer, i, pp. 755–6. The Pope declared that the episcopal statutes were good in themselves, but, in deference to Henry's wishes, he had put off the confirmation of them. Meanwhile, he urged the King to respect the liberties of the Church of his Kingdom.

[3] T. Wykes, *Chron.*, p. 128, *R. S.* " Sine consensu et voluntate d. Papæ et cardinalibus ecclesiæ Romanæ, cujus vassallus Rex Angliæ fore dinoscitur, hujus momenti sacramentum præstare non potuit."

lessened the King's power and freedom ; but he was careful to add a proviso that any such ordinances as guaranteed the liberties of the Church were not to be considered void.[1]   The bull of April 13 was soon followed up by two others addressed to the Archbishop of Canterbury and others bidding them absolve all who had taken these unlawful oaths, and compel the magnates to obey the King.[2]

Within three weeks after the dispatch of the latter of these letters, Alexander IV. had breathed his last, and the further defence of Henry was left to Urban IV.

IRELAND.

Various relations between Alexander and the Bishops of Ireland.

There is nothing very striking in the relations between Alexander IV. and Ireland. We see him giving its bishops permission to build cathedrals,[3] to raise loans,[4] or to supplement small revenues by collecting tithes.[5] He confirms some episcopal elections [6] and annuls others [7] ; settles questions of precedence among them [8] ; and to some of them grants indults concerning Provisions.[9] Others again are instructed to proceed against abuses. The archbishop of Armagh is to deal with the clerics of his diocese who, without papal dispensation, are holding a plurality of benefices with the cure of souls [10] ; and the bishop of Raphoe is bidden even to invoke the secular arm to deal with certain serious evils.   On a visit to the Pope, the bishop had told him that there were a number of men in his diocese who worshipped idols, intermarried with their kinsfolk by blood or marriage, and when rebuked called in question the authority of

---

[1] Rymer, i, 405, Rec. ed.
[2] Epp. of April 29 and May 7, ap. Rymer, i, 722 f.
[3] Bliss, *Calendar*, i, 312.   [4] *Ib.*, p. 355.
[5] *Ib.*, p. 343.   [6] *Ib.*, p. 313.
[7] *Ib.*, p. 333.   [8] *Ib.*, p. 324.
[9] *Ib.*, p. 321.   [10] *Ib.*, p. 330.

the Apostolic See, and plotted against the lives of those who rebuked them. The bishop must proceed against them by ecclesiastical censure, and, if expedient, call in the aid of the secular authority.[1]

The Irish were also called upon by the Pope to contribute their tithes to King Henry, along with their fellow subjects in England, Wales, and Gascony.[2]

In Ireland, as elsewhere, the civil authorities were encroaching on the privileges of the Church. We find Florence, archbishop of Tuam, and the clergy of Ireland generally, complaining to King Henry that the Church was being so robbed of its rights and liberties that unless he applied a remedy it would be ruined. We know that the King ordered Prince Edward to look into the grievances complained of,[3] and to apply a remedy. That anything effective was done we may well doubt; for only a few years later we learn from a letter of Alexander to the abbot of Tintern, the prior of Afthissel (or Athassel) and the archdeacon of Ferns that the archbishop of Dublin had complained to him that the Justiciary of Ireland and his councillors were infringing insufferably on the liberties of the Church, especially in his diocese. The archbishop complained that various matters including pecuniary cases [4] that affected him were decided by the secular courts; and, without their sanction, the Justiciary and his officials will not permit the execution of the archbishop's sentences. To his excommunications they oppose the King's authority and coerce ecclesiastics by the sequestration of their goods. In consequence of these representations, the

Encroachments by the secular power.

---

[1] *Ib.*, p. 329, or in full ap. Theiner, *Mon. Hibern.*, p. 71. It would be interesting to know if these idolators were descendants of the Danes.

[2] Bliss, *ib.*, p. 314.

[3] *Cal. of docs. relating to Ireland* (1252–84), n. 460, July 30, 1255.

[4] In 1266 we see Prince Edward ordering that only pecuniary cases connected with wills or marriage were to be brought before the ecclesiastical courts. See *Historic documents of Ireland*, p. 179, *R. S.*

Pope orders his correspondents to admonish these officials, under pain of ecclesiastical censures, from interfering with the liberties of the Church.[1]

The Annals of Ireland at this period do not add much to the information on its ecclesiastical affairs which is to be gathered from the Papal Registers. However, they do tell us that Tomaltaih (Thomas, bishop of Elphin) went to Rome in 1259, and that, as archbishop of Tuam, he came back with the pallium and with great privileges for his Church. Well deserving is he of mention, for we are assured that he was " the most eminent in all Erin for wisdom and knowledge, for hospitality and nobility, for munificence, and for distributing jewels and valuables to all in general ".[2]

SCOTLAND.

Gameline of St. Andrews.

Owing to differences between Alexander IV. the Pope of Rome and Alexander III. the boy king of Scotland or his guardians, rather more, perhaps, that is of interest is known about this Pope's relations with Scotland than with Ireland. As a mark of his goodwill towards them, Alexander conferred various privileges on Scotland's King and Queen. To the latter he granted an indult by which she might have the services of the Church performed for her privately by her chaplains in any place in Scotland that might be under an interdict.[3] To the King he confirmed all the privileges which had been granted by the Apostolic See to him or to any of his predecessors, as well as all the ancient and reasonable customs of his realm.[4] Noting that he also granted

---

[1] *Ib.*, p. 170 ff., Apr. 18, 1260. *Cf. ib.*, p. 172 ff., for letters of Urban IV. to the same effect.

[2] *Annals of Loche Cé*, i, pp. 431, 485, *R. S.*, *The Annals of the Kings of Ireland*, by the Four Masters, i, p. 373, ed. O'Donovan.

[3] Bliss, i, 310.

[4] *Ib.*, p. 351.

a privilege in the matter of Provisions to the bishop and chapter of Moray,[1] and that Alan, the Durward, Doreward (" Hostiarius ") of Scotland, the King's brother-in-law, tried to obtain the earldom of Mar on the strength of what were alleged to be forged papal letters,[2] we may pass to the matters that caused some controversy between the Pope and the King.

On the first of July, 1255, Alexander IV. addressed a letter to Master Gameline, papal chaplain [3] and chancellor of the King of Scotland. Granting him a dispensation on the score of illegitimacy, the Pope urged him to accept the burden of the See of St. Andrew's to which he had been elected, to go to his church, and to govern it prudently.[4] At the same time he instructed the bishop of Glasgow, with two other bishops who were to be named by the bishop-elect himself, to consecrate him.[5] On the last day of the same month he gave permission to the bishop-elect to retain first for one year and then for two years the benefices which he had held before his election. This indult was granted " in consideration of his church, and the repairs of which it and other buildings were in need." [6]

But though " the King and his counsellors " had approved of the election of Gameline,[7] they sought to

---

[1] *Ib.*, p. 365. They were not to be compelled by papal or legatine letters to make provision to anyone of a canonry or prebend, unless special mention were made of this indult.

[2] *Ib.*, pp. 349, 351.

[3] He had been named " papal chaplain " by Innocent IV. in 1253. *Cf.* Theiner, *Mon. Hib.*, p. 59.

[4] Bliss, i, 318.

[5] *Ib.*, p. 319. Three weeks later (July 20) at the request of the King and Gameline, bishop-elect, Alexander decided that no prejudice was to arise to the prior and chapter of St. Andrews from their having, under protest. admitted two of the Keledei (Culdees) to take part in the election of their former bishop, David de Bernham. *Ib.*, p. 320.

[6] *Ib.*, and p. 321.

[7] *Chron. de Mailros*, an. 1254.

prevent his consecration, which did not take place till
December, 1255.[1] Soon after this, in the following
year, Gameline was banished (1256). According to
the Chronicle of Melrose the opposition of the King
and his counsellors to Gameline was caused by his refusal
to " acquiesce in their wicked designs, and because he
scorned to give them money as if for the purchase of
his bishopric ".[2] Then " as Scotland had cast him out,
and England refused him a passage through her territories,
he went by sea to France, and thence boldly proceeded
to the court of Rome against his adversaries ", who
promptly plundered the goods of his see.[3]

At this time the Scottish King was merely a boy of
thirteen, and was in the hands of Alan the Doreward
(*Hostiarius* as he is styled in the papal bulls), and a party
whose interests were English. It would seem that it
was his opposition to the unpatriotic conduct of this
party that brought trouble on Gameline. The envoys
of this faction followed Gameline to the Pope. But
Alexander " having heard and examined the sides. . . .
with his own lips pronounced that the bishop was guiltless
of all the accusations which had been unjustly brought
against him . . . He excommunicated his accuser, and
those who had plundered his see ".[4] He then commissioned the bishop of Dunblane, the abbot of Melrose
and others to promulgate throughout the Kingdom of

---

[1] *Ib.*, an. 1255.

[2] *Ib.*, an. 1256. As far as the King was concerned, he opposed
Gameline only because the party in whose hands he was opposed him.
Hence Fordun, *Scotichron.*, l. vi, c. 43, writes : " Quodammodo rege
invito."

[3] *Ib.*, *Mailros*.

[4] *Ib.*, an. 1257.   For papal documents issued in the course of
Gameline's suit at Alexander's courts see Bliss, i, p. 350 ; and *Reg.*,
ii, n. 2232, July 20, 1257, and n. 2233.   In the former letter, the Pope
insists that Gameline's property must be restored to him before the
King's charges against him are investigated.

Scotland a general excommunication of the King's counsellors, and, if they continued contumacious, they were to be excommunicated by name. The general sentence was promulgated at Stirling, and as that failed to produce any effect, the commissioners proclaimed the particular excommunication at Kambuskinele (Cambuskenneth).[1]

" Now when the nobility of Scotland," continues the chronicler, " of whom the leader was Walter Cumin (or Comyn) perceived that their King was the constant associate of men who had been excommunicated, and becoming apprehensive that the whole land would be placed under an interdict, they made a rising," and seized the person of the King at Kinross.[2] Alan fled to England, and Gameline, despite our King, who in the interest of his party in Scotland had ordered the Wardens of the Cinque ports to seize him if he landed in any of them,[3] was recalled from his banishment and restored to his see." [4] Gameline died in possession of it in 1271,[5] and is highly praised by Fordun.[6]

The same year in which Gameline returned to Scotland (1258), his consecrator, William de Bondington, bishop of Glasgow, died. Master Nicholas de Moffat, archdeacon of Teviotdale, was elected in his stead, and confirmed by the King. When, however he went to

John of Cheyam.

---

[1] *Chron. de Mail.*, an. 1257.

[2] *Ib.*

[3] Rymer, i, 652, Jan. 22, 1258, Henry, who had not listened to Alexander's request to support Gameline (ep. Dec. 16, 1256, ap. *ib.*, p. 615) gave out that the bishop was plotting against his son-in-law : " quædam impetravit, ad curiam Romanam in exhæretationem fiiii et fidelis nostri Alexandrı." On this affair see also *Cal. of docs. relating to Scotland*, nn. 2037, 2104, 2107, 2110 2112.

[4] *Mailros*, an. 1258.

[5] See p. 18 of that most excellent book of reference, Dowden's *The Bishops of Scotland*.

[6] L. x, c. 23. In the midst of these factions among the nobility, it is not easy to be sure which was the patriotic party.

Rome he failed to secure the confirmation of the Pope.
This, according to the Chronicle of Melrose, was due
" partly because he was unwilling to pay a sum of money
which the Pope and the cardinals demanded of him",
but evidently more " because those who had accompanied
him, apparently for his assistance ", opposed him.   The
ringleader of these, says the same chronicle, was Robert,
bishop-elect of Dunblane, who hoped to be chosen for
the See of Glasgow himself, if the election of Nicholas
was quashed.   In this, however, he was disappointed,
for the Pope himself chose for the see John de Cheyam,[1]
archdeacon of Bath, and papal chaplain (June, 1259).
King Alexander was not pleased at the setting aside
of his nominee, and wrote (1260) to beg the Pope to revoke
the provision of John, pointing out, moreover, that it was
against the customs of kingdom for him to grant the
temporalities of his see to a bishop before he had taken
the oath of fealty.   Pope Alexander, however, refused
to revoke his nomination, but decided that the
new bishop was to present himself under a safe conduct
to the King, and was to receive the temporalities
from him after he had taken the oath.[2]   This arrangement satisfied the King—the more easily that King
Henry had assured him that there was no legal means
of upsetting what the Pope had done [3]—and Master John

[1] *Chron. de M.*, an. 1259. *Cf.* ep. Alex. June 13, 1259, ap. Rymer, i,
683 f.   The Pope appoints him " by the plenitude of his apostolic
power ".

[2] *Cf.* the Pope's letter of May 21, 1260, ap. Bliss, i, p. 372, or in full,
ap. Theiner, *Mon. Hib.*, p. 86.   Dowden, *l.c.*, pp. 304–5, states that
among the documents found in the castle of Edinburgh in 1282, was a
bull of the Pope directing John to render fealty to the King before
receiving the temporalities.   He quotes *Acts of the Parliaments of
Scotland*, i, 108.

[3] Ep. of March 6, 1260, ap. Rymer, i, 697 f., Henry had written to
Alexander at the Pope's request. *Cf. Cal. of docs.* : *Scotland*, i, pp. 423,
428–9, 431.

" having obtained permission from the King of Scotland, entered into the Kingdom and was kindly received by him. He was then conducted to his see, where he was enthroned in state ".[1]

As in England, so also in Scotland, there were difficulties about the raising of money. On May 16, 1255, Alexander issued a bull extending the grant to our King Henry of " the twentieth of all the ecclesiastical revenues of the Kingdom of Scotland " for a second term of three years.[2] The grant was made " for the assistance of the Holy Land ". The Scots, however, when it became known to them, as of course it must have done, that their money was going to be used to increase the influence of their powerful neighbour, raised all manner of difficulties against the carrying out of the papal concession. So much so that Henry tried to pacify them by assuring their King that the concession should not engender any prejudice against his rights or those of his successors.[3] This, however, was not enough. Papal intervention was necessary. Alexander wrote to Rostand, his nuncio in England, and bade him tell the Scottish people that they might either help him in the matter of his Sicilian debts or pay Henry the twentieth. The nuncio was to set before them a statement of the expenses he had incurred " for the defence of ecclesiastical liberty, but especially for the Sicilian affair ". Children must help their mother in her difficulties, and therefore, if the Scottish clergy did not choose to pay the grant to Henry, they must help the Pope. Rostand must compel payment.[4]

Pope Alexander had also to protest against his name-

Trouble about the money " for the Holy Land ".

The jus spolii.

---

[1] *Chron. de M.*, an. 1260.

[2] Rymer, i, 552. *Cf.* the letter of May 17, 1259, *ib.*, p. 553.

[3] Ep. Feb. 10, 1256, ap. *ib.*, p. 582.

[4] Ep. Sept. 27, 1256, ap. *Cal. of docs.* : *Scotland*, i, p. 403, n. 2065 (*cf.* 2066) ; or ap. Rymer, p. 608. *Cf.* the following letter also.

sake of Scotland's exercising the outrageous custom of the *jus spolii*, or of taking possession " of the movable estate of deceased bishops ". Alexander accordingly declared that, as there was neither custom nor right for the practice, it must be strictly prohibited (1259).[1] It seems, however, that such a *custom* at any rate had existed, and later it was alleged [2] that " bulls were granted sanctioning the practice, if it was founded on established custom ".[3]

FRANCE.

The peace with England, 1258.

Perhaps the most important of the relations between France and the Holy See was the share taken by the latter in the peace made between France and England in the year 1258. It has been spoken of already in these pages,[4] and at the time was described as the greatest work of Alexander IV. It is alluded to now once again because one of the rare diplomatic notes of the Middle Ages has come down to us in connexion with it. We have seen it stated by Alexander's nuncio in England that " the three Kings " of England, France, and Germany desired a legate to ratify the treaty of peace. The document containing the request of St. Louis for a legate was discovered in the French national archives, and published by Delaborde. It is most interesting on many counts. It shows the zeal of the saintly monarch for the good name of the Church ; that he was concerned at the smallness of the number of the cardinals and that he gave the Pope a very broad hint as to the necessity of creating some new ones. The document opens by informing the Pope that peace has been agreed upon between the three Kings ; and, that though the fact is

[1] Ep. Nov. 20, 1259, ap. Theiner, *Mon. Hib.*, n. 212, p. 82.

[2] *Act. Parl. Scot.*, i, append. to preface, p. 2, ap. Dowden.

[3] So writes Dowden in another of his estimable books : *The medieval Ch. of Scotland*, p. 196.

[4] *Cf. supra*, p. 81.

not public, the King of France makes it known to him. The King understands that his brother of England is about to ask for a legate, and therefore he himself asks that the legate may pass through France, and be present at the ratification of the said peace. "The Lord King" specially requested a legate to be sent who was a sincere friend of himself and of his Kingdom, and to whom he could safely entrust his secrets. The King would like John Gaëtani Orsini, cardinal-deacon of St. Nicholas *in carcere Tulliano*,[1] and he understands he would be welcome to the others. If he cannot come, then the King asks for " the lord of Tusculum ", Eudes of Châteauroux, or the lord Hugo, of the title of Sta. Sabina. If, however, the King of England should request another cardinal, then the King asks that if England is to have a special cardinal, then he would like one, and, if possible, " the lord of Tusculum."

The note proceeds to state that, if a promotion of cardinals is to take place, the King asks that it may take place before the departure of the aforesaid cardinals, or be put off till their return. An affair of such importance as the creation " of such columns of Holy Church, and such lights of the whole world " ought not to be carried into execution without the counsel of those great and good men who are specially interested in the matter. The King, moreover, begs that, " when the creation does take place, those be named cardinals who are animated by zeal for the cause of God, who are eager for the salvation of souls, and who detest avarice. For they ought to be the model of honour and Christian holiness to all the prelates of the Church both of high and of low degree."[2]

A hint that cardinals and good ones should be created.

---

[1] Afterwards Nicholas III.

[2] These representations were not ill-timed, as Alexander himself had to rebuke the avarice and insolence of some of his envoys. *Reg.*, i, nn. 1323 and 1325.

In fine, as the King of France has a large sum to pay to England, he begs the Pope to order the churches of the Kingdom to help him.[1]

BOHEMIA.

Přemysl
Ottokar II.,
1253-78.

If St. Louis of France was the most powerful sovereign in Western Europe at this time, the most powerful in the East of Europe was Přemysl Ottokar II., King of Bohemia, known in some of the Chronicles as " the golden King " or " the iron King ". By their defeat of the Tartars at Olmütz (1241), the Bohemians had saved not only Moravia, but, as their historians believe, even Europe. The ruler of a strong nation, Ottokar was, like St. Louis in the West, a strong supporter of papal power.[2] In 1255 Alexander named him Captain-general of the Crusaders who had been drawn together to combat the pagan Prussians whose cruelty was as revolting in the thirteenth century as it is to-day.[3] It must be confessed, however, that the vengeance taken on them by the Crusaders was as ruthless as the original brutality of the Prussians. However, they did their work, and many of the Prussian chiefs were terrified into accepting Christianity.[4]

Ottokar asks
the Pope to
confirm his
treaty with
Hungary.

It is thought that it was on account of this successful campaign that some of the German electors wished, in the following year (1256) to make him King of the

---

[1] See the original, ap. *Bib. de l'école des Chartes*, 1888, p. 632 ff. Though the relations between France and Alexander were in the main very friendly, still he found it necessary to threaten with excommunication all who should subscribe to laws and customs against ecclesiastical liberty. Ep. to the French episcopate ap. *Reg.*, ii, n. 2068.

[2] G. E. Maurice, *Bohemia*, p. 81.

[3] Potthast, 16153-5. " To-day " is March, 1917.

[4] See various Bohemian Chroniclers ap. Emler, *Fontes. Rer. Bohem.*, vol. ii, 293 ; iii, 474, 566, etc.

Romans.[1] Ottokar, however, like many others, declined the proffered honour. He preferred vaguely to recognize our weak Richard of Cornwall, and to pursue his plans for the aggrandisement of Bohemia. These plans brought him into collision with Béla IV., King of Hungary,[2] and his allies Daniel, Prince of Kief, and many others. The Hungarians were severely defeated at Kressenbrunn on the river March (1260), and had, in coming to terms with the redoubtable Ottokar, to yield Styria to him. In a letter which the Bohemian King sent to the Pope, he asked him to confirm the treaty which he had made with Béla. The letter is an interesting one, and deserves to be quoted on many grounds. " To the most holy Father and Lord in Christ, by the grace of God the lord Pope Alexander the Fourth, the supreme Pontiff of the Holy Roman Church, Premysl Ottokar, by the same grace, Lord of the Kingdom of Bohemia, Duke of Austria and Styria, and Marquis of Moravia. Since the escape of his sheep from the wolves brings delight to the good shepherd . . . we have thought it right to tell your Paternity of the serious war which by God's will we have waged against Béla and his son Stephen, illustrious kings of Hungary, and against those who had come to their aid, Daniel, King of Russia . . . Boleslaus Duke of Cracow . . . and an innumerable multitude of savage men, such as Cumans and Slavs, . . . and even of schismatics, such as Greeks and Bulgarians . . . and of Bosnian heretics. We would also tell you of the victory given

---

[1] *Chron.*, ap. *ib.*, iii, 566. The native chroniclers tell us of an Order called " of the Blessed Martyrs ", which was approved of by Alexander IV., and whose brothers first appeared in Prague in this year (1256). *Ib.*, p. 474.

[2] Innocent IV. in 1254 worked hard to keep the peace between Bohemia and Hungary, the more so that he was on such very good terms with Béla that that King urged a marriage between his son and a niece of the Pope. *Cf.* Theiner, *Mon. Hung.*, i, pp. 226–30.

us by heaven, and of the peace made by us, after our victory, with the said Kings." Ottokar goes on to tell the Pope how he met the enemy on the river March which marks the boundary of Hungary and Austria ; how, breaking a truce, the enemy attacked him unexpectedly ; and how putting all his trust in God, he completely defeated them. Then, though he might have overrun all Hungary, thinking it better to have a good neighbour than to destroy a rebel, and by devastating Hungary, to open a way for the Tartars, he made peace with Béla : "We beg then that the terms of the treaty which, authenticated by their seals has been sent to your Apostleship, may be ratified by the Apostolic See, and, by apostolic patronage, be confirmed for ever." [1]

Divorce and coronation of Ottakar II., 1261.   The next request which Ottokar made to the Pope was for a divorce from his first wife the aged Magaret, widow of Henry VII., King of the Romans.[2]   This he appears, ultimately at least, to have obtained.[3]   He then married Cunegunda, daughter of Rostilas, duke of Bulgaria, and was solemnly anointed and crowned with her at Prague

---

[1] Ep. ap. *Kronika Marignolova*, ap. Emler, *l.c.*, iii, p. 569 f. "Prenotate itaque composicionis formam vestro apostolatui sub eorum sigilis petimus a sede apostolica communiri, et in œvum apostolico patrocinio roborari." Also ap. *ib.*, p. 315 ff.

[2] The son of the Emperor Frederick II. One of the grounds of the application for the divorce was "sterilitatis causa", in connexion with which cause the Bohemian Chroniclers tell a story as to how Ottokar proved he had the full powers of a man. *Cf.* ep. of Alex. IV., Oct. 21, 1260, ap. Rod., iii, n. 509, as bearing on the story.

[3] *Cf.* ep. of Urban IV., Apr. 20, 1262, ap. Rod., iii, n. 518, p. 481. "Episcopi convenerunt et de consensu sedis apostolicæ divortium . . . celebraverunt." See the Chronicle of Brother Peter, ap. Emler, iv, p. 11. *Cf.* also *ib.*, p. 351, and especially the important *Pulkava Chronicle*, ap. *ib.*, v, 144, 152 f. The German chronicler, Hermann of Altaich, an. 1261, ap. Böhmer, *Fontes*, ii, p. 517, declares that M. was repudiated "sine judicio ecclesie". He moreover describes Rostilas as King of Russia. See also the German chronicles, *Ann. Aust. contin. Garstense,* p. 600 ; and the *Contin. Sancruc.*, p. 645, ap. *M. G. SS.*, ix.

by the bishops of Prague and Olmütz, who had been commissioned by Alexander to do so (1261).[1]

But for the exigences of time and space much could be told of Alexander's action in other countries. As it is, just to emphasize how completely the Pope was head of the European commonwealth, we may note his efforts to keep internal peace in Sweden, his confirming a new coinage in Aragon, and his permission to Theobald (Thibaut) count of Champagne to take the title of King of Navarre, and to be crowned when he chose.[2]

Sweden, Navarre, and Aragon.

---

[1] Ep. Oct. 6, 1260, ap. Rod., iii, p. 469 ff. This ceremony was usually performed by the archbishop of Mainz, but at this time Werner, the occupant of the see, had not yet been confirmed by the Pope. *Cf.* the Bohemian chroniclers ap. Emler, ii, 297 ; iii, 571, etc.

[2] Potthast, 16151 ; 17437, and *re* Navarre 17468 and 17482. The bishop of Pampeluna was given the right of crowning the Kings of Navarre. *Reg.*, ii, n. 2285.

CHAPTER V.

THE RELIGIOUS ORDERS—JOACHISM AND WILLIAM OF ST. AMOUR.

The university of Paris. The seculars against the religious.

ALL the earliest biographies of Alexander[1] tell us that he condemned two books, one by William of St. Amour against the new Orders of SS. Dominic and Francis, and the other a Franciscan document known as *The Eternal Gospel*. Whatever concerned the Friars was always of the greatest interest to Alexander. He was so much attracted to them that it might almost be said that the greater number of his bulls were concerned with them, granting them privileges of one sort or another.[2] Hence no life of him would be complete that did not say something of the two famous books just referred to.

At first the appearance of the Friars as teachers was welcomed in the lecture rooms at the University of Paris.[3] But, as they increased in numbers, influence, and learning, and it was seen that the greater devotion to duty on the part of the *regular* professors, and the greater learning especially of the Dominican lecturers, were attracting to them the greater number of the students, the secular

[1] E.g., that of Bernard Guidonis, ap. *R. I. SS.*, iii, p. 593. *Cf.* Salimbene, *Chron.*, pp. 53, 300, 454–5.

[2] He at once (Dec. 22, 1254) recalled the decree of Innocent IV. (P., 15562) that took away their most important privileges. Potthast, 15602, *cf.* 16129. See 15669 for his interest in the Dominican rule ; 15714 and 15960 for a grant of a papal palace to the Franciscans ; 15826 for indulgences offered to those who support them ; and 15950, 16059, 16063–4, 16080, 16081 for other privileges.

[3] *Cf.* the letter of Honorius III., Feb. 27, 1220, ap. Denifle, *Chartular. Univer. Par.*, i, 95. *Cf.* what was said by the University itself, 1254, ap. *ib.*, p. 253.

professors were filled with jealousy. It was there " that
the shoe pinched ", to quote the actual words of a contemporary Dominican.[1] If, however, on the one hand,
the secular professors were jealous of the success of the
Friars, it is not unlikely that the religious, conscious
of their superior virtue, learning, and popularity, gave
way somewhat to pride, and made no adequate effort
to soothe the feelings of men whom they were perhaps
justly causing to take a second place, but who, after all,
as the founders of the University, had their rights, and
were entitled to consideration.[2] However this may be,
a quarrel to the death sprang up between the secular
masters [3] and the Friars. According to the former,
the Friars set at naught the institutions and customs
(institutis aut cæremoniis) of the University, and when
the Chancellor and the whole University had passed
a decree, the Friars set their own will above the University.
They decided to lecture in Theology without the licence
of the Chancellor or the University, and that they alone
should examine their professors. Such, at any rate,
is the statement of the action of the Friars as given by

[1] *De Apibus*, i, c. 10, p. 181, ed. Douais, 1605. The same author
says that one of the secular professors afterwards acknowledged that
he had nothing against the Friars except their intellectual superiority.
Ib., p. 178, ap. Mortier (*Hist. des Maitres Généraux*, i, p. 437), whom
along with Rashdall, *Universities of Europe*, i, p. 369 ff., and Bondatti,
Gioachinismo e Francescanismo nel Dugento, p. 112 ff., 1924 (a very
valuable book), I mostly follow in this affair of the University.

[2] The words of Richer († *c.* 1267) somewhat bear out this view.
" Prædicatores dicebant ab eis questionum diffiniciones debere proferi,
quia *pocior scientia in personis ordinis* vigeret . . . Clerici vero
econtra asserebant se *antiquitus* magistros et definitores habuisse, qui
scolarum et scolarium rectores extiterant. *Gesta senonensis ecclesiæ*,
iv, c. 44, ap. *M. G. SS.*, xxv, p. 328.

[3] It must be borne in mind that *secular* does not here mean *lay*. All
the students and professors of a University were then *clerics*. *Secular*
is here opposed to *Regular*, which denotes connexion with a religious
Order governed by a written rule (regula).

a member of the Benedictine Order [1] which was itself
rather jealous of what it regarded as upstart religious.

The Masters
commence
the attack on
the Friars,
1252.

In February, 1252, the secular masters began the
attack on the Friars by issuing a regulation which hit
a number of religious Orders, and another which aimed
at the Dominicans especially ; for, as they were essentially
an Order devoted to learning, they were made to bear the
brunt of the attack on the regulars. They had at this
period two theological lecturers (magistri regentes) and
two schools. The regulation against them decided [2]
that each religious Order was to be content with one
school and one master.[3]   The breach between the secular
and the regular professors was widened by the refusal
on the part of the latter to share in a *strike* to which
the others had agreed. Fresh legislation against the
Orders followed (Sept., 1253) [4] ; and, as the religious
professors would not submit to it, they were denied
communion with the other professors.[5] The result of
this drastic action was an appeal to Rome. Innocent
IV. espoused the cause of the Friars. He declared that
their virtues made them worthy of honour both from
God and man ; and he ordered " the masters and the
university of the scholars at Paris " to reinstate the
religious professors.[6]

---

[1] The author of the *Annals of Burton*, p. 347.   Both he and Matthew
Paris show a strong bias against the Friars. A similar dispute sprang
up in the pontificate of Clement IV. between the University of Oxford
and the Friars Preachers. It is dealt with by H. Rashall in " The
Friars Preachers *v.* the Univ. of Oxf." (1311–13), in *Collectanea*, 2nd
series, ed. M. Burrows, Oxf., 1890, p. 193 ff.

[2] " Hanc autem ordinationem Universitas approbavit, et sigili
sui munimine roboravit." Denifle, *Chart.*, i, p. 227.

[3] " Prædicti magistri ordinaverunt ut singula religiosorum collegia
singulis magistris actu regentibus et unica scola de cetero sint contenta."
Ib., p. 228. *Cf.* Thos. of Cantimpré, *De Apibus*, ii, c. 10, n. 32.

[4] *Ib.*, n. 219, p. 242 ff.

[5] *Cf.* the letter of Innocent IV.,❘July 1, 1253, ap. *ib.*, p. 247.

[6] *Ib.*, and ep. of Aug. 26, ap. *ib.*, p. 249.

Peace was, however, not restored. On the contrary, the tension was aggravated by the issue on the part of the University of a pamphlet, addressed " to the prelates of the Church and to all scholars ", in which the action of the Friars and especially of the Preachers with regard to the University regulations, was attacked in strong terms (Feb. 4), 1254).[1] The manifesto asserted that the Dominicans had obtained possession of two chairs of theology in an irregular manner ; and pointed out that, as the statutes limited the number of such chairs to twelve, and as the canons of Paris had a right to three, there would soon not be a single one left for the clergy of the world, if action such as that of the Friars Preachers were tolerated. The University had therefore decided that they were only to have one chair, and this decision they had refused to obey. In like manner, too, they contumaciously refused to obey a regulation which the University had drawn up for the preservation of its privileges. It was clear, concluded the pamphlet, that the University had been nursing a serpent in its breast which had stung it.

Innocent IV., however, was not a man to submit to have his orders trifled with ; and he accordingly summoned the Masters of the University to appear before him. Four of their number were selected to represent them. At the head of this deputation was William of St. Amour, a canon of Beauvais, who showed himself the irreconcilable enemy of the Friars.[2] It would appear that the arguments of William made some impression upon the Pope. At any rate, without however issuing

Innocent annuls the privileges already granted to the Friars.

---

[1] Ap. Denifle, *ib.*, pp. 252–8.

[2] *Cf.* ep. Inn. IV., July 13, 1254, ap. Denifle, i, 265. "Cum . . . Clerum Parisiensem et prælatos ecclesiæ, quorum se defensorem dicebat, contra ordinem concitasset (W. of St. A.), etc." *Catal. gen. O.F.M.*, ap. *M. G. SS.*, xxxii, p. 663. *Cf.* ep. of the Dominican General, Humbert de Romanis, ap. Denifle, i, n. 273, p. 309.

any decision on the subject of their position at the University, Innocent, possibly somewhat hastily, issued a decree, a week or two before his death, by which he revoked the most important parochial privileges which had been granted to the Dominicans and the Franciscans (Nov. 21, 1254).

It is, of course, quite possible that this decree had no connexion with the University question. However, whether it had or not, it was withdrawn a few weeks later by Innocent's successor, Alexander IV. (Dec. 22, 1254).

Innocent's bull is withdrawn by Alexander, who issues one in favour of the Friars, 1255.

The eloquence and, possibly, the just arguments of St. Amour were lost upon Alexander who on April 14, 1255, issued his famous but somewhat verbose bull " Quasi lignum vitæ " which settled the questions in dispute between the seculars and Regulars of the University in favour of the latter.[1] By it, the Dominicans would be able to keep their second theological chair, as the Pope decided that " vested interests " were to hold good, and that the Chancellor might, as he had done before, grant the licence to teach to such as were found by him to be competent. With regard to the oath to be taken on admittance to the University, it was not to bind to secrecy when that secrecy could not be kept without danger to souls. As for suspension of lectures, the Dominicans had indeed to obey a University order for such suspension. But such an order was not to be issued except with the consent of two-thirds of the members of each Faculty [2]; and, as the regulars could dominate

---

[1] Ap. Denifle, i, p. 279 ff. The Pope has decided : " aliqua ex . . . ordinationibus . . . a vobis editis . . . moderanda providimus, cetera vero . . . resecanda." P. 282.

[2] A suspension of lectures could be ordered " dummodo due partes magistrorum theologice facultatis, et eodem modo due partes magistrorum singularium facultatum reliquarum, videlicet canonistarum, physicorum, et etiam artistarum (the faculty of Arts), suum super hoc voluerint præstare consensum." *Ib.*

the theological faculty, they could thus block professorial strikes if they thought fit [1] Finally the papal decree ordered the restitution of the Dominican theological professors to the fellowship of the professors generally.[2] The bishops of Orleans and Auxerre were commissioned to see to the execution of the decrees contained in " Quasi lignum vitæ ".[3]

Rome had spoken and, as the secular professors showed no sign of submission, the two bishops excommunicated them. The University as such could not but submit. There was, however, no power which could compel men to go on teaching or to remain in Paris, and of this the secular Masters reminded the Pope. In an outspoken manifesto they told him they would rather renounce their corporate privileges, and even leave Paris itself and return to their own hearths where they could enjoy their native liberty, than be forced to admit the preachers to their society. They accordingly urged the Pope to annul the sentence of excommunication passed against them, " an unarmed band of foreigners " as they described themselves, and to restore to them the liberties which they had enjoyed at the time of his accession. This manifesto was signed by all except the Dominican professors, and, " seeing that they had no common seal, as they were now separated from the college of the University," it was

Strong opposition to " Quasi lignum ".

---

[1] This was pointed out in the professional reply (" Radix amaritudinis ") to the " Quasi lignum " (Oct. 2, 1255, ap. D., i, n. 256, p. 292). " Cum enim magistrorum saltem theologie pars major quam tertia de canonicis Parisiensis ecclesie et fratruum aliorum conventuum Parisien. maxime occasione dicte ordinationis semper existat, etc."

[2] *Cf.* a papal mandate on the subject to theological professors in particular. Apr. 14, 1255, ap. Denifle, n. 249.

[3] *Ib.*, n. 248. Thomas of Cantimpré, in his collection of pious stories *De Apibus, l.c.,* p. 179, says that the seculars could not be overcome by any arguments or by the words of the Holy Fathers. To subdue them it took the judicial sentence of the lord Pope and all his Curia. It must be observed that Thomas was a Dominican.

sealed " with the seals of the four Nations which have
long been recognized in Paris ".[1]

" The Perils
of the Last
Day " and
" The
Eternal
Gospel ".

There is some reason to believe that both the famous
books which Alexander condemned were mentioned in
this manifesto. The manifesto declares that the regular
Masters in order to decry William of St. Amour had
maliciously attributed to him a pamphlet against the
authority of the Pope whose private life from his youth
upwards had been so strikingly distinguished.[2] It is
thought that this refers to the " Treatise on the perils of
our times ", which appears after all to have been really
the work of St. Amour.   It is certain from the pamphlet
itself that it was written in 1255, and a Vatican MS.
of it closes with the words : " Here endeth the book
written at Paris against hypocrites and false religious
by the Burgundian William of St. Amour in the year of
our Lord 1255." [3] The pamphlet was a bitter attack on
the Mendicant Orders and contained various utterances
injurious to the authority of the Pope.[4]   Though this
production did some harm to these bodies, the lustre
shed upon them at this moment by the learning, teaching
ability, and virtues of Albertus Magnus, and SS. Thomas
Aquinas and Bonaventure was such that they attracted
so much sympathy and support that they could easily
vanquish any attack, however calumnious. Indeed, they
had at this time such well deserved influence both with

[1] The manifesto is dated Oct. 2, 1255, ap. *ib.*, n. 256, p. 292 ff. The
four Nations were the French, Normans, Picards, and English.

[2] " Fratres . . . quod ipse . . . personam vestram infamie non
patentem (utpote cujus ab ipso puerili evo semper rutilans fama corus-
cavit) ore maledicto diffamasset contra vos libellum famosum . . .
confinxerunt." *Ib.*, p. 294. *Cf. ib.*, n. 288, p. 331 ff., Oct. 5, 1256, for
the bull in which Alexander condemns the Treatise.

[3] *Cf. ib.*, p. 296, n. 6.

[4] The pamphlet " De periculis novissimorum temporum," is printed
among the works of St. Amour, *Operas* Constance, 1632, and under a
false title in Browne's *Fasiculus rerum*, vol. ii, p. 17 ff.

Pope Alexander and St. Louis, both at the court of Rome and in the Palace of the King, that there was perhaps a natural, if unconscious tendency in both those rulers to incline the balance of justice in their favour. However, both St. Thomas,[1] and St. Bonaventure wrote triumphant refutations of the work of St. Amour, who wrecked what was just in his cause by endeavouring to support his position not simply by sound arguments but by throwing mud at his opponents. His work was condemned by the Pope, and solemnly burnt both at Anagni, and at Paris in the presence of St. Louis (1256), who expelled St. Amour from France.[2]

If the Regulars were able, seemingly with truth, to father the " Tractatus de periculis " on to St. Amour, the Seculars, despite their efforts to do so, were unable to saddle the Friars Preachers with " The Eternal Gospel ". It is true that in their manifesto, when St. Amour and his

The Eternal Gospel.

---

[1] In the Parma ed. (1874), vol. xv, or in that of Vivès, vol. xxix (Paris, 1876), the *Apology for the religious Orders* of his Thomas is made up of his Opusculum i: "Contra impugnantes Dei cultum et religionem" and Opusc. iii : " Contra pestiferam doctrinam retrahentium homines a religionis ingressu." They were translated (*An apol. for the rel. Orders*, by J. Procter, London, 1902. They were probably written *c.* 1267, and it may be noted that they do not mention W. de St. A. by name.

[2] *Cf. Catal. Generalium O.F.M.*, ap. *M. G. SS.*, xxxii, p. 663 ; *Phil. de Perusio ep. de cardinal. protect.*, *ib.*, p. 681 ; Salimbene, *Chron.*, *ib.*, pp. 300 and 454, and ep. Alex., Aug. 3, 1257, etc., ap. Denifle, i, pp. 362 and 363 ff. It is William of Nangis who tells us that the book was burnt before the Pope. *Chron.*, ad an. 1255 ; and also Thos. of Cantimpré, *De Apibus*, ii, c. 10, n. 23. As we learn from a letter of Pope Clement IV. to William (Oct. 18, 1266, ap. Denifle, i, p. 459), he pretended to modify the views set forth in the *De periculis* in another work (probably *Liber de Antichristo et ejusdem ministris*). The Pope, who had read a portion of it, tells him that though parts of the new book are in appearance more tolerable than the other, " it is much the same in spirit " : " Qui (the new book) licet interdum alias auras circinet, veterem tam multum sapit." The work in Martène and Durand, *Ampless. Collect.*, vol. ix, which bears the name of Nicolai Oresme is thought to be this production of W. of St. Amour. *Cf.* Kingsford, in his introduction to John Peckham's answer to W., p. 16, Aberdeen, 1910.

party speak of the possible destruction " of the Empire of Peter ", foreshadowed in *The Eternal Gospel*, they assigned that idea " to the prophecies of the heresiarch Joachim ".[1] But they succeeded, apparently, in getting many to believe that " the Preachers compiled a certain book of the Gospels ".[2] The book here referred to is, indeed, a compilation, but it was the work neither of Joachim nor of the Dominicans. It was put together by brother Ghiradino of Borgo San Donino, one of the Franciscan acquaintances of Brother Salimbene. To three genuine works of Joachim,[3] he added an introduction (*Liber introductorius*) and glosses of his own.

Through his mystic interpretations of the Bible, and his forecasting of the future from the records of the past, Abbot Joachim of Fiore was regarded by many as a prophet. He himself had disclaimed any prophetical power ; but his statements with regard to the proximate coming of Antichrist and of a new spiritual era took a great hold on many minds. He was supposed, too, by some to have fixed the year 1260 as the date of the beginning of this era.[4] But for the elaborations of

[1] P. 296. This idea of the possible failure of " Peter's Empire " is not Joachim's ; for, as may be seen, *supra*, vol. x, p. 439, note 1, Joachim declared that the " Church of Peter which was the throne of Christ, would never fail ". It was one of Ghiradino's additions to Joachim's books.

[2] The words of Richer, *Gesta Senon. Eccles.*, iv, c. 44, ap. *M. G. SS.*, xxv, p. 328. *Cf.* Mat. Par., *Chron.*, v, 598, who relates the history of this affair with his usual inaccuracy. *Cf. ib.*, pp. 506, 528.

[3] The *Concordia Novi ac Veteris Testamenti, Apocalypsis Nova*, and the *Psalterium Decem Chordarum*.

[4] Others, for instance, a certain Brother Hugo," who was a great Joachite, and had all the books of the abbot Joachim well written out (de grossa litera)," maintained that Joachim did not assign fixed dates,. " non limitavit omnino aliquem certum terminum licet videatur quibusdam quod sic." Salimbene, *Chron.*, pp. 236–9. When the year 1260 passed, and nothing extraordinary happened, Salimbene himself gave up all belief in Joachism, and decided to believe no more than what he could see. *Ib.*, pp. 302 and 455.

Brother Ghiradino (or Gherardo), the mystic musings of
the abbot of Fiore would never have come to world-wide
fame.   In his speech, too, the brother maintained that
Alfonso X. of Castile was Antichrist,[1] and that the works
of Joachim constituted *The Everlasting Gospel* which
was to be interpreted by the spirituals among the Friars,
seeing that Pope and Church were shortly to disappear.[2]

It is only fair to add that the *Introductorius* is no longer The E.G. a
extant, and that it would seem that, at times, what are useful
given as extracts from it are rather conclusions, more or weapon for
the seculars.
less warranted by its text.   In any case, its appearance
at this moment from a *Regular* source put a useful
weapon into the hands of the secular masters against the
Mendicant Orders.   Moreover, as the "Eternal Gospel"
was well received by a number of Friars, St. Amour
and his friends were able with some show of justice to
contend that it represented the general feeling of the two
Orders.   They wished, declared St. Amour, to replace the
Gospel of Christ by "that cursed Gospel which they call
the Eternal Gospel".[3]

Brought to the Pope's notice, the *Liber Introductorius*, Alexander
after being duly examined by three cardinals, was adheres to
his bull.

[1] Salimbene, *Chron.*, p. 456.

[2] Ghiradino's *Liber Introductorius* is only known by the report of
the commission of cardinals which examined it, ap. Denifle, *Das
Evangelium æternum*, ap. *Archiv. fur Litteratur . . . des Mittelalters*,
i, Berlin, 1885.   The author of the *Romance of the Rose* (see note below)
gives the reason for the scarcity of the *Liber Int.*

[4] . . . What since became of it
None know, for those of whom 'twas born
Have hid it until time be worn."

Vol. ii, p. 165, Eng. trans.

[3] "Legem Christi conculcari, et tolli per Evangelium illud maledictum,
quod appellant Evangelium æternum."   Ed. Brown, p. 39.   *Cf.* the
Apocalypse, xiv, 6 : "And I saw another angel flying through the
midst of heaven, having the eternal gospel."   The *Introductorius*
appeared in 1254.

condemned.[1]   These disputes and condemnations in
connexion with a University with its thousands of
eager minds made a great sensation, and were discussed everywhere. Each side had its strong partisans.
Jean of Meun, in the famous *Romance of the Rose,*
prays :—

> " God starve me of good meats and wine
> Unless his book (St. Amour's) in accord be
> With Paris University. . . .
> Let those who scoff at him scoff still
> And grumblers grumble as they will
> For my part, I shall ever hold
> His name in honour. . . ." [2]

His condemnation of Ghiradino is as strong as his
advocacy of St. Amour. The Everlasting Gospel was :—

> " The prime exemplar of a book
> So vile that by the devil's crook
> It well were written . . . .
> Men are exhorted there to slay
> All those who Peter's rule obey :
> But howsoever they assail
> His law, hell's gates shall not prevail
> Against it, but it still shall stand,
> A beacon unto every land,
> And those who hold it fast shall be
> God's people everlastingly." [3]

Public feeling ran very high, and the Preachers
especially often suffered personal violence at the hands of
the student supporters of the secular Masters.

Unshaken, however, by the resistance offered to his
decree, Alexander continued by ordinance after ordinance
to enforce his " Quasi Lignum ". He was so insistent
because he considered the Friars an ornament to the

---

[1] Ep. Oct. 23, 1255, ap. Denifle, *Chart.*, i, n. 257, p. 297. *Cf.* n 258,
Nov. 4, 1255, in which Alexander bids the bishop of Paris proceed
cautiously in carrying the Pope's condemnation into effect. He does
not wish any harm to come to the Friars Minor from the said condemnation : " et obloqutores et emuli non possint exinde sumere contra
ipsos materiam detrahendi."

[2] Eng. trans., ed. Ellis, vol. ii, p. 153. *Cf. supra*, vol. ix, p. 38 f.

[3] *Ib.*, pp. 162-6.

University.[1] No professor was to be given a licence to teach who would not subscribe to it [2] ; opposition to it was to be punished by excommunication [3] ; and William of St. Amour and other ringleaders of the opposition to the Friars were to be expelled from France.[4]

These strong measures, supported by St. Louis, were not without their effect, and some of the secular leaders, such as Eudes of Douay and Christian of Beauvais, made their submission to the Pope.[5] The Dominicans were not ungrateful for the efforts made in their behalf by the Pope and the King ; and their General, Humbert de Romanis, ordered special prayers for them.[6] By degrees the opposition of the secular masters was beaten down. In April, 1259, a letter of Alexander enables us to see that peace had been practically re-established [7] ; and before that year was out we find him granting various privileges to the University.[8] Whilst, then, their papal patron lived, the victory of the Friars over the University was tolerably

Some of the secular masters submit, 1256.

---

[1] Ep. Nov., 1256, *ib.,* p. 344.

[2] Ep. Dec. 7, 1255, ap. Denifle, n. 259, i, p. 298. *Cf.* n. 298.

[3] *Ib.,* n. 262. *Cf.* nn. 263, 269, March 3, 1256 ; 270, same date. (This letter praises the chancellor for giving '' Thomas of Aquinas '' licence to teach) ; 271, Apr. 4 ; 272, 275, etc., 300, Jan. 13, 1257.

[4] Ep. to St. Louis, June 27, 1256, ap. *ib.,* n. 272, p. 324. The sentence of exile against W. of St. A. was repeated Aug. 11, 1257. *Cf.* Potthast, n. 16977. Alexander's interest in the University may be seen from his sending his nephews there. *Cf. ib.,* n. 283 ; and n. 296 for his great praise of it.

[5] See their act of submission, *ib.,* n. 293. *Cf.* nn. 317, 319–20.

[6] *Ib.,* n. 311.

[7] Ap. *ib.,* n. 331. '' Intellecto Parisiense studium pacifice agere, ac vigere circa scolasticam disciplinam, necnon et Universitatem ipsius directis pro ejusdem conservatione studii mandatis apostolicis debita reverentia humiliter paruisse, gavisi sumus vehementer.'' Subsequent letters, however, show that the peace was not absolute. *Cf.* nn. 332 ; 226–9, 342, etc., 353–5.

[8] *Cf.,* e.g. *ib.* 349, Aug. 7, 1259, where he grants their servants the same immunities as were enjoyed by the masters and the scholars. *Cf.* n. 350 f.

complete. After his death, however, the University was gradually able for the most part to render nugatory the privileges he had bestowed upon the Regulars, [1] and to assert its paramount position.

That the advance towards peace and order was, indeed, distinctly gradual is very clear from an interesting passage in Roger Bacon's *Compendium studii Philosophiæ*, written in 1271. In his rather over bitter style, the friar asserts that the Seculars have for some forty years back ceased to study theology and philosophy, and so have not written any theological works. They have simply placed themselves at the feet of young inexperienced masters of the two Orders. As a consequence, the Orders have become conceited,[2] and the result has been quarrels, mutual abuse, and appeals to Rome. These quarrels, concludes the caustic Franciscan, are still going on, and will go on till either Antichrist comes, or some excellent Pope shall put an end to the whole difficulty with the aid of a General Council.

[1] *Cf.* Rashdall, *Universities*, i, p. 389 f. To the works on this subject cited here and in vol. x, p. 435 ff., add a delightful essay, " Joachim of Flora and the Everlasting Gospel," by E. Gardner, ap. *Franciscan Essays*, Aberdeen, 1912 ; and *S. Bernadino of Siena*, by A. G. Ferrers Howell, pp. 2–14. London, 1913 ; F. Tocco, " L'Evangelo Eterno " ap. *Studii Francescani*, p. 191 (Naples, 1909).

[2] " Elevent cornua in studio et appareant miri modo." 1. 5, ap. *M. G. SS.*, xxviii, p. 580.

CHAPTER VI.

THE LATIN AND GREEK EMPIRES IN THE NEAR EAST.
CYPRUS. THE TARTARS. AFRICA.

IF neither the world nor its ordinary order was near its Last days of the Latin Empire of Constantinople. end during the pontificate of Alexander, the same cannot be said for various important institutions on its surface. Before Alexander's death the Tartars had put an end to the Caliphate of Bagdad (1258), and, within a few months after it, the Greeks of Nicæa had destroyed the ill-starred Latin Empire of Constantinople.

Though Innocent III., under whom the latter institution took its rise, strongly condemned its origin, both he and his successors accepted the situation and endeavoured to make the best of it. They strove to support " the Empire of Romania " in the hope that it might serve as a reliable base of operations for the recovery of the Holy Land, and as a lever to move the Greek Church to return to union with that of Rome. But their efforts had largely been thrown away. The curse of its evil birth seemed to cling to the Latin Empire. But, though its last hour was at hand, Alexander continued the policy of his predecessors, and made some effort to relieve the dearth of men and money from which it suffered.

He had not been Pope for many weeks when he Alexander supports the Latin Empire of the East. addressed a letter to the bishop of Argolis and other occupants of Grecian Sees. After saying that he had been thinking how he could help " the Empire of Romania ", and that he had heard that Achaia and Morea were in great need of assistance, he urged his correspondents to see that all the clergy, both bishops and priests, exempt and non-exempt, contributed funds for their defence.[1]

He also took steps to obtain from the aforesaid bishops an annual sum of five hundred marks for the patriarch of Constantinople, as the hostility of the Greeks had so diminished his revenues that he could not support his position. Both in Church and State the Latin Empire of Constantinople was at its last gasp.[2]

He strives to keep the peace among the Franks.

The Latins in Greece were exposed to the attacks of the Greek State of Epirus, on the one hand, and of that of Nicæa on the other. Yet, despite their perils from the implacable Greeks, the Latins would not keep the peace among themselves. At this time the ambition of William Villehardouin, Prince of Achaia, was the main cause of trouble among the Franks of Greece. Desirous ultimately of uniting " all the Frankish baronies " under his over-lordship,[3] he was at this moment (1255) at war with the rulers of Eubœa (Negroponte) about the dowry of his wife (†1255). This brought him into collision with Venice, which claimed a suzerainty over the island. On this Pope Alexander, " in order that the Greeks in the Empire of Romania might not become more powerful against the Catholics, urged the combatants from zeal for the faith and from reverence for the Roman Church to desist from their enterprises, lest he should have to take severe measures against them." [4] Alexander's protests were not listened to. Robbed of his conquests in Eubœa by the Venetians, William allied himself with the ambitious Michael Palæologus, who had usurped the empire of Nicæa after the death of Theodore Lascaris II. (August,

---

[1] Ep. Jan. 2, 1255, ap. Raynaldus, an. 1255, n. 74.

[2] *Reg.*, vol. ii, n. 2072, July 15, 1257. " Contra ipsum patriarchum ac alios negotium Constantinopolitani imperii prosequentes eorundem Grecorum feritas fortius invalescit."

[3] Rodd, *The Princes of Actaia*, i, 192.

[4] Dandalo, *Chron.*, l. x, c. 7, ap. *R. I. SS.*, xii, p. 363.

1258). This naturally roused Alexander still more, and he bade William dissolve the alliance or he would instruct the bishop of Modon (Methone) to compel him by Apostolic authority to do so.[1] The barons of " new France " were a lawless company, but possibly on this occasion the Pope's representations were heeded.

At any rate, the Prince of Achaia took for his third wife Anna,[2] the daughter of Michael II., Despot of Epirus (1259), and in company with troops from Manfred, Michael's other son-in-law, joined himself to his father-in-law against Palæologus. It was a question as to whether the Despot or the usurper was to become the leader of the Greek people and to grasp the prize of Constantinople. A battle in the plain of Pelagonia, south of Ochrida, and treachery settled the question in favour of the usurper. The Despot's army was defeated by the troops of Palæologus, and William Villehardouin, the most powerful of the Franks in the East, was taken prisoner (October, 1259). This disastrous battle sealed the fate not only of the Latin Empire of Constantinople, but also of the Franks in Greece.[3]

Great defeat of the Franks at Pelagonia, 1259.

It would seem that, when the Prince of Achaia broke off his alliance with Michael Palæologus, and that usurper, who had set aside John IV., the child heir of Theodore II., and who had had himself crowned emperor of Nicæa (December, 1258), he found himself faced with the formidable coalition of the Despot of Epirus and his sons-in-law, and turned to Alexander. In his usurpation, the Pope's favour would be a support to him in face of the opposition of his own patriarch Arsenius who was loyal to his pupil John. It was desirable, therefore, to placate the Pope, and by

Palœologus turns to the Pope, 1259.

---

[1] *Ib.*, p. 364.

[2] She was the sister of Helen, the wife of Manfred. *Cf.* Sanudo, *Istoria del Regno di Romania*, p. 107, ed. Hopf.

[3] *Cf.* Miller, *The Latins in the Levant*, p. 111 ff.—a delightful book ; and Rodd, *l.c.*, p. 205 ff.

holding out to him prospects of re-union, to prevent his taking disagreeable steps, if Constantinople should fall to him. However, all this may be, it appears from a comparatively recently discovered letter [1] that " After the rudder of the ship of the state was put into our hands we straightway sent ambassadors to Pope Alexander IV. to treat with him about peace ". Michael informs the Pope of his coronation, and begs his support against the coalition which has been formed against him. The fact that his enemy Manfred was opposed to the Greek emperor might naturally have induced Alexander to use his influence in Michael's behalf. But whether the discourteous manner in which his envoys had been treated by the " Pope Emperor ", Theodore Lascaris II.,[2] had turned Alexander against the Greeks of Nicæa, or simply because he had no taste for the game of politics and war, he does not appear to have taken any action in behalf of Palæologus. He made no difficulty, however, only a few weeks before he died, in acknowledging him as Emperor. Addressing him as such, he interceded with him for the release of two merchants of Lucca, who had been

---

[1] N. Festa, ap. *Bessarione*, vol. vi, p. 532, cited by Norden, *Das Papsttum und Byzanz*, p. 382. The letter was drawn up by Manuel Holobolus, and was dispatched to Clement IV. Manuel was for a time secretary of M. Palæologus, and then spent part of his time in banishment in a monastery. He was a learned man, and, as he knew Latin, the Dominican Simon of Crete addressed him a letter on the Procession of the Holy Ghost.

[2] *Cf. supra*, vol. xiv, p. 231. On the ecclesiastical authority claimed by Theodore, see Miss Gardner, *The Lascarids of Nicæa*, ch. xi. The *Annals of Orvieto*, ap. *R. I. SS.*, t. xv, p. 154, new ed., thus briefly allude to Alexander's embassy to Greece : " D. frater Constantinus, de ordine Predicatorum, episcopus urbevetanus, legatus d. Pape ivit (1256) ad Greciam, et ibi post multa bene gesta, dormivit in Domino." In vol. iv of the new *Cambridge Mediæval Hist.*, p. 609, this Dominican bishop of Orvieto is metamorphosed into " Orbevieto bishop of Civitavecchia", where there had been no bishopric since the eleventh century.

taken prisoners by the Greek prefect.[1] Had Alexander favoured either side, he would probably have reaped some advantage. His relations with Michael Palæologus supply us with another instance of his weakness of character resulting in grave loss to the causes he had at heart.

After that lovely island had been conquered by Richard Cœur-de-Lion, it passed by the King's gift into the family of Lusignan. As the island was now in the hands of Franks, it was but natural that a Latin hierarchy should be set up. Accordingly, by the authority of Pope Celestine III. (1196), a Latin metropolitan was established in Nicosia, and three suffragan sees were subjected to it. We are told that the Pope was not prepared to establish the hierarchy till he was assured by the King (Amaury) that funds would be forthcoming for its proper maintenance, and the native historian, Machéras, who tells us this, avers that the funds were taken from the established Orthodox Greek Church.[2]

Cyprus.

Between the Greek bishops thus robbed and the Latin bishops endless quarrels ensued ; especially as, for the safety of their position, the Frank rulers were anxious to bring the Greeks into subjection to their own hierarchy. In the main, the Popes supported the Frankish sovereigns and their bishops. Honorius III., for instance, decided [3] that where in one diocese there was a Latin and a Greek bishop, the latter could not be allowed to remain in the diocese as a bishop. In the case of Greeks who had returned to the unity of the Church, he was anxious, he declared, to preserve their rites and customs as far as possible, but it was monstrous that one diocese should

" Uniat " Greeks subjected to Latin bishops.

---

[1] Potthast, n. 18080, Apr. 2, 1261.

[2] *Chronique de Chypre*, pp. 19–20, French trans. Celestine's bull is dated Feb. 20, 1196.

[3] See his bull " Licet diligentia " of Dec. 30, 1221, ap. *Bullar. Rom. Pont.*, iii, 382.

have two bishops. The Greek priests and deacons, therefore, must submit to the Latin bishops in whose diocese
they lived.[1]

As time went on, more pressure was put on the Greek
clergy to induce them to acknowledge the supremacy
of the Pope. Eustorgius (Eustorge de Montaign), archbishop of Nicosia, had been very active in this matter,
and the Greek bishops, or some of them, after asking for
time to deliberate, availed themselves of the delay,
stripped their churches of their valuables and fled to
Armenia. Thereupon Gregory IX., consulted as to what
should be done, bade the archbishop consecrate Latins
for the said sees.[2]

Better treat-
ment of the
Greeks by
Innocent IV.
Under Innocent (IV.) the Magnificent, a better time
dawned for the Greeks under Latin domination. On
June 5, 1247, he sent to Armenia, Greece, etc.,
Bro. Lawrence, a Franciscan, as his legate, to deal " as
an angel of peace " with all questions between the
Greeks and the Latins in those parts, and to protect the
former from molestation.[3] In dealing then with those
Greeks " who dwelt in the kingdom of Cyprus ", he had

[1] Rev. J. Hackell, *A History of the Orthodox Church of Cyprus*, p. 85,
would appear to have wholly misunderstood this bull which he quotes
from Raynaldus, *Ann.*, 1222, n. 8. He says, quite wrongly, that it
was concerned with suppressing the Greek sees in the island, which
numbered fourteen. It was, in fact, concerned with Greeks who had
returned to the unity of the Roman Church. If they were in a Latin
diocese they must obey the Latin bishop, and could not be allowed
to have a bishop of their own in that see. The Greek sees were reduced
from 14 to 4 under the legate Pelagius, cardinal-bishop of Albano, on
Sept. 14, 1222. See the famous " Summa " of Alexander IV. of July 3,
1260, ap. Raynaldus, *Ann.*, 1260, n. 37, and especially the bull of
Honorius III. (Jan. 21, 1223) in which he confirmed the doings of that
self-opiniated man. Ap. Mas. Latrie, *Hist. de Chœpre*, ii, 45.

[2] Ep. of Apr. 13, 1240, ap. Raynaldus, *Ann.*, 1240, nn. 44-5.

[3] Ap. *ib.*, 1247, n. 30 ff. " Ideoque mandamus, quatenus Græcos . . .
auctoritate Apostolica protegens, turbari eos violentiis, vel quibiscum-
que molestiis non permitas."

ordered the recall of the Greek archbishop from exile.
Encouraged by this sign of friendliness, the Greeks
formulated their grievances and sent them to Innocent.
Some time after their return, as we learn from the Pope's
letter to his legate Otho (Eudes of Châteauroux), cardinal-
bishop of Tusculum,[1] the Greek bishops had of their own
accord (sponte) offered submission—manual obedience,
as Innocent expressed it—to the Roman Church. At the
same time, their archbishop requested that, as formerly,
he should have the right of canonically instituting the
ancient fourteen Greek sees of the island, and that, subject
to the Holy See and not to the Latins, they should enjoy
the same privileges as the Latins. They requested,
therefore, that they should be allowed to exercise the
same jurisdiction over their Greek subjects as they had had
" before they left (resilirent) the Roman Church ", and
that the tithes from the Greek monasteries, and even
certain tithes from the Latins should be assigned to the
Greek hierarchy. Finally, appeals from the Greek bishops
were to be carried not to the Latin bishops but to the
Pope. Realizing that only local knowledge could give a
satisfactory answer to these requests, Innocent ordered
Cardinal Otho to deal with them on the spot.

In pursuance of his broad-minded policy, it would
appear that Innocent IV., setting aside the bull of
Celestine III. (or the interpretation put upon it) which
decreed that Nicosia should be the metropolitical see,
allowed the Greeks to elect Germanos Pesimandros as a
metropolitan for themselves.[2] Moreover, a year or two
later, declaring how dear to his heart was the union of all
Christians,[3] he again proclaimed that, as some Greeks had
returned " to the devotion of the apostolic See ", it was

The Greeks
elect a
metropolitan
for them-
selves, 1252.

---

[1] Ep. July 21, 1250, ap. *ib.*, 1250, n. 41.

[2] For all this see the " Summa " of Alexander IV. of 1260, *l.c.*

[3] Ep. " Sub catholicæ professione " of March 6, 1254, ap. *Bullar.
Rom.*, iii, 580.   " Hæc inquam, unio sive connexio cordi nostro

right and proper to tolerate, as far as the law of God would permit, their rites and customs " in order that we may keep them in their obedience to the Roman Church ". He then proceeded to adjudicate upon certain points connected with Catholic faith and the administration of the Sacraments which the legate Otho had put before him as matters upon which there was disagreement between the Greeks and the Latins. At the close of his bull, he especially laid it down that the Latin metropolitan of Nicosia and his suffragans should not interfere in the enforcing of his decrees, but only the legate, who, in virtue of his apostolic authority, was also to punish any such interference as the Pope had condemned.[1]

The *Constitutio Cypria* or *Summa Alexandrina*, 1260.

Unfortunately, not all the Popes have been as courageous and as broad-minded and clear-sighted as Innocent IV. was. On his death, the ambition of the Latin metropolitan of Nicosia, Hugh de Fagiano, reasserted itself. He at once attacked the position of Germanos. It was, he averred, a flagrant violation of the regulations of Celestine III. The dispute came before Alexander IV., who, despite the fact that Germanos and his suffragans had promised obedience to the Roman Church,[2] settled the question in a way that did little credit to his ability as a statesman, not to say even to his sense of justice.

It is true, " in order that he might join the Greeks and Latins," as he said, " by the bonds of mutual love," he began by fixing the boundaries of the dioceses. He

inæstimabilis gaudii rorem infunderet, si varias gentium nationes ejusdem observantia fidei in unam acceptabilem Christo populum adunarent."

[1] " Memoratis autem archiepiscopo Nicosien., et ejus suffraganeis latinis firmiter auctoritate nostra præcipias, ut eosdem Græcos super præmissos contra hujusmodi provisionem et deliberationem nostram, non inquietent aliquatenus, nec molestent." *Ib.*

[2] See his own bull of July 3, 1260, ap. Raynaldus, 1260, n. 37.

" irrefragably " decreed that within the four Latin dioceses and under the metropolitan of Nicosia the four Greek dioceses should be fixed as follows. In the diocese of Nicosia the Greek see should be at Solia, in Paphos at Arsinoë, in Famagusta at Karpasso, and in Nimosia (or Limassol) at Levkara (or Amathus).[1]

But in each case the Greek bishop was in a subordinate position to the Latin, who had the right of confirming his election and of receiving from the newly elect an oath of obedience before he put him in possession of his see. Serious questions, however, connected with translation or punishment of Greek bishops were to be left to the Holy See. Moreover, if Greeks attacked the rights of the Latin bishops, they could themselves proceed against them. The Greek bishops, too, had to attend the diocesan synods of their Latin ordinaries, and observe their decisions, while the Latin bishops had a right " to visit " the Greeks in their respective dioceses. The Greek metropolitan Germanos was to retain his powers during his lifetime, but they were to end with him.[2]

This " Constitution " remained in force till the capture of Cyprus by the Turks in 1571, and the consequent expulsion of the Latin hierarchy. The Greeks then once more got a metropolitan of their own ; but they were to find that, if the Latins had scourged them with whips, the Turks were to scourge them with scorpions. One cannot help feeling, however, that if they had been treated more liberally by the Latins, a real union of heart and belief between the two peoples might have resulted.

---

[1] In the *Chronique d'Amadi*, p. 85, ed. R. Mas Latrie, Paris, 1891, we read in Nicosia, " el vescovo greco de la Solia," in " Bapho ", " il greco di Arsinoë " ; in " Farmagosta ", " il greco di Carpasso " ; and in " Limisso ", " il greco di Amathonda."

[2] See the " Constitutio " of July 3, 1260, ap. Raynaldus, *Ann.*, 1260, n. 37 ff.

THE TARTARS.

The fall of
Baghdad,
1258.

To all such as were looking forward to the destruction
of the old order of things about the year 1260, the news
of the fall of Baghdad must have seemed a sure presage
of the more general destruction that was soon to follow.[1]

During the year 1242 the Tartars for the most part
withdrew from Europe.[2] But their appallingly devastating
expeditions did not cease in Asia, and in 1258 Europe was
profoundly stirred by the news that Baghdad had been
captured by Houlagou, the lieutenant and brother of
Mangu or Manghou Khan, the third successor of the
terrible Chingiz-Khan. The last of the Abbaside Caliphs,
al Mutasim, was slain, and the greater part of his splendid
city burnt to the ground.[3]

Writing of Baldach (Baghdad) some hundred years
later, the traveller, Ludolph of Suchem,[4] says : " In
this city there are now the richest and best merchants
under heaven, neither is there in any place in the East
so much and so many different kinds of merchandise
as there. In this city used to dwell the Caliph, that is the
successor of Mahomet, to whom the Saracens render
obedience in all things, even as do the Christians to the
Pope, the successor of St. Peter. I will tell you somewhat about the loss of this city of Baldach, according as
I have read thereof in the chronicles and histories of the
Kings of Armenia,[5] and have heard from a right truthful

---

[1] To be writing about a fall of Baghdad in the month of March,
1217, is particularly interesting for an Englishman, inasmuch as at this
moment the British flag is flying over that ancient city.

[2] *Cf.* supra, vol. xiv, p. 183 ff.

[3] See Osborn, *Islam under the Khalifs of Baghdad,* chap. iv ; and G. le
Strange, *Baghdad under the Abbasid Caliphate,* ch. xxiv, Oxford, 1900.

[4] Or Suthem, i.e., Sudheim near Lichtenau.

[5] He is supposed to refer to " Haithoni, *Armeni Hist. Orientalis,*
ap. Vincent of Beauvais, *Speculum Historiale.* In the old French translation of the *Relation de Hayton,* written in 1307, ed. Backer, the story
of the fall of Baghdad is told on pp. 177 ff.

knight who was there at the time. In the year of our Lord 1258, when the Tartars had conquered all the kingdoms of the East, Ayco,[1] the then King of Armenia, of his own accord proceeded to the great Khan, the Emperor of the Tartars, to visit him. Ayco was kindly received by him, because so great and singular an honour had been shown him, that kings should of their own accord visit him, and come to meet him, whereat he was much pleased, and honoured the king with many presents. In process of time, when the King of Armenia was about to return home, he asked the Emperor to grant him five boons. First, that the Emperor and all his people should become Christians; second, that there might always be peace between the Tartars and Armenians; third, that he would destroy all the churches of Mahomet and consecrate them in honour of God; fourth, that he would aid him to recover the Holy Land and restore it to the Christians; and fifth that he would besiege Baldach and destroy and bring to nought the Caliph, the successor of Mahomet, and his name. To all these demands the Emperor willingly agreed, and consented, and fulfilled them in every respect, save only the fourth demand, which was hindered by his death. With regard to the fifth demand, that he should destroy Baldach and the Caliph, he charged his brother Haloon, who then had conquered Persia, that as soon as he had settled the kingdom of Persia, and provided for its safe-keeping, he should join the King of Armenia in besieging Baldach. This he willingly did, and had no sooner settled the affairs of Persia than he removed himself to the great city of Nineveh, rested during the winter, and when the month of March came, went with the King of Armenia

---

[1] Ayco is one of the innumerable forms of the name of Hetoun, Haithon, etc., King of Armenia († 1271), whose journey to Mongolia and back (1254–5) is here alluded to. It is given ap. Bretscheider, *Medieval Researches*, i, p. 164 ff.

to Baldach, and besieged the Caliph. They took the city on the thirteenth day." [1]

We know also from another traveller, William of Rubruquis, that Mangu Khan was one of those Khans reported to be Christians. William of Rubruquis, however, was much better informed than Ludolph of Suchem, and he added : " But in very deede themselves are no Christians." [2] Fortunately, too, there were at this time many who were under no delusion as to the intentions of the Tartars. They knew that they had but one idea, and that was to subdue the whole world. Letters poured into the West to inform its leading men of what had happened to Baghdad, and envoys came to demand their help. The Grand Master of the Templars, Thomas Berardi, writing from Acre, March 4, 1260, to Brother Amedeus, " the preceptor of the houses of the Temple in England," reminds him that for many years back he has been telling him of the terrible advance of the Tartars. Now, however, he continues, they are knocking at our very gates, and are so numerous and powerful that they are irresistible. ". . . They have subdued the Persians and the Medes, the Assyrians and the Chaldæans, the Turks, Armenians, and Georgians, and other great nations, and now, unhappily, they have suddenly and unexpectedly seized that great, most famous and most powerful city of Baghdad, and they have put to the edge of the sword the Caliph, i.e., the Pope of the Saracens, their leader and lord, along with his children, his enormous household, and many of the inhabitants." [3] The Grand Master goes on to inform his

---

[1] *Liber de itinere Terræ sanctæ* (1336–41). We have used the translation of A. Stewart, ap. *Palestine Pilgrims Text Soc.*, London, 1895.

[2] *Cf.* c. 19 of the old English version of William's *Voyage*, ed. Beazley, p. 214, London, 1903.

[3] " Ac etiam carnibus Caliphæ, i.e., Papæ Saracenorum, ducis et domini eorundem, una eum liberis . . . in ore gladii sui crudeliter devoratis." Ep. ap. *Annal. de Burton*, p. 492.

correspondent that some of the Christian States, like
Antioch, terrified by the deeds of the Tartars, had already
offered them tribute. The Templars would, however,
hold their strong places to the very last. Envoys had been
sent to Spain, France, and Germany, to tell their peoples
that unless help were sent quickly " the whole of
Christendom in these parts would be subjugated ". In
the defence of the great cause the Templars were prepared
to pledge the whole of their church plate, and to sacrifice
their lives.[1] The King of England must be asked to help
them with money.

A little later (April) the Grand Master and many others
wrote to Henry directly.[2]

The first, of course, to be asked for help was the Pope,
and to him all looked for guidance.[3] Accordingly before
the close of the year (1260), Alexander sent letters to the
rulers of Christendom, both ecclesiastical and secular,
informing them of what the Tartars were doing, and
bidding them consider the best means of resisting them.[4]
Of these numerous documents we will look at the one he
addressed to our Prince Edward.[5] He tells him that it
behoves everyone to know of the doings of the Tartars
" who have sprung as it were from the hidden depths of
hell". They have destroyed the chief cities of the
Saracens, Aleppo, Damascus, and Baghdad, and have
slain the Caliph their Prince ; they have subjected the

Alexander summons the nations to deliberate. 1260.

---

[1] " Imo potius nos et honorabilis conventus noster circa defensionem
Christianæ fidei magno stamus desiderio exsolvere naturæ debitum."
Ib., p. 494. When one reads the foul charges that were brought against
the heroic Templars some fifty years later, it is well to have such
words as these in one's mind.

[2] Epp. of Apr. 4 and 5, ap. Rymer, i, 698–700.

[3] *Cf.* Hermann of Altaich, *Chron.*, an. 1261, ap. Böhmer, ii, p. 517.
Cf. Potthast, 17732.

[4] *Cf.* his letter to the archbishop of Canterbury and the clergy of his
province ap. *Annal de B.*, p. 495 ff.

[5] Ep. Nov. 17, 1260, ap. Rymer, i, p. 716. *Cf.* Potthast, 17964–5.

Christian kingdom of Armenia, and the Christian cities of Antioch and Tripoli, and they have even shed much Christian blood in Europe. All, then, must consider well how this awful evil may be met ; for the Tartars spare no one, are not bound by any treaty, and merely pretend to be well disposed to Christians, in order the easier to overcome them. He cannot well call a General Council to consider the matter, as so many difficulties have to be overcome in summoning one, and time presses. The magnates, therefore, of the land must be called together and consulted as to what steps should be taken. Envoys should then be sent to him for the octave of SS. Peter and Paul (1261), to tell him of the result of their deliberations, " so that the Apostolic See may in such such serious circumstances, adopt such measures as the public safety may require."

Local assemblies held to discuss the Tartar question, 1260–1.

In response to these and similar letters, local councils were held in different countries. Whatever may have been done in England, distracted as it was with the discord between the King and the Barons, in France, at any rate, we know that it was decided that prayers should be increased, and luxury in dress and food diminished ; that blasphemy should be punished and that all sports should cease, but that men should occupy themselves in the use of the bow, and in the management of artillery.[1] Unfortunately, however, Alexander died on May 25, and when the octave of SS. Peter and Paul arrived, the Holy See was vacant.[2]

---

[1] Will. of Nangis, an. 1260. Cf. Salimbene, *Chron.*, pp. 402–3, for a synod at Ravenna. The prelates were summoned " ut de facto Tartarorum aliquid ordinemus, sicut mihi (the archbishop of Ravenna) et aliis metropolitanis d. Papa mandavit."

[2] Cf. *Annal S. Rudbert*, ap. *M. G. SS.*, ix, p. 795. Reverence for the once great and flourishing Church of Africa compels me to record the faint traces that one finds of its survival during this dark period of its history. On March 18, 1255, Alexander named the Franciscan Lupus, bishop of Marocco, his legate, throughout Africa. Cf. Potthast,

The active,[1] if not always strong, career of Alexander
IV. had come to an end.

n. 15752, or Eubel, *Bullar. Francisc.*, n. 763, and the note thereto
which shows that Alexander had a considerable amount of intercourse with him, but that most of Lupus' work was in Spain. This
was due to the fact that Alfonso X., the Learned, King of Castile and
Leon, was contemplating a Crusade against the Saracens of Africa,
and Lupus was commissioned by the Pope to preach it in Spain. The
King tried to induce our Henry III. to take part in the expedition with
him, but want of funds caused Alfonso to abandon the enterprise. *Cf.*
Potthast, 15855, 16065–6, etc.

[1] *Cf.* Baldwin of Ninove who says that Alex. ruled the Church
" strenue ". *Chron.*, ap. *M. G. SS.*, xxiv, p. 544. For the doings of
Alexander regarding Prussia and the Baltic provinces, and many other
places to which we have made no reference, see Tenckhoff. He also
issued a number of Decretals some of which are included in the *Liber
Sextus Decret.* of Boniface VIII. *Cf.* Ptolemy of Lucca, *Hist. Eccles.*
lib. xxii, c. 17.

URBAN IV.

A.D. 1261–1264.

Sources.—Differing in this respect from that of Alexander IV., the Register of Urban IV. is now completely printed in three volumes, *Les registres d'Urbain IV.*, by J. Guiraud, Paris, 1901. A fourth volume began to appear in 1906. It is to contain a number of letters hitherto not printed which were never registered, but which the editor found in different libraries in Europe. This part of the fourth volume is already published. The second part, which is to contain tables and indexes, though in 1906 said to be " sous presse ", has unfortunately not yet (1927) issued from that press. Mons. Guiraud has done his work most satisfactorily, as he has printed in full all the documents which are of importance. Urban's Register is arranged more scientifically than its predecessors. The bulls of this Pope were not all written down simply in chronological order. They were classified. There was an exchequer or treasury Register (Registum Camerale), which Guiraud has given in his first volume, a Register dealing with benefices and privileges (Registum de litteris beneficiorum et aliarum gratiarum concessarum), which occupies Guiraud's third volume, and a general Register which is to be found in his second volume.

We possess two contemporary *lives* of Urban, one in prose and one in verse, of which sufficient use has not always been made, perhaps because the prose *life* was not published by Muratori, and is not easy to obtain. They were published originally by Papirius Masson in his *Lives of the Popes* (*De episcopis Urbis*, Paris, 1586). These *lives*, the one in prose by Gregory, a nephew of P. Gregory IX., dean and then bishop of Bayeux, the other mostly in indifferent leonine verse by Theodoric Vallicoloris (or Thierry of Vaucouleurs),[1] were written at the instigation of

---

[1] Hence he sings :—

    " Gregorius prosam fecit, versus ego, glossam
      Qui volet apponat, sic mea musa sonat."   P. 16.
ed. A. Assier. Theodoric wrote 15 years after the death of Urban.
    " Post obitum cujus (Urban) annis ter quinque paractis
      Cum studio vigili scribitur iste liber." *Ib.*, p. 46.

Urban's nephew, Ancherus, who afterwards became cardinal-priest of Sta. Prassede († 1286).[1] The former was written about the time of the battle of Tagliacozzo, i.e., soon after August, 1268, the latter some time afterwards. The copy of Theodoric's work which was kept at Troyes was a transcript made by Gerard, grand-nephew of Urban, 15 years after that Pope's death. Copies of both works were preserved in the archives of the chapter of Troyes, and were lent by the canons to Masson, who inserted them in his book. He did not, however, send the MSS. back to the canons, but only a copy of his own volume. What became of the originals is not known. A small edition of the two *lives* was reprinted at Troyes in 1854 by A. Assier from the edition of Masson, and the verse *life* was printed by Muratori (*R. I. SS.*, iii, pt. ii, p. 405 ff.). We shall quote from the edition of Assier.

Modern Works.—Their usual keenness to make known the glories of their great men has caused many Frenchmen to devote their attention to the career of Urban IV. One of the earliest of the modern *lives* of Urban is that by Courtalon-Delaistre (*La vie du P. Urbain IV.*, Troyes, 1782. Assier (p. 4) praises a *life* by Magister (*Vie du P. U. IV.*, Troyes, 1854) which I have not been able to find. The fullest modern *life*, somewhat uncritical and vague in its references, is that by É. Georges (*Hist. du P. U. IV.*, Arcis-sur-Aube, or Paris, 1864). He is an enthusiastic panegyrist. Comparatively recently Le Vicomte Oscar de Poli (*Le P. U. IV.*, Paris, 1903) has issued a most detailed study on the family and arms of Urban, and has succeeded in dissipating some mistakes usually made in these matters. With reference to

---

[1] He was buried in his titular church in which may still be seen part of his beautiful tomb, ascribed by some to Arnolfo di Cambio, but by others perhaps more probably to the Comnati. We give the epitaph from Ciaconius, *Vitæ Pontif.*, i, p. 719, corrected from the version in Delaistre, p. 201.

> " Qui legis Ancherum duro sub marmore claudi,
> Si nescis, audi quem nece perdis herum.
> Treca parit puerum, Laudunum dat sibi clerum.
> Cardine Praxedis titulatur, et istius ædis
> Defuit in cœlis, largus fuit atque fidelis.
> Dæmoniis a telis serva Deus hunc quoque cœlis,
> Anno millesimo centena bis et octuageno
> Sexto, decessit hic prima luce Novembris."

Theodoric naturally dedicated his poem to Ancherus : " Inclita de Patruo do tibi gesta tuo." P. 15.

special episodes in Urban's career, we may cite K. Hampe's *Urban IV. und Manfred*, Heidelberg, 1906. This little work is said to be useful especially on account of the use of documents drawn from the inedited *Formulary* of Richard of Pofi [1]; but these documents were themselves taken from Urban's Register which is now in print. It must, however, be noted that, without evidence, Hampe lays the continuance of the Sicilian trouble at the door of Urban. See also L. Fumi, *Urbano IV. e il sole Eucharistico*, Rome, 1896, and Daunou's sketch of Urban in *Hist. littéraire de la France*, vol. xix., pp. 49–66, Paris, 1838.

[1] *Cf. English Hist. Review*, Jan., 1898, p. 137.

CONTEMPORARY SOVEREIGNS.
(See under Alexander IV.)

CHAPTER I.

THE PRE-PONTIFICAL CAREER OF JAMES OF TROYES.
HIS ELECTION AS POPE. HE FAVOURS LEARNING, MAKES
CARDINALS, RECOVERS CHURCH PROPERTY, AND DOES
MUCH FOR THE CITY OF ORVIETO.

The youth and early manhood of James of Troyes.

FOR a beginning of this biography one may adopt the simple words of Urban's earliest biographer, Dean Gregory : " There was a man of venerable life by name James (Jacobus, *Jacob*), who from his boyhood had an old head on his shoulders, and who, as his name imports, *supplanted* sins and vices, and in their stead planted the virtues. Gradually growing from one virtue to another, he merited to reach the height of the supreme pontificate. Thinking then that his career would prove a fine example to posterity, I have briefly set it forth." [1]

According to the conclusions of de Poli (which, however, cannot be accepted), James of Troyes was the son

---

[1] P. 7. De Poli tried to prove that there is no ground for the general assertion that he was called James *Pantaleon*. He observes correctly that the earliest authorities always call him James of Troyes (de Trecis) before he became Pope ; and he believes that his true name was James Langlois ; that he was called " of Troyes ", not from his natal city, but from his mother's family ; and that he belonged to a *bourgeois* branch of the House of Courpalay. He has proved that he was entitled to a coat of arms. Gregory, however, implies, p. 7, that his name " of Troyes " was taken from the city : " huic siquidem de catholicis orto natalibus Trecarum civitas nomini proprio cognomen adjecit." And as for the " Pantaleon " Röhricht, *Regesta Hierosol.*, n. 1304, Aug. 17, 1261, has published a document which settles the question in favour of the common tradition. We give the document as it appears in Röhricht : " Viterbii, vacante Romana ecclesia.—Jacobus *Pantaleonis*, patriarcha Hierosolymitanus, G(uillemo) abbati de Monasterio, quocum Parisiis theologiæ studiis olim se dederat, congratulatur, quod in expiscopatum Laudunesum evectus fuerat." (Paris, Bib. nat., M.S. lat., 17193, fol. 188–9, s. xvii, cop.)

of H. (Hyacinth ?) of Courpalay, called Langlois, and of
Lancenne de Troyes, lady Langlois (dominæ Anglicæ).[1]
It is certain, at any rate, that his name was Jacques
Pantaleon, and that he was born in Troyes, the capital of
Champagne [2] (perhaps about 1185), and in the parish
attached to the Benedictine monastery of our Lady.
He was baptized in its church of St. Stephen.[3] The position
of his family shows that he was not, as is commonly said,
the son of a poor cobbler. This assertion is first found in
the forged *Istoria* of Ricordano Malespini [4] ; and, if the
cobbler story has any foundation at all we may conclude
that the father of James of Troyes, obviously a man of
position, was a worker or dealer in leather in at least a
comparatively large way. James had certainly one
brother, the father of cardinal Ancherus, and a sister,
Agnes, who was abbess of Montluisant (or Monte Luca)
in Perugia [5] when he became Pope. Naturally glorying
in his promotion, she had written to congratulate him.
Replying to her kind letter, he had assured her that he
was unequal to the burden of the daily care of the

[1] *Le P. Urb. IV.*, p. 183. Urban tells us himself that his mother
was buried in the Cistercian monastery of our Lady *in Pratis* near
Troyes. Potthast, 18640.

[2] Theod. '' Urbe Trecensi natus '', p. 18.

[3] See Urban's letter of Sept. 9, 1263, to the bishop of Troyes in which
he notifies him that he is sending him 400 marks for various purposes.
One hundred has to go to make provision for an anniversary mass for
himself, and then 100 marks has to go to each of the following churches :
the cathedral in which he was educated, the church of St. Stephen in
which he was reborn by baptism, and the church in which his mother
was buried. Potthast, n. 18640. The monastery and its church of St.
Stephen seem to have now disappeared ; but, when Courtalon-Delaistre
wrote his *life* of Urban, the font in which he was baptized was still to
be seen, bearing the inscription :

"Hic fuit ablutus pura baptismatis unda
Jacobi Urbanus nomen et inde tulit." P. 4.

[4] Ap. *R. I. SS.*, viii, p. 997.

[5] A convent in which, some years ago, I found pining to death an
English sister, a victim of the barbarously cruel expulsion from France
of the female religious orders.

universal Church. "In the very midst of the happy circumstances that attended our election, the worry of business overtook me. I have become involved in difficulties of all kinds that have poured in upon me, so that I cannot find a quiet hour free from anxiety. Even when I sleep, the silence of the night brings no rest to my troubled heart. Hence you should rather grieve for me than rejoice. . . . Do you then, child, who, far from the tumults of the world, sit in peace at the feet of the Lord, help me, . . . I beg you, with all the prayers you can." [1]

Education and preferment.

The foundations of his education were laid at the cathedral school of Troyes,[2] where a good voice helped his advance in the musical branch of the *quadrivium*.[3] Then, whilst still very young,[4] he went to the University of Paris, where he had a very distinguished career as a student. In due course, he became a doctor both in the liberal arts, and in canon law, very proficient in theology and an impressive preacher.[5]

When he returned to Troyes, the fame of his learning and good life caused the bishop of Laon to make him first a canon of his cathedral, and then his archdeacon.[6]

[1] Potthast, 18136, Sept., 1261, or in full, ap. Raynald, an. 1261, nn. 16 and 17.

[2] Potthast, 18640.

[3] Theodoric, p. 18.

[4] Gregory, p. 7, says: "adhuc puerulus." *Cf.* Röhricht, *Regest. Hierosol.*, n. 1304.

[5] *Ib.*, and Theodoric, p. 18 . . ."divini præco fidelis Verbi." His connexion with the University of Paris led him afterwards to favour not only it (*Reg.*, ii, n. 360), but also those of Padua (Potthast, 18772) and Palencia (*Reg.*, ii, n. 240).

[6] G., p. 8; T., p. 19. In eloquent words he tells us himself what he owed to the Church of Laon. Ep. Dec. 28, 1262, Potthast, n. 18337, or Raynaldus, an. 1261, n. 8. "Hæc ecclesia nos olim per nostræ successus ætatis fovit ut mater, pavit ut nutrix, protexit ut tutrix, edocuit ut magistra, et sicut benefica honoravit. Hæc statum nostrum primulum, primo canonicatus præbendæque beneficio, et prostea archidiaconatus adauxit, etc."

Whilst connected with the church of Laon, he appears
to have drawn up a cartulary of the Church of Our Lady
in that city [1] From Laon he was called to be archdeacon
of Liège.

He had now severed his connexion with his native
city ; but, like a true Frenchman, he never forgot it.
Following, as he said himself, the example of Gregory
the Great and Gregory IX., he determined after he
became Pope to erect and endow a church for twelve
canons and a dean on the site of his father's house,
and to dedicate it in honour of Pope Urban the Martyr.[2]
The work was entrusted to John Langlois, a citizen of
Troyes, who is supposed to be a relative of the Pope,
and who must have possessed some of his ability.[3] At
any rate, a church was at length built with a very fine
exterior, and of extraordinarily light construction—
so light indeed that to some the interior with its great
expanse of glass presents a rather frail appearance.
Still the effect produced by the brilliant colouring of
its large area of stained glass, and by the delicacy and
daintiness of its details has caused the Church of St. Urban
of Troyes to be generally regarded as one of the remarkable
churches of a land of striking and lovely churches.[4]

We may see further proof of his love for his native
city in his offer of an indulgence to all such as contributed

[1] He would seem to have been at Laon in 1233. The title of his
compilation was : " Cartularium ecclesiæ S. M. Laudunensis a Jacobo
de Trecis canonico." De Poli, p. 146.

[2] Ep. May. 20, 1262, Potthast, n. 18328. *Cf. Reg. Urb. IV.*, iv, p. 47,
and dean Gregory, p. 12 ; and Theodoric, p. 38.

 " Præterea miram construxit in urbe Trecensi
 Ecclesiam dominus dictus in æde patris."

Urban's *Reg.*, iii, p. 426, n. 2528, gives the appointment of a canon
for his new Church.   Clement IV. speaks of Urban's church " quæ in
fundo sive solo suæ paternæ domus est ". Ep. Sept. 24, 1265, ap.
Martene, *Thes. nov.*, ii, p. 204. *Cf. ib.*, n. 155, p. 208.

[3] De Poli, pp. 14, 77.

[4] *Cf.* A. Babeau, *St. Urbain de Troyes*, Troyes, 1891.

to the completion of its cathedral,[1] and in his forbidding any legate to lay an interdict on any of its churches unless special mention were made of his indult,[2] or, except on the same condition, to summon for trial outside of Troyes any of its clerical or lay inhabitants.[3]

Legate in Poland, 1248-9.

Whilst still archdeacon of Liège, and bearing the title of chaplain of the Pope, he was sent as legate into Poland. Writing after he had become Pope to Anselm, bishop of Warmie or Ermland in Prussia, he tells him that when he occupied a lower position he was sent as legate to Poland, Pomerania, and Prussia, and that, whilst in those parts, he issued certain decrees concerning " the salvation of souls, the divine worship, the utility of the Churches and clerical decorum ". He had made these constitutions, he said, at a council at Wratislav (Breslau) (Oct. 10, 1248), and had enjoined their observance upon the bishops who were present at the council. Anselm is exhorted by the Pope to see that they are inviolably observed.[4] The Annals of Poland also tell us of this council ; and all are careful to record that the legate gave the Poles permission to eat meat from Septuagesima to Quinquagesima Sunday ; for, they say, in imitation of the custom of the primitive Church, the Poles were wont to abstain from flesh meat during that period.[5]

At this same council, the legate also brought forward the needs of the Roman Church caused by the oppression of Frederick, and in the Pope's name asked the assembled Fathers for a third of all their ecclesiastical revenues. Though agreeing that the matter was urgent, they thought

---

[1] Potthast, 18582. [2] Reg., i, n. 107. [3] Ib., n. 108, p. 28.
[4] Ep. June 3, 1263, Potthast, n. 18553. Cf. Reg. Inn. IV., vol. i, n. 4075 ff., Nov. 19 ff., 1247, for the bulls of Innocent in connexion with the appointment of James de T. as his legate in Poland, etc.
[5] Kronika, c. 84, an. 1248, ap. Bielowski, Mon. Polon., ii, p. 565. Cf. ib., pp. 805, 877 ; iii, pp. 14, 49, 168-9, etc.

that they could not subscribe more than a fifth for three years, which was paid up loyally in one sum.[1]

By mandates dated Nov. 22, 1247,[2] James of Troyes had also been commissioned to try to make peace in Prussia, where furious fighting was going on between, on the one side, Swantopelk, duke of Pomerania, a fierce ambitious noble who had assassinated his liege lord, Lesko the White, duke of Poland, and who had allied himself with such Prussians as had been recently converted to Christianity, and, on the other side, the Teutonic knights, weakened by their struggles against the Tartars, and Przemyslas, duke of Great Poland and others. The legate was successful in this pre-eminently Christian work of making peace. His biographer says that, while keeping his hands clean from presents, he calmed strife, and made peace,[3] and that Innocent confirmed his work.[4]

As we learn from a letter of James himself after he had become Pope, this commission did not begin well. He tells us that, whilst archdeacon of Laon, he was sent by Innocent into Germany. A number of knights, however, set upon him on his entrance into the country, robbed him of his money, horses, property, and kept him for a time in captivity.[5]

Innocent somewhat later on also employed his chaplain, James, in his efforts to secure the imperial crown for William of Holland (1251). Praising him for his diligence in executing the commissions which had been entrusted

Legate in Germany, 1251.

---

[1] *Kronika*, c. 85, ap. Bielowski, ii, p. 566. *Cf.*, however, a letter of Innocent IV., March 19, 1248, ap. *Cod. diplom. Poloniæ*, i, p. 225, wherein he remits the fifth for one of *two* years, at least in the case of the archbishop of Gnesen.

[2] Potthast, 12771–3. *Cf.* Theiner, *Mon. Polon.*, i, p. 45, n. 92 ff.

[3] Theod. "Lites sedavit, pacem stabilivit, ab omni Muneris excutiens accipiente manus." P. 19.

[4] Ep. Oct. 22, 1249. Potthast, n. 13840.

[5] Ep. July 9, 1264, ap. Raynaldus, an. 1264, n. 30. *Cf.* Theod., p. 19. As Urban IV., James pardoned these robbers most graciously.

to him, the Pope urged him to approach the Princes of
the Empire in company with brother Theodoric, a Master
of the Teutonic Knights " who knew German ", and to
exhort them to do homage to William, King of the
Romans.[1]

Bishop of
Verdun and
patriarch of
Jerusalem.

On the death of John of Aix, bishop of Verdun (Aug. 10,
1252), James of Troyes, " an honourable, literary, pious,
and capable man," became bishop of that important
see, through a " provision " of Pope Innocent IV. (1253).[2]
A few years later a decree of Alexander IV. made him
patriarch of Jerusalem (c. Sept., 1255).[3]

In both these positions he conducted himself as a true
bishop. He improved both his clergy and his people
by word and example, and laboured to clear his diocese
of debt, and to protect it from the oppression of the
powerful.[4] Whilst patriarch he had a most difficult

---

[1] Epp. of Feb. 18, *Reg.*, ii, nn. 5288-9. *Cf.* nn. 5284, 5300, 5309,
5316.

[2] *Ann. S. Vitoni Virdun.*, ap. *M.G.SS.*, x, p. 528. *Cf.* the bull of
Innocent IV., Dec. 18, 1253, *Reg.*, iii, n. 7124. Innocent praises
" Jacobum de Trecis, archidiaconum Laudunensem . . . virum utique
litteratum, morum honestate conspicuum, consilio providum, et in
spiritualibus et temporalibus circumspectum acceptum nobis et
fratribus nostris sue probitatis merito." *Cf.* Gregory, p. 8 ; Theodoric,
p. 19.

[3] *Ib. Cf.* ep. Alex. IV., Oct. 5, 1255, ap. *Reg.*, vol. i, n. 842 ; and
epp. of Dec. 7, 1255, ap. Raynaldus, *Ann.*, an. 1255, n. 66 ; G. and T.,
ib., and *Catal. Pont. Laudunens.*, ap. *M.G.SS.*, xxii, p. 374. The last-
named authority says that he resigned the archideaconate of Liège.
Hence, as it is said that he was made bishop when he was archdeacon
of Laon, it must be presumed that he was archdeacon of the two
churches for a time.

[4]　　" Exemplo, verbis clerum correxit, ovesque
　　　Tradita multiplicat quinque talenta sibi.
　　　Exoneravit enim prædictæ debita multa
　　　Ecclesiæ, quibus, hæc plurima damna tulit,
　　　Contra magnates patriæ solitos per abusus,
　　　Capere proventus ecclesiæque bona
　　　Restitit, ecclesiæ terras et castra potenter
　　　Ejus defendit virga potente manu." Theod., p. 20.

situation to face.[1] Although there was peace during his patriarchate between the Christians and the Moslems, there was unhappily civil war. In Palestine, as all over the East where their galleys reached, the Genoese and Venetians were fighting for trade supremacy. Moreover, there were quarrels between the great military Orders ; and the Tartars, fresh from the destruction of Baghdad [2] were threatening Moslem and Christian alike In addition to the difficult work which this state of affairs brought upon the Patriarch of Jerusalem, Alexander commissioned him to negotiate with the Tartar chief Houlagou, who had asked the Pope to be received into the Church and to be baptized.[3]

Despite the calls on his time made by all these important occupations,[4] he contrived to write an account of the Holy Land which we are assured was almost entirely copied by Christian Adrichomius, a geographer of the sixteenth century, in his *Theatrum Terræ Sanctæ . . . cum tabulis geographicis,"* Coloniæ Aggripinæ, 1593.[5] Among his authorities Adrichomius gives that of " Jac. Pantaleonis, Galli, Patriarchæ Hierosolymitani ", and adds (p. 287) that he flourished in 1247.

---

[1] Some of his acts as patriarch will be found in Röhricht, *Register Hierosol.*, n. 1243, etc., 1244*b* (in the supplement), etc.

[2] *Supra*, p. 124 ff.

[3] *Cf.* ep. of Alex. to Houlagou ap. Raynaldus, an. 1260, n. 29 ff. The Pope says that John cf Hungary, who styled himself the chief's envoy, assured the Pope " quod tu ad salutem dirigens vota tua votive desideras, secundum . . . doctrinam quam S. Romana ecclesia fatetur et prædicat, sacri baptismatis unda renasci ". According to Hayton (ed. de Bacher, p. 180 ; *cf. supra*, vol. xiv, p. 178), Houlagou's brother Mangu Khan had already been baptized.

[4] *Cf.* Röhricht, *Reg. Hierosol.*, n. 1269, Oct. 9, 1258. for the peace which he brought about between the military orders.

[5] Georges, p. 120. This same author thinks it likely that it was, whilst patriarch, that James Pantaleon composed the fine commentary on the *Miserere* psalm, which is assigned to Urban IV., in the *Bib. Vet. Patrum*, ed. de la Bigne, i, p. 109, Paris, 1634. Georges, pp. 121–54, translates the commentary.

The difficulties with which James Pantaleon had to
contend were in some cases greater than he could solve
by his own authority ; and so he was driven to seek that
of the Pope. Moreover help was needed "against
the ferocity of the Tartars."[1] Accordingly, he set sail
from Palestine towards the end of the year 1260 or the
beginning of the year 1261, landed at Venice, and found
the Pope at Anagni.[2] Warmly welcomed by Alexander,
he accompanied him to Rome, where, as we have already
stated, he quelled civic troubles. The patriarch then
went with the Pope to Viterbo, and was there when
he died.[3]

After Alexander's body had been solemnly laid to
rest in the cathedral at Viterbo, only eight cardinals
assembled to elect a successor to him. Their names are
given us by Theodoric [4] ; and they were : Eudes (Otho)
of Châteauroux, cardinal-bishop of Tusculum ; the
Hungarian Stephen, cardinal-bishop of Palestrina [5] ;
the Dominican cardinal of Sta. Sabina, Hugh of St. Cher ;
John Tolet (or of Toledo), the English Cistercian cardinal
of St. Lawrence in Lucina ; and the four following
cardinal-deacons, Richard Annibaldi, of St. Angelo ;
Octaviano Ubaldini, of Sta. Maria in Via Lata ; John
Gaetano Orsini, of St. Nicholas, afterwards Pope Nicholas
III.; Ottobono of Fieschi, of St. Hadrian, afterwards
Pope Hadrian V.

Unfortunately, however, for some time these few
cardinals could not come to any decision. From an
interesting but unfortunately mutilated letter of one of
his agents (John of Hemingford) to Henry III., it would

---

[1] *Annal. S. Rudbert. Salisburg.*, ap. *M. G. SS.*, ix, 795.

[2] Gregory, p. 8. If he found the Pope at Anagni, he must have arrived
there before Nov. 10, 1260, on which day Alexander was back in Rome.
Cf. Theod., p. 20.

[3] Gregory, p. 9.   [4] P. 17.

[5] Some say he was absent in Hungary.

appear that one cause of the delay in making the election, was the refusal of the English Cistercian cardinal and of Hugh of St. Cher, the Dominican cardinal, to accept the burden of the Papacy.[1] At length the cardinals looked outside their own body, and they unanimously elected the Patriarch of Jerusalem,[2] who *took* rather than *was given*, the name of Urban IV. (Aug. 29, 1261).[3] On the following Sunday (Sept. 4) the new Pope was solemnly blessed and crowned in the Church of the Dominicans at Viterbo.[4]

Before and after his coronation, Urban issued letters telling the story of his election, and asking for prayers.

Urban announces his election to the world.

[1] At least that is how it would appear that one should understand the following : " Noverit vestræ dominationis sublimitas quod ecclesia Romana pastoris solatio destituta a 25 die Maii usque ad diem Decollationis S. Johannis Baptistæ . . . (here are some undecipherable words) . . . monachos . . . (more such words) . . . totum habentes intra se caritatem et dilectionem mutuam, et reputantes se tam humiles et indignos summi pontificatus honore, quod dicto die patriarcham Jerusalem oriundum (another blank) d. regis Franciæ in Romanum pontificem elegerunt." Ap. *Royal letters, Henry III.*, ii, p. 188.

[2] Greg., p. 9 ; Theod., p. 17. Ep. of Urban himself, Sept. 5, 1261, ap. *Reg.*, vol. ii, p. 2 ; *Mon. Pat. Chron. = Annal. S. Justin. Patav.*, ap. *R.I. SS.*, viii, p. 715 ; Saba Malaspina, ii, c. 5, ap. *ib.*, p. 803.

[3] Several of the chroniclers speak as though it was the cardinals who had styled James Pantaleon, Urban. But Urban tells us himself that the Popes took a new name when they were elected, and that he himself took the name of Urban because it was on the feast of St. Urban I., Pope and martyr (April 25), that he was elected. *Cf.* ep. May 20, 1262, ap. Martène, *Thesaurus nov. anecdot.*, ii, p. 3. *Cf.* Hemingford ap. *Roy. Let.*, ii, 189. " Assumpto nomine Urbanus, etc." ; and *Chron. Pont. Mant.*, ap. *M. G. SS.*, xxiv, p. 216, which says that James " gave himself the name Urban ". We need not believe the story of Urban's election which is found in one copy of Villani's Chronicle. He says that when the Cardinals shut up in Conclave could not agree as to whom to elect Pope, they resolved to choose the first cleric who knocked at the door of the Conclave. It chanced that J. Pantaleone was the first to do so.

[4] See Urban's letter of Sept. 12, 1261, ap. Potthast, 18121 ; *Ann. of Burton*, i, 499. " Corona et imperiali diademate coronatus ad palatium sibi deputatum recessit." *R. Let.*, ii, 189.

He says that he hesitated very much indeed (vehementer) about placing " his weak neck beneath the intolerable yoke of the apostolic ministry ", but that he accepted it, lest he might seem to be opposing the will of God, and lest he might destroy the harmonious unity of the electors.[1]

Henry III. congratulates the Pope on his election, 1262.

Among the letters of congratulation which were sent to Urban that of our King Henry III. has been preserved. After pointing out that God had at length rewarded the long continued tearful supplications of His people for a successor to Peter, the Fisherman of souls, he declared that that successor was a man who in subordinate positions had used to the best advantage the talents that had been given to him. He assured Urban that it was due to the disturbed state of the realm that he had not congratulated him earlier ; and he begged him in conclusion to give favourable attention to what his envoys would have to say to him about the Crusade and other matters which concerned his kingdom.[2]

The new Pope a patron of learning.

There was now seated upon the throne of Peter another learned Pope, a worthy successor in this respect of Gregory IX. and Innocent IV. He was, moreover, a pastor of learning, and a friend of learned men. He made the mathematician, Campanus of Novara, one of his chaplains, and accepted the dedication of his *Theorica planetarum*. " Lo ! Holy Father," cried the grateful scholar, " you pass sleepless nights and spend your days in anxious thought, and you scatter your money as if it were mere dirt." [3] " You have raised Philosophy from the dust— philosophy which, deprived of all aid from our prelates— had been wont to sit in beggary . . . To you with your

---

[1] Ep. 1, Sept. 5, ap. *Reg.*, ii, p. 1, *cf.* ep. 2, *ib.* Cf. Potthast, 18120, for a letter issued with an imperfect bulla before " consecrationis insignia fuerimus assecuti ". *Cf.* also 18133–6 ; and 18270, April 13, 1262.

[2] *Royal Letters*, ii, p. 206, March 20, 1262.

[3] Ap. H. Grauert, *Magister Heinrich.*, p. 465, Munich, 1912.

vigorous intellect, with your polished mind, and with your brilliant knowledge, to you as a lover of beauty alone does philosophy come securely and gladly, for it knows that it is being ca'led not to a foreign land but to its own." [1]

After his dinner, which he often took in the company of a number of learned men, Urban was fond of making them sit round him, and of listening to them discussing different questions which he proposed to them. It would appear to have been at his command that St. Thomas Aquinas left Paris, and taught in Rome. At any rate, it was certainly at his command that the Saint did "many things and wrote much", for of this we are assured by one of his students, Ptolmey of Lucca,[2] and have proof in the dedication of some of his works to him. Dedicating his *Catena Aurea* to Urban, the saint said : "In your studious zeal, most holy Father, it has pleased your Holiness to entrust to me the Commentary on the Gospel of St. Matthew. I submit it to be examined and corrected by the decision of your supreme authority. It is the joint fruit of your solicitude and of my obedience. Deign to accept it, so that, just as the order to write it came from you, the final appreciation of its value may be pronounced by you, as rivers return to the source whence they have sprung." The first of the *Opuscula*, too, of St. Thomas (ed. Lyons, 1562) is addressed to

---

[1] *Cf.* the dedication of his work on Mathematics made by the same author to the Pope, cited by Tiraboschi, *Storia della lett. Ital.*, iv, p. 147. Campanus declares that he owes all to Urban. "Gratia Domini mei Urbani sum id quod sum." It is interesting to note that from this dedication we can see how the cardinals were already distinguished by the *hats* which had been assigned them by Innocent IV. Campanus speaks of them as "illud venerabile *Capillorum* (*sic.*) vestrorum Collegium".

[2] *Hist. eccles.*, l. xxii, c. 24. ap. *R. I. SS.*, xi, p. 1153. *Cf.* the *Annals* of the same author, p. 81, ed. Firenze, 1876. "Hic ad petitionem et mandatum Urbani P. glossavit Evangelia."

Pope Urban, and is directed against the errors of the Greeks : " Opus contra errores Græcorum."

The Pope had sent him a book in which there were many extracts from the Greek fathers bearing on the disputes between the Latins and the Greeks, and in accordance with the wishes of the Pope, the Saint himself drew up a treatise from the Greek Fathers, setting fcrth the Catholic Doctrine on the Procession of the Holy Ghost ; on the unique position of the Pope in the Church ; and on Purgatory.[1]

Nor was it the fault of Urban that we have not more from the glowing pen of St. Bonaventure, seeing that he urged him to literary work which only his arduous duties of Minister-General prevented him from executing.[2] The great cause of learning owes much to Urban IV., who may justly be regarded as one of the forerunners of the Renaissance.

His character generally.

Besides being learned, Urban was, according to his biographers, pure, kind, munificent, and courageous, a careful administrator, a lover of honour, freedom, and law, and so pious that he shed tears whenever he said Mass. In short, as one of his panegyrists declares, " he was full of all goodness." [3] We are also assured, and this appears to be borne out by the recorded actions of his life, that he was keen to reward virtue and learning,[4] and that it was by the will of God that he rose to the Papacy gradually through all the ranks of the clergy, in order that he might learn how to rule.[5]

First creation of cardinals, 1261.

The facts of his election had taught Urban some of the

[1] He concludes : " Hæc sunt, pater sanctissime, quæ ex auctoritatibus doctorum Græcorum secundum vestram jussionem excepi, et exponenda et ad confirmationem veræ fidei inducenda."

[2] *Ib.*, p. 1153.   [3] Grcgory, p. 13.

[4] " Quos animi virtus, morumque scientia, fama extulit, hos voluit multiplicare bonis." Theod., p. 18.

[5] " Ut dominus factus, dominari sçiret, et ejus
Compatiens servis, sciret utramque viam." *Ib.*, p. 19.

evils that naturally follow from the College of Cardinals
being allowed to decrease considerably in numbers.
Accordingly, he had barely time to look round with the
necessary care to make a suitable selection,[1] before he
made his first promotion of cardinals. This took place,
if we are to believe Roger Lovel, one of the agents of our
King Henry in Rome, on Christmas eve,[2] but, if we are
to suppose that the Pope followed the usual custom,
the promotion will have taken place on Ember Saturday
(December 17). And if it is true that a Pope may be
measured by the cardinals he creates, Urban must be
allowed to be a great man, as three of the first seven
cardinals he made afterwards became Popes—Guido
Fulcodi or Gui le Gros (Clement IV.), Simon de Brion,
sometimes wrongly called " de Brie " (Martin IV.), and
Jacobo Savelli (Honorius IV.).[3]

It has been just said that Urban had had barely
time to make a careful selection when he chose his first
group of cardinals ; and so it happened that it was
urged that he had made one unhappy choice. Such
accusations were made against Simon Paltinarius, a canon
of Padua, and administrator of the see of Aversa, that
the Pope had to decide not to give him the red hat till

---

[1] Writing to Guido Fulcodi, one of those who were first created
cardinals, he speaks of the anxiety felt by himself and the cardinals in
looking out for proper candidates for the cardinalitial dignity. " Opus
enim est, cum de talibus agitur ; curam assiduam, sollicitam operam,
et vigile studium adhiberi." Urban wanted men of great devotion,
judgment, discretion, large-mindedness, and virtue. They were to
form one body with the Pope, to be the columns of the Church and the
bearers of its burdens. Ep. ap. Martène, *Vet. SS. ampl. coll.*, ii, 1256.
Potthast, 18224.

[2] Ap. *Royal Letters,* ii, p. 204, Feb. 6, 1262.

[3] Both Theodoric, p. 21, and Lovel, *l.c.*, have preserved the names
of these seven cardinals. *Cf. Chron. mon. Patav.*, ap. *R.I.SS.*, viii,
pp. 715–16.

the said charges were cleared away.[1] Investigation, however, justified Urban's choice, and we find him naming cardinal Simon of S. Martino *rector* of the Duchy of Spoleto and of the March of Ancona.[2]

Second creation of cardinals, 1262.

In May [3] or, if on Ember Saturday, then on June 11, 1262, Urban added seven more members to the College of Cardinals, one of them being his nephew Ancherus. Of the fourteen cardinals created by him, half were Frenchmen, and half Italians ; and of the second creation one was Henry of Susa, the famous canonist, always spoken of as *Hostiensis*, from his see of Ostia.

Finance.

On his election Urban found himself not only without sufficient cardinals to enable him to carry on the work spiritual and temporal which the Church at this period was called upon to do, but also in the same pressing want of money as his immediate predecessors. Being pre-eminently a practical man, he made it one of his chief concerns to improve his financial position.[4] To render his endeavours more systematic, he formed a financial division (regestum camerale) of his Register. He then dispatched his envoys into the different countries to collect the dues that were owing to the Roman Church.

[1] Lovel, *l.c.*, who calls him by mistake " Adversanus ", says he was a friend of Cardinal Ottobono. *Cf. Reg. Urb.*, ii, n. 39, Jan. 9, 1262, and n. 48, Feb. 7, 1262. However, we find him († 1277) subscribing as cardinal-priest of St. Martin in Jan., 1263 ; for, as we learn from the *Annals of St. Justin*, ap. *M. G. SS.*,xix, 181, after the accusations had been examined, " the pristine splendour of Simon's character was re-established." It was at this creation of cardinals that the English cardinal John Tolet (incorrectly printed Soletanus in *Royal Letters*, ii, p. 189) was promoted to be cardinal-bishop of Porto.

[2] Potthast, 18917–18, May 21, 1264.

[3] Gregory, p. 9.

[4] Writing (June 13, 1264) to the Archbishop of Braga, Urban tells him how he at once tackled the difficulties in front of him : " solertem et efficacem inter alia dantes opem et operam, ut Romana ecclesia relevaretur a grandium et gravium sarcina debitorum, quibus eam multipliciter invenimus obligatam." *Reg.*, i, n. 463, p. 129.

Magister Synitius, for instance, in whose "fidelity and discretion" he had full confidence, was sent "to the parts of Aragon and Spain and other regions" (Portugal, Barcelona, etc.), to collect the arrears due to the Roman Church, from the Kings and others of those countries.[1] He was, moreover, furnished with a list "of all the monasteries and churches in the parts of Spain, and in the provinces of Bordeaux and Narbonne" which were tributary (censuales) to the Roman Church, and with an account of the sums due from each.[2]

Writing a few months before his death to the arch-bishop of Tarragona and his suffragans, Urban tells them that his early efforts had almost relieved the Roman Church of its load of debt, when the renewal of the violence of its persecutors forced him to contract debts again.[3] To safeguard the orthodox faith and to defend the Church, its faithful adherents (fideles), and ecclesiastical liberty against the attacks of tyrants, he had had to contract great debts, in order to raise troops.[4] He accordingly begs the bishops to help him in his efforts to raise the necessary money.

Urban at first clears the Roman Church of debt, but has to burden it again.

The work which Magister Synitius was commissioned to do in Spain, was being done by Magister Albert in Germany, and he was ordered to compel archbishop and bishop alike to pay what they owed to Rome.[5] Money was to be collected in Hungary, Poland, and Bohemia,

---

[1] Ep. March 21, ap. *ib.*, n. 455. *Cf.* 456–71.

[2] *Ib.*, n. 465. The lists were given "sicut in registris ejusdem Romanæ ecclesie continentur," i.e., the *Liber Censuum*.

[3] *Cf.* what Clement IV. says of this in his ep. of Aug. 1, 1265, to Charles of Anjou, ap. Martène, *Phes. nov.*, ii, n. 116, p. 174. " Quamvis noster . . . prædecessor tunc habens multa reposita, quæ in hæc tempora forsitan reservabat, coactus fuerit ante tempus universa consumere . . . sine fructu."

[4] Ep. June 27, 1264, ap. *Reg.*, i, n. 463. " Tandem, urgente necessitate compulsi, coacti sumus magna contrahere onera debitorum."

[5] Ep. Oct. 15, 1263, ap. *ib.*, n. 483–90.

and to be sent to Venice,[1] and the archbishop of Torres, the metropolitan of Sardinia, was directed to collect all that was due to the Church of Rome in that island. We may in a word take it for granted that the energetic Pope reminded every country of the Catholic world of its pecuniary obligations to Rome, and even to the College of Cardinals,[2] and that he did all in his power to ensure payment.

In his handling of money, Urban showed himself a thorough man of business. It would appear that some of his predecessors had allowed themselves to be imposed upon ; and, without much examination, had paid over to the money-lenders of Rome, Siena, and Florence such claims as they had presented. Urban, however, suspecting that he was being called upon to pay more than was really owing, had the accounts thoroughly overhauled, with the result that while the debts due were paid, money accumulated in the pontifical treasury.[3] He would not, however, pay the excessive claims which the greedy Roman bankers alone refused to abate, and to show his displeasure with them, he would not visit the city.[4] He took care, however, we are assured that the poor of Rome, and his household there did not suffer by his absence. All such were treated by him more generously than they had been before.[5]

---

[1] Potthast, Sept. 26, 1261, n. 18131.

[2] Ep. Oct. 23–8, 1261, to Magister Albert, ap. Rodenberg, i n. 513. *Cf.* ap. *Reg.*, i, n. 121, etc., for letters ordering bishops elect to pay different sums to the Apostolic treasury. There is here question of the *servitia*. *Cf. supra*, vol. xiv, p. 238 f.

[3] " Conjiciens igitur præfatus Papa, quod ultra
Sortem legitimam plura darentur eis (the *mercatores* of Siena, etc.),
Consuluit super his prudentes, veraque solvit
Debita, etc." Theodoric, p. 22–3.

[4] " Unde nec accessit dominus prædictus ad urbem
Quamis nollet eis jura negare sua." *Ib.* This is the only reason assigned by a contemporary for Urban's not going to Rome.

[5] *Ib.*

With the money which his intelligent management He redeems
and re-
covers and careful expenditure put into his hands, Urban not merely redeemed the estates belonging to the Roman Church
lands. Church which his predecessor or predecessors had had to pledge, but he even added to its property.[1] He insisted that Nicholas of Anagni, a nephew of Gregory IX. " of happy memory ", should give up the custody of the castle of Monte Fumone which he had formerly entrusted to him[2]; he forbade the alienation of the castle of Giulianello, east of Velletri,[3] and he struggled hard but in vain to prevent Peter de Vico usurping Bieda and other estates belonging to the Church which, by the will of Peter, count of Anguillaria,[4] and sometime Prefect of Rome, were to return to the Church.[5] Some of the property and proprietary rights of the Church such as those usurped by Raynaldus Rubeus, a nephew of Alexander IV., could only be recovered by force of arms.[6] He had also to employ force against James de Bisenzo, of which place there are now no traces. In July, 1262, finding the heat of Viterbo very oppressive, Urban sought " the quiet roofs " of the commanding height of Montefiascone. From the hill above the town Urban could look down on the glorious lake of Bolsena, " the great lake of Italy," with its two islets standing out like bosses from the polished steel surface of a great round shield. These islets, Martana and Bisentina, belonged

---

[1] *Ib. Cf.* pp. 25–6, 27–8.

[2] *Lib. Censuum*, i, p. 567, ed. Fabre, July 8, 1263.

[3] *Ib.*, p. 565 ff., Jan. 18, 1263.

[4] The arms of this now extinct family may still be seen on the well in the piazza of Bieda.

[5] Ep. Apr. 24, 1263, ap. *Reg.*, i, n. 237. *Cf.* n. 231 ; and Theod., pp. 30–1.

[6] He had usurped property and rights in the districts of Ferento, Ferentinum, a few miles north of Viterbo, Trevi, etc. :

" Ac in eum surgens armis animoque virili

Perdita restaurat cuncta potente manu." *Ib.*, p. 24. *Cf.* p. 25.

to the Roman Church, but they had been usurped one
by Peter de Vico, and the other by James de *Bicquo*,[1]
i.e., Bisenzo. Finding that remonstrance was thrown
away on these barons, Urban bought back Martana,[2]
and recovered its larger compeer, Bisentina, by force.[3]
Then he fortified the latter, and called it Urbana.

He builds
and destroys
fortifications.

Bisentena was far from being the only place fortified
by the discerning eye of Urban, who was everyday
proving himself more and more like his splendid predecessor from France, Calixtus II. To keep the peace
in the Umbrian vale, he built a strong castle in Trevi
(the ancient Treba or Trebia, not far from Spoleto),[4]
"one of the steepest places imaginable." He also built
a citadel in Montefiascone, a place he did not leave
without restoring its exceptionally curious old church
of St. Flaviano, and beautifying its buildings generally.[5]
From an inscription in Cappelletti, we learn that on
October 14, 1262, Pope Urban, in the time of Prior Philip,
"with his own hands," in presence of several cardinals,
archbishops, and bishops, consecrated in St. Flavian's

---

[1] "Insula Marchana falso detenta colore
    A dicto Jacobo perdita pene fuit." Theod., p. 27. *Cf.* Theiner,
Cod. Diplom., ep. Nov. 15, 1263, i, p. 144.

[2] Theod., pp. 25–6.

[3] "Armatos illic transmittit qui sine marchæ (*sic*)
    Acquirunt turrim, restituuntque sibi." *Theod., ib. Cf. Ann.
Urbevet.*, ap. *M. G. SS.*, xix, p. 270.

[4] "Huic (his citadel) Trebium nomen, quod structum mansit Asylum
    Ecclesiæ, terror hostibus ejus erat." *Ib.*, p. 24.

[5] "Inveniens igitur habitacula millia, turrim
    Construit, et reparat bellificando domos." *Ib.*, p. 26. In
L. Delisle's extracts from this chronicle (ap. *Notices et extraits*,
vol. xxvii, pt. ii, p. 210) for "millia" there is the better reading
"vilia". *Cf. ib.* for his recovery and fortification of "Castrum
Marchæ", which his predecessor had pledged to Peter de Vico, of whom
more will be said presently. See also ep. Aug. 4, 1263, ap. Theiner,
l.c., p. 153, *re* the building of a citadel on a suitable eminence in the
Castrum S. Gemini in the Duchy of Spoleto.

an altar in honour of our Lady, Pope Urban and other saints.[1]

But Urban was not content with erecting fortresses in places suitable for the pontifical government. He took care to destroy such as were inimical to it.[2] He was careful, however, to recompense those who were true to the Church but who might have been injured in any way by such destruction. All, therefore, we are assured, admired the man who after wormwood gave honey, after war, peace.[3]

Throughout, too, the whole of his too brief pontificate he kept a watchful eye on the Communes who were always attempting to strengthen themselves at the expense of the rights of the Pope. The Communes of Velletri, Narni, etc., were forbidden to molest their weaker neighbours, or to seize property belonging to the Holy See.[4] Other Communes had to be forbidden

He endeavours to ward off encroachments of the Communes.

---

[1] *Le chiese d'Italia*, v, 630. *Cf.* A. K. Porter, *Lombard Architecture*, iii, 61, Yale and Oxford, 1917, and the local historian, G. de Angelis, *Commentario su l'origine de Montefiascone*, Montef., 1841, a poor production.

[2] As Theodoric quaintly observes, p. 25,

" Sicut construere quod prodest credo necesse,
Sic ego destruere quod nocet esse reor."

[3] " Admirando virum qui post absynthia mella,
Post guerram pacem distribuebat ita." *Ib.*, p. 25. Theodoric tells us, pp. 27–31, of other places which he recovered.

[4] Ep. Dec. 28, 1261, ap. Theiner, *l.c.*, n. 264. " Cum igitur Rocca seu Castrum Larianum sit demanium sedis apostolicæ speciale, Universitatem vestram . . . monemus . . . quatenus homines Castri ejusdem . . . nullatenus offendatis." This is addressed to the Podestà, the Council, and the Commune of Velletri. *Cf. ib.*, nn. 268 (Bologna) ; 286 (Spoleto) ; 305 (Narni), and 306 (Siena). Cf. n. 271 against Spoleto for seizing the " terra Arnulphorum " which belonged to the Roman Church. Against Spoleto Urban had to employ force, sending Guiscarde de Petra Sancta against them. He had been made Rector of the Patrimony in Tuscany in July, 1263. *Cf. ib.*, p. 151.

" Unde Spoletanos non spontè venire coëgit,
Ad Papæ metas ecclesiæque manus." Theodoric, pp. 28–9.

to alienate their lands or rights,[1] or to make alliances,[2] or to elect their officials without the consent of the Holy See,[3] or, in certain cases, to elect any others for their officials than natives of their districts.[4] Finally, he strictly forbade the formation of Communes to the prejudice of the rights of the Church.[5]

Urban arrives in Orvieto, 1262.

It has just been stated that Urban left Viterbo in 1262 for Montefiascone in order to avoid the heat. After the summer had passed, he proceeded northwards, and arrived at the strong city of Orvieto in October, 1262. There he remained, seemingly in the episcopal palace,[6] almost to the day of his death. Among his other doings in that fascinating city, he consecrated to St. Dominic on the first Sunday in May, 1264, one of the first churches, if not the very first church consecrated to that Saint.[7] During his stay at Orvieto, Urban is credited with having added to the episcopal palace the portion which now forms its centre, and is justly regarded as its most perfect part.[8]

Although Urban never went to Rome, but spent most of his time at Orvieto, and therefore devoted most of the time and money he could spare to its adornment, he did not altogether forget the architectural needs of his episcopal city. As we have already noted he continued the work of his predecessor in repairing the Lateran[9]. Moreover an extant inscription on the door of

---

[1] Theiner, l.c., n. 266.
[2] Ib., n. 287. Cf. nn. 269, 278.
[3] Ib., n. 308.
[4] Ib., nn. 289 and 297.
[5] Ib., n. 290.
[6] Potthast, 18858.
[7] Ann. Urbevet., p. 129. Ap. R. I. S.S., t. xv, new ed.

[8] According to Ciaconius, Vitæ Pont. Rom., i, p. 717, Urban adorned Orvieto with many public and private buildings; but, according to the editor of the Annales Urbevetani, xv, pt. v, p. 155 n., new ed. of R. I. SS., he is wrong in attributing to that Pope the papal palace in the locality called Soliano near Sta. Maria Prisca, the walls of which were still standing when he wrote.

[9] Cf. supra, p. 54.

the church of S. Urbano in the modern via Alessandrina
informs us that the church and monastery connected
with it were built by Urban at the request of Jacoma,
daughter of Pietro Bianchi, on the site of her parental
palace (1264).[1]

[1] " †Anno ab incarn. D. MCCLXIV
    Ind. VII. mens. Aug. Die xxv. Urbanus
    Papa Quartus hoc monasterium
    Fierri fecit ad preces Jacobe filie
    Petri Blanci in domo patris sui.
    Ave Maria gratia plena." Ap. Armellini, *Le Chiese di Roma,*
p. 170.

CHAPTER II.

THE KINGDOM OF SICILY, AND THE INTERREGNUM IN THE EMPIRE.

Action against Manfred during the vacancy of the See, 1261.

As the power of King Manfred of Sicily had been greatly enhanced by the Ghibelline victory of Montaperti (1260),[1] the College of Cardinals, during the vacancy of the Holy See, found it necessary to continue Alexander's work of opposition to him. Accordingly on July 4, 1261, in order to make a stand against the Tuscan League which had been formed in Ghibelline interests, "the cardinal-bishops, priests, and deacons of the Roman Church" urged the Podestà and people of Perugia to exert themselves on behalf of their mother the Church, and to help those of the Duchy of Spoleto who were resisting the encroachments of Manfred.[2]

Manfred sends envoys to Urban, 1262.

Although that astute Prince had no intention of giving up his designs against the liberty of the Church in Sicily, or seemingly, against the States of the Church, and even against the whole of Italy,[3] he lost no time in sending

---

[1] *Cf. supra*, p. 39 ff.

[2] Potthast, 18119. *Cf.* Theod., p. 31 :—

> " Perfidus Hubertus Palavicenus et inde
> Manfredus Guelphis multa tulere mala.
> Hostes ecclesiæ sceleratos hi scelerati
> Semper foverunt per scelus atque nefas."

Cf. Gregory, p. 9. Urban's *Register*, i, n. 38, shows him confirming an award of the College of Cardinals.

[3] " Meinfridus spurius sibi vendicavit
> Christi patrimonium ; diu prophanavit,
> Quia cardinalibus aurum propinavit." *Chron. rhytm. Austr.*,
ap. *M. G. SS.*, xxv, p. 365. *Cf.* Brunetto Latini, *Li Tresors*, l. i, pt. ii, c. 98, " Et pensa (Manfred) en son coer, et lit prendome li tesmoignierent que Manfrois aroit et penroit bien toute Italie, se il n'estoit qui li contredesist."

envoys to the new Pope. But Urban found their offers
delusory.[1] One of these offers as we learn from Roger
Lovel, one of the agents of our King at Rome, was a
pecuniary one. Roger informs Henry that, about the
feast of the Conversion of St. Paul (Jan. 25, 1262), envoys
came from Manfred and offered the Pope and the cardinals
three hundred thousand ounces of gold, and the annual
tribute of ten thousand ounces if he would accept the
situation and recognize their master as King. The Pope,
however, would not acknowledge the usurper,[2] for he did
not believe that he was any more sincere than his father
in his offers of peace.[3] And when Manfred induced
James King of Aragon to negotiate with the Pope on
his behalf, Urban urged him not to listen to his fraudulent
suggestions, and not to allow himself, in his belief in
Manfred's straightforwardness, to be involved in his
deceits.[4]

One of the "suggestions" to which Urban was
particularly anxious that James should not listen was
that he should agree to a marriage between his son
Pedro and Constance, the daughter of Manfred. That
Prince had already strengthened his position by his
marriage with Helen, daughter of Michael, the Despot
of Epirus, and he endeavoured to strengthen it still more
by a matrimonial alliance with Aragon. He hoped to be
able to use Aragon against Charles of Anjou. It was in

Urban strives in vain to prevent the marriage between Pedro of Aragon and Constance, 1262.

---

[1] "Licet enim post vocationem nostram ad apostolatus officium ad
nos plures nuntios destinarit . . . nulla tamen per ipsos nisi delusoria
quaedam audivimus nec digna relatu." Ep., Apr. 26, 1262, to James I.
of Aragon. *Cf.* Theod., *ib.*

[2] Ep. Feb. 6, 1262, ap. *Royal Letters*, ii, p. 204 f.

[3] He calls his "oblationem pacis" . . . "proculdubio simulatam."
Ep., Apr. 26, 1262, just cited, ap. Raynaldus, *Annal.*, 1262, nn. 9–15.

[4] *Ib.* "Tu credens ipsum in veritatis simplicitate procedere . . .
Celsitudinem tuam affectuose rogamus, quatinus sinistris ejus
suggestionibus non prestes auditum nec ipsius fraudibus te patiaris
involvi."

vain that Urban pointed out to James the crimes of Manfred, and declared that it would be a disgrace if he allied himself to his family.[1] James was as ambitious as Manfred, and the marriage was duly celebrated at Montpellier on June 13, 1262[2]—the bride being described as " the most beautiful, the most accomplished, and the most honourable that could be met with ".[3]

St. Louis refuses the Aragonese alliance.

Although this marriage was not to the liking of Urban it had at least one consequence which pleased him. A letter written by him to St. Louis of France shows him praising that monarch for refusing to ally his son with the daughter of King James of Aragon, after he heard that he had become the father-in-law of Manfred, " a manifest persecutor of the Church ".[4]

Urban cites Manfred to appear before him, April 6, 1262.

Altogether dissatisfied with Manfred's attitude, Urban, in presence of a great multitude of people on Maunday Thursday, solemnly summoned him to appear before him on the first of August, 1262. The vassal was cited to answer to his lord on various charges which were made against him, and the formal citation was affixed to the door of the cathedral of Orvieto.[5] The charges against Manfred were set forth at length in this citation which is unfortunately lost. Some of them are, however, repeated in a letter of the Pope. Manfred, " formerly Prince of Taranto," was accused of having through his Saracens destroyed the city of Ariano (west of Benevento) in 1257 ; of having basely slain Thomas of Oria and

---

[1] *Ib.*

[2] See the marriage contract ap. *Hist. gen. de Languedoc*, iii, p. 556. *Cf. ib.*, p. 496-7.

[3] Muntaner, *Chron.*, c. 11. *Cf.* Desclot, *Cron.*, c. 51, and Saba, ii, c. 6.

[4] *Ep. c.* Aug., 1262, ap. Raynaldus, 1262, nn. 17–19.

[5] *Ep.* Nov. 11, 1262, *Reg.*, ii, n. 151, or Rod., iii, n. 527 ; Saba, ii, 7 ; and *Contin. Jamsillæ*, p. 591, which in the main is the same as Saba, but written in the interests of Manfred. Both ap. *R. I. SS.*, viii. *Cf.* Hemingford to Henry in a letter which in Shirley is wrongly referred to the year 1254 ; ii, p. 105.

Thomas of Salice, having cruelly and treacherously murdered Peter of Calabria, count of Catanzaro, of having shed the blood of " many of the faithful " ; of having set at naught the censures of the Church, of embracing Mohamedanism and of consorting with Saracens ; of overtaxing his people, and of having compassed the death of Conrad Brussarius, the envoy of Conradin.[1]

Manfred lost no time in putting in a defence, through his agents, for he was very desirous that the papal negotiations with Charles of Anjou should proceed no further. Accordingly, when the final hearing of his case was postponed to November 18, he declared that he would like to appear in person and asked that a safe-conduct should be granted him.[2] As Urban was anxious that his action should not be open to hostile criticism,[3] he granted the request, and on November 11 issued the safe-conduct on condition that Manfred came with a limited following.[4] This limitation Urban declared he was bound to make, as Manfred had already laid violent hands on the March of Ancona and other territories belonging to the Church. The King must, therefore, swear not to injure the lands of the Church when he came to the Pope, and not to come with a suite of more than eight hundred persons, of whom about a hundred might be armed. If he came with a larger number, it would show that he was not working for peace, and it would then be necessary to regard him as a heretic.[5]

The event showed that Urban's suspicions were well

---

[1] Ep. just cited, addressed to " the faithful of Christ ". Urban hints at his having murdered his brother, etc. : " ac super dira nece proximis sibi sanguine illata per ipsum."

[2] Ep. cit., and Saba, *l.c.*

[3] " Ut processus noster nequeat aliquorum detractorum morsibus vel obloquiis subjacere." *Ib.*

[4] *Ib.*   [5] *Ib.*

founded. Manfred came "magnificently with a great
force of cavalry" to the borders of the papal territory,[1]
ready, if need should arise, to overcome force by force.[2]
Led astray by the interested advice of certain barons
who had been enriched with the property of exiles which
they knew would have to be restored in the event of
peace, Manfred would not agree to the demands of the
Pope. The negotiations came to an abrupt termination,
and Manfred, under sentence of excommunication,
returned to Apulia, furiously (fremens) resolved to overthrow the papal party.[3] He had lost his opportunity
of making peace, and securing his recognition by his
suzerain. Later on, when he seems to have really wished
for peace, he could not obtain it.[4] Urban had made
up his mind that Manfred could not be trusted, and that
there was nothing for it but to deprive him of the
Kingdom.

Intervention of Baldwin II., 1262-3. It may be added that the intervention of others was
as little able to bring about a peace between the Pope

---

[1] *Contin. Jamsil.*, p. 591.

[2] Saba, "Paravit tamen se Rex ipse magnifice, ut, si expediret,
non solum curiales, sed et posset terrigenas, casu accidente, viribus
superare." L. ii, c. 7, p. 806. And yet throughout Manfred always
professed to regard the Roman Church as "the teacher and mistress—
magistra et domina, of the Christian faith." See a letter of his to the
Pope, ap. Martène, *Thes. Anecdot.*, ii, 91 ff.

[3] Saba, ii, 7. Saba is in this chapter more than usually obscure.
Cf. Theodoric,

"Hinc cum tractatus simulatos dictus inisset
Manfredus, dicto patre favente tamen,
Nil veri tenuit, imo perjuria verbis
Ipsius, et fraudes actibus ejus erant." P. 31.

It is clear from a letter, July 2, 1263, of the ex-emperor Baldwin
to Manfred, that neither he nor the French believed that Manfred was
in earnest about peace. Ep. ap. Martène, *Thes. Anecdot.*, ii, p. 23 ff.

[4] Saba, *l.c.* "Cum autem postmodum visus est velle sub exquisitis
cum omni diligentia pactis Sedis ejusdem se subjicere voluntati, ejus
humilitatem tunc repudiavit ecclesia, quæ se sibi tempore congruo
humiliare nequivit."

and Manfred as the direct negotiations between them.
After the Greeks again took possession of Constantinople
(July, 1261) its feeble Latin Emperor Baldwin II. fled
first to Greece and then into Apulia and thence into
France.[1] His object in his journeys from one royal court
to another was if possible to obtain men and money from
the Pope, the King of France, etc., to enable him to recover
his lost kingdom.[2] He arrived in Apulia (1262) whilst
Manfred was making overtures to the Pope for peace.
Taking advantage of Baldwin's necessities, Manfred
promised to help him if he could secure recognition of his
position from the Pope, and bade him go to Urban, and
assure him that, if the Pope would make peace with him
" or at least a truce," he would make the exiled monarch
again master of Constantinople. After that, if he will
grant me Apulia, I will endeavour to wrest Jerusalem
from the pagan. Baldwin agreed readily enough to
Manfred's wishes, found his way to Urban, and laid them
before him. " But gentlemen," continues the Venetian
historian da Canale, " the Pope would not give any
definite reply to the proposals." [3] Although Urban
would not listen to Manfred, he graciously received two
envoys from the Doge, Renier Zeno, to whom also had
Baldwin notified his misfortunes. Finding from them that
Venice was prepared at her own expense to transport to
Constantinople all who would take up arms for its

[1] Sanudo, pt. ii, p. 115, ed. Hopf.

[2] *The Chronicle of Morea*, p. 31, ed. Buchon, says that " he hoped to
be helped by the Pope . . . and by the King of France ". *Cf*. Martino
da Canale who tells us the same in his quaint French. " Mes il (Baldwin)
ne demora gueres en la Moree ; anceis s'en ala en Puille por aler a
Monsignour l'Apostoille, et d'ileuc en France, por li secors demander."
C. 189, p. 498.

[3] *Ib.*, c. 191. " Saches, signore, que Monsignor l'Apostoille ne
respondi a ces paroles ne si ne quoi."

recovery, he agreed to preach a crusade in Baldwin's behalf.[1]

From Urban the exiled emperor, in company with one of the Venetian envoys, Marco Giustiniani, proceeded to France, and at the court of Louis learnt why the Pope would not hearken to Manfred's protestations or proposals. Writing from Paris (July 2, 1263) to Manfred, from whom he hoped so much, Baldwin informed his friend that he was grieved to find that a number of the advisers of Louis were of opinion that the Sicilian had no other aim than to deceive the Church, and that he had no real wish for peace.[2] Baldwin, accordingly advised Manfred to send an envoy to Louis to justify himself, " unless indeed you know you are guilty, a thing which we do not in the least believe." He then earnestly exhorted his correspondent to do all he possibly could to make peace with the Pope, and he promised that he would use all his influence in his behalf.

Serious negotiations with Charles of Anjou, 1263-4.

From this letter, which fell into the Pope's hands, he was more than ever convinced of Manfred's bad faith. Accordingly, fully aware that, with such feeble resources as the Holy See had at its diposal, he was no match for Manfred, and seeing clearly that no help was to be got from England,[3] Urban now threw all his energy into realizing the idea of his predecessors, and securing the co-operation of Charles of Anjou. Accordingly, " when,"

---

[1] *Ib.*, c. 192. " L'Apostoille i promist la cruis et la solucion a tos ciaus que donera li secors." Here we may note that our author winds up his narrative about Baldwin that he got nothing but words from all to whom he went : " Saches, signore, que aces li fu promis, et petit atendu." C. 193.

[2] It was said : " Hæc erat vestra intentio, ut Ecclesiam ipsam possetis decipere, et mala voluntas quam habetatis circa Ecclesiam satis fuerat manifesta." Ep. ap. Martène, *Thesaurus*, ii, p. 24.

[3] Though in 1261 Henry continued to push Edmund's claims on paper. *Cf.* his letters to St. Louis, etc., ap. Rymer, i, p. 730 f.

to use the words of an old chronicler,[1] " he perceived that the papal rights had been seized, and that everything was going from bad to worse, then, urged on by his own views and by the complaints and exhortations of the exiles, and because he thought that there was need of greater force to overcome the power of Manfred, and that there was only one remedy for such evils, he resolved to call into Italy, Charles the brother of Louis, King of the French, a man of great talent in war, and on just and lawful grounds to grant him the Kingdom of Sicily, which was in the hands of Manfred." [2]

He therefore instructed his agents in France, especially his notary, Master Albert, to push the negotiations with Charles and his brother. Albert, who had been sent by him into France to find out the views of Louis and Charles on the situation, but who, whilst the negotiations with Manfred gave some hope of bringing about a settlement, had been forbidden to take any final steps,[3] was now urged to action. Especially was he to show Louis that neither Conradin nor Edmund of England had any right to Sicily; and that, in supporting Charles, he would not injure the rights of anyone.[4] Besides instructing Albert to allay the scruples of Louis, Urban also bade him try to obtain, on the best terms he could, the consent of Charles to come to his assistance and to accept Sicily.

Accordingly, on June 17, 1263, he sent Albert a set of conditions which were to be offered to Charles in the

Urban sends different sets of terms on which Charles could have Sicily, 1263.

[1] Leonardo Bruni (or L. Aretinus, † 1444) *Hist. Florent.*, lib. ii, p. 44, ap. *R. I. SS.*, t. xix, pt. iii, new ed.

[2] Urban's biographer, Gregory, says, p. 11, that he called in Charles "sapienter providens ad ejusdem regni (Sicily) regimen". *Cf.* Theod., pp. 31-2.

[3] Ep. of Oct. 25, 1262, ap. *Reg.*, ii, n. 146, "Verumtamen ad firmandum quicquam non procedas."

[4] Ep. probably at the very close of the year 1262, ap. Raynaldus, an. 1262, n. 21 ; Potthast, n. 18440.

first instance.[1] With the exception of Benevento and its
district, the Terra de Lavoro, and a few other places,
Charles was to have Sicily and the territories " on this
side of the Farus [2] up to the borders of the territories
of the Roman Church. But he was not to have any manner
of control, as Senator, Rector, etc., over any of the
belongings of the Church. On the other hand, he was to
pay a tax to the Pope of two thousand ounces of gold,
and when he had established his power over the Kingdom,
he was to pay fifty thousand marks sterling. Further,
every three years, he was to present to the Pope a fine
white palfrey, as an acknowledgment of his suzerainty.
He had, moreover, to agree to perform the other duties
of a vassal, by paying homage to and defending his lord,[3]
and by supplying him with troops for a limited time when
called upon to do so. Moreover, Charles and his heirs
had to swear that the Empire and Sicily should never be
united, and that they would never hold any large portion
of Italy in addition to Sicily (dominium Lombardie vel
Tuscie seu majoris partis earum). They were also to
guarantee full freedom to the Church in the Kingdom,
and to restore what had been taken from it. In addition,
the barons of the country were to enjoy the *status* which
they had had in the days of William II., and while all
exiles were to be recalled and to have their property
restored to them, all political prisoners were to be
released.

A second document, of the same date, authorized
Albert to accept an annual tax of ten thousand ounces of
gold in case Charles should insist on having the Terra di
Lavoro, and the other places south of the boundaries of
the territory of the Church, except Benevento and its

[1] *Reg.*, ii, n. 269, June 17, 1263 ; or Rod., iii, 539.
[2] *Cf. supra*, vol. xi, p. 211 n.
[3] The oath of allegiance is given in full in the document n. 269,
p. 120.

district, which was not to be ceded to Charles. Further,
failing direct heirs, Charles might be authorized to leave
the Kingdom to one of his brothers. In like manner,
should occasion arise, Albert was commissioned to allow
a number of other minor modifications.[1]

Albert was also instructed to inform Charles that, if the
papal conditions were accepted, the Pope would give
ear to his requests, and grant him a tenth of all the
ecclesiastical revenues of the Kingdom of France, the
county of Provence, and the provinces of Lyons, Vienne,
etc., for three years for the Sicilian affair. He would,
moreover, cause a crusade to be preached in those
countries, and in Lombardy and the states of the Church
against Manfred and his Saracens, and would grant to
those who took part in the expedition the usual Palestine
indulgences. Finally he would agree never to recognize
Conradin or any descendant of Frederick as Roman
emperor.[2]

It need hardly be said that Charles was as anxious for
favourable terms as the Pope. Long negotiations ensued
between them, and the original conditions laid down by
Urban had to be considerably altered in favour of the
lord of Provence. During the course of these negotiations
various circumstances, which will be related presently,
operated to Charles' advantage.

Whilst Urban was working to secure the co-operation
of Charles of Anjou against Manfred, he did not cease to
act against him as far as he could by his own resources.
He strove by exhortation and every other means in his

Urban's
efforts
against
Manfred.

---

[1] *Reg.*, ii, n. 270.
[2] *Ib.*, n. 272, June 26, 1263. Soon after this, July 6, 1263, he absolved
Philip, the son of Louis, from an oath which his mother had induced
him to take not to help Charles. He had been induced to take the oath
more from the easy-going habits of youth than from mature judgment.
"Ad que potius juvenilis etatis facilitate, quam animi judicio es
inductus."

power to detach supporters from Manfred. He ordered all encouragement to be given to the *Judge* of Arborea, who was trying to wrest Sardinia from Manfred,[1] he worked hard to withdraw Pisa from its alliance with him [2]; and he raised troops in Italy and elsewhere to help such places (e.g., Pesaro) as wished to hold out against the usurper.[3]

The offer of Sicily definitely withdrawn from Henry, 1263.

About this time, too, Urban definitely withdrew the offer of Sicily to Edmund of England. It had long been absolutely clear that there was no possibility of Henry's ever taking any efficient action against Manfred. Urban, accordingly, dispatched to England Bartholomew Pignatelli, archbishop of Cosenza, to explain to Henry that it was quite impossible for the Holy See to wait for his intervention any longer.[4] Henry and Edmund were told how Pope Alexander had in vain awaited the armed assistance of " the high throne of the Kingdom of England, and the great power of the English nation " ; and how the non-arrival of this help had caused great loss to the Holy See. Manfred, not content with seizing the Kingdom of Sicily, had begun to lay his greedy hands upon the March of Ancona, and other territories belonging to the Church, and even, at length, upon a part of Tuscany that belonged to the Roman Empire.[5] Henry is therefore asked, as he himself cannot

---

[1] Ep., July 14, 1263, ap. *Reg.*, ii, n. 321.

[2] Potthast, 18586, July 14, 1263. *Cf. ib.*, 18700, and *Reg.*, iii. Append. ii, nn. 2831–3.

[3] Ep. to the Podestà of Pesaro, July 15, 1263, ap. Rod., iii, pp. 529–30. " Nos . . . stipendiare milites, ubicumque per Italiam strenuos possumus invenire, et alias etiam magnificum congregare exercitum non cessamus." *Cf. ib.*, ep. July 11, 1263, ap. *ib.*, p. 525 f.

[4] Various letters from July 25–30, 1263, ap. *Reg.*, ii, n. 296–303.

[5] " Manfredus, occupatione ipsius regni Sicilie non contentus, ad Anconitanam Marchiam et quamplures alias terras de patrimonio ipsius ecclesie, et demum ad quamdam partem Tuscie que Romano imperio subjacet, avidas et occupatrices manus extendens . . . ecclesiam . . . affligit." Ep. July 28, 1263, n. 297. In another letter to

help, not to do anything to hamper the action of the
Holy See in seeking assistance elsewhere. Four months
were, however, granted him within which time he could
make good any claims he had in the matter. Henry's
relations, however, with his barons at this moment were
such that he was powerless to do anything even for
himself. His connexion with the Sicilian affair was,
fortunately, to all practical purposes now at an end.[1]

This point in favour of the interests of Charles of Anjou
was followed by others which forced the Pope to offer
him still more favourable terms in return for his
acceptance of the Sicilian crown. All during Urban's
pontificate, intrigues had been going on in Rome for the
Senatorship. Richard of Cornwall, candidate for the
Empire, was aiming at it,[2] and so also were Manfred and
his son-in-law Alfonso. Suddenly, to the surprise of
everyone, the " boni homines ", " the good men and true ",
who had been governing the city since the death of the
last Senator, elected Charles of Anjou Senator, not for
one year as usual, but for life (c. the beginning of August).[3]

Events which favoured better terms for Charles. He is elected Senator, 1263.

Henry of the same date, n. 302, the Pope does not fail to tell him that,
when he was reading " the volumes of the Annals of the Roman Church,
and the *Regesta* of his predecessors, he perceived his devotion to that
Church. What were these ' annalium R. E. volumina ? ' "

[1] It was not, however, till June 26, 1265, that Henry appointed
plenipotentiaries to renounce Sicily for himself and Edmund, if they
saw fit. Rymer, i, p. 815.

[2] Rymer, i, 728–9, and *supra*, p. 29. *Cf.* Theod., *in vit. U.*, p. 32.

[3] Saba, L. ii, c. 9, p. 808 ; Will. of Nangis, *Chron.*, an. 1263, i, p. 225 ;
Theod., *l.c.* ; Potthast, ep. Aug. 11, 1263, n. 18621. According to
Theodoric, the Romans fixed the feast of St. Michael as the date of
Charles' arrival in Rome, but afterwards prolonged it to the feast of
Pentecost, June 8, 1264. And, as a matter of fact, Charles' vicar
appeared in Rome some two or three weeks before the last mentioned
date. Brunetto Latini, *Le Tresors*, l. iii, pt. ii, c. 5, p. 583, ed.
P. Chabaille, gives a letter in old French purporting to be from the
Romans to Charles—" li governierres de Rome o tout lor conseil salut,"
etc., to Charles. " Nos, par le commun assentment de la ville, avons

This unexpected event had been brought about chiefly by the efforts of Richard Annibaldi, cardinal-deacon of St. Angelo. As he was a member of a Ghibelline family, the historian Saba Malaspina was quite at a loss to explain his conduct. However, he tells us how the cardinal expended large sums on Charles' behalf, and how, contriving to expel from the City the greater portion of the Ghibelline nobility, he brought about the election of Charles as perpetual Senator. At the news of this election Urban was both pleased and alarmed. He was pleased that the senatorial power should be in the hands of a strong friend, but he was alarmed at the idea that it should be in such hands for a long period. Were it to remain so, his own authority in the City would be reduced to nothing, and he would be in the Senator's power. He accordingly wrote to Charles to say that he would be glad if he accepted the government of the City ; but at the same time he reminded him that the election of the Senator belonged to the Pope, and that he would never allow anyone to hold the senatorial office for life. Should, then, there really be question of his accepting the office for life, he must take a secret oath to the Pope's representative, the notary Albert, to lay it down when called upon by papal authority to do so.[1]

The fortune of war favours Charles, 1263-4.   Charles' hope of obtaining the crown of Sicily from Urban more or less on his own terms was further strengthened by the success of Manfred's forces in the field. Whilst the intrigues and negotiations just recorded were in progress, fighting was going

establi que vos soiez senatours . . . de Rome, de ceste prochienne feste de la Touz Sainz jusqu'à i an." But it not clear whether Latini himself composed this letter as a model, or whether he used a genuine letter to serve as a model.

[1] Ep. just cited. *Cf.* n. 18622, wherein Urban gives the notary Albert power to absolve Charles from any oath which he may have taken to hold the office for life.

on in various parts between the papal party and the adherents of Manfred. In the March of Ancona the troops of the Church were successful, and Manfred's nephew Conrad was taken prisoner (1262 ?).[1] But great trouble was brewing for the Pope in Tuscany. The Ghibelline nobles, who had been expelled from Rome and the Germans in that province gathered round Peter de Vico, " Proconsul of the City," [2] whom we have seen possessing himself by force of fiefs which ought to have reverted to the Pope. This noble, besides his *Castrum de Vico*, had several other castles in the neighbourhood of Rome,[3] and belonged to the family which had by hereditary right long provided Rome with its prefects, and hence styled itself " de Præfectis or Præfectani ".[4] Peter himself is described as " Prefect of the City of Rome ".[5]

Despite the efforts of the Guelfs under Pandulf of Anguillara, Peter took possession of Sutri, in the early spring of 1264, while, perhaps somewhat earlier (February 2, 1264), one of his associates, Guithius of Bisenzo, murdered the Pope's nephew, Guischard, the *rector and capitaneus* of the Patrimony of St. Peter.[6] Manfred, too, about this time, tearing himself away from

[1] Saba, L. ii, c. 8, p. 807. Conrad afterwards escaped. *Cf.* Theod., p. 28, and ep. of John of Hemingford, ap. *Royal Letters*, ii, pp. 105–6.

[2] " Sane de Vico Petrus memoratus adhæsit
  Manfredo, Papæ foedera nulla tenens." Theod., p. 34. *Cf.* Saba, ii, c. 10, pp. 808–9.

[3] " Qui (P. de V.) in maritimis partibus Urbi vicinis, et alibi per districtum Urbis plura castra tenebat." Saba, *ib.*

[4] In 1248, Apr. 30, Innocent IV. addressed a letter " Prefecto Urbis, Petro Bonifatii, Amatori quondam Gabrielis de Prefectis, dominis de Vico et aliis Prefectanis". Ap. Theiner, *Cod. Dipl.*, i, n. 233.

[5] In *Memoir. Potestat. Regiensium*, ap. *R. I. S.S.*, viii, p. 1128, where we are told that he died in Dec., 1268.

[6] *Annal. Urbevet.*, ap. *R. I. S.S.*, t. xv, pt. v, pp. 129, 146, 155. *Cf.* ep. Urb., July 14, 1263, ap. Theiner, *Cod. Dip.*, i, p. 151 ; epp. of Feb. and March, ap. *Reg.*, ii, 757, 764 ; and Theod., pp. 35 and 44, where " Gaufridi " no doubt stands for " Guischardi ".

his pleasures, held a diet at Naples to deliberate on the resistance to be offered to Charles. Among other resolutions, the diet decreed that the Genoese captain Percival Doria, should be sent with a great army into the Duchy of Spoleto.[1]

Fighting in the March and in Tuscany.

This renewed activity of Manfred soon made itself felt in the March of Ancona and in Tuscany ; and in both of those districts the tide of battle ebbed and flowed. There were successes for the Guelfs [2] and successes for the Ghibellines. The Guelfs recovered Sutri, and under James Cantelmi an army of Romans in the pay of the Pope [3] besieged the castrum de Vico (May, 1264).[4] But Manfred ordered the force under Percival Doria which was moving against the Duchy of Spoleto to march to the relief of Vico. At the same time he collected an army on the papal frontier of Campagna. Tired of the siege, afraid of the armies of Manfred, and anxious about their crops, the Romans, " with their wonted inconstancy," says the Pope, raised the siege and returned home in June, 1264.[5]

---

[1] Saba, *l.c.*

[2] *Cf.* Theod., pp. 36–7, " Alter (a Ghibelline noble) Cum Gibellinis pluribus ense cadet."

[3] Ep. July 17, 1264, ap. Martène, *Thes. Anecdot.*, ii, p. 82 ff. The Pope had to pay " de camera nostra ".

[4] *Ib.*, Saba, l. ii, c. 11, p. 809. *Cf.* ep. Urban, May 30, 1264, ap. Theiner, *Cod. dip.*, i, n. 304, to James Cantelmi, the Vicar of Charles of Anjou in Rome.

[5] *Ib.*, " Cum recolligendarum frugum tempus instaret, . . . ab ejusdem castri obsidione discedunt." Saba, this is one of the very few indications of time given us by Saba. The dearth of chroniclers at this period makes it very difficult to fix the exact dates of many of the events of Urban's reign. It may be noticed that the Roman Saba, anxious for the military reputation of his countrymen, says that they showed their wisdom in abandoning the siege, " usi consilio saniori." The Frenchman, Theodoric, however, thinks they were very ill advised in doing so : " Nam licet hoc (the castle of Vico) leviter everti posset, iniquo Consilio Romam plebs dominante redit." Pg. 37. *Cf.* the important letter of Urban, July 17, 1264 (ap. Martène, *Thes. Anecdot.*, ii, 82), addressed to Simon de Brion.

Although Percival Doria was accidentally drowned soon after the retreat of the Romans from Vico, and his amy lost all courage,[1] the indomitable Peter de Vico inflicted a severe defeat on a numerous papal army made up of men to whom Urban at Orvieto had given the Cross against Manfred, and of a number of Lombard knights sent by him to support the count of Anguillara. This defeat took place in the neighbourhood of the Cimmian hill-city of Vetralla, and resulted in the capture of Pandulf.[2]

This conspicuous success still further fired the zeal and enterprise of the Ghibelline supporters of Manfred. Eager to prevent the arrival of Charles of Anjou, they watched the seas with " a multitude of galleys ", while their German allies, as though sure of final success, openly flaunted their banners within sight of Rome.[3] Manfred fanned their enthusiasm with liberal supplies of money. Regretting now, so we are assured, that he had not closed with Urban's peace offers, he strove to make it impossible for Charles to come to the Pope's assistance by the time he had promised. Should he be successful in this, he had hopes of being able to become reconciled to the Church.[4]

Manfred's want of courage.

Acting in Manfred's name, but without waiting for the co-operation of his friends, the daring Peter de Vico set out one night from Cervetri, managed to break into the Trastevere through some houses which he had once held there, and which were seemingly insufficiently guarded. Then, rapidly crossing the island of the Tiber,[5] he fortified

---

[1] *Ann. Urbevet., l.c.*, p. 130 ; Saba, ii, c. 12 ; Theod., p. 41 ; Gregory, p. 10.

[2] Saba, *ib.*, pp. 810–11 ; Theod., pp. 42–3 ; and the letter of Urban to Cardinal Simon.

[3] Saba, ii, c. 13.

[4] *Ib.*, " Rex Manfredus postea ejusdem ecclesiæ, cujus jam eum pœnitebat non paruisse mandatis, reconciliare se posset affectibus."

[5] Saba, whom we are still following, calls it by its old name of " insula Lycaonia ".

himself in the district called " Piscinula ", between the island and the church of St. Cecily, wherein is the church of St. Benedetto in Piscinula. At once attacked by Charles' Vicar, James Cantelmi, and his Provençals, he would, nevertheless, have held his own but for the help and encouragement given to them by John Savelli, who from the island attacked de Vico in the rear. Practically the entire troop of the rash noble was slain or captured, whilst he himself and three followers, with the greatest difficulty, escaped to Cervetri.[1] Despite this setback, the military situation ought to have been in Manfred's hands, but he was " indolent and vain-glorious ",[2] and was hence wholly incapable of so strengthening his position that Charles would never have ventured to leave Provence. As the Campanians on his front stood firm, he himself, giving up all thoughts of fighting, returned to Apulia, " in order to resume his wonted pleasures," and left to his adherents the task of subduing the Guelfs by force of arms, and of seizing the Pope in Orvieto if they could.[3]

Urban did not live to see the arrival of Charles and the downfall of Manfred ; but it was not very long after his death that his policy matured.

Charles of Anjou, after fresh concessions, agrees to attack Manfred.

As the reader will no doubt have gathered from the preceding narrative, the election of Charles as Senator of Rome, and the warlike activity of the Ghibelline party

[1] Saba, ii, cc. 13 and 14. The brief account of this stirring episode given by Andrew of Hungary, *Descriptio*, c. 11, is not so reliable or so good.

[2] So is he justly described by Mr. C. W. P. Orton, *Outlines of Medieval Hist.*, p. 324, Cambridge, 1916. The praise given to Manfred by Gregorovius and other German authors is misplaced.

[3] *Cf.* Urban's letter of July 17 to Cardinal Simon de Brion, frequently cited : " Suis consuetis delitiis potiturus," ap. M., ii, p. 83. " Manfredus . . . ad obsidendum nos et curiam nostram in civitate Urbevetana in qua personaliter residemus, cuncta suæ pravæ intentionis studia dicitur convertisse." *Ib.*, p 85.

had, long before the summer of 1264, compelled Urban
to make more concessions to Charles of Anjou in order to
secure his intervention. The Pope had certainly displayed
great energy against that party. He had caused a crusade
to be preached vigorously against Manfred [1] ; and he had
raised troops and paid mercenaries to fight against it.
But the financial strain alone was more than he could
bear. The expenses of the campaign involved him in
payments to the amount of a thousand marks a week. [2]
Besides, owing to the success of Manfred's Germans and
the Ghibellines at Montaperti, and the subsequent
adhesion to their party of nearly the whole of Tuscany, [3]
the Pope found himself to a very large extent cut off
from communication with the Catholic world. Charles
of Anjou, therefore, was Urban's only hope ; and hence,
through the notary Albert, he made first one and then

---

[1] Epp. March 27, May 20, 1264, ap. *Reg.*, ii, n. 778, and n. 633. In this
latter he notes that the Church has usually been accustomed to raise
her voice in behalf of the Holy Land, but that now she has to raise her
voice in behalf of her own freedom (" de propria liberatione sollicita ")
threatened by degenerate sons—by Manfred who shows by his life and
conduct how far removed he is from the Christian faith. Urban then
shows that by the King's action and by that of others like him, communication is cut off between the faithful and the teacher of catholic
faith and the guardian of ecclesiastical liberty—" dum ad nos et eandem
ecclesiam (the Roman), magistram veri dogmatis et catholice fidei, ac
tutricem ecclesiasticæ libertatis, etc."

[2] *Chron. min. Erphord*, ap. *M. G. SS.*, xxiv, p. 203.

[3] " A.D. 1261 status Thusciæ totus est mutatus, quia tota Thuscia
imperialis, præter Lucam et exiticios Florentinos ad partem ghibellinam
convertitur." . . . " A.D. 1263 . . . Urbans P. videns se undique hostibus
vallatum, Carolum comitem Provinciæ . . . advocat in subsidium suum
et Ecclesiæ." Ptolemy of Lucca, *Annales*, pp. 80 and 82. *Cf.* the Pope's
letter, n. 633, quoted in the note above. *Cf.* also ep. Apr. 25, 1264,
ap. *Rod.*, iii, n. 591. " De ejus (the kingdom of Sicily) divitiis magna
pars mundi corrumpitur, ecclesie patrimonium laceratur, et vie nostre
et ad nos venientium ex parte jam maxima sepiuntur." See also Will. de
Nangis, *Chron.*, an 1264, for the last point.

another concession to him.[1] Declaring that now all evil
no longer came, as Jeremiah said, from the north (i, 14),
but from the Kingdom of Sicily, and that, under ordinary
circumstances, he could not have any other Prince
supreme in Rome except the Pope,[2] he notified Charles
that he was prepared to assent to his being Senator
for a time in order that his access to the Kingdom might
be thereby simplified. Finally, at the request of Charles
himself and of his brother St. Louis, he dispatched to
France Simon de Brion, cardinal-priest of St. Cecily,
as his legate to arrange definitely the conditions on
which Charles was to be acknowledged as Senator,
and as King of Sicily (May, 1264). The legate was to
be allowed considerable latitude in the matter of the
modification of terms. He was to be allowed, for instance,
gradually to reduce the requirement of an annual tax
of ten thousand ounces of gold to one of two thousand.
On the other hand, however, he was to put an end to
all negotiation rather than agree that Charles should be
Senator for life. He was not to consent to the Count's
holding the Senatorship for a longer term than five years,
nor to his holding the Kingdom of Sicily and the Senatorship at the same time.[3] The Count was, however, to
be allowed a tenth of all the ecclesiastical revenues

---

[1] Potthast, n. 18715, ep. Nov. 18–19, 1263 ; nn. 18750–1 ; n. 18768,
Jan. 7, 1264 ; Jan. 9, nn. 18773–4. Ptolemy of Lucca, *Annales*, an.
1263, says that the Pope gave Sicily to Charles : " quia progenies
Frederici ex delicto ejus unumet(?)a feudo ceciderat ipsse, et genus .
ejus totum."

[2] Ep. Apr. 25, 1264, *l.c.*

[3] *Ib.*, i.e., ep. Apr., 1264, ap. Rod., iii, p. 580 ff., which is called :
" Diffinitio inter fratres (the cardinals) super Senatu Urbis et regno
Siciliæ dando . . . Carolo." For other documents connected with the
commission of Card. Simon see *ib.*, n. 592–603. In a letter to Charles
himself, ep. May 3, 1264, ap. *ib.*, n. 590, Urban tells him plainly that
he cannot be Senator for life.

of France for three years[1]; and when it was imposed all were to be informed of the great spiritual and temporal advantages which would follow to the Roman Church, and to the universal Church, and especially to the Holy Land and to the empire of Constantinople if the Church, through a Catholic ruler, secured full power in the Kingdom. The Roman Church would not then have so frequently to lay financial burdens on the ultramontane Churches in order to cope with her necessities. The patrimony and the tax from the Kingdom would suffice for her needs.[2]

The long negotiations about the Kingdom of Sicily came to an end at last. Charles resolved to accept the proffered crown; and, at the request of the Guelf party in Rome, at once dispatched a Vicar to Rome to represent him as Senator (May, 1264). Gaucelin, the first one whom he sent, died shortly after his arrival in Rome, and was succeeded by a Provençal, James Cantelmi or Gantelmi.[3] The Vicar had but a few troops with him, and, had Manfred shown any courage, he would not have been able to resist him. Still the position of the Pope was dangerous enough.[4] The Ghibelline party, if not Manfred himself, was securing its hold on the March of Ancona, was threatening the Duchy of Spoleto, was all powerful in imperial Tuscany, and had a footing too in papal Tuscany. Urban longed for the coming of Charles; and was fearful lest anything should occur to prevent it. In his anxiety he forgot the secret code in which he had agreed to write to Charles[5]; but he

[Marginal note: Charles sends a Vicar to Rome, 1264.]

---

[1] Card. Simon got the tenth for Sicily at a council held in Paris. *Cf. Ann. Norman.*, ap. *M. G. SS.*, xxvi, p. 515.

[2] Ep. May 3, 1264, ap. *ib.*, n. 594, p. 586 ff.

[3] *Cf.* Saba, ii, cc. 10 and 11. The similarity of these names has caused confusion between them. *Cf.* Andrew of Hungary, *Descripti o vict.*, c. 10.

[4] *Cf. supra*, 168 ff.

[5] Ep. to Charles, July 28, 1264, " Ceterum quia propter occupationes multas oblivioni tradidimus illa secreta vocabula, sub quibus tibi

did not forget to warn him against assassins whom it was said that Manfred had sent into France to murder him.[1]

Moreover, he did not forget that, if Percival Doria was drowned, his army was still in existence ; and so to oppose it he dispatched his marshal, Boniface of Canossa, with a thousand men, and three cardinals to stir up the Spoletans against it.[2]   Nor, in fine, did he forget, even within a few weeks of his death, to urge his legate, cardinal Simon de Brion, to do all in his power in conjunction with the cardinal-bishop of Sabina, Guy Fulcodi,[3] and with the notary, Master Albert, to expedite the departure of Charles.[4]   One of his last acts was to implore Margaret, the wife of St. Louis IX., to make friends with Charles [5] ; and Louis himself to advance money to his brother, so that the Sicilian expedition might be rapidly forwarded.[6]

'Death of Urban.

Urban, however, did not live to see the success of his efforts.   He died on Oct. 2, 1264, and Charles did not sail up the Tiber till May 21, 1265.

THE INTERREGNUM IN THE EMPIRE

Condition of the Empire during the interregnum.

If the tranquillity of the Church during the days of Urban IV. was disturbed by such luxurious and ambitious tyrants as Manfred and by such lawless nobles as Peter de Vico, the peace of the Empire during the interregnum

---

scribere debebamus ; ideo si tibi sub prædictis vocabulis non scribimus, non mireris."   Potthast, n. 18993, from Martène, *Thes. Anecdot.*, ii, 86.

[1] *Ib.*

[2] *Cf.* Urban's letter ap. Martène, *Thes.*, ii, 82 ff.   The cardinals had no great success " propter maliciam et perfidiam incolarum ".   But Simon of S. Martino, who was sent at the same time as legate to the March of Ancona, was much more successful. *Ib.*

[3] Afterwards Clement IV.

[4] Ep. to Simon, Sept. 4, 1264.   Potthast, n. 19010 from Martène, *l.c.*, p. 87.

[5] Ep. Sept., 1264, Pott., n. 19021.

[6] Ep. to Louis, *ib.*, 19022. *Cf. ib.*, 19024.

was disturbed by a similar class of men. Strong in their inaccessible castles, the nobles robbed the traveller and the merchant and " behaved with the greatest insolence ".[1] Brunetto Latini, who was himself a sufferer from the lawlessness of the times,[2] tells us that, according to Merlin and the Sibyl, the empire had to come to an end with Frederick II., but that he did not know whether it was meant that the imperial dignity was to pass with him from his family or from the German people.[3] Both of Latini's suppositions may be said to be correct. Frederick was not only the last Hohenstaufen emperor, but he was also the last head of the Holy Roman Empire who was emperor in anything but name.

It has been already told how, on the death of Frederick, the German electors, only concerned not to have an efficient ruler, chose, some of them, first Richard of Cornwall, and then, others of them, Alfonso X. of Castile. It has also been told how Alexander IV., anxious above everything for a peaceful life, would not take the responsibility of an attempt to put an end to the schism, but left the question to be faced by his successor. The claim of Richard, if only from the fact that he had several times been in Germany and had been recognized by many of

---

[1] " Cum . . . medio tempore (during the period between the death of the emperor Frederick II., 1250, and the election of Rudolf of Hapsburg, 1273) in partibus Alemanie et aliarum circumjacentium per diversos spoliatores viarum et nobiles ipsius terre fuerint insolentiæ quam plurimæ perpetrate, etc." Godfrey of Ensmingen, *Gesta Rudofi*, ap. Böhmer, *Fontes*, ii, p. 111. Perhaps the real author of these annals was Ellenhard, procurator of the fabrick of the Church of Strasburg, †1304. The connexion between these two authors has not been cleared up ; but it is thought that Ellenhard inspired Godfrey to write or furnished him with the material or both.

[2] He was driven from Florence by the Ghibelline party after Montaperti : " Et avec els (the Guelf party) en fu chacié maistres Brunez Latin ; et si estoit il par cele guerre esiliez en France quant il fist cest livre." *Li Tresors*, l. i, pt. ii, c. 99.

[3] *Ib.*, c. 94.

its people, would seem to be the better founded. Had
he not written to tell the citizens of London that at
Aix-la-Chapelle he had " received the sceptre of the Holy
Roman Empire and the crown thereof ? " [1]

However that may be, both candidates endeavoured
to obtain papal support for their position. Especially
did Alfonso strive to secure the patronage of Urban.
But Urban refused to give his favour to either of the
rivals, the more so that, though each of them was anxious
to win a verdict from him in his favour, the two of them
would not formally agree to submit their claims to his
judgment.[2]

A letter, written by the Pope a month or two later,
shows that he was not indifferent to the situation, for
he wrote on June 3, 1263, to the ecclesiastical electors
to say that he was glad to hear that there was a prospect
of the difficulty being settled by a fresh election. At
the same time, however, following in the footsteps of
Alexander IV., he strictly forbade them to think of
choosing Conradin.[3]

Nothing came of the idea of a new election ; but
the rivals at length agreed to submit their claims to
the decision of Urban, who duly summoned the claimants

---

[1] *Cron. maiorum Lond.*, an. 1256, p. 26 ff., ed. Stapleton. Riley's
translation, p. 28 ff. In a letter, Aug. 16, 1262, to Alfonso of Castile,
Henry declared that the Roman Church recognized Richard as King,
but that, as the question of the Empire was under examination by it,
he could not consistently with the fidelity he owed that Church move
at all in the matter in dispute. " Non possemus, salvo fidei et fidelitatis
vinculo, quibus eidem Ecclesiæ astringimur, super hoc aliquid
attemptare." Rymer, i, p. 749.

[2] Urban refused (ep. Apr. 17, 1263) to favour Alfonso " præsertim
cum tam tui quam præfati comitis (Richard, Earl of Cornwall) nuntii
apud sedem apostolicam constituti se nolle in hoc ipsius sedis subire
judicium frequenter duxerint proponendum ". Rod., iii, p. 481.

[3] *Ib.*, p. 488 ff., or *Reg.*, ii, nn. 104, 109. *Cf.* Theod., p. 37.

> " Advertens dictus hinc Papa quod Imperialis
> Mundo deerat honor, hunc revocare cupit."

to appear before him on May 2, 1264.[1] Before that date, however, Richard of Cornwall was in arms helping his brother King Henry III. against the barons; and, within a few days after it, was captured by the Barons at the battle of Lewes (May 13, 1264). Under the circumstances, it was obviously impossible for Richard to appear before the Pope on May 2.[2] Accordingly, despite the efforts of Alfonso to obtain a decision in his favour, owing to the failure of his opponent to put in an appearance at the prescribed time,[3] Urban put off the hearing of the case for another year.[4] Before the time appointed by him, he had departed this world, and the affair had finally to be settled by Gregory X. after the death of Richard of Cornwall (1272).[5]

[1] Cf. his ep. of Aug. 27, 1263, ap. Rod., iii, n. 560, n. 561, and Reg., ii, n. 358. Cf. Gervase, Contin., ii, p. 231, R. S.

[2] Theod., p. 38 :—

" Richardus minime venit nec misit, ab ejus
    Hostibus, et dicto Simone (de Montfort) captus erat."

[3] Ib.

[4] Ib., " Sed quia tunc aberat pars altera, terminus alter
    Assignatur eis, sufficiensque dies." Cf. Potthast, n. 18931 ; in full ap. Reg., ii, n. 712, Aug. 26, 1264.

[5] Cf. Ellenhard (or Godfrey of Ensmingen), Gesta Rudolfi, ap. Böhmer, Fontes, ii, pp. 111–12.

CHAPTER III.

THE BRITISH ISLES, MISCELLANEOUS DEEDS OF URBAN.

APART from the ordinary business connected with the government of the Church in England, including many dispensations to hold more than one benefice, and not a few " provisions ", Urban's intercourse with it and with the country itself was chiefly concerned with money matters, and with giving aid to Henry against the barons.

The straits to which the Pope was reduced by Manfred and the Ghibelline party, and the many important concerns in which he was interested, caused him to be in great need of money. Very naturally, therefore, he turned to England to get some. There was money in England even in Urban's reign ; and he appealed to its bishops " to assist the Roman Church in her necessities caused by defence of ecclesiastical liberty and by the business of Sicily ".[1] England, moreover, owed him money. In 1262 he had to complain that the annual tax of one thousand marks due to the Holy See had not been paid for two years [2] ; and, on August 26, 1263, he had to instruct one of his nuncios to put pressure on the King on account of its non-payment. By next Michaelmas, said the indignant pontiff, the tax " will have been due for three years ".[3]

---

[1] Ep. to the Bishop of Ely, Jan. 21, 1262, ap. *Calendar of Papal Registers*, i, p. 382. *Cf.* epp. of Jan. 23, etc., 1262, ap. *ib.*, pp. 383–4.

[2] Epp. of Dec. 13, 1262, ap. *Cal.*, i, p. 380. *Cf.* ep. July 25, 1263 ; *ib.*, p. 379.

[3] *Ib.*, p. 387. *Cf. ib.*, pp. 384 and 385 for Urban's efforts to recover that share of the late Master Rostand's property which he had left to the *camera* (treasury) of Alexander IV. He had also difficulty in getting money due from the will of Aylmar, bishop of Winchester, *ib.*, p. 380.

Urban also wanted money for the now defunct Latin Empire of Constantinople. With the connivance of the Genoese, whom trade rivalry had made enemies of the Venetians who were the mainstay of the Empire, the Greeks regained possession of Constantinople on July 25, 1261. The weak emperor Baldwin fled to Italy, and began the second of his European begging tours. In concert with the Venetians he implored the help of the Pope, and then he approached other sovereigns of the West, in the hope of inducing them to assist him to recover the lost city.[1]

Urban, overwhelmed by the news of the loss of Constantinople,[2] took up Baldwin's cause at once. The Genoese were excommunicated,[3] and every effort was made to prevent them from assisting Michael Palæologus, now installed in the Queen of Cities. To help the Greek emperor, so Urban insisted in a letter to the Genoese, was not only to oppose the Latins in the East, but to oppose the Roman Church and the Catholic faith.[4] He called upon the Churches to help Baldwin,[5] and roused

---

[1] Dandolo, *Chron.*, x, c. 7, ap. *R. I. SS.*, xii, p. 370. Marino Sanudo tells of the Venetians "mittentes ad d. papam et ad alios barones fideles quos ad istud negotium valere credebant conquirendi imperium Romanie". Fragmentum ap. Hopf, *Chron. gréco-roman.*, p. 173. *Cf.* Martino da Canale, *Cron. Veneta*, c. 189, p. 499. "Anzi se ne andò in Puglia per condursi a Monsignore lo Apostolo . . . e mandò sue lettere a Monsignore il Doge pregandolo inviasse suoi messagi a M. lo Apostolo, etc. *Cf.* c. 192, p. 503. See also Mar. Sanudo, *Vite de' Duchi di Venezia*, ap., *R. I. SS.*, t. xxii, p. 560, and ep. Urban (June 5 ? 1262), ap. *Reg.*, ii, n. 131.

[2] Ep. June 5, 1262, to Louis, ap. Raynald., an. 1262, n. 40. "Nos ex rumore hujusmodi, veluti ex quodam terrifico sonitu vehementer attoniti, etc."

[3] *Ann. Gennen.*, ap. *R. I. SS.*, vi, p. 529.

[4] Epp. Jan. 19, 1263, ap. *Reg.*, ii, n. 132, and May 7, nn. 228-30, ap. *ib.* *Cf.* nn. 719-21. When too late, the Genoese renounced the Greek alliance and were absolved, n. 756, Feb. 11, 1264. *Cf.* nn. 850-2 ; June 15-22, 1264.

[5] *Cf.* epp. Jan. 23, 1263, to the French bishops, ap. *ib.*, n. 187.

the warlike William of Villehardouin, Prince of Achaia, against Michael, and bade the clergy of his Principality help him with money.[1] We have evidence, too, that he ordered the Poles to be urged to take up arms in behalf of the Latin cause in the East,[2] and that the French were exhorted to co-operate with the Venetians in an endeavour to recapture Constantinople, or at least to save the Latin principalities in Greece.[3] He even authorized Baldwin to offer some of the money collected for the needs of the Latin Empire to such of the French nobility as would promise to help him.[4] Finally, in May, 1264, he made a special appeal to the French to save their countrymen in " new France ",[5] as Honorius III. had called Greece.

England will not contribute.

No great results, however, followed Urban's efforts. St. Louis was interested in the situation,[6] and William of Villehardouin, lately released from a Greek prison, measured swords not unsuccessfully with the Greek Emperor.[7] But the West in general was apathetic, and England in particular, about which we are immediately concerned, would do nothing. After Trinity Sunday, " at the command of the lord Pope," the clergy met his nuncios, Leonard and Berard, at Westminster (May, 1263). They would not, however, contribute anything " either from the revenues of the Kingdom or from those of the Church ". They pleaded general poverty, brought about by the dissensions with which the country was

---

[1] Ep. Apr. 27, 1263, ap. *ib.*, nn. 231–2.

[2] Ep. May 21, 1262, Potthast, 18332.

[3] Epp. June 5, 1262, ap. *Reg.*, ii, nn. 131–2.

[4] Epp. June 7–20, 1262, ap. *ib.*, n. 133–7. *Cf.* Potthast, n. 18465, Jan. 12, 1263, for a note of warning against the designs of Palæologus sent to the King of Cyprus.

[5] Epp. May 13, 1264, ap. *Reg.*, ii, 577–9.

[6] Potthast, *c.* Nov., 1262, n. 18440.

[7] *Cf.* Miller, the *Latins in the Levant*, p. 120 ff.

torn, and by the failure of the crops. It was their duty, they said, to help their liege lord and themselves first.[1]

Probably, however, the real reason why the efforts in Baldwin's behalf failed was the Pope himself. He was more anxious for the reunion of the Greek Church than for the recapture of Constantinople. This the wily Palæologus knew; and he acted accordingly. Besides being afraid that the Pope would direct a crusade against him, he was in trouble at home, as he had been excommunicated by the venerated patriarch, Arsenius, for blinding his ward, John Lascaris (1262).[2] Declaring that there were other Churches whence he could get pardon,[3] he sent several letters and embassies to Urban at different times,[4] regarding which it may suffice to state here that they had the effect of causing the Pope to check the progress of hostilities against him.[5] The policies of Palæologus and the Pope were both very simple. When the Emperor thought it would strengthen his usurped position at home, he entertained Urban with proposals for uniting the Greek and Latin Churches; but when he believed that he could accomplish his purposes without recourse to papal interference, then he ceased to cultivate the support of Rome. On his side,

Reunion proposals.

---

[1] *Flores hist.*, ii, 478, *R. S.*

[2] Pachymeres, l. iii, c. 14, p. 201 ff., ed. Bonn; and Niceph. Gregoras, l. iv, c. iv, p. 93.

[3] Pach., *l.c.*, c. 1, p. 255. "ἀλλ' εἰμὴ παρ' ὑμῖν μετανοίας θεσμοί, ἀλλαχοῦ τῶν ἐκκλησιῶν εἰσί, καὶ προσδραμοῦμαι ταύταις, καὶ παρ' ἐκείνων θεραπευθήσομαι."

[4] *Ib.*, l. ii, c. 36, pp. 168–9, and l. iii c. 18, p. 209 f.; and epp. Urb. ap. Potthast, 18399, c. July, 1262, and July 8, 1263, ap. *Reg.*, ii, n. 295, and July 28, nn. 322 ff., etc.

[5] Ep. Aug. 1, 1263, ap. *Reg.*, ii, 325, to Will. of Hardouin. *Cf.* Lebeau, *Le Bas Empire, l.c.*, n. 20. For the sake of greater clearness we shall treat under the *life* of Gregory X. of the negotiations regarding *reunion* initiated by Mich. Palæologus, which, during his pontificate came to a successful termination; and of their subsequent collapse, through the action of his son Andronicus II, under Martin IV.

Urban was naturally disposed to support the cause
of Baldwin against the Greeks ; but gave up opposition
to him when he had any reason to hope that Palæologus
was in earnest in his wish to reunite all Christians under
one shepherd.   Then it was " do you, my son, meanwhile
cease from attacking Palæologus ".[1]

Urban and the Holy Land.   Urban's deepest concern, however, was not with the
re-establishment of the Latin Empire of Constantinople,
but with the desperate position of the Latins in the
Holy Land.   It was on that account that he had come
to Europe ; and, though, aware that the question of
the Eastern Empire was intimately bound up with that
of the Latin Kingdom of Jerusalem, it was care for the
well-being of the latter that filled his heart.   It was
because the Sicilian affair interfered with his work for
the Crusade, that Urban declared that all evil came from
it, and not from the North as Jeremiah proclaimed
(i, 14).[2]   In 1260, Palestine was overrun by the Tartars,
and in the following year by the Mamelukes of Egypt
who had driven out the Tartars.   Towards the close of
1260 (Oct. 23), Beibars Bandukdary (Ruku eddin
Beibars), a second Saladin in ability at least, became
Mameluke sultan of Egypt.   In the next two years he
was ravaging the territory of Christian Antioch.   If then
the prospects of the Holy Land were bad when the
patriarch James Pantaleon left it, they were worse when
he mounted the chair of Peter as Urban IV.   However,
he took up the matter with his characteristic vigour.
He preached a new crusade himself to a great multitude
of people,[3] and caused the Franciscans and other preachers
to make known the miserable condition of the Holy Land
throughout Europe.[4]   The need of an immediate crusade

---

[1] Ep. 325 just cited.   [2] Ep. Apr. 25, 1264, *Reg.*, ii, 386.
[3] *Chron. min. Erphord.*, Nov. 18, 1262, ap. *M. G. SS.*, xxiv, p. 202.
[4] Ep. May 11, 1262, Potthast, 18310.

was proclaimed in Lombardy,[1] Germany,[2] Denmark,[3] Norway,[4] and France.[5]

In England, Urban entrusted the preaching of the Cross to Walter, bishop of Worcester, and he called upon the archbishops, bishops, and other prelates in England to assist him in his task and to collect a subsidy for the Holy Land.[6] The subsidy that Walter was empowered to collect was a yearly hundredth of all church revenues in England for five years. He was, at the same time, authorized by preaching indulgences and dispensations to incite, or, by announcing censures, to compel all to assist in the crusade—any papal indults to the contrary notwithstanding.[7] The bishop of St. Andrew's was ordered to do likewise in Scotland, and the Bishop of St. David's in Wales.[8]

Walter of Worcester is entrusted with the preaching of the Crusade. in England.

Although, only a month or two before he died, Urban wrote to the Christian leaders in Palestine about the Crusade which was being prepared,[9] he did not live long enough to see the results of his efforts. And, as far as England was concerned, during the years of his pontificate it was so taken up with its own internal difficulties, that no help could be expected from it for any cause, however, worthy.

To these troubles we must now turn. In the preceding biography, it was told how Henry III., taking advantage of the want of statesmanship displayed by the Barons in their attempt to govern the country, declared his inten-

Urban absolves Henry from his oath to observe the Pro- visions of Oxford, 1262.

---

[1] *Ib.*, 18314; 18351–4.

[2] *Ib.*, 18491. "In Germany, Bohemia, and all the other lands to which the Teutonic tongue extends."

[3] *Ib.*, 18321; 18664 ff.

[4] *Ib.*, 18686, 18692; Hungary, 18663. *Cf.* other letters to Sweden, etc., *ib.*, pp. 1514–15.

[5] *Ib.*, 18525, etc.   [6] Bliss, *Calendar*, i, p. 379.

[7] *Ib.*, p. 394.   [8] *Ib. Cf.* p. 384.

[9] Röhricht, *Regista Hierosol.*, July 17, 1264, n. 1332a.

tion no longer to be bound by the provisions of Oxford,[1] and obtained a bull from Alexander IV. deciding that he was not bound by his oath to the barons. As Alexander died before his bull could be published in England, Henry dispatched John of Hemingford and Roger Lovel to the new Pope. They were to beg him to renew the decision of his predecessor, and to find some remedy for the troubles in England.[2]

Supported by the English cardinal, John Tolet (or of Toledo), and by Cardinals Ottoboni and J. Gaetano Orsini,[3] the King's envoys worked hard in his interests. Their first interview with Urban they reported to Henry as most satisfactory, for the Pope had declared that only irrefragable evidence (evidens necessitas) would ever lead him to issue any decision adverse to the King.[4] The Barons, however, were well represented at the papal curia, and their asseverations caused Urban to hesitate.[5] But, despite the efforts of their opponents, the King's envoys, at the cost of much toil and money, gained the day[6]; and, on February 25, 1262, Urban issued a bull absolving the King and his family from the oaths they had taken to observe the Provisions of Oxford, on the ground that they interfered with the King's liberty.[7] As soon as Urban's bull reached England, Henry caused its

[1] " Statuta facta Oxoniæ quæ provisiones appellant," as the legate Guy of Sabina calls them. Ep. ap. Rymer, i, p. 799.

[2] Letter, Oct. 26, 1261, constituting these men his procurators, Ry., i, 729. Cf. ep. Jan. 1, 1262, where he states that he does not acknowledge other envoys sent under the great seal, now no longer in his keeping. Pg. 736. Cf. a similar letter to the cardinals. Pg. 737. See Flores hist., ii, 392, and 401, R. S.

[3] Afterwards Hadrian V., and Nicholas III. respectively.

[4] Loyal Letters, ii, p. 188, which letter must be dated Nov. or Dec., 1261, and not Sept. Cf. ib., p. 104, ep. 501, which must be dated after Nov. 11, 1262.

[5] Ib., ep. 556, p. 189. " Scio enim . . . (a few illegible words) magnatum Angliæ sunt in curia literas procurantes contra vos."

[6] Ib., epp. 559 and 561, Feb. 6 and May 14, 1262, respectively.

[7] Ap. Rymer, i, p. 742.

contents to be made generally known. " During Lent,"
says the London Chronicle of its mayors and sheriffs,[1]
" the King, caused to be read at St. Paul's Cross a certain
bull of Pope Urban . . . which confirmed the bull of Pope
Alexander his predecessor, who had previously absolved
the King and all the others of the oath which they had
made in the Parliament at Oxford. . . . The King also sent
his writ throughout all the cities of England, commanding
that no one should gainsay such absolution, and further
that, if anyone should in deed or word presume to do
the contrary . . . he should be taken and not liberated
without the order of the King."

But the bull of Urban did not put an end to the internal
troubles of the land. During the course of this year
(1262) the real leader of the Barons, Simon de Montfort,[2]
returned to England (Oct. 16), and, to counterbalance
the effect of Urban's absolution, produced what purported
to be a letter of that Pope to the Barons. This document
was read at a meeting in London, presided over by its
bishop, Philip Basset, then Justiciar of England. It
declared that the Pope had granted the absolution under
a false impression, and that he absolutely recalled it.
The historian who gives us this information adds that
against the wish of the Justiciar, Simon forwarded this
letter to the Barons.[3] As no trace of it, however, is to be
found anywhere, and it is opposed to Urban's known
action, it may be taken for granted that Basset objected
to its circulation, because it was a forgery.[4]

The settlement of the dissensions between the King and Barons referred to St. Louis, 1263.

---

[1] *Cron. maiorum*, p. 49 ; Eng. trans., p. 53. *Cf.* the writ, May 2,
1262, ap. Ry., i, 746.

[2] The latest biography of *Simon de Montfort*, by S. Bateman
(Birmingham, 1923), though carefully founded on the original sources,
is somewhat spoilt by the insertion of trifles in the midst of the
narration of important events.

[3] *Contin. Gervas.*, ii, p. 217.

[4] Bémont, *Simon de Montfort*, p. 198 n., goes so far as to deny that
Simon came to England at all in Oct., 1262.

However this may be, it is certain that the struggle
between the King and his Barons still went on. At
length in utter weariness both parties agreed to refer the
whole matter to St. Louis (Sept., 1263).[1] According to
the Annals of Tewkesbury, the French King was disposed
to give judgment in favour of the Barons ; but, " deceived
by the serpent-like cunning of Eleanor, Queen of
England," he decided in favour of the King.[2] At any
rate, whether because, like the Pope, he was naturally,
if unconsciously, biassed in favour of a vassal, or whether
because he was convinced that existing law and custom
was with the King, he declared (the Mise of Amiens),
principally, he said, in view of the Pope's condemnation,
that the Provisions of Oxford were invalid (Jan. 23,
1264).[3] The award of Louis was confirmed by Urban
in a series of bulls from March 16 to March 25, 1264.[4]

In connexion with these awards, it may, we believe,
well be doubted whether either the Pope or the Saint
understood the deep discontent which the arbitrary
conduct of our weak King and his extensive favouritism
of foreigners had engendered in this country. The latter
cause especially was probably not fully grasped by them.
Nationalism, whether for good or for evil, was developing
in all the countries of western Europe ; but, owing to
our insular situation, it was developing much faster in
England than on the continent. Not unnaturally,
this was not adequately comprehended either by Urban
or Louis ; nor did they realize how this growth of national
spirit was bringing about fresh aspirations after liberty
which had the sympathy of the best men in the realm.
Not knowing how much such churchmen as Grosseteste
were in touch with Simon de Montfort, they regarded

---

[1] Rishanger, p. 11 ; *Flores hist.*, ii, 485.
[2] *Ann.*, 1263, i, p. 176 ff.
[3] Rymer, i, 776 ff.   [4] *Ib.*, p. 781 ff.

him as an agitator and a foe of Church and State alike.
It was " de Montfort and his false followers who were
the cause of the whole trouble.   They had deceived the
people and especially the pestiferous city of London ". [1]
Accordingly Urban and Louis, both of them suzerains
of Henry, in forming their judgments on the quarrel
between him and his Barons, looked upon the matter
almost entirely from the point of view of feudal law such
as they found it.   Vassals were opposing their overlord.[2]
That was enough.   The Pope, indeed, while refusing
to confirm certain episcopal regulations because Henry
had declared them prejudicial to his rights, had had to
acknowledge that they were good and just,[3] and Louis,
in deciding against the Barons, had had to proclaim that
he had no intention of interfering with the liberties which
they had acquired previously to the issuing of the Provisions of Oxford.[4]   But neither of these great men had
understood that the time had come when they should
have looked at the whole question in the light of those
liberties, and not in the light of the letter of feudal law.

Before the French King's sentence had been delivered
against the baronial cause ; indeed, about the time when
the King and the Barons were making their final arrangements with Louis to act as arbitrator between them,
Urban had decided to make an effort himself to put an
end to the sad state of unrest in England.   For this
purpose, he named as his legate in England, Ireland,

Urban names a legate to work for peace, 1263.

---

[1] No doubt in this language of Urban's biographer we may recognize
the view of the papal curia :—

" Simon de Monteforti, falsique sequaces
    Ejus sunt tanti causa suprema mali.
  Alliciunt primo populum fallaciter, inter
    Quos urbs pestifera Londoniensis erat." Theodoric, p. 33.

[2] *Ib.*, " Servis in dominos male conspirantibus."

[3] Ep. Jan. 30, 1263. " Quæ (the bishop's statutes), licet ex sui forma
viderentur honestatem et justitiam continere, etc." Rymer, i, 756.

[4] *Ib.*, p. 778.

and Wales, Guy Fulcodi, cardinal-bishop of Sabina (Nov. 22, 1263). In dispatching him to England, he furnished him with ample powers by means of some fifty bulls, addressed to Guy himself, and to the great ones of England and France.[1]

War between the King and the Barons. The battle of Lewes, 1264. Before Guy, whom Urban eulogizes most warmly,[2] had time to act, a crisis had come about in England. Despite the promises they had made, Simon and his party would not accept the decision of Louis, and, though many of their adherents fell away from them in consequence, they appealed to the verdict of the sword. They were completely successful in this appeal, and at the battle of Lewes, May 14, the royal army was beaten, and the King himself and his brother, Richard of Cornwall, were taken prisoners.

Action of the papal legate, 1264. In the long negotiations for a settlement of the affairs of the country which followed the battle of Lewes, an attempt was made on the part of the Barons to placate the Pope by naming the legate Guy one of the arbitrators to adjust the relations between the King and the nobles. The captive monarch was made to subject himself to his jurisdiction.[3] But Guy was not thus to be won over.

---

[1] Bulls dated November and December, 1263, ap. *Reg.*, ii, nn. 581–630, p. 294 ff. Theodoric says, p. 34, that Guy was sent to help Henry, whom Urban knew to be " just, faithful, and pious, and whose land was free from heresy."

" Cujus non hæresi. terra notata fuit."

[2] Guy was described to Prince Edward (ep. Nov. 18, 1263, n. 584) as " virum utique laudabilium meritorum claritate conspicuum, eminentis dono scientie preditum, multis insignitum virtutibus et in magnis et arduis multipliciter approbatum ". He is also praised by our own historians, whether royalist, like Wykes (p. 155), or revolutionary, like the author of the *Flores Hist.*, ii, 500.

[3] Ep. Sept. 11, 1264. " Nos autem omnia et singula quæ ipsi ad . . . observationem pacis ejusdem ordinaverint rata habemus et accepta ; subjiciendo nos jurisdictioni et cohertioni (*sic*) venerabilis G. Sabin. episcopi, Apostolicæ sedis legati, ut ipse per sententiam excommunicationis . . . nos . . . compellere possit, si forte ordinationi prædictorum . . . præsumpserimus contrahere." *Rymer*, i, 796. *Cf.* other documents, pp. 797–8.

He had meanwhile gradually been making his way to the north coast of France [1] with the usual state of a cardinal-legate ; and " having the power of both swords. With the (spiritual) sword he was to depose the bishops who should refuse to excommunicate the Barons, and with the (temporal) sword to disinherit some thirty of the latter ".[2]

For the relations of cardinal Guy Fulcodi with the Barons of England there has recently become available, through the discoveries of L. Delisle [3] and others, the Register of his legation.   As this document, so important for the history of England, seems to have escaped the notice of writers in this country, it will here be drawn upon at some length.[4]

He notifies his coming to England, 1264.

Although it was before the end of the year 1263 that Urban commissioned Guy to try, in his place, to bring back law and order to England, it was not till May 8, 1264, that he landed at Nice in Provence.[5]   The disordered state of Italy, through the widespread Guelf and Ghibelline faction fights, had prevented Guy from moving for some time.   Thanks, however, strange to say, to the good offices of the Ghibelline chief, Oberto Pallavicini, he reached Genoa, whence he took ship.[6] From Nice he wrote to tell King Henry, Simon de Montfort, and the English bishops that he had been

---

[1] For some of the work done by him during his journey through France, see Nicolas, *Clémens IV.*, p. 101 f.

[2] *Ann. de Dunstap.*, iii, p. 233.

[3] L. Delisle, *Collections de M. Jules Desnoyers*, Paris, 1888.   *Cf.* J. Heidemann, *P. Clemens IV.*, 1st part, Münster, 1903. " Das Legations register," p. 183 ff. ; Nicolas, *Clément IV.*, p. 107 ff.

[4] It is given in its entirety by both Heidemann, p. 194 ff., and Nicolas, p. 558 ff.   With brief notes and original documents it contains over fifty pieces.   It will be quoted as *Leg. Reg.* or *L.R.*   It even escaped the notice of Abbot (now Cardinal) Gasquet in his *Henry III. and the Church*, where he has brought so much to light.

[5] *L.R.*, n. 1.   [6] *Ib.*, nn. 1, 2, 19c, ed. H.

appointed legate in England, that he expected to arrive
in Paris about the octave of Pentecost,[1] and that, from
that city, he would send them particulars as to his arrival
in England (*c.* May 25).[2]   Accordingly, when he reached
Paris, he sent messengers to the same persons to ask for a
safe-conduct to England, as he had heard much of the
disturbed state of the realm.   He told them that he wished
to come to them " as an angel of peace, and like an angel
to work among the Angles ".[3]

Moreover, he decided to send on before him the archdeacon of Agde and other envoys to prepare the way for
his arrival.   But, whilst they were waiting at Witsand
for the safe-conducts which had been sent for, they
received a letter (about the beginning of July) [4] from the
messengers whom the cardinal had sent to England
to the effect that, as soon as they had landed at Dover,
their letters had been taken from them.   They had even
been partially stripped in the search for others, and had
been told that they would be killed if they were introducing any letters to the detriment of the country.
They had also heard it argued that, if the cardinal was
coming to make peace which they could make themselves,
his coming would not be necessary.

The Barons
decline to
allow Guy
to land in
England.
This letter was followed by a close letter addressed
to the cardinal (*c.* July 27), by the " Earls, Barons,
Knights, and communities of the Kingdom of England ".
It was sealed with four round seals, one of which bore
the figure of a shield with a lion and the words " Simonis
de Monteforti " upon it.[5]   The letter informed the
cardinal that his proposed coming had been discussed

---

[1] That feast in 1264 fell on June 8.

[2] *L.R.,* n. 2.

[3] *Ib.,* nn. 2–8.   " Ad pacem in regno Angliæ reformandam a sede
apostolica destinati pacis angelum implere proponimus et angelice
inter Angelicos . . . conversari." Pg. 197, ed. H.

[4] Ap. *ib.,* n. 12.   [5] *Ib.,* n. 13, p. 200.

in a parliament at London,[1] and that it had been decided not to receive on this occasion either him or his envoys. His coming might endanger the peace which had been arranged, and it was against the privilege of the Kingdom that a legate should enter it unless he had been asked for. Moreover, they had decided not to allow any of the bishops to go to the cardinal, unless it had been agreed by all parties concerned that they were not to publish any decree against the country or any of its people. However, if the cardinal was desirous of treating with them, he might come to Boulogne or some such French seaside place, and they would send envoys to him to show him the justice of their cause and their loyalty to the Apostolic See.[2] They also suggested that, if the legate was anxious for peace he should prevent the King of France from aiding the party opposed to the Barons.[3]

The bearers of this letter made great efforts to excuse the attitude of the Barons; and declared that they would strive to induce them to send envoys to Boulogne to treat with the cardinal about peace and about his coming to England. They further urged the cardinal to write to the Barons.[4] To this Guy agreed, and sent the Barons a close letter in which, after upbraiding

[1] Reference is made to the Parliament of June 24, at which the prelates, barons, and *communitas terræ* were present, and at which ordinances " for the peace of the Kingdom " had been drawn up. *Cf.* Parry, *The Parliaments of England*, p. 43.

[2] " Et cum ad vos venerint (the envoys of the Barons), et facti nostri veritatem, fidem et devotionem, quam erga sedem apostolicam semper habuimus et habemus ad plenum cognoscere facient," etc. *L.R.*, n. 14, p. 100.

[3] Eleanor, Henry's wife, was raising an army on the continent to invade England. It was encamped near Boulogne, and when Guy went thither, he was near it. *Cf. Annal. S. Pauli London.*, ap. *M. G. SS.*, xxviii, p. 550, and *Chron. de Bello, ib.*, p. 554.

[4] *L.R.*, n. 15. The Barons' envoys were to come to Boulogne in fifteen days. *Cf.* n. 18, p. 207.

the English for their ingratitude towards the Apostolic
See, and for their forgetfulness of what they owed to
their suzerain, he scouted the notion that the Pope could
not send a legate to a country unless he was asked to do
so ; declared that he had endeavoured to prevent the
gathering of an army to invade the country, and agreed
to go to Bologne.[1]

Guy sum-
mons the
bishops of
England to
appear
before him.
About the same time that this close letter was dispatched to the Barons, the legate laid the whole state
of the case before a large gathering of people at Amiens,
and bade the bishops of England come over to him before
September.[2]

Meanwhile the cardinal made his way to Boulogne ;
and, as the Barons did not send any envoys, he proclaimed
publicly, in the Church of St. Mary (Aug. 12), that he
would excommunicate them if they did not permit him
to enter England before the first of September.[3] Before
that time too they must restore the King to his full
liberty and authority, and abjure the statutes of Oxford
" which they call Provisions ".

Three or four days later the King sent to Guy the

---

[1] *Ib.*, n. 16. " Si gens Anglorum . . . (apostolicæ) sedis dominium,
quo regi dominatur et regno, reverenter attenderet, ad insolentiam
erigi non deberet. Est enim gens illa peculiaris populus et thesaurus
gratissimus alma sedis." Guy contrasts the barbarous manner in which
his messengers had been treated with the manner *curialiter* in which
even the Tartars had received papal envoys. With regard to the asserted
privilege about the reception of a legate, he reminds them that, even if
it had been granted, a Pope is not necessarily bound by the doings of his
predecessor " of whom he is not the heir but the successor ". Besides,
the King had earnestly begged for a legate.

[2] *Ib.*, n. 18, p. 204 ff., especially says Wykes, p. 156, Walter de
Cantilupe of Worcester, Walter of Sandwich of London, John Gervase
of Winchester, and Stephen of Bersted of Chichester, who were the
chief episcopal supporters of Simon de Montfort.

[3] *Ib.*, nn. 19, 20. He proposed to excommunicate " barones Angliæ,
quorum consilio regnum regitur vel subvertur . . . Londonenses, et
babitatores quinque portuum." Pg. 215.

conditions of peace (forma pacis) which he had had to accept.[1] This agreement, as wholly subversive of the royal and apostolic authority, the legate refused to ratify, and blamed the bishops for accepting (Aug. 17). He pointed out that it set at naught the decision of King Louis, confirmed by the Pope,[2] and he declared positively to a deputation from the Barons[3] that he could not alter his decision not to accept the " forma pacis ".[4]

The month of August was drawing to a close, and still there was no sign of the coming of the bishops. However, before the close of the month, messengers arrived from some of them with a patent letter which bore the seal of the bishop of London. The bishops in question began their letter by assuring the cardinal that his holiness and wisdom would be of the greatest advantage to England in its disturbed condition, and that they would be glad to meet him. But, apart from the fact that their lives and property have been threatened if they go to him,[5] they cannot reach him because ships have been denied them.[6] They further declared that they cannot compel the Barons to give way by ecclesiastical censures, " as they are not feared in the customary manner." Besides they really cannot understand why

The bishops come late.

---

[1] The *forma pacis* may be read ap. Rymer, i, 793 ff. ; or Stubbs, *Select Charters*, p. 412, ed. of 1876. It is dated June, 1264.

[2] *L.R.*, nn. 21–3.

[3] *Ib.*, nn. 24 and 25. It had been sent, it was said, to show the devotion of the Barons to the Holy See : " Ut tamen devotionis zelum et affectionis puritatem, quam erga apostolicam sedem et ejus missores sincero corde gerimus, plenius agnoscatis . . . excusatores nostros . . . destinamus, etc.," p. 222.

[4] *Ib.*, n. 26, Aug. 22–3.

[5] This they had already asserted. *Cf.* n. 23, and the letter, n. 26, of the cardinal to the Barons : " Miramur autem non modicum quod prælatos ad nos venire non sinitis, prout scribunt, cum id vobis prohibere non liceat." Pg. 225.

[6] The royalist writer, Wykes, p. 156, says that the bishops themselves suggested the refusal of the ships.

the legate will not ratify the articles of peace, seeing
that the King's counsellors, whom the legate calls so
many Kings, are no more rulers of the King than the
cardinals are of the Pope.[1]

To this Guy returned a prompt reply.[2] He cannot
accept the peace, because, as he had already said, it
would deprive the King of all power. He then told
the bishops that he was astonished that they could not
see this, as it was perfectly plain to the King of France
who had said that he would rather be a ploughman than
a King under such terms.[3] With regard to what they
had argued about the Vicar of Christ, and his cardinals,
it is perfectly true that he takes their advice, but then
he is not bound to follow it.[4] He reminded them that
the Pope had direct dominion over England,[5] and that
it was better that he should get information about its
state from them than from strangers. The fact was
they were cowards (homines timorosi). Nevertheless
he will remain at Boulogne till September 9, and they
should come to him before that date.

Bishops and
Barons at
length come
to Boulogne.
However, September the first passed and the Barons
had not sent the required permission for the legate to
enter England, and September the eighth also passed,
and the bishops had not appeared in Boulogne. But

---

[1] Ep. n. 28. "Summus pontifex etiam nos (the bishops), sicut et
ceteros S.R. ecclesiæ cardinales sibi ut fratres et conjudices facit in
proferendis judiciis assidere, . . . et tamen plures papas penitus
abnegamus." Pg. 227.

[2] n. 29, still before the end of August.

[3] "Andivimus dicentem christianissimum regem Franciæ, cum
hujusmodi formam pacis audiret, quod mallet post aratrum glebas
frangere, quam hujusmodi principatum habere." Pg. 230.

[4] "Quid de Christi vicario nobis obicitis ! habet utique cardinales
et eorum consiliis utitur, non ligatur . . . Ejus enim libertatem in summo
supremum reputamus honorem." Ib., p. 229.

[5] "Videte . . . ut in eo (England) Romana ecclesia directum
dominium habeat." Ib., p. 230. Cf. pp. 212, 215.

excuses of one sort or another had been sent ; [1] and, at length, the bishops of London, Worcester, and Winchester, who had thought of appealing to the Pope against the legate, took a sounder view of the situation (saniora meditantes), and crossed over to Boulogne. With them came the Justiciar, Hugh le Despenser, and a few other nobles (Sept. 24).[2] There also appeared envoys from queen Eleanor and Prince Edward.[3]

When the envoys met in the presence of the cardinal, it seemed at first as if an agreement was going to be brought about, but the Queen's representatives insisted on standing by the award of St. Louis, as modified if necessary by the same monarch or by the cardinal. To this, however, the envoys from England declared that they had no power to consent [4] ; and several of them went home for further consultation.[5]

They cannot come to an agreement.

On October 2 they returned with a fresh treaty of peace, which they declared had been agreed upon between the King and the Barons. They were, however, unable to produce the actual document. Fear of the people of Boulogne, said the envoys, had caused the sailors to put to sea in a hurry ; and they had taken the document and other things with them.[6] Annoyed at what he regarded as shuffling, the legate issued a mandate to the bishops of England to excommunicate the Barons, if they were not reconciled to him in a fortnight.[7]

There was, however, no hope of the Barons and the legate coming to any understanding. Their points of view were too divergent. The Barons knew that the word of the King could not be relied on, and that it was

---

[1] *Ib.*, nn. 30–8.
[2] Wykes, p. 156. *Cf. Cron. maiorum*, p. 69 ; Eng. trans., p. 4 ; *Ann. de Dunst.*, p. 234 ; *L.R.* n. 39.
[3] *L.R.*, 1. 41.
[4] *Ib.*, nn. 42–3.
[5] *Ib.*, n. 43.
[6] *Ib.*, p. 239.
[7] Ep. of Oct. 2, n. 44.

necessary that they should have some control over their wayward sovereign. The cardinal, as representing Henry's suzerain, the Pope, who was resolved to stand by his chief vassal,[1] looked upon the controlling barons as rebellious subjects, who were false to their liege lord. And he was confirmed in his view when he found it was shared by France, and even by other " parts of Europe, such as Brittany, Guienne, and Spain ".[2]

The envoys of the Barons did not return to Boulogne,[3] nor would they accept another concordat drawn up by the cardinal.[4] The result was that the legate, " perceiving the hardened malice of the Barons of England," [5] excommunicated Simon de Montfort, and his adherents,[6] and ordered the excommunication to be proclaimed throughout France,[7] as well as in England.

The English clergy appeal to a general council.

There was, however, very little chance of the knowledge of the excommunication being circulated in England. When the bishops who carried the bull of excommunication landed there, they were seized. The bull was torn up by the Wardens of the Cinque Ports, and thrown into the sea, and the bishops were threatened with death if they published any sentence against the Barons.[8] But, of course, some account of the situation leaked out.[9] Thereupon, those of the bishops who were on the side of

---

[1] *Reg.*, iv, append. i, n. 2838.

[2] *Flores Hist.*, ii, 501 f.

[3] *L.R.*, n. 45. They, however, sent over a knight to Witsand, who would not land but threw overboard a box full of letters for the legate.

[4] *Ib.*, n. 46.   [5] *L.R.*, n. 49.

[6] *Ib.*, n. 50, Oct. 20, or ap. Rymer, i, 798.

[7] *L.R.*, n. 52. *Cf.* n. 53, the last document of Guy's register.

[8] Wykes, p. 157. He expresses a doubt as to whether it was not with their own consent that the bishops were seized. His royalist sentiments led him to think little of the bishops' conduct : " sic eorum præceps vesania indevotos pontifices et perjuros mutos reddidit et elingues." *Cf. Flores Hist.*, ii, 500.

[9] Rishanger, p. 31 ; *Cron. maiorum*, p. 83, Eng. trans., p. 88.

the Barons appealed to the Pope or to a general council [1]
—an appeal subsequently approved by the clergy
generally.[2] Nevertheless, the Barons, through their
captive King, made a last effort to pacify the legate.
Henry was instructed to notify him that he was
making known to his friends in France the state of his
realm, and was assuring them that he had learned " by
experience that the business for which the legate was sent
to England could in these days be better conducted by
lenity and kindness than by ecclesiastical coercion ",
and he begged him " to act graciously in the matter to the
honour of God and the peace of the realm (November 18,
1264) ".[3] With this letter, which had no effect upon
Guy, all intercourse between him and the Barons came
to an end ; but the legate did not soon forget the contempt
with which he accused the English of having treated him. [4]

Meantime, however, Urban IV. had died (October 2), Death of
and the new Pope (February 2, 1265) was no other than Urban, 1264.
the legate himself, who was credited by some of our
historians with remaining hostile to the Barons because
they had refused him admission into England.[5]

As there is nothing in the relations between Urban Patrick
and Scotland or Wales that calls for any particular O'Scanlan.
attention, we may, if only for the sake of spreading a
correction, mention the name of Patrick O'Scanlan.
In Rymer's *Foedera*, under the date of November 5,
1363, a bull is assigned to Urban V., which ought to have
been printed under the date of November 5, 1261, and
assigned to Urban IV. The itinerary alone of the two

---

[1] *Gervase contin.*, ii, pp. 239–41.

[2] *Ib. Cf. Flores Hist.*, ii, 501 ; *Ann. de Dunstap.*, p. 234.

[3] *Calendar of Patent Rolls*, Henry III., vol. v, p. 474.

[4] *Cf.*, ep. *Clement IV.*, Apr. 1, 1265, ap. Martène, *Thes. nov.*, ii,
p. 115, n. 33. He recalls " contemptum quem Anglici erga personam
nostram, dum essemus in minori officio constituti. . . . ostenderunt."

[5] *Gervase, l.c.*

Urbans makes this absolutely certain. The bull confirms
the translation of Patrick O'Scanlan from the See of
Raphœ to that of Armagh.[1] Urban was not quite satisfied
with the new Primate. Two years later (1263), he is
urging him to collect the papal taxes and to inquire into
what had been collected by John of Frosinone, once the
Pope's nuncio in Ireland. The Pope writes that he
considers that the archbishop has been negligent in these
matters, and reminds him that, when in Rome he had
promised to attend to them.[2]

The feast of Corpus Christi.

Urban's biography may well be now brought to a
close by an account of his institution of the feast of
Corpus Christi. His bull, *Transiturus*, ordering the
observance of the feast, was issued within a few weeks
of his death ; and, owing to the extraordinary increase
of the external cult of the Sacrament of the Blessed
Eucharist in our times, it links him to them in a remarkable
manner.

When archdeacon of Liège, Urban had come in contact
with the mystic St. Juliana, a religious of Mont Cornillon.[3]
Through her ardent devotion to the Sacrament of the
Altar, she conceived a great desire to see established a
special feast in its honour. In accordance with her
wishes, Robert, bishop of Liège, ordained the celebration

---

[1] Mr. J. A. Twemlow, in calling attention to this, reprinted the
document in *Otia Merseiana* from the original in the Public Record
Office, Papal bulls, Box 61, n. 4.

[2] Theiner, *Vet. Mon. Hib.*, p. 91.

[3] There are two versions of the bull in which Urban instituted the
feast of Corpus Christi. The one, addressed to the whole hierarchy,
which begins " Transiturus de hoc ", and which is to be found in the
various *bullaria*, and is cited in part by Raynaldus ; the other, which we
quote below and which begins " Transiturus de mundo ". In the former
version Urban alludes to this intercourse : " Intelleximus autem olim
dum in minori essemus officio constituti, quod fuerat quibusdam
Catholicis revelatum festum hujusmodi generaliter in Ecclesia
celebrandum." Ap. Raynaldus, an. 1264, n. 27, or *Bullar. Rom.*, iii,
707, ed. Turin.

of such a feast in his diocese (1246). His successor, Henry Guelders, at the instigation of Eve, a disciple of St. Juliana, urged the Pope to order its celebration by the whole world.[1] Urban listened very readily to the request, and on August 11, 1264, issued his famous bull on the subject.[2] It begins by recalling our Lord's institution of " the supreme and magnificent Sacrament of his Body and Blood ", and by reminding us what a sweet memorial it is of His love. By it, Christ is still with us, under another form indeed, " but truly in his own substance." By it he has become our food, and the Giver is given to us in His gift. " This bread is eaten, but not transmuted ; it is in no way changed into the consumer, but if it be worthily received the recipient becomes like to it."

The bull then declares that it is desirable, especially in order to confound heretical folly, to set aside a day upon which the institution of the Blessed Eucharist may be specially honoured, because on Holy Thursday, the day on which it was actually instituted, the attention of the faithful is taken up with the Passion of our Lord. The bull, therefore, prescribes that the Thursday after Trinity Sunday shall be set aside for specially honouring the Body of Christ. On that day " let faith dilate in thanksgiving, let hope leap with joy, let charity be moved to the depths with gladness ".[3] The bull concludes by offering to such as were present at Mass on that day, and had confessed their sins and were truly sorry for them, a hundred days' indulgence.[4]

[1] Cf. Georges, Urb. IV., p. 29 ff. ; p. 478 ff., and Raynaldus, Annales, an. 1264, n. 27 f., whom Georges follows as usual. Cf. Hoesemius, Chron., p. 38 f.

[2] Reg., ii, n. 874, p. 423. Cf. Theod., p. 39 ; Ann. S. Vitoni Virdun., ap. M. G. SS., x, 528 ; a sermon of St. Thomas of Aquinas, Opusc., 57. The bull is addressed to the hierarchy of the patriarchate of Jerusalem.

[3] Bishop Hedley's version of a few words of this eloquent bull : The Holy Eucharist, p. 267, London, 1907.

[4] Cf. the letter, Sept. 8, which Urban wrote to Eve to tell her that

It was also stated in the bull that a new " office "
was forwarded with it.   This " office ", one of the very
finest in the glorious liturgy of the Church, was written
by St. Thomas Aquinas at the command of the Pope.[1]

Art soon connected Urban with the Blessed Sacrament.
In the first half of the fourteenth century the curious
church of St. Flaviano, at Montefiascone, which had
been restored by Urban himself, was adorned with
frescoes.   They were brought to light again quite recently
(1896) ; and one of them showed the portrait of a Pope
with his right hand raised in the act of blessing, and with
a sun upon his breast.   An inscription above the figure
" Beatus Urbanus P.P." showed that the painting was
meant to represent Urban IV.   By a striking coincidence,
it was brought to light on the vigil of the fifteenth
Eucharistic Congress, which was celebrated at Orvieto.
The fact that our Lord is often referred to in the Scriptures
and in the Fathers as " the sun ", and that in the same
church of St. Flaviano is an antique sculpture of a chalice
and host with a sun above it, is more than sufficient to

the desire of her heart had been accomplished.   Potthast, n. 19016,
or in full in a French translation ap. Georges, *l.c.*, p. 487 f.   It is to be
noted that neither in the bull of institution, nor in any contemporary
author is there any mention of " the miracle of Bolsena " in connexion
with the introduction of the Feast of Corpus Christi.   *Cf.* the *Catholic
Encyclopædia*, vol. xi, art., Orvieto, on the miracle.   It is, however,
alluded to in a bull of Clement VI. (Feb. 13, 1344), in which, in
response to the wishes of the people of Orvieto who had built the first
oratory in honour of the institution of the feast, and in honour of a
miracle worked there, he increased the indulgences offered by
Urban IV.   " Quod cum in ecclesia Urbevetana post institutionem dicti
festi, de ipso primum oratorium constructum fuerit, et propter
quoddam miraculum quod ibidem extitit," etc.   *Cf.* the bull " Et si
devota ", ap. *Archiv. Vat.*, *Reg. Vat.*, *Clem. VI.*, *communium* an. ii,
lib. iii, vol. 159, p. 423, ep. 1762 ; *Reg. Avin.*, 76, p. 300.

[1] Ptolemy of Lucca, *Hist. Eccles.*, l. xxii, cc. 21-4, ap. *R. I. SS.*, xi,
p. 1153 f.   " Officium de Corpore Christi fecit ex mandato Urbani."
Cf. P. Mandonnet, *Des écrits de S. Thoma d'Aquin*, p. 127 ff.

show that the sun depicted on the breast of Urban is a type of the Blessed Sacrament, is a " eucharistic sun ".[1]

In less than a month after the issue of his bull con- *Last illness* cerning the feast of Corpus Christi, Urban left Orvieto *and death of* *Urban.* (September 9),[2] owing to a difference with its people, fanned no doubt by Manfred, who was planning to seize him in this city.[3] Like every other Italian city of any importance, Orvieto was at this period engaged in extending its authority over its less powerful neighbours, and that, too, very often without any reference to the rights of the overlord. Accordingly, during the years 1257–62, we find Guittius and his sons James, Nicholas, and Tancred, submitting their fiefs of the island of Martana, Capademonte, etc., to Orvieto without any regard to the rights of the Pope.[4] When, therefore, Urban requested that Capudemonte should be handed over to him, the people of Orvieto refused to do so (1264).[5] Naturally annoyed at this, Urban at length left their city, the more readily that, owing to the plots of Manfred, he felt he was living among " scorpions and serpents ",[6]

---

[1] *Cf.* L. Fumi, *Urbano IV. e il sole eucaristico*, Rome, 1896.

[2] Theod., " Septembris die nona discessit ab ipsis (the people of Orvieto)

Tudertum veniens, membra quietis egent." Pg. 44.

[3] See the oft-cited letter (July 17, 1264) of Urban to the cardinal legate in France, Simon of St. Brion, ap. Martène, *Thes. anecdot.*, ii, p. 82 ff.

[4] *Cf. Regesto degli Atti del commune* (of Orvieto), nn. 56, 66, 68–70, ap. *R. I. SS.*, t. xv, pt. v, pp. 106–8, new ed. *Cf.* Theod., p. 27, and *supra*, p. 169.

[5] *Ann. Urbevet.*, 1264, ap. *ib.*, p. 155.

[6] Ep. to Simon just cited. Urban tried to console himself with the hope of the coming of Charles of Anjou by the feast of St. Michael, and, in that hope, he went on incurring expenses for military purposes, though they had now reached 200,000 Sienese pounds. *Ib.* From a letter of Clement IV., Feb. 28, 1265, to the same cardinal, we learn that certain Sienese merchant-bankers in France were reckoned " inter familiares ", " among the household " of Urban IV. Ap. Martène, *Thes. anec.*, ii, 101.

and that he suspected the Orvietans of sympathizing with the murderer of Guischard, the rector of the papal patrimony in Tuscany.[1] Making his way towards Perugia, he had to rest at Todi, for he was taken ill on August 27, at the time of the appearance of a great comet.[2] After resting a few days at Todi, he descended the steep hill on which it is perched, and appears to have only increased his illness by eating some figs.[3] However, he reached the commanding height of castrum Diruta, on the left bank of the Tiber but was not able to ride far beyond it. Taken from his horse, he was placed in a litter, and carried to Assisi, where he lay, getting gradually worse, for a fortnight. Then, as the cardinals saw he was certain to die, they caused him to be conveyed to Perugia. There in the Church of St. Peter, " the great-hearted " [4] pontiff received the last sacraments and died at dawn on the following Thursday (October 2, 1264), at the time when the comet, " as though it knew its death," finally faded from view.[5] He was buried with great honour in the Cathedral of S. Lorenzo [6]; but unfortunately his tomb, said to have been sculptured by Giovanni Pisano, was destroyed, according to Vasari, in 1437, when the cathedral was enlarged at that time. But though his

---

[1] Theod., pp. 35, 43–5 ; *supra*, p. 169.

[2] *Cf.* Theod., pp. 44–5, *Ann. Urbevet., l.c.*

　　　" Tudertum veniens est gressus pondere fessus

　　　　Insolitusque labor debilitarat eum." Theod., p. 45.

All the chroniclers speak of the extraordinary comet.

[3] *Ann. Urbevet., l.c.,* " Et in via comedit ficus, et infirmatus est." He would appear to have been suffering from constipation. " Ejus siccari cœperunt interiora." Theod., *l.c.*

[4] " Il fut de mult grand cuer." A continuator of William of Tyre, lxxvi, c. 6, ap. Migne, *Pat. Lat.,* t. 201.

[5] Theod., p. 46. " Quo moriente, velut mortem cognosceret ejus, Apparens minime stella comata fuit." *Cf. Contin. Sanblasiana,* ap. *M. G. SS.,* xx, p. 336 ; and *Cron. Pont.,* ap. *ib.,* xxxi, p. 225 ; Gregory, p. 13.

[6] Amalricus, *Vit. Urb.,* ap. *R. I. SS.,* ii, pt. ii, p. 405.

tomb has perished, a fragment of the epitaph may still
be seen in the Museum at Perugia. Delaistre [1] cites it
from an ancient manuscript, which says it was composed
by Thomas of Aquinas.

Archilevita fui Pastor gregis et patriarcha
Tunc Jacobus, posui mihi nomen ab urbe monarcha
Nunc cinis, exigui tumuli concludor in archa
Te sine fine frui tribuas mihi summus hierarcha.

In our biography of Innocent III.,[2] relying on Bonazzi, History of
we gave a somewhat inaccurate account of the subsequent the tomb of
Urban IV.
history of the body and tomb of Urban IV. During the
rebuilding of the cathedral in the fourteenth and fifteenth
centuries, the sepulchral monuments of Innocent III.,
Urban IV., and Martin IV., were destroyed, and the three
bodies were placed together in an iron casket (cassa). [3]
This was opened in 1587, in the presence of the historian
Crispolti,[4] who says that he saw therein two bodies
clad in chasubles of an antique pattern, and wearing
mitres, rings on their fingers, and other pontifical
ornaments. He saw also some other bones enveloped in
cloth ; and Chouiller [5] gives reasons for believing that
they were those of Martin IV. In 1615 Bishop Comitoli
removed all the remains from the casket, and placed them
in the mausoleum we have already described.

Theodoric, from whom alone we learn most of what we Praise of
know concerning the last days of Urban, expresses his Urban.
belief that, on account of his merits, Urban is in

---

[1] Pp. 183–5 ; Georges, p. 517. *Cf. ib.*, p. 518, for the translations of
Urban's body.

[2] Vol. xii, p. 302.

[3] *Cf.* P. Pellini, *Istoria di Perugia*, i, p. 296, ed. Venice.

[4] *Perugia Augusta*, p. 68.

[5] *La vie du P. Martin IV.*, p. 27 f. Ap. *Revue de Champagne*, Jan.,
1878, from whom we have taken these particulars. He in turn cites
Canon Coffinet, " Recherches sur les restes mortels du P. Urbain IV."
Ap. *Mém. de la Soc. academique de l'Aube*, t. xxi, p. 1857.

enjoyment of eternal happiness. But his biographers, Theodoric and Gregory,[1] do not stand alone in praising Urban. He was by various contemporary authors [2] declared to have been a most Christian and honourable man, and to have been elected for the increase of the Catholic faith.

[1] *L.c.*, " Hic Urbanus, patrum pater, mitis, pius, benignus, munificus, gratiosus et omni bonitate refertus."

[2] *Cf. Gesta Henrici archiep. Trev.*, ap. *M. G. SS.*, xxiv, pp. 416, 453, and Gaufridus de Collone, *Chron.*, ap. *ib.*, xxvi, p. 620, " Vir laudabilis, simplex et honestus," etc. The backbiting tongue of Salimbene, however, spared neither Urban nor his nephew Ancherus. Pg. 170.

CLEMENT IV.

1265–1268.

Sources.—Up to date (1928), Monsieur E. Jordan, under the auspices of the French School of Athens and Rome has published the first vol. of his *Les Registres de Clément IV.*, Paris, 1904 ff. This volume contains not only the register of Clement IV., strictly so-called, but also, in various appendices, other letters of this Pope which the editor has found in different manuscripts. Unfortunately, neither he nor any of the other editors of this splendid series, has endeavoured to give us all the known letters of the Popes they deal with. One has therefore to search for them in many different publications. As far, however, as Clement is concerned, the principal documents issued by his chancery which are not contained in his Register have been published by Martène in the second volume of his *Thesaurus novus Anecdotorum*, Paris, 1717. The most striking feature of the letters of Clement is their historical character. Perhaps more of the history of his time can be gathered from them than from those of any of the Popes we have hitherto treated of. Apart from the light they throw upon his own character, upon his energy and vigour, his disinterestedness, his clear-headedness, and his moral courage, they depict for us on the one hand the dying struggles of the Holy Land, in the grip of the infidel, and, on the other, the relaxing of that grip on Spain. They unfold to us the establishment of the Angevin dynasty in the Kingdom of the Two Sicilies, the collapse of that of the Hohenstaufen, and the preparations of the last of the Crusades. In a word, they are a source of first-class historical importance.

In the " Formulary " or " Dictamina " of Richard de Pofi of the Chancellary of Pope Honorius III. who finished his work in 1286, there are some 450 bulls which Richard extracted from the Registers of Urban IV. and his successors. They are difficult to deal with as Richard has omitted the names of the Popes and the dates. But Monsieur E. Jordan has been able to place about a hundred of them, and has dealt with those which concern Clement IV. and his Italian policy and with the expedition of Charles of Anjou.[1]

Some of the letters of Clement are also printed in full in G. del Giudice, *Codice diplomatico del regno de Carlo I. e II. d'Angiò*, 3 vols., Naples, 1863.[2] Very important, too, as a collection of the sources for the history of the Papacy and Sicily, is B. Capasso, *Hist. diplomatica Regni Siciliæ* (1250–66), Naples, 1874 ; but it unfortunately ends with March, 1266. Light is also thrown on Clement's pontificate by the thirty-six letters of his legate, Cardinal Ottoboni, in England. They are published in the *English Historical Review*, Jan., 1900, vol. xv, p. 87 ff.

The outstanding feature of the *life* of Clement IV. was his intercourse with Charles of Anjou, the brother of St. Louis IX., King of France. As the French chroniclers naturally took a special interest in him, and looked upon him with the same favourable eye as did their Guelf brethren in Italy, we may naturally look for valuable information from them. To those of whom mention has already been made, we will add here only the monk of St. Denis, Primat, who, in Latin, continued the *Speculum historiale* of Vincent of Beauvais.[3] The original Latin chronicle, going from 1259–85, has been lost ; but a French translation of the work of this contemporary writer was made by Jean du Vignay, whilst Jeanne of Burgundy was Queen of France (1316–22). This valuable work has been published in full ap. *R. F. SS.*, xxiii, p. 5 ff., and partially by Brosien ap. *M. G. SS.*, xxvi, p. 628 ff.

Of capital importance in connexion with the " Sicilian affair " and Charles I. of Anjou are the extracts which C. M. Riccio has published from the rich Angevin archives of Naples. Unfortunately his productions were published somewhat erratically and in small editions, so that they are hard to find. (1) *Alcuni*

---

[1] E. Jordan, " Notes sur le Formulaire de R. de Pofi," pg. 329 ff., in *Études d'hist. dediées a G. Monod.*, Paris, 1896. *Cf. Eng. Hist. Rev.*, Jan., 1898, p. 137.

[2] *Cf.* the same authors *Del cod. diplom. angioino apologia*, Naples, 1872, and P. Durrieu, *Étude sur les registres du roi Charles I.*, Paris, 1886 ; 2 vols. The second vol., p. 165 ff., contains an itinerary of Charles I., which completes the *Itinerario di Carlo I. di Angiò*, by C. M. Riccio, Naples, 1872.

[3] William of Nangis drew very largely upon Primat for his *Life of St. Louis* and his other works.

fatti riguardanti Carlo I. di Angiò, Naples, 1874, give us facts of his career from 1252 to 1270 ; (2) *Il regno di C. di A. negli anni* 1271–2, Naples, 1875 ; (3) then the other years of his reign till his death appeared in the *Archivio Storico Italiano*, third series, t. xxii, 1875, p. 3 ff., p. 235 ff., and subsequent vols. From " Jan., 1284, to Jan., 1285," had already been published as *Diario Angioino*, Naples, 1875. *Il regno* may sometimes be procured as an *extract* from the *Archivio*. The same author's *Saggio di codice diplomatico*, two vols. with supplements, Naples, 1878–9, gives documents in full regarding Charles I. and subsequent Angevin rulers till the close of the dynasty in 1434. Further extracts from the Archives regarding Charles and his successors will be found in Riccio's *Stridi storici su' fascicoli Angioini*, Naples, 1863 ; *Studi storici fatti sopra 84 Registri Angioini*, Naples, 1876 ; *Nuovi studi riguardanti la dominagione Angioina*, Naples, 1876 ; *Notizie storiche tratte da 62 Registri Angioini*, Naples, 1877.

Ch. Merkel has grouped together the evidence of contemporaries on the Italian expedition of Charles in his *L'opinione dei contemporanei sull' impresa Italiane di Carlo I. d'Angio*, Rome, 1889, and he concludes that public opinion was in his favour, and against Manfred, p. 8, *cf.* p. 163.

Modern Works.—The work of J. Heidemann on *Papst Clemens IV.* is unfortunately not yet complete. The first part only, treating fully of the pre-pontifical career of Clement, has hitherto been published : " *Das vorleben des Papstes und sein legationsregister*, Münster, 1903. Canon Nicolas, as the result of the useful employment of his leisure hours for seventeen years, has produced a full but not too critical biography of " un pápe saint-Gillois ", under the title of *Clément IV.*, Nîmes, 1910.[1] Many

---

[1] He explains, p. x : " Le vif désir de voir l'Église donner la sanction supréme au culte, rendu de temps immémorial au pape Clément IV., a été le seul mobile de notre audacieuse et téméraire entrepreprise " ; and on p. xiii, " En écrivant cette histoire . . . nous n'avons eu qu'un seul désir, qu'un seul amour, celui de la vérité historique." Two seventeenth century writers wrote *lives* of Clement IV. The first of these was written by the Jesuit, Claude Clement, from which La Mure, canon of Montbrison, extracted a second. Last century M. Mazer compiled a fresh biography from the *Thesaurus* of Martène, but only an analysis of it has been published in the *Mémoires de l'Académie du Gard* (1808). In *Position des Thèses* (École nationale des Chartes), Paris, 1883, there are the *outlines* of an *Essai sur la vie de Cl. IV.*, by A. Corda.

writers have illustrated different episodes more or less closely connected with the life of Clement, e.g., P. Brayda, *La responsabilità di Clemente IV. e di Carlo I. d'Anjou nella morte di Corradino*, Naples, 1900, and G. del Giudice, *Il giudizio e la condana di Corradino*, Naples, 1876,[1] and his *Don Arrigo di Castiglia*, Naples, 1875 ; G. Colasanti has treated of Charles' crossing the Liris at Ceprano in 1266 in his " Il passo di Ceprano " ap. *Archivio Rom. di storia patria*, 1912, vol. xxxiii, p. 1 ff.[2] We may also cite P. Egidi, *Viterbo*, Naples, 1912 ; C. Pinzi, *Il palazzo papale di Viterbo*, Viterbo, 1910 ; and F. Cristofori *Le Tombe dei Papi in Viterbo*, Siena, 1887. In connexion with Clement's efforts to protect trade (Potthast, 19900) we may quote : G. Yver, *Le commerce dans l'Italie meridronale au XIIIe et au XIVe siècle*, Paris, 1902. Finally, Dounow in his article on " Clément IV." in the *Hist. litt. de la France*, vol. xix, p. 92 ff., analyses his letters.

[1] Del Giudice concludes : " Ma era destinato dalla Providenza, che col sangue di quell' infelice vittima, la Chiesa acquistar dovesse la sua *indipendenza*. . . . Il ghibellinismo imperiale che voleva rendere onnipotente lo Stato ed assoggettare i popoli e la Chiesa, fu colla distruzione degli Hoenstaufen, affievolito e depresso." Pg. 119.

[2] On p. 316 of the same review it is stated that other authors differ from the Professor, and do not believe that any resistance was offered to Charles at Ceprano. In a previous number of the review (1910, p. 313 ff.), G. Presutti, from a newly discovered bull of Clement (June 9, 1268, is able to throw fresh light upon the Colonna family : " I Colonna di Rioffredo."

CONTEMPORARY SOVEREIGNS.

(See under Alexander IV.)

CHAPTER I.

THE EARLY CAREER OF GUY FULCODI. HIS ELECTION
AS POPE.

On the right bank of the soft milky waters of the Little Birthplace Rhône, there stands the ancient town of St. Gilles; and family of Guy Fulcodi. and, in one of its narrow streets opposite its famous abbey church, there is shown a three-storied mediaeval house adorned with fine sculptured work. Tradition marks this out as the home in which Guy Fulcodi was born [1] some time before the beginning of the thirteenth century.[2] Guy had the good fortune to be the son of a father who was at once virtuous and distinguished both by birth and talent. His name was Pierre Fulcodi.[3] Guy had several brothers and sisters, of whom Mary, who married the

[1] Nicolas, p. 24. Clement, commending St. Gilles to Louis, tells us, ep. July 18, 1266, ap. Martène, ii, 371, he was born there : " quæ nobis ortum dedit." *Cf. ib.*, p. 629.

[2] At any rate, in 1268, when he died, he is described as " plenus dierum ". *Chron. pont. et imp. Mantua.*, ap. *M. G. SS.*, xxiv, p. 217.

[3] Guy " fu estrait de chevalier et de bonnes gens ", says a contemporary continuator of William of Tyre, *Belli sacri hist.*, l. xvi, c. 7, ap. Migne, *Pat. Lat.*, t. 201. *Cf.* an ancient Chartreuse chronicle ap. Martène, *Vet. SS. ampliss. coll.*, vi, p. 177, " Iste (prior Jocelin, † 1233) recepit ad ordinem Petrum Fulcerii (i.e., Fulcodii) patrem f. r. d. Clementis IV." On the strength of the *Chronicle* of St. Antoninus, various authors (e.g., Nicolas) say that Guy's mother was called Germana. But in *tit.* xx, c. 1, p. 186, of the ed. of 1587, the passage seems to refer to Guy's sister. After saying that Guy was well disposed to the Dominicans, the Saint continues : " Cujus *germana* devotissima mulier et affectuosissima ordini," saw the Holy Ghost in the form of fire descend on the brethren in General Chapter as Guy himself told the General. Guy himself related this vision of his *sister* in a letter to the Friars Preachers of Montpellier. The letter has been preserved by Gerard de Frachet in his *Vitæ Fratrum*, i, c. 6, or p. 42 ff. in Conway's English translation. It belongs to 1247. It must be noted also that Guy F. was not called *Grossus* or *le Gros*. *Cf.* Nicolas, p. 11.

Lord of Tarascon, had at least three sons and a daughter.
To or about each of these Guy wrote at least one letter
when he was Pope.[1] One or two of these letters have
become very famous, as they reflect great credit upon the
strictly upright character of their writer. The first of
these in the order of time is the one which he addressed
to his nephew, Peter, only a few weeks after his election

Clement is
opposed to
nepotism.

as Pope. We give it in its entirety. " To our beloved son,
Peter of St. Gilles." " It is true that there are many who
rejoice at our promotion ; but what is bringing joy to
many is only bringing to us fear and tears, because we
alone fully understand the greatness of our burden. In
order that from this you may learn how to conduct yourself we would have you realize that you should be more
lowly. For it is not becoming that what greatly weighs
us down should puff up those who are related to us,
especially as the glory of this world passes like the
morning dew. We do not wish that either you or your
brother [2] or any of our relatives should come to us without
receiving a special mandate from us. If they do they will
have made their journey to no purpose, and will return
home in confusion. Do not, moreover, endeavour on
account of our position to marry your sister into a higher
rank of life ; for you will not secure our favour nor our
support. If, however, she marries the son of a simple
knight, we will help you to the extent of three hundred
pounds of the money of Tours. But, if you aim higher,

---

[1] To Peter, ep. March 7, 1265, ap. Mart., ii., n. 21 ; to Alphantus
or Alphonsus, *ib.*, n. 256 ; to Rostanus (Rostaing), *ib.* ; to Alvicia (or
Adelaide), *ib.*, n. 631, p. 590 ; *cf.* n. 632 and n. 21. He also wrote a
well-known letter to a nephew, Raymond Alfred, the son of his sister
Egidia. *Ib.*, n. 403, p. 423. Against nepotism Alvares, *De planctu
ecclesiæ*, ii, p. 48, quotes the " felix exemptum " of Clement IV.,
" papa provincialis."

[2] This brother was very likely the knight Alphantus, whose offer
of service Clement refused saying that he had no post to offer him, and
that " his court was not for soldiers but for clerics ". Ep. ap. M., ii,
n. 256, p. 300 f.

you need not hope for a single penny from us. And even this offer we would have kept secret, and known only to you and to your mother. Know, too, that we would not have any of our relatives puffed up by reason of our elevation ; but we would have both Mabel and Cecily [1] marry the men they would have done had we remained a simple cleric. See Gilla (no doubt his sister Egidia), and tell her not to change her abode, but to remain at Suyusa, and to dress modestly and simply. Nor must she venture to address to us recommendations in anyone's behalf, as they would be rather hurtful than helpful to the person for whom they were presented. And if some offer her gifts for this purpose, she must refuse them if she would keep our goodwill. Greetings to your mother and brothers. The letters we have sent to you and to our friends we have not sealed with a (leaden) bulla, but with the seal of the Fisherman,[2] which the Roman Pontiffs

[1] These were Guy's daughters. One of his letters which, as Pope, he wrote to Cecily is extant. Ep. ap. *ib.*, n. 634 (*cf.* 635), p. 591. He can think of nothing fresh to say to her : " nisi quod Dominum timeatis." A fourteenth century writer, John Hocsemius, a canon of Liège, who wrote *Gesta Pontificum Leodiensium*, 1246–1348, Brussels, 1927, says, p. 41, that many of the great nobles of Provence sought Cecily's hands, and that Clement used to reply to them : " It is the Pope you want, not Cecily. She is the daughter of Guy Fulcodi, and as such you do not want her." And, as a matter of fact, Cecily did not marry but entered a convent. The same author says that Clement would not even give one of his brothers, who was a priest, a better parish. Ed. G. Kurth.

[2] This appears to be the first mention of this seal—" sub piscatoris sigillo " ; or, as it was expressed by Martin V., and later Popes, " sub annulo piscatoris—under the ring of the Fisherman." This ring shows engraved upon its stone St. Peter seated in a boat fishing, i.e., casting his nets into the sea. *Cf.* Barbier de Montault, vol. iii, *Le Pape*, p. 236 f. The use of this seal for *briefs* only dates from Nicholas V., 1447–55. A *brief* is defined to be an apostolic letter or constitution, sealed with the seal of the Fisherman on red wax, in the superscription or address of which the Pope takes the title, not of " servant of the servants of God ", but of " Pope ", e.g., " Nicolaus Papa V." *Cf.* Mas Latrie, " Les éléments de la diplom. pont.," ap. *Rev. des Quest. hist.*, Apr., 1886, pp. 448–9.

are wont to use in their private letters. Given at Perugia
on the feast of SS. Perpetua and Felicitas." [1] He warned
another of his nephews that, if he fulfilled his desire and
came to see him, he would have to return home again
very quickly.   Then, after impressing upon him the
dangers of the roads, he finished his letter by reminding
him that great state was expected to be shown by nephews
of a Pope, and that, while he disliked such display, if
his nephew attempted it, he would not have money enough
to keep it up ; and, if he did not attempt it, he would
be despised. [2]

In this same letter he told Alphantus that, for the same
reason, he did not wish another of his nephews,
Rostannus, to come to study at Bologna. [3]   He would
rather he completed his studies at Montpellier.

To another relative, Peter Raymbaldus, who had
written to ask his advice as to the lord from whom he
should seek his knighthood (cingulum militare), he replied
that he had long turned his mind from such questions.
However, " lest you should imagine that you are
altogether forgotten," we would advise you to apply
to the lord of Narbonne ; but, if you aim higher, and look
to the palaces of Kings, " which we do not regard as a
mark of great prudence," we would suggest the King of
Aragon. " You must not, however, expect that we will
write or speak to anyone for you. Advantages which we
seek not for ourselves we will not seek for others, no

---

[1] Ep. 21, ap. Mart., ii, p. 110 f.   Cf. ep. 384, where Clement tells his
correspondent to notice in that letter the " seal of the fisherman ".

[2] Ep. 256, ap. ib., p. 300 f.

[3] Ib. " Eum studere Bononiæ nolumus, cum ibidem nec ad nostrum
honorem nec ad suum posset aliquatenus sustentari." Cf. n. 403 for
similar advice to another nephew. To one of his own brothers who was
a priest, Clement refused to give a better parish (cf. Martène, Amplis.
col., t. v, p. 106, cited by Heidemann, p. 4) ; nay, hearing, on his death-
bed, that the bishops of France had given him three prebends, he
ordered him to resign two of them. Martinus Pol., ap. L.P., ii, 456.

matter how nearly related to us they may be." [1] Lest, however, it should be thought that Clement was " a hard man ", and had no love for his relatives, it must be noted that his correspondence shows he was anxious to hear about their welfare, and gave them affectionate paternal advice. [2]

Pierre Fulcodi, Guy's father, who had devoted himself to the study of law and had risen high in the service of Raymond V. and Raymond VI., counts of Toulouse, showed the depth of his religious feeling by becoming a Carthusian on the death of his wife. He died with a great reputation for piety in 1232. [3]

Pierre Fulcodi.

Intending to bring up Guy in his own profession, his father sent him to Paris, after he had finished his preliminary education at the abbey opposite his house. [4] At the University Guy had a very distinguished career. He made such progress both in canon and in civil law that he became known as the " lord of laws ". [5] One of his close friends both in the lecture room and in his lodgings at Paris was a certain Armann. Because he was a " louias homs ", Guy never forgot his old friend ; and

Guy Fulcodi, student and advocate.

---

[1] Ep. 270, ap. M., ii, p. 315.

[2] Ep. 47, ap. *ib.*, p. 123 ; and ep. 316, p. 357, where, though "fixum habemus quod de nostra actum extitit conscientia ", he thanks the Bishop of Beauvais for conferring a prebend on his nephew. *Cf.* epp. 631–4, p. 590.

[3] Nicolas, pp. 15–18.

[4] According to Nicolas, p. 22 f., Guy went to fight the Moors when 18 years of age, and took up the study of law in consequence of a very serious wound which prevented him from continuing to serve as a soldier. It is true that St. Antoninus in his *Chronicle*, p. 186, and others call him " miles ", but I do not know on what original authority Nicolas rests when he says that he fought in Spain as a " miles " (knight).

[5] *Chron. S. Petri Erford*, ap. *M. G. SS.*, xxx, 402, " Dominus legum." *Cf.* the contemporary continuator of William of Tyre, already quoted, from Migne, *Pat. Lat.*, t. 201, p. 1046, " Estoit grand clerc en droit, et estoit avocat le meilleur de la terre." *Cf.* Ptolemy of Lucca, *H.E.*, ap. *R. I. SS.*, xi, p. 1161.

when afterwards Armann was elected to a bishopric, Clement insisted upon his accepting it, and gave him several dispensations which were necessary for his obtaining it.[1] This noble quality of loyalty, " not at all common among men of his profession," says the chronicler, we are quoting, made Guy as true to the institutions and places with which he had come into close contact as to his friends and benefactors. Hence his declaration of special love for Paris, on account of its containing such a glorious fount of knowledge, and of its sending forth men so conspicuous in learning.[2] Hence, too, the interest he showed in St. Gilles and its abbey,[3] and his efforts to protect the church of Narbonne of which he was afterwards archbishop.[4]

Guy becomes the counsellor of St. Louis. At what date Guy married, and at what dates his two daughters 'were born does not appear to be known. We do know, however, that his name appears in a public document for the first time in 1241 [5] ; that his reputation

[1] Ep. Dec. 6, 1266, to Armann ap. M., ii, 431, " Qui si quidem olim Parisius noster in domo fuisti socius et in scholis." Cf. ap. ib., epp. 73, 576, where he exhorts a widowed friend not to marry again but to become a priest.

[2] Cf. ep. May 27, 1266, to his legate Simon in which he blames masters and scholars of the University for abusing papal privileges granted to it. Ap. Denifle, Chartular. Univer. Par., i, p. 446 f.

[3] Epp. 286 and 351 re the monastery which " dum conditionis nostræ status circa minora versabatur officia, nos multipliciter honoravit " ; 552, 701 ap. M., ii. He also gave a silver seal to this monastery, Potthast, 19535.

[4] Cf. ep. 58, " Caritas insolubilis, quæ ad ecclesiæ Narbonensis honorem et commodum nostram vertit sollicitudinem incessanter, quotiens ejus statum prosperum intelligimus, vultum et animum nostrum exhilarat, etc." When necessary, however, he did not hesitate to blame the archbishop of Narbonne. Cf. epp. 108, 576, ap. M., ii.

[5] The document records the homage paid by the count of Toulouse to the bishop of Albi. One of the witnesses is " Guido Fulcodii ", ap. Hist. de Languedoc, iii. Preuves, p. 401. It is said that his name is to be found on a charter of March 12, 1236, recording a donation made by Douce, the lady of Mourmoiron to Peter de Cairana, master of the house

as "a consummate jurist"[1] grew apace; and we may presume that the death of his father at any rate put him into more easy circumstances.[2] Serving the counts of Toulouse, Raymond VII., and Alfonso, his legal attainments soon brought him to the notice of King Louis, who attached him to his court, and soon made him one of his most trusted counsellors.[3] Though thus favoured by the King, he would never allow justice to be warped in favour of the great. He is credited with saying that the judge must, indeed, listen to the pleading of the advocate, but the advocate himself must listen still more attentively to the voice of his conscience[4]; and a fourteenth century historian, John Hocsemius, writes: "He would never at the expense of justice defer to any King, so that he was honoured, feared, and loved by everyone."[5]

Extant documents prove that Guy Fulcodi was, in his legal capacity, employed by King Louis as late as 1256.[6] As he then became a cleric, we may assume that his wife died about this same period.

---

of the Templars at Orange. Other acts of February 9, 1237, and of May 14, 1239, are also said to bear his name; but I am unable to state where these documents are to be found.

[1] Ptolemy, l.c.

[2] In ep. 286, ap. M., ii, p. 325. Clement, though he declares his disinclination to mention such things, has occasion to complain of injury done to his patrimony by an abbot of St. Giles.

[3] "Advocatus in utroque jure, in Curia regis Ludovici sancti gratiam habuit in conspectu ejus; unde et ipsum de suo secreto fecit concilio." Ptolemy, H.E., l. xxii, c. 29. Cf. ep. 56, May 8, 1265, ap. Mart., ii, p. 128.

[4] Nicolas, p. 29, quoting a seventeenth century author.

[5] Gesta pont. Leod., p. 42.

[6] For a full account of the career of Guy as a lawyer, see Heidemann, pp. 9–45; and Nicolas, pp. 27–61. The documents proving that Guy was a layman till 1256 are given by the latter on p. 57. But for them we might have concluded from the Cron. S. Barthol., ap. M. G. SS., xxi, p. 225, that he left the world somewhat earlier; for it says: "Qui (Guido) infra xiii annos fuerat laicus, uxoratus, clericus. . . . archiepiscopus . . . et papa."

The epitaph of Clement IV. informs us that he became a cleric and archdeacon of Le Puy soon after the death of his wife.[1] About a year afterwards, he was elected by the chapter of Le Puy to be their bishop; and their choice, at first rejected, was subsequently confirmed by Alexander IV., October 19, 1257.[2] Almost exactly two years later, on the death of James, archbishop of Narbonne (October 5, 1259), Guy was elected to succeed him " by compromise ", i.e., by the selection of a few to whom the right of choice was made over by the rest of the Chapter (October 10, 1259).[3] During the whole of Guy's episcopal life as a French bishop, he remained one of the counsellors of the King, and was constantly employed by that monarch to transact important business.[4] During the whole of that period, what is most striking among his recorded episcopal acts is the number of times he was called upon to act as arbitrator. It was what we may call his passionate love of justice that caused men to seek him out to judge between them. And it was this love of justice combined with his legal knowledge that caused the inquisitors in Languedoc to seek from him the solution of a number of difficulties that occurred to them in the course of the performance of their duty. Guy's replies to their questions, given in his private capacity, are clear and well supported by arguments,[5] and at the same

[1] " Qui viduatus ea, mox Christi sorte petitus," ap. Cristofori, Tombe, p. 15.

[2] Ep., an. 3, t. 25, ep. 668. Cf. Ptolemy of Lucca, l.c., etc. On his doings as bishop of Le Puy, see Heidemann, pp. 45–59 ; and Nicolas, pp. 61–71.

[3] Baluze, Concilia Galliæ Narbonensis, p. 161 ff., has preserved the deed of election. Cf. William de Nangis, sub an. 1264, the other chroniclers, and Clement's own letters, epp. 58 and 108, ap. M., ii.

[4] Cf. a decree of St. Louis entrusting business " to our beloved and faithful subject, Guy, archbishop of Narbonne." Nov. 9, 1260, ap. Vaissète, Hist. de Languedoc, iii, Preuves, p. 550 f., ed. 1737.

[5] Donais, Documents pour servir à l'hist. de l'Inquisition, i, p. lxxvii, Paris, 1900.

time show he was no rabid persecutor of heretics. He always inclines to the side which favoured the accused, even in cases where " others had written to the contrary " and insists that the proofs of a man's heresy must " be clearer than the day ".[1]

The distinguished position which Guy Fulcodi had so long occupied in the Church and State of France could not escape the notice of such an alert person as Urban IV. Accordingly, among the great men promoted by that pontiff in his first creation of cardinals, was the archbishop of Narbonne (December, 1261) [2]; and about two years later the same Pope named him legate for England (November, 1263).[3]

Guy becomes cardinal-bishop of Sabina.

The cardinalitical dignity was far from being sought by Guy. He tried to evade it, and put forth the plea that he was bound to the see of Narbonne. Urban, however, would not listen to his excuses. " Considering," he said, in reply to Guy's representations, " that the public good must be preferred to private, and being unwilling that, under pretext of the church of Narbonne, the honour of the Apostolic See, which is the head and mistress of all the churches, should suffer, we cannot yield to your entreaties." [4]

Urban at once availed himself of the advice of the new cardinal; and his register records the transmission of letters on Guy's recommendation without their having

---

[1] *Cf.* the questions and answers ap. Nicolas, pp. 78–87. On these replies and on the other events of Guy's archiepiscopate, see Heidemann, pp. 59–83. *Cf.* C. Douais, " Les sources de l'hist. de l'inquisition," ap. *Rev. des Quest. hist.*, t. xxx, 1881, p. 382 ff.

[2] Urban's poetical biography, Theodoric writes :—
    " Huic archipræsul Narbonæ nomine Guido,
        Cui successit ei secula jure regens." Pg. 21. On the diocese of Sabina, and Clement's connexion with it, see G. Tomassetti and G. Biasiotti, *La diocesi di Sabina*, Rome, 1909.

[3] *Cf. supra*, p. 190.

[4] Potthast, 18441.

had to be submitted to all the ordinary formalities.[1]
The high esteem in which he held Guy is made very plain
in the letters which he addressed to him or about him
when he appointed him legate in England. In the letter
to Guy in which Urban informed him that he had named
him legate, " in the parts of England, Wales, and Ireland,"
he declared that it was " in view of the abundant graces
that had been confirmed upon him by God that he had
deliberately turned his eyes towards him, in order that
he might send a strong man where strong things had to
be done, and that he might lay a heavy burden on his
stout shoulders ".[2] And writing about a month later to
St. Louis, he tells that monarch that he is sending for the
legation in England a man after his own heart, a man full
of wisdom and virtue, and a man who from intimate
service is well and favourably known to the King himself.[3]

But, as may be seen at length in the biography of
Urban IV., despite the high character of Guy, his legation
was not a successful one, as he was too completely imbued
with the knowledge of canon and feudal law, and perhaps,
too little acquainted with the state of public opinion in
England, to take a sufficiently clear and broad view of the
situation.

Guy is elected Pope, 1265.

Guy's legation was approaching its final collapse when
Urban IV. died (October 2, 1264). At his death there were
twenty-one cardinals, and of these eighteen were soon
shut up in conclave at Perugia. Of the remaining three

---

[1] *Cf. Reg. Urb. IV.*, vol. ii, p. 177 n. " De consilio d. . . . episcopi
Sabinensis, hæc littera transivit sine audientia."

[2] *Ib.*, n. 581, Nov. 22, 1263. *Cf. Chron. maiorum Londin.*, p. 83 ;
Eng. trans., p. 88.

[3] *Ib.*, n. 586, Dec. 12, 1263. It was by Urban's orders (so Clement
tells us himself, ep. 652, May 31, 1268, ap. Martène, *Thes. nov. anecdot.*,
ii, p. 604), that " in the episcopal hall " of the bishop of Maguelonne,
in presence of a large number of doctors and scholars assembled for
the purpose, he gave a cleric " the licence to teach by the tradition of
a book ", " et librum tradidimus solita solemnitate servata ".

Guy and Simon de Brion were in France, and Simon
Paltinieri of S. Martino was in his " Rectory ", the March
of Ancona, which, on account of the troubles fomented
in it by Manfred, he could not well leave.

According to Martinus Polonus, the cardinals were
strictly confined by the Perugians.[1] But the intention in
confining them, to wit, that they might the more quickly
come to a decision, was not fulfilled. Month after month
passed by, and no Pope was elected. We are, however,
assured by one of the cardinals in conclave that, whatever
were the causes of their want of agreement, their
discussions never became violent. Their discord was
healthy.[2] No doubt Manfred of Sicily had his friends
among the cardinals. It is probable also that the two
candidates for the Empire had each his supporters, and
it is possible that the worldly Philip, archbishop of
Ravenna, who hoped to be elected, had his partisans in
the Sacred College.[3] At length on February 5, one of the
youngest of the cardinals proposed that the method of
election " by compromise " should be again attempted.
This was at last agreed to, and the two cardinals chosen
to make the election nominated the absent Guy Fulcodi.[4]

---

[1] " Perusinis cardinales pro electione pape cicius facienda ipsos
recludentibus et strictissime artantibus. Similiter fecerunt in creatione
Clementis IV." Chron., an. 1216, ap. M. G. SS., xxiii, p. 438. See also a
letter of cardinal Ottoboni written about Jan. 1, 1265, and published
by K. Hampe, Neues archiv., xxii, 368. " Omnes unus tenet carcer
inclusos, unumque votum est ad salubre propositum, una mensium
trium et eo amplius cohabitacio."

[2] The letter just cited, p. 367, " Salubri discordia decertamus."
Ottoboni was apparently writing to the cardinal of S. Martino.

[3] " Multum affectabat habere papatum," says Salimbene, who knew
him well. Chron., p. 401. He adds that he hoped to be elected, because,
during the course of the election discussions, his name was mentioned in
some way " quod aliquid interdum dicebatur de eo ad istam materiam
pertinens." Cf. p. 433.

[4] Cf. a letter of Clement himself to the archbishop of Colocza soon
after his accession. It was published by Hampe, ap. N. Archiv., xxii,

Meanwhile, Guy himself was making his way towards Perugia through France and Italy. We are not told when he heard of the death of the Pope. From the gossip of Salimbene, however, we learn incidentally that the death of Urban was known in Ravenna on October 6 or 7,[1] and so we may conclude that Guy knew of it about the same date in the following month. As in duty bound, he at once turned his steps towards Perugia ; but, as the experience of his journey to France had taught him the dangers of the route, he took the precaution of travelling as a private person, seemingly as a monk.[2] Either because he had to take measures to avoid falling into the hands of any of the adherents of Manfred, or because he wished to lessen the chances of his being elected Pope, Guy travelled very leisurely. On his journey he appears to have transacted no little business. We find him on January 5, 1265, writing to Charles of Anjou regarding his Vicar in Rome, James Cantelmi. After some sarcastic allusions to " the magnificent acts, thundering words, and terrible deeds of the Romans ", the cardinal pointed out to Charles that the Vicar he had sent was not a man of sufficient character, and had not been supplied with money enough to rule the Romans. He begged Charles to send at once a really capable and experienced man.[3]

Before Guy reached Piacenza, he had heard of his election to the Papacy (February 5). On his arrival in that city, mindful of the kindness shown him by the Ghibelline leader, Oberto Pallavicini, when he was on his

---

1897, p. 406 ff. Guy tells us he was returning from Gaul when he was elected—" qui tunc omisso legationis officio, quod propter obstinatam perfidiam et contumaciam pertinatiam rebellium Anglicorum nolentes nos ad legationem istam admittere." Ep. Feb. 22, 1265.

[1] *Chron.*, p. 433.

[2] *Cf. supra.*, p. 191, and Salimbene, *ib.*, p. 479, " Sub habitu persone private." *Cf.* p. 469 ; and Ptolemy of Lucca, *Hist. eccles.*, l. xxii, c. 30, " Occulte . . . sub habitu monachali."

[3] Ep. 1, ap. M., ii, p. 97 f.

way to England, the Pope elect sent word to him that, if
he would become reconciled to the Church and to God,
and would suffer men to live in peace, he would in turn
recommend him to the mercy of the Pope. The offer was,
however, made in vain; for, says our informant,
Salimbene : " He that teacheth a fool is like one that
glueth a potsherd together" (Ecclus., xxii, 7).[2] As
Clement himself afterwards said, the marquis was drunk
with Apulian gold, and would not hearken to the words
of salvation.[3]

When at length, after paying a visit to the shrine of St. Francis at Assisi, Guy presented himself before the cardinals at Perugia, sometime after February 5, he protested his unfitness for the burden which they wished to place upon him.[4] They would not, however, listen to his excuses, but pressed him so hard that he at length gave way.[5] He was crowned in the cathedral of Perugia, probably on February 22, as that day was a Sunday and the feast of St. Peter's chair at Antioch.[6] The new Pope took the name of Clement, because he was born on the feast of St. Clement, and had received many blessings on that day.[7]

Guy strives to decline the honour, but is crowned.

[1] *Chron.*, p. 479. *Cf.* p. 469.

[2] Ep. 120, ap. M., ii, p. 178 f. " Cum Pelavicino multipliciter attento nihil profuimus. Nam auro inebriatus Apuliæ, verba salutis non recipit."

[3] " Noluit ire ad accipiendum papatum nisi prius visitaret ecclesiam b. Francisi de Assisio." Salimbene, p. 470.

[4] See Clement's own letters of Feb. 22, 1265, announcing his election to the archbishop of Sens, the King of France, etc., ap. *Reg.*, i, nn. 1 and 2 ; *cf.* ep. ap. *N. Archiv.*, t. xxii, p. 408. " Sed ipsi (the cardinals) nullum omnino excusationis nostre suffragium admittentes nobis reclamantibus . . . jugum apposuerunt apostolice servitutis."

[5] Ptolemy of Lucca, *Hist. Eccles.*, xxii, c. 30. " Post multam precum instantiam sibi porrectarum cum lacrymis."

[6] Others give Feb. 17, e.g., Theiner, *Cod. Diplom.*, i, 617.

[7] This interesting little item we learn from Clement's reply to a letter of congratulation addressed to him by Alfonso of Castile and Leon. *Cf.* Raynaldus, *Ann.*, 1265, n. 9.

In accordance with custom, Clement, assuming the device : " Oculi mei semper ad Dominum " (Ps. xxiv, 15), announced his election to the Catholic world, and begged for prayers.[1] He told how, though all unworthy, he had been elected one of those pontiffs who, through their succession, were destined by God to keep alive the presence of the Redeemer, and he entreated his correspondents to pray that by his acts he might give glory to God, and bring blessings on Christendom.[2]

Congratulations poured in upon Clement from all quarters—from his own friends and relations and from the heads of states. Among the latter, Béla IV. wrote to offer him his profound homage. Signing himself " King of Hungary, Dalmatia, Croatia, Rama, Servia, Galicia, Lodomeria, and Cumania ", he expressed his belief that God had blessed the earth in choosing him to feed the flock of the Lord by the authority of the Prince of the Apostles, whose faith and position he held. When he had heard of the election of one of whose love of justice and mercy, and of whose zeal for the faith he had already heard so much, he was greatly rejoiced, and felt impelled in his own difficulties to turn to such a worthy " successor of Peter and Vicar of Jesus Christ." [3]

What the Hungarian monarch here tells us of the high character of Clement on the testimony " of very many persons who loathe lies ", is corroborated by the general

[1] *Reg.*, i, nn. 1, 2. In his letter (April 23, 1265) asking the prayers of the Dominicans, he says he is learning every day in the book of experience the difficulties of his office ; but, though frightened by his own weakness, he trusts in the divine help. Ep. ap. Ripoll, *Bullar. Ord. FF. Prædicator.*, i, 450, Rome, 1729.

[2] *Ib.*, n. 1, Feb. 22, 1265.

[3] Ep. March 28, 1265, ap. Raynaldus, an. 1265, n. 6. " Audito eo, quod personam vestram . . . divina providentia sacræ Urbi et orbi pariter præfecisset, affecti sumus hilares." Béla had had trouble with his son King Stephen, and begged the Pope to confirm the agreement (compositionem et ordinationem) to which he had come with him. *Ib.*

verdict of his contemporaries. After what we know of
his success as an advocate, we are not surprised to learn
that he had a good voice and was a good singer ; that he
was an excellent preacher, and that, from his knowledge
of law, he should be set down as an " all-round churchman—generalis clericus ".[1] He was, moreover, a man of
very ascetic habits, and in his long abstinence from flesh
meat, in his use of a hard rough bed, and, of coarse cloth
next his skin, he imitated the austerities of the Dominicans
to whom he was much attached.[2] Altogether, he led a
most holy life, and we are assured that it was the general
belief that this holiness of his was the reason why God
put an end in his time to many of the evils which were
distressing the Church.[3]

---

[1] Ptolemy of Lucca, *Hist. Ec.*, l. xxii, c. 38, ap. *R. I. SS.*, ix, p. 1161,
" Generalis clericus fuit, videlicet, jurista summus, prædicator egregius,
cantor palcherrimus, concionator sine pari."

[2] *Ib.*

[3] So says even Rishanger, *Chron.*, an. 1268, p. 61, *R. S.* So also
notes Martinus Polonus, ap. *M. G. SS.*, xxii, p. 441. *Cf. Ann. clerici
Paris*, ap., *ib.*, xxvi, p. 583. " Magnus clericus, et optimus pacificator " ;
Ann Posnan., ap. *ib.*, xxix, p. 464. " Justus judex . . . sanctissimus."
Catal. Pont. Rom., *contin. Laudunensis*, ap. *ib.*, xxii, p. 371. " Vir
summe sapiencie discretionis, et probitatis, vitam quasi sanctam
duxit quamdiu fuit in apostolatu."

CHAPTER II.

CHARLES OF ANJOU AND THE KINGDOM OF SICILY TO THE DEATH OF MANFRED († MARCH, 1266).

Urban IV. and Charles of Anjou. SHORTLY before his death, Urban IV. had secured from Charles of Anjou a definite undertaking to fit out an expedition for the conquest of the Kingdom of Naples ; and equally before his death a vicar of Charles, as Senator of Rome, had taken up his residence in the city.[1] But he died before Charles himself crossed the Alps ; and it was left to his successor, who continued his policy, to welcome the arrival of the Count in Italy.[2]

Clement IV. continues the policy of Urban IV., 1265. Getting in touch at once with the papal legate in France, Cardinal Simon de Brion, Clement bade him proceed without delay to Provence in order to push on the Sicilian affair,[3] and, at the same time, he renewed the extensive legatine powers which had already been conferred upon him.[4] He then, after notifying our King that he had now no claim to the realm of Sicily, as he had for so long a time made no effort to make it his own,[5] confirmed the fief of the Kingdom of Sicily to Charles of Anjou, subject to some thirty-five conditions.[6] In the document setting

---

[1] Cf. supra, p. 175 ff. [2] Saba, ii, 15.

[3] Ep. Feb. 26, 1265, ap. Martène, ii, p. 101.

[4] Epp. of March 1, etc., ap. ib., p. 104 ff. ; March 19, etc., p. 111 ff. Cf. Reg. Clem. IV., append. iii, n. 1426 ff., for the letters relative to the legation of the cardinal of Sta. Cecilia.

[5] Ep. Feb. 26, 1265. Potthast, n. 19037, and Capasso, n. 438. See the letter cited in the next note.

[6] Ep. Feb. 26, 1265, a very lengthy document, signed by the Pope and sixteen cardinals, and printed in full by Saint-Priest, Hist. de la conquête de Naples, vol. ii, pp. 332–64. A summary of it is given by F. Moise in his ed. of the chronicles of Muntaner and D'Esclot, ii, p. 1191.

forth this confirmation, Clement shows, at no little length, as a result of a careful inspection of the registers of the Roman Church and the legal " processes " of Innocent IV. and others concerned in the affair, that the English Edmund had no right to Sicily,[1] but that the Pope had a right to assign to Charles the fief of Sicily. This Clement then proceeded to do, laying down that he must in person come before him or his representative before the next feast of SS. Peter and Paul (June 29, 1266), in order to receive the said fief.[2] The conditions on which it was to be given him have already been set forth in connexion with the agreement of 1263. They include the payment of homage and an annual tax, an agreement not to interfere with the States of the Church, and not to allow the union of Sicily with the Empire or with any notable portion of Italy. They also contained guarantees of the freedom of the Church and people in Sicily. Charles was further to agree to lay down the Senatorship of Rome within three years. Finally to guard against accidents, Charles was to furnish two signed copies of the concordat.[3]

At the same time, while bidding him continue to preach the Crusade against Manfred,[4] Clement urged his legate, the Cardinal of Sta. Cecilia, Simon de Brion, to exhort Charles to hasten his departure.[5] But the point which most exercised the mind of the Pope regarding the

Money difficulties worry the Pope.

---

[1] " Ecclesiæ Romanæ diligenter perquisitis et inspectis regestis, et ipsius Innocentii papæ ac prædicti notarii processibus super eodem regno circa prædictum Eadmundum habitis, perfecte visis et examinatis, etc." *Ib.*, p. 339.

[2] *Ib.*, p. 341.

[3] *Ib. Cf.* epp. March 27–8 ap. Mart., ii, pp. 115–16. All modifications of the earlier agreement were in favour of Charles.

[4] Epp. March 20–1, ap. *ib.*, pp. 113–14, nn. 30, 32. *Cf.* his letter of Nov. 2, 1265, to various bishops and to the Dominicans and Franciscans in France to preach against Manfred, " the virulent offspring of a poisonous race." Ep. ap. Ripoll, *Bullar. FF. Prædic.*, i, 460.

[5] Ep. April 14, ap. *ib.*, p. 122, n. 45.

Sicilian question was that of finance. He had, indeed, other matters to think of concerning that question, such as the healing of the quarrel between Charles and the Queen of France,[1] but the monetary side of the expedition worried him perpetually. His predecessor had declared in the July of 1264 that he had already expended two hundred thousand pounds of the money of Siena in keeping up the fight against Manfred.[2] Clement, then, might well declare in the following year that he had no money, and might well impress upon his legate the necessity, "for the time being of spending laborious days and sleepless nights" in raising the tenth throughout France, in order that they might procure money.[3] The legate was to grant subsidies to Charles out of the tenth[4] ; and King Louis was to be asked to advance money to him on the security of the same source.[5] Clement assured the King that Charles' expedition would prove beneficial to the Holy Land, to the Latin Empire, to the peace of Italy, and to the tranquillity of the whole Church.[6] This was the Pope's real belief. With Manfred and his Saracens ever pressing him closer and closer, he felt, as he told Simon de Brion, that "among the great and difficult matters which weighed upon his heart, which crushed him with anxious care, and which cruelly rent his mind, the final and happy termination of the Sicilian

---

[1] Ep. May 8, ap. *ib.*, p. 128, n. 56.

[2] Ep. July 17, 1264, ap. *ib.*, p. 85, n. 56.

[3] Ep. May 19, *ib.*, p. 132, n. 60.

[4] Epp. May 30-1, *ib.*, p. 118-19, nn. 39-40. *Cf.* Saba, ii, 14.

[5] Ep. March 28, 1265, ap. *Reg.*, n. 224.

[6] *Ib.* As pay, Charles offered to the knights ten solidi and 30 pounds for equipment (ad preparandum), and to the crossbow men (balis tariis) five solidi and 15 pounds for equipment. *Cf. Notæ S. Martini Lemov.*, an. 1265, ap. *M. G. SS.*, xxvi, p. 438. Both Charles and his wife pledged all they possessed to raise money. "Ma costoro pativano gran difetto di denaro pe' loro bisogni, perlochè Carlo impegnava e vendeva quanto più potea." *Cron.*, del D'Esclot, c. 53.

affair concerned him most of all."[1] Hence he brought
all the pressure he could to break down the opposition of
many of the French clergy to the payment of the tenth
for the purposes of Charles of Anjou. There was the
hundredth for the Holy Land, urged the malcontents,
and now there is the tenth for Charles. But, retorted the
Pope, you agreed in full council to pay the tenth,[2] and
it is too late now for anyone to go back. The Roman
Church will not profit by the money. It is all to be given
to Charles, and is needed for the safety of Christendom.
Pay, then, peacefully.[3]

Further, when Charles' Vicar in Rome pressed Clement
for money, he replied : " You ought to know, for it is
known to euery one, that I did not find any money at all
in the papal treasury."[4] And yet he pledged the credit
of his treasury, such as it was, and of the Roman Church,
to borrow some for him.[5]

At any rate, the Pope gave Charles all the financial
help that he could, and a late author, the historian and
poet, Galeotto del Carretto, goes so far as to say that
Clement found most of the money for the French
expedition.[6] However unlikely that may be, Charles,

Charles sets out for Italy, 1265.

[1] Ep. Feb. 26, 1265, *ib.*, p. 101, n. 3. lt is the letter in which Clement
entrusts to Simon the negotiations with Charles.

[2] " In dandam decimam in pleno consilio (concilio ?) consensistis,
vel aliis consentientibus tacuistis." Ep. July 13, 1265, *ib.*, p. 157, n. 94.

[3] *Ib.*, n. 95. Complaint was also made of the number of legates
passing to and fro. Well, replies the Pope, that is rendered necessary
by the cases which have to be settled. At any rate, speaking for myself,
I never found anyone who was not glad to see me when I was a legate.
" De nobis autem dicimus confidenter, quod per vos transitum facientes,
in nullius facie legimus, quod graves ei ad videndum essemus."
L.c., ep. n. 94. Saint-Priest avers : " C'est à Naples que le saint-
siége était menacé non seulement dans sa dignité, dans son pouvoir,
mais dans son existence," ii, p. 129.

[4] Ep., an. 1265, ap. Mart., ii, p. 107, n. 13.

[5] Ep. 51, ap. *ib.*, p. 126. *Cf.* n. 55 ; and Riccio, *Fatti di Carlo I.*, p. 6.

[6] " Quasi la maggior parte alle spese del Papa " ; ap. *Mon. Hist.
Pat.*, iii, p. 1153, in his *Chron. di Monferrato*. The chronicle is brought
down to 1530.

with the approval and help of his brother, St. Louis,[1] got together money enough to make a start. Arranging for the great mass of his army, when ready, to march overland to Rome, he himself set sail from Marseilles with a picked company in some eighty ships, great and small,[2] about the middle of May.

Manfred's preparations.
Meanwhile, Manfred had not been altogether idle. Uberto Palavicini was commissioned to prevent the land forces of Charles from advancing through Piedmont, and Guido Novello, with an army of Germans and Italians, drawn from the Ghibelline cities of Siena, Pisa, etc., was to watch Tuscany.[3] His " immense " Sicilian and Pisan fleet, after endeavouring to block the mouth of the Tiber with stones and beams, was to try to intercept Charles' fleet and capture its chief.[4]

Later on, May 24, 1265,[5] he tried the effect of words, and addressed a very long, obscure and declamatory letter to the Senator and people of Rome. In the bombastic style of many of the letters of his father, Frederick II., he boasted of possessing under God and his victorious Eagle not only most of the provinces of Italy, but of ruling over Sardinia, and the islands of the Tunisian sea, and of holding the greater part of Romania and of having

[1] It has been sometimes asserted that St. Louis did not approve of Charles' expedition. The contemporary *Livre de la conqueste de l'Amorée* shows that the reverse is the fact, and that the holy King thanked God that his brother had the will to undertake the arduous enterprise. *Cf.* c. 426 ff., ed. J. Longnon, p. 164 ff., Paris, 1911, and Buchon, *Chron. étrangères*, p. 139 f., Paris, 1841.

[2] Ep. May 20 or 21, 1265, ap. Mart., ii, p. 134, n. 62. *Cf.* n. 57, and Will. of Nangis, ap. *R. F. SS.*, xx, 418.

[3] *Cf. Annal. Ubervetani*, an. 1265, ap. *R. I. SS.*, t. xv, pt. v, new ed. *Cf.* Manfred's letter to him ap. Capasso, n. 464.

[4] Saba, ii, 17. *Cf. Life of St. Louis*, ap. *R. F. SS.*, t. xx, p. 421.

[5] After Charles' arrival in Rome, but, seemingly, before that fact was known to Manfred.

more money and men than anybody in Christendom [1] ;
and he declared his intention of coming to Rome " the
head of the world ", and of restoring to it the right of
electing to the Empire which had been usurped by the
Church of Rome. Also in the language of his father, he
attacked the Pope, who, not content with being the
successor of St. Peter and the Vicar of God in spiritual
matters, wished to bind also in temporal matters. But
his great-grandfather, Frederick I., by bursting into
Rome, and by placing without any clerical intervention,
" the imperial crown upon his magnificent head," [2]
had shown the way to deal with such claims. And so he,
the heir of such power and blood, was not going to suffer
" any German, Spaniard, Englishman, Frenchman, or
Provençal " to rule the Roman people. He therefore
exhorted them " under the protection of the wings of
our thundering power " to drive away the Vicar of the
Count, and to prepare for his speedy coming to make
Rome once more the mother of Empire. [3]

The knowledge of Manfred's preparations ; of the
uncertain loyalty of the Romans, especially as he had no
money to give them [4] ; of the progress of Manfred's
party in the March of Ancona ; and of the massing of
the King's German troops on his frontier in the neighbourhood of Tivoli, filled the Pope with anxiety.

---

[1] " Nos vero qui sub Dei dextera victricis aquile nostre signis
clarissimis non solum singulas quasi regiones Ytaliæ possidemus, etc."
Ep. ap. Capasso, n. 460, p. 277.

[2] " Imperii coronam per se ipsum et principes suos edicto proposito
quod nullus assisteret clericorum . . . suo imposuit magnifico capiti."
Ib., p. 283.

[3] " Sub tuicione alarum nostræ tonantis potencie." Ib., p. 284.
" Data Fogie 24 madii octave Indictionis."

[4] Cf. ep. n. 11, ap. M., ii, p. 107. " Cum . . . nec circa nos habeamus
nec militiam, etc." Cf. ib., nn. 45, 47. " Gens enim sua (the Provençals)
in Urbe est in magna discrimine et nisi celeri succurratur auxilio,
procul dubio amittetur." Cf. the continuator of the so-called Jamsilla,
ap. R. I. SS., viii, p. 595.

Charles
arrives in
Rome.

This anxiety was somewhat lessened when he had heard, and was able to announce that, despite bad stormy weather, the fleet of Charles had been seen in Porto Veneris on May 15.[1] Although the storm continued, Charles again put to sea, and reaped the reward of his courage. Trusting to the dam at the mouth of the Tiber being strong enough to keep out the Angevin's fleet, and fearing to be driven on to the shore, Manfred's admiral put out to sea, and thus failed to intercept the Count. Fortunately for Charles, his fleet discovered the dam before they struck against it. His captains cast their anchors, and were successful in being able to fix them. Then preferring, no doubt, " to touch the soil of Rome even as a dead man," rather than to fail to touch it at all by the date he had promised, the indomitable Count left his ship and put to shore in a small boat. Fortune favoured him once more, and he reached land in safety (May 21).[2] Shortly afterwards the storm subsided, and his galleys, removing the obstacles that had been placed in the mouth of the river, were successfully towed up stream.[3]

Charles is
escorted to
Rome.

The unexpected news of Charles' landing spread like wildfire, and " all the nobles of Rome " hastened to Ostia

---

[1] Ep. n. 62 just cited.

[2] We follow here the reliable narrative of Saba, ii, c. 17, ap. *R.I. SS.*, viii, p. 815. " Eadem durante procella, Karolus quamdam sagittariam ascendens. imminente sibi periculo personali terram petiit, cupiens forsitan vel extinctus adimplere quod jurando spoponderat, etc."

[3] *Ib. Cf. Contin. Jams.*, ap. *ib.*, p. 597, " Galli sui . . . ut moris est trahuntur ad Urbem." See also Andrew of Hungary, *Descript. vict.*, c. 13. On the coming of Charles to Ostia and Rome see the quaint rhyming old Italian chronicle of Buccio de Ranallo (written *c.* 1355), p. 8, ed. V. de Bartholomæis, of which, for curiosity's sake, we quote a few lines :—

> " Re Carlo primo di Francia dalla Chiesa chiamato
> Venne con multa genté d'arme adcompagnato
> Contra de re Manfredo per averlo caciato
> Et per santa Ecclesia repunere in estato."

to meet him, and escorted him in the first instance to St. Paul's outside-the-walls. Hither, a day or two later, came the Roman people, both cleric and lay, bearing palm-branches and singing "Hosanna! Blessed is he that cometh in the name of the Lord" (May 23). In this style the Romans conducted the Count in triumph to Rome, and "to the Church and palace of St. Peter".[1] Impressed by his warlike yet gracious appearance, the people, not content with offering him their acclamations, gave him presents and willing homage, and by the celebration of games gave him an altogether unprecedented welcome.[2]

The man whom the Romans welcomed with such enthusiasm was in many ways worthy of it. Far was he from being the contemptible "Charlie"—little Charles, Carlotto[3]—that the adherents of Manfred thought him before they felt the weight of his right arm. As the Apulian monarch was soon to find, he was, to use the words of the famous Florentine historian, Villani, " the most capable captain of his age, a man endowed with every gift of body."[4] He was, moreover, says the same writer, wise and prudent in counsel, brave, great-hearted, and of high purposes, firm in adversity, faithful to his promises, steadfast in carrying out every great undertaking which he took in hand, liberal to knights in arms, brief of speech but of remarkable activity, taking no pleasure in minstrels or jesters, chaste as a monk, and a

(margin note: Charles of Anjou.)

---

[1] Ep. 75, May 27, to Cardinal Simon, the Rector of the Duchy of Spoleto and the March of Ancona, ap. M., ii, p. 136. *Cf.* Saba, *l.c.*, p. 815, and *Contin. Jamsil.*, p. 597.

[2] Ep. 75. " In conspectu omnium gratiosus . . . alii cum muneribus, alii vero cum laudibus et omnes suum obsequium ei liberaliter offerentes." *Cf.* Saba, ii, cc. 17–18.

[3] G. Villani, *Hist.*, vi, 90, ap. *R. I. SS.*, xiii, " Conte Carlo, il quale per dispregio chiamavano Carlotto."

[4] *Ib.*, c. 89. Giovanni V., who died in 1345, was probably born in the last years of the reign of Charles of Anjou, † 1285.

Catholic. He was a man, too, who slept little, saying that time spent in sleep was time lost. But he was also harsh and cruel, much feared by the Kings of the earth, ambitious of power and territory, and greedy of money to enable him to carry on his wars.[1] As the Romans looked upon him in the year 1265, he was a man of forty-six years of age, tall and well-built (bene nerboruto), of an olive-coloured complexion and large-nosed. He looked much more the King than any of his followers.[2]

Manfred.   Against such a man what chance of success had the dainty, Sybaritic dilettante Manfred of Sicily? According to the historian just cited in connexion with Charles, his opponent Manfred, always clad in green raiment, was handsome, liberal, courteous, and gracious, a musician and a singer, so that he was much liked, and was made much of by his admirers. The wealth which he had inherited from his father, Frederick II and from King Conrad his brother, and which he had wrung from a rich country, enabled him to buy from poets favour and praise which his character could never have acquired. Still, it must be allowed that his appreciation of literature and love of learning won for him some really disinterested esteem.[3] But, adds Villiani,[4] he was in every way

---

[1] vii, c. 1. "Molto vegghiava e poco dormiva, e usuava di dire, che dormendo tanto tempo si perdeva . . . Curioso d'acquistare terra, signoria, e moneta."

[2] As Buccio sings :—

    " Lo re Carlo fo prencepe de multe gratie plino
      Et della soa persona fo quasi uno paladino." Pg. 11–12.

[3] For this reason and on account of Manfred's imperialistic connexions and aspirations, Dante does not hesitate to call this bastard, "fortunately—begotten, benegenitus," and to speak of "the nobility and righteousness of his character ' and his disdain of what was "bestial " '." De Vulgari Eloquentia, i, c. 12. According to Tiraboschi, though Manfred loved poetry and poets, no poem of his has come down to us. Lett. Ital., l. iii, c. 3.

[4] Hist., vi, c. 46. "Come il padre, o più fu dissoluto in lussuria in ogni maniera."

even more dissolute than his father ; an epicurean, who
cared neither for God nor His saints, but only for bodily
delights, loving to have around him buffoons, minstrels,
and beautiful concubines.[1] Moreover, he was an enemy
to Holy Church and to the clergy, taking possession of
the churches as his father had done.[2]

Such an effeminate fop, a distinguished predecessor
of the degenerates who in our own time associated with
Oscar Wilde, could not but be stupefied when he heard
of the safe landing of the warrior, Charles of Anjou—
the more so that he found himself deceived by flattering
astrologers in whom, also like his father, he had fondly
trusted.[3] The stupefaction of Manfred was to a large
extent shared by his followers. On the mere rumour
of the Count's landing, even the redoubtable Peter de
Vico and the Annibaldi promptly withdrew from the
Sabina,[4] and Clement felt able to assure cardinal Simon,
legate in the March, that Manfred's troops would soon
leave his territory (as they would be recalled to defend

Some effects of the arrival of Charles in Rome.

---

[1] *Ib. Cf. ib.,* c. 88. " Elli si stava quando in Cicilia e quando in
Puglia, a gran diletto, seguendo vita . . . epicura, renendo più concubine,
vivendo in disordinate lussurie." Even Dante, *Purgat.*, cant. 3, sub
fin, makes him say : " My sins were horrible." On the character of
Manfred see also Saba, i, c. 3 and c. 5, p. 795.

[2] *Cf.* the *Acts* of Guy of Melloto, bishop of Auxerre, a warlike prelate,
who contributed to the victory of Charles at Benevento. " Paterni
sceleris imitator Manfredus . . . regno Scicilie (*sic*), proprio Petri
patrimonio, et ducatu apuliæ occupatis, res ecclesiasticas dampnabiliter
detractabat, evertebat ecclesias, et fugabat prælatos." Ap. *M. G. SS.*,
xxvi, p. 589.

[3] Saba tells us, ii, 19, how not only was Manfred's admiral stupefied
(stupefactus), but also Manfred himself : " Cepit mente fremescere, et
animo conturbari . . . vehementissime obstupescit." For the way in
which Astrologers and knaves of that species deceived him, see *ib.*,
cc. 16 and 20. " Veniunt igitur ad Regem Augures, assistunt Astrologi,
assunt Harioli, currunt Haruspices, et festinant Divini." *Cf. Contin.
Jamsil.*, pp. 597–8.

[4] *Ep. Clem.*, May 20 or 21, 1265, n. 62 ap. Mart., ii, p. 134.

the Kingdom),[1] and that the roads to Rome had become so secure " that the highwaymen (itinerum aggressores) seem to have been buried rather than merely terrified." [2]

Delay of Charles in Rome.

As a matter of fact, Charles was at first not in the least formidable. The Pope had imagined that he had a great army with him [3]; but he soon found that he had only a small force, and was without money and horses. He at any rate quickly realized the weakness of the Count's position; and, had the King of Sicily, who must have heard of the smallness of the French force, been a man at all, Charles' Sicilian expedition would have had a swift and disastrous termination.[4]

As it was, Charles, who had brought with him only a thousand men, picked troops it is true, could do nothing but wait the arrival of his forces coming by land. Meanwhile, Manfred collected a large army.[5] He recalled his Germans whom he had sent to different parts of Italy in order to support the Ghibellines; strove to induce fresh ones to come from Germany; and, by eloquent words, endeavoured to animate his followers to make a stout resistance. But his brilliant descriptions of the cruelty of the French only shook the confidence of his barons; and they began to enter into negotiations with Charles and the Pope.[6]

Charles is reprimanded by the Pope.

During his enforced stay in Rome, Charles was not idle. He improved the efficiency of his followers by procuring them a supply of the very best horses, and he

---

[1] *Ib.*   [2] Ep. May 27, n. 65.

[3] " Ipse vero megnam militiam secum ducit." Ep. 62, just quoted.

[4] Ep. 68, June 3. " Carolum . . . ad Urbem venisse noveris pecunia carentem et equis : unde cum nec persona comitis nec negotium quod agitur sit in tuto, nisi ei pecunia celeriter ministretur, etc." Charles had only a thousand men with him. *Cf.* Saba, ii, 18.

[5] Saba, ii, c. 20. *Cf.* ep. 120 ap. Mart., ii, p. 178.

[6] Saba, cc. 21 and 22. " Futuri casus præmeditatione perterriti (some of Manfred's adherents), tractatum per nuntios tam cum Comite prædicto, quam cum Apostolica Sede dolosius ineunt."

laid himself out, not unsuccessfully to conciliate the Roman Ghibellines.[1] But he came near to seriously offending the Pope. Acting as if he was lord of Rome, he presumed to take up his abode in the Lateran palace. This brought upon him a sharp reprimand from Clement. " Although we are sincerely attached to you, still we cannot keep silence when we contemplate the dangers that threaten the Church, entrusted to us, and we prefer to practise prevention rather than cure. On your own authority, and, seemingly, without the excuse of necessity, you have done what no devout Prince has hitherto done. At your bidding, it is said, your followers have made bold to enter the Lateran palace . . . Now this we would wish you to know without any shadow of doubt that we could never be content to allow any Senator of the city, no matter what might be his rank or title to favour, to occupy either of our city palaces. We have to look to the future, and we are unwilling that the singular prerogative of the Church, over which we unworthily preside, should be lessened in our time, especially by you, whom we have summoned for its honour and glory. Do not my beloved son, take this in bad part ; but, as you are in a city of spacious palaces, be ready to go to another one, and do not imagine that you are being driven in dishonour from our palace. We are rather considering your dignity. . . . For it cannot be that, for a small advantage to yourself, you would wish to inflict a great and irreparable injury on us." [2]

---

[1] Saba, ii, 18, and iii, 2. *Cf. Contin. Jams.*, p. 600, ap. *R. I. SS.*, viii. However, even by Aug. 5, 1265, Clement stated that a large number of Charles' men were without horses. Ep. n. 120, ap. M., ii, p. 178 f.

[2] Ep. June 18, 1265, ap. Mart., ii, 141 f. " Cum nec tibi placere debeat pro tua utilitate tam modica, nos ingens et irreparabile subire discrimen." *Cf.* ep., n. 572, ap. *ib.*, p. 547, where Clement says that when he protested Charles left the papal palace which he had taken possession of.

Leaving aside the question as to whether Charles had any other higher motive in undertaking this enterprise than that of an adventurer, he certainly could not afford to quarrel with the Pope in any case. He accordingly left the Lateran, and is thought to have taken up his abode at the *Quatuor Coronati* on the Celian hill ; presumably with the Benedictines attached to that interesting church.[1]

Charles is invested with the Senatorship and with the Kingdom, June, 1265.

The "palace" incident, promptly closed, scarcely even ruffled the surface of the solid agreement between Charles and the Pope. A few days after the writing of the letter about the Lateran, Charles was solemnly invested with the Senatorship of Rome,[2] and with the Kingdom of Sicily (June 21 and 28). The former was conferred upon him on the Capitol, and the latter, by means of "the banner of the Church", in front of the high altar of the Lateran basilica by cardinals Annibaldo, Richard of St. Angelo, John of St. Nicholas, and James of Sta. Maria in Cosmedin, who had been specially commissioned for the purpose.[3]

---

[1] At any rate, one of Charles' decrees is dated : "Rome ap. SS. Quatuor, 14 Oct." Ap. Del Giudice, *Cod. dip.*, i, n. 23. We may note here that this letter was but the first of a series in which Clement had to protest against the doings of either Charles or his officials.

[2] Villani, *Hist.*, vii, 3, says he was made Senator of Rome " by the will of the Pope and of the Romans ". He was invested with the Senatorship in the inner cloister of the monastery of Aracœli (Sta. Maria di Campidoglio). Gregorovius, *Rome*, v, pt. ii, p. 369 n., says that Lelli, *Storia di Monreale*, ii, 11, shows that " Archbishop Gaufrid of Beaumont was a witness of Charles' assumption of the office of Senator". *Cf.* Baldwin of Aven., *Chron. Hanon.*, c. 241, " Li douna (Clement) le senaterie de Roume," ap. *M. G. SS.*, xxv, p. 459 ; Primat, c. 14 ; Will. de Nangis, *Chron.*, an. 1265, especially *Vie de S. Louis*, ap. *R. F. SS.*, t. xx, p. 421, *Annals of Vendôme*, ap. *Eng. hist. Rev.*, Oct., 1898, p. 699 ; and *Chron. Cav.*, ap. *M. G. SS.*, v, 194.

[3] See the bull of Clement of Nov. 4, 1265, confirming their work, and setting out at large the conditions on which the kingdom of Sicily was granted to Charles. Ap. Mart., ii, p. 220 ff. *Cf. Reg.*, i, iv, n. 411, and nn. 819–21. The date of these last two letters must be anterior to

After the solemn investiture, Clement did all he could The Pope helps Charles. to help Charles, especially with money. In the first place, at the new King's request, he allowed three out of the four cardinals to remain in Rome to assist him with their advice.[1] Then he exerted himself to the utmost to get him money and support of every kind. He bade cardinal Simon send him all the sums he could from the French tenth[2]; urged the Friars to preach the crusade against Manfred in the March of Ancona[3]; exhorted Charles not to be discouraged by difficulties, and suggested that he should try to raise money in Rome, where there was plenty of it.[4]

Although, at this period, Clement was so poor that How the Pope raised money for Charles. at times he had barely enough for his daily needs,[5] and hence had not enough money to support the cardinals,[6] and although he could not draw for money on England, financially exhausted by reason of the struggles between De Montfort's party and the King; nor on France groaning under the weight of the tenth for the Sicilian affair; nor on Spain which, subdivided among many Kings, "was not sufficient either for itself or them; nor on Germany

June 21. *Cf.* the letter addressed to the four cardinals in Mart., ii, pp. 223-4, epp. 72, 75, and 79. Ottoboni of St. Hadrian, one of the *five* cardinals mentioned in the letters of the *Register*, 819 ff., did not take part in the investiture, as he had been sent to England in the meanwhile. The commission was then entrusted to the remaining four mentioned in the text.

[1] Ep. June 27, 1265, ap. M., ii, p. 146. But Clement required the return of Richard, *ib.*, p. 143, n. 75.

[2] Ep. July 7, 1265, ap. *ib.*, p. 151. [3] Ep. July 10, Potthast, 19252.

[4] Ep. July 11, 1265, ap. M., ii, p. 153. "Mutum quæri fecimus quantum possumus . . . Vide, fili, quid in Urbe poteris reperire, ubi sunt plures abundantes in sæculo multas divitias obtinentes."

[5] Ep. July 30, *ib.*, p. 172. "Ea premimur paupertate ut ipsis quotidianis et domesticis sumtibus minus plene respondere possimus."

[6] Ep. Oct. 30, *ib.*, p. 218. "Nec possunt de nostra quæ satis tenuis est camera sustentari." *Cf.* epp., nn. 160 and 180, and especially n. 125, where he emphatically declares that he has not "an inexhaustible fount of money".

exhausted by the imperial schism, and scarcely obedient [1]; nevertheless, after much anxious consultation with the cardinals,[2] he agreed to allow the revenues and possessions of the Churches of Rome to be pledged up to the sum of a hundred thousand pounds,[3] in order that the King might raise a loan. From the revenues thus offered, those of the Lateran, St. Peter's, the titular churches, St. Gregory's, and the hospitals were to be excluded ; and it was, moreover, expressly declared that among " the possessions of the Churches " were not to be included the churches themselves, the houses in which those who served them lived, nor the lands attached to them which were known as their *castra*.[4]

The Pope also helped to keep Charles informed of the doings of Manfred, telling him of efforts he was making to capture Tivoli, if not by force then at least by treason,[5] but at the same time begging him not rashly to engage the enemy with his small force. He must await the arrival of those who are coming over the Alps to his assistance.[6]

The months that elasped between the arrival of Charles himself in Rome and that of his reinforcements were a time of cruel dread to the Pope. He awaited the news of their coming over the Alps with the anxiety with which Hannibal awaited the approach of Hasdrubal.[7]

---

[1] Ep. Feb. 12, 1266, *ib.*, n. 267, p. 313. *Cf.* nn. 116, 354.

[2] Ep. Aug. 3, 1265, to the cardinals in Rome, *ib.*, p. 176.

[3] Epp. nn. 120, 122, and 136–7, 163, 181, *ib.*

[4] See the letters in the last two notes.

[5] Epp. July 13, n. 96, ap. M., ii, 160, and n. 137, Aug. 25. *Cf.* also his gaining over Peter de Vico to the cause of Charles, and his efforts to stop reinforcements coming to Manfred by sea. *Cf.* E. Jordan, quoting from the *Book of forms* of Richard de Pofi, pp. 321–3, ap. *Etudes d'hist dédiées à G. Monod.*

[6] Epp. July 18, 1265, ap. *ib.*, nn. 103–4.

[7] Ep. to St. Louis, Nov. 12, 1265, ap. M., ii, 240, n. 170. "Cum multa pendeant ex adventu ultramontanæ militiæ, quam de die in diem nos et fratres nostri suspensis animis cum universis hujus terræ fidelibus expectamus, etc." *Cf. ib.*, n. 173.

The King was no less anxious, and together they strove to facilitate their advance. Charles made alliances against Manfred with Obizo II., marquis of Este and Ancona, and with other barons and communes in Lombardy,[1] and Clement sent the archbishop of Cosenza to help to smooth the way for the march of Charles' troops.[2]

But the more the Pope saw of the situation the more he felt that the one need of Charles was money. His daily expenses, according to Clement, had by August 5 risen to a " thousand pounds of Provins,[3] or, as we believe, of Tours ",[4] and by October 19 " to twelve hundred pounds and often more of the money of Tours ",[5] i.e., about one hundred and eight thousand francs.[6] Whence this formidable sum was to come gave both Clement and Charles the greatest concern. Even if the loan of one hundred thousand pounds of Tours which Charles tried to float on the security of the possessions of the greater part of the Roman Churches had been successful, it would not have sufficed. Charles already owed some forty or fifty thousand pounds, and out of the residue not much would have been left after the Roman merchant-bankers had secured their enormous interest.[7] But Clement's fears about the success of the loan were well

Money, the great need of Charles.

---

[1] See the treaty of alliance ap. Del Giudice, i, p. 39, n. 11, Aug. 9, 1265. *Cf.* n. 14, Sept. 7, for a treaty with Genoa and other cities. The Lombard allies : " in perpetuum adherebunt parti Ecclesie et dicti dom. Regis."

[2] Epp. Sept. 23, nn. 151-2, ap. M., ii, 203. *Cf.* Potthast, nn. 19404-5, and ep. 120, ap. M., ii, p. 180, for Clement's efforts to secure a safe passage " through the land of Genoa ".

[3] On this money see *supra*, ix, p. 151 ff.

[4] Ep. Aug. 5, n. 120, ap. M., ii, 178.

[5] Ep. Oct. 19, ap. *ib.*, n. 165.

[6] *Cf.* H. Wallon, *St. Louis*, p. 505 f. It should be observed that the money of Tours was held in the highest esteem at this period.

[7] Ep. Aug. 23, 1265, ap. M., ii, n. 136, p. 190. *Cf.* Riccio, *Alcune fatti*, document of Sept. 27, 1265, p. 6, dated " in hospitio nostro *SS*. Quat. Coronatorum ".

founded.[1] Charles could only raise thirty thousand
pounds, to which personal appeals from the Pope could
add only fourteen thousand more.[2] The bankers were
not satisfied with the way in which the tenth was being
paid in France, and some of them had been bribed by
Manfred not to lend to Charles.[3] Where then was the
much-needed money to come from? Clement declared
that he had no concealed treasure; and he emphatically
stated that he was not prepared to use the means which
some advocated to get it.[4] He moreover repeated to
Charles what he had already said about the disturbed
state of the different countries being reponsible for his
want of money. "In England there is opposition,
in Germany hardly anyone obeys, France groans and
grumbles, Spain suffices not for itself, Italy gives no help,
but plays one false." He, accordingly, suggests to
Charles that he should sell what movables he has in
Provence, mortgage (des ad firmam) his revenues there
for some years, and, above all, appeal to his brother,
St. Louis, for financial help.[5] Both directly,[6] and
indirectly through his legate Simon of the title of
St. Cecily, did he himself support Charles' appeal to the
King of France. Indeed his letters to Simon are one
long exhortation to him to press St. Louis and indeed
all on whom the Church or Charles had any claim for
money.[7]

---

[1] Ib., ep. 165, p. 214.   [2] Ep. 17 or 18 Nov., ap. ib., n. 181.
[3] Ep. 181, p. 242. Cf. Andrew of Hungary, Descriptio, c. 32.
[4] Ep. Aug. 1, ap. M., ii, n. 116, p. 174. Cf. ib., n. 120, p. 175, " Nec
enim thesaurum habemus, nec acquirere volumus inhoneste, nec
honestum credimus, quod multi licitum judicarent."
[5] Ep. 116. On how " Italia . . . emungit " see ep. Aug. 5, ib., n. 120.
[6] Epp. to St. Louis, July 18, n. 105, Nov. 12, n. 179 ; Nov. 16 or 17,
n. 181. In this letter he tells Louis that, if he does not help, and Charles
has to return, he will, trusting to get help from God, bare his back to
the scourge ; and, if need be, face prison and death.
[7] Cf. epp. to Simon (Nov. 16 or 17), nn. 182–8.

How far these appeals to the French King for pecuniary His army sets out for Italy, 1265. assistance were answered, does not appear to be known. It seems certain that he encouraged men to join Charles [1]; but whether he assisted Charles to any great extent with money is perhaps doubtful. That important commodity was particularly scarce in the Middle Ages, and the heart of Louis was set on another Crusade for which he would need all his monetary resources. At any rate whether he helped his brother with money or not, Charles' lieutenants raised a large force in France, and set out for Italy in the month of October [2]. Soon, as Saba tells us, " the gleaming standards of the lilies were shining among the mountains, and in the plains on this side of them."[3] Crushing some obstacles and eluding others; helped by the marquis of Montferat, and opposed by Palavicini, the host of Charles descended the Alps, swept through Lombardy, and, to avoid encountering the strong Ghibelline forces of Tuscany, marched through Romagna and the March of Ancona, and reached Rome in December.[4]

About the time of the arrival in the city of his wife Charles crowned King of Sicily, 1266. and the main body of his army, Charles, strengthened by Guelf reinforcements, pushed on the negotiation with the Pope regarding his coronation as King of Sicily.

---

[1] Ep. of Clement to Charles, July 11, 1265, ap. M., ii, n. 89, p. 154. Reliable report asserts "quod ... Rex Franciæ ... pro te factus est prædicator, barones et alios ad tuum subsidium excitans et invitans ".

[2] Will. of Nangis, *Chron.*, i, p. 299.

[3] L. ii, c. 15, p. 813.

[4] *Ib.* Cf. *Chron. Sic.*, pp. 4–5, ed. De Blasiis ; *Chron. de rebus in Italia* (= *Ann. Placentini Gib.*), pp. 254–5, ed. Huillard-Bréholles ; Villani, *Hist.*, vii, 4 ; *Ann. Genuen.*, ap. *R. I. SS.*, vi, p. 535 ; and Salimbene, *Chron.*, p. 470, who saw Charles' troops on the march. The *Annals of Bergamo* tell us that they descended from the mountains about Nov. 11, ap. *M. G. SS.*, xxxi, p. 334 ; and that there were among them a great company of men from Picardy, " who fear not death."

For various reasons, among others to avoid his creditors,[1] Clement did not wish to leave Perugia in order to crown Charles at Rome, nor did the Count desire to leave Rome for Perugia. The Romans had told Charles that, if Clement refused to crown him in Rome, they would take his refusal as an insult to themselves. " What next ! " exclaimed the indignant Pope, " the coronation of the King of Sicily is our affair. Neither by law nor by custom does it appertain to the Romans, and yet they feel aggrieved when they have in no way been wronged. Is the pontifical authority so dead that popular outcries (propter populares) are to disturb both it and the curia ? Know, my son " (he is writing to Charles), " that our cities and fortresses may be taken from us, but never our defence of our freedom. . . We are, however, quite willing to entrust this power of crowning you to another, so that you may not incur their hostility ; and though it is more becoming that you should receive the crown from us as we are so near, we are not so greedy of honour but that we prefer to consult your needs rather than to secure it at the cost of danger to you and yours . . . For the time we put the world before the city—præferimus orbem urbi . . . If then you come here, we shall all be glad, and we will place the crown upon your head. If you cannot come, we will send some cardinals to crown you, and we would suggest the Epiphany (Jan. 6) as a suitable day." [2]

When it was at length decided that Charles and Beatrice should be crowned by cardinals in Rome, Clement sent word to him, as a final piece of good news for his corona-

---

[1] Writing on Apr. 24, 1264, Clement expressed a hope of visiting Rome in the following winter, " si cum creditoribus nostris Romanis convenire poterimus." Ep. 261, ap. Mart., ii, p. 315.

[2] Ep. Dec. 20, 1261, ap. M., ii, n. 195. Cf. nn. 203 and epp. of Dec. 29, ap Del. Giudice, i, pp. 81–5, about the cardinals who are to crown Charles.

tion, that, by the extraordinary step of pledging the
plate, in fact the whole treasury of the Church, he had
hopes of getting fifty thousand pounds of the money
of Tours from the bankers.[1] At the same time, he warned
him not to keep his army too long in Rome, lest there
should be trouble with the Romans, and also to beware
of attempts on his life.[2]

On the day suggested by the Pope (Jan. 6), the five Coronation
cardinals, who had been commissioned for the purpose,[3] of Charles, 1266.
made their way in solemn state to St. Peter's, in order
to perform the first merely regal coronation that had
ever taken place therein. They were Rudolf, cardinal-
bishop of Albano, Ancherius, cardinal-priest of Sta.
Prassede, and the cardinal-deacons Richard, Godfrey,
and Matthew. A great multitude of people filled the old
basilica to which Charles and his wife were escorted by
the Roman nobles with the utmost pomp. Within the
church, the King and Queen were anointed by the bishop
of Albano ; and the cardinals in the Pope's name received
Charles' liege homage for the Kingdom of Sicily. In
the oath that he took, Charles, styling himself " King of
Sicily and of the Duchy of Apulia and of the Principality
of Capua ", proffered homage " for the Kingdom of Sicily,
and for all the territory on this side of the Pharus to the
confines of the territories of the Roman Church,
all which Kingdom and territory, except the city of

---

[1] Ep. Dec. 31, 1265, ap. M., ii, n. 210.

[2] *Cf.*, on this point, the anonymous monk of Padua : " Coepit . . .
Principi insidias præparare . . . procurando . . . per assasinos . . . ut
gladio vel veneno auferret de medio Ecclesiæ defensorem." *Chron.,
Ann. S. Justinæ*, ap. *R. I. SS.*, viii, p. 725. See also Andrew of Hungary,
Descript. vict., c. 20. He tells of the capture of a would-be poisoner.

[3] *Cf.* the Pope's letter to them of Dec. 29, 1265, ap. Capasso, n. 501.
They were to receive from Charles the homage (ligium homagium)
due to the Roman Church.

Benevento and its district, have been ceded to us by the said Church." [1]

Then, by way of marking his sense of the favour bestowed upon him, and, as he himself said, to imitate the practice of the Frankish Kings, his predecessors, he ordered an annual grant of fifty ounces of gold to be paid to the canons of the chapter of St. Peter's from the Customs or other legal dues belonging to the crown in the city of Naples.[2] In return they were expected to offer Masses for him during his life and after his death.

Trouble with Charles' officials.

Now that Charles had been duly crowned, the Pope, at any rate, must have been keenly anxious to see his Provençal followers out of Rome, and their chief at a safe distance on his throne at Naples. Clement had to complain of the high-handed action of Charles' urban vicar in [3] and out [4] of Rome both before and after the arrival of the King himself. He had to complain to Charles that the frequent serious charges " of perverse conduct " brought to him against his followers " were gall and wormwood " to his soul. He, accordingly, begged Charles to have a care for the honour of the Church, as he had ever had a care for his, and not to

[1] *Cf.* the public instrument (Jan. 6) of the five cardinals, ap. Del. Giudice, i, n. 33. See also Saba, iii, c. 1 ; *Chron. Cavense*, an. 1266.

[2] *Cf.* the grant ap. Del. G., n. 34. In notes on pp. 90–1, Del. G. gives several documents showing how the payment of this grant was enforced by Charles and his successor. In return for this donation, Charles lays down the number of masses he wishes to be said for him.

[3] *Cf.* ep. 13 ap., Mart., ii, p. 107. This letter is not dated but was no doubt written before the arrival of Charles in Rome. The Pope complained that the Vicar had broken into the Lateran Church, and, in contempt of the rights of the clergy, had himself put an offending priest in fetters.

[4] Epp. Jan. 7, 1266, to the cardinals in Rome and to Charles himself regarding the Vicar's ill-treatment of the people of Castrum Asperæ (Aspra) in the Sabina, because they had refused to receive one of Charles' followers (de tua familia) as their rector. Nn. 214–15, ap. M., ii, pp. 263–4.

content himself with saying that he and his followers were only doing what the Roman Senators had done before. Leaving out of the question what others had done he reminded the King that " he had not summoned him in order that he might copy the evil doings of others, nor to swallow up the rights of the Church, but in order that, content with his own rights, he might defend first and foremost the Roman Church, and then other churches." [1]

Clement had even to complain of the arbitrary conduct of Charles himself. Setting at naught the rights of ecclesiastics, and of the Pope himself, the King, so Clement had been informed, had caused an abbot with his retinue to be prevented from making his way to the papal court. Charles was warned that he must allow the abbot to proceed.[2] He was also warned that, if he hoped for success in the field, he must abandon the tyrannical ways he had not unfrequently displayed both in his own territories and also in Italy.[3] Money difficulties also made the Pope anxious to see Charles master of Naples. " I have neither mountains nor rivers of gold " wrote Clement to the King ; " and, however great is the need, I can do no more. I have been as liberal as I could, and what I can conveniently do that I will do. But as my means are exhausted, and the bankers are tired of lending, I cannot see why you continue to trouble me, unless indeed you want a miracle. But my virtue is not sufficient to enable me to convert earth or stones into money." [4]

But if the Pope was anxious to get Charles out of

Charles himself anxious for battle.

---

[1] Ep. 215, just quoted.

[2] Ep. Jan. 10, 1266, ap. M., ii, p. 266, n. 217. *Cf.* n. 218.

[3] Ep. Jan. 11, n. 219. *Cf.* ep. Feb. 24, n. 233, to Charles. " Audimus quotidie quæ non placent vel si vera sunt, quia mala ; vel si falsa sunt quia falsa."

[4] Ep. 225 ap. Mart., ii, p. 274.

Rome, the King was, at any rate, equally anxious to subdue Manfred. He too, of course, felt the financial strain of his position, and he knew that Manfred was intriguing to make peace with the Pope, and that he had already had too much time to make defensive preparations. He knew, indeed, that Clement had rejected Manfred's latest overtures, couched, as the Pope had said, rather in bombastic than in regal style. He knew that " the once Prince of Tarento " had been told that there was a time for everything, and that the time for making peace had gone by.[1] All this, no doubt, he knew well enough ; but he did not know how long the Pope could hold out against Manfred, if he professed his sorrow for the past, and his readiness to comply with all that Clement might require. Then too he was anxious for an early campaign in order that Manfred might not have further time to prepare resistence.[2]

Manfred's preparations.

Meanwhile, what time he could snatch from his carnal pleasures, Manfred spent, not in making a bold attack upon Charles before his main army had arrived, but, for the most part, merely waiting to be attacked. His Ghibelline allies and some of his lieutenants indeed were not inactive. In Lombardy, Pellavicini was harassing the great Guelf city of Milan ; in Tuscany Ghibelline Sienna was waging war on Guelf cities beyond its borders ; and, in the March, the Ghibellines, though not making much progress were contriving to keep it in a state of

---

[1] Ep. 226 to Manfred, *ib.*, p. 274 f. " Verum sciat Manfredus quod fuit tempus in quo gratiam repulit, cui parata per omnia videbatur, et quæ postmodum haberi non potuit, tempore minus opportuno quæsita." *Cf.* ep. 232 of Feb.

[2] Charles' whole army felt like its chief. " Romam veniunt quidem inopes, et laboribus fatigati ac expensis oppressi et ideo eorum prompti spiritus violento appetitu ad bella eos accelerant." *Contin. Jamsil.*, p. 600. *Cf.* Saba, iii, 1 and 3.

unrest.[1] But Manfred himself did very little. He sent
to Germany for two thousand horse,[2] and with large
forces, partially under his own command,[3] beset
the frontiers of the papal states.[4] Both he and his
generals met with some slight successes, especially in
the neighbourhood of Tivoli. But he himself soon left
the field of battle,[5] and was content to fortify the banks
of the rivers covering Capua, Ceprano, and Benevento,[6]
and to listen to his astrologers assuring him, with regard
to one of the small initial successes gained by his troops,
that it was a sure augury of his final victory.[7]

A fortnight after his coronation Charles was ready
with the blessing of the Church upon him,[8] to take the
field (Jan. 20, 1266). Advancing along the Latin Way
through the valley of the Sacco, he reached the river
Liris which, says Saba, separates the Kingdom from
Campania.[9] From the archives of Naples, we learn
that, on this march, Charles was accompanied by the
legate, cardinal Octavian. When they reached the
boundary stones fixed between " Insula Pontis Scelerati
which is in the Kingdom and Ceperano which is in
Campania, the cardinal said to Charles : ' Your kingdom
begins here.' He then blessed him, and saying :
' Advance in God's name,' he left him, and returned to
Rome. This spot was known as La Colonella from a
column of marble which had been set up at the confines
of the two states, and here Frederick II. had built a city
known as Citta Nuova." [10]

The Battle of Benevento, 1266.

---

[1] Ep. of Clement, Aug. 25, 1265, ap. M., ii, p. 190, n. 137. " Marchia
satis volubilis nullum penitus habet statum."

[2] *Contin. Jamsil.*, p. 599.　　　　　[3] Ep. 137 just cited.

[4] *Monachi Patav. Chron.*, ap. *R. I. SS.*, viii, p. 725.

[5] Ep. 137. Clement speaks of Manfred's disappointment in not
having Tivoli betrayed to him, and then of his capture of Matrice
(Amatrice), 12 miles from Norcia.

[6] Saba, iii, 3.　　　　　[7] *Ib.*, ii, 16.　　　　　[8] Saba, iii, 3.

[9] *Ib.* ; *cf. Contin. Jamsil.*, p. 600.　　　[10] Riccio, *Alcuni Fatti*, pp. 7–8.

First
successes.

Either through Manfred's incompetence or, possibly, through the treachery of some of his followers, neither the river nor the strongholds about it were seriously defended.[1] Charles had accordingly no great difficulty in entering the Kingdom, but quickly capturing Rocca d'Arce and San Germano, he made haste to come in contact with the main army of Manfred. On his march, he was joined by a number of the Apulian nobles, who impressed by the rapidity of his initial successes, and, it is said, tired of the tyranny of Manfred and his Saracens, abandoned their master.[2]

If adequate resistance was not offered to Charles at the Liris, still less was offered to him at the Vulturno in front of Capua, where Manfred had boasted that he intended to give battle.[3] The fact was that, as soon as Manfred learnt that Charles had no intention of trying to force the strong bridge at Capua, but was marching towards Telese in order to cross the river higher up, he abandoned all thoughts of fighting at Capua, but made his way to Benevento in order, if necessary, to be able to retreat into Apulia.[4]

Battle of
Benevento,
1266

Flushed with their victories, the troops of Charles

---

[1] *Ib.*, *Cf.* Andrew of Hungary, *Descriptio*, c. 32–6; Ep. Clem., March 25, 1266, ap. M., ii, n. 257, *cf.* n. 240, 244; Riccio, *l.c.*, p. 8. Villani, vii, 5, and Dante, *Inferno*, xxviii, 15.

" And those the rest whose bones are gathered yet
　　At Ceperano, there where treachery
　　Branded the Apulian name . . ." See G. Colasanti, *Il passo di Ceprano*, p. 74 ff.

[2] *Mon. Patav. Chron.*, p. 726. See also a letter sent to the nobles of Anjou after the battle of Benevento. It tells how during Charles' march: " Non paucis etiam Comitibus, militibus et baronibus Manfrido relicto. ad eundem illustrem Regem confluentibus." Ap. Del. Giudice, *Cod. diplom.*, i, p. 110 n. It is Menko, *Chron.*, ap. *M. G. SS.*, xxiii, p. 531, who speaks of " the tyranny ".

[3] Ep. of Charles to Clement, ap. *ib.*, or M., ii, p. 283, Feb. 26, 1266, " A Capua quoque, ubi se jactabat velle resistere, confusus abcessit."

[4] Andrew, cc. 39–40; Villani, vii, 7.

in hot pursuit, riding their horses almost to death, pushed
across the mountains by Alife and Telese towards Benevento. When they came in sight of Manfred's army,
they were anything but in a condition to fight. The
rapidity of their march had left both men and horses
short of food. Nevertheless, Charles was not prepared
to listen to terms of peace or to conditions for a truce.
When, as it is said, they had been offered earlier by
Manfred, he had replied to his envoys : " Go and tell
the Sultan of Lucera that this day I will send him to hell,
or he shall send me to heaven." [1] On this occasion,
however, Manfred was perhaps more ready to fight than
Charles. He had just received a reinforcement of eight
hundred German cavalry [2] and was all eagerness to
fight. Under the circumstances, however, his desire
for battle was foolish, as time was on his side. Accordingly
his army, wholly unable to face the religious enthusiasm
that animated many at least of the wearers of the red
and white cross,[3] and weakened by treachery, was utterly
defeated, and he himself slain, Feb. 26, 1266.[4]

[1] Villani, vii, 5.   [2] The letter to the nobles of Anjou just cited.
[3] The author of the *Majus Chron. Lemovicense*, ap. *R. F. S.S.*, xxi,
p. 771, tells us that cardinal Simon gave Charles' Crusaders a cross :
" et unum brachium crucis erat album et aliud rubeum." The religion
of many of the Crusaders is well seen in the career of Guy of Melloto,
bishop of Auxerre, who with raised " mailed fist, elevata manu loricata",
pronounced the words of absolution before the battle, and " being
not unmindful of episcopal modesty " contented himself with charging,
and with killing the horses of Manfred's men. *Cf.* contemporary *Annals*,
ap. *M. G. SS.*, xxvi, pp. 581–6.   The fact that Manfred showed great
favour to the Moslems, and that the greater part of his officers were
Moslems, as were also a very large portion of his soldiers, did no little
towards firing the religious enthusiasm of the troops of Charles. The
facts showing Manfred's proclivities towards the religion of Mahomet
are given us by the Arab chronicler, Djemaleddin, who went on an
embassy to him. Ap. Michaud, *Bib. des Croisades*, iv, p. 482 n.
[4] *Cf.* the letters, Feb. 26 and March 1, of Charles to the Pope ;
ap Del. Giudice, i, pp. 110–14 ; and various letters of Clement, March 8,
etc. Ap. Mart., ii, p. 287 ff. *Cf.* Saba, iii, 6–11 ; Villani, vii, 8–9, etc.
Both Saba and Villani speak of treachery against Manfred.

" In Sicily we first may see
Lord Mandred, who by treachery
Long time unchallenged kept the land,
Till Charles of Anjou's mighty hand
O'ercame him, and there reigns to-day,
Where no man dares dispute his sway.
This good King Charles from Manfred took
His kingdom not alone, but strook
The life from him, when he, with sword
Fine tempered, on the battle sward
Where first they met assailed him, high
On towering war-horse mounted : ' Die,
Shalt thou ', he cried, ' for check and mate
I give thee ' ; but soon met his fate
Amid his goodly company,
By arrow-stroke, death pierced, fell he." [1]

These words of Guillaume de Lorris are an indication
that, in other countries besides Italy, was there joy over
the defeat and death of Manfred.   In the latter country,
at any rate, a Ghibelline author assures us that his death
brought " great exultation and gladness among Italians,
i.e., among the clergy and those who are known as the
Church party ; but it brought sorrow and distress to
the partisans of the Empire ". [2]

---

[1] *Romance of the Rose*, line 7014 ff.   Vol. i, pp. 237–8 of F. S. Ellis'
translation, London, 1900. I have taken the liberty to alter the position
of four words.

[2] *Chron. de rebus in Italia*, pp. 257–8.   Among the troubadours of
Provence, Aimeric of Peguiliain (1205–70), who is stated to have
died " a heretic ", wrote in his usual style a " complaint " on the
death of Manfred :—

" All honour, every deed by man well wrought
Were wasted all, and all did perish quite
That day when to an end was sadly brought
Bold Manfred's life, of woman born the best ;
The valiant King, of manhood's pride the crest,
The hope, the deepest joy of all the good.
I know not how fell death his life's blood could
Have ta'en. Oh cruel death to strike him down
Whose death did all that's best in life discrown." See the original
in Merkel, *L'opinione*, p. 49.

Of this sorrow we have proof in the lamentations The burial of Manfred, 1266.
which Saba and Villani put into the mouths of some of
Manfred's counts, on the finding of his body, a day or
two after the battle. " Alas ! Alas ! " they cried, " slain
is the lamb, our King, our leader, and our lord, who chose
rather to die with his people than to live without them.
Now our life must be called death rather than life. Oh
that one sword had killed us along with him." [1]

As he died under sentence of excommunication, his
body was buried not in consecrated ground, but close
by a ruined church, near the bridge over the Calore,
and the French soldiers in sympathy erected a cairn
over it.[2]

The day after the battle, Charles wrote to tell the Charles' success published to the world.
Pope that he had joined battle with " the public enemy,
Manfred ", " in the name of Him on whose work they
were engaged " ; that his opponents had been completely

---

[1] Saba, iii, 13.

[2] Saba, *ib.* Charles himself told the Pope, ep. March 1, ap. Del.
Giudice, i, n. 41, " Ego naturali pietate inductus corpus ipsum, cum
quadam honorificentia sepulturæ, non tamen ecclesiasticæ tradi feci."
Maurinus de Maurellis, a citizen of Benevento, says Manfred was buried
" secus Caloris fluvium ad pontem."   Ap. *Vatic. Cod. Barber. Lat.*,
2062, f. 17. This is the contemporary authentic account of his burial.
But certain Ghibellines ("it was said by some " is the phrase of
Villani, vii, 9) added that " by the command of the Pope ", Bernard
Pignatelli, bishop of Cosenza, disinterred the body and buried it
by the banks of the Verde (i.e. the Liris). " This, however," says
Villani, " we do not affirm." The story, made much of by the Ghibelline
Dante (*Purgat.*, cant. iii) condemns itself. If the bishop had wished
further to dishonour Manfred's body, he would not have troubled to
transport it from the Calore to the Liris. Modern *Ghibellines* also have
cherished the story and " the priestly hatred " (Balzani, *The Popes
and the Hohenstaufen*, p. 244) of " the low-minded bishop Pignatelli,"
(Gregorovius, *Rome*, v, 394) is duly held up to scorn.   Both these
authors fail to tell their readers how this *cruel* bishop induced Charles
to spare the lives of several of Manfred's nobles after the battle :
" Quibus Rex . . . ad preces B. de Pignatellis . . . vitae veniam . . .
indulserat." Saba, iii, 17, p. 832.

defeated ; and that so many had been killed that the field of battle could not be descried for the number of dead lying upon it. He had, moreover, taken a great number of prisoners, and though, at the moment, he did not know what was the fate of Manfred himself, he had every reason to hope that he would be able to " bring back the Kingdom of Sicily to its traditional devotion to the Roman Church ", and that his efforts would promote " the honour and glory of God, the exaltation and peace of the Church, and the prosperity of the people of the Kingdom ".[1]

A day or two later Charles was able to inform the Pope of the death of Manfred,[2] and Clement himself published broadcast the news of the King's success.[3] The Pontiff was at pains to impress upon his correspondents that he rejoiced, not in the slaughter of men, but in the humbling of the pride of bad men, and in the exaltation of the good. Moreover, in one of his terse eloquent passages, he showed that he expected that not only would the church of Sicily benefit by the victory of Charles, but also Italy, the Latin power in eastern Europe and the Holy Land :   " As a result of this battle, despoiled churches are indemnified, innocent exiles are recalled, perfidy falls but faith arises, Tuscany blooms forth once more, the whole of Italy revives, Achaia is inspirited, the Holy Land breathes once again." [4]

The results of Charles' victory.

Although many of these expectations were never realized, immediate tangible results favourable to the Papacy did follow from the victory of Charles. His military success was complete.   Not only did Manfred's wife,

---

[1] Ep. Feb. 27, 1766, ap. M., ii, n. 236, or Del. G., i, p. 110.

[2] Ep. March 1, ap. Del. G., n. 41.

[3] Epp. nn. 238–40, 244, 257 all of March, 1266, ap. M., ii, p. 285 ff.

[4] Ep. n. 240, March 8. The Archives of Naples show that Charles frequently restored to Churches property that Frederick II. had wrested from them. Cf. Riccio, *Alcune Fatti*, p. 28.

children, and treasure fall into his hands, but the
Saracens of Lucera submitted to him; and practically
all opposition to him ceased, not only on the mainland
but also in the island of Sicily itself.[1] With regard to the
rest of Italy, Clement was able to report the collapse of
almost the whole of the Ghibelline resistance. The March
of Ancona had returned to its allegiance ;   Florence and
Arezzo had accepted terms ; and even Pelavicini and
Pisa had offered conditions of peace, which the Pope
felt strong enough not to accept at once as not sufficiently
favourable. Genoa alone did not show itself disposed to
make peace with the victorious Guelfs.[2]

But in the midst of the triumph of the Guelf cause, Trouble
the fly was not wanting to the ointment. After the rout about the
sack of
of Manfred's army in front of Benevento, the victorious Benevento.
troops of Charles, mad with want of food, with the
shedding of blood, and with lust for gold, poured into the
city. Excesses of every kind were perpetrated by them.
They spared neither age nor sex, neither private dwellings
nor the house of God. And that, too, not merely in the
first heat of victory when they might have been easily
infuriated by the belief that the people had helped
Manfred, but for over a week.[3] Bitterly did the Pope
upbraid Charles for the way in which he had outraged

---

[1] "Totum regnum obedivit Carolo." *Ann. Cavenses*, 1266, ap.
M. G. SS., iii, p. 194. *Cf.* Saba, iii, 12 ; Villani, vii, 10 ; Cronichi
di Sichilia, p. 177, and epp. 257 and 278, ap. Mart., ii, To help the
pacification of Sicily, Clement at once sent thither, along with Philip
de Montfort, the Vicar of Charles, the Archbishop of Cosenza, " whom
we have translated to Messina." Ep. 257.

[2] Epp. 257 and 278 of March 25 and Apr. 8. On the submission of
Florence see also n. 264, Apr. 13, 1266 (with the submission of Florence
" the gate of Tuscany was opened—janua panditur ad salutem totius
Tusciæ ") ; n. 288, May 16 ; n. 345, July 27 ; 409–12, Nov. 20–2.

[3] Saba, iii, 12. "Cædes, cæsorumque prædatio vix adhuc die
quiescit octava." *Cf.* epp. Clem., nn. 254 and 262, ap. Mart., ii, pp. 298
and 306 ; and Marinus de Maurellis, *ubi supra.* Even some of the clergy,
" who were rejoicing over the victory which had been gained, were slain."

God and man, and the respect due to a city that belonged to the Holy See. With good reason, he indignantly urged, will our mutual foes predict future ill-treatment from such a cruel beginning. Well may they ask what sort of a son has the Church chosen, seeing that he injures her in her best loved possessions. Charles must humble himself before God, and make due satisfaction to the outraged city.[1]

Nor did Clement leave the matter of restitution altogether to Charles' initiative. Not in the least pacified by the valuable presents which the King sent him,[2] he appointed Rudolf, cardinal-bishop of Albano, his legate in Benevento and its district, and commissioned him to enforce the restitution, if necessary, by ecclesiastical censures.[3]

As no more appears to be found on this subject in the extant correspondence of either Clement or Charles, and as Charles is known a few weeks later to have sent to the Pope a privilege sealed with a golden bull for the rector and people of Benevento, granting them certain liberties and favours,[4] we may presume that the King made the required restitution.

---

[1] Ep. 262, April 12.   [2] Saba, iii, 14.   [3] Ep. 254, March 25.
[4] July 3, 1266, Potthast, n. 19719.

CHAPTER III.

CHARLES OF ANJOU AND THE KINGDOM OF SICILY FROM
THE DEATH OF MANFRED (1266) TO THE DEATH OF
CONRADIN AND OF CLEMENT HIMSELF (1268).

So decisive was the battle of Benevento that, for the Charles
time at least, the Ghibelline cause at once completely resigns the Senatorship.
collapsed throughout the length and breadth of Italy
and Sicily.[1] Clement could congratulate himself that
through the restoration of the temporal power, the
Papacy would be able to enjoy a little repose. It only
remained for Charles to resign the Senatorship of
Rome, and the Pope would be really independent.
Accordingly, with a view to returning to his capital,
Clement left Perugia (April, 1266), and, passing through
Orvieto, went to Viterbo, with the intention of entering
Rome in the winter, " if he could come to some agreement
with his Roman creditors." [2] Moreover, he refused
Charles' request to be allowed to retain " the dominion
of the city " for some time longer, even in the interests
of the Pope himself. He had urged that " de jure " the
right of appointing the Senator lay with Pope, and had
begged that he would for a time longer secretly confirm
his position as Senator. But when Clement had pointed
out that de facto the right, however unjustly acquired,
belonged to the Roman people, and that it should not

---

[1] *Cf. Gaufred. Malaterræ Contin.*, ap. *R. I. SS.*, v, 606, really the
work of Bro. Conrad of Palermo in 1290. *Cf. ib.*, i, pt. ii, p. 279, whence
we learn that Messina raised the standard of Charles on March 13,
1266, and that Count Philip of Montferat came to Sicily as Charles'
vicar on Apr. 1.

[2] Ep. Apr. 24, 19266, n. 271, ap. Martène, ii, p. 315.

be taken away from them without proper judicial proceedings,[1] the King gave way, and resigned the Senatorship. He, moreover, urged the Roman people to respect the Pope's rights in this matter.[2] However, whether from ambition or from real concern for the interests of the Pope, Charles was not well pleased at having to resign, and Clement had to complain that, for some time, the royal officials kept their positions, and that, even after his resignation, the King had sent letters to him styling himself Senator as usual.[3]

The new Senators.

Clement was, however, to learn by bitter experience that it would probably have been better for him if he had hearkened to Charles' request, and had left him " the dominion of the city " until his power had been thoroughly established. On the resignation of the King, Rome, " with its liberty restored to it " at once forgot law,[4] and elected two senators, Monaldeschi of Orvieto and the Roman, Luca Savelli, the father of Pope Honorius IV., who died during his year of office.[5] These men are set down by Clement as behaving like robbers and thieves, both inside and outside the city.[6] But, as we shall see, after these two undesirables had been succeeded by the Spaniard, Henry of Trastamare (Don Arrigo of Castile) brother of the would-be emperor Alfonso of Castile, Clement was glad once again to acknowledge Charles of Anjou as Senator. The Spaniard, though a cousin of Charles, was to prove one of his worst

---

[1] Ep. May 15, 1266, ap. M., ii, n. 285.

[2] Ib. Hence the resignation of Charles took place before May 15.

[3] Ib.

[4] Ep. June 15, n. 310, ap. ib., p. 353. " Ecce Roma suæ reddita libertati in sua conversa jam viscera nescit legem."

[5] Cf. the inscription on his tomb in the right transept of the Church of S. Maria in Ara Coeli or in Capitolio. " Hic jacet Dns. Lucas de Sabello pat. Dni Ppe. Honorii, Dni Johis, et Dni. Pandulfi, qui obiit dum esset Senator Urbis " A.D. MCCLXVI.

[6] Ep. 310.

enemies, and, through the support he was to give to
Conradin, was almost able to ruin his relative.

Meanwhile, however, tolerably well satisfied with the Trouble in the King-
state of affairs in Italy, rejoicing that " Sicily had dom, 1266.
arisen from the dead, and that Tuscany, and the
Marquis Pelavicini, with the peoples of Cremona and
Piacenza, and other nobles of his party, had bowed to
the will of the Church ",[1] Clement now devoted his
attention to promoting the interests of a Crusade for the
benefit of the Holy Land.[2] He also strove to clear off
the mortgage he had put upon certain possessions of the
Churches in Rome [3]—the more so that those " robbers
and thieves ", the two Senators were trying to foreclose
the mortgages.[4]

Whilst the Pope was thus employed, Charles, by his
avarice and tyranny, and possibly even by unwise
leniency, was preparing trouble both for Clement and for
himself. The King began well. At a parliament held in
Naples, he proclaimed a general amnesty [5] ; but, in order
to reward his numerous French followers, he greatly
increased the taxes, and placed his supporters in positions
of authority, endowing them with the fiefs of the
conquered.[6] On the other hand, no doubt in the case of
nobler souls who would not stoop " to wring from the
hard hands of peasants their vile trash ", or who would
not accept lands that belonged to others, Charles allowed
many to return to France whom he should have retained

---

[1] Ep. May 15 or 16, n. 288, ap. M., ii, p. 327.

[2] Epp. 293–4 and 300 ap. *ib.*

[3] Epp. 301–4, 309.

[4] Ep. 310.   [5] Saba, iii, 15.

[6] *Ib.*, iii, 15–16. *Cf.* Villani, vii, 10. One result was in the words of
Villani, " Che in poco tempo appresso tutti i Baroni del Regno di
Puglia e gran parte di quelli di Cicilia fecero le comandamenta del
Re Carlo." Another was that in every dispossessed noble il Re had a
bitter enemy.

in Italy, but whom his avarice prevented from rewarding from the royal possessions.[1]

Avarice, we know, has often its explanation in extravagance ; and in the letters in which the Pope blames Charles for greed of gold, he also blames him for reckless expenditure.[2]

Possibly, too, those French and Provençal officials who remained with Charles were more tyrannical than their master. At any rate, they committed offences against the people which called forth frequent strong protests from the Pope, and which he declared that God would not endure. " As I have learnt," wrote Clement to the King, " from religious men worthy of belief, your officials do not fear openly to perpetrate robberies, adulteries, rapine, and exactions of every kind. And since you do not correct or punish these enormities when they are reported to you, you are of a truth defiled by the sins of others. Who can sympathize with that poverty of yours, when you profess that you cannot or know not how to support yourself from the revenues of a Kingdom whence the great Frederick, once emperor of the Romans, was able immensely to enrich himself and his followers, and even though he had greater expenses than you, was further able to satisfy Lombardy, Tuscany, both the Marches, and Germany." [3] Furthermore, the Pope had to

---

[1] It was for this shortsightedness that he was often blamed by Clement. *Cf.* ep. 288, 332, 380, and 462. In the last letter the Pope blames Charles for unfeeling neglect of friends—among others the Italian troubadour Sordello " qui emendus esset immeritus, nedum pro meritis redimendus ", and yet was allowed " to languish " at Novara.

[2] Ep. 462, where he tells his legate to warn Charles " ut . . . expensis inutilibus parceret ". *Cf.* ep. 471, " Et regem Siciliæ pauperem esse noveris, et inordinate consumere bona sua."

[3] Ep. 530, Sept. 15, ap. M., ii, p. 524, " Sane cum regnum tuum pessime laceretur a tuis, tuæ adscribitur culpæ." *Cf.* ep. n. 380, Sept. 22, 1266, in which he warns Charles not to keep what belongs to another, nor to delay the course of justice. Of the King's ministers

blame him for his haughty manner of dealing with his subjects ; for treating the ecclesiastics of his Kingdom contrary to the agreement he had made with him [1] ; for unduly proroguing his parliaments [2] ; and for not realizing that, in the Saracens, Greeks, Germans, and great maritime cities, he had perchance fewer friends than secret enemies " who cannot love you nor your nation ".[3]

The result of his lust of money, and of his haughty disregard of the rights of others displayed by Charles and his officials,[4] was that the régime of Manfred began to be regretted. Now that he was dead, only his bright qualities were remembered. The man whom his former subjects had regarded as a rapacious wolf was now thought of by them as a gentle lamb. Then they proceeded to carry their complaints of " the hard and insupportable dominion of the French " to all the enemies of Charles throughout the length and breadth of Italy.[5] Finally a number of those whose lives Charles had spared at the request of the papal legate,[6] repaired to Germany in order " to rouse the sleeping whelp ",[7] i.e., the young Conradin,

Appeal to Conradin against Charles, 1266.

it is commonly stated " quod tibi subtrahunt et tuis auferunt quidquid possunt " ; ep. 432 (Feb. 5, 1267), in which he tells him that if he is poor, it is because he neglects his estates (massaria or massaritia or massarum is a farm), and " hæc est enim vita regum Siciliæ ". His taxes are turning all his people against him, and will involve both himself and the Pope " in extreme confusion " ; epp. 433, 462, 471, 504 (a splendid letter full of good advice for the good government of a country) ; etc.

[1] Ep. nn. 343, 380, 433, and 462.

[2] Ep. 315, May 21 or 22, ap. M., ii, p. 356.   [3] Ep. 332.

[4] Cf. Anon. Chron. rythm., ap. M. G. SS., xxv, p. 366.

[5] Saba, iii 16.

[6] William of Nangis expresses a great regret that Charles had not put them all to death, " qui secundum leges pœnam mortis debuerant incurrisse." Gesta S. Ludovici, ap. R. F. SS., xx, p. 426. Cf. Villani, vii, 10.

[7] Saba, iii, 17. Cf. Jamsil. contin., p. 610 ; and Barth. de Neocast., c. 8 ; Villani, vii, 23 ; Hermann of Altaich, an. 1268.

now 15 years old, the only legitimate survivor of the offspring of Frederick II. The envoys were successful in their quest. Against the advice of his mother, who was naturally opposed to the idea of a mere boy undertaking such an arduous enterprise, but relying on the support of his uncle, Louis the Severe, Duke of Bavaria,[1] the youthful Conradin declared that he would make the attempt to recover his father's Sicilian crown.[2] He accordingly, signing himself King of Jerusalem and Sicily, issued a manifesto to all the German Princes. In it, after denouncing both the Popes, to whose guardianship when " an unweaned babe " he had been committed, and also his uncle Manfred, who had been false to him,[3] he declared his intention to fight for the recovery of his father's crown. As his efforts were to be directed against Charles and not against the Pope, whom he regarded as his father and lord,[4] he begged the Princes to urge Clement to lay aside his " fury " against him.[5] At the same time, however, he tried to secure the help of the Sultan Bibars, the enemy of the Christian name.[6]

Action of the Pope against Conradin, Sept.–Nov., 1266.

Through the publication of some manifesto or letters similar in tone to the one just mentioned, Clement was

---

[1] *Ann. S. Rudbert*, an. 1267, ap. *M. G. SS.*, ix, 798.

[2] *Cf.* Villani, *l.c.*, and Conradin's own manifesto ap. *Chron. Siciliæ* c. 34, ap. *R. I. SS.*, x, p. 824 ff.

[3] Manifesto, p. 825. " Reciprocavit (Manfred) ad se negotium dicti regni, mentitus est regnicolis mortem nostram . . . pseudo-regem se fecit."

[4] " Non ut adversus eumdem Pontificem generalem contrarium aliquid cogitemus, quem patrem reputamus et dominum." *Ib.*, p. 827.

[5] This particular manifesto was only issued after May 23, 1268, when Clement named Charles Vicar of the Empire. With the manifesto compare ep. n. 471, ap. M., ii, p. 472.

[6] *Cf.* Reinaud, *Chron. arab.* in *Biblioth. des Croisades*, iv, pp. 515–16, and Mas Latrie, *Traités de Paix*, pp. 134–5. *Cf. Ann. Cavenses*, an. 1267, ap. *M. G. SS.*, iii, p. 194 f., for the rising in his behalf of the Saracens in Lucera.

made aware that Conradin was aiming at setting aside
both the claimants to the Empire, and at dethroning
Charles of Anjou. He therefore addressed a letter
(September 18) to Wernher, archbishop of Cologne, and
to other ecclesiastical princes in Germany. In it he
pointed out how the fact that the ungrateful "house of the
impious Frederick once emperor of the Romans" had
scourged the Church was well known, not merely "to
the churches and princes of Germany", but to the world.
By a just judgment, he had been deprived of the empire
and of Sicily, and, owing to the death of his sons, there
was left only "one little spark in a house of so great a
name". This was Conradin, "young indeed in years,
but, as we have heard on good evidence, of premature
wickedness." Plotting with enemies of the Church from
Lombardy, the March, Tuscany, Apulia, and Sicily,
he was aiming both at the Empire, although there were
already two candidates for it, and he himself was ineligible
from want of age, and, moreover, at the throne of Sicily,
although Charles of Anjou had been constituted its true
King by the Apostolic See.[1] All such as should help
Conradin to accomplish either of these purposes were
declared excommunicated, and Conradin was warned
that the power which, on account of his wrongdoing had
deprived his grandfather of the Empire and of the
Kingdom of Sicily, could deprive him also of the Kingdom
of Jerusalem, and of any other dignities which he might
possess. Two months later this letter was included in a
process against Conradin, which, in order to ensure its

---

[1] With these aims of Conradin the Pope became acquainted from
letters of his, sealed with a royal seal, which he had himself seen.
"Literas suas disseminat sub sui expressione nominis . . . typario
regie majestatis empressas." *Cf.* the first "process" against Conradin
issued by Clement, Nov. 18, 1266, ap. Rodenberg, iii, p. 667 ; Potthast,
n. 19815.

publicity, was affixed to the door of the Cathedral of
Viterbo.[1]

Clement
does not
fear the
coming of
Conradin.
Although Clement took these prompt measures against
Conradin, it would appear that he did not expect that
the lad would make any serious attempt on Sicily.
Hence, as he told cardinal Simon of St. Martini, when
he had heard from him that certain men from the March
had sent envoys to their " idol, the youth Conradin ",
he was not much concerned by their traitorous conduct.
He merely thought they were very stupid to suppose
that Charles, who had recently defeated a wise and rich
King, was not more than a match for a " naked poor
boy ".[2]

Month followed month, and the rumours that Conradin
was preparing to make an armed descent on Sicily
became more persistent ; but still Clement does not
appear to have believed that there was real fire behind
the smoke.   It is true that he continued to take some
precautions.   He warned, for instance, various Guelf
cities of the designs of Conradin.[3]   In strong language
he told the Florentines that the poisonous offspring
of the snake was infecting various parts of Tuscany
with his noxious breath.   " The improvident youth
Conradin " was sending Guido Novello and other traitors
into Tuscany to bribe and cajole men to declare for him.
They were said to be busy hiring German mercenaries,
and making treaties.   He, however, had urged Charles

----

[1] The *process* was dated Nov. 18, 1266, ap. Rod., *l.c.*, p. 666 ff. :
" Ut autem hujusmodi processus ad omnium notitiam deducatur,
cartas sive membranas continentes eundem in hujus majoris ecclesiæ
Viterbiensis civitatis appendi . . . hostiis . . . faciemus." P. 670.
It should be noted that the *process* opens with a statement of the great
judicial care with which the sentence of deprivation against Frederick
had been passed.

[2] Ep. Oct. 16, n. 392, ap. M., ii, p. 416.

[3] Epp. 450–1.

to send troops into Tuscany,[1] and to go thither himself in order to expel these disturbers of the peace. Further, as the Empire was vacant, he took upon himself to name the King, " Peacemaker general (paciarium generalem)," not, they must notice, " Party-supporter (panciarium)." [2] Still, months after the dispatch of this letter, Clement continued to assert that, though reports of the coming of Conradin were becoming more frequent, he believed they would again die down, as they had done before, and that he would not come into Italy.[3]

Meanwhile, however, he made it known to Conradin that, if he did not give up his pretentions, he was to be regarded as excommunicated,[4] and he summoned him to reply in his presence before the feast of the Apostles SS. Peter and Paul (June 29) to charges made against him. Then on Nov. 18, as Conradin, so far from abandoning his pretensions, had entered Verona in arms, Clement before a great number of people in the cathedral of Viterbo solemnly declared that he and his followers had incurred the said sentence of excommunication ;

Conradin is excommunicated, April, 1267.

---

[1] *Cf.* ep. 427, ap. M., ii, p. 440, Jan. 18, 1267. *Cf.* S. Terlizzi, *Le realzioni di Carlo I. con la Toscana* (1265–85), Rome, 1906. An extract from the *Atti del Congresso*, Rome, 1903.

[2] Ep. 450, Apr. 10, 1267. *Cf.* Thos. of Tuscany, ap. *M. G. SS.*, xxii, p. 520 : " Paciarium eum vocat, mandans ut omnes ad pacem recipiat, qui ei voluerint obedire." *Cf.* epp. Clem., nn. 492, 494, 512, ap. Mart., ii, p. 499 f. In the first of these letters he says he has made Charles " pacis servatorem " ; and that, in making the appointment, he was following the example of his predecessors who made such appointments when the Empire was vacant or was inoperative (imperio fluctuante). He had arranged for Charles to lay down this office within a month after the settlement of the Empire. *Cf.* epp. June 4, nn. 589 to 591, ap. *Reg.*, i, p. 200 f.

[3] Ep. 530, p. 524, Sept. 15. " Si venerit in Italiam, quod non credimus, etc." *Cf.* ep. 464, May 11, 1267.

[4] *Reg.*, i, n. 601, p. 206. " Alioquin ipsum ex nunc excommunicationis sententia innodamus." Apr. 14, 1267, i.e., Maunday Thursday, the day on which excommunications were wont to be pronounced.

and that Conradin was moreover deprived of his Kingdom of Jerusalem.[1] These decisions were again solemnly renewed on the Maunday Thursday of the following year (April 5, 1268).[2]

Charles at Viterbo, and in Tuscany, 1267.
However, although Clement was convinced that there was no immediate prospect of Conradin's being able to make an armed descent on Italy, he saw the trouble that his agents were causing, and realized how the hope of his coming was everywhere giving life to the Ghibelline party. He was, accordingly, glad when Charles himself appeared before him at Viterbo (April, c. 25). The arrival of the King north of Rome, produced an immediate effect on the political situation. Florence and some other Tuscan cities received him, and named him their podestà for six years, and Clement soon felt justified in asserting that " the Ghibelline power was much depressed ",[3] and that, " though great things were reported about Conradin, they did not seem to him to present any appearance of truth, although they were not altogether to be set at naught." [4] Still, even if Clement was further able to say that, through his envoys, the cities of Lombardy, with the exception of Pavia, were making peace with

[1] See the second *process* against Conradin, ap. *Reg.* i, n. 602, p. 207 ff., Nov. 18, 1267. *Cf. Ann. S. Rudbert*, ap. *M. G. SS.*, ix, 798–9.

[2] *Ib.*, n. 690 ff., p. 250 ff. The Senator of Rome, Henry of Castile, the city of Pisa, etc., were also proceeded against in a similar way, Apr. 5, 1268. Conradin's excommunication had also been renewed on Feb. 28, 1268. *Ib.*, n. 689, p. 249, for his reopening the wounds which Frederick and his " damned brood, dampnata progenies "had inflicted on the Church and its territory. Against the attacks of Conradin and such traitors as Galvano Lancia, Clement was resolved to defend Charles," the strenuous athlete of our Redeemer, and indefatigable right arm (pugil) of the Church." On May 17, 1268, Conradin was declared for ever ineligible for any kingdom. *Cf.* further *processes* against him and his supporters. Ap. *Reg.*, i, n. 699 ff., p. 263 ff.

[3] Ep. 462, *c.* May 11, 1267, " Jam multum depressa est potentia Gibellina." *Cf.* epp. 464, 471, and 512.

[4] Ep. 464, May 11.

each other, and that, as the Empire was vacant,[1] he was
thinking of making Charles, *Captain* of Tuscany, he was
nevertheless driven to admit in confidence to cardinal
Simon de Brion that Charles was trying. Charity,
he said, and the possible peril in front of us, compel
us to love him as much as we can, but he is poor and
extravagant, burdensome to the churches and to all his
subjects, gracious to nobody, and unreliable when it
comes to the point with regard to his promised help
for the Holy Land. " I greatly fear that he will
do very few things well, as he is busy with a great
many." [2]

Among the many schemes which were then occupying
the attention of the ambitious Charles of Anjou was
one for recovering the Latin Empire of Constantinople.
His attention was directed to it by his coming into
possession of Epirus which Helen had brought as a
dower to her husband Manfred, as well as by the appeals
of Baldwin II. Hearkening to the latter, he made a
treaty with the ex-emperor at Viterbo in presence of
the Pope, May 27, 1267.[3] The act, still preserved
in the archives of Naples, sets forth that " in the presence
of our most holy father and lord, by divine providence
Pope Clement IV., who consented thereto, and gave
weight to it by his authority ", it was agreed that, in
return for concessions of territory and of rights of
suzerainty over parts of the Empire, Charles should aid
Baldwin to recover it, and that his daughter Beatrice,
when of marriageable age, should marry Baldwin's son

Charles' treaty with Baldwin.

---

[1] Clement declares that it is well known that " the pacific preservation of the Empire when vacant belongs to him—cujus (the Empire)
ad nos dum vacat, pacifica conservatio noscitur pertinere." Ep.
June 4, 1267, ap. *Reg.*, i, n. 589.

[2] Ep. 471, May 23, 1267.

[3] Henry of Castile was also with the Pope. Ep. May 15, 1267,
M. ii, 468.

and heir Philip.[1]   The attack of Conradin, however, and,
later on, the Sicilian Vespers, prevented Charles from ever
being in a condition to push his ambitious designs on Constantinople by giving help to Baldwin.

Action of the
Pope and of
Charles in
Lombardy
and Tuscany

Though the Pope and Charles may have been convinced
that the coming of Conradin was highly unlikely, they
had no difficulty in seeing that Ghibelline influence
was reviving everywhere, in Tuscany, Lombardy, and
in Rome itself.   To combat this, energetic measures
were taken by both.   In the first instance, Clement
named (July 8) as a new legate in Lombardy and Dalmatia
the warlike archbishop of Ravenna, Philip Fontana,
who, according to Salimbene, was feared by his men-at-
arms as the devil.[3]   The archbishop, who replaced two
who had been sent in 1266, and were reported to have
done much good,[4] was commissioned to reconcile the
Ghibellines to the Church.   About the same time, too,
both the Pope and Charles were successfully using the
sword.   Guido de Pileo, "captain of the Patrimony,"
recovered Bolsena from Orvieto ; and its people swore
allegiance to the Roman Church.   He also recovered
the mountain-city of Aquapendente,[5] which was the last
city of the States of the Church on the road to Siena.

---

[2] Cf. the treaty ap. Del. Giudice, *Diplom.*, ii, p. 30 ff.   *Cf. Chron. of
the Morea*, pp. 147–52, ed. Buchon.   There is no need for us to say more
about this treaty, as it never came to anything.   See on it, Rodd, *The
Princes of Achai*, i, p. 241 ff.   Philip and Beatrice were married at Foggia
in 1273.   See also C. du Fresne, *Hist. de l'Empire de Constantinople*,
lib. v, c. 49, p. 87, ed. Venice, 1729.

[3] *Reg.*, i, nn. 487–8, pp. 154–5.   The first letter is analysed in Raynaldus,
an. 1267, n. 21.   Salimbene, p. 399.

[4] *Chron. de rebus etc.=Ann. Placent.*, pp. 260 and 271.   Ambassadors
from Cremona, Piacenza, Milan, and Brescia told the Pope of the good
the two legates had done.   The Ghibelline chronicler who tells us this
fact, adds that Philip F. was sent " to complete the mischief (malum)
which the two were unable to accomplish ".

[5] *Annales Urbevet.*, an. 1267.   Various other *castra* in the neighbourhood followed the example of Bolsena.

Not far from the last-named city, then a centre of the Ghibellines, Charles too was fighting. About the same time as the appointment of archbishop Fontana as legate, the King had commenced the siege of Poggibonsi (*c.* the middle of July, 1267).[1]

It was whilst Charles was besieging this ally of Siena, that the rumours of the coming of Conradin became still more persistent. Though Clement was even yet not disturbed by these reports as they had hitherto proved false, and because, as he said, he was ready to face such troubles as God might send him,[2] he was, nevertheless, anxious about the state of things in Rome. The two Senators who had succeeded Charles of Anjou, and had shown themselves so objectionable to the Pope,[3] became at length through their support of the nobility hateful to the people also. Under the leadership of Angelo Capocci, the people rose, deprived the two of their power, which they placed in the hands of Angelo and of a number of men chosen from each of the *seven* regions.[4] But as " Captain of the City ", Angelo, even though he had the support of the Pope, was soon in difficulties. Nor were they lessened by a rumour, which he made known to Clement, that they had even been caused by him. In replying to Capocci, the Pope told him that the rumour was a lying one, and that he was so distressed at the troubles in the city that he was sending two bishops to help to quell them. He begged the Captain, as " a peace-loving and modest man, mindful of the devotion

Trouble in Rome.

---

[1] *Ann. Placent.*, p. 273, ed. Huillard-Bréholles. *Cf.* also *Ann. Urb.*, *l.c.*

[2] Ep. 16 or 17 Aug., 1267, ap. Mart., ii, n. 521. " De adventu juvenis Conradini multa dudum audivimus, quæ sicut hactenus æstimavimus, sic et probavimus esse falsa."

[3] *Cf. supra*, 258 f.

[4] *Contin. Jamsil.*, p. 611. " Per quem (Aug. 6) contra Urbis Magnates cœperunt populi quibusdam viris de qualibet Regione VII. electis secum adjunctis, etc." *Cf.* Saba, iii, 19.

which his family had ever exhibited to the Roman Church ", to co-operate with the bishops.[1]

Capocci was unable to hold his own ; and he was bidden, no doubt by the party of the nobles, to resign his authority, and name a Senator. To the annoyance of " very many of the nobles ; and of some of the cardinals who already had their suspicions of his good faith " ; Henry of Castile, then with the Pope at Viterbo, was the man selected by the Captain.[2] The Infante, Henry of Trastamara or of Castile, son of Ferdinand III. of Castile, was the younger brother of Alfonso the Wise, one of the claimants to the title of King of the Romans, and was a cousin of Charles of Anjou. Banished from Castile for treason, he became a soldier of fortune,[3] and for some years served under the Sultan of Tunis against the Moors.[4] Stirred up by the bold enterprise of his kinsmen, he placed his money, his sword, and a company of Castillians at the disposal of Charles (1266).[5] The King received him gladly ; and, according to Villani,[6] it was through his influence that he was elected Senator. He also recommended him to the Pope, who it is said, put him in charge of the fortresses of Tuscany.[7] Whether

---

[1] Ep. July 9, n. 479, ap. Mart., ii, p. 489.

[2] *Contin. J.*, and Saba, *l.c.* Gregorovius, *Rome*, v, 403, calls Capocci a Ghibelline, but it does not appear that there is sufficient authority for the assertion.

[3] *Cf. Mon. Patav. Chron.*, ap. *R. I. SS.*, viii, p. 729. Clement gives Henry the title of *Infans*. *Cf.* G. del Giudice, *Don Arrigo, Infante di Castiglia*, Napoli, 1875.

[4] He was the man fixed upon by Henry III. to uphold in arms the claim of his son Edmund to the crown of Sicily. *Cf.* Rymer, *Fœdera*, i, p. 631.

[5] Villani, vii, 10.

[6] Will. of Nangis, an. 1266, also notes, if too strongly, Charles' influence in obtaining the senatorship for Henry.

[7] The authority is that of a late author L. Bonincontrius, fl.1475, *Hist. Siciliæ*, p. 5, ed. Florence, 1739, cited by Gregorovius, v, p. 405. " Arces quæ in Etruria ecclesiæ Rom. erant, tutandas suscepit."

this is so or not, there is no doubt that Henry of Castile was just as ambitious as Charles of Anjou, and rathei more unscrupulous.[1] Among his other ambitions was the obtaining of the suzerainty over Sardinia, which belonged to the Holy See, and which was also coveted by Charles and by James of Aragon. So well too did he manage the cardinals that he succeeded in having his claims discussed in consistory.[2]

Meanwhile, however, before the Sardinian question became acute, a question arose about the marriage of Henry. With a view, no doubt, to strengthening Charles' claims in Greece, efforts were made to bring about a marriage between a daughter of Michael, despot of Epirus, and the Senator. Through his wife, Helen of Epirus, Manfred had obtained suzerainty over Dyrrachium, the island of Corcyra, and various towns on the mainland opposite to it.[3] It is possible that it was to this particular daughter (Helen) of Michael that Clement and Charles wished to marry Henry.[4] However that may be, both the Pope and Charles were apparently in earnest in their endeavour to bring the marriage about, as the former especially was convinced that it would prove advantageous to the cause of the Latin Empire. But the negotiations for some unknown reason, perhaps the secret jealousy of Charles of Anjou, came to nothing; nor did any result

Question of the marriage of Henry.

---

[1] Will. of Nangis, *Chron.*, an. 1266, says he was : " Nimium callidus sed sceleratissimus et in cultu fidei catholicæ non diligens prosecutor." Saba, iii, 18, attributes to his stay in Tunis his adoption of Moslem beliefs ; and he adds that even the Sultan of Tunis at length suspected him of treason.

[2] Saba, *l.c.*

[3] *Cf.* Miss Gardner, *The Lascarids of Nicæa*, pp. 243-4.

[4] *Cf.* ep. of Charles to Henry, Oct. 27, 1266, ap. Del. G., i, p. 193 ff., and epp. of Clement to Charles and to Henry himself both of Jan. 5, 1267, epp. 422 and 423, ap. Mart., ii, p. 437-8. Del. Giudice, *Don Arrigo*, p. 10 ff., thinks the daughter referred to may be Helen herself, Manfred's widow.

follow subsequent ones to effect a union between Henry and the daughter of the redoubtable James, King of Aragon,[1] the sovereign whom Clement had constantly to rebuke for his matrimonial offences.[2]

Trouble between Henry and Charles *re* Sardinia.

Whilst these negotiations regarding a suitable wife for Henry were in progress, and were seemingly being conducted in good faith, a matter arose which had much to do with fierce enmity breaking out between the Senator and Charles. The internal state of Sardinia had long been very unsatisfactory. The island had for a considerable period been in a state of disorder through the rivalry of the Genoese and Pisans who were both aiming at the practical possession of the island. There was, accordingly, arising among the more peacefully disposed citizens a conviction that it would be best if they brought in a strong outsider to keep order, just as so many cities in Italy had been compelled to call in podestà's from without. As soon as this desire became known, James of Aragon, Charles of Sicily, and Henry, the Senator, at once became candidates for the position. The Pope was now in a most awkward predicament. As overlord of the island, he would be called upon to favour one of the candidates, and would probably make enemies of the other two. It may be doubted whether he really desired to see any one of them lords of the isle. At any rate, he began by urging Henry not to proceed in the matter. He told him that, after consultation with a Genoese knight, he had come to the conclusion that he should not attempt the enterprise. It would be very

---

[1] Ep. May, 15, n. 467, *ib.* Del. Giudice, however, *l.c.*, attributes the failure of the negotiations to Charles' jealousy of Henry.

[2] E.g. epp., July 5, 1266, n. 323, p. 362 ; Jan. 16, 1267, n. 426, *ib.*, p. 440 ; also n. 437, p. 448. He had refused to grant James a divorce as early as Feb. 17, 1266, n. 230, p. 277, and we find him upbraiding the King for imposing "bovage" and other taxes on the churches ; ep. ap. Raynaldus, an. 1266, n. 32. " Agit nec immerito."

costly as he would have to fight against the Pisans who, owing to their geographical position, could most advantageously attack any who should attempt to make a descent upon the island.[1] Some six months later, Clement found a good reason to put an end to the aspirations of all the candidates. As early as August 19, 1266, he had agreed to remove a sentence of excommunication from the Pisans only on condition of their making no further attempts to extend their sphere of influence in the island, especially in the direction of the *Kingdom* (judicatus) of Torres.[2] Twelve months after this, however, he informed the three rivals that he had lost Torres, and that, as the gate of entry to the island was now closed, he could not sanction any further action in the matter. He preferred to lose for a time longer what he had already lost, rather than that serious differences should arise between such important persons.[3]

Serious differences had, however, already arisen between two of the rival candidates for Sardinia, between Henry and Charles. The quarrelsome Henry had not been true either to his brother of Castile, or to the Sultan of Tunis. He was, as we shall see, to be false also to Conradin. His idea was to get him out of the way after he had defeated Charles, and then to get himself crowned King of Sicily in his stead.[4] It would scarcely be expected, therefore, that he should be found true to the Pope and to Charles. On the ground of the Sardinian affair or some other, he had hardly entered Rome as its Senator when he openly showed his hostility to Charles;

Other causes of quarrel between Henry and Charles.

---

[1] Ep. Jan. 5, 1267, n. 423, p. 438.

[2] Ep. n. 337, p. 373.

[3] Ep. July 23, 1267, n. 507, p. 509. "Illam partem amisimus, judicatum scilicet Turritanum, per quem dare poteramus ingressum ei qui conveniret nobiscum." *Cf.* E. Besta, *La Sardegna medioevale*, p. 235 f., and ep. 519, Aug. 13.

[4] So at least says Saba, iv, 7, who had a very low opinion of Henry.

and, to embarrass him, abruptly demanded the repayment of money he had lent him.[1] But, although we find Clement urging Charles to remove this source of quarrel between them by repaying the money,[2] we are assured by Saba that the question of the money was only an excuse, and that the real cause of the quarrel between the cousins was the senator's jealousy of Charles' success.[3]

Henry
begins to
favour
Conradin.

Be that as it may, he was at no pains to conceal his hostility to Charles or his determination to make himself really master of Rome. He even sent to offer Conradin his support and that of the Romans, assuring him, "quite falsely" (mendaciter), that "all Italy" was longing for his coming; that the support of the Ghibellines, at least, would be given to him, and that he would "infallibly" defeat the French.[4]

Clement soon realized that he was wasting his time in trying to persuade Henry to keep the peace with the King.[5] Within a few weeks after Henry's entry into the city, he had written to forbid the nobles and people of the Tuscan patrimony and of the Sabina to pay any attention to the pretensions of the Senator.[6] A little later, he had occasion to communicate his suspicions of him to Charles,[7] and to warn the King's Vicar to watch

---

[1] According to Ricobaldi, ap. *R. I. SS.*, ix, p. 136, Charles would not repay the money he had received from Henry, nor fulfil the promises which he had made to him. *Cf.* D'Esclot, *Cron.*, c. 60, p. 609, ed. Buchon, who calls Henry 'N'Anrich' and makes Charles say, "Per ma fe! ço dix Carles, vos podets anar lla hon vos vullats, mas del tresor yo ara nous en retre gents."

[2] Ep. Sept. 26, 1267, ap. Mart., ii, n. 537. *Cf.* ep. 555.

[3] Saba, iii, 19.

[4] *Ib.*   [5] Ep. July 26, 1267, n. 508.

[6] Ep. 514, July 30. *Cf.* ep. 523.

[7] Ep. 518, Aug. 13, 1267. He tells Charles that to his complaints Henry "verba verbis reddiderit". *Cf.* ep. 532, Sept. 17, where he tells him that Henry is mounting great engines of war on the towers of Rome.

the passes of the Kingdom against a possible attack from Henry.[1]

Meanwhile whilst Charles was still besieging Poggibonsi, Conradin, "with a small force and with little sense," starting for Italy on September 8, entered Verona on October 21.[2] His banner also, through the connivance of the Senator Henry, had been publicly elevated in Rome by Galvano Lancia, a few days before (Oct. 18).[3] Even after Conradin had actually started for Italy, Clement was still sceptical about his intention of joining issue with Charles.[4] Nevertheless, as the rumours of the Germans' coming were rapidly becoming more and more emphatic, he began to be anxious about the military position of Charles. He was too far away from the Kingdom. Clement was convinced that he ought to return to it at once, especially in view of the fact that he had such an enemy as Henry in his rear.[5] The Pope, moreover, expressed his willingness again to recognize Charles as Senator for a time, if he could contrive to subdue Henry who was moreover styling himself "captain-general of Tuscany",[6] and mounting great engines on the walls of Rome.[7] To add to these dangers, Ghibellines, under Henry's brother, Frederick, had made a descent on Sicily proper, with a force of Germans, and Saracens, and

Conradin enters Italy, 1267.

---

[1] Ep. Aug. 26, ap. Del. G., ii, p. 63.

[2] *Chron. de rebus = Ann. Placent.*, p. 271 ; *Ann. Mellicenses*, an. 1268, ap. *M. G. SS.*, ix, 509 f. *Cf. Regest. Imp.*, v, pp. 895–7.

[3] See Clement's letter, Oct. 21, to "the Rectors of the Roman Fraternity", ap. Potthast, 20147. *Cf.* Raynaldus, an. 1267, nn. 17–18. *Cf.* ep. of Cl., n. 556, Nov. 16, ap. M., ii, p. 540, where he speaks Henry "Galvanum Lanceam in Urbem cum armatis, expanso Corradini vexillo inducens ". See also n. 569.

[4] Ep. Sept. 15, n. 530.

[5] *Ib. Cf.* nn. 532 and 566.

[6] Ep. Dec. 17 to Charles, n. 568, ap. *ib.*, p. 547. " Scias, fili quod si potes Senatum Urbis acquirere ad tempus competens, tolerabimus."

[7] Ep. Sept. 17, to Charles, n. 532.

of men from Tunis,[1] and the Senator Henry was concluding an alliance (Nov. 18 ff.) with the Communes of Pisa
and Siena and their Ghibelline allies.[2]   Charles, however,
boldly continued the siege of Poggibonsi, even after he
was certain of the advent of Conradin into Italy.   The
place fell into his hands on Nov. 28.[3]

Action of Clement on hearing of the arrival of Conradin.
Sometime in October Clement learnt for certain that
Conradin, " the seed of the basilisk," had entered Italy.[4]
He at once resolved to send a legate, as soon as he could
find a suitable one, with full powers (generalem legatum)
to Germany, in order that he might stir up opposition
to Conradin in that country.[5]   He then issued processes
or condemnatory proclamations against the invader,[6]

[1] *Ib.*, " Illud vero iterato concludimus, quod et scripsimus tibi
nuper, ut ad Lombardiam intrandam nullatenus te involvas." *Cf.* ep.
559.

[2] *Cf.* documents in *Siena-Roma*, Siena, 1895, n. 28 ff., p. 37. A
document, n. 246, p. 167, in Kern, *Acta Imperii*, Tübingen, 1911, shows
that relations between Clement and Siena had been strained. King
Charles afterwards made the Sienese pay for the alliance. *Cf.* n. 32
in *Siena-Roma*.

[3] *Ann. Urbevet.*, ap. *R. I. SS.*, t. xv, p. 157, new ed. *Cf.* ep Clem.,
n. 582 ; and Simone della Tosa, *Annal.*, p. 140 f.

[4] Epp. 546, Oct. 26 ; 548, Potthast, 20172.

[5] Epp. 546, 583.

[6] Nov. 18, Viterbo, ap. *Reg.*, i, n. 602.   This " sentence " he dispatched to the " Rectors of the Roman fraternity " to be published
in the city.   Ep. 561, Nov. 26, ap. Mart., ii, p. 544.   The Pope's first
letter to the " Fraternity " against Lancia is dated Oct. 21, and may
be read in full ap. *Liber Censuum*, ii, p. 15.   The *Fraternitas Romana*,
an association of the clergy of the city of Rome not attached to the papal
court was fully developed in the twelfth century, acquired its greatest
powers in the fourteenth century, and began to decay in the same
period.   In the twelfth century, by means of papal privileges and by
gradually acquired rights, the association exercised through its chiefs,
its rectors, many of the powers which were afterwards exercised by
such different functionaries or bodies as the papal vicar (vicarius
apostolicus), the tribunal of the ecclesiastical vicariat of Rome, and
the chamberlain of the clergy.   These rights were the surveillance of
the services performed in the churches, the management of clerical

and against the Senator [1] who, he had already assured Charles, was feared " like lightening ",[2] and whom he denounced for imprisoning a number of Guelf Roman nobles, including Angelo Malabranca, John Savelli, and other relatives of cardinals, driving their families out of their homes, and then fortifying them along with St. Peter's and the Vatican.[3] He moreover encouraged the Hospitallers to take up arms against the enemies of Charles, though, as he said, he was aware that by their vows they were only to fight the Saracens. This he did, on the ground that these enemies were worse than the Saracens, and with help obtained from the Saracens of Tunis, were disturbing the peace of Sicily.[4]

Further, to strengthen Charles' position in Tuscany, " which for a long time had been cruelly torn with internal dissensions," he proceeded to increase his power, at least as far as higher titles may carry increased authority, " within the boundaries of Tuscany which were subject to the Empire." He had already named

funerals and of religious processions, the distribution of the *presbyterium* (donative), the execution of papal decrees regarding the personnel of the clergy, the right of excommunicating such as, summoned before their tribunal, did not present themselves, the right of judging in first instance differences which arose among clerics—everything in fine which concerned the economical and moral interests of the city clergy. *Cf.* G. Ferri, " La Romana Fraternitas," ap. *Archivio Rom. di storia patria,* 1903, p. 414 ff., from which this note is directly taken. For daily business, the rectors met in the church of St. Thomas " de Fraternitate " or " in capite molarum ", or S. Tommaso a Cenci by the island of the Tiber. *Cf.* Armellini, *La chiese di Roma,* p. 572. The main body of the Roman Fraternity usually met at S. Salvatore in Pensili near the circus Flaminius. The account of the *Frat.* in Armellini, *l.c.,* p. 20 ff., is not so good as that of Ferri.

[1] N. 566, Nov. 16, ap. M., ii, p. 540.

[2] Ep. n. 532, Sept. 17.

[3] *Cf.* epp. 556, 559 (Nov. 23), and 563. *Cf.* Saba, iii, 20. " D. Henricus omnes nobiles Urbis Guelfos una hora simul in Capitolio ad instar piscium quando plures uno tractu capiuntur, etc."

[4] Ep. 541, Oct. 15, 1267. *Cf.* ep. 559, " Pars magna Siciliæ rebellavit." *Cf.* Saba, iii, 18, iv, cc. 2 and 3. See Del. Giud., ii, p. 81 n.

the King, *Paciarius* of that district. Now as disorder, he complained, was growing therein, " we who have the care of the unsettled Empire constitute you its Vicar-general in those regions." [1]

He was anxious also to increase Charles' power by a suitable second marriage, as his first wife Beatrice had died in July, 1267 ; and he suggested the daughter of James of Aragon. [2]

Finally, in view of the pretensions of the Senator who, styling himself Captain-general of Tuscany, was expecting troops from there with which to attack the Kingdom, he kept begging Charles to return to it forthwith. [3] At the same time, however, he showed himself most anxious to make a peaceful arrangement with the Senator, so as to avoid coming into open conflict with the Romans. [4]

Charles at length returns to the King-dom, 1268.

Events, however, did not move as the Pope would have had them. Despite some attempts at dissimulation, the Senator took care that Rome was more and more committed to the support of Conradin. [5] Charles, moreover, even when master of Poggibonsi, would not return " to make headway against the troubles which had arisen

---

[1] Ep. 625, p. 587, Feb. 15, 1268, *cf.* ep. 626. John, xxii, in his second indictment (*processus*) of Louis of Bavaria, appeals to this action of Clement IV., and to similar action of Clement V. Ap. Mart., ii, p. 650.

[2] Ep. 568, Dec. 17, 1267 ; but in March, 1268, the Pope had to tell Charles of her death. Ep. 610. *Cf.* ep. 644 on Charles' new marriage.

[3] Ep. Dec. 14, 1267, n. 566. *Cf.* epp. of Jan. 14, n. 572 ; of Jan. 25, n. 592, and of March 28, 1268, ap. Raynaldus, an. 1268, n. 3 ; or *Reg.*, i, 1337. See particularly ep. Feb. 7, n. 602.

[4] Epp. 554, 558, 559 of Nov. 13, 20, 23. In the last letter which he wrote : " Nos quantum possumus guerram fugimus Romanorum sed timemus ne et nos et regem Siciliæ cum iisdem finaliter male concordare possimus." *Cf.* ep. 569, Dec. 18, in which he tells Henry that if Manfred, could not resist Charles, he must not expect that Conradin will be able to. *Cf.* also ep. 572, Dec. 28 ; 573, 602-3.

[5] See the treaty made between the city with Pisa and the other Ghibelline cities of Tuscany, Nov. 18, 1267, ap. Del. G., ii, n. 18. *Cf.* ep. Clem., n. 559, ap. Mart., ii, p. 542 f.

in his Kingdom, both on the mainland, and especially in Sicily, of which he had already lost a great part." The fact was that the King, angry with the Pisans for negotiating with Conradin, who with Louis, duke of Bavaria and other German nobles was still at Verona, proceeded to make war upon them. This, wrote the Pope to the legate Simon in France, has displeased me very much. One can only hope that his idea may have a happy issue.[1]

Meanwhile at Verona the youthful Conradin, for some time at least, cannot have been regarding his position as altogether satisfactory. He had, indeed, been promised the assistance of Pavia to enable him to reach Pisa, inasmuch as a number of Apulian nobles had promised him large sums of money when he should reach that city.[2] But, on the other hand, the Duke of Bavaria, the count of Tyrol and others were very urgent for him to return to Germany with his whole force.[3] Then, when inflamed with the hopeful ardour of youth, Conradin refused to listen to their advice, the Duke and the Count, influenced we are told by the excommunication issued by the Pope, abandoned their young leader, and returned to Germany.[4] Undeterred, however, by this serious

---

[1] Ep. 582, Feb. 14, 1268. Despite the fact that the Pisans had become reconciled to the Pope, and had deposited 30,000 pounds with him as security for their loyalty to the Roman Church (mandatis Ecclesiæ observandis firmiter) they appear to have been very ready to join Conradin, *Chron. Pisan.*, ap. *R. I. SS.*, vi, p. 196. *Cf. Chron. de rebus, etc.=Ann. Placent.*, p. 274 f. Even the victories which Charles had gained over them, and which forced them to make a treaty with him about the beginning of 1268, did not suffice to prevent them from supporting Conradin. The Pope had conceived the greatest hopes from this success of Charles. He believed it would make Conradin withdraw, and confound the Senator and the traitors in Sicily. Ep. Jan. 22, 1268, n. 599.

[2] *Ann. Placent.*, p. 274.   [3] *Ib.*

[4] Ann. S. Rudb. ; John of Victring, etc., cited by Böhmer, *Regest. imp*, v, n. 4848a. *Cf.* ep. 606 of Clement to Ottocar, King of Bohemia,

blow, Conradin boldly set out for Pavia (Jan. 17, 1268), where he remained about two months (Jan. 20–March 20). At the last-named date, he left that city where Clement believed he was dreaming his time away, oppressed by want of everything,[1] and reached Pisa on April 5,[2] where he received an enthusiastic reception.[3] The successful way in which Conradin, eluding the troops of Charles who occupied posts between Pavia and Pisa, got to the coast, and thence, by boat, reached the great maritime city of the Ghibellines, alarmed the Pope. Nor was his anxiety lessened by a knowledge of the fact that Conradin, in imitation of his grandfather, had tried to secure the help of the Mameluke Sultan Bibars.[4] Moreover, even if he knew that the young Prince had not obtained much from him except words, he knew that, with Moslem help, Sicily was being withdrawn from the allegiance of Charles, and that, although they had been well treated by Charles, the Saracens of Lucera were in rebellion against their King.[5]

Clement now redoubled his appeal to Charles to return to the Kingdom. Alarmed at length himself, the King made his way to Viterbo, and remained with the Pope nearly the whole of April (4–30).[6]

---

in which he denounces the folly and bad faith "of the Dukes of Bavaria who with more childish thoughts than those of the boy" led him into Italy and then deserted him. March 28, 1268. *Cf.* n. 608.

[1] "Corradinus Papiæ somniat egestate depressus, et gentem habens modicam, etc." wrote Clement on March 16, 1268. Ep. 614, p. 581. In ep. 620 he announces his arrival in Pisa, "in die cœnæ Domini." *Cf. Ann. Placent.*, p. 278 f.

[2] Roncioni, *Istorie Pisane*, p. 562.

[3] *Ann. Placent.*, an. 1268, p. 279. *Cf. Chron. Pisan., l.c.* Ep. Clem., n. 620.

[4] Makrizi, ap. Michaud, *Bib. des Croisades*, iv, p. 516. See *supra*.

[5] Ep. Feb. 12, 1268, n. 605, p. 575. *Cf. Chron. Placent.*, p. 279.

[6] *Cf.* epp. 620, p. 585, Apr. 12, and ep. 630, p. 589, May 1, 1268. *Cf. Chron. de rebus = Annal. Placent.*, p. 279.

Both Clement and the King at once turned their Charles'
attention to Rome, as the Senator Henry (Don Arrigo) failure and
had completely got the upper hand of the Guelfs. A success in
popular assembly at which were present " the consuls of Rome.
the merchants and the heads of the Arts (priors of the
guilds) ", and which, as usual, was held in the Church
of our Lady on the Capitol (or in Aracoeli), had concluded
a treaty with Pisa, Siena, and the Ghibellines of Tuscany
against Charles (Nov. 18 and Dec. 1, 1267).[1] On the
other hand, Clement had had to inform the King that
he had completely failed to secure a footing in the city.[2]
It was clearly therefore necessary for Charles to attempt
to prevent the Senator from being able . to introduce
his rival into Rome. Accordingly, after Clement had
renewed his excommunication of Conradin and of all his
contumacious supporters, and had, in the event of Henry's
continued opposition promised Charles the Senatorship
for ten years,[3] the King dispatched to the Eternal City
a force of some two thousand men, partly French and
partly Italians with such Guelf nobles as the count of
Anguillara. But he had completely underrated the
power of the Senator. With the Ghibelline nobles,
Jacopo Napoleone, Peter de Vico, some of the Anibaldi,
and his vicar, Guido de Montefeltro, Henry fell upon
Charles' force, and completely destroyed it, April 23.[4]

[1] Cf. documents in Gregorovius, Rome, v, pp. 420–2, from the
Archives of Siena.

[2] Ep. Sept. 17, 1267, n. 532, ap. M., ii, p. 526, " Scias tamen post
collationes diversas, nos adhuc nullum aditum invenisse."

[3] Documents from April 1 to 5, ap. Del Giud., ii, p. 142, Reg., i, n. 689 ff.;
Potthast, n. 20310 ; and Raynaldus, Annal., 1268, n. 4 ff. Cf. G.
Villani, vii, 23.

[4] Ann. Placent., p. 279. Cf. epp. Clem., nn. 636, 638, 662, of May 4
and 11, and June 13, 1268 ; Del G., ii, p. 160 n., doubts, as it appears
to us without sufficient reason, the truth of this Roman expedition,
which rests, he says, on the sole testimony of the Ghibelline Annals of
Piacenza. But the Annales Normannici, ap. M. G. SS., xxvi, p. 516,
after speaking of some of Henry's excesses, add : " Unde ad ipsum
debellandum ex jussu pape rex Sicilie exercitum mittit."

Alarmed by this defeat and by the rebellion of the Saracens of Lucera, Charles at length hearkened to the repeated exhortations of the Pope,[1] and withdrew to his Kingdom in order to undertake the siege of the Saracen stronghold (April 30).[2] The road was now open for Conradin to enter Rome. Envoys came thence to urge him to come without delay.[3] The youthful leader answered the call. Charles' marshal in Tuscany was defeated at the bridge de la Valle d'Arno, June 25 [4]; and the Pope from the walls of Viterbo, to which for his protection he had summoned assistance from Perugia and Assisi,[5] descried the large Ghibelline army devastating the district on its march to Rome.[6]

But Clement was not in the least daunted by the successes of Conradin; and he strove to inspire Charles' followers with a spark of his own courage. Writing to Guido Guerra, the count Palatine of Tuscany, and to Charles' Vicar and the Florentines, on the defeat of the King's marshal, he reminds them that it is not the time to think of misfortunes, but of facing the enemy with greater bravery and spirit. " Let not then your faces fall on this account; nor let your courage droop, but

---

[1] Repeated as late as the close of March. *Cf.* ep. of Clement ap. Del Giud., ii, p. 140 ff. " Usque ad contristationem litteris inculcatis monuimus, adjuravimus et rogavimus, mandata precibus annuentes, quod dimissa in Tuscia parte militie cum residua rediret ad regnum."

[2] Ep. 649, May 28, 1268. *Cf.* ep. 650.

[3] *Ann. Plac.*, p. 280.

[4] *Cf.* Conradin's letter announcing the fact to the Lombards, ap. *ib.*, or Del Giud., ii, p. 157 ff.; or *Ann. Placent., l.c. Cf.* ep. Clem., 669, July 4 ; and epp. 672, 677, 684. Villani, vii, 24, describes the site of the battle as at the bridge at Valli which crosses (*cf.* 664) the Arno near Laterino.

[5] Epp. of June 13 and July 15, nn. 663 (*cf.* 664), and 675, ap. M., ii, pp. 609, 616, or Del G., ii, p. 160 ff.

[6] " Corradinus ipse per faciem summi Pontificis et dominorum cardinalium . . . non erubescit cum copiosa Gebellinorum multitudine pertransire." Saba, iv, 6.

like men full of faith and virtue, take heart of grace, and resist the enemy like men." [1] And James de Voraigne, then provincial Prior of the Dominicans of Lombardy, who was present on the occasion, tells us that, when all were in fear, the Pope, preaching in their Church on the feast of Pentecost, bade them not be frightened because " we know that this youth is being led by evil men like a lamb to the slaughter ; and we know that, after the articles of faith, there exists no higher knowledge than this.[2] "

Meanwhile, however, if the Pope did not lose heart, matters continued to go against his ally, King Charles. On July 24, Conradin made a triumphal entry into Rome, and that city, at heart Ghibelline, says Saba,[3] gave him a reception beyond all comparison more magnificent than that which it had accorded to Charles of Anjou.[4] A Ghibelline fleet, which had left Pisa a few days before this " quasi imperial " reception of Conradin, in order to co-operate with him, sailed to the island of Ischia (Aug.) ; and, after perpetrating the most atrocious cruelties there, made its way to Sicily.[5]

Supplied with money which the Senator had procured by plundering the churches,[6] and joined by him and by many of the Romans, Conradin left Rome (Aug. 18), The battle of Tagliacozzo, August 23, 1268.

---

[1] Ep. 669, July 4, 1268, ap. M., ii, 613. *Cf.* ep. 672.

[2] *Chron. Januense*, c. 6, ap. *R. I. SS.*, ix, p. 50. Geoffroy de Courlon (*Chron.* an. 1262), among others, gives a slightly different version of the Pope's *prophecy* as he calls it : " Factum Corradini tam quam fumum transiturum, et ipsum tam quam ad victimam intraturum."

[3] iv, 6, " Naturaliter imperialis existit."

[4] *Ib.* *Cf. Contin.* of Will. of Tyre, ap. P.L., t. 201, p. 1046.

[5] *Cf.* documents in Del G, ii, p. 170 f. *Cp. Chron. de rebus = Ann. Placent.*, p. 281 ; Barthol. de Neocast., c. 8.

[6] Saba, iii, 20–1 ; *Contin. Jamsil.*, p. 613 ; Thos. of Tuscany, ap. *M. G. SS.*, xxii, p. 522. Henry even seized the deposits of money which for safety's sake many people were in the habit of entrusting to different churches. *Cf. Annal. Norman.*, ap. *M. G. SS.*, xxvi, p. 516. Ep. Clem., 635, May 3, 1268.

and followed the road towards the Abruzzi which had been taken by Charles when he marched against Manfred.[1] His plan was to effect a junction with the Saracens of Lucera. Charles, however, on hearing that his enemy had left Rome, raised the siege of Lucera,[2] and promptly advanced to meet him. The two armies joined battle on the plain of San Palentino (Valentino), a few miles from Tagliacozzo. The decisive contest which took its name from this town resulted in the total defeat and flight of Conradin ; and, with his death, in the end of the Hohenstaufen line, and of the German power in Italy (Aug. 23).[3]

On the field of battle (in Campo Palentino) and on the very day of the battle, Charles wrote to tell the Pope of the great victory he had gained. He would have the sovereign Pontiff arise, eat of the fruit of his son's hunting, thank God for the favours He had granted, and at length find rest from his toils. After having unfolded to the Pope in some detail the course of the battle near Lake Fucino, Charles assured him that his victory had been so complete that the number of the slain at Bene-vento was not to be compared with that at Tagliacozzo. The King closed his letter by saying that, of the fate of Conradin and the Senator he was at the moment quite ignorant.[4]

As soon as he had received the King's letter, Clement himself sent on the good news of Charles' victory to others, and endeavoured to increase the fruits of it by

---

[1] *Ann. Placent.*, p. 282 ; Saba, iv, 7 ; Villani, vii, 25.

[2] *Cf.* Del G., ii, 175, for a diploma which shows how the Saracens after Charles' departure roused the neighbouring country against him. See *ib.*, p. 178, for other documents concerning other risings in the Terra di Lavoro against Charles.

[3] Salimbene, p. 476 ; Saba, iv, 8–12 ; Villani, vii, 26–7.

[5] Ep. of Charles, ap. Martène, ii, p. 624, n. 690. He speaks of the present letter " quæ statim post victoriam scriptæ fuerunt." The letter is also printed in Del G., ii, p. 185 ff.

forbidding the cities of the Patrimony to receive the fugitives from the battle.[1] He urged the devoted sons of the Church to thank God for the victory, and to felicitate him and the Roman Church on it.[2]

After the battle, the unfortunate Conradin fled at once to Rome, where he hoped to find protection, and perhaps to be able to rally his broken forces, and to form a new army. Henry's Vicar, Guido de Montefeltro, held the Capitol, and Ghibelline nobles held the Colosseum, the island of the Tiber (called of St. Peter) refortified by Peter de Vico, and the fortress of Jacobo Napoleone, known to the people as *Arpacata*, built amid the ruins of Pompey's theatre, and situated in the Campo di Fiore. This fortress bristling with towers, says Saba, he had, "as the leader of the Ghibellines," been allowed to construct by the favour of the Senator, Henry.[3] The Ghibellines held also the Castle of St. Angelo, the Vatican, and the fortified palace of Stephen Alberti.[4] Although the party of the Church "only held the (castellum) which is called "Guastum", no doubt the fortified mausoleum of Augustus in the hands of the Colonnas,[5]

Capture of Conradin and his chief followers.

[1] Ep. Aug. 26, n. 692, to the people of Rieti.

[2] Ep. *ib.*, n. 693. *Cf.* 694. Villani tells us how in the plain of Tagliacozzo, Charles caused an abbey, our Lady of Victory, to be built wherein prayers might be said for the repose of the souls of those who had perished in the battle. *Chron.*, vii, 27.

[3] Saba, v, 6. It was destroyed by order of Charles : " Hanc quidem fortericiam turrificatam circualiter per ejusdem Regis Vicarium Guelfi Urbis dirui funditus procurarunt." He also tells us of the fortifying of the island of the Tiber and its approaches by Peter de Vico : " Quædam etiam turres quas Petrus Romani in capite pontium Judæorum et trans Tyberim pro fortificatione insulæ Lycaoniæ fecerat " —and of their destruction in the same way.

[4] *Annal. Placent.*, p. 283.

[5] *Ib.* The passage is corrupt : " Pars ecclesiæ habebat tantum (here some word—castellum, montem ?—is omitted ; or perhaps *tantum* may stand for castrum) qui appelatur Guastum." Now the *Mirabilia Urbis Romæ*, n. 22, states : " Ad portam Flammineam fecit

it was rapidly increased by the Guelfs who flocked back to the city after Conradin's defeat. The star of the unfortunate youth was seen to have set. Even the Senator's Vicar, would not give him refuge in the Capitol. He had to quit Rome. After vainly attempting for a brief space to find a secure place of refuge, he made for the coast ; and, with a few companions, put to sea from the little port of Astura, on the river Stura, near Cape Circello. But, if his hope was to reach Pisa, it was doomed to disappointment. John Frangipane, the lord of Astura, pursued, captured, and brought back the fugitives to his castle. Along with Conradin, were Frederick of Baden, duke of Austria, Galvano Lancia and his son, with some others. Overawed by fear, or moved by money or devotion to the Guelf cause, Frangipane made over his captives to Charles.[1] Certainly considerable pressure was brought to bear upon him on the one hand by the King's admiral, Robert de Lavena, to induce him to yield his prisoner to him and his master, and on the other hand, by Jordan, cardinal-deacon of SS. Cosmas and Damian,[2] rector of Campania, in behalf of the Pope's claim to the prisoner.[3] It would appear that Frangipane merely resisted the pressure for a time, in order to increase the ransom money which he claimed for his prize. At any rate, Cornadin and his companions (though he begged in vain to be delivered to " the Romans ", i.e., to the Cardinal),[4] fell into the hands of Robert and then of Charles, somewhat before the middle

Octavianus quoddam castellum quod vocatur Augustum." P. 106, ed. Urlichs, *Urbis Rom. Topog. Guastum*, is probably one of the many corruptions of *Augustum*, like Austa, Lagusta, etc.

[1] *Ann. Placent.* = *Chron. de rebus*, p. 283 ; Saba, iv, 13–15 ; *Mon. Patav. Chron.* = *Annal. S. Justin. Patav.*, pp. 729–30, ap. *R. I. SS.*, viii ; Villani, viii, 29.

[2] J. Piruntus de Comitibus Terracinæ.

[3] " Qui officio Rectoriæ Comitatus Campaniæ per Sedem Apostolicam fungebatur." Saba, iv, c. 15, p. 851.

[4] B. de Neocast., c. 9. He asked " si eum Romanis restituat ".

of September. On the fourteenth of that month the Pope wrote to the cardinal-bishop of Ostia, the famous canonist, Henry of Susa (Hostiensis) to tell him that he had heard from cardinal Jordan and other reliable sources that Charles was holding as prisoners " Conradin, the duke of Austria, Galvano (Lancia) and his son Galiotto, Henry, once Senator of the City, and Conrad of Antioch ". He added that Charles was already at Præneste on his way to Rome.[1]

Charles, meanwhile, had been gradually drawing nearer to the city. On his march, he had caused the Lancias, who had shown themselves traitors to him, to be put to death, and had received the deputation of three cardinals whom Clement had sent to him from Viterbo to invite him to be Senator of Rome.[2] On September 16 Charles, as its Senator, made his triumphal entry into Rome, received from its fickle people a splendid reception,[3] and, amidst the acclamations of the multitude, ascended the Capitol which Henry's Vicar had sold to the Guelfs for four thousand pounds of the money of Provins.[4]

Charles enters Rome, Sept., 1268.

---

[1] Ep. 695, Sept. 14, 1868, ap. M., ii, p. 627. On the 12th, Charles himself had given the same information to the King of France. Ep. ap. Del G., ii, p. 198.

[2] *Ann. Placent.*, p. 283. Ep. of Charles, ap. Del G., ii, p. 214. In this letter Charles tells of those whom he has in prison : " Conradin, etc. Galvanum Lancia, ejusque filium, jam in capitali pena condempnatos." No doubt the words about the death penalty only refer to the two Lancias. Salimbene, p. 476, and the *Mem. Potest. Reg.*, perhaps also by Salimbene, ap. *R. I. SS.*, viii, 1127 ; *Mon. Patav. Chron.*, ap. *ib.*, p. 730, who adds, with other authors, that a great many other traitors were put to death after the battle : " Hos (proditores quamplures) omnes transfugas regia severitas fecit subire sententiam capitalem." Already on Sept. 12, Charles had told his brother, St. Louis, that he had been elected Senator for life " by the unanimous assent of the Roman people ". Ep. ap. Del G., ii, p. 198 ff. But Clement limited the period of the Senatorship to ten years. See *infra*, under Nicholas III.

[3] *Mon. Pat. Chron., l.c.*

[4] *Ann. Placent., l.c.*, Del G., vol. ii, gives several letters of Charles, dated " in arce Capitolii ". E.g., p. 206.

In Rome, Charles was occupied in firmly establishing his power in the city; in raising money for which he had to pledge his crown,[1] and in preparing to compass the death of the unfortunate youth Conradin. Furious no doubt at the way in which he had been traitorously treated by the Ghibelline chiefs whose lives he had spared after Manfred's death, and irritated at the way in which the Ghibellines in Tuscany were striving to spread evil reports against him, and to belittle his victory with the object of concealing the misfortunes which had befallen their cause at Tagliacozzo,[2] the King resolved that Conradin should be put to death. It was, moreover, asserted by some about the time, and has, in the face of evidence to the contrary, been repeated since, that Clement also " desired . . . the death of the last descendant of Frederick II., because he wished to put an end for ever to the claims of the house of Hohenstaufen ".[3] But Villani, also about the same time, declared that he did not " give faith to this, because Clement was held to be a holy man " [4]; and we do not believe it now because historical evidence is against the assertion.[5]

---

[1] Ep. Sept. 28, ap. Del G., ii, p. 212.

[2] The important letter of Charles to the commune of Lucca, ap. *ib.*, p. 214. He says he understands from their letters how the bitterness of the envious: " de persona nostra sinistra seminare conatur, et indulte nobis de Conradino et sequacibus suis finali victoria derogare."

[3] Gregorovius, *Rome*, v, p. 451.

[4] vii, 29.

[5] Similarly the saying put into Clements' mouth that "life for Conradin would mean death for Charles " is, says, Huillard-Bréholles, *Recherches sur l'hist. des Normands*, p. 151 n., rejected by all impartial historians. Speaking of the accusation generally, Brayela, *La respon-sibilità di Clemente IV.*, p. 6, says: " Tutti i cronisti sincroni, siano guelfi che ghibellini . . . non accennano ad una menoma circostanza che avesse potuto dichiararlo inquinato di tale uccisione." This asser-tion is unquestionably true. Without note or comment one and all say with the *Annals of Genoa*, Charles " condemned Conradin, the Duke of Austria, etc., to death, and beheaded them."

Whether or not because he suspected Charles' merciless intentions, Clement at first wished that Conradin should be brought before himself to be judged.[1] But to this the King would not agree, no doubt on the ground that it was his Kingdom that had been invaded.

Charles' first step towards the accomplishment of his resolve to compass the death of Conradin was to obtain from Clement the dispatch of a number of cardinals to absolve the young Prince from excommunication.[2] By this means he secured the withdrawal of his prisoner from the jurisdiction of the Pope. He then summoned to Naples in order to try, or perhaps merely to acquiesce in the condemnation of the young Suabian prince, two syndics from each of the more important cities of the Terra di Lavoro and the principality of Capua, " in order that what he had determined to do to Conradin might be regarded as the verdict of the men of the country

---

[1] Pipino, *Chron.*, ap. *R. I. SS.*, ix, 684 ; and Ricobaldi of Ferrara, *Hist. imp.*, p. 137, ap. *ib.*

[2] Saba, i, 15. If we are to believe the authors of the *life* of Blessed Ambrose Sansedoni of Siena († 1287), it was Conradin himself who through that saintly man begged that he might be freed from the excommunication which Clement had laid upon him. See his biography, ap. *Acta SS.*, t. iii, 20, Mart., c. 39, p. 189. Ambrose was much employed in various missions by the Popes. In pleading Conradin's cause, he used the parable of the prodigal son, and Clement replied : " Ambrosi, tibi dico quod misericordiam volo et non sacrificium." A later French chronicler, Geoffroy de Courlon, *Chron.*, an. 1268, declares that a report ran (dicitur) that Charles asked Conradin what he would have done with him had he been the captive. " I would have beheaded you," replied Conradin. Whereupon Charles, " You have answered without prudence, and have decided your own fate." Even if Conradin never gave such a reply, still, to judge from the way in which his great-grandfather Henry VI. treated the last Norman princes of Sicily, and much more from the way in which he beheaded (contra honestos mores) during the battle his prisoner, Charles' marshal, because owing to his being dressed like him, he believed him to be Charles himself (Saba, iv, 10), we may safely conclude that they express his intention.

rather than his own." [1] The exact import of the words
of Saba who gives us this information is not clear, and
may mean hardly more than what is said on the subject
by Bartholomew of Neocastro. He tells us that Charles
summoned the chief men of the country in order that
they might see perish by the sword one whose escape
would cause still greater trouble. [2]

Jurists
decide in
Conradin's
favour. However this may be, there is no doubt that the
Angevin tried to get a legal opinion in favour of his right
to put Conradin to death. He summoned a number of
men learned in the law, and asked them whether the
German King and his associates could be legally condemned
to death. They had taken up arms against a lawful
King, and had plundered and burnt monasteries. There
was much discussion among the lawyers, but the verdict
of the majority (plurimorum), especially that of the
famous jurisconsult, Guido de Suzaria, [3] was favourable
to Conradin. They decided that he had but tried to
recover a kingdom which be believed to belong to him
by hereditary right ; and that as there was no proof
that he had ordered the destruction of the monasteries,
it was to be presumed that they had been destroyed
as is usual in war time by irresponsible persons. Of
course, in such debates there will always be found
differences of opinion, springing either from honest but
ill-informed conviction or from a wish to please the
powerful. Charles, therefore, found a minority who
favoured his wishes, and who declared that he

---

[1] Saba, iv, 16. They were summoned " pro Corradini sententia
. . . ut non suum quod acturus erat de Corradino judicium videretur,
sed potius hominum de contrada ".

[2] C. 9. " Primates regni sollicitat ut visuri accedant ferro modico
fore multandum, quem indulta vita posset eripere, et esset error
priore deterior."

[3] On this jurist, a professor at the time of civil law in Naples, *cf*.
Del Giudice, *Diplom.*, ii, p. 231 ff.

might legally condemn Conradin and his associates to death.[1]

Embracing this latter servile or wrong-headed opinion, Charles caused the unfortunate Prince and his companions to be tried and condemned to death by the syndics whom he had summoned for the purpose.[2] Accordingly, on October 29, 1268, the head of the last of the Hohenstaufen fell beneath the headsman's axe in the market place of Naples. With Conradin were executed Frederick, duke of Austria and several others[3] ; while the Infante Henry, owing to his powerful connexions, was confined in first one fortress and then another till the year 1291.

Death of Conradin, 1268.

Although it may be true to say with Saba, that the unfortunate youth Conradin suffered for the sins of his grandfather, Frederick II., it is certain that in putting him to death, Charles committed, even if not a crime, at least a great political blunder, and outraged the ideas of chivalry.[4] The youth and beauty of the unhappy Prince appealed to the imagination of friend and foe alike ; and, whatever sympathy he may have lost by his appearance in arms, like our own Charles I., he more than regained by his death. His blood inspired

[1] Ricobaldi, *l.c.*, who is at pains to inform us that what he related about the last days of Conrad he had learnt from one who, in the company of Guido de Suzaria had seen and heard what he narrated to him. " Hæc ego quæ scripsi accepi a Joachimo Judice cive regio (*sic*) tunc in comitatu, etc."

[2] " Volebat quod prædictorum periret judicio et eorum sententia sancirentur, quorum spolia occupare . . . intentarat. Factumque est ita, etc." Saba, iv, 16. *Cf. Chron. Normanniæ*, ap. *R. F. SS.*, xxiii, 220.

[3] Ricobaldi, *l.c.*, Saba, iv, 16. Bart. de N., c. 9 ; *Annales Mantuan.*, ap. *M. G. SS.*, xix, p. 25, " per sententiam datam per judices," Charles beheaded Con., and imprisoned Henry ; Jac. de Vorag., ap. *R. I. SS.*, ix, p. 50, Guillaume Puylaurens, *Chron.*, p. 171, ed. Beyssier, says Charles beheaded Conradin, etc. : " non absque legis peritorum sententia."

[4] Brayela, *l.c.*, p. 42 ff., has shown that Charles was within strict legal right in putting Conradin to death.

apologists and poets, whose words did more for the Ghibelline cause than for the Guelfic did the joy and moral reflections of some few of his enemies.[1]

The last letters between Clement and Charles, and the end of the Saracen power at Lucera, 1268–9.

Having failed in his attempt to be the arbiter of Conradin's fate, Clement apparently made no further attempt to interfere between Charles and his enemy. His own life was all but over, and very little further communication passed between him and the Sicilian King. On the day before the execution of Conradin (October 28), the Pope wrote to tell Charles that he had received a communication from the duke of Burgundy and others, begging him to dissuade the King from again attacking the Saracens of Lucera before their arrival with fresh troops. Clement, however, makes it clear that he would prefer that the robber stronghold should be destroyed at once if the undertaking will not involve too great a risk.[2] However, it was not till the August of the following year that Charles succeeded in finally breaking the power of the Saracens of Lucera.[3]

On the day following the death of Conradin (Oct. 30), Clement commends two noblemen to the King,[4] and

---

[1] The Templar of Tyre in his Chronicle tells of the joy at Acre on the reception of the news of the defeat and death of Conradin, though he says graciously that " la feste ne fu faire par mavaisté nulle, mais pour appaiser sainte yglise pour le roy Charle, que estoil defendeor de sainte yglise et sanatour, et l'autre (raison fu) que Dieu le vost ensi consentir pour desheriter les heirs de l'empereor et ses fis, le roy bourat et Manfrè ". *Les gestes des Chiprois*, p. 190. *Cf.* the *Romance of the Rose*, v, 7100 ff., which, after telling " how both these men (Conradin and the Infante) ' Like caitifs fled the combat ' " exhorts men to reflect on their fate for making war " 'Gainst holy Church their nurse ". *Cf.* Huillard-Bréholles, *Recherches*, p. 153, quoting troubadours, etc., against Charles, and in favour of Conradin.

[2] Ep. 706 ap. Mart. ; or 79 ap. Del G., ii, 230

[3] *Cf.* Del G., iii, p. 37, n. 15 and n. 72, Aug. 28, 1269 ; Riccio, *Alcuni Fatti*, pp. 43, 54, 69 ; and P. Egidi, *La Colonia Saracena di Lucera*, p. 49 ff., Naples, 1912.

[4] M., ep. 709, or Del G., ii, p. 233.

on Nov. 8, there is a formal acknowledgment that the tribute due to the papal treasury from Charles for Sicily had been received on the feast of All Saints (Nov. 1) instead of on the feast of St. Peter.[1] But there is no record among the Pope's letters of any communication having passed between the Pope and Charles after the news of Conradin's death could have reached Rome.[2] Such a fact alone may lead one to suppose that Clement disapproved of the King's treatment of his foe; and, if there is no evidence in his letters on the matter one way or another, we are definitely assured by Villani[3] that Charles " was greatly blamed by the Pope, by his cardinals and by all good men " for his treatment of the unhappy youth.

It is even possible that he may already have been too ill to attend to anything very closely; for, " full of days and holiness," [4] he departed this life at Viterbo, exactly one month after the death of Conradin (Nov. 29). Already, in 1266, we find him complaining to St. Louis of the ills of old age,[5] and showing his feet and legs to the famous physician, John of Procida; but humorously

Death of Clement, 1268.

---

[1] *Reg.*, n. 718. There are similar receipts, etc., connected with the payment of this tribute (8,000 ounces of gold) of the following years during the vacancy of the Holy See—" Sede Vacante ". *Cf.* nn. 719-22. In addressing " the sacred College of cardinals " Charles signs himself: " King of Sicily, of the Duchy of Apulia, and of the Principality of Capua, Senator *Alme Urbis*, Count of Anjou, Provence and Folcalquer, and through the Holy Roman Church Vicar-general of the Roman Empire in Tuscany."

[2] Even in days of Sixtus V., it took four days for a well-mounted horseman to cover the distance between Rome and Naples. *Cf.* Hübner, *Sixtus V.*, i, 99–101.

[3] *Chron.*, vii, 29.

[4] *Chron. Pont. et Imp. Mantuan.*, ap. *M. G. SS.*, xxiv, p. 219. *Cf.* his biography in Muratori, *R. I. SS.*, iii, p. 595. " Clemens P. IV., vir totius providentiæ præ cunctis generationis hujus, obiit Viterbii, etc." The continuator of William of Tyre, calls his death " grant damage ", ap. *Pat. Lat.*, t. 201, p. 1046.

[5] Ep. 288, May 16, 1266, M., p. 327.

declaring that he preferred to be tortured by the Supreme Physician to taking John's medicine ! [1]   He was seized with his last illness on the feast of St. Cecily (Nov. 22), and died on the vigil of the feast of St. Andrew.[2]   The end, it appears, came rather suddenly.   He was seized, says another authority, with an acute fever in the middle of the night between the twentieth and twenty-first of November, and died a little after dawn on November 29, when, says the author we are following, " it is firmly believed that the holy angels received his soul." [3]

Dispute over the possession of his body, 1268-74.

The earthquake which took place at this time, and which was popularly connected with the death of the Pope,[4] may rather be regarded by us as a symbol of the commotion which was made over his dead body.   During his life, Pope Clement had had a great affection for the Dominican Order,[5] and had expressed a desire that his corpse should rest in their church.[6]   After the funeral service at the Cathedral, the body of the deceased pontiff was accordingly conveyed with due pomp to the then new Dominican church of Santa Maria in Gradi, to which he had himself probably added the lovely Gothic cloister that is still so much admired.   That a suitable tomb might be made for the late Pope, the papal chamberlain, the archbishop of Narbonne, summoned that same " Roman citizen ", the *marmorarius* Peter di Oderisio, who was called to London to make in Westminster Abbey the

---

[1] Ep. 298, June 5, 1266, M., p. 339.

[2] Salimbene, *Chron.*, p. 475.

[3] See a note in a copy of the *Sentences* of Peter Lombard, MS. Paris, Lat. 15707, published by K. Hampe, *N. Archiv der Gesellschaft*, xxiii, 1898, p. 613.

[4] *Chron. Min. Erford.*, ap. *M. G. SS.*, xxiv, p. 213. According to the *Chronicle* of the monk of Padua, the earthquake took place in the beginning of November, ap. *R. I. SS.*, viii, p. 730.

[5] Ptolemy of Lucca, H. E., xxii, c. 38, ap. *R. I. SS.*, xi, p. 1161.

[6] " Qui (Clement) apud ecclesiam dictorum Prioris et Fratrum (O.P.) elegerat sepulturam," said his successor Gregory X.   Ep. July 31, 1274, ap. Ripoll, *Bullar, O.P.*, i, p. 520.

beautiful Cosmati tombs which to this day bear his name.[1] The monument designed by Peter consists of three parts, a basement upon which rests a sarcophagus of smaller dimensions, and a canopy supported by twisted columns of marble.

Both contemporary and modern authors unite in praising Clement, acclaiming him " as one of the most austere, learned, and pious Popes who have ever mounted the throne of St. Peter ".[2] He was most abstemious

Character.

[1] *Cf.* ep. Greg. X. (*ib.*, p. 525), to Richard, cardinal-deacon of S. Angelo : " Sua nobis " of July 31, 1274. That Peter di O. was the maker of the tomb we learn from Papebrock, *Propyl. ad. mensem Maii*, p. 54 **. In his time there were to be read to the right of the epitaph : " Petrus Oderisii sepulchri fecit hoc opus." The said epitaph in leonine verse (at the back of the monument above the figure of the Pope), after calling upon the reader to behold the little space required for a great Pope, and assuring him that contemplation of a successor of St. Peter reduced to a little dust will cause him to cease from seeking the joys of this world, gives a brief sketch of the career of Clement till, by being elected Pope he might be considered as raised to the stars. The last verses exhort the passer-by to pray that he might attain everlasting joy.

> " Lector fige pedes admirans quam brevis edes
> Pontificem quartum Clementem contegit arctum.
> En datur in cineres Petri successor et heres,
> Cujus si memor es, mundi non gaudia queres.
> Hinc inde primum, quem sic successus opimum
> Reddidit, ut fertur, miles probus efficeretur.
> Taleque sortitus nomen, jurisque peritus,
> Virginis unius fuit unicus ipse maritus ;
> Qui, viduatus ea, mox Christi sorte petitus
> Anitiensis ita dignus fuit Archilevita.
> Præsul ibi factus, post Archiepiscopus auctus,
> Utque Deo gratus vir Cardinibus sociatus.
> Papatus nomen Urbis sucepit et omen.
> Sic sublimatus, sic denique clarificatus,
> Perficiendo gradus, censetur ad astra levatus,
> Annis sex denis octo cum mille ducentis
> Transactis Christi, Clemens tumulo datur isti.
> Agyos quare qui transis corde precare,
> Ut finalis ei det gaudia summa diei."

[2] Pinzi, *Storia di Viterbo*, ii, 246-7. As for his contemporaries, besides those already cited, we may adduce Ricobaldi, who, though

in the matter of food, observing in this respect the rules
of St. Dominic [1] ; but, if thus " severe to himself ", he
was, we are told, indulgent (pius) towards others ".[2]
Without a peer in preaching the word of God, he sang
with the most refined taste.[3] In a word " throughout
all the period of his pontificate he is said to have lived
practically the life of a Saint ".[4] " So upright was he in
everything that," in the words of the chronicler Hocsemius,[5] " he would never defer to Prince or King, and was,
therefore, loved and feared by all. Especially was he
beloved by St. Louis, once his lord, and the two were
wont to encourage each other in the exercises of a holy
life."

somewhat of a Ghibelline declares that no worthier Pope governed
the Holy See in this age. *Chron.*, ap. *R. I. SS.*, ix, 181. Pinzi, in
his judgment prescinds from politics " all infuori d'ogni politico
rispetto ".

  [1] Ptolemy of Lucca, *H.E.*, xxii, c. 38.

  [2] Jordanus of Osnabruck, ap. Raynaldus, *Annal.*, an. 1268, n. 54.

  [3] *Ib.*, " Cantor delicatus, in concionando non habens socium."
Ptolemy of Lucca's words are just those of Jordanus.

  [4] *Ib.*, and *Catal. pont. Rom. cont. Laud.*, ap. *M. G. SS.*, xxii, p. 371.
Cf. supra at the end of Chapter I.

  [5] *Chron.*, c. 6, p. 42.

CHAPTER IV.

THE INTERREGNUM OF THE EMPIRE. RICHARD OF CORNWALL AND ALFONSO X. OF CASTILE. CRUSADES AND ARMENIA. THE GREEK CHURCH. THE TARTARS. ART, ETC.

THOUGH Clement, no more than his predecessors, was destined to settle the dispute between Richard earl of Cornwall and Alfonso X. of Castile for the Empire, he had to enter into it. On account of the troubles in England between Simon de Montfort and King Henry III., Urban IV. had had to put off the hearing of the claims of the two candidates.[1] As the complaints about the vacancy of the Empire continued to make themselves heard, and as the difficulties in England had been lessened by the battle of Evesham and the death of de Montfort (Aug., 1265), Clement fixed the Friday after the Epiphany of 1267 for adjudicating on the quarrel, and bade Richard present himself before him on that date either in person or by proxy (Apr. 30, 1266).[2] This notice proved to be too short, and on May 9 in the following year (1267) the Pope addressed letters to the rivals fixing the day after the feast of the Annunciation (March 25, 1268) as the trial day. Meanwhile he ordered the examination of witnesses to begin ; and, to save time and expense, he ordered that the examination should take place at different centres, at Frankfort, Paris, Burgos, and Bologna.[3] It would appear, however, that the candidates,

Clement bids the candidates for the Empire appear in 1267.

---

[1] Cf. *supra*, p. 178 f.   [2] Ep. 415, *Reg.*

[3] Potthast, 20002, from Raynaldus, *Annal.*, 1267, n. 22. *Cf.* a series of letters of Sept. 17, 1267, addressed to various dignitaries, authorizing them to receive the depositions of the witnesses in the above named cities. *Reg.*, nn. 596–600.

especially Alfonso, were more anxious to settle their claims by intrigue than by fair trial.[1] The situation became strained, and if Clement showed some signs of favour to Alfonso, he had to impress upon him that he could no longer tolerate the unbecoming and hurtful obstacles that were being thrown in the way of an authoritative settlement of the dispute.[2] It was, as we have said, apparently Alfonso who, because his claims were inferior to those of Richard, intrigued and spent all the more to secure the brilliant phantom of the imperial crown.[3] But both aspirants were jealous or suspicious of the Pope as well as of each other, and when Clement named Charles of Anjou to be Peacemaker and Imperial Vicar in Tuscany he had to assure both of them that he had not bestowed the Empire on Charles.[4] Further, to explain his own position, he sent to Alfonso extracts from the Register of Innocent III., so that he might see what had happened in the case of the double imperial election at that time.[5]

---

[1] Alfonso at once pretended that even this last prorogation gave too short a time. Writing on Oct. 23, 1267, to Alfonso on the subject of his complaint, Clement reminded him that the further prorogation gave him nearly another year, and that he ought not to call the time short if he considered " si pericula mundi circumspicis, si scissuras imperii, si detrimenta continua, confusionem Italiæ," etc. Ap. Mart., n. 445, p. 534.

[2] Ep. June 5, 1267, Potthast, 20031, from Raynaldus, *l.c.*, n. 26. In this letter Clement tells Alfonso that his chaplain (variously called R. de Orabazan, Maphazan, Mahazan), who knows his mind, will let him know certain secrets. Perhaps these ambiguous words may show some inclination on the part of Clement to support the claims of Alfonso.

[3] Mariana in his famous *History of Spain*, Bk. xiii, c. 5, allows this. Jofré de Loaisa in his *Chronicle of the Kings of Castile* (1248–1305), tells of the enormous sums of money (expensas fere incredibiles) which he gave to the Germans and others who favoured his candidature. C. 7. Published by A. Morel-Fatio in the *Bib. de l'école des Chartes*, 1898.

[4] Epp. of June 15, 1267. Potthast, 20049, Del Giudice, ii, pt. i, 49.

[5] Ep. June 17, 1267. Potthast, 20051, Mart., n. 490.

But, despite all his wishes, Clement could not bring the negotiations to a head. Another prorogation of the hearing of the case became necessary ; but in granting it, and this time it was fixed for Dec. 18, 1268,[1] the Pope expressed himself strongly on the troubles which the long vacancy of the Empire was causing. Still, despite the fact that the procurator of Richard of Cornwall was pressing hard for a decision,[2] Clement felt bound to grant Alfonso the required prorogation, as sickness and other obstacles had prevented one of his agents from communicating with him, and another had been robbed and murdered in Tuscany.[3]

Another prorogation.

Richard, however, was not the only one who was irritated at the constant delays which Alfonso was causing. The electors in Germany were getting restless, and spoke of having a fresh election. Fearful lest the election of a new candidate would only make matters worse, Clement, a few weeks before he died, wrote to Ottocar, King of Bohemia, in response to a communication from him, begging him not to consent to the desire of the other electors for a fresh election, and pointing out that the delay was due not to the Holy See, but partly to the bad will of the two candidates, and partly to circumstances out of man's control. Such were the imprisonment of Richard of Cornwall by the Barons of England, the death of Pope Urban IV., and the accidents to the procurators of Alfonso.[4]

A wish for a fresh election.

Whether " the great jurist ", as Clement is called, would have had an opportunity in the December of 1268 of displaying his great skill in adjudicating the

Death of Clement.

---

[1] Ep. May 18, 1268, *Reg.*, n. 704 ; or ap. Rodenberg, n. 688. The continued vacancy was " grandium discordiarum parens et gravium procuratrix insidiosa discriminum, etc."

[2] " Petitionem repetens frequenter ipsius electi nomine (i.e. in the name of Richard of Cornwall) iteratam, petebat instanter predictum negotium finaliter absque ulteriori dilatione decidi." *Ib.*

[3] *Ib.*   [4] Ep. Nov. 7, 1268, ap. Raynaldus, an. 1268, nn. 43-6.

claims of Richard and Alfonso to the Empire, cannot be said, for this " most holy Pope " [1] died in the same month in which he wrote to Ottocar.

Continuing the work of his predecessors, Clement ever strove to guard and propagate the faith. To those peoples who would have the sword, the Pope tried to let them have the sword, and so exhorted the Dominicans and other religions in the East and North of Europe to be constant in urging the Christians in those parts to take up arms to defend their fellow Christians against the Prussians and other savage heathens in Livonia, Courland, and Prussia.[2]

Clement also vigorously supported the efforts of Alfonso X. of Castile against the Moors of Spain and Africa. He not only tried to get help for the Spaniards from Italy, from the maritime Republics of Genoa and Pisa,[3] but he caused the crusade against them to be preached in the kingdoms of Aragon and Majorca,[4] and granted the King a tenth of the ecclesiastical revenues of his own country and Portugal.[5] He had the good fortune of being able to see some result of his work, and was able to congratulate James I. of Aragon and Alfonso on their victories over ben Alamar, the King of Granada. He rejoiced, so he assured Alfonso, that the Moor's " iron neck " had at length been bent beneath his yoke.[6]

[1] So is he called by Saba, iv, 20.

[2] Epp. of 1265, Potthast, nn. 19097 and 19146. *Cf.* nn. 19163–4, and *supra*, vol. xiii, p. 212 f.

[3] Ep. June, 22, 1265, Pot., n. 19220, from Wadding, *Ann. Minor.*, iv, 250.

[4] Ep. May 23, 1265, Pot., n. 19156, from Raynaldus, *Ann.*, an. 1265, n. 32.

[5] Ep. June 24, 1265, Pot., n. 19228 ; Mart., n. 77. *Cf.* also *Reg.*, nn. 15–17, 19.

[6] Ep. Oct. 23, 1267, Mart., n. 545, to Alfonso. The successes referred to by the Pope were those in Murcia, including the capture of Murcia itself in 1266. *Cf.* Muntaner, *Chron.*, c. 17, and c. 65 of that of

After " the day of salvation had dawned " on Sicily, and, as Clement further expressed it, that country was peacefully subject " to the sway of Charles, our most dear son in Christ ",[1] Clement was more free to devote his attention to the needs of the Christians in the Holy Land. The Sultan of Egypt, Bibars (or Baibars) was conducting a most successful campaign against them. His troops had defeated the Tartars who had been operating against the Moslems in northern Syria (1265), and he himself, after taking Cæsarea and other places in the same year, had returned to Palestine with great forces in the following year. Clement was alive to the danger threatening the remains of the Latin Kingdom. Already in May he had dispatched earnest letters " to all the nobles of Gaul ", and to Thibaut, King of Navarre.[2] He told them that a terrible trumpet call had resounded in the East telling of woes past and of dire troubles to come. He told them how Cæsarea " the metropolis of Palestine " had fallen, and that the Sultan of Babylon (Egypt) was aiming at " completely exterminating the small remnant of Christianity " in those parts. He urged them to get ready for action at least by the following March. He bade his legates explain to the people how the Holy Land was attacked at one time by " the savage and damnable Tartars ", and at another by the Saracens.[3] He granted ecclesiastical tithes to

---

d'Esclot. Murphy, *The Hist. of the Mahometan Emp. in Spain*, p. 138, London, 1816. The Pope's letter to James of Aragon was dated July 5, 1266, Mart., n. 323. Clement availed himself of the opportunity afforded him by this letter to exhort James to lead a more chaste life. " O quantam in tua gloria ponis maculam ! " On this latter subject Clement sent a more severe letter, Jan. 16,1267, Mart., n. 426. *Cf. James I. of Aragon*, by Swift, p. 115, n. 1, p. 17.

[1] Ep. June 6, 1266, Mart., 300, to card. Simon de Brion.

[2] Epp. May 28, 1266, Mart., nn. 293-4.

[3] *Cf.* ep. July 30, 1266, to Simon de Brion, Mart., n. 348. *Cf.* the following letters.

S. Louis IX. and to the count of Flanders and other nobles. He tried to stir up the English [1] and Germans as well as the French,[2] and bade Richard, cardinal-deacon of St. Angelo, discuss the matter with Charles of Anjou who " of all the Princes of the world was the one who could give the quickest help ".[3] Clement's warnings were certainly needed, for even Jaffa and then Antioch fell (May 28, 1268) before his death ; but, despite " the letters he sent to all Christians to co-operate in the expedition " of St. Louis,[4] that chivalrous monarch could not get ready for war till the year 1270.

With all his anxiety for armed intervention in favour of the Holy Land, Clement very plainly told James I. of Aragon, who had written to say that he was preparing " to vindicate the wrongs of the Crucified ", that " the Crucified " would not accept his service till he had amended his unchaste life.[5]

---

[1] The Pope was well seconded in England by his legate Ottoboni Fieschi (afterwards Pope Hadrian V.), who, preaching in St. Paul's, induced many to take the cross including Theald or Theobald, archdeacon of Liège (afterwards Gregory X.), who had come to England with the cardinal legate. *Cf. Flores Hist.*, iii, 14 *R. S.*

[2] *Cf.* epp. Oct. 19--21, 1266, Mart., 396 ff. To encourage those to give money who could not fight, the Pope offered a plenary indulgence to such as should contribute a quarter of their property. *Cf. Mémoire de la Chambre des comptes*, ap. *Hist. lit. de France*, vol. xxxiv, p. 507 n.

[3] Ep. ap. Mart., n. 396.

[4] Menko, *Chron.*, ap. *M. G. SS.*, xxiii, 554.

[5] Ep. Jan. 16, 1267, Mart. 426. "Alias enim complacere non poteris Crucifixo, nec injurias ejus redimere, si ab ejus injuriis ipse nolueris abstinere." How prophetic were Clement's words was proved by the sequel. Deceived by Tartar promises of help, and urged also by Michael Palæologus, James set sail for the East (1269), but he soon returned, induced not by a storm, but there is reason to believe by the persuasions of that very Doña Berenguela whose evil connexion with the King Clement had denounced. *Cf.* Swift, *l.c.*, pp. 117–19. Clement was more successful in another course of royal immorality. He had occasion to blame Queen Isabella d'Ibelin, the widow of Hugh II., King of Cyprus (†aged 14, Dec. 5, 1267), for her notoriously scandalous life. He exhorted her to marry rather

In his zeal for the welfare of the Christians in the Armenia. Holy Land, Clement also strove to excite Hayton I., King of Lesser Armenia (1226-69), to do his best for the Christian cause, and he recommended to him especially the Knights Hospitallers who had suffered very much at the hands of Bibars.[1] Unfortunately, however, the same Bibars soon after inflicted the greatest losses on Hayton's Kingdom [2] (1266) ; and it became necessary for Clement to express to the King his sympathy for his troubles, and to assure him of the help of the West, especially of King Louis of France,[3] and, at the same time, to urge the Greek emperor Michael Palæologus,[4] and the Christian chiefs in Palestine to give help at once to the Armenians.[5] No help was forthcoming at the moment, however, and Hayton, having had to make a disastrous peace with Bibars, resigned in favour of his son Leo, and died a monk.[6]

Here passing over Clement's relations with the Greek The Greek Church and with the Tartars, because the former will be Church and treated of under the pontificate of Gregory X., and the the Tartars. latter under that of Nicholas IV., and, passing over also, from want of space, his work for the pacification of the Church in Denmark, through Guido cardinal of

---

than burn. See his letter ap. L. Deslisle, *Notices et Extraits*, t. xxvii, pt. ii, p. 124 ff. She listened to his wise advice and married several times, to the English noble, Raymond the Stranger, to Nicholas, the German, lord of Cæsarea, and lastly to William Barlas.

[1] Ep. July, 1265, ap. Mart., n. 111, or Galanus, *Conciliat. eccles. Arm. cum Roma*, i, 388.

[2] *Cf.* Hayton, *Fleur des hist.*, p. 189, ed. De Baeker.

[3] Ep. May 17, 1267, ap. M., n. 470, or G., p. 391, where it is abridged.

[4] Ep. ap. M., n. 469.

[5] Ep. to the patriarch of Jerusalem, to the Grand Masters of the Templars, etc., *ib.*, n. 468.

[6] M. 1270. *Cf.* Galanus, p. 394 f., or Tournebize, *Hist. de l'Arménie*, p. 212 ff.

St. Lawrence in Lucina,[1] we may here just briefly call attention to a few isolated facts which may throw light on Clement's character or administration.

Various acts of Clement.
Several of Clement's letters show his love of learning. Thanking the bishop of Vicenza for the gift of a book, he assured him that he could not have sent him anything which would have pleased him more. "For God," he said, "had long ago granted me the grace of always wishing to learn, and of always finding joy in the learning of the wise."[2] This zeal for learning naturally drove him to seek the society of the learned,[3] and to read the works of the learned; and so we shall see shortly his earnest wish to procure the works of the famous English Friar, Roger Bacon.[4]

William of St. Amour.
In writing of the relations between Alexander IV. and William of St. Amour, we quoted a letter of Clement to that uncompromising opponent of the Mendicant Orders.[5] Bulæus, in his *History of the University of Paris*,[6] says that Clement recalled him from exile. If there is no proof of that,[7] the letter of Clement to him, on the receipt of a new book from him, was at least kind. In it he gave proof of great moderation. He had not only, he wrote,

---

[1] Guido was sent at her request to make peace between Margaret, the queen regent of Denmark, and its hierarchy (Potthast, 19182 ; cf. 19189–91), to get help for the Crusaders against the pagans in Livonia (*ib.*, 19194 ; cf. 19204–10 for various powers granted him as legate), and to defend the rights of the Church against King Eric (*ib.*, 19910 ; cf. 20138). The Pope had occasion to blame this legate for greediness. Not content with the extensive legation assigned to him, he wanted England. *Ib.*, 19499, or Mart., n. 209 : "nunc ad illam portionem anhelas . . . Angliam." The activities of Clement in Denmark can also be seen from the *Regesta diplomatica hist. Danicæ*, p. 77 ff. Copenhagen, 1889. *Cf.* Allen, *Hist. de Denmark*, i, p. 170 f.

[2] Ep. 318, M., ii, 358.

[3] Hence he had as his chaplain the Dominican Orientalist, William of Moerbeke. *Cf.* Gregorovius, *Rome*, v, pt. ii, p. 618.

[4] See *infra*, p. 327.   [5] *Supra*, p. 109 n.   [6] T. iii, p. 677.

[7] *Cf.* Crevier, *Hist. de l'Université de Paris*, ii, p. 29, Paris, 1761.

read part of it already, but he undertook to read the whole
of it himself, and to have it read by competent persons
before passing any judgment upon it. But he gave him
to understand that it might be a long time before such
judgment could be pronounced, as he was more than
usually overwhelmed by the presence of business from
all parts of the world.[1] Both Pope Clement and William
himself († 1272) appear to have refrained from writing
any further on the subject.

Clement's learning was not merely academic. It
led him to aim at results of practical utility. He insisted
on the isolation of lepers,[2] he took measures for the
protection of trade, and he fostered bridge-building.[3]
In his work for the encouragement of trade, he took under
the protection of the Apostolic See all honest traders
in the countries round the Baltic, especially in the case
of ship-wreck [4]; he endeavoured to secure protection
for the persons and goods of the merchants of Lucca [5];
and he authorized King Louis IX. of France to impose
a moderate duty on the imports and exports of his new
port of Aigues-Mortes; but, in view of its being the only
port in his dominions suitable for pilgrims, the duty was
not to be increased in the future.[6] In his letter to Louis
on the subject, he hinted plainly to him that it was within
his competence as a sovereign to impose such a duty

Practical results of Clement's learning.

---

[1] Ep. Oct. 18, 1266, M., ii, p. 417, n. 394. Molinier, *Les sources de
l'hist. de France*, iii, p. 135, names the book sent to Clement :
Collectiones catholicæ et canonicæ scripturæ. Crevier, *l.c.*, very justly
observes that in his zeal for the interests of the University it is a great
pity that William did not properly distinguish between the cause
and persons, and that in resisting pretensions, he did not render
greater justice to merit.

[2] *Bullar. Rom.*, iii, p. 742, n. 7, ed. Taur.

[3] Ep. 457 ap. M., ii, p. 461. He praises those engaged in the work,
and offers an indulgence to those who contribute to it.

[4] Potthast, 19990.   [5] Ep. 275, ap. M., ii, 317.

[6] Ep. 379, ap. *ib.*, p. 405, or *Reg.*, n. 1128. The Pope was personally
acquainted with the site, and speaks very critically about it.

without appealing to the Pope. But it appears that the
King had taken into account the general watch over
such imposts which the Popes had always exercised.
If, on the other hand, Louis wanted to know how it was
that the Roman Church was possessed of the fief of the
county of Maguelonne, he was promptly told to be
content with his rights and broad domains, and not,
by listening to the idle words of dreamers, to trouble the
Roman Church.[1]

As a Frenchman, Clement could not but be interested
in art; and, if we are to believe Vasari, he summoned to
Viterbo the famous sculptor Niccolà Pisani.[2] With his
aid, he restored, among other things, the church and
monastery of the Friars Preachers, and we may believe
that it was with his aid that he added to the palace
which the city had already built for the Popes.[3] It
was from the loggia of this palace, which, with its delicate
trefoil arches, is one of the beauties of the city, that

[1] Ep. Sept. 16, 1266, ap. M., ii, n. 376, p. 401. At the same time he
assured its bishop that he had nothing to fear from Louis, as he had
explained the situation to him. However, he took occasion to forbid
the bishop striking Moslem money (miliarenses). He was injuring
the King of France if his money is not struck in his fiefs. Besides,
"what Catholic ought to strike money bearing the inscription
of Mahomet?" Finally, what right had he to strike the money of
others? Ep. 377, ib. To-day Maguelonne is one of the "Dead
Cities of the South of France". Cf. C. Enlart, *Villes Mortes du Moyen
Age*, p. 31 ff., Paris, 1910.

[2] See Vasari's *Life of Nicolà and Giovanni Pisani*.

[3] See the inscription which recorded the completion by the city
of the papal palace :—

"Rainerius Gattus, jam ter capitaneus actus
Edem papalem struit istam pontificalem."

In the upper part of the present episcopal palace of Viterbo
I was in 1918 shown remains of the old papal palace ; and, in the
bishop's garden, remains of the hall which fell down and caused the
death of Pope John XXI. Cf. Pinzi, *Il Palazzo papale di Viterbo*,
pp. 3–5, Viterbo, 1910. Della Tuccia in his *Chronicle of Viterbo*, p. 31,
says that the Viterbese built the palace in the hope of inducing the
Popes to take up their abode in their city.

Clement watched Conradin and his army marching to disaster. If Clement did not do more in the domain of art, it was because he was so short of money. He had so many interests to subsidize,[1] and the Church was so poor that some of the cardinals had not even the means to support themselves becomingly.[2] Nor could money be got from the different countries. Instead of getting help from England, he has to help its King in the midst of his difficulties ; France is drained for the Sicilian expedition ; Spain has not enough for itself and its Kings ; and Germany, torn with the schism, cannot help anyone.[3]

But Clement was zealous for the spread of the faith, and full of delicate feeling, as well as learned. We shall see him anxious for the conversion of the Tartars ; and we find him earnestly exhorting the Dominicans to preach the Gospel to the nations generally.[4] He was most sympathetic in settling the differences between those around him. If he has to chide Richard, cardinal-deacon of St. Angelo, for his rashness in denouncing as traitors men who were loyal to the Holy See, he lets him know that, at his request, he has stopped some process against Matthew, cardinal-deacon of Sta. Maria in Portico, and if what is said against this rector of the Patrimony of St. Peter should prove to be true, he will act justly but mercifully.[5] But, on the other hand, to teach him not to be too ready to blame the administration of others, he quietly informs him that places under

Clement's treatment of others.

---

[1] Spain, Constantinople, the Holy Land, Prussia, etc. See ep. 113, ap. M., ii, 172.

[2] *Reg.*, n. 440.   [3] Ep. Apr. 14, 1266, n. 267, ap. M., ii, 313.

[4] Epp. nn. 235, ap. *ib. Cf.* 19937, Potth. See the *Annal. Aust., Hist.*, ann. 1264–79, ap. *M. G. SS.*, ix, pp. 650 and 699 ff., for what he did for the Austrian Church through Guido, cardinal of S. Lorenzo in Lucina of whom it is beautifully said : " S. Ecclesiæ studuit prodesse potius quam praeesse." P. 650.

[5] Ep. 67, May 28, 1265, ap. M., ii, 138.

his rule, such as Corneto, Spoleto, and Città Castellana, not to say, such persons as Peter de Vico, have offended him more grievously than places under the rule of others.[1]

Cardinal Radulfus had evidently intimated to Clement that he had written to him rather curtly, the more so that he (the cardinal) had had occasion to write of some favours which the Pope had granted to certain unworthy persons. In his reply Clement assured the offended Cardinal that, if his letter had wounded his feelings it had not been his intention to hurt him. The fault must be attributed to the scribe who finally drafted the letter.[2] He goes on to assure the Cardinal that it had never been his desire to bestow honours on unfit persons, or " unworthily to promise dignities to the unworthy ". He proceeds then to deal with certain cases about which Radulfus had complained. He denied, for instance, that he had done more for the famous physician, John of Procida, than to write " temperately enough " in his behalf " to the King and to you ", at the request of certain cardinals (fratrum nostrorum). He assures Radulf that he has no wish to see " that man of blood, the count of Acerra, because, if he came, he would be able to make friends in the curia ; for there he would find men who would to-morrow support the devil himself if he came with money.[3]

[1] *Ib.*

[2] Ep. June 5, 1266, ap. *ib.*, n. 298, p. 339 ; *cf.* n. 315. Card. R. had, at the request of Louis IX., been sent to France for the business of the Crusade. He succeeded Simon de Brion, who had conducted the Sicilian negotiations. *Cf. Chron. Normandiæ*, p. 220, ap. *R. F. SS.*, xxiii.

[3] " Haberet vel sibi faceret aliquos amicos in curia, qui diabolo cras assisterent cum muneribus venienti." *Ib.* We have said nothing about the *Pragmatic Sanction*, supposed to have been issued by St. Louis in behalf of the so-called "liberties of the Gallican Church ". The said document is an acknowledged forgery of the fifteenth century. *Cf.* C. Gérin, *La Pragmatique Sanction de S. Louis*, Paris, 1870.

This is perhaps the less shocking at this period because The papal bankers. not only was the Pope so short of money that he had not enough to meet his ordinary daily domestic expenses,[1] but some of the cardinals had nothing and others not enough for their decent maintenance.[2] Clement, however, strove to bear his grinding and anxious poverty with patience ; and, as he said, abstained from every shadow of extortion or money-grabbing.[3]

Still, of course, large sums passed through his hands for the purposes of the Crusades and of the Latin Empire of Constantinople as well as for those of the Apostolic See itself. To deal with these sums, he employed, like his predecessors, certain banking firms of North Italy. Not only were they employed to negotiate loans for him, but also to collect [4] and transmit to him sums due to the Holy See on various counts.[5] The firm usually employed by Clement was that of Bonaventura di Bernadino of Siena. How useful these bankers were to the Holy See will be readily understood. Those employed by it were taken under its special protection, granted various privileges and, as " mercatores Papæ " or " campsores Cameræ Apostolicæ ", had an official position in the Papal household.[6]

[1] Ep. July 30, 1265, ap. M., ii, p. 172, n. 113. *Cf.* n. 60.

[2] Ep. Nov. 12, 1265, ap. *ib.*, p. 240, n. 180. " Propter fratrum inopiam . . . nuper decrevimus singulis fratribus indigentibus, *si nihil* omnino habeant, 300 marcas redituum commendare . . . sed minus habentibus eamdem quantitatem supplere." *Cf.* n. 194.

[3] Ep. of August, 1265, ap. *ib.*, p. 186, n. 133 ; *cf.* nn. 13, 201–2.

[4] *Cf. Reg. Clem.*, nn. 753, 755, 756, 794, 796.

[5] *Cf. ib.*, nn. 747–8, 798, 803, etc. As a rule monies raised that did not belong directly to the Apostolic See (e.g. collections for the Crusade), were kept in the country in which they were raised, till they were assigned to Crusaders in that country by the Pope.

[6] Hence, if ever they failed to act justly, the reputation of the Holy See suffered. *Cf.* Nicholas, pp. 425–40, and Jordan, *Le S. Siège et les banquiers ital.*, Bruxelles, 1895, and his *Les origines de la Domination Angevine en Italie*, pp. 515–59.

CHAPTER V.

THE BRITISH ISLES.

Clement
sends
cardinal
Ottoboni to
England,
1265.

WHEN, as Bishop of Sabina, Clement had been sent as his legate by Urban IV. to try to make peace between Henry III. and the Barons of England, his last act had been to excommunicate Simon de Montfort and his adherents (Nov., 1264).[1] Because he had been prevented by the Barons from landing in England, our historians, who were their partizans, declared that he nourished a perpetual dislike to the English.[2] But, though he felt the contempt with which they had treated him " when he was in a lower office ",[3] still the assertion of the baronial historians was not well founded ; for he declared that, as Pope, he was no less anxious to give some help to England than he was when he had been appointed legate to it by his predecessor.[4] If it is true that, failing to comprehend that the cause of the Barons was largely the cause of liberty,[5] he had unduly favoured the King, he had, at any rate, erred with his one-time sovereign and friend, St. Louis, and with continental opinion generally. With most politicians abroad, he had regarded Simon and his adherents simply as rebellious vassals,

[1] *Cf. supra*, p. 198.

[2] *Contin. Gervase of Cant.*, ii, 242, *R. S.*

[3] Ep. March 23, 1265. *Cf.* ep. Nov. 29., both ap. *Cal. of Pap. Reg.*, i, p. 419.

[4] Ep. May 4, 1265, *ib.*, p. 426.

[5] And so the author of the *Song of Lewes*, vv. 189–90, declares that if Simon were confounded, " most of the people would be confounded, and the greatest part of the realm would be put in peril." The country was well nigh desolate, but the cornerstone of its salvation was " the truly wonderful religion of Simon ", vv. 263–5.

and he continued when Pope to regard them in the same light.[1] Almost immediately on his accession, he had received appeals for help from Henry and his Queen, Eleanor. He promised to send a legate to England; but, " remembering the contempt with which the English had treated him when in a lower office," he had resolved to wait for a month before doing so, in the hope that they would in the meantime have come to a better frame of mind.[2] When he had left the north of France (Nov. 18, 1264), the baronial party was completely master of the situation in England; and, as it continued to remain so, Clement at length sent to England the legate who, he hoped, would put a term to its insolence.[3] The person he selected for that difficult task was Ottoboni Fieschi, cardinal-deacon of St. Hadrian, afterwards Hadrian V., who is spoken of by James de Voragine as a man " of great wisdom and experience ".[4] On May 4, Clement commissioned him to continue the legation begun by himself, and to be a messenger of peace in England, Ireland, Scotland, and Wales; for the glorious realm of England was the dearer to him as it had of old held such sincere faith in God, was so munificent in His worship and was so devoted to the Roman Church that she was in turn so closely bound to it as to feel in herself

---

[1] Hence the English royalist historians regard it as a special dispensation of God that he who had been treated ignominiously by the English should be made Pope, and so get the power " to punish the wicked and to reward the devoted ". Wykes, *Chron.*, p. 157, *R. S.*

[2] Ep. March 23, 1265, ap. *Cal. P. R.*, i, 419; or ap. Mart., ii, p. 115, n. 33. " *Cum sit nobis cordi negotium Angliæ*, nec a nostra memoria possit excidere indecens et probrosa depressio . . . regis Angliæ," etc.

[3] *Ib.* " Qualem requirat protervias eorum."

[4] *Chron. Genuense*, c. 9 ap. *R. I. SS.*, ix, p. 52. In the following letter Clement " speaking from experience " praises Ottoboni's prudence and benignness, and says that the Roman Church can ill spare his absence.

all its joys and all its sorrows.[1] In concluding this inspiring mandate to the cardinal, he declared that he would ratify such sentences as he should think fit to pronounce.

About the same date, (May 4-12), the Pope issued a number of other documents, some addressed to the new legate and others to Henry III. and his Queen, to the English hierarchy, to the King and Queen of France, etc. Ottoboni was authorized to support Henry by a crusade if necessary, and, indeed, by every means in his power. A little later (June 8), he was also authorized to grant Henry a tenth for three years of all ecclesiastical revenues in England, Ireland, and Wales ; and, with the consent of King Alexander, in Scotland.[2] He was also commissioned later to institute proceedings regarding the bishops of Worcester, Lincoln, London, and Ely, and to suspend them if they continue to act against the King. He was moreover, in general, provided with faculties to meet all emergencies.[3]

About the same time (Sept. 13, 1265), Clement authorized him to pay over to the King the balance of the tenth of ecclesiastical property which de Montfort, for his own purposes, had begun to raise whilst his sovereign was in his power.[4] The Pope, " to whom the care of all kingdoms and Kings has been committed

[1] Ep. ap. *Cal.* i, p. 426, or Theiner, *Mon. Hib.*, n. 245, p. 96. " Ad regnum Angliæ inclitum tanto nobis et fratribus acceptius, quanto magis se ab olim exhibuit erga Deum fidei puritate sincerum . . . ac in ipsius veneratione devotum, eo intime caritatis affectu Romana semper ecclesia fervit, ut ejus velut propriis afficeretur incommodis, etc." He goes on to profess both his past *and his present* affection for the whole country.

[2] *Cf. Cal. P. R.*, i, 419, 426-9, 566-7, and Theiner, *l.c.*, pp. 98-9. *Cf.* also in Clement's *Register*, n. 40 ff., p. 12 ff., n. 115 ff., p. 26 ff. ; *Gervase Contin.*, ii, 242.

[3] *Cf.* Gasquet, *Henry III. and the Church*, pp. 401-3. *Cf.* ep. of Sept. 19, 1265, ap. *Cal., l.c.*, p. 435.

[4] Rymer, i, pp. 817-18.

by God," also declared all pacts entered into "under the King's name ", when he was in the same subject condition, null and void.[1]

Meanwhile, in England, events were moving to Henry's advantage. Simon de Montfort was ambitious and dictatorial. His party began to break up, and Prince Edward escaped from confinement (May, 1265). The royalists flew to arms ; the military genius of Edward asserted itself, and on August 5, at the battle of Evesham, Simon and his eldest son were defeated and slain. *Battle of Evesham and the landing of Ottoboni in England, 1265.*

Before the battle, Clement had heard of the discord that was dividing the barons ; and he had written to Ottoboni to urge him, on the one hand, to hasten to England, not allowing excessive love of his native land [2] to detain him ; and, on the other, not to be satisfied with any " false peace ". There was nothing for it but that " the pestilent man and all his offspring " should be driven from England.[3]

Before the arrival of Ottoboni, a peace, if not " false ", at least very hard, had been imposed by the royalists on the vanquished at a Parliament at Winchester (Sept. 8). Estates had been freely confiscated. The " disinherited " remained in arms ; there was fighting and bloodshed everywhere, and the fruits of the victory at Evesham were largely lost. It became necessary for Clement to urge the claims of mercy. Throughout the year, *The Pope's help for the vanquished.*

---

[1] *Ib.*, pp. 818-19. " Confœderationes, promissiones, conventiones . . . et pacta omnia, per eosdem Regem et Edwardum detentos taliter in suæ libertatis . . . præjudicium, cum præfatis Symone . . . vel fautoribus suis . . . inita, cassamus . . . et viribus decernimus omnino carere." *Reg. Clem.*, n. 228. *Cf. ib.*, 955, or ap. M., ii, n. 148.

[2] Ottoboni himself in a letter to Henry III. ap. *E. H. R.*, p. 89, attributes the lateness of his arrival to ill-health and the necessity of travelling by a roundabout way to avoid enemies.

[3] Ep. July 19, ap. M., ii, p. 166, n. 106. " Benedictus Deus, qui vertiginis spiritum miscuit inter Anglicos, viam tibi præparans, quæ multis difficilis videbatur . . . Curre, igitur . . . nec te nimis teneat soli natalis allectiva dilectio."

even up to the early part of September, still in ignorance of the successes of the Royalists, he had been working hard for the King's cause.[1] In the Cathedral at Perugia, he had on Holy Thursday, in the presence of a great number of people, solemnly renewed the sentences which, as legate, he had pronounced against the Barons.[2] But, when once he learnt that victory had been secured, mercy to the vanquished became his cry. Letters were at once sent to King Henry, Prince Edward, and the Earl of Gloucester.[3] In each of them he urged that clemency strengthens authority[4]; he adduced the example of our Lord's forgiving those who crucified Him, and he assured the King that he would win over more by gracious pardon than by strict justice which, while repressing the malice of a few, would irritate many. Especially did he beg the King, for the love of Him whose ministers on earth they were, not to lay hands on the Bishops who had opposed him.

At length on October 29 or 30,[5] cardinal Ottoboni with Queen Eleanor landed at Dover.[6] He came, " as he himself said, " to restore peace to the realm. After he had presented his credentials, he was honourably received by the King whose cause he favoured. At first, says the authority we are quoting, he tried to make peace ; but then turned to plundering, and devoted all his

---

[1] *Cf.* various letters in Rymer, *Fœdera,* i, pp. 817–25.

[2] Ep. Sept. 24, 1265, *ib.*, p. 825.

[3] Epp. Oct. 4–6, 1265, *ib.*, pp. 827–9.

[4] Ep. to the King, p. 828. " Clementia firmat imperium." Very strongly and very beautifully did he write to Prince Edward : " You are cruel towards yourself when you are cruel towards your people." Pg. 829.

[5] This is the date furnished by the *Winchester Annals*, p. 103, *R. S.* Wykes, p. 179, gives Oct. 29, *R. S.* Most of the *Annals* say " about the feast of All Saints ".

[6] He had written to the Bishops and King to prepare them for his coming. *Cf.* his letters ap. *E. H. R.*, 1900, pp. 87–8.

attention (prorsus inhiabat) to collecting money.[1] The course of this narrative will show that Ottoboni not merely tried to make peace, but was highly successful in his mission of mercy, and that the other assertion of our anonymous author is a merely gratuitous partisan statement. If modern English historians do not repeat our author's calumny, they do not appear to do any more justice to the Cardinal's great work for the peace of the land than he did.[2]

The cardinal's first act was, in response to an appeal from the clergy and people of London, who promised " to obey the church ", to remove " piously " the interdict which Cardinal Guy had laid upon their city.[3] Then with the King, in whose company he mostly remained during his stay in the country, he went to London, and was solemnly received at St. Paul's (Nov. 10).[4] He then summoned before him, at a Council which he held on December the first [5] " in the northern part of the new abbey Church of Westminster, " the episcopal supporters of Simon de Montfort, the bishops of London, Lincoln,

Ottoboni's first acts.

[1] The continuator of William of Newburgh ap. *Chronicles of Stephen, etc.*, ii, pp. 549, 551, 553, *R. S.* This continuation was compiled by a monk of Furness Abbey *c.* 1290.

[2] The authors of vols. ii and iii of *A History of the English Church*, barely mention his name, though his *Constitutions* " still retain the force of law in the ecclesiastical courts ". Even Tout, *The Political Hist. of England*, iii, pp. 128–32, does not do full justice to the legate's work. J. R. Green, however, in his essay : *The Ban of Kenilworth*, does realize how Ottoboni brought with him " the calm wise policy of Rome " Pg. 198 ; and the Rev. C. H. Hartshorne in his " The Parliament of Kenilworth " in the *Archæological Journal* of 1864, p. 145, attributes peace " mainly . . . to his sage and considerate advice."

[3] *Annal. Lond.*, i, p. 71, ap. *Chronicles of Edward I., R. S.* ; also *Ann. de Oseneia*, p. 180, *R. S.*, which do not state the matter quite accurately.

[4] *An. L., l.c.* ; Wykes, *Chron.*, p. 180, *R. S.*

[5] " In crastino b. Andreæ," and " post festum S. Andreæ Ap. ", say the *Annals* of Osney (p. 180), and Winchester (p. 103) respectively. The *Flores Hist.*, iii, 9, *R. S.*, which speak of the coming of the cardinal " in his scarlet robes " do not give the date of the Council.

Winchester, and Chichester.[1]   The meeting was stormy.
There was " much altercation ".   The legate attacked
the bishops for siding with the King's enemies ; and the
bishops no doubt contended that they had but fought
for the people's rights.   In the end, the Legate suspended
them.   Then in the spring of the following year (March,
1266), as they appealed to Rome, he bade them, in
accordance with instructions he had received from the
Pope, present themselves before him within three months.[2]

From a letter of Clement to Ottoboni, dated
May 8, 1266, we learn that he had received a
considerable number of letters from the Cardinal,
telling him of the condition of England, and of
what he had done in this matter of the bishops.
He rejoiced to hear from him that the inhabitants of
the Cinque Ports, whom he flatly designates as " sea-
robbers ", had been reconciled to the King.   Though
he is in " bitter " need of the Cardinal's presence, he
trusts that nothing will deter him from completing the
work he has so well begun.[3]

Meanwhile, Walter de Cantilupe of Worcester, being
at the point of death, wrote to the Legate to confess
that he had done wrong in supporting Simon, and to
beg for absolution.   This he obtained before his death
(February 12, 1266).[4]   Of those who went to face the

---

[1] *Ann. of O.*, p. 181, *Ann. of Dunstable*, p. 240.   Their names in
the order of the text were Henry of Sandwich, Richard Gravesend,
John Gervais, and Stephen Berksted.   The *Flores Hist.*, *l.c.*, omit
Lincoln, as does the *Chron. Maiorum*, pp. 83–4 ;   Nic. Trivet, *Annals*,
p. 268, adds the name of Walter of Worcester, as do the *Flores*.
Our historians at this period are as confused as the times.

[2] " Recepto prius rescripto sedis Apostolicæ."   Wykes, p. 185.
Cf. ep. dated Nov. 12, 1265, ap. *Reg. Clem.*, n. 978.

[3] Ep. ap. M., ii, n. 278, p. 319.   *Cf. Gervase Contin.*, ii, 244.   As
usual, he gives him news.   He tells him of the complete defeat and
death of Manfred, and expresses his wish to decide between Richard
and Alfonso lest Conradin should be elected.

[4] *Flores, l.c.*, but *cf. Gervase Contin.*, ii, 243.

Pope, namely, the bishops of London, Lincoln, Winchester, and Chichester, the bishop of Lincoln soon submitted ; and so, says one of our historians, " obtained mercy and not justice." [1] The others, seemingly, would not allow that they had done wrong, and remained as it were in exile (quasi exulantes) for years at the papal court. There the bishop of Winchester died (Jan. 20, 1268),[2] and the bishops of London and Chichester did not get back to England till 1272 or 3.[3]

Meanwhile the legate, having spent Christmas at Northampton with the King and Queen,[4] proceeded in the summer to Kenilworth, in which castle some of the leaders of the party of Simon de Montfort and a number of the " disinherited " had shut themselves up. The siege of the castle began in June, and the Legate appeared before it in the following month, and for a fortnight strove in vain to make peace between the King and the " disinherited ".[5] At length, he was driven, " in his red cope," to excommunicate the besieged, who only replied by mockery. One of them, " who was a quointe man," dressed himself as a legate, and from the castle walls presumed to excommunicate the King and the legate himself.[6]

The Award of Kenilworth, 1266.

[1] *Flores, l.c.* ; *Ann. of O.*, p. 182. It should be remembered that the author of the *Flores* and of the *Chron. Maiorum* were, along with Wykes, supporters of the Royalist party, whereas the Baronial cause was upheld by Robert of Gloucester and Rishanger (as the author of the Continuation of Matthew of Paris, *R. S.*, and of a *Chronicon*, Camden Soc.) and by the compilers of the Annals of Melrose, Dunstable, Osney, and Waverley. Whence it will be seen that the monasteries favoured the Barons.

[2] *Osney, l.c.*, and *Reg. Clem. IV.*, n. 1327.

[3] The *Annals of Worcester*, ap. *Anglia Sacra*, i, 499, or ap. *Monast. Annal.*, iv, p. 464, *R. S.*, gives 1273 as the date of the return and death of the bishop of London. At any rate, he had been absolved by Gregory X. on May 31, 1272. *Cf.* Posse, *Analecta Vaticana*, n. 683, p. 54. Chichester was absolved on Nov. 26, 1272 ; *ib.*, n. 709.

[4] *Ann. of Winchester*, p. 103.   [5] *Ann. of Waverley*, p. 371, *R. S.*

[6] *Rob. of Gloucester, Chron.*, v. 1357 ff. " The quointe (quaint) man was a clerk and a surgeon."

But Ottoboni was far from deserving any man's mockery. He was working all along in the interests of both parties, and was finally instrumental in bringing about the famous " Dictum (Award or Ban) of Kenilworth ". At a parliament held before Kenilworth (Aug. 24), the legate " brought about the appointment " of twelve magnates, four bishops and eight barons to make an ordinance regarding the state of the Kingdom, and the position of the " disinherited ".[1] This he contrived to bring about, despite the furious opposition of those who held the property of the " disinherited ". They threatened him with violence ; but were silenced by excommunication " as disturbers of the peace by holding the property of others ".[2] Finally Ottoboni himself and Henry of Almaine were named the ultimate referees in case of disagreement among the members of the Committee.[3]

---

[1] *The Chronicle of Abingdon*, p. 557, ed. J. O. Halliwell, text and translation. That the appointment of this committee was due to Ottoboni is also directly stated as due " to the wisdom of the cardinal ", and " to his instance " by the *Flores Hist.*, iii, 12, and the *Ann. of Winchester*, p. 104, respectively. See also the following notes.

[2] *Cf.* Rishanger, *Chron.*, p. 57, ed. C. Soc. " Legatus . . . nititur ut ipsis et aliis exhæredatis terræ suæ restituantur, marchionibus (the Marchers) contradicentibus et minas tumide minis accumulando quod in ipsum legatum insurgerent."

[3] *Cf. Ann. de Dunst.*, p. 242 ; *Ann. de Wav.*, p. 372 ; Rishanger, *Chron.*, p. 57. " Legato quoque et d. Henrico filio regis Almanniæ, per eos xii sic data est potestas ut si quid ex ordinatione predictorum xii virorum remaneret, quod perfectione et mutatione indigeret suo possent judicio conformare." These words are repeated practically *verbatim* in ep. 23 of Ottoboni, pg. 109. *E. H. R.* These letters of Ottoboni are most disappointing. For the most part they consist of generalities regarding the sad state of the country and the Cardinal's difficult task. The MS. from which Miss R. Graham published these letters is of the early fifteenth century. From the omission of titles, addresses, dates, etc., " we infer," she writes, " that the scribe was compiling a collection of Formulæ." Pg. 87, I am disposed to think that they are nothing more than exercises, and not genuine letters of the Legate.

The twelve got to work without delay, and many were the points which Ottoboni and Henry had to settle before the Award of the twelve was ready for publication.[1] That the *Dictum* might be proclaimed with the utmost solemnity, not only were the barons summoned to meet in Parliament at Northampton on October 27, but, by the authority of the Legate, all the superior clergy.[2] The *Award* was published by the Legate after his sermon. The " Disinherited " were not to lose their lands. They could redeem them by payments varying in proportion to their offences, and, if the *Dictum* restored his rights to the King, he was to see to the strict administration of justice, and to observe those liberties of the Church and State to which he had sworn.[3]

After the close of this most important parliament, the Legate continued his good work of pacification. When, in December, the Castle of Kenilworth finally surrendered, the lives and goods of its gallant defenders were spared at the cardinal's intercession.[4]

In the very midst of all these serious political troubles, Ottoboni found time to attend to a request of the Masters and Scholars of Oxford University. In 1254 Innocent IV. had taken the University under the protection of

Ottoboni gives privileges to Oxford University, 1266.

[1] Rob. of Gloucester, v. 1397, notes how the twelve " often. disagreed ". *Cf.* Green, *l.c.*, p. 215. E. F. Jacob in his *Studies in the period of baronial reform and rebellion*, does justice to the work of Ottoboni. He concludes : " If the detailed Provisions of the *Dictum de Ken.* are not his, the credit for its inception and its interpretation must in great part belong to him. Pg. 170–1, Oxford, 1925.

[2] Rishanger, *Chron.*, 57, *C. S.* The final proclamation of the *Ban* of Kenilworth was made at Coventry, Nov. 1. *Cf. Ann. of Waverley*, p. 372 ; of *Osney*, pp. 190–1 ; and of *Dunstable*, p. 243 ; *Chron. of Abingdon*, p. 557, and *Chron. Maiorum*, p. 88.

[3] *Cf.* Green, *l.c.*, where the *Dictum* is treated of at length, p. 218 ff. It shows that the Legate was no blind partisan of the King.

[4] *Chron. of Abingdon*, p. 557. Previously, the younger Simon de Montfort had submitted to the arbitration of the Legate among others Rishanger, *Chron.*, p. 42, *R. S.*

the Holy See.   In response to the request he had received,
Ottoboni confirmed the privilege of Innocent, and granted
an indulgence of twenty days to all who should attend
the three masses which were wont to be said at Oxford
for the Pope, the Roman Church, the Royal family
and the benefactors of the University (July, 1266).[1]

Trouble in
London,
1267.

After spending Christmas with the King at Osney,[2]
the Legate proceeded to London, and kept the feast of
St. Edward (Jan. 5) with him also.[3] He then betook
himself to his ordinary residence, the Tower. He continued, however, to devote himself ceaselessly to the
work of pacification, without, as he said, refusing any
toil.[4] Much remained for him to do that was by no
means easy of accomplishment. He had summoned
to a conference with him the powerful Gilbert de Clare,
Earl of Gloucester, whom he had every reason at this time
to regard as favourable to the cause of the King and of
peace. But the Earl was treacherous, and advanced on
London with a large force which he had secretly gathered
together (March, 1267).[5] Apprised of his approach,
the citizens became alarmed, and took counsel with the

[1] *Munimenta Oxon.*, i, p. 32, *R. S.* Boniface VIII. exempted the
University from all local ecclesiastical authority (June 12, 1300,
ib., p. 78 ff.), and Urban V. even decided that the election of the
Chancellor need not be confirmed by the bishop of Lincoln. *Ib.*,
p. 228, Nov. 8, 1368.

[2] *Ann. of Winchester*, p. 105.

[3] Rishanger, p. 46, *R. S.*, p. 59, *C. S.* Henry showed his gratitude
to the Legate by setting him on his throne during the banquet. " In
prandio vero Legatum in sedili regio collocavit." R., p. 46.   Mr.
Bateman, *Simon de Montfort*, p. 260, who wonld appear to have no
conception of the part our historians assign to Ottoboni in the
settling of our country, says (but without citing any authority) there
was " general indignation " because "the Legate was placed in the
royal seat, and served before the King." Henry, we take it, was the
best judge of what he owed the Legate.

[4] " Nec timentes pro re hujusmodi quemcunque subire laborem."
Ep. xvi, p. 105.

[5] Rob. of Gloucester, v. 1427 ff. *Cf. Ann. London*, p. 77.

Legate as the King had commanded them to do.[1] But Ottoboni had full trust in the Earl, and permitted his entry into the city. He soon perceived, however, what a mistake he had made when he found himself besieged in the Tower. Although Earl Gilbert failed to take the Tower,[2] much mischief was done in the city before the King and Prince were able to collect a sufficient force to induce him to ask for peace (June).[3] In presence of the Legate, the Earl swore never again to bear arms against the King, and to offer such security to him as should be determined by the Pope.[4] But at the same time the author of the *Annals of Osney* avers that many contended that Gilbert's seizure of London improved the position of the " Disinherited ", who were in many cases able to recover their estates without having to pay fines. The rest of them, including those who had held out in the island of Ely, submitted to the King on the basis of the Award of Kenilworth.[5]

Thus about the middle of the year (July), peace was once more restored to the exhausted land,[6] and a certain unanimity to the utterances of its historians. Both royalist and baronial writers at once begin to grumble at the taxes. After the peace, says the Osney annalist, " both the lord King and his son began to extort vast sums of money both from the clergy and from the laity,

Peace and taxation, 1267.

[1] *Chron. Mai.*, p. 90.

[2] According to Wykes, p. 201, the Legate animated its few defenders to a vigorous resistance : " ad motus bellicos animavit."

[3] To raise money the King empowered Ottoboni to pledge his jewels and plate for his " most urgent " business, March 28, 1267, ap. *Cal. of Patent Rolls Henry III.*, vol. vi, p. 50, *cf.* p. 133.

[4] See the Treaty in Rymer, i, 841. Each party " acceptans expresse quicquid summus Pontifex super securitate . . . duxerit ordinandum ". *Cf. ib.*, p. 849 ; *Chron. Mai.*, p. 93 ; John de Oxenedes, *Chron.*, p. 212, *R. S.* ; Wykes and the *Annals of Osney*, p. 205 f. ; *Flores*, iii, 14 ff. ; Rishanger, *Chron.*, p. 57, *R. S.*

[5] Pg. 206–7. *Cf. Ann. de Wint.*, p. 105.

[6] *Ann. de Oseneia*, p. 207 ; Wykes, p. 210 ; *Flores*, iii, 6.

so that many were more harassed in the days of peace
than in the time of war." [1]

Among the measures to strengthen the King's position
that Ottoboni was authorized by the Pope to take, was
the granting to him of a tenth of his ecclesiastical revenues
for three years.[2]   The raising of the money was seriously
discussed at a Parliament that had been held at
St. Edmundsbury in the early part of the year (February,
1267). It would seem that there was considerable
opposition to what Wykes calls " the unheard of grant "
which the Pope, " exceeding, if it is right to say so,
rather than exercising his plenitude of power," had
granted to the King.[3] However, the grant was made
in the end ; and was, according to Wykes (who was
another Matthew Paris in his denunciations of monastic
taxation), pushed by the Pope in his own interests
as well as in those of the King. He looked forward, says
Wykes, to getting out of the proceeds the tribute money
which had not been paid during the period of the troubles.
Certain it is that whilst, on the one hand, the Pope
assigned 60,000 pounds (of Tours) to the Queen out of
the tenth,[4] there is extant an order of King Henry to
pay Pope Clement 7,000 marks of the arrears of the
annual grant.[5]

[1] Pg. 207. How many Englishmen are in the same condition
to-day ! The Royalist Wykes, however, speaks only of the action of
the Pope in the taxation, pp. 212–14.

[2] *Supra*, p. 312. Not for seven years as Rishanger, p. 47, *R. S.*,
says by mistake. Elsewhere, however, in the same chronicle, p. 51,
and in his other, p. 61, *C. S.*, he gives the proper term of years. *Cf.*
Wykes, p. 213. When the Osney annalist, p. 198, says that by the
Pope's authority the English church began to pay the tenth in 1266,
he appears to refer to the beginning of what we call the year 1267.
Cf. the *Annales of Dunstable*, p. 244.

[3] Pg. 213. The accounts in the two chronicles of Rishanger, p. 50,
R. S., and p. 60, *C. S.*, are identical.

[4] Ep. July 15, 1267, ap. Rymer, i, p. 842 (ed. 1704).

[5] *Ib.* Record ed., i, 473. *Cf. Reg.*, n. 786, June 22, 1266. Wykes
tells how the Pope sent over Master Simeon to England to look

But the good work accomplished by Ottoboni was
not yet finished. Llewellyn, prince of North Wales,
had helped the party of Simon de Montfort, and had to
be dealt with. Accordingly, in company with the King,
the legate went towards the principality in September.[1]
In making peace between Henry and the Prince, for
which he had laboured long and earnestly, Ottoboni
secured his property for Llewellyn,[2] as the King had
given him all power in the matter.[3] Llewellyn was also
to be recognized as " Prince of Wales ", but had to do
homage to Henry.[4]

When he had thus satisfactorily settled the last detail
in the way of perfect peace for the State, Ottoboni,
having spent Christmas with the King at the abbey of
Hyde,[5] met the clergy of England in Council at St. Paul's
in London, April 23, 1268. There, to bring order into
the Church, which as the Cardinal said, had, with the
State fallen from its high place, he published a number
of Constitutions.[6] With the previous ones of the legate

[marginal notes: Peace with Llewellyn, 1267. — Council of London; Ottoboni's Constitutions, 1268.]

after his financial interests, and ordered the religious houses of
England to pay him " procurations " at the rate of 7 solidi a day.
Wykes complains of the falling off of morals and the piling up of
taxation after the Civil War, just as Englishmen are complaining to-
day after the Great War. Wykes complains, too, of the fresh valuation
on which the tenth was to be raised. The " Simeon " of Wykes is no
doubt the " master *Sinicius* " appointed by Clement to collect the
annual tribute and the other papal dues in England on May 23,
1266. *Cf. Reg.*, nn. 764–71

[1] *Cf.* documents in Rymer, i, pp. 843–7.

[2] *Cf.* the *Annals of Winchester*, p. 105, ep. of Ottoboni, 35, p. 118.

[3] " Nos (Henry), pacis semitas amplectens, ven. Patri Ott. S.
Adriani Diac. Card. Apostolicæ Sedis Legato, componendi, et
compositionem firmandi prout sibi videbitur expedire . . . cum
præfato Lewelino . . . plenam . . . concedimus potestatem." Sept. 21,
1267. Rymer, p. 843.

[4] *Cf.* the decision of Ottoboni, *ib.*, p. 845 f., Sept. 29.

[5] *Ann. de Wint.*, p. 106, where there was a fierce fight between the
abbots' and the legate's men.

[6] The Kingdom of England : " Quod diebus proximis a gloriæ
suæ culmine . . . exciderat." *Cf.* the preface to his *Constitutions,*

Otho, they became the basis of all future ecclesiastical legislation in Catholic England. Many of them, notes Lingard, " which regard commendams, residence, dilapidations, repairs, and the plurality of benefices still retain the force of law in the ecclesiastical courts." His legislation against pluralities provoked much opposition from *some* [1] of the clergy, and they talked of appealing to the Pope.[2] But, after private conversation with the Legate, they withdrew their appeal ; and so he, who had presided with " the glory of magnificent power ", says a Chronicler,[3] ordered his Constitutions to be " observed inviolate ".[4]

The Legate preaches the Crusade, June, 1268.
There still remained one more task for the Legate. He had been commissioned by the Pope to appeal for help for the Holy Land. As the King and the magnates of his realm were to hold a Parliament at Northampton, Ottoboni betook himself thither, and set forth the desperate condition of the Holy Land with such eloquence that Prince Edward and Prince Edmund for his father,[5] " and many other magnates received the cross from him ".[6] Among these " other magnates " was Tedaldus

p. 78, printed with the notes of John of Athona at the end of Lynwood's *Provinciale*, ed. Oxford, 1679.

[1] B. Cotton, *Chron.*, p. 143, says " all ".

[2] Wykes, pp. 215–16.

[3] *Ib.* " Cum magnificæ potestatis gloria."

[4] *Ib. Cf.* Contin. of W. of Newburgh : " nullo reclamante," p. 553. *Ann. de Wintonia*, p. 106. " Varias constitutiones et statua præcepit observari." On the " pluralities " legislation of Ottoboni, *cf.* Maitland, *Canon Law in England*, p. 20 ff. We may note that Ottoboni was not successful in imposing legislation on Scotland. No doubt on the ground that Scotland was immediately subject to the Holy See, and because, as they held, Ottoboni could not show that he had been sent out by Pope Clement for the special purpose of legislating for Scotland, the King and bishops refused to admit him into Scotland or to accept his laws. *Cf.* Fordun, *Scolichronicon*, x, cc. 22 and 24, pp. 106, and 108 ; and Wilkins, *Concilia*, ii.

[5] The Pope had, April 9, 1268, *Reg.*, n. 609, absolved Henry himself from his vow to take the Cross. The state of the country forbade his leaving it.

[6] *Ann. de Wint.*, p. 107 ; Rishanger, p. 59 ; *Ann. de Osen.*, p. 216.

(or Theobald), archdeacon of Liège, afterwards Pope
Gregory X., who had come to England in the suite of
the Legate (June 24).[1] When, however, at the request
of Ottoboni and King Henry, Pope Clement wrote to
the Scotch bishops to urge them to pay to King Henry
a tenth of the Scotch ecclesiastical revenues for the
purposes of the Crusade, King Alexander and his clergy
replied that the money was needed for their own Crusaders,
of whom, indeed, not a few " with great joy " set out not
long after.[2]

Ottoboni's task was at length finished, and he was
ardently desirous of returning home and seeing " the face
of his father " the Pope.[3] There had been times when the
difficulty of the work which he had to do had well nigh
overwhelmed him, and he had implored Clement to
recall him. The Pope had had to encourage him.
He declared to him that to give up the work he
had commenced would result " in the overthrow of
the whole realm, the death of the King and Queen and
their children, and the irrevocable loss to the Roman
Church of so noble a fief ".[4] He bade him stick to the
ship ; for the barque of Peter, no matter how tossed
about, cannot, like other ships, be wrecked. " If you
remain and succeed, all the merit will be yours, and you
will reflect glory on us and on your brethren."

Ottoboni remained, but continued to wish to return [5] ;

*Ottoboni
leaves
England,
1268.*

---

[1] Cf. *Flores*, iii, 14.

[2] Fordun, *l.c.*, c. 24, p. 109.

[3] Ep. Ott., 26, p. 112 ; *cf.* ep. Clem., 559, of Nov. 23, 1267, ap. M., ii,
542.

[4] Ep. 289, May 16, 1266, ap. M., ii, 328. " Si terram deseris, et
sinistrum, quod absit emergat tibi totum ab omnibus imputabitur."
In concluding his letter the Pope tells his legate that he has put off
deciding the case of the bishops till he has received further information
regarding the condition of the realm. *Cf. infra*, p. 353, for further light
on the idea that England might be lost to the Holy See.

[5] *Cf.* ep. Clem., 559, " Tibi ad reditum spiranti." He had had to
endure ill-health and " unspeakable " trials of mind in his work for the

so that, at length, at the close of the year 1267, Clement felt constrained to leave the question of further stay or return to Ottoboni's own judgment. He acknowledged that his presence in the curia would be very useful to the Roman Church, and that, unless spoilt " by the usual levity of the English people ", he had well accomplished the delicate negotiations that had been entrusted to him. Hence, as he must know the state of England better than the writer, he leaves his future action to his conscience. He goes on to say that he has heard that he has made a vow to make a pilgrimage to St. James of Compostella. He may certainly go thither; but, if his vow should weigh heavily on him, he is ready to commute it. Should he, however, decide to go to Spain,[1] the Pope bids him make a careful inquiry into the state of the Church there, and make him a report thereon when he returns. He concludes his letter by giving him various items of news. King Charles is still besieging Poggibonzi, and he has made him " Peacemaker of Tuscany ", against the Sienese and other Ghibellines with whom the Senator Henry of Castile is trying to form an alliance. Henry has seized John Savelli, some of the Anibaldi, etc. Conradin is at Verona with a small army; but has nearly all Lombardy against him.

Ottoboni's conscience assured him that he had earned a right to a rest; and at the council he earnestly (devote) requested permission to return home.[2] This could not reasonably be any longer refused him, and he left the

---

good of the realm; " labores corporis graves . . . indicibiles mentis molestias." See his fine letter of July 7, 1268, to the clergy of the Northern Province, in which he extols the blessings of peace and begs the clergy to help the Disinherited to pay their fines. Ep. ap. *Northern Registers*, p. 15, *R. S.*, or ap. *Register of Archbp. Giffard*, p. 97 ff., Surtees Society.

[1] " Statum ecclesiarum Hispaniæ qui multum collapsus est."

[2] John of Oxnead, *Chron.*, p. 213.

country about the middle of July[1] with, say Wykes and others meanly, a number of swollen money bags.[2] If ever the labourer was worthy of his hire it was the legate Ottoboni Fieschi, who left our country rejoicing that the King's majesty was re-established, and the liberty of the subject assured.[3]

When, as legate of Urban IV. to England, Guy Fulcodi had resided in the north of France (1264), he had heard much of the novel views, powerfully set forth, of the English Franciscan friar, Roger Bacon († 1294), and he had endeavoured to obtain a fair copy of the work (opus . . . scriptum de bona littera) which he believed that the friar had already published. When Guy became Pope Clement IV., he wrote to Roger ; and after thanking him for the communication he had received from him, commanded him to send him the work, despite any superior's prohibition to the contrary. He also bade him secretly and without delay to make known to him what should be done to remedy the state of things against which he had spoken.[4]

In complying, after the lapse of some time, with the Pope's request, Roger explained that, contrary to the belief of His Holiness, the book asked for had not been as yet composed. Up to the time of receiving the Pope's

---

[1] The *Annals of London*, p. 79, give July 5 ; Oxnead, p. 213, July 13 and Wykes, p. 219, " about the feast of S. Margaret, virgin (July 20)."

[2] *Ann. de Os.*, p. 217–18 ; Rishanger, p. 59, *R. S.* ; Wykes, " tumentibus sacculis."

[3] Ep. Ott., 36, p. 119. " Et regnantis solium consurgat, et inferiorum gradus suis locis coopti proprie libertatis securitate lætentur." The author of the *Annals of Winchester* says that Ottoboni did many more " mirabilia " than he records. Among them were his relations with the monastery of Stratford de Langthorne, on which see Miss R. Graham, *English Hist. Rev.*, April, 1918, p. 213 ff. The cardinal's departure was regretted immediately. *Cf.* ep. to him of arch. Giffard of York, *Reg. of W. G.*, p. 157, Surtees Soc., 1904.

[4] Ep. June 22, 1266, ap. *Thes. nov.*, ii, p. 358, or Brewer, *Fr. R. Bacon Op. ined.*, i, p. 1, *R. S.*

request, he had only written an odd chapter or two,
nothing fit for " your wisdom ".[1] One reason for this
was the fact that, by the rule of the Franciscan Order,
its members were not permitted to write books to be
communicated to others unless commanded by their
superiors, and moreover he could not have got a fair
copy of a book made except by employing transcribers
unconnected with the Order, and they would have copied
the works for their own purposes or those of others
without regard to his wishes, as authors' works, he
declared, are now very often pirated in Paris by the
dishonesty of the transcribers.

Then, after the reception of the Pope's letter, there
had been great difficulty from his superiors. They knew
not of the Pope's order, and he, as His Holiness had
enjoined secrecy, could not inform them of it. Expense
also was a serious item, to which the Pope, with all he
had to think about, did not advert. It was only reverence
for the Vicar of Christ that made him persevere in the
midst of such difficulties.[2]

Roger sends
three works
to the Pope,
1267.

From the day, however, that he received the papal
mandate, Roger devoted himself with such energy to
putting down in writing the results of years of scientific
thought and experiment, that, in about a year and a half,
he had composed and dispatched three important works
to Pope Clement. " Such a feat," says Mt. Brewer, " is
unparalleled in the history of literature." [3] They were
his *Opus Majus*, *Opus Minus*, and *Opus Tertium*,[4] of

---

[1] Even the *Opus Majus* which Bacon ultimately sent to the Pope
was only a preliminary treatise ("tractatus præambulans " or a
" persuasio ") to the work on all branches of knowledge which he had
at first hoped to write—his *Opus principale*.

[2] *Cf. Opus Tertium*, cc. 2 and 3, pp. 13–16 ; and Brewer, *Introduction*,
p. xv.

[3] *Ib.*, p. xlv.

[4] The *Opus Magnus* alone, edited by Dr. S. Jebb in 1733, and not
including the seventh part on Ethics, ran to 474 pages in folio. The

which the second and third were introductory to the
first. The *Opus Majus* " embraced the entire scope of
the physical sciences as then understood ",[1] and, like
the other two, was dedicated to the Pope, and sent to
him, also like the other two, by the youth John of London.[2]
John, who had been trained by Roge rfrom his youth
upwards, was chosen by him because, for that very
reason, he could explain the friar's methods and experi-
ments to the Pope, who from his position could not have
much leisure to devote to study.[3]

Roger composed what is generally described as his
second work, the *Opus Minus*, lest, on account of the
dangers of the roads, the larger work might be lost, and
also to explain and to serve as an abridgment to his
chief work. He wished that the Pope whose occupations
were many and weighty should have a sort of epitome
by means of which he could recall to his mind the conclusions of the wise.[4]

The Opus Minus.

new edition of *The Opus Majus of Roger Bacon*, by J. H. Bridges,
Oxford, 1897–1900, runs to three volumes.

[1] Brewer, *l.c.*, p. xlvi. *Cf.* Bacon's *Compendium studii philosophiæ*,
c. 3, p. 414, ap. *ib.* " Unde ad imperium d. Clementis . . . collegi in
tractatu speciali electas sententias scripturæ, etc. . . . et præposui
omnibus libris quos misi, etc."

[2] Hence in sending the Pope the *Opus Tertium*, Roger says he has
already sent " to the magnitude of your wisdom two works ". *Ib.*, p. 3.
Of these three works Bacon sent fair copies to the Pope ; but John
also bore other treatises of which he was to get fair copies made if the
Pope wished to read them. See the same, *Op. T.*, p. 270. He also sent
the Pope a treatise " On Rays " separate from the *Op. Majus*, but
whether a fair copy or not is not stated. *Op. T.*, p. 227.

[3] *Cf. Op. Tertium*, c. 19. " Quoniam vero a longis temporibus fuit
vestra sapientia negotiis ecclesiasticis et curiis variis rerum publicarum
occupata, atque sedes apostolica non permittit hominem vacare multo
studio, etc." Pg. 60 ff., ed. Brewer. *Cf.* pp. 111, 221, 270, and *Op.
Minus*, ap. *ib.*, pp. 315–16, regarding the " youth " John, and also the
" letter preface " of Roger found by Dom (now Cardinal) Gasquet,
and published in the *English Hist. Rev.*, xii (1897) : " Non solum
adolescens hic potest vestre sanctitatis occupationibus in opere quod
mitto deservire." Pg. 516–17.

[4] *Op. tert.*, p. 5.

There is no little controversy as to the order in which the three works just enumerated were published ; and the discussion on the subject has even led to the denial that the *Opus Minus* and the *Opus Tertium* were ever actually sent off to the Pope at all.[1]

Unfortunately, owing to the state in which the manuscripts of Bacon's works has reached us, we do not know the precise form in which they left his hands. The *Fragment* of one of Roger's works found and published by Dom, now Cardinal, Gasquet would have thrown much light on the subject if it were certain to which of the three works in question it belongs. Siding with those authorities who believe it belongs to the *Opus Minus*, we believe that the said work was the first one sent to the Pope. He had found that the composition of his principal work (scriptum principale) which was to have been written on the same lines as the subsequent *Opus Majus* was going to take longer than he had anticipated [2] ; and so, not to keep Clement waiting too long, he sent off to him the *Opus Minus*. It was to serve as a *compendium* to the larger work (*Opus Majus*) that was to follow, as a table of contents, so that he would know clearly what he had to expect in that work, and as an explanatory introduction to it.[3]

[1] P. Mandonnet, " R. Bacon et la composition des troi ' Opus ' " in *Revue Néo-Scolastique de Philosophie*, Feb. and May, 1913, Louvain, tries to prove that the *O.M.* and the *O.T.* were never dispatched to the Pope, that the *Opus Majus* was not sent before the beginning of 1268, and that Gasquet's *Fragment* was the " letter preface " to the *Opus Majus*.

[2] It is clear that, when the *Opus Minus* was written the *Opus Principale*, at any rate, was not finished. " Sicut nec potuit *scriptum principale* propter impedimenta celsitudini vestræ præparari, sic propter impedimenta nec potuit adhuc propter operis prolixitatem." *Op. Min.*, p. 315. *R. S. Cf.* the " letter preface " : " Quamvis autem scriptum principale non transmitto." Pg. 503, Gasquet. *Cf.* p. 501.

[3] Hence in the *Op. T.*, after speaking of the magnitude (quantitas) of the main work (principalis scripturæ), he says that he thought of

The *Opus Majus* itself (the substitute for his proposed *Opus Principale*) was finally sent off to the Pope towards the end of the year 1267 ; and was followed soon after by the *Opus Tertium* (1267).[1] In the beginning of the last-named book Bacon wrote : " To the magnitude of your wisdom I have sent two works. Of these one is the chief (principale), and in it owing to my respect for your highness and the dignity of your office by which advantage for the whole world must be procured, I endeavoured, as far as difficult conditions (impedimenta) allowed and my memory permitted, to draw the dictates of philosophy to their farthest conclusions (ad ultimam potestatem)."

Then, after declaring that he had composed his second work (i.e., the *opus minus*) to serve as a complement to elucidate the first, he adds that he had written a third work (the *opus tertium*) to throw light upon and to perfect each of the others.[2] He proceeds to express his astonishment that the Pope should think of asking words of wisdom from one who was unknown to the great world ; that " the head of the Church " should deign to seek information from the " unworthy sole of its foot ", and

---

drawing up (1) a *compendium* to the *Opus Majus* : " Cogitavi ut sub quodam *compendio* videretis quod latius in *Majori Opere* est diffusum." Pg. 5, *R. S. Cf.* p. 67 (2). A table of contents to it : " Necesse fuit ut aliud opusculum formarem in quo *principalis scripturæ intentionem* aperirem." If as we suppose the " letter-preface " belongs to this *Opus Minus*, then it certainly does forecast the contents of the *Op. Maj.* (3). An explanatory introduction to it : " Ideoque velut *introductorium* volui secundam parare scripturam quatenus difficultas primi operis mitigetur." *Ib.* The " first work " of which he speaks here is the *Op. Maj.* ; first in time of commencement and importance, but not of completion and dispatch. *Cf. Op. T.*, c. 21, p. 67 f. Here the *Principalis Scriptura* is the *Op. Majus.*

[1] And even then he regrets in it that he has not been able to send exactly what the Pope required, namely, " Ut scriptum philosophiæ mitterem principale." *Op. T.*, c. 17, p. 58.

[2] *Op. T.*, p. 6, *R. S.*

that " the Vicar of our Saviour and the lord of the whole earth " should condescend to beg of me " who am scarce worthy to be numbered amongst its parts ".[1] The difficulties, he continues, in the way of the studious in these days are so great that they can only be removed by the special intervention of the Pope. " But where such authority manifests itself, there can be no difficulty, since it penetrates the heavens, opens purgatory, treads down hell, and enfolds the whole earth." [2] Praised then be God for putting on the throne of his Kingdom a wise ruler interested in learning ; for Clement's predecessors " occupied with other concerns of the Church, and much oppressed by contumacious tyrants " have had no leisure for learning.[3] At present, especially, the cause of science can be advanced only by the support of such a patron as the lord Pope, the Emperor, " or some magnificent King like that of France (St. Louis IX)." [4] Bacon, therefore, earnestly begs Clement to take great care of his health, and not to be too abstemious, nor to be too much given to watchings [5] ; for he is the Pope from whose virtue and extraordinary knowledge of the law [6] we may look for the return of the Greeks to the faith, the conversion of the Tartars, the destruction of the Saracens, and the formation of the one fold with its

---

[1] *Ib.*, p. 7, *R. S.* He continues for many more sentences in the same strain : " Sol sapientiæ mundum irradians, vas admirabile opus excelsi, hominem ignorantiæ multiplici caligine involutum, . . . sapientum jubet exprimere monumenta."

[2] *Ib.*, p. 8.

[3] *Ib.*, pp. 9–10

[4] *Op. T.*, p. 24, *R. S.* *Cf.* p. 86.

[5] For after all, he wisely adds " piety " is of greater worth than bodily mortifications : " quia exercitatio corporis ad modicum valet, pietas autem ad omnia, ut dicit apostolus." *Ib.*, p. 87.

[6] " Nunquam fuit Papa qui ita veraciter sciret jus sicut vos ; nec credo quod erit aliquis." *Ib.*, p. 86.

one shepherd.[1]   From his authority too must come the reform of the Calendar.[2]

With regard to the three works which Bacon sent to Pope Clement, it should be noted that they are largely concerned with pleas for new methods in studies. The friar begged for more experimental work in physical science, and in literature for a thorough knowledge of the original languages in which the Scriptures and the great works of the philosophers were written. Thoroughly convinced of the unity of knowledge, he sketched the main outlines of its great branches.

As, however, we have no proof that Clement ever read the rather undigested mass of the masterful friar's writings, or that they exerted any influence over him, the subject need not be pursued by us any further. In fact we do not know even that the poor friar was ever as much as thanked for his laborious efforts, still less if he was reimbursed for the money expended on their production.   Certainly the Pope's messengers did nothing to help Roger to the acquisition of that money [3] the getting of which had brought him much confusion and his friends no little loss.[4]

The death of Clement was certainly a misfortune for Roger. The worthy friar had written a great deal, and that too very hastily ; he had not kept his scientific facts and theories rigidly apart from those of philosophy and theology ; and he had, not unnaturally, offended many by his sweeping condemnation of not a few of their favourite authorities, and by his reckless declamations against all classes of both ecclesiastical and civil society.[5]

Imprisonment and death of Roger.

[1] Bacon declares that for forty years it had been prophesied that such a Pope would arise in these times. *Ib.*

[2] *Ib.*, p. 212. *Cf. Op. Min.*, p. 321. We may note that, in this latter work, Bacon adds that improved texts of the Sacred Scriptures must be sought for from the same source. *Ib.*, and p. 342.

[3] *Op. T.*, pp. 15–16.   [4] *Op. Majus*, pp. 2 and 58.

[5] *Cf.* his *Compend. stud. philos.*, p. 398 ff., *R. S.*

However, whilst Clement's successor, " the most blessed Gregory X., held the supreme authority," his books, as he tells us himself, were not gainsaid ; but, after that Pontiff's death, certain " great ones—famosi—in the Church " strove to have them burnt. But " by a most beautiful miracle " they were saved.[1]

Still, the final result of his rashness was that " the Minister-General of the Franciscans, Jerome of Ascoli (afterwards Pope Nicholas IV.), on the advice of many brethren, condemned and rejected the doctrine of the English brother, Roger Bacon, . . . which contains many suspect innovations, by reason of which Roger was imprisoned ".[2] The friars were also commanded to repudiate his teaching, and Pope Nicholas III. was asked to suppress it by his authority.[3] This was about the end of the year 1277 ; and it is believed that Roger remained under a mild kind of imprisonment almost to his death in 1292.[4]

THE VACANCY OF THE HOLY SEE.

The cardinals who took part in the conclave, Dec. 1, 1268–Sept. 1, 1271.

At the time of the death of Pope Clement there were twenty cardinals,[5] of whom Radulfus, bishop of Albano,

---

[1] *Op. Maj.*, part i, c. 9, ap. *M. G. SS.*, xxviii, p. 571.

[2] *Chron. XXIV General O.M.*, p. 360, ed. Quaracchi, 1897.   [3] *Ib.*

[4] The standard work on this original thinker is perhaps still *R. Bacon, sa vie etc.*, by E. Charles, Bordeaux, 1861. But as some of his works have been published since then, one should read the Prefaces to H. Rashdall's *R. B. compend. studii theol.*, Aberdeen, 1911 : A. G. Little, *Part of the Op. Tert. of R. B.*, Aberdeen, 1912 ; R. Steele, *Op. hactenus ined. R. B.*, Oxford, 1910–13, 3 vols. ; and the *Essays* contributed on the occasion of the seventh centenary of his birth, ed. A. G. Little, Oxford, 1914 ; H. G. James, *The Life and Work of R. B.*, London, 1914, a very bright essay by Rev. J. G. Vance, " R. B.," in *Dublin Rev.*, Oct., 1914, and J. H. Bridges, *The Life and Work of R. Bacon*, London, 1914. Despite Bacon's free criticism of many things ecclesiastic, Mr. Bridges feels called upon to point out that he was " intensely papal ". Pg. 166.

[5] Document of 1269 ap. Raynald, 1269, n. 7. In connexion with this election, reference is sometimes made to Loserth : " Akten über

was in France on the business of the Crusade of St. Louis. As his mission was confirmed to him by the College of Cardinals, and as he died during the Crusade in Tunis (August 11, 1270), he took no part in the conclave for the election of the new Pope. The work of electing a successor to Clement, therefore, was commenced by the following nineteen cardinals. Stephen, bishop of Palestrina, Otho of Tusculum, John Tolet " of Toledo ", the English Cistercian, bishop of Porto, Henry, bishop of Ostia ; the cardinal-priests, Simon of St. Martin, Ancherus of S. Prassede, Guido of St. Lawrence in Lucina, William of St. Mark, Simon de Brion of S. Cecily (afterwards Martin IV.), Anibaldo of the Twelve Apostles ; the cardinal-deacons, Richard of St. Angelo, Octavian of S. Maria in Via Lata, John of St. Nicholas in Carcere (afterwards Nicholas III.), Ottoboni Fieschi of St. Hadrian (afterwards Hadrian V.), James Savelli of S. Maria in Cosmedin (afterwards Honorius IV.), Godfrey of St. George in Velabro, Hubert of St. Eustachio, Jordan of SS. Cosmas and Damian, and Mathew Orsini of S. Maria in Portico. Of these nineteen two died during the long interregnum (*Jordan at the end of* 1269 and *Stephen July* 9, 1270), and Henry became so ill that he could take no further part in the election (June, 1270).

Now, according to the Ghibelline Annals of Piacenza,[1] eleven of the cardinals, Richard of the Anibaldi, Octavian, Hubert, etc., favoured the imperial party, whilst John Gaetani, Ottoboni, and others favoured King Charles. One section wanted a foreign Pope (de ultramontanis partibus), and the other an Italian Pope and an Emperor, so that " as is right and proper one may hold sway over the world in spiritual matters,

die Wahl Gregors X." in *Neues Archiv. der Gesellschaft,* 1895, vol. xxi, p. 309 ff. Hanover. But Loserth simply gives a notice of a certain MS. in which occur the acts printed in Raynaldus and elsewhere.

[1] Otherwise the *Chron. de rebus, etc.,* p. 293.

the other in temporal". A Norman chronicle speaks of three parties,[1] and other authors [2] of the ambition or partisanship of the individual cardinals.

The cardinals begin the election. Whatever were the party or private feelings that animated the cardinals in the year 1268, they proceeded to elect a new Pope on the second day after the burial of Clement. They adjourned in this case, not to the Cathedral but to the papal palace, under the protection of the Podestà and of the Captain of the People ; and, after the Mass of the Holy Ghost had been sung, they began the work of election.[3] They were not enclosed as now ; and, at first at least, appear to have returned to their homes in the afternoon or evening, as the case might be.

St. Philip Benizi to be Pope. It was soon apparent that they could not agree to elect one of their own number; and at length they began to talk of choosing the saintly general of the Servite Order, Philip Benizi.[4] It is said that he had come to Viterbo to exhort the cardinals to elect a Pope without further delay ; but, on hearing of their intention to elect him, he fled and hid himself forthwith.[5]

If the saintly Servite did not exhort the cardinals to do their duty, we may note here that that task was

---

[1] *Chron. Norman*, ap. *R. F. SS.*, xxiii, 220 : "ut duæ partes non possent in aliquem promovendum convenire, sicut electio papæ requirit."

[2] Our own Roger Bacon, *Compend. studii philosop.*, p. 399, *R. S.*

[3] *Cf. Ordo Rom. XII*, of Cencius, n. 77, ap. *Pat. Lat.*, t. 78, p. 1097. "Tractant de electione, perserutata omnium cardinalium voluntate."

[4] Hence he is represented with a tiara at his feet. *Cf.* his *life* in Butler *Lives of the Saints*, viii, 301, and Cristofori, *Il conclave del* 1270, pp. 10, 15, 129, 214.

[5] See also G. Signorelli, *Viterbo nella Storia della Chiesa*, p. 260. This is a valuable book, and I have made much use of it ; but the work of F. Cristofori (*Il conclave del* 1270 *e l'assassinio di Enrico di Cornovaglia-Cornwall*, Viterbo, 1888) is a confused conglomeration of material, useful and useless, most inaccurately printed.

undertaken by Vincent, archbishop of Tours.[1] After modestly asserting that he had no wish to teach the cardinals their duty, he said that his conscience urged him to tell them of the five bitter things which men were saying about them for not giving the Church of Rome a head. They say you are guilty of causing infidelity, scandal, bad example, manifold loss, and rancour or hatred. Infidelity; because the Church has no shepherd, heresy and unbelief are on the increase; for it belongs to the Pope alone to define what must be believed, what not believed, and to condemn errors. Then you yourselves know full well what scandal this long vacancy is causing. Not only the little ones are scandalized, but also those in high places; and yet you must remember that "it were better for him who has scandalized one of these little ones, if a mill-stone were hung round his neck and he were plunged in the depth of the sea". Think next of the bad example you are setting to other churches. After your example, they need not be ashamed of discord and negligence in their elections. What loss also to churches is your conduct causing! They lack defenders of their rights, and their spiritual needs are not being provided for. Lastly, you are causing rancour; for it cannot be that such things can go on without breeding enmities. Then, throwing himself on his knees, the archbishop, with tears in his eyes, humbly implored the cardinals to put an end to the delay.

---

[1] See a MS. of Monte Cassino, Cod. 21, Sec. xiii, f. 163 v., possibly an autograph. A copy of this MS. was most obligingly given me by Abbot Amelli. Internal evidence shows that the discourse had reference to this election. It refers to an election at Viterbo, and to the presence in the city of Guy and Simon de Montfort. Vincent was archbishop of Tours from 1257 to 1270 († Sept. 19), and he is said to have addressed the College of Cardinals on Thursday (quinta feria), Aug. 14. Now in 1270 August 14 (19 Cal. Sept.) did fall on a Thursday. We print the interesting portion of this document in an appendix.

Speaking in reply for the whole College, Otho cardinal-bishop of Tusculum, said that he knew full well that a very great deal more than what the archbishop had put forward was being said against them. They could offer no excuse ; but they trusted that God would not abandon His Church, and they thanked the archbishop for stimulating them to do their duty.

But the words and tears of the worthy prelate were thrown away, More than another year was to elapse before the disgraceful vacancy was filled at length.

The Viterbese begin to give the cardinals trouble.

If not at first, at least later on, the cardinals agreed to be enclosed.[1] But even then they could not come to any decision, and the Viterbese, getting restless, began to annoy them seriously. During the first half of the year 1270, there were constant recriminations between the cardinals and the people. On January 3, the cardinals called on the Podestà and the other civic authorities to keep the agreements they had entered into with them ; and five days after they excommunicated the Podestà, Corrado d'Alviano.[2] Despite promises of amendment on the part of the Commune,[3] the annoyances continued. At Pentecost (June 1) the election was still undecided, and the English cardinal, John Tolet (" of Toledo "), is said, with dry humour, to have suggested that the roof of the palace should be uncovered to give the Holy Ghost freer access to them.[4] Whether acting on this alleged hint or not, the Viterbese, while threatening to cut off the cardinals' food supplies, actually did uncover the roof ; and, on June 6, we find the cardinals, in a document

---

[1] Cf. Ptolemy of Lucca, Hist. Ecc., xxiv, 1, notes that at this period the " reclusio . . . erat spontanea, ut de electione aliorum Prælatorum contingit ".

[2] See Garampi's extracts from the lost register of Bassus, ap. Cristofori, l.c., pp. 108–9, 181–2, and 186–9. In document 36 on p. 187 the vi should be attached to the Ides and not to 1270.

[3] Doc. of Apr. 11, ap. Cristofri, l.c., p. 182.

[4] Cf. Vit. Greg. X., by B. Guidonis, ap. R. I. SS., iii, p. 597.

dated from " the uncovered palace " threatening to lay
Viterbo under an interdict and to excommunicate and
fine the chief civic authorities if they did not proceed
to recover the palace, to put an end to the annoyances
complained of, and, for a time at least, to allow cardinals
Simon of S. Cecily, Annibaldi, and Ottoboni to leave
the conclave in as much as they were ill.[1] These and
other threats produced the desired effect, and on August
22 (?) the new Podestà Albert and the civic authorities
swore to cease disturbing the cardinals for the future.[2]

Meanwhile, however, the worry and discomfort had *Hostiensis leaves the conclave.*
such an effect on Henry, cardinal-bishop of Ostia, that,
after he had renounced all his rights to take part in the
election, his brother cardinals granted him permission
to leave the Conclave altogether (June 8).[3] Soon after
this Stephen of Palestrina died (July 9), with the result
no doubt that the Viterbese were confirmed in their
undertaking to molest the cardinals no longer.

Whether Charles of Anjou was or was not at the *The action of Charles of Anjou.*
back of the disorderly conduct of the people of Viterbo
with a view to thus hurrying on the election or to putting
pressure on the party opposed to him, it is certain that
he kept sending agents to the Curia " on the King's

---

[1] See the document printed in full by Cristofori, pp.337–43. "Datum
Viterbii in discooperto palatio Viterbien. Epatus., die veneris ante
tertiam. VIII Idus Junii, A.D. 1270, Aplica. sede vacante."

[2] See the document (mutilated) in Cristofori, pp. 343–4. *Cf.* p. 181.
As cardinal Stephen's name is appended to this document, and he
died July 9, the date " Aug. 22 " should probably be June 22.

[3] The cardinals require that the Podestà and the Captain of the
people shall permit Henry " de Palatio in quo sumus inclusi . . . exire ".
Again : " Given from the uncovered Palace—Datum in Palatio
discooperto." Later, Henry himself described the state of things at
Viterbo in his Commentary on the Decretals. He tells how the people
shut up the cardinals in a house which they uncovered, and, moreover,
deprived them of their private rooms : " in una domo incluserunt,
ipsam discooperiendo et eis privatas cameras subtrahendo." Ed. 1581,
vol. i, f. 91, cited by Signorelli, p. 261, and more completely by
Cristofori, p. 127.

business ", and kept granting favours to different
cardinals.[1] At the same time, by putting off the payment
of the tribute due from Sicily, or by only paying part of it,
he helped to keep the cardinals in great want of money.[2]
They were, some of them at least, in such great straits
that they wrote abroad for help. Cardinals Richard
of the Anibaldi (Hanibal, as Archbishop Giffard calls
him) and Matteo Rosso wrote more than once for
pecuniary assistance to the Archbishop of York. But,
as we learn from Giffard's letter to his agent in Rome,
Richard de Nedham, he had had to refuse. Owing to
the recent troubles in England, which, he thought,
were likely to be made worse by the departure of Prince
Edward for Palestine, money was most scarce in England.
However, in the letter we are quoting, he bade his agent,
while making the most of the archbishop's own pecuniary
difficulties, give cardinal Richard twenty-five marks,
and cardinal Matteo ten pounds or ten marks, and express
his regret that he could not do more.[3] So pressed were

[1] See quotations from Minieri Riccio, *Reg. Angioino*, 1269 and 1270,
ap. Signorelli, *l.c.*, p. 263, nn. 17 and 18. See also Del Giudice, *Cod.
Diplom.*, iii, n. 92, for " our dear friend " Godfrey of St. George in
Velabro, and n. 139 for our " bosom friend—præcordialis amicus
noster ", Richard of St. Angelo. Ottoboni, Jordan, " his most cordial
friend," and Henry are also favoured.

[2] Del Giudice, *l.c.*, i, pp. 174–5.

[3] *Cf.* his letter of Nov. 3, 1271, ap. *Letters from Northern Registers*,
p. 39 f., *R. S. Cf.* his *Register*, p. 144 f., *Surtees Soc.* At that date he
could have heard of the election of Gregory X., and it appears to me
that, in this very letter, he shows that he knew of it. Both Raine and
Brown in the above editions speak as though Giffard had not heard of
the election. But he tells his agent to give " with considerable circumspection—cautius ", 100 marks to the lord Pope, " statim in sua
creatione " which might mean that the new Pope had not been elected ;
but at the end of the letter he says he will give more instructions to his
agent, " as soon as he hears of the arrival of the elect, in whose good
will (specialitate et gratia) we believe we can trust, unless he changes
the kind manner (modum . . . et affectum), to which he gave expression
towards England—nisi modum mutet quem pretendit in Angliam et

the cardinals for money, that they had to pledge the great gold ring which King Charles had given to Clement IV.[1]

Still they could not or would not agree. However, they continued to keep a watch over the affairs of the Church, and we find them in the course of the year 1270 trying to continue the work of Urban IV. and Clement IV. for the reunion of the Greeks,[2] and to protect ecclesiastics from the encroachments of various communes.[3] Meanwhile St. Louis of France had died in Tunis (1270) at the head of the last of the great Crusades; and when his son, the new King of France, Philip the Bold, accompanied by Charles of Anjou reached Viterbo (March 10, 1271),[4] the cardinals were as far as ever from being agreed. The two Kings, Baldwin, ex-emperor of Constantinople, and his son, and Henry of Almaine, the nephew of the King of England, and other magnates, most respectfully but earnestly besought the cardinals to end the danger to the Church which the long delay was causing.[5]

affectum." The "arrival", of course, refers to his return from Palestine. *Cf.* W. Giffard's letter to the cardinals " true servants of God and rulers of the Church—cives Apostolici Dei vere domestici, ordinatores ecclesie, etc.," in which he excuses himself from paying his triennial visit to Rome. Ep. pp. 159-60 in his *Register.* See also *ib.* for his letter to cardinal Richard excusing the smallness of the present he had made him; and also to card. M. Rubens, p. 244 and p. 144.

[1] Garampi (from the regist. of Bassus), *Sigillo della Garfagnana,* p. 81, n. 6, cited by Signorelli, p. 263 n.

[2] Potthast, 20505-6. *Cf. infra,* p. 404.

[3] *Ib.*, nn. 20508-9, and Signorelli, pp. 264-5, notes.

[4] See the itinerary of Charles in Durrieu, *Les Archives Angev.*, ii, 172.

[5] Will. de Nangis, *Gesta Phil.*, iii, ap. *R. F. SS.*, xx, p. 484. " Quos (the cardinals) rex cum reverentia et honore visitans, cuilibet dato pacis osculo, ut secundum Deum ad regendum sanctam ecclesiam idoneum pastorem eligerent, monuit simpliciter et oravit." *Cf. Contin. Chron. Martinus Polonus,* ap. *M. G. SS.*, xxiv, p. 251; *Ann. Genuenses,* ad an. 1271, ap. *R. I. SS.*, vi, p. 553: " Quod tali Christi Vicario sacrosanctæ Romanæ ecclesiæ providere curarent, qui Deo esset acceptabile, etc." *Chron. de Primat,* ap. *R. F. SS.*, xxiii, p. 86. The

Whilst the Kings were, to no purpose, trying to induce
the cardinals to elect a Pope, they and all Europe were
horrified by the news that in their very midst, in the
Church of St. Silvestro, Henry of Almaine had been
foully murdered, when he was hearing Mass, by Guy de
Montfort, then Vicar of King Charles in Tuscany, and
his brother Simon.   Having slain the defenceless Prince,
the assassins, completely to avenge the murder of their
father, the great earl of Leicester, dragged the bleeding
corpse from the church, and dashing it down in the square
in front of them, made off to the stronghold of Aldobrandini,
called the Red, count of the Maritima, and Guy's father-
in-law [1] (March 13).   It is hinted by at least one of our
historians [2] that Kings Charles and Philip were privy
to the atrocious crime.   But their letters to Prince Edward
and King Richard written immediately after the murder
do not seem the work of guilty men,[3] and Charles' first

presence of Baldwin and his son is proved by a document in Del Giudice,
Cod., ii, p. 41. Philip III. himself gave an account of what took place
to the abbot of St. Dennis ap. D'Achery, *Spicilegium*, iii, 669, and ap.
Cristofori, p. 219.

[1] *Flores Hist.*, iii, 21. The Viterbese some time after caused a picture
of the assassination to be painted on the wall of the Church.
Unfortunately, it has perished, but the author of the *Flores* has
preserved the inscription that was placed below it. The last two lines
ran :—

> " Urbe Viterbina fuit in ejus carne ruina
> Celi regina precor ut sit ei medicina."

The savage deed is mentioned by all the chroniclers of the age.
Because it took place before March 25 it is said in many chronicles to
have taken place in 1270. The flesh of the murdered Prince, separated
from the bones, was buried at Viterbo " between two Popes " (*Annal.
Halesienses*, ap. *M. G. SS.*, xvi), Clement IV. and Alexander IV., in
the Cathedral of S. Lorenzo. *Cf.* St. Clair Baddeley's " The English
murder at Viterbo ", at the end of his *Queen Joanna I.*, London, 1893.

[2] Wykes, *Chron.*, p. 242. He speaks of the Kings' " ignorantibus vel
forte conniventibus ".

[3] See the letter of Charles in Rymer, i, 870. He said that he had ordered
his new Vicar in Tuscany to pursue and capture the murderers. Philip's
letter is quoted in Blaauw, *The Barons' Wars*, p. 307, from a MS.

act was to order the confiscation of all Guy's property in the Kingdom.[1]

The cardinals in conclave forthwith excommunicated the murderers,[2] but the intervention of Gregory X., urged on, it is now said, by Edward I., was necessary before they were in any way brought to justice (March 1, 1273).[3]

Even the tragic outrage just related did not put an end to the differences among the cardinals. More months slipped by, and the Church still cried in vain for a Pope. At length, on September 1, after a conclave of two years and ten months, they agreed that the election should be made " by compromise ", and accordingly selected Simon of St. Martino, Guy and Richard, Octavian, John of St. Nicholas in Carcere, and James of Sta. Maria in Cosmedin to elect the new Pope.[4] A number of Franciscan historians pretend that the cardinals gave over their right of election to St. Bonaventure. While this is

Election of the arch-deacon of Liège by compromise, Sept. 1, 1271.

But, as the pursuit was, to say the best of it, unsuccessful, Edward never forgave Charles. However, as Guy's father-in-law was of the powerful family of the Anguillara, who had strong fortresses on the Lago di Bracciano and elsewhere, it was probably anything but easy to seize the murderers.

[1] Riccio, *Il regno*, pp. 11–12. " Qui Comes Guido *et fratres* incontinenti privati fuerunt a dicto rege Karulo omni honore, beneficio, et bonis." The contemporary Guido de Corvaria, *Hist. Pisanæ*, ap. *R. I. SS.*, xxiv, p. 679.

[2] Wykes, *l.c.*

[3] Gregory's bulls in Rymer, i, 890 ff., and in Gregory's *Register*, pp. 209, 210–15. *Cf. infra*, p. 369. The church of S. Silvestro, now del Gesù, has been declared " a national monument" and the inscription from the *Flores* has been set up on the epistle side of the altar. *Cf.* C. Pinzi, *I mon. di Viterbo*, p. 73 ff.

[4] See the official document in Raynaldus, an. 1271, n. 8. Either from illness or disgust the English cardinal had retired to his chambers; but he gave his assent to the " compromise ". According to the *Chron. de rebus*, three were of one party and three from the other, and the election was made by five out of the six. But the numbers and names of the cardinals given are unreliable.

certainly false, it is possible that the Saint may have suggested the name of Tedaldus to them, and they may have accepted his suggestion.[1] At any rate, the six cardinals did elect Tedaldus (Thedaldus, Theobald) Visconti, archdeacon of Liège, as their official pronouncements prove.[2]

Then, having contracted a loan for the purpose,[3] they dispatched a solemn embassy, headed by the Archbishop of Corinth, to the archdeacon (at the moment in Acre with Prince Edward) to inform him of his election, and faced as best they could the hard things which were deservedly directed against them.[4] Of these gibes there was popularly ascribed to " the white cardinal " the one which mocked them for having by their dissensions caused a mere archdeacon to be set over them.[5]

The satisfaction of the world at large at the termination of the long vacancy is well reflected in the communication on the subject made by Charles of Anjou to his Vicar in Sicily. He announces to him the date of the election ; calls it a day of joy for the whole world on which it behoves all men to rejoice and be glad ; and bids

---

[1] *Cf.* Wadding, iv, 329 ff.

[2] Ap. Raynaldus, *l.c.*, nn. 9–11. " Eslurent un sage clerc prodome et de bonne vie . . . sire Theals." *Cont. of Will. of Tyre*, ap. *P. L.*, t. 201, p. 1046.

[3] Sept. 12, 1271, ap. Cristofori, p. 181.

[4] Pipinus, *Chron.*, ix, p. 700. That the archbishop of Corinth was the head of the embassy is stated in *Chron. Erphord.*, Contin. iii, p. 688, ed. Holder-Egger. The ships for the envoys were supplied by King Charles. *Cf.* C. M. Riccio, *Della dom. Ang.*, p. 8.

[5] " Fertur per saltum noster Tedaldus altum

    Invidia fratrum fit pater ille patrum." The *Contin. of Will. of Neuburgh*, ap. *Chron. of Stephen*, ii, p. 561, *R. S.* The distich is given in somewhat different forms; e.g., in Rishanger, ad an. 1272, p. 71, *R. S.*

    " Papatus munus tenet, archidiaconus unus

      Quem patrem patrum, fecit discordia fratrum."

The serious historians, e.g., Herman of Altaich, simply say that God " permitted " the disagreement of the cardinals " ad malum totius Christianismi ".

him make known the good news to all. On his coming
from the Holy Land, the new Pope will probably land
at some port in the Kingdom. He must be honoured
more than he himself would be ; and the roads repaired
for his journey.[1]

---

[1] See the document (and similar ones were sent to all the great
officials of the Kingdom) ap. C. M. Riccio, *Della domin. Angioina,*
p. 2 and p. 31.

Bl. GREGORY X.

1271–1276.

Sources.—In one volume (Paris, 1892 ff.) M. M. J. Guiraud and L. Cadier have published the Registers of both Gregory X. and John XXI., but, so far (1928), it would seem that their work is not finished. There is no introduction to the letters of Gregory and no index to either register. Unfortunately the Register of Gregory is like most of the others. Unlike the interesting Register of Clement IV., it does not contain a large number of letters giving items of news on the important events of the moment. Its documents, when not treating of the Crusades, are simply concerned with the details of ecclesiastical government in every land. It contains 656 letters, but with three appendices of documents drawn from the collections of the notary Berard of Naples, and other sources, the number is raised to 1090.

In his *Istoria eccles. di Piacenza*, vol. ii, Piacenza, 1651, P. M. Campi published an anonymous contemporary *life* of Gregory (*Anon. C.*). It was written about 1290, certainly before 1297. After a short rhetorical introduction it begins the story of Gregory's career by telling of his taking the ecclesiastical habit under Gregory IX. It occupies about seven folio pages in Muratori (*R. I. SS.*, iii, pt. i, p. 599 ff.), who reprinted it; and, of the seven pages, it devotes about two to a list of Gregory's virtues and miracles. It is a simple narrative of the doings of a single-minded man, to which the shorter *lives* of Bernard Guidonis (*ib.*, p. 597 f.) and of Amalricus Angerius (*ib.*, pt. ii, p. 424 f.) add hardly anything new.

The original documents concerning the relations between Gregory and Rudolf of Hapsburg are to be found in : M. Gerbert, *Codex epist. Rudolphi*, Saint Blaise, 1772, and J. Schwalm, *Rudolfi regis Constitutiones* in *M. G. LL.*, Hanover, 1904.

Modern Works.—The notice of Gregory which Campi himself gave in his *Istoria* from the *Anon. C.* and other sources was by S. Petrasancta translated into Latin and republished, Rome, 1655. A fuller *life* (*Istoria del Pont. il B. Gregorio X.*, Rome, 1711) was published by A. M. Bonucci, and at the end of his work there is printed the *B. Gregorii X. relatio* prepared by three auditors of the Rota for his canonization and addressed to Urban VIII. Another *Relatio ad f. m. Gregorium* for the same purpose had already (Piacenza, 1624) been published by the above-named P. M. Campi. In 1876, P. Piacenza published a *Compendio della storia del B. Gregorio X.*, Piacenza, from these modern lives. Finally G. Mischi in the *Bollettino Storico Piacentino* wrote " Gregorio X. nella cronaca inedita di un Vescoro Aretino ". The bishop was Bened. Falconcini (1704–24). But the "inedited Chronicle" throws very little new light on the career of the Pope.

Different episodes of his life have been illustrated by a number of scholars. German writers have naturally treated of his relations with Rudolf of Hapsburg, e.g., A. Zisterer, *Gregor X. und Rudolf Hapsburg*, Freiburg-im-B., 1891.[1] A. G. Tononi has written a few pages on " Relazioni di Tedaldo Visconti (Gregorio X.) coll'Inghilterra 1259–71 " in *Archivio Storico per le provincie Parmensi*, 1902, Parma, 1905.[2] In the *Revue d'hist. ecclés.*, 1921, April and following numbers, M. Viller has written a valuable paper " La question de l'union des Églises entre Grecs et Latins (1274–1438) ". Perhaps if the learned author had observed a more strictly chronological order, the paper might have been more readily useful. The Papacy and France during the reign of Philip III. (1270–85) may be studied in L. Leclèrc, *Les rapports de la Papauté et de la France sous Philippe III.*, Bruxelles, 1809.

[1] The following which I have not examined are also cited in the same connexion, Walter Fritz, *Die Politik der Kurie unter Gregor X.*, Berlin, 1894 ; and H. Otto, *Die Beziehungen Rudolfs von H. zu P. G. X.*, Innsbruck, 1895.

[2] The same author has written *Il b. G. X. nelle sue attinenze colla basilica di S. Antonio in Piacenza*, Piacenza, 1876.

CONTEMPORARY SOVEREIGNS.

WESTERN EMPIRE.
The great interregnum, 1254–73.
Rivals.
Richard, earl of Cornwall,
Alfonso X. of Castile, 1257–72.
Rudolf of Hapsburg, 1273–91.
ENGLAND.
Henry III., 1216–72.
Edward I., 1272–1307.

EASTERN EMPIRE.
Michael VIII., Palæologus, 1259–82.

FRANCE.
Philip III. (the Bold), 1270-85.

CHAPTER I.

THE EARLY LIFE OF TEDALDO VISCONTI. HIS ELECTION
TO THE PAPACY.

THE "noble "[1] Tedaldo Visconti, a scion of the noble Family of
T. Visconti. house[2] of the Visconti of Piacenza, which may or may not have been connected with that of the more famous Visconti of Milan, was born in 1210,[3] but of parents whose names are unknown.[4] However, in Riccio's extracts from the Archives of Naples, we read of William and Henry Visconti, nephews of Pope Gregory, and of his very near relatives the noble Pelavicini of Peligrino.[5]

We are assured that Tedaldo's early years gave promise of his future greatness, that he held a canonry in the basilica of St. Antoninus in his native city, and that, as soon as he had acquired sufficient knowledge" of the liberal arts and Canon Law ", he

---

[1] " The actions of this *noble man* were indeed those of conciliator and a prince of peace," says Gregorovius, *Rome*, v, ii, p. 461. His name is variously written, Thedaldus, Tedaldus, Thealdus, Tealdus, or Theobaldus ; and our historian Wykes says he was commonly called Tyardus (pg. 246, *R. S.*).

[2] Truly does his biographer (*Anon. C.*) write, p. 509 : " Nobilis quidem genere, sed moribus nobilior."

[3] *Cf.* " a very old " document cited by Ciacconius. *Vit. PP. RR.*, ii, p. 185.

[4] Such is the statement of the older and more recent biographers of Gregory ; hence it would appear that that of Gregorovius, *l.c.*, p. 460, to the effect that he was " the son of Uberto, and nephew of Otto Visconti, archbishop of Milan " can scarcely be accepted. On the Visconti of Piacenza, see P. Piacenza, *Compend.*, pp. 1–12. Bonucci gives as his probable paternal mansion the house which in his time stood by the Church of S. Silvestro in Piacenza and was even then called " Palazzo del Papa ". Pg. 7.

[5] *Il regno*, 1271-2, pp. 84–112.

attached himself to the household of James Pecoraria, cardinal-bishop of Præneste, for he had heard much of his holiness (1236).[1]   In his journeys as Legate of Gregory IX. in France and Germany, the cardinal took Tedaldo with him as the steward of his establishment ; and that one, " so pleasing to God and acceptable to man," should not lack ecclesiastical rank, the legate named him archdeacon of Liège (1238–41).[2]   When, however, the cardinal set out to attend the council summoned by Gregory IX. in order to consider the conduct of Frederick II., the archdeacon was taken ill, and so avoided the fate of his master who, with so many other prelates on their journey to Rome, was seized and imprisoned by the emperor (1241).[3]

Greatly distressed at the misfortune of his friend and patron, Tedaldus set out for Italy as soon as he had recovered his health, and exerted himself to the utmost to obtain the cardinal's release. For, says his biographer, " love makes the heart sick till it attains the object beloved," and, as the tongue of man, he continues, is quite incapable of expressing the joy Tedaldus conceived when his friend was released (1243), he has to pass it over in silence.

Refuses the bishopric of Piacenza, 124

Soon after his release, the cardinal endeavoured to have the archdeacon appointed to the bishopric of Piacenza. A certain James, a Dominican, had, on the death of bishop Giles (May, 1242), intruded himself into the see, or was, in some way, " not canonically instituted." [4]   Tedaldus, however, refused the post lest, as his biographer assures us, if he accepted it, he should have

---

[1] *Anon. C.*, p. 599 ; *cf.* Parma, 1877.

[2] *Ib. Cf* G. Tononi, *Storia del Card. Jac. Pecoraria*, p. 136 and p. 153 ff. ;G. Tononi, *Il b. Greg. X. nelle sue attinenze colla basilica di. S. Antonino*, Piacanza, 1876.

[3] *Anon. C.*, p. 599. *Cf. supra*, vol. xiii, p. 308 ff.

[4] *Cf.* Potthast, ep. n. 11203 (Dec. 18, 1243). *Cf.* n. 11594.

been thought to have worked for the displacement of one who had been his friend.[1]

When the cardinals set out to assist at the thirteenth ecumenical council of Lyons, Pecoraria remained in Rome to celebrate the approaching feast of St. Peter. But to the grief both of the Romans and especially of Tedaldus, he died before the festival (June 25, 1244).[2] Much distressed at his patron's death, Tedaldus resolved to devote himself to study and to the work of the ministry at Liège. Hence he refused a number of earnest invitations from various cardinals who wished to engage him in their service.[3] However, when he passed through Lyons on his way to the University of Paris, he was received with the greatest cordiality by his friend the famous Philip, bishop-elect of Lyons. You have been sent by God, he declared, to show me how to comport myself with the Pope and the cardinals at the Council. Philip was so insistent on his remaining with him that, despite his wishes to the contrary, he yielded ; and, according to his biographer, won the praise of all by his administrative ability.[4]

At the conclusion of the council, Philip let him depart with great reluctance. He then betook himself to his studies at Paris, and not only " stored up in his heart " what his Professors taught him, but put in practice the

The Council of Lyons, 1245.

Study and work, 1245–65.

---

[1] *Anon. C.*, p. 600.   [2] *Ib.*

[3] *Anon. C., ib.* " A quampluribus de Cardinalibus, ut cum eis vellet morari, et eorum socius fieri instantius invitatur, etc." This shows that when he was elected Pope, he was not such an unknown person as some modern writers suppose.

[4] *Ib.* Philip must have attached Tedaldus in some way to his diocese ; for, when Pope, he spoke of himself as a " special member " of the Church of Lyons : " de cujus corpore nos olim . . . speciale membrum fuisse recolimus " (Posse, *Analecta Vat.*, n. 688 says " spirituale membrum "). *Reg.*, n. 37, P. Piacenza, *Compendio*, p. 18, quotes a bull of Gregory of 1274, in which he calls himself *a canon* of Lyons : " Memores uberum Ecclesiæ Lugdunensis quæ olim nos, tunc ipsius Canonicum, tractavit ut filium." Cf. *Reg.*, n. 601, Apr. 22, 1275, where he speaks of his long residence in Lyons as one of its canons.

good lessons that he had learnt. " Knowing that virtue was to be preferred to learning, and that faith not to be dead must be informed by good works." [1] Whilst he was at Paris, St. Louis, whom the archdeacon's biographer calls " the mirror of faith, and an elegant example of very good work ",[2] honoured him to such a degree that men wondered how it came about that he took such notice of a man who held no great office. But, adds the biographer with pride, " the King knew what he was doing," and both from what he heard and what he saw himself, he knew that the spirit of God was with him.[3] That was known also by the people of his archdeaconry at Liège. So hard did he work for the reformation of the clergy and laity entrusted to his charge that we are solemnly assured that, as long as their memory lasts, they will never forget his uprightness and the bright light of his piety.[4]

How it was that the archdeacon left Liège, to which he had gone after studying at Paris, and, as we shall narrate immediately, took the cross in France, we learn from other sources. The people of the city were oppressed and scandalized by Henry de Gueldre, its evil-living bishop. Unable to oppose him, Tedaldus left the place and went into voluntary exile in France ; but, when he became Pope, he supported the people by deposing him, and replacing him by John, bishop of Tournay.[5]

Accompanies Ottoboni to England, and takes the cross, 1265-8.

When St. Louis began to make active preparations for his last Crusade, Tedaldus, though then some fifty-five years of age, thinking that it was not right that the laity should display more zeal in that matter than the clergy,

---

[1] *Anon. C., ib.*

[2] In turn the archdeacon had the greatest affection for the King. See his letter of March 4, 1272, regarding his canonization ap. Raynaldus, *Ann.*, 1272, n. 59. " Quem vivum pura mente dileximus."

[3] *Ib.*   [4] *Ib.*

[5] *Cf.* Potthast, n. 20777, and sub 20, 859. *Chron. Imp. et Pont. Barav.*, ap. *M. G. SS.*, xxiv, p. 225 ; Baldwin. Ninov., *Chron.*, ap. *ib.*, xxv, p. 545 and *Chron. Hanon.*, p. 431. For the terrible sequel of Henry's career see John de Thilrode, *Chron.*, ap. *ib.*, pp. 561, 573.

took the cross himself, and was getting ready for departure, when a very different task was assigned him. His worthy biographer, a man evidently more remarkable for simple piety than for political insight, tells us very positively that the realm of England was at this time very near ruin, and that " there was a strong suspicion that a schism against the Roman Church was being hatched therein.[1] For Simon de Montfort, " in order that he might be the real King (solus regnaret)," had, with many bishops and barons taken up arms against his Sovereign, and had presumed to imprison him. Seeing that when Simon was exiled as a traitor from France, Henry had received him, had honoured him, and had given him his sister in marriage, the Earl was thus guilty of detestable ingratitude against his benefactor.[2]

Accordingly Clement IV., " pitying the King and the realm," sent thither cardinal Ottoboni, and urged him to take with him the archdeacon of Liège, as a man of " great prudence (sani consilii) ", beloved and trusted by the King, the Earl and the Bishops (1265). He was favourably known to Henry III. because he had helped to bring about peace between him and St. Louis of France.[3] Tedaldus accordingly accepted the cardinal's invitation to accompany him ; and his biographer, at any rate, does not hesitate to ascribe the peace that was brought about in England as much to the foresight of the archdeacon as " to the authority of the Legate ".[4]

When, at the close of his mission to England, Ottoboni preached a new Crusade, the archdeacon again took the cross.[5] In the following year (Dec. 28, 1269), he deposited

The Archdeacon goes to Acre, 1271.

---

[1] Pope Clement himself gave a voice to this wild idea. *Cf. supra,* p. 325.

[2] *Ib.,* p. 601.

[3] *Cf.* two letters (1259–60) of Henry to Alexander IV. ap. Shirley, *Letters of Henry III.,* ii, pp. 143, 150, *R. S.,* Rymer, i, 695.

[4] *Ib.* [5] *Supra,* p. 324.

with St. Louis the sum of twenty-four marks of gold for his crusading expenses.[1] He did not, however, for some reason, accompany the King to Tunis; but, on hearing of his death (Aug., 1270), he proceeded to Acre where he joined Prince Edward. Here he so distinguished himself by the zeal with which he inspired the Crusaders to fresh endeavours that some of them said that he would be or ought to be Pope.[2] It was at this time that the contemplation of the dire straits to which the Christian remnant in Palestine was reduced, made him henceforth a man of but one idea. Europe must be roused to reconquer Palestine.[3]

Tedaldus is elected Pope and returns to Italy, 1271-2.

Hence, when word was brought to him that, as his biographer believes, " by divine inspiration," he had been elected Pope, he realized that his chance of freeing the Holy Land had come. He at once set out for Italy, though the season was unsuited for sailing, escorted by a small fleet supplied by Charles of Anjou (Nov. 18). However, by the mercy of Him " who commands both the winds and the waves ", he landed safely at Brindisi whence he had set out for Palestine (Jan. 1, 1272).[4]

Meanwhile, the agents of the different sovereigns of Europe had sent the news of the election to their respective masters. One of these, Henry of Isernia, the notary of Ottocar, King of Bohemia, wrote to say that a Pope had been elected who like the morning sun would dissipate the darkness that enveloped the world,

[1] See the document ap. *Bib. de l'école des Chartes*, 1858, p. 285 f. The gold was " inpalleola ".

[2] *Anon. C.* Prince Edward arrived in Acre, May 9, 1271. *Cf. Les Gestes des Chiprois*, p. 199.

[3] Hence in writing to Prince Edward (see next note) he tells him how he hastened from Brindisi to Viterbo without stopping even at Rome, that he might the sooner take measures for the help of the Holy Land.

[4] *Ib. Cf. Chron. Placent.*, p. 337 ; Gregory's letter to Prince Edward of March 31, 1272, ap. Ripoll, *Bullar.*, i, p. 505 ; *Reg.*, 918 ; *Cont. Will. of Tyre*, lib. xxvi, c. 7.

to wit, Theobald Visconti of Piacenza.[1] As soon as he
had received his envoy's letter, Ottocar wrote to congratulate the cardinals on listening to his request as he
had frequently begged them to elect to the Papacy one
who would be able to deal with men and things.[2]

When the newly elect reached Brindisi, he was received
as the Vicar of God on earth with great enthusiasm ;
and, after a brief delay needful for the procuring of
horses and other necessaries for himself and his suite,
he set out for Benevento where he was met by King
Charles (Jan. 20). As he passed through the kingdom
of Naples on the way to the frontier of the Papal States
he was accompanied by the King, who to show him honour,
as " his father in Christ, and special Lord ", acted as his
groom when he came to any important place.[3] Whether
the King was or was not pleased at the election to the
Papacy of a noble Italian ecclesiastic, he at any rate
evidently tried to make a good impression on him.[4]

At Ceperano, the frontier town of his States, the
newly elected Pontiff was met by a number of the
cardinals ; but Charles also appears to have continued
to accompany him until they reached San Germano at
the foot of Mt. Cassino.[5]

Reaches Viterbo.

---

[1] Ep. 2, ap. Dolliner, *Cod. epist. Ottocar*, ii, Vienna, 1803.

[2] *Ib.*, ep. 3, p. 7, " ad oportune nostre peticionis instantiam."

[3] *Anon. C.*, p. 601. " Ei (the Pope) per loca insignia Regni sui,
per quæ ipsum contigebat transire, ad extractoris offitium exhibens
reverenter." " Extractoris " is evidently " statoris ". · See Charles'
mandate to his justiciaries " quod mittant pecuniam quia obviam
ituri sumus in occursum SS. Domini nostri Summi Pont. qui de Accon
recessit, et transiturus est per Regnum nostrum, quia ipsum tractare
debemus honorifice tamquam in Christo patrem, etc., et hoc non potest
exequi sine magnis expensis." *Cf.* C. M. Riccio, *Nuovi Studii riguard.
la domin. Angioina*, p. 14, Napoli, 1876.

[4] Riccio, *Il regno*, 1271–2, pp. 37, 39, 44 -5, 59, etc.

[5] His itinerary shows that he was at S. G. from Jan. 25–30, 1272.
Hence one sees again the worthlessness of historians' " conjectures ".
Saint Priest, *Hist. de Conquête de Naples*, iii, 267, " Là (Ceperano), il

Before he had entered his own territory, a deputation
from the leading men in Rome had waited on him,
and had earnestly begged him to come thither at once.[1]
Anxious, however, to get to Viterbo to consult with the
cardinals on the state of the Holy Land, without the
slightest delay, he refused their request for the moment,
and pushed on to Viterbo which he reached on
February 10.[2]

Gregory is
invested,
and at once
appeals for
the Holy
Land. He was at once invested with " the grand mantle ",
and elected to be called Gregory, because he had great
devotion to the first Gregory and his feast (March 12)
was drawing near.　When asked by the cardinals whether
he would be crowned in Viterbo or Rome, he is said to
have replied : " You know my dearest brethren that
Constantine the ruler of the world, when in Rome, placed
his crown upon the head of Pope Silvester, as a mark of
temporal authority.　Hence reason, justice, and decency
demand that, in Rome, the Church should, in my unworthy person, be duly crowned." [3]

Meanwhile, though wearied with his journey, he immediately began to work to obtain help for the Christians
in the Holy Land.　For eight days on end he sat discussing the matter with the cardinals, and decided that
something must be done to secure permanent assistance
for the Holy Land, and that for that purpose he must
summon a General Council.[4]　In the meantime, to obtain
immediate assistance for the hard-pressed Christians, he
wrote to Philip of France.　Announcing his election to
him, he tells him that he is sending him the first fruits of

prit congé du pape ; car il n'avait pu obtenir la permission de
l'accompagner à Rome, pour assister à son couronnement." Pure
imagination !　He did assist at the coronation. See *infra*, p. 356.

[1] His letter to Prince Edward just quoted.

[2] *Vita B. Guid.*, p. 597.

[3] " Manto papali vestitus, ex ejus arbitrio prodiit, quod vocaretur
Gregorius." *Anon. C., ib.*

[4] See the letter to Edward.

his letters, begs him to receive the archbishop of Corinth [1]
who, like himself, " had seen and as it were touched with
his hands," [2] the miseries of the Christians of the Holy
Land, and implores to send them immediate help. As
he has not yet been consecrated, he tells the King not to
be astonished if the *bulla* appended to his letter does not
bear his name.[3] On the same date (March 4), letters
were dispatched on the same subject to the count of
Savoy, the archbishop of Rouen and others. The
Templars were urged to borrow twenty-five thousand
marks to help the King should he not be liberal enough in
the matter of men and ships, and the bishops of France
were asked to provide the archbishop of Corinth with
thirty solidi of Tours per day for his necessary expenses.[4]

He also begged the Venetians, the Genoese, the Pisans,
and the people of Marseilles each to furnish immediately
three fully equipped galleys ; moreover, he implored
the Genoese to prevent any of their subjects from giving
any manner of help to the Saracens,[5] and the bishops of
England to obtain financial assistance for Prince Edward
in order to enable him to cope with the difficulties into
which " his service of the Crucified " had thrown him.[6]

When he had finished these preliminary steps for his
Crusade, he proceeded to Rome which he entered on
Sunday, March 13.[7] He was able to enter it with security
as, during the vacancy of the Holy See, the Guelfs, with

Gregory crowned in Rome, March 27, 1272.

---

[1] He had been the envoy of the cardinals to Gregory.

[2] Ep. to the Queen mother, Margaret of France, March 4, 1272,
ap. Raynaldus, n. 5.

[3] Potthast, 20510, and Raynaldus, n. 5.

[4] Potthast, 20512 ff. ; *Reg.*, 342–8.

[5] *Reg.*, n. 351 ff., pp. 137–8, March 31, 1272.

[6] *Reg.*, n. 186, Sept. 30, 1272. *Cf.* the *Register of Archbp. W. Giffard*,
p. 39 ff. These letters to the bishops of England are of a later date,
but, from his known friendship with Edward, we may be sure that he
interested himself in his behalf from the beginning of his pontificate.

[7] *Ann. de Winton*, ii, 111.

the aid of the Vicar of King Charles, had broken the power of the Ghibellines, especially by destroying the great tower known as Arpacata which their leader Jacopo Napoleone had erected in the Campo di Fiore, and other towers which Pietro di Romano possessed at the head of the bridge " of the Jews " and on the Island.[1] Gregory was ordained priest on the following Saturday,[2] and next day week was consecrated, sang Mass, and was crowned.[3] After the ceremony in St. Peters, he went with his crown on his head, and, says his biographer, like a bride all aglow in silk and gems, and with King Charles and the ex-emperor Baldwin [4] acting as his grooms, to take possession of the Lateran. In that palace was held the customary state banquet at which the King, also we may be sure, magnificently attired, for he had demanded special supplies of money for the ceremony,[5] served the Pope with the first course.[6]

Gregory announces his election and receives congratulations.

After receiving the homage of Charles for the Kingdom of Sicily, Gregory sent notices of his election to the great ecclesiastics and sovereigns of the Christian world.[7] In them he declared that he had only accepted the burden of the papacy, lest by refusing to place it on his shoulders —too feeble indeed for its weight—he should prolong the evils caused by the long vacancy ; and he earnestly begged for prayers to enable him to bear the burden he had assumed.

[1] Saba, v, 7.   [2] Chron. de rebus, p. 337.

[3] Ib., B. Guidonis, l.c. ; Anon. C., etc.

[4] Glassberger, Chron., p. 84, is the authority for the presence of Baldwin, and before him Chron. Erphes. min., p. 685, ed. Holder-Egger.

[5] See his demand for money " ut interesse possimus consecrationi d. Summi Pontificis ". Riccio, l.c., p. 13, and in his Della dominazione, p. 3.

[6] Anon. C., p. 602.

[7] Potthast, nn. 20517–18, Reg., nn. 1–2, 971, of March 28, 1272 ; Raynaldus, 1272, n. 9 ; Rymer, i, 879. Besides the circular letter, Gregory sent (March 31) the special letter to Prince Edward already quoted.

Among the letters of congratulation which he received
on his elevation was one from Walter Giffard, archbishop
of York. It was written (February 24) before it was
known what name the newly-elected Pope had taken,
and hence at the close of the letter the archbishop begs
him to excuse the omission of his name at its head.[1]

" To the most holy Father and Lord in Christ (Gregory)
by God's grace, Sovereign Pontiff, Walter, Primate, etc.
Kissing with devout obeisance of mind and body, the
blessed feet.

" The House of the Lord, which as the ' Stone of
Help ' [2] is divinely built upon the foundation of the
Apostles and Prophets, namely the Holy Roman, Catholic,
Church, which has obtained the princedom (*principatum*)
not merely by decrees of Councils, but by the Gospel
teaching of Our Lord and Saviour Jesus Christ.

" In Blessed Peter and his successors, it has at all
time received the form of sacred doctrine and the state
of security, so that what branches owe to their trunk,
what the individual members owe to the head from
which soundness is imparted to the whole body, what
rivers owe to the source from which they flow, what
rays of light owe to the sun from which they proceed—
that, all Christian churches throughout the world owe
to the eminence of the Apostolic See."

He informs the Pope that the news of his accession
has been hailed with filial joy by " the English Church,
which is so much the more devoted to the Apostolic
See, as it is conscious of the manifold benefits which
she has received from it".

" In addition, Holy Father," he continues, " I devoutly

---

[1] The letter may be read in *Letters from Northern Registers*, p. 42,
R. S. We make use of a translation which appeared in the *Tablet*,
Oct. 15, 1910. Among others who wrote to congratulate him was
Felicitas, the wife of Baldwin of Avesnes, *Reg.*, n. 931.

[2] 1 Kings, vii, 12.

commit and submit to your lordship, myself who am,
albeit the very least, still a spiritual plant of the Roman
Church, and all that the said Church has placed in my
charge, even though it indeed be yours, and could not
be more yours than it is. Make use of it, therefore,
according to your pleasure, for I am and shall be most
ready to anticipate your commands and your interests.
I profess that I owe to you all that a servant can owe
to his lord, a disciple to his master, a son to a father." [1]

[1] *Cf.* also the most respectful letter which he sent on March 25, 1271,
to the Pope, "who was to be elected" in order to excuse his not coming
to Rome for his triennial visit ; and also the declaration of the English
clergy in general (Jan., 1272), when they declared that " in this (helping
Prince Edward with a tenth), and in all other matters, they desired to
fulfil the wishes and desires of the lord Pope ". Wilkins, *Concil.*, ii,
24, ap. Gasquet, *Henry III. and the Church*, p. 418. Giffard's letter of
March is to be found in full in the *Letters from N. Reg.*, p. 35. *Cf.* his
Register, p. 156, *Surtees Soc.* Among others who wrote to congratulate
the new Pope was the well-known notary of the papal chancellary,
Berard of Naples. *Cf. Notices et extraits*, t. xxvii, pt. ii, p. 101 ff.,
Paris, 1879.

CHAPTER II.

GREGORY'S EFFORTS FOR PEACE IN TUSCANY AND
LOMBARDY. THE COUNCIL OF LYONS (1274), AND
THE STORY OF THE MAKING AND UNMAKING OF THE
UNION BETWEEN THE GREEK AND LATIN CHURCHES.

EATEN up with zeal for the Holy Land,[1] Gregory put the situation of the Christians therein before the cardinals. Impressed with the Pope's earnestness, they agreed after much discussion that a General Council should be called, and that the Clergy should be taxed for the Crusade, as the laity would be called upon to offer both their goods and their lives. At first, however, they could not agree as to the place where the Council should be held, as some wanted it in Rome, and others in some transalpine city.[2]

Gregory
summons a
General
Council,
1272.

In order then that no time should meanwhile be lost, Gregory issued circular letters (March 31, 1272) to inform Christendom that a General Council was to be held on the first of May, 1274.[3] It was called to treat of the situation in the Holy Land, and the union of the Greeks. The body of the Church, wrote the Pope, was mutilated by the loss of such a noble member as that of the Greek people, and his own eyes had seen how " by the unspeakable Saracens " the Christian people were slaughtered as though there was no one to help or have pity on them. He would, in due course, make known the place where the Council was to be held, but in the meantime all were exhorted to give careful thought to the objects for which the Council was summoned. The bishops were

---

[1] " Quem Terræ Sanctæ zelus comederat." *Anon. C.*, p. 602.
[2] *Ib.*   [3] *Reg.*, nn. 160–1, p. 53 ff.

also exhorted to consider carefully whatever needed
reform or correction, to commit the same to writing and
to bring it before the notice of the Council. All who are
summoned must come to the Council, and not try to
find vain excuses for absenting themselves.[1] All archbishops, bishops, abbots, priors, deans, archdeacons,
provosts, and other ecclesiastical prelates were summoned
to attend the Council, and Kings too were earnestly
urged to be present at it.

In the following March, the reports on points needing
reformation which Gregory had asked to be drawn up,
were ordered to be forwarded to the apostolic see six
months before the date fixed for the Council.[2] Finally
the nations were informed on April 13, 1273, that Lyons
had been chosen as the place where the Council was to
be held.[3] Even the King of Armenia is asked to come
and to send at once copies of the acts of the Council of
Nicæa and other councils which are said to exist in
Armenian, and with them learned men who can translate
them from Armenian into Latin.[4]

Promotion
of cardinals,
1273, June 3.

A little later, in order that he might have the assistance
of one of the most famous men of his day, he named
St. Bonaventure, the Minister-General of the Franciscans,
cardinal-bishop of Albano, and, exhorting him to accept the
dignity in the spirit of humble submission, he bade him come
to him without delay.[5] The holy and learned Franciscan
was appointed cardinal along with four other distinguished

[1] " Nullus igitur . . . fallacium excusationum velamento se muniat."
Ib., n. 160. The notice to Henry III. is in Rymer, i, 881. *Cf. Bullar.
Rom.*, iv, 14, ed. Taur.

[2] *Cf.* epp. of March 11, 1273, ap. Potthast, n. 20685 ; Theiner,
Mon. Hung., i, 294.

[3] Potthast, 20716–17. *Bullar. Rom.*, iv, 16 ; *Anon. C.*, 602.

[4] Potthast, 20722 Apr. 20, 1273.

[5] *Ib.*, 20746, from Wadding, iv, 381, June 3, 1273. He bids the
Saint " huic provisioni nostræ in humilitate spiritus, sine cujusquam
difficultatis obice acquiescas ".

men, Petrus Julianus, archbishop of Braga, master in Arts, Medicine, and Theology, the famous Petrus Hispanus, afterwards John XXI. (he became bishop of Tusculum), Pierre de Tarentaise, a Dominican, master of theology, archbishop of Lyons (bishop of Ostia and grand penitentiary) ; Bertrand a S. Martino, archbishop of Arles (bishop of Sabina), and Guglielmo Visconti, archbishop of Aix, nephew of the Pope, and a distinguished jurisconsult (bishop of Præneste).[1] In his bull of nomination of Bonaventure, the Pope had declared that it was his aim to promote to the cardinalitial dignity men " whose lives should instruct the living, whose good repute . . . should refresh those who should hear of it, whose wisdom would assist him in doubt, and whose prayers would win for him the help of God ".[2] It is because in this promotion that he acted on these principles that the historian calls it " most praiseworthy ".[3]

Gregory[4] spent the interval between his summoning the Council and his celebration of it, in striving to make peace everywhere, to arouse interest in the Holy Land, and to terminate the interregnum in the Empire. Wars in Europe and the Empire without a head were not conducive to a successful Crusade.

Efforts to make peace, especially in Lombardy and Tuscany.

To conciliate the Ghibelline cities of Lombardy he restored to them ecclesiastical rights of which, owing to

---

[1] *Anon. C., ib.,* B. Guidonis, p. 597 ; Eubel, *Hierarchia Cathol.,* p. 9. Ciacconius says that another nephew of the Pope, John Visconti, and Theobald of Ceccano, abbot of Fossannova, were also made cardinals ; and, according to Cardella, *Mem. de Card.,* ii, p. 8 f., they were promoted at the General Council of Lyons.

[2] Ep ap. Wadding, iv, 381.

[3] B. Guidonis, *l.c.,* " quia honestas et valentes personas assumpsit."

[4] In this matter of making peace between the Guelfs and Ghibellines, Gregory's policy was followed by his immediate successors. Butler, *The Lombard Communes,* p. 365, writes : " The Popes who reigned from 1271 to 1280, and Nicholas IV., who reigned from 1288 to 1292, on the whole strove to reconcile the two parties, or at least to hold the balance even."

the support which they had given to Frederick II., Conrad, and their adherents, they had been deprived. He restored to Milan, especially, because, as he said, it had returned to its loyalty to the Church, its rights in the matter of freedom of election to its bishopric, abbacies, etc.[1] But to those cities which persisted in maintaining a Ghibelline attitude, and in displaying hostility to King Charles, he would not only not make any concessions, but he renewed the decrees against them published by his immediate predecessors (Apr. 12, 1272). Such cities were especially Siena, Pisa, Pavia, and Verona, and they were given till September, 1272, to come to terms.[2] By that date, however, none of the said cities had made any submission, but, before proceeding to extremities, Gregory gave them a further period of grace till the feast of the Purification (1273).[3]

Pisa gave way, and the Dominican, John of Viterbo, was commissioned to absolve the city from the censures under which it lay, and to reconcile it with the Curia on all counts—save and except the Sardinian question.[4] Siena appears to have followed the example of Pisa,[5] but, despite another extension of the time in which they might obtain favour,[6] Pavia and Verona continued in opposition. Consequently, Gregory, now in Lyons awaiting the assembly of the General Council, in presence " of a great multitude of the faithful ",[7] not only renewed

[1] Kaltenbrunner, *Actenstücke unter Rudolf I.*, n. 1, Vienna, 1889; *Reg.*, n. 741.

[2] *Reg.*, nn. 162–5, Apr. 21, 1272. *Cf.* epp. *Reg.*, 182–4, June 2, 1272, renewing the preceding.

[3] *Reg.*, nn. 203–6, Nov. 18, 1272.

[4] *Reg.*, n. 309, May 21, 1273. *Cf.* nn. 742–4, 1025. *Cf.* Guido de Corvaria, *Hist. Pisanæ*, ap. *R. I. SS.*, xxiv, p. 780.

[5] For Ghibelline supremacy came to an end in Siena in 1269–70. *Cf.* E. G. Gardner, *The Story of Siena*, p. 19 f., London, 1902.

[6] *Reg.*, nn. 310–11, May 18, 1273.

[7] *Reg.*, n. 480, March 29, 1274, against Verona. *Cf.* n. 481, for a similar decree against Pavia.

the excommunication and interdict already launched
against Verona and Pavia, but forbade other cities to
have intercourse with them.   This took place on Maunday
Thursday ; and he warned the recalcitrant cities that
unless they submitted before Ascension Thursday (May 10)
he would deprive them of their episcopal sees, and call
on Catholic Princes to take the field against them.   To
these extremities he was loth to go, but as no sign of
surrender came from the two cities, he simply went on
renewing to the end of his life the sentence just detailed.[1]

Among those whom Gregory employed to promote
peace in Lombardy (where the Genoese were at enmity
with Pisa and with Venice, and the Venetians with
the Bolognese) [2] was his nephew, Guglielmo Visconti,
archbishop of Aix.   He was instructed to use apostolic
censures, in short, every means in his power to induce
the perturbers of the peace of Lombardy, and the
Spaniards and Germans who were helping them, to
come to terms.   If he could not make a permanent peace,
he must try to make truces for a time.   A General
Council had been summoned to further " the inestimable
good " of the peace of the world, and, for its assembling,
peace and the consequent security of the roads were of
the first importance.[3]

Peace for the sake of the security of the roads

Gregory also aimed at promoting internal peace in the
great cities of Italy.   In Florence, which was now becoming
very powerful, the dominant Guelfs had expelled the
Ghibellines, but, through the agency of Jean de Verceil,

---

[1] *Reg.*, nn. 483–4, Ascension day, 1274. In these documents, Gregory
declares that the business of the General Council prevents him from
giving full attention to the case of the cities. *Reg.*, nn. 572–3, Nov. 18,
1274 ; and nn. 640–1, Holy Thursday, Apr. 11, 1275, Still mercy.

[2] Potthast, 20637.

[3] *Reg.*, n. 752, May 15, 1272. He had summoned a council " et sive
in Ytalia sive ultra montes ipsum celebrari contingat, venturis ad illud
viarum est præparanda securitas ". *Cf.* nn. 753–9.

Master-General of the Dominicans,[1] negotiations for a settlement were in progress when Charles' vicar in Tuscany, and the Guelfs brought down upon themselves indignant letters from the Pope for not treating the Ghibelline nobles fairly in the meanwhile.[2] Later on we shall see how the peace that the Dominican and the Pope managed to effect was again broken. Gregory also strove to bring internal concord to the unstable Genoese,[3] and even in the city of Lyons which had been selected for the Council, he had to work for peace between the people and the clergy of the cathedral. He sternly forbade the populace to interfere with the seigniorial rights of the archbishop.[4]

Piacenza.

Of more personal interest to Gregory was the condition of his native Piacenza, of which he had taken cognizance immediately after his coronation.[5] Its fights with Parma and, afterwards, its internal factions, had reduced it to the verge of ruin.[6] Some time previously, it had abandoned its " traditional alliance " with Milan and the Guelf party ; but, as it had recently expelled its Ghibelline chief, Oberto Pelavicini, Gregory wrote to Milan in its behalf, and named as his legate to bring it

[1] Gregory used this virtuous man a great deal in his efforts to pacify Italy. See his letters to him in Kaltenbrunner, *Actenstücke*, pp. 7 and 9. *Cf.* Mortier, *Hist. des Martres-Généraux*, ii, p. 1 ff.

[2] *Reg.*, nn. 767–9, or Kaltenbrunner, nn. 6–7, p. 9 ff. Villari, *Hist. of Florence*, p. 253, scarcely realizing it would seem that, after all, Florence was only a very small section of the areas to which Gregory was striving to bring peace, believes that he favoured the Ghibellines to reduce the power of Charles of Anjou.

[3] Kaltenbrunner, *l.c.*, p. 4.

[4] Ep. ap. Ripoll, *Bullar. O.P.*, i, p. 511, n. 11, April 10, 1273 ; Potthast, n. 20715.

[5] Potthast, 20519, March 20, 1272.

[6] Gregory speaks " of the perilous condition of the state (civitatis) of Piacenza, de cujus subversione verisimiliter timetur ". Ep. to Raymond della Torre, bishop of Como (1261–73), ap. Kaltenbrunner, n. 8, pp. 13–14. Speaking generally, the della Torre family were Guelf leaders of the Milanese people.

peace, the bishop of Como, Raymond della Torre. It would appear that he failed to do so, and that the Pope's nephew, the archbishop of Aix, who entered Piacenza on June 21, 1272, also completely failed to make peace between Count Ubertino de Lando (or de Andito), the leader of the Ghibelline nobles and the people. Accordingly, the Ghibelline chronicler accuses him of working not in the interests of peace, but in those of Charles of Anjou.[1] However that may be, the legate excommunicated Ubertino,[2] and when, later on (Jan., 1274), the people of Piacenza made a treaty with the count, the Pope not only urged them not to ratify it, because in its terms there was no mention of compensation for injuries inflicted on the King of Sicily and on various churches,[3] but himself took measures against Ubertino.[4] The truce between Ubertino and the Commune did not last long, and, for years after Gregory's death, the same state of things continued. Intervals of fighting between the two were followed by intervals of peace.[5]

Gregory had left Rome to avoid its intense summer heat, and had betaken himself to the charming hill-city

Arrival of Edward at Orvieto, 1273.

[1] *Chron. de rebus*, or *Placent*, p. 340. Unfortunately the letter addressed to Raymond is undated, so that one cannot be sure of its relation to the mission of G. Visconti. *Cf.* Kaltenbrunner, n. 13, p. 22, for Gregory's letter to the people of Piacenza. He upbraids them for the weakness of their action towards Ubertino, when they had braved "imperialibus insultibus".

[2] *Chron. de rebus*, p. 340. Against this excommunication, Ubertino at once appealed to the Pope.

[3] *Chron. de rebus*, p. 345 ; ep. Greg., March 12, 1274, Potthast, 20802 ; *Reg.*, n. 341, p. 133. Gregory assured the people of Piacenza that, from the very beginning of his pontificate, he had had hardly anything more at heart than that peace should be made with the count.

[4] March 29, 1274, *Reg.*, p. 203. May 10, 1274, *ib.*, p. 206 ; Apr. 11, 1275, *ib.*, p. 278, n. 643. As usual Gregory's shows himself averse to taking the severest measures. *Cf. Chron. de rebus*, p. 345.

[5] See *Chron. de rebus*, 352, 377, 381-3.

of Orvieto, where he had arrived on June 26, 1272.[1]
He was still there when word reached him that Prince
Edward and his wife had returned from Palestine and
had reached Trapani in Sicily. After the famous attempt
to assassinate him had failed (June, 1272), he made a
truce with the Moslems, and left for England on his
recovery from his wounds (Sept. 22).[2] As soon as news
of their landing reached Orvieto, Gregory wrote to the
Prince to tell him how pleased he was at the rumour
which had reached him that God had brought him safely
out of so many perils to Trapani. After a brief exhortation to him to serve God who had done so much for him, he
tells him how happy he would be to receive him if he could
come to him. He bids him, however, consult his own
convenience; but again assures him that he would be
glad to have an opportunity of showing him his paternal
affection (Nov. 22, 1272).[3]

When the Pope wrote this, neither he nor Prince Edward
knew of the death of the latter's father (Henry III.),
which had taken place a few days before (Nov. 16). No
sooner, however, did news of the event reach Gregory,
than he wrote to Edward, now King of England, to
sympathize with him on his father's death,[4] and feeling
now that it would on all counts be desirable to see the
new King, he wrote to tell his wife that he expected them,
and urged her also quietly to lead her husband in his
trials to conformity to God's will, as he had himself
tried to do.[5]

---

[1] *Annales Urbevet*, p. 132, ap. *R. I. SS.*, xv, pt. v (new ed.). The date
is thus expressed " die dominica quinta exeunte mense junii ".

[2] The Templar's *Gestes des Chiprois*, n. 382, p. 201. " Dont (the
poisonous wound) il fu bien guary, la mercy Dieu ; et se party à 22
jors de Setembre, et a la outremer en sa terre."

[3] *Reg.*, n. 893. *Cf.* n. 897 to Charles of Anjou, who had sent him
certain intelligence of Edward's arrival in Sicily.

[4] *Reg.*, n. 895, Jan. 8, 1273.

[5] *Reg.*, n. 896. *Cf.* also Rymer, i, pp. 888–9.

The new King accepted the Pope's invitation to visit
him. He had been honourably received by King Charles,[1]
and by the Romans, when he made a solemn entry into
their city (Feb. 5, 1273). On his approach to Orvieto he
was met by the cardinals and all the magnates who
chanced to be at the papal court, and afterwards was most
warmly welcomed by the Pope himself (Feb. 7).[2] Needless
to say, the first subject discussed by the English King
and Gregory, formerly Edward's friend now his lord, says
our historian,[3] was the perilous condition of the Holy
Land. One result of their conversation on this matter
was that Edward obtained from the Pope a tenth for
three years from all the clergy of England without
exception.[4]

The next subject discussed was the murder of Edward's
cousin, Henry of Almaine [5]; and the King begged the
Pope " formally to condemn " both Aldobrandini and
Guy.[6] Gregory at once took up the matter with vigour.
Before a large number of people he cited Guy de Montfort,
the Red Aldobrandini his father-in-law, and their
supporters to appear before him within fifteen days ;
and he explained that the vacancy of the Holy See and
his own but recent election had, to the detriment of
justice, prevented earlier action in the case. Safe conducts
were offered them to come to the papal court (March 1,

(margin note: Edward asks for the punishment of Guy de Montfort.)

---

[1] Ever since Edward's arrival in Sicily, Charles had made every
effort to receive him well. *Cf.* Riccio, *Il Regno*, 1871–2, pp. 84,
100 ff., 112–13.

[2] *Cf.* Wykes, *Chron.*, p. 254. His chronological data cannot be
reconciled. See also *Flores Hist.*, iii, 29. The Continuator of Will. of
Newburg, says Edward, was in Rome in Lent, and followed the devotion
of the " stations ". " Quadragesima ad Stationes." Ap. *Chronicles
of Stephen*, ii, p. 564, *R. S.* The directions given by Charles to his
Vicar in Sicily as to the reception to be given to Edward are most
honourable to himself. *Cf.* his instructions, ap. M. Camera, *Annali
delle due Sicilie*, i, p. 314. Naples, 1841.

[3] *Flores H.*, just cited.   [4] Wykes, *l.c.*

[5] *Cf. supra*, p. 342.   [6] *Flores, l.c.*, and *Chron. de rebus*, p. 312.

1273).[1] That the culprits might have no opportunity of pretending that they were ignorant of the citation, Gregory ordered it to be affixed to the doors of the cathedral of Orvieto, and ordered his agents to publish it in other neighbouring places.[2] The summons to attend the papal court was accordingly served on Aldobrandini, who protested his innocence,[3] and through him on Guy.[4] The latter in a letter, dated March 7, and addressed to the Pope who " by divine providence presides over all men ", ventured, while professing his readiness to accept the Pope's sentence, even if excessive, to declare that, if the cause of his action was considered, the language which the Pope had used about it was too severe.   He asked that a safe conduct be granted him to go to the papal court, and to return from it, and finished by averring that before the issue of this citation, he had " frequently, undertaken to offer satisfaction to God and Holy Church in accordance with the will of the Pope ".[5]   In a second letter, he emphatically denied that he had killed Henry, and added that, if he had done so, there was cause enough either to excuse him altogether or to lessen the gravity of his act.[6]   He referred, of course, to the brutal massacre of his brother Henry after he had been taken prisoner

[1] *Reg.*, n. 210.   " Submurmurat justitiæ non modicum ex tanta delatione detractum."   These words do not appear in the copy of the letter in the Register, but in the copy of Rymer, i, 890.   Copies of some of the other documents relating to this affair are given in the same collection, i, 891, and ii, pp. 4, 17.

[2] *Cf. Reg.*, epp. 210–17, for Gregory's orders to different officials to publish this citation, and their replies that they have done as ordered, before the people at large, summoned " ad sonum campanæ ac voce preconia " (ep. 211).

[3] *Reg.*, 217.

[4] *Ib.*, 211.   One of his officials tells the Pope how to reach Aldobrandini ;   he had to go " per loca deserta et nemorosas solitudines ".

[5] *Reg.*, n. 218.   Under this number are included three letters of Guy, dated 7, 9, and 14th March.

[6] *Ib.*, p. 84.   " Ego nego, et constanter inficior me predictum Henricum occidisse."

at Evesham, and he protested that the Pope was being hounded by King Edward to violate justice. He accordingly prayed that his trial should be put off till Edward had left Italy. But it must be allowed that he showed the weakness of his cause, when he began to hint at an appeal from the Pope " to a future Council ".[1] In a third letter (March 14) Guy says that " it is commonly thought " that on account of his special friendship for the King of England, the Pope has made the case of his friend his own, and that it is the influence of the King of England that has turned him against the writer, and caused him unduly to favour the King. He again asked that his case should not be heard whilst the English King was with the Pope, and definitely declared that, if this request were not granted, he appealed to a future council.[2] He also again denied that he had killed Henry, and urged that, if he had he had a most just right to do so. He further pretended that Edward had said openly that, all securities notwithstanding, he would kill him, if he had the chance.

Needless to say then, Guy did not follow the example of his father-in-law,[3] and present himself before the Pope within the prescribed time. Accordingly, on April 1, 1273, in a very long document, Gregory published his sentence against Guy and his supporters. He related the facts of the case which, he said, were absolutely certain, and, during the vacancy of the Holy See had been acknowledged by Guy himself in his efforts made at that time to obtain mercy. The safe-conducts which the Pope had offered to Guy and to any whom he wished

Gregory condemns Guy.

---

[1] *Ib.*

[2] *Ib.*, p. 85. " Alioquin ipsam (causam meam) ad examen sacri futuri concilii detuli, et nunc defero, me at mea ipsius concilii ordinationi et judicio supponendo."

[3] The Red Count took an oath before the Pope and Edward that he had not consented to Henry's death. *Cf.* John of Oxnead, *Chron.*, p. 222, *R. S.*, and *Flores Hist.*, iii, 29. *Cf. Reg.*, n. 338, Sept. 3, 1273.

to defend him were abundantly sufficient to ensure their safety. Then, brushing aside all worthless excuses, Gregory declared Guy an outlaw (infamis), and gave strict orders to all authorities to seize him, and to send him to the Pope to be imprisoned. He placed under an interdict any territory which might willingly receive him (terram que sibi obediet) and excommunicated Guy himself and his accomplices in the foul deed.[1]

Guy submits and is imprisoned, 1273–83.

Safe, however, in the fortress of his father-in-law at Soana, or in some sanctuary, Guy was for a time able to brave the sentence, and, when in June, first Edward and then the Pope left Orvieto for France, Guy was still at large.[2] However, when on his journey to Lyons, Gregory reached Florence, Guy, backed by the prayers of his wife and many friends, implored the Pope to permit him to come to him. This request, in order to try him, as he explained to Edward, Gregory refused. But when he had just left Florence (August), Guy with some friends appeared before him at Santa Croce. Barefooted, clad simply in the penitential shirt, and, with a halter round his neck, he made a complete submission to the Pope, and begged for imprisonment, if only he were pardoned. At first Gregory would not listen to him, and when Guy retired to Bologna, Gregory forbade anyone, under the severest penalties, to harbour him.[3] At length, however, he relented, and ordered him to be imprisoned in a papal fortress, and guarded by Charles of Anjou.[4]

[1] See the document in full, ap. *Reg.*, n. 219, or Rymer, ii, p. 4 ff. Gregory draws out at great length all the disabilities involved in the outlawry and excommunication, and even declared Guy's descendants to the fourth generation incapable of holding ecclesiastical offices. Cristofori, *Il conclave de* 1270, cites (p. 248) a copy of the condemnation preserved in Lambeth Palace. *Cf. Flores Hist.*, iii, 29–30.

[2] Edward crossed the Alps on June 7. *Cf.* Wykes, *Chron.*, p. 255 ; *Flores, l.c.*, and Gregory left Orvieto for Lyons, June 5, 1273.

[3] *Cf.* the letter of an English envoy, ap. Kern, *Acta Imperii*, n. 2, p. 2.

[4] See ep. Greg. to King Edward, Nov. 29, 1273. *Reg.*, n. 814, or Rymer, ii, 17.

Although, in the following year, Gregory hearkened to his request, and absolved Guy from the excommunication under which he lay, he would not release him from prison.[1] The unhappy man remained in prison for eleven years, and was then released by Pope Martin IV., who made use of his military talents.[2] Adhering to Charles of Anjou in his struggle with James of Aragon for Sicily, Guy was taken prisoner,[3] and died in prison at Messina (1291).

Whilst waiting for the assembling of the Council, Gregory also strove to clear the ground for the election of a King of the Romans, who would be generally recognized, so that there might be an Emperor to head the united forces of Christendom against the Moslem. One of the candidates for the imperial crown, Richard, earl of Cornwall, had died on April 2, 1272, so that the only candidate then in the field was Alfonso X. of Castile. He accordingly promptly sent envoys to the Pope to push his claim, and to beg him to prohibit the electors from making a fresh choice. But Gregory was not in the least favourable to his candidature. It was clear on the one hand that with the Moors and his own discontented nobles,[4] he had enough to do in Spain, and on the other that there was no hope whatever of the Electors agreeing to accept him. Gregory, therefore, in a document of some length, and no little complication of language, countered the arguments of the Spanish envoys (Sept. 16,

Candidates for the Empire; (1) Alfonso X.

---

[1] Ep. July 23, 1274, ap. *Bullar. O.P.*, i, p. 520 ; *Reg.*, 383.

[2] Rishanger, *Chron.*, an. 1283, p. 105, and Pipinus, etc., and Potthast, n. 22022. May 11, 1283, or in full ap. Cristofori, *l.c.*, p. 159. In his letter the Pope says he has appointed him to the command of the Army of the Church at the suggestion of Philip III. of France.

[3] In 1287. *Cf. Chron. Parm.*, ap. *R. I. SS.*, t. ix, pt. ix, new ed., and Pipinus, *Chron.*, ap. *R. I. SS.*, ix, 726.

[4] *Cf.* Mariana, *Hist. of Spain*, 1. 13, cc. 9 and 10 ; Colmeiro, *Reyes Christianos en Castilla*, p. 121 f., Madrid, 1893 ; Burke, *A Hist. of Spain*, i, 265.

1272). He pointed out that an imperfect election of one
candidate was not made good by the death of another.
The right of those who had elected the late King Richard
to elect another if they thought fit could not be interfered
with ; and, as the King's envoys were not empowered
to modify their petitions, they could not be admitted,
at least as they stood.[1]

(2) Philip
III.

In the Curia then, there was clearly no wish to support
Alfonso ; indeed, there might well be even distrust of him,
as his brother Henry had been so stout a supporter of
the Ghibelline party. Of this, at least, coldness towards
the Spanish King, Charles of Anjou made use. He knew
that there was no hope of the Empire for himself, so he
threw in his influence in behalf of his nephew, Philip III.,
King of France. The King of France was becoming the
most powerful sovereign in Europe, and Philip had
already shown that he had inherited the Crusading zeal
of his father. So eager was he to undertake another
Crusade that Gregory found it necessary to temper his
enthusiasm, and to urge him to more careful preparation
before further action.[2] But, although Charles gained
the support of cardinals Ottoboni and Simon de Brion,
and though he tried to fire the ambition of Philip, and
they tried to move the Pope, Gregory could not be
prevailed upon to encourage the candidature of the French
King for the Empire in any way.[3] He was determined
not to hamper the free choice of the electors. But if
we can trust an anonymous Italian who in the beginning
of the fourteenth century added notes to the text of the

[1] *Reg.*, n. 192, or ap. Theiner, *Cod. Diplom.*, i, p. 175, where the
document is better punctuated.

[2] Potthast, n. 20654 ; Raynaldus, *Annal.*, § 7–9.

[3] *Cf.* Langlois, *Philippe le Hardi*, pp. 63–71. This plan of Charles
of Anjou is only known by two documents—one a memoir addressed
to Philip by Charles, and the other a report addressed by Master
Nicholas of Senlis also to Philip. They have been published by Figeac,
Mélanges, i, 652 ff. Potthast, 20752

French chronicler, Géraud de Frachet, Gregory wished to see Philip Emperor. Although the Pope's letter to the electors is not extant, it is certain that he bade them choose a King of the Romans within a limited time[1]; and "note carefully", says the Italian scribe, "that that Pope was most eager for a Crusade, and that as at that juncture there was no Emperor, he thought of making the King of France Emperor. Hence he ordered the Electors to choose within a month anyone they desired. He believed that the Electors could not come to an agreement within that space of time, and he thought within himself that he would choose the King of France." The anonymous author assures us that Gregory's idea was sound, for the Emperor must be a rich and powerful man, and in all Christendom the King of France has no equal.[2] It is hardly likely, however, that Gregory would so play into the hands of the ambitious Charles as to wish that his nephew should be Emperor in the West, when he knew that Charles was aiming to make himself Emperor in the East.[3] However, whatever were the wishes of Gregory, the Electors, as we shall see, astonished the world by suddenly choosing Rudolf, count of Hapsburg (Oct. 1, 1273).

If, however, Gregory was fortunate enough to see the end of the long interregnum in the Empire before he left Italy, he was not fortunate enough to leave complete peace behind him when he crossed the Alps. He had

Gregory in Florence, June, 1273.

---

[1] "Præcepit principibus ut regem eligerent infra terminum anni." *Ann. Elwacenses*, an. 1272, ap. *M. G. SS.*, x, p. 38. *Cf. Ann. Aust. Contin. Vindob.*, " monitis," Greg. X., ap. *ib.*, ix, p. 704 ; "ad indictum et mandatum d. Pape," ap. *ib.*, p. 800, etc. See *infra*, p. 455.

[2] Cited by Langlois, *Philippe*, p. 69. L. Delisle, *Notices et extraits*, vol. xxxv, p. 380, quotes this as from the chronicle of an anonymous Dominican of Parma, who, he not unnaturally suspects, may have been a Frenchman.

[3] *Cf.* L. Leclèrc, *Les rapports de la Papauté et de la France sous Philippe III.*, Brussels, 1889. His first thesis is that Gregory IX. was opposed to the candidature of Philip for the Empire.

arrived in Florence from Orvieto on June 18, and had
been received with honour by the Florentines, having
entered their city with King Charles, the Emperor
Baldwin, and a number of lords and barons. He took
up his abode with his court in " the palaces " of the
Mozzi, merchant bankers " for the Pope and the Church ",
who "in a little time had come to great riches and state ",
and whose palaces, we are told,[1] were "at the head of the
Rubaconte Bridge on the further side of the Arno".
He at once devoted himself to make peace between
the Guelfs and Ghibellines of that important city. After
" great toil and anxiety ", says his biographers,[2] he
succeeded in making peace between the factions—a peace,
however, which the Ghibelline chronicle declares was
hard for the Ghibelline exiles.[3] Finding, says Villani,
that this good city of Florence was being ruined by
factions, the Pope determined that the Ghibelline exiles
should be recalled, and that peace should be made
between them and the Guelfs. He goes on to tell how great
wooden stands were erected for the notables on the sands
of the Arno by the head of the Rubaconte, now alle
Grazie, bridge, and that the people of Florence all gathered
round them. Then on July 12, Gregory, with the King
and Emperor, and the barons and gentlemen of the
Court, pronounced his sentence which had to be observed
under sentence of excommunication. Representatives
of the two parties had to kiss each other on the mouth,
and to give securities and hostages ; all the castles which
the Ghibellines held had to be given into the hands of

---

[1] Villani, *Chron.*, vii, 42.   The firm of Mozzi was well known in
England, as the money collected for Gregory's Crusade was ordered
to be deposited with their agents in England. *Cf. Calendar of Papal
Registers*, i, pp. 585, 598, 600, 604.

[2] P. 602.

[3] *Chron. de rebus*, p. 344. *Cf.* Guido de Corvaria, *Hist. Pisanæ*,
p. 681.

King Charles, and the Ghibelline hostages had to go into the Maremma in charge of the Red Count with whom we are already familiar.[1]

On the same day, Gregory laid the foundation stone of a church which was to be built by the Mozzi, and called it after his own name.[2]

Four days after this, he left " the good city " of Florence suddenly, though, says Villani, he had resolved to spend the summer there, because its situation pleased him " by reason of the convenience of the water and the pure air " and the comfort which the court found there. He left it in anger because the peace he had laboriously made was rudely broken. The Ghibelline representatives who had remained in the city to complete the treaty of peace were assured that King Charles' marshal, at the request of the leading Guelfs, had resolved to cut them in pieces if they did not depart forthwith. Villani, does not pretend to know whether there was any truth in the assertion or not, but the Ghibellines believed, or pretended to believe, what they had been told, left the city and broke the treaty. Gregory was naturally very angry, and, in his turn, left the city, laid it under an interdict, and " continued in great wrath with King Charles ".[3]

He leaves it in anger, July 16.

[1] Villani, *l.c. Cf. Chron. de rebus, l.c.* ; a report of an English envoy at the papal court, ap. Kern, *Acta imperii,* p. 2 ; *Annali di Simone della Tosa,* p. 144, ed. Firenze, 1733. The sentence of the Pope is given at length in the *Bullarium,* vol. iv, p. 19 ff., ed. Turin. " Actum Florentiæ supra litus Arni juxta pontem qui vulgariter dicitur Robaconti, 4 idus Julii." The date in Villani July 2 is a mistake for July 12.

[2] Villani, *l.c.* From the inscription of the façade of the Church, it is clear that the date was July 12. " Luce duodena Julii radiante serena." Bonucci, p. 101, gives the whole inscription :—

> " Gregorio Decimo Papa, Sancti sub honore
> Gregorii Primi, pro Christi fundor amore.
> Hic Gibellinæ cum Guelfis pace patrata
> Cessavere minæ sub qua sum luce creata,
> Luce, etc."

[3] Villani, *l.c.* ; *Anon. C.,* p. 602 ; and Thos. Tuscus, *Gesta imp.,* p. 523, ap. *M. G. SS.,* xxii.

At first, leaving Charles behind him in Florence, Gregory went with cardinal Ottaviano Ubaldini to Mugello near Florence. He was received with great honour by the Ghibelline Ubaldini who owned most of the Val di Mugello, as the valley of the Sieve on the way to the pass of La Futa was then called. Gregory, no doubt, thus showed favour to this Ghibelline cardinal [1] and his family to prove to them that he sympathized with them for the way in which the Ghibelline representatives had been treated in Florence.

Proceeds to Bologna.

After a short stay in Mugello, Gregory moved on towards Bologna to promote the sacred cause of peace between that famous city and Venice. Arrived at Santa Croce in its neighbourhood,[2] in view of his impending departure from Italy, he nominated Aldobrandini, bishop of Orvieto, his Vicar in Campania, the Maritima, the March of Ancona, the Duchy of Spoleto and Tuscany.[3] Here he fell grievously ill, and did not reach Bologna till September 20.[4] He lodged in a palace by the Church of St. Michael in Bosco on a hill just outside the city, whence he had a splendid view of the whole neighbourhood.[5] This time, the quarrel between the two

[1] Dante places him in hell. *Cf. Infer.*, x, 121, and his commentator, Benvenuto da Imola, writing on this passage, says that once when denied a sum of money by the Ghibellines, the cardinal burst out : " If I have a soul I have lost it many times for the Ghibellines." The *Annals of Verona* call him an imperial partisan, and say that he had been the chief promoter of Gregory to the Papacy. *Cf.* ed. C. Cipolla, p. 415, ed. Venice, 1890.

[2] According to the report of the English envoy quoted above, *Santa Croce* was a *castrum* of cardinal Ottaviano, and was 30 miles from Bologna.

[3] Ep. Aug. 20, ap. Ripoll, *Bullar. O.P.*, i, p. 517.

[4] *Chron. de rebus*, p. 344. The English envoy did not expect him to see the end of the year.

[5] " Et hospitatus est ad S. Michaele in Buscho . . . I Bolognixi feceno pace con Veneciani Nel quale tempo el p. Gregorio venne a Bologna." *Corpus Chron. Bonon.*, pp. 187–8, ap. *R. I. SS.*, xviii, pt. i, new ed.

cities concerned, not the party factions of Guelf and Ghibelline, but trade and access to the Adriatic; and peace was effected by the devoted work of the Pope's agents, the Franciscans. They had brought about meetings of the envoys of the two cities in various places, and even before the Pope, and at length their unwearied efforts were crowned with success.[1] Peace was the result. Although, as he says, he was not accustomed to preaching, the contemporary Venetian chronicler could not contain himself when he reflected on all that the friars had done on this and other occasions to make peace. "All the world," he says, "should praise them and hold them dear. All such as have the care of souls should act in this way . . . for you know well that the prelates of Holy Church have to render an account to our Lord Jesus Christ of the souls entrusted to their keeping ; . . . and to them he has given a good reward for watching over them, i.e., the titles and firstfruits which belong to the Church." [2]

When he had confirmed the peace brought about by the Franciscans, Gregory turned west again, and, passing through Modena, Reggio, and Parma,[3] he reached his native city of Piacenza on Oct. 2. Here, with a view to making peace between the Guelf and Ghibelline factions, he tried to get in touch with the leader of the latter faction, Ubertino de Lando. If we are to believe the

Gregory visits his native place, etc.

---

[1] In the quaint French of the contemporary Martino da Canale, *Cron. Veneta*, c. 309 : "Assemblerent les mesages de Venise avenc les mesages de Boloigne, que devant l'Apostoille que en autres teres."

[2] *Ib.*, c. 311. "A cui il a done mult grant sodee por garder iaus." *Cf.* Hodgson, *Venice*, etc., p. 165 ff.

[3] At Reggio he stayed at the monastery of St. Prosper outside the walls of the city, and gave to its sacristy a pallium with the scene of the Nativity of our Lord worked on it. *Cf.* A. Miliolus, *De Temp.*, p. 543, ap. *M. G. SS.*, xxxi, and *Chron. Reg.*, p. 7, ap. *R. I. SS.*, xviii. At Parma he stayed "ad Religionem veterem", i.e., in the monastery of the Canons regular of St. Mark of Mantua. *Cf. Chron. Parm.*, ad an. 1273.

Ghibelline Chronicle of the city, intrigue prevented
Ubertino from meeting the Pope at Piacenza ; but, as
he also failed soon after to meet him at Milan or at the
abbey of Morimondo, his next halting place, we may
conclude that he had no wish to see him.[1]

Gregory at
Milan.

After a stay of a few days at Piacenza, Gregory made
his way by Lodi to Milan, which he reached on Oct. 8,
taking up his abode by the fascinating old basilica of
S. Ambrogio.[2] Here again he was in the midst of party
strife which he tried in vain to quell. By the support
of the Ghibelline Oberto Pelavicini, the Torriani who
professed to stand for the people had made themselves
supreme in the great city of Milan ; and, when in 1263
Otto Visconti, a scion of a noble family who had large
estates round the southern end of the Lago Maggiore,
was made its Archbishop, they refused to recognize him.
He at once placed himself at the head of the party of the
nobles, and the struggle was still going on between the
parties when Gregory arrived on the scene. He had
intended to take Otho with him into the city, but the
Torriani objected, so that Gregory was forced to bid
Otho·remain for the moment at Biella. When in the city,
the Pope completely failed to effect any reconciliation.
Indeed it would seem that threats were uttered against
him, if he attempted to establish the Archbishop in the
city, and he had to be content with promising Otho to
reinstate him on his return from Lyons. Faction ran so
high that, in order to escape assassination, Otho found it
advisable to follow the Pope to Lyons. On his return
from the Council, Gregory was equally unable to restore
him, so that Brother Stephanardus declares that the

[1] *Cf. Chron. de rebus*, p. 344. On the abbey of Morimond, between
Benasco and Abbiategrasso (18 miles from Milan), see D. Sant' Ambrogio
"La Badia di Morimondo," Milan, 1891, an extract from *Archivio
Storico Lombardo*, 1891.

[2] *Annal. Mediol.*, c. 45, ap. *R. I. SS.*, xvi, p. 672.

Pope's want of firmness in supporting his hero was a disgrace to him.[1] It may be that, in this case, Gregory went too far in tolerating violence ; but his one aim was to promote peace everywhere by peaceful means in order to secure the success of his one end—the Crusade. In any case on his journey to the Council, he had neither the time nor the means to force the party which had then control of Milan, to receive their archbishop into their midst.

But he went on his way with a heavy heart, for he was distressed to have to leave Italy still a prey to warring factions.[2] Making arrangements, however, to continue his work for the spread of peace on his return, he crossed the Alps, and passing through Chambéry, he reached Lyons about the middle of November. He was met by the King of France, Philip III., "with a great and noble company," who after treating with him on the affairs of his kingdom, and on the canonization of his father, Louis IX., departed with the Pope's blessing. But he left behind him soldiers to guard the Pope and the Council, set over them his own kinsman, Himbert of Beaujeu ; and gave over to the Pope for the same purpose three strong castles.[3]

Gregory at Lyons.

---

[1] " Dedecus hoc aule est grandisque injuria deni, Gregorii, tantum facinus qui sidere clauso, Dissimulat, legi metuens obsistere seve." *De Gestis in civit. Mediol.*, l. ii, ap. *R. I. SS.*, ix, pt. i. The Dominican Stephanardus de Vicomercato († 1297) wrote of the doings of Otho in rather inflated verse. *Cf. Annales Mediol.*, c. 45, ap. *R. I. SS.*, xvi ; and G. Flamma, *Manip. Florum*, c. 310, ap. *ib.*, xi.

[2] See his letter to the Podestà and people of Milan, ap. *Reg.*, 772, or Kaltenbrunner, *Actenstücke*, p. 46 : " Si adesset nobis opportunitas temporis, si concilii necessitas nos ad assumpti continuationem itineris non urgeret, tanto libentius reformando Lombardie statui pacifico vacaremus, quanto non solum ex antiquarum partium generali discordia, verum etiam ex singularibus germinatis ibique disidiis majora heu imminent animarum pericula, etc." *Cf. Anon. C.* " Flevit super illam (Lombardy)".

[3] Will. of Nangis, *De gest. Phil. III.*, ap. *M. G. SS.*, xxvi, p. 671. *Cf. Hist. reg. Franc. contin. Paris.*, ap. *ib.*, p. 609. *Grandes Chron. de France,*

Received also by the people of Lyons, as though, says his biographer,[1] they had suddenly found a most valuable treasure, Gregory at once, despite infirmities aggravated by the hardships of his journey,[2] commenced to work for the success of the approaching Council and the Crusade. He urged on collections for the Holy Land in France,[3] carried on negotiations in its interests in all directions, and also continued his labours in the cause of peace.[4] He did all that lay in his power, as will be seen presently, to facilitate the coming of the Greeks to the Council, and he begged Edward to hasten or defer his coronation, so as not to hinder his own or the bishops of England from coming to the Council.[5]

Council of Lyons, 1274. At length on May 1, 1274, the prelates of Christendom met for the Council so ardently longed for by Gregory, and the number and importance of the representatives, cleric and lay, of every land which he saw around him gave him every reason to hope for great results from such a gathering. Owing to the diverse data furnished by contemporaries who no doubt estimated the numbers they give at different moments of the duration of the council it is impossible to give the average number of the prelates attending it. Certain Austrian annals assure us that almost all the rulers of the Church were present at it.[6] From other authors, it may be said that there assembled no fewer than five hundred bishops, sixty abbots,

Philipple III, c. 18. (The King ordered that "l'aposole eust trois chasteaulx et deffensables"), and *Chronographia Reg. Franc.*, ed. Moranville, i, p. 2.

[1] *Ib.*

[2] Ep., Nov. 18, 1273, Posse, n. 762. *Cf.* n. 766.

[3] *Ib.*, nn. 763–6.

[4] *Ib.*, nn. 766–7, 772, 775, 777.

[5] Rymer, ii, 20, Dec. 1, 1273. *Cf. ib.*, p. 29, where, for the sake both of his body and soul, Gregory begs King Edward not to take part in a tournament, May 15, 1274. *Cf.* p. 30.

[6] *Ann. Aust. contin. Lamb.*, ap. *M. G. SS.*, ix, 561. *Cf. Ann. S. Rudberti*, ap. *ib.*, p. 800.

and about one thousand inferior prelates, including procurators of chapters, etc.[1] Among the bishops, we must reckon " nearly all " those of our own country.[2] The Grand Master of the Templars was also present in person ; but the Grand Master of the Hospitallers by proxy. Although James of Aragon was the only sovereign present in person, there were " innumerable envoys " of other ruling princes, and although, most unfortunately, the greatest of mediaeval philosophers, St. Thomas of Aquinas, died on his way to the Council, his renowned contemporary St. Bonaventure was present at it, and did much by his sweet character, to reconcile the Greeks to the Church. It is worth adding, too, that " Ultima Thule " took part in this great assembly. Even though Iceland was too poor to bear the expenses of a journey of one of its bishops to Rome, it was represented by Sighvat, canon of Nidaros (Trondjhem), who at one time had lived at the papal court. He represented bishop Arni of Skalholt ; and, as we learn from a letter of Nicholas de Tracia, whose business it was to examine the papers of those who represented bishops at the Council, Sighvat did his work well.[3]

After proclaiming on May 2, a three days fast for all the prelates,[4] the Pope himself formally opened the first

First Session May 7.

---

[1] *Otto Fresing. cont. Sanblas.*, ap. *ib.*, xx, 337. Ptolemy of Lucca, *H. E.*, xxii, c. 3, gives 70 abbots.

[2] *Annal. Furnes.*, ap. *M. G. SS.*, xxviii, 558. On the questions of the date, numbers, etc., of the Council see the note in Raynaldus, *Ann.*, 1275, n. 1. We know the names of the cardinals present from a document, ap. *ib.*, 1278, n. 47—bishops, Peter of Ostia and Velletri (Innocent V.), Peter of Tusculum (John XXI.), John of Porto, Bonaventure (St.) of Albano ;—Priests, Simon of St. Martin, Ancher of S. Prassede, William of St. Mark, Simon of S. Cecily—deacons, Ottoboni of St. Adrian (Hadrian V.), Hubert of St. Eustachio, James of S. Maria in Cosmedin, Godfrey of St. George in Velabro, and Matthew of S. Maria in Portico.

[3] *Cf.* the contemporary *Saga* of Bp. Arni Thorlakson, c. 10, ap. C. C. Rafn, *Antiquités Russes*, ii, p. 363, Copenhagen, 1852.

[4] Potthast, sub. 20818, from Mansi, *Concil.*, vol. xxiv.

session of the fourteenth General Council in the Cathedral
of St. John on May 7. The chief event of this session
was the Pope's sermon from the words in St. Luke
(xxii, 15) : " With desire have I desired to eat this
Pasch with you," in which he treated of the threefold
object of the Council—help for the Holy Land, union
with the Greeks, and the reformation of morals. Gregory
spent the interval between the first and second sessions
in exacting promises from the prelates to agree to a tax
of a tenth of their revenues for six years for the benefit
of the Holy Land. At the second session (May 18),
after another sermon from the Pope, articles of faith
touching the Procession of the Holy Ghost were issued.[1]

Consulta-
tions with
James I. of
Aragon.
The interval between the second and the third session,
Gregory again passed in hard work. He had specially
begged James I. of Aragon, as a soldier experienced in
wars against the Moslem, to attend the Council in order
that he might give it the benefit of his knowledge in
this matter.[2] The old warrior lets us know how much
the invitation gratified him, and tells us of the splendid
reception he received when he approached the city of
Lyons. He was met by the cardinals, by the Master of
the Templars, by those who held the city for the Pope,
and by bishops and barons, and so great was the throng
of people who accompanied him that it took him " from
morning till noon " to traverse a league. Arrived
before the Pope " I did him that reverence which Kings
pay to a Pope according to established custom ".[3]

For the history of the Council, James' *Chronicle* is
most interesting, as he gives us summaries of some of
Gregory's fervent exhortations in behalf of the Holy
Land, and of the advice that he and others gave to the
Pope as to what should be done at once. He tells of the

---

[1] Potthast, sub. 20830. Hefele, *Conciles*, vi, p. i, p. 170, new ed.
[2] *Cf.* his *Chronicle*, c. 513, vol. i, p. 638. *Cf.* J. Forster's Eng. trans.
[3] *Ib.*, cc. 524–5.

plenary indulgence granted by Gregory to all who took
part in the Crusade, and of his reminding his listeners
that there was no pardon to be got for sins of robbery
or usury unless full compensation were made to those
who had been wronged.[1] He advised the Pope to send
out to the Holy Land at once five hundred knights and
two thousand foot soldiers to hold the castles till the
main body of the Crusaders could come to their assistance.
In promising pecuniary help, the glorious old braggart
declared that he would "not give less than he who
gives most"; and, while asking the Pope to grant him
the tithes of his kingdom, he concluded : "For the rest,
I say that if you yourself go beyond the sea, as you have
proposed, I will accompany you with a thousand knights."[2]
Among the other advisers of the Pope there was less
enthusiasm as well perhaps as a little less brag ; but, to
show his appreciation of the Spanish monarch's goodwill,
Gregory ordered that throughout Christendom a special
prayer should be offered for the King at Mass, and that
such clerks as were not priests should pray that God
would give him health to fulfil all that he had promised
to do "for the honour of God and of the Church".[3]
Gregory, however, refused to crown him, as he would
not agree to pay the tribute which had been promised
by his father Pedro the Catholic, and which was in
arrears to the extent of eleven thousand "sous tournois".
The King was indignant. "He had done such service to
God," he said, "and to the Church of Rome" that such
trifles ought not to stand in his way.[4]

Before leaving the city, James had another interview
with the Pope in which he prayed for the release of
Henry of Castile. Though the Pope in reply declared

---

[1] *Ib.*, c. 529.
[2] *Ib.*, c. 531.
[3] *Ib.*, c. 539.
[4] *Ib.*, cc. 536–8.

that Henry had spoken against him, and that he was not aware that he was still in prison, he promised to speak to Charles of Anjou in his behalf.[1] The King also begged the Pope to hear his confession, and ingenuously informs us that he enumerated not only his sins, but also " what I remembered of the good deeds I had done ".[2] Then he returned to Catalonia with the Pope's blessing, but without having accomplished very much.

Confirmation of the election of Rudolf.

Also before the third session, the Pope brought forward the position of affairs with regard to the Empire—the election of Rudolf (Oct. 1, 1273), and the continued claims of Alfonso X. As we shall see, more at length later on, the claims of the latter were rejected, and the election of Rudolf solemnly confirmed.[3]

Venaissin ceded to Gregory, 1274.

Another event also took place at this time which was destined to have a most important bearing on papal history. It was the completion of the negotiations which led to the cession of the comtat Venaissin to the Pope. This territory exclusive of, but around Avignon, on the left bank of the Rhone between the provinces of Dauphiné and Provence, i.e., between the Isere and the Durance, had been originally ceded to the Holy See by Raymond VII. (the Younger) in 1229, as a result of the Albigensian wars.[4] Stated by some modern writers to have been restored to Raymond in 1234 by Gregory IX.,[5] but

---

[1] *Ib.*, c. 540 f.

[2] *Ib.*, c. 542.

[3] *Catal. pontif. Laud.*, ap. *M. G. SS.*, xxii, p. 371.

[4] See clause 13 of the treaty of 1229, ap. Vaissette, *Hist. gen. de Languedoc*, iii, p. 370 ff., ed. 1737. " Quant aux païs et domaines qui sont au-delà de ce fleuve (the Rhone) dans l'empire, avec tous les droits qui peuvent m'y appartenir je les ai cedez précisément et absolument à perpetuité à l'église Romaine entre les mains du légat."

[5] *Ib.*, p. 376. *Cf.* pp. 583–5. For correspondence on the subject between Gregory and Louis IX., King of France, and Raymond himself, *cf.* Potthast, nn. 8888–90, 8896, 9367.

emphatically claimed as his by Gregory X.,[1] it was at this time, at any rate, definitely ceded by King Philip to the Holy See.[2] The first Rector (or governor) of the province appointed by Gregory was William de Villaret, prior of the hospital of St. Giles of the Order of St. John of Jerusalem.[3]

The third session of the Council was held on June 7; Third and, after a sermon by Peter of Tarentaise, cardinal- session, June 7. bishop of Ostia, a number of decrees were issued to lessen delays in the matter of elections to bishoprics,[4] to put a stop to certain abuses of procurations,[5] and to regulate various points connected with excommunication and interdict.[6] Then, as the exact time of the arrival of the Greeks was not known, no date was fixed for the holding of the next session, but the prelates were informed that in the meanwhile they were at liberty to go anywhere within six miles of the city.

In a little over a fortnight from the close of the third The Greek session of the Council, the Greek envoys arrived at Lyons unites itself (June 24). Before, however, relating what took place with Rome. between them and the prelates of the West, we must go back a little and relate the events that led up to their presence at Lyons, and to the Union of 1274. Further, when that Union has been described, we will proceed to tell how it soon came to an end, so that the story of this most important event may not be broken.

---

[1] Cf. ep. Nov. 21, 1273, ap. Raynaldus, 1273, n. 51. " Terra Venesina . . . Romanæ ecclesiæ *cujus est propria* . . . dimittenda."

[2] Cf. Sanudo, *Hist. Hierosol.*, lib. iii, c. 12, n. 13, ap. *ib.*, " Philipus . . . reddidit summo Pontifici comitatum Venesi, quem longo tempore ab ecclesia sui tenuerunt prædecessores." Cf. John Longus, *Chron. S. Bertin.*, ap. *ib.*, or M. G. SS., xxv, 857. The city of Orange and its district was not included in the C.V. (*cf.* Debombourg, *Atlas Chron. des états de l'Église*, pl. 8 ff.), and the city of Avignon only became the property of the Popes by purchase in the days of Clement VI.

[3] Pot., n. 20817, Apr. 27, 1274. *Cf. Reg.*, Nicholas III., n. 227.

[4] *Cf.* Cap. 3, 4, 5, 6, 7, 8, 9, etc.

[5] C. 24.

[6] Cc. 29, 30. *Cf.* Potthast, sub. 20843.

Relations
between
Urban IV.
and Michael
Palæologus.

One of the things which Gregory X. had especially at heart was the reunion of the East and West.[1] When he was in Palestine it had been brought home to him very strongly how fatal to the interests of Christianity was the disastrous separation between the Greek and Latin churches. It was one of the principal causes of the ill-success of the Crusades, and was an almost insurmountable obstacle to the propagation of the Christian faith in the East. These results would not have been so pronounced had there been a mere separation between the two churches ; but the more or less natural cleavage between East and West, between the Greek and Latin mind, purposely intensified by Photius, had been much widened by subsequent Greek insincerity and Latin violence. Throughout the period of the Crusades, the Greeks had endeavoured to exploit the prowess of the Latins in their own interests, and the latter had prostituted that prowess by the capture of Constantinople, and the establishment of their ill-starred Latin Kingdom. Before the seizure of their capital, the Greeks had affected to look down upon the uncultured Latins, and the Latins in turn to despise Greek effeminacy. The unfortunate triumph of the latter in 1204 had further embittered the ill-feeling between the two races.[2] The Greeks spoke with contempt even of the Latin Church services, and of the

---

[1] Important on this subject is the recent work of C. Chapman, *Michel Paléologue*, Paris, 1926. It is strange that the author accepts as authentic such documents as *Conspiration de Jean Prochyta* without calling attention to the fact that all such documents connected with J. P. are rejected as spurious by many first-class authorities.

[2] Hence, in the *Disputatio* between the Latins and Greeks at Nymphæa in 1234, the Greeks attempted to justify the contemptuous disregard of the Latin Mass by the outrageous manner in which *Latin* soldiers had behaved on that occasion. See Golubovich's more accurate version of the *Disputatio* ap. *Archiv. Francaise. Hist.*, 1919, p. 451.

Latin style of singing [1] ; and the Latins retorted by speaking of the Greeks as "White Saracens ".[2] And while the ignorant and the fanatics on both sides abused each other they knew not why, the educated Latins regarded the Greeks as schismatics for refusing to recognize the primacy of the Pope, and as heretics for denying the Procession of the Holy Ghost from the Father and from the Son ; and the Greeks, in a similar position, accounted the Latins heretics for asserting this Procession, and schismatics for cutting themselves off from them.

However, despite all the difficulties in the way, the Popes never ceased trying to bring the Greeks back to Unity ; while, on the other hand, temporal conditions were ever making the more farseeing of the Greek Emperors equally anxious for the same result for political reasons. When Emperor at Nicæa, Michael Palæologus, threatened by a coalition between Michael of Epirus, Manfred and William of Achaia, had wished to enter into negotiations with Rome. His efforts, perhaps through the feebleness of Alexander IV., came to nothing ; but in 1261 an unexpected change in the political world again made him anxious for the friendship of the Pope. In that year, through the co-operations of Greeks within the city, through the selfish support of the Genoese,[3]

The Greeks recapture Constantinople, 1261.

---

[1] Eustathius, the metropolitan of Thessalonica († c. 1193), besides contemptuously alluding to the Latin Mass : " τὰ ἑαυτῶν ἐτέλουν," speaks of the Latins trying to drown the chanting of the sacred Greek liturgy by a raucous bawling of profane songs, and declares that they had no respect for sacred vessels, places or persons. Cf. De Thessalonica Urbe a Latinis capta, c. 115; cf. c. 98 ff., ap. Pat. Græca, t. 136. Throughout this work, Eustathius speaks as though the Latins in general were simply savages. See especially, cc. 135–6 and 139.

[2] G. Pachym., Hist., v, 10.

[3] It is William of Nangis who tells us how the Genoese, through (commercial) jealousy of the Venetians, helped the Greeks. Chron., ad an. 1261. In 1261, to obtain the aid of the Genoese, Michael, by the treaty of Nymphæum, had agreed to give them the commercial privileges which the Venetians had enjoyed from the commence-

and through the absence, on an expedition, of the greater part of the Latin garrison, the Greeks, by surprise, recaptured Constantinople; and Michael Palæologus made his triumphal entry therein on the Feast of the Assumption of our Lady (August 15).

Palæologus at once sends envoys to Rome. The Latin emperor Baldwin II. had meanwhile fled to Italy, and thence, seeking help everywhere, he had made his way to Spain and France, and ultimately to the ambitious Charles of Anjou, whom the Greeks regarded with reason as a forceful and exceptionally able man.[1] With the ambitious Count, he would appear, if Pachymeres has not antedated events, to have come to some understanding which, some years later (May 27, 1267), was sealed by the formal treaty of Viterbo, and cemented by the betrothal of his son Philip to Beatrice, the baby daughter of Charles.[2] By this treaty Baldwin ceded to *King* Charles, as he was then, practically all his rights in the Byzantine Empire.[2]

If animated only by trade rivalry with Genoa, preparations for an attempt to recover Constantinople were at once commenced by Venice.[3]

ment of the Latin Empire, in Constantinople, Salonica, etc., and various islands. See Muralt, *Chron. Byz.*, 1261, n. 14. *Cf. Chron. Mon. Patav.*, ap. *R. I. SS.*, viii, 716–17. Hence the remonstrances of Urban IV. with the Genoese, and his final excommunication of them for siding with Michael (*cf.* ep. of Jan. 19, 1263, ap. *Reg.*, vol. ii, n. 182, p. 72; *ib.*, nn. 850-2, p. 409); and hence, on the other hand, Michael's complaint to the Pope about his endeavouring to withdraw from him the friendship of the Genoese: "quorum amicitiam nos tibi subtrahere velle conquereris" wrote Urban, ep. of July 28, 1263, ap. Wadding, iv, p. 206. See also *Annal. Januenses*, ap. *M. G. SS.*, xviii, p. 243 ff. On the capture see Niceph. Gregoras, iv, 2; G. Pachym., ii, 27, and the more accurate account of G. Acropolita.

[1] "Σοβαρῷ καὶ ὑπὲρ τὸ μέτρον φρονοῦντι." G. Pach., ii, 32; *cf.* iv, 29, and N. Greg., v, 1, and Villani, *Chron.*, vi, 88, vii, 1. "Feared by all the Kings of the earth."

[2] See the treaty ap. Del Giudice, *Cod. Diplom. di Carlo I.*, ii, p. 30 ff., Pachym., ii, 32; N. Greg., vi, 1. The marriage between the two took place in 1273.

[3] *Cf.* Muralt, *Chronog. Byzantine*, vol. ii, nn. 5, 7, 8, pp. 403–4.

Under no delusion as to the gravity of the situation, the Byzantine monarch began without delay to look to the fortifications of his capital, and sent off envoys to the Pope.[1] According to Pachymeres, the first envoys were Nicephoritzes and Alubardes, who had been Baldwin's secretaries, but who had gone over to his rival. When they landed in Italy, the Greek historian tells how, in defiance of the law of nations, they were seized, and how the former was skinned alive, and the latter only escaped a similar fate by successful flight.[2] But, as no allusion whatever is made to these ambassadors or their fate in the official correspondence of either Urban or Palæologus,[3] we may safely conclude that they were not authorized envoys from the Emperor; but that, whilst travelling on their own account, they were caught and proceeded against as spies or traitors. Michael's real envoys, as we shall see presently, reached the Pope quite safely.[4]

Urban's first recorded intercourse with the Emperor was in connexion with the arbitrary conduct of a Greek official. Following up the action of Alexander IV.,[5] he asked the Emperor to cause the official at Adramytteum (Edremit) to restore the money he had taken from certain citizens of Lucca.[6] Then, somewhat later, under the

Urban takes action against Palæologus, 1262.

---

[1] It is certain that he sent off letters to the Pope on the subject of ecclesiastical union immediately after the capture of Constantinople. See ep. *Imperialis excellentiæ* of July 28, 1263, sent by Urban to him: "Nam licet statim capta Constantinopolitana urbe alias nobis epistolares litteras miseris, etc." Ap. Wadding, iv, 202.

[2] G. Pach., ii, 33 and 36, ed. Bonn.

[3] Unless indeed they were the bearers of the letters mentioned in note 1.

[4] In general terms, G. Pachymeres frequently says that the emperor endeavoured to win over the Pope by embassies and by presents both to him, to certain cardinals and to such as he thought had influence with him. "πρεσβείαις καὶ δεξιώσεσι . . . τὸν πάπαν . . . ἐξεμειλίσσετο." iii, 18. *Cf.* v, 8.

[5] Ep. of Apr. 2, 1261, ap. Potth., 18080.

[6] *Ib.*, n. 18158, ep. of Nov. 22, 1261, from *Hist. Pat. Mon.*, i,

influence of Baldwin and Charles, Count of Anjou, he took up the cause of the former with great energy. Letters of his are extant in which we see him stirring up the Poles and the French to take up arms for the recovery of Constantinople. He tells how grieved he was to hear of the loss to the Church of that great city which had been won back to Catholic unity.[1] Already, he continues, the Catholics therein are being harassed, and already are preparations being made to attack the other Latin Principalities in Greece. The loss of the city is fatal also to the success of the Crusades for the recovery of the Holy Land. The West must rise and win the city back.[2] A month later he is authorizing Baldwin to promise and to give certain sums of money to those Frenchmen who are willing to help him.[3]

He receives the envoys of Palæologus, 1262.

However, soon after the dispatch of this letter to the ex-Emperor, i.e., towards the end of June, there arrived in Orvieto the envoys of Michael Palæologus, namely the monk Maximus Alufardus, Andronicus Muzalo and Michael Abalantes.[4] To the messages which they

---

[1] *Cf.* his letter of June 5 to St. Louis of France : " stupidos sensimus sensus nostros," ap. Raynaldus, *Ann.*, 1262, n. 39 ff. *Cf. Chron.,* Danduli, ap. *R. I. SS.*, xii, p. 369, " mœrore stupefactus."

[2] Ep. May 21, 1262, to the Dominicans in Poland, ap. Ripoll, *Bull. Ord. Prædicatorum,* i, p. 422, Rome, 1729. A similar bull to the Franciscans in France may be seen, ap. L. Wadding, *Annal. Minorum,* iv, 175, Rome, 1732. See also *Reg. Urb.*, vol. ii, n. 131 ff., p. 46.

[3] June 20, 1262, Potth., n. 18361 ; *cf.* Raynaldus, *Annal. eccles.,* 1262, § 43.

[4] See Urban's letter to M. Pal. of July 28, 1263, ap. Wad., iv, 202. A narrative of these events may be read in *Hist. polemica de Græcorum schismate,* by L. Cozza, 4 vols., Rome, 1719. Some would identify the monk Alufardus with Alubardes the one-time secretary of Baldwin II. Bréhier, ap. *Cambridge Med. Hist.,* iv, p. 609, believes that " a common hostility to Manfred " decided the Emperor and the Pope to take up the question of the union. But after the great defeat of Manfred's father-in-law at Pelagonia (1259), and, with the fear of Conradin's party over him, it is hard to see how the Sicilian usurper can have inspired much fear into Palæologus at that moment.

brought by word of mouth and to the letters which they presented, and which he caused to be translated from Greek into Latin, Urban straightway sent off a brief reply to the effect that he would in due course by special messengers send word to the Emperor as to what he had been able to arrange for the joint advantage of the Roman Church and of his majesty.[1]

This was followed about a year later by a long letter to " Palæologus, illustrious Emperor of the Greeks ", sent by the hands of four Franciscans, Simon of Alvernia, Peter de Moras, Peter de Crista, and Boniface of Ivrea.[2] In his lengthy reply to "his Imperial Excellency ", Urban expressed his contentment that the Emperor had recognized him as the successor of St. Peter, and as his spiritual father. He was anxious, indeed, to see the Greeks in communion with the Latins, so that all the sheep of the Lord under one shepherd might be fed with the doctrine of salvation ; and he would, he declared, have sent off his envoys to the Emperor before had there not been great delay in getting them together from distant lands, and had not certain rumours reached him of his attacking the territories and subjects of that most devout son of the Church, William of Villehardouin.[3] However, he continued, he had at length dispatched four religious and learned men as Angels of peace, to bring about peace and unity, especially that unity which results from subjection to the successor of St. Peter to whom were given the keys of the

Envoys and letter sent to Palæologus, 1263.

---

[1] Ep., without date, ap. Wad., iv, 181 f., c. July, 1262.

[2] Ep. *Imp. excellent.*, ap. *ib.*, p. 202 ff. It is dated in Wadding, July 28, 1263, but in the *Register*, vol. ii, p. 134, n. 295, July 18, 1263.

[3] A letter of Jan. 12, 1263, ap. Potthast, n. 18465, or *Reg.*, vol. ii, p. 76, n. 188, shows Urban actively engaged in frustrating the designs that M. Palæologus was meanwhile endeavouring to bring to a head in Cyprus. Further, during the course of the year 1263, the Greek navy was seizing islands that were in the hands of the Latins. *Cf.* G. Pach., iii, 15.

Kingdom of heaven. For it was through him that, when
other churches were defiled by heresy, the Roman
Church remained ever immaculate [1]; and, as is averred
by the writings of certain Greek Fathers, all Catholics have
to submit to the Apostolic Throne of Rome, and receive
from it the light of truth. He accordingly exhorted the
Emperor to show by deeds that he gave that homage to
the Holy See which he had professed in words, and he
assured him that great would be to him the advantages
of that submission both in the spiritual and in the temporal
order. With the reincorporation of so important a
member as the Greek Church, the whole body of the
Church would become stronger, and would therefore
impart fresh vigour to each and all its members. Hence,
too, would the Greek Empire receive from the See of
Peter the same assistance in the preservation of its external
and internal peace as the other nations which depended
upon it. After declaring that it was a grave crime not
to obey the Roman Church, he proceeded to show that
the results of the disunion between the two Churches
had brought about great temporal evils. Then, apolo-
getically, he added that if, at times, the Latins had
attacked the Greeks, it had not always been through
greed, but that, by the lesson of misfortune, the Greeks
might acquire the light of truth, and that if, at times,
as often happened in wars, certain wicked Latins had
profaned the churches of the Greeks, such evil conduct
must not by reasonable men be imputed to the whole body
of the Latins. In conclusion, he beggéd the Emperor
to receive well the envoys, whom he had sent to treat
about the dogmas of the faith, the rites of the Church,
and peace and concord with the Empire, and, meanwhile,
to cease all hostilities against the Prince of Achaia.

[1] " Cum postmodum aliarūm ecclesiarum nonnullæ fuerint
hæreticorum errore fœdatæ, Romana ecclesia cujus idem beatus Petrus
magister extitit, immaculata remansit." *Ib.*, p. 205.

Letters, of the same date as the above, gave to the papal legates all the necessary faculties for reconciling members of the Greek Church to the See of Rome, and required all clerics, whether secular or religious, and all secular Princes to give every kind of assistance to them.[1] About the same time also (August 1) he wrote to inform William of Villehardouin that he was sending certain friars to Michael Palæologus " who accounts himself Emperor of the Greeks " to bring him back, " *if he ever can be brought back*," to the unity of the faith. He went on to beg him in the meanwhile to refrain from hostilities against Michael, as he had in turn exhorted Michael to refrain in the meantime from attacking the Prince of Achaia.[2]

It would appear that the Greek Emperor was not altogether satisfied with the legates sent him by the Pope. Perhaps they were not sympathetic or had not a sufficient knowledge of Greek [3] to influence the people, or, possibly, were not in a position to give satisfactory assurances as to the pacific intentions of the count of Provence. There was ever before the troubled eyes of Michael Palæologus the menacing figure of Charles, count of Anjou.[4] At any rate, " after the winter " of 1263-4, he sent a letter to the Pope, whom he always proclaimed as his spiritual father and the first of bishops,[5] in which he told him that he had recently come in contact

Request of Michael for a fresh legate, 1264.

---

[1] Epp. ap. Wad., iv, 210-13, or *Reg.*, ii, p. 149 ff., n. 322.

[2] Ep. ap. Wad., iv, 212.

[3] This is the point specially insisted on by the Emperor in his letter : " In omnibus rationibus," *Reg. Urb.*, n. 748. He says that because there were not a sufficient number of interpreters able to grasp the thoughts of both parties, no agreement could be come to, and strife of all kinds arose.

[4] *Cf.* G. Pach., v, 8, 9.

[5] *Ib.*, v, 8: " ἔχειν δὲ καὶ αὐτὸν τοῦτον πατέρα πνευματικὸν, καὶ λογίζεσθαι ἀρχιερέων ὄντα τὸν πρώτιστον." In this letter the Pope is saluted as " the father of our Empire ", and " the prince of all bishops and doctors of the universal Catholic Church ".

with Nicholas, bishop of Crotone.[1]　As this man was by
birth a Greek and by education a Latin, and hence
spoke both languages perfectly, and was moreover
an able theologian, he was most suitable to carry on
the negotiations between the two Churches which,
by a comparison of the Greek and Latin Fathers, he
had demonstrated to the Emperor were at one in their
beliefs.[2]　For this reason, after having unfolded to him
his aims, Palæologus begged to send him to the Pope
with a request that he would in turn confer with him,
and send him back to Constantinople with other legates.[3]
No doubt the principal object that the Greek Emperor
had in view in the dispatch of Nicholas was to urge the
Pope not to suffer Charles to make war " upon Christians
who were of the same Church ".[4]

The religious
and political
acts of
Palæologus.

Whilst bishop Nicholas was making his way to Italy
with Michael's letters and instructions, the Emperor
continued working for his own ends in his conduct both
of ecclesiastical and civil affairs.　Whilst his troops
did not cease their efforts to expel the Latins from
what had formerly been Greek territory, he himself did
not relax his endeavours at least to convince the papal
envoys that he was in earnest in his desire to effect the
union of the two Churches.　He was active in this direction
for reasons of personal as well as of public advantage.
He had been excommunicated by the Patriarch Arsenius
(1262) after that prelate had discovered that he had blinded

---

[1] Nicholas of Dyracchium, who had once been a member of the papal
camera (treasury).　G. Pachymeres, v, 8, says that he was " a learned
theologian and bilingular ", i.e., that he spoke both Latin and Greek
fluently.

[2] He had proved to me, wrote the Emperor, that the Roman Church
" ea fere nobiscum sentientem ".　Ep. ap. *Reg. Urb.*, vol. ii, p. 356,
n. 748, or ap. Wadding, iv, p. 223.

[3] *Ib.*

[4] Such are the words put into his mouth by G. Pach., v, 8.

his ward, John Lascaris, the rightful heir to the throne.[1]
He expected that the prospect of his submitting the
Greek Church to the see of Rome would make Arsenius
willing to remove the excommunication from him, in
order to induce him to pause in his march towards
reconciliation with the West. Michael also made every
effort to induce the Greek ecclesiastics to have frequent
intercourse with the papal legates, and to admit them
to all the sacred functions, among others to the *stations*,
and to a participation of the blessed bread which was
distributed at the end of Mass.[2]

In his reply to the letter of the Greek Emperor presented
to him by bishop Nicholas,[3] the Pope, after summarizing
or rather repeating the Emperor's letter, declared that,
though he thought that Simon of Alvernia and his other
envoys were sufficiently capable of dealing with the
situation, he willingly complied with the Emperor's
wishes and therefore added Nicholas,[4] and brothers
Gerard of Prato and Rainer of Siena to those other
envoys. In turn, he implored the Emperor not to be
slack in his efforts to conclude the union.

Urban sends fresh envoys to Constantinople, 1264.

At the same time, while prohibiting action against
the Greeks on the part of Charles of Anjou,[5] he did not
cease to work for peace between the Venetians and the
Genoese; for, as he said, by their discord " were the
seas reddened with Christian blood, the condition of
the Holy Land (in face of the Moslem) greatly weakened,
and that of the Empire of Constantinople almost completely

The last relations of Urban with the Greeks, 1264.

---

[1] G. Pach., iii, 14.

[2] *Ib.*, v, 8: " ἐν μεταλήψει τοῦ θείου ἄρτου ὃν ἀντίδωρον λέγουσιν."
Cf. N. Greg., v, 1 and 2.

[3] Ep. " Mediator Dei ", May 23, 1264, ap. *Reg.*, ii, p. 405, n. 848.
In Wadding, iv, 225 ff., this letter is dated June 22, 1264.

[4] Urban's metrical biographer naïvely says :—
" Mittitur a dicto domino (Urban) Cotronensis eidem (Palæologus)
Præsul, et articulis omnibus imbuat hunc." P. 26.

[5] G. Pach., v, 8.

ruined ".[1] By his action in detaching the Genoese from
the service of the Greek Emperor, and by his words
when he insinuated his doubts as to whether Palæologus
could ever be brought back to Catholic unity, Urban,
up to the very end of his life, gave proof that he understood the selfish motives that animated that ruler.
Consequently, whilst doing all that lay in his power by
compliance with Michael's wishes to further such good
intentions as he might have, he did not lose sight of
the necessity of clearing the way for possible action
against him in the future.

Palæologus
sends envoys
to Clement
IV.

A few months after the dispatch of the letters regarding
the relations of Venice and Genoa, Urban breathed his
last (October 2), and was succeeded by Clement IV.,
another Frenchman (February 5, 1265). As soon as the
news of his accession reached Constantinople, the
Emperor at once sent envoys to him in order to assure
him of his zeal in the cause of unity.[2] In these continued
negotiations with Rome, Michael, with a view of reconciling
his people to his policy, constantly brought forward
what had happened under the Emperor John III. Ducas
(Vatatzes).[3] He pointed out that then the Greeks had

---

[1] Ep. June 20, 1264, ap. *Reg.*, ii, p. 409. n. 852. *Cf.* nn. 850–1.

[2] The letter they bore has been published by N. Festa in the original
Greek in the periodical *Bessarione*, An. iv, p. 48, and separately as
Let. ined. di M. P., Rome, 1899. It begins: " Ἦν ὅτε., Fuit tempus
cum." The Emperor extols the time when Greeks and Latins were one
in faith ; deplores the miseries that have supervened since their division ;
tells how, in love of peace, he had already corresponded with Alexander
IV., and Urban IV., and how their deaths had distressed him ; rejoices
that Clement has been constituted by God " a worthy successor of the
throne of the chief, Peter ", and exhorts him to work for Union, whilst
he himself condemns the harm done by " the mad Photius " and other
Greeks, and undertakes, without infringing on the Divine ordinances, to
respect all that emperors or Councils have confirmed to the Pope,
saving " the authentic prerogatives of the Church of New Rome ".

[3] *Cf. supra*, vol. xiv, p. 222 ff.

professed themselves ready to obey the Pope, and insert
his name in their diptychs, if only he would not help
the Latins in Constantinople.[1]

Another Greek writer of this period, whether under
imperial inspiration or not we would not venture to say,
also stressed the advances made to Rome by Vatatzes.
This was George Metochita, archdeacon of S. Sophia of the
school of Beccus, who was exiled in 1282 and died in prison
after 1308. In his *Historia dogmatica* [2] he observes that the
great emperor Vatatzes, who flourished a little before
his time, amidst all his other occupations, regarded
his work for the union of the Churches as of first importance.
He tells of the envoys from Rome whom he received,
and those whom he sent thither, and appeals to men
who were still living and could tell the story. Especially
does he dwell on the splendid embassy he sent to Rome,
on the important bishops who took part in it, including
the patriarch Manuel, a man of the greatest virtue, and
on the state officials who went with it. Those among them
who were priests pronounced the name of the Pope
during the celebration of the Liturgy, " according to
ancient custom," and they did the same on their return :
" so that it was understood that if any other privilege
of old pertained to the Pope, it should be acknowledged." [3]
He concludes his remarks about the negotiations of
Vatatzes by saying that the religious questions were
agreed to by all the ecclesiastics of the time. The negotiations, he adds, fell through because the Pope could
not guarantee the surrender of Constantinople.

But Palæologus was animated, as we have said, by
reasons of private as well as of public utility in his dealings
with Clement and the Popes of this period. He was still

(margin note: George Metochita on Vatatzes.)

---

[1] G. Pach., v. 10.

[2] i, c. 20, ap. Mai, *Nova Pat. Bib.*, viii, p. 27.

[3] " ὡσαύτως καὶ λοιπὸν εἴ τι προνόμιον ἀρχῆθεν ὑπῆρχεν ἀπονενεμημένον
αὐτῷ, τοῦτο ἦν ἐνδεδομένον, etc."

writhing under the excommunication which the patriarch
Arsenius had laid upon him, and could not be induced
to remove.　Unable to endure the burden any longer,
he took advantage of an accusation made against the
patriarch to depose him, and send him into exile (1266).[1]
But, though he was absolved by his friend, Germanus
of Adrianople, whom he had advanced to the patriarchate,
he thereby brought fresh difficulties on himself.
Many very properly regarded the deposition of Arsenius
as unjust, and cut themselves off from communion with
Germanus.　Finding it impossible to heal the fierce
schism of the Arsenites, Germanus resigned his see
(September 14, 1267), and the Emperor's confessor,
Joseph, was made patriarch in his stead.[2]　But a schism
had been commenced which was to endure, and to cause
trouble in Constantinople for many years.

Messages of Clement to Constantinople.
Meanwhile Pope Clement had dispatched his legates
to Michael in response to those whom the Emperor
had sent to him (1266) [3]; and he had also weighed the
report of Urban's envoys who had brought back with them
the profession of faith which they had received from the
Emperor.[4]　However, not till the beginning of the year
1267 did Palæologus send ambassadors to the Pope to
request his acceptance of the said *profession*.　What kind
of reception Clement gave to the *scriptura*, as he calls
the profession, and how far the Greeks were in earnest
in these negotiations may be judged from the letters
which he addressed to the authorities in Church and State
at Constantinople.　They bear the date of March 4, 1267.

[1] *Ib.*, iv, cc. 4–8, Arsenius died in exile, Sept. 30, 1273.

[2] *Ib.*, cc. 21 and 23.　It would seem that Joseph had schemed against
Germanus to obtain his place.　*Cf.* Muralt, *Chronog. Byzant.*, ii, nn. 3,
4, 6, 7, p. 417.

[3] To the sending of these envoys and their long delay at the imperial
court, Clement refers in his letter of March 4, 1267, p. 272.　See next note.

[4] *Cf.* Clement's letter of March 4, 1267, ap. Wadding, iv, 269 ff.,
or *Reg. Clem.*, vol. i, p. 199, n. 585.　King Charles of Anjou saw to the
safe return of the Greek envoys.　*Cf.* Del Giudice, *Cod. diplom.*, i, p. 299.

In his letter to the Emperor, Clement told him with
what pleasure he had received his nuncios and his letters
treating of the Union which he had so much at heart,
and how he had been requested to approve of " a certain
writing " which Urban's returning envoys had presented
to him. He added that the envoys had accepted it in
as much as they could not get what they wanted, and
had promised to try to induce the Pope to accept it.[1] He
had, however, along with his cardinals, examined it with
care, but had found it unsatisfactory, if only because it
was very ambiguous. Hence he could not accept it;
and he thought that his action would the less surprise
the Emperor, seeing that it would appear that he did
not himself attach much importance to it, as for three
years he had not mentioned it either in his letters to him,
or to his envoys, and even now had not empowered his
nuncios to discuss it. Consequently, as all should be
clean and explicit that concerns faith upon which our
salvation depends, he sent the Emperor a plain summary
of the belief of the Roman Church to be accepted by him
and his people, so that they might all return to the
bosom of their mother, the Roman Church. After
unfolding the doctrine of the Church on the Blessed
Trinity, the Church, Purgatory, and the seven Sacraments,[2] he laid down that the Roman Church had received
" the full and complete primacy and principality of
the whole Catholic Church ", and that that primacy is
vested in the Roman Pontiff, the successor of St. Peter,
to whom it was given. To the Pope all questions arising

---

[1] " Cum non possent (Urban's envoys) ad plenum assequi quod
volebant, volentes tandem obtinere quod poterant, in quamdam tecum,
ut dicitur, convenere scripturam, certos articulos continentem." *Ib.*

[2] With regard to the Eucharist, while saying that the Roman
Church uses unleavened bread, he does not condemn the use of leavened
bread : " Sacramentum Eucharistiæ ex azymo conficit eadem Romana
Ecclesia . . . docens quod in ipso sacramento panis vere transub-
stantiatur in corpus, etc." p. 273.

about the faith must be referred for his decision ; to him
can appeals be made, and to him all Prelates are subject.
These truths, as wholly certain, he had no intention of
submitting to the Council which the Emperor had
expressed a wish to hold in his territory.   However,
he had resolved to send able envoys to Constantinople
who could explain and defend them, and the Emperor
in turn might send those to Rome who wished for further
enlightenment on them.   He had given a copy of this
Profession of Faith to the Emperor's nuncios.   If it is
accepted, he will then fall in with the desire for a Council.[1]

It was this lucid profession of the Catholic faith that
was referred to throughout the whole of the rest of these
negotiations.

In his letter to the Greek Patriarch, Clement begged
him to strive to bring the Emperor and all his people
back to that unity which they had professed to desire.[2]
A few months later, in order to fulfil his promise of sending
learned men to Constantinople to expound the doctrine
professed by the Roman Church, he begged the Master-
General of the Dominicans to send him three brothers
who might, by their exposition of the Catholic faith,
bring back the Greeks to Catholic unity, or, by exposing
their deceits, save the Pope from being called to judgment
by God on their account.   The General, he said need not
search the whole Order for men, because the Greeks
profess to seek not argument but demonstration, and
because, after all, their arguments are as weak as reeds.[3]

---

[1] This letter was followed by another (May 17, 1267) in which he
again exhorted Michael to return to ecclesiastical unity, and to join
the French in helping the Holy Land.   *Reg. Clem.*, Append., ii, p. 404,
n. 1201.

[2] Ep. ap. *Wad.*, iv, p. 275 f., or *Reg.*, i, p. 199, n. 586.   As the name
of the Patriarch is not cited, it is not clear whether the letter was
addressed to Germanus or to Joseph.

[3] Ep. June 9, 1267, ap. Ripoll, *Bullar. Ord. Præd.*, i, p. 485.   A week
or two before, May 17, he had written to ask the Greek Emperor to
assist the Holy Land.   Ep. 469, ap. Marten.

None the less, it may be added, he caused another Dominican, the great doctor St. Thomas Aquinas, to write a book to refute them.[1]

Whether the Dominican mission was dispatched or not, nothing of any importance towards the completion of the desired union had been effected when Clement died (November, 1268), and there ensued the regrettable vacancy of the Holy See of nearly three years. Taking advantage of there being no Pope to restrain his ambition, Charles of Anjou, since the battle of Benevento (January, 1266), King of the two Sicilies, began to make active preparations for an attack on Constantinople; for, on May 27, 1267, he had concluded a treaty with Baldwin II., the ex-emperor of Constantinople, by which in return for the suzerainty of Achaia, and various lordships, he agreed to help the exile monarch to recover his throne. And, moreover, with an eye to the future, his daughter Beatrice was betrothed to Baldwin's son, Philip.[2]

Death of Clement. Negotiations between Palæologus and Louis IX.

Frightened as ever of Charles, the Greek Emperor, hardly knowing what to do, turned to St. Louis of France, and implored him to put pressure on his brother to prevent him from attacking the Greeks.[3] Knowing, moreover, the great zeal of the saintly monarch for the Christian faith, and feeling that he could work upon that to interest him still more in his behalf, Michael proposed to him that he should constitute himself arbiter between the Greek and the Latin Churches, and he promised that he would abide by his decision.[4] Conscious, however, that the union of Churches was not his affair, Louis at once explained

---

[1] Cf. Hefele, *Hist. des Conc.*, vi, pt. i, p. 156, ed. 1914.

[2] See the treaty ap. Del Giudice, *Cod. dip. di Carlo I.*, vol. ii, p. 30 ff., or in Buchon, *Chron. étrangéres*, p. 148 ff.

[3] G. Pach., v, cc. 8–10. The *Genoese Annals* (ap. *M. G. SS.*, xviii, p. 264) tell of the arrival in Genoa in 1269 of envoys from M. Palæologus to interview the Pope.

[4] Cf. the letter of the Cardinals (May 15, 1270, sede **Vacante**), ap. Wadding, iv, 303 ff.

the situation to the cardinals who, during the Vacancy of the Holy See, were ruling the Church. They in turn, after thanking the King for the information he had sent them, and at the same time begging him to do all in his power to promote the cause of union,[1] communicated with Rudolf, the cardinal-bishop of Albano, who was the papal legate in France for the affair of the Holy Land. They explained to him the state of the case as made known to them by St. Louis,[2] and what had been done by Popes Urban IV. and Clement IV. Then, entrusting to him the future conduct of the affair, they sent him a form of oath according to which the Emperor and his people had to swear to observe the Profession of faith which Pope Clement had drawn up. However, as both the King and the Cardinal died this very year (1270) in Tunis, they were unable to do much towards compliance with the new scheme of the Greek Emperor.[3]

Gregory X. receives the congratulations of Michael.

At last, however, the long vacancy of the Holy See came to an end (September 1, 1271) by the election to the supreme Pontificate of Thedald or Theobald of the Visconti of Piacenza, archdeacon of Liège, and papal legate in Syria. One of the first things which the new Pope Gregory X. did after his election had been announced to him was to write to Michael Palæologus to urge him to work for peace between the two Churches. And, if we are to believe the Greek historian, Pachymeres, the

---

[1] See their letter to Louis, *ib.*, p. 306. The Cardinals do not conceal from Louis that in the past the Greeks have not been in earnest in their negotiations about the unity of the Churches, and that their present earnestness is problematical: "si *forsan* appareat dictos Græcos, efficaciter velle procedere in præmissis, etc."

[2] "Ipse namque Imperator, ut suis verbis . . . utamur, se velle Regem eumdem arbitrum in hoc constituere asserens, promittebat quidquid idem Rex super hoc diceret se plane ac inviolabiliter observaturum." Ep. of the cardinals to Rudolf cited above; and the first ep. of Gregory X. to Michael, ap. Wad., iv, p. 347.

[3] Ep. of Greg. X., Oct. 24, 1272, ap. Wad., iv, 348, or *Reg. Greg.*, i, p. 67, n. 194.

Emperor, again through fear of Charles of Anjou, gladly
listened to the Pope's exhortations[1] and with renewed
energy resumed his peace propaganda. In congratulating
the new Pope on his election, he expressed his regret
that he had not had the satisfaction of seeing him on
his way to Rome, and said that the bearer of his letter
would let the Pope know his reverence for the Roman
Church, and his wish to heal the schism.[2]

On October 24, 1272, by the hands of Jerome of Ascoli, He replies to
afterwards Pope Nicholas IV., and three other Franciscans them, 1272.
" men poor in spirit, but rich in faith ", Gregory sent a
long reply to the greetings and professions of the Greek
Emperor. Ever a lover of peace, he expressed a hope that
he could now do more to promote it, especially by bringing
the Greek and the Latin Churches once more together.
For this end among others, he had notified (April 1, 1272)
the princes and prelates of the Catholic world that he
would hold a General Council on May 1, 1274. Then,
after recounting at length all that Urban and Clement
and Michael himself had done towards effecting the union,
he begged him to send nuncios to the Council with full
powers, and furnished with letters from himself, from the
Patriarch, and from some of the more distinguished
prelates, stating that they acknowledged the Primacy
of the Roman Church, and accepted the Profession of
Faith sent by Pope Clement.[3]

In other letters, he invited the Patriarch Joseph and
various Greek bishops to the Council, gave instructions
to his legates, begged all princes and prelates to help
them, and asked Charles of Anjou to issue letters of safe

---

[1] G. Pach., v, 11, an. 1272.

[2] The Emperor's letter sent by the famous Minorite, John Parastron,
is summed up in Gregory's letter, " Qui miseratione ineffabili," just
cited.

[3] Ep. of Oct. 24, cited above. *Cf.* the letter of Michael, " Quoniam
missi," ap. Wad., iv, 389.

conduct for the envoys of the Greeks, and to facilitate
the journey of his legates to Constantinople.[1]

The Pope's
envoys are
received in
Con-
stantinople,
1273.
With the reception of the Pope's envoys in Constantinople, and Michael's fresh exhortations to unity, great
excitement began to manifest itself in the Greek capital.
Even with the Greeks, the character of Gregory stood
high,[2] and they knew that, if the Emperor was only
moved by fear of Charles, " Gregory's party " was
actuated by a real love of peace and the unity of the
Churches. They knew, too, that the Latins thought it
disgraceful that two great peoples should be divided over
" certain small matters ",[3] and that both of them had
enough to do to combat the enemies of the cross of Christ.
Pachymeres goes on to single out the work done for the
union by another agent of the Emperor, a Franciscan,
a Greek by birth, who had resided in Italy, and whom
the historian calls John Parastron. He was, he says, well
skilled in Greek, and most desirous of the union of the
Churches, so that he was wont to say that he would
willingly give his life if the cause of peace could be
thereby promoted.[4] He was employed by both the

[1] Epp. to Joseph, etc., ap. Wad., iv, pp. 352–5, or Reg., l.c., nn. 195–8.
See Charles's letter of Oct. 26, 1272, to his officials in Apulia and Brindisi,
bidding them furnish the Pope's envoys and their suite with ships
" at the expense of our Court ", so that there may be no delay in their
voyage " to the parts of Romania ". Ep. ap. Wad., iv, 378.

[2] G. Pach., v, ii, "ἀνδρὸς διαβεβοημένου εἰς ἀρετὴν καὶ ζηλωτοῦ τῆς
ἀρχαίας τῶν ἐκκλησιῶν εἰρήνης καὶ ὁμονοίας"; and "ἄνδρα τῆς
εἰρήνης . . . καὶ ἐπιθυμίας τῆς κρείττονος." Pg. 371, ed. Bonn.

[3] Pach., ib., p. 370.

[4] Ib., p. 371. Cf. ib., vol. ii, p. 22. By Western historians J. Par.
is called J. de Balastri or Palastro. According to Bro. Glassberger
(fl. 1508), Chron., p. 88, he died a holy death at Constantinople, whither
he returned after the Council of Lyons ; and, in consequence of the
numerous miracles he wrought on the day of his death, the Greek
Emperor and the Greek prelates frequently urged the Pope to canonize
him. Cf. p. 86, ed. Quaracchi, 1887. Gregory X. speaks of him as :
" John called Belastro." Reg. Greg., Append. i, n. 866. On this Greek
Minorite, see especially G. Golubovich, Biblioteca Bio-bibliografica dell'
Oriente Francescano, i, p. 283 ff., Quaracchi, 1906.

Emperor and the Pope. When in Constantinople, he treated the Greek rite, continues the Byzantine historian, with the greatest respect, and used to tell the Latins and the Greeks that there would be no difficulty in making peace if the former would remove the addition to the Creed, and if the latter would accept the reasons which the Latins advanced for inserting it. Moreover, he is said to have added that both those who held that the Holy Ghost proceeded from the Father and the Son, and those who maintained that He proceeded from the Father through the Son had become somewhat deranged by over-scrutiny of the mysteries of God. But if any agent of the Emperor or legate of the Pope went so far in the way of diplomacy as to use such language, it had no effect on the intractable Greeks. They roundly declared that the monk was merely " attempting to gloss over the daring addition to the Creed ", that there was the greatest danger in swerving ever so little from the path of orthodoxy, and that the Latins were the only ones to blame for adding to the Creed.[1]

With a view to bringing about a better understanding *An abortive* between the two parties, the Emperor called a meeting *assembly,* of the Patriarch, the bishops, and some of the clergy, *1273.* and laid before them the story of the union which had taken place under Vatatzes and the patriarch Manuel.[2] Hitherto, according to the narrative of Pachymeres, the Greek ecclesiastics feeling sure that nothing would come of these negotiations with Rome, had followed the Emperor's lead, had paid court to the Latins in Constantinople ; and in general had acquiesced in all their ruler's doings.[3] Now, however, they began to realize that there was more earnestness in the air, and

[1] *Ib.*, p. 372.
[2] *Ib.*, p. 374 ff.
[3] *Ib.*, v, 10.

they turned to the archivist (chartophylax) John Veccus, a man of deserved reputation for learning and virtue,[1] to reply to the Emperor. Fórced to speak by the Patriarch, the archivist's answer resulted in the abrupt breaking up of the assembly by the Emperor, and in imprisonment for the bold speaker. [2]

Veccus embraces the cause of the Union, 1273.

Whilst with the aid of a number of learned men whom he had won over to the cause of the union, Palæologus ceased not to strive to impress on the people that the Latins were free from heresy,[3] he, or one of his advisers, called to mind that, when this question of union had been agitated some twenty-five years before under Vatatzes, Nicephorus Blemmydas had collected many passages "from the sacred writings" which seemed to favour the teaching of the Latins. His work was accordingly given to Veccus in prison, and he applied himself to the study of it.[4] Being considerably impressed by the passages "inasmuch", says Pachymeres, "as he was single-minded and a lover of truth," [5] he asked to be supplied with the books from which the extracts had been culled. Whereupon the Emperor ordered his release from prison, and gave instructions that he should be given the books

---

[1] *Ib.*, v, 12, p. 376. See also N. Gregoras, who says he was " a man above all his contemporaries in ability, eloquence, and learning, and was a man too of great beauty of form and feature. He had a remarkable talent for dealing accurately and quickly with every question that was put before him, so that he was regarded as a shining light in governmental and learned circles ", v, 2, p. 128, ed. Bonn. Ephræm, who wrote about the middle of the fourteenth century, also bears testimony to the learning of Veccus : " ἀνὴρ σοφός τις, ἐντεθραμμένοις λόγοις." V. 103257, p. 414, ed. Bonn. On Veccus see P. Souarn, "Tentatives d'union avec Rome," in the *Échos d'Orient*, t. iii (1900), pp. 229 ff. and 351 ff.

[2] Pach., v, 12 and 13 ; and N. Greg, *l.c.*

[3] Pach., v, 14.

[4] N. Greg., p. 129, and G. Pach., v, 15, pp. 380–1. The earlier writer is also the fuller.

[5] " ἀπλοῦς ὢν καὶ φιλαλήθης." P. 381.

which he desired in order that he might study them at his leisure. At length, says the same contemporary historian, he came to the conclusion that the only thing that could be alleged against the Latins was the addition of a word to the Creed ; and that, as far as the doctrine involved in that one word was concerned, Greek Fathers, like Saints Cyril and Athanasius, were in agreement with the Latins about it. They had argued that the Holy Ghost proceeded from God the Father " through the Son " not " progressively, but efficaciously ".[1]

Whilst Veccus was devoting himself to the study of the Greek Fathers, the patriarch Joseph, not having made any profound study of the question, was exploited by a designing monk, and about the time that Veccus had decided that it was his duty to work for the union of the Churches, Joseph was induced to write against the Latin position, and to take an oath that he would never consent to the Union, and would resign if it took place.[2]

Strong now in the support of Veccus, and, at the moment of the learned professor Holobolus,[3] the Emperor resolved to make complete submission to the Holy See. He accordingly sent a letter to " the most holy and blessed Lord Gregory, Pope of Old Rome, Supreme Pontiff of the Universal Church, Successor of the Apostolic See, and his most Reverend Father ", subscribing himself, " Michael in Christ our God faithful Emperor . . . the

Greek envoys to be sent to the General Council, 1273.

---

[1] " ἐν τῇ τῆς τριάδος τάξει τὸ πνεῦμα γινώσκεσθαι μὴ προοδικῶς ὂν ἐκ θεοῦ δὶ υἱοῦ, ἀλλὰ ποιητικῶς."—" fieri non posse ut in Trinitatis ordine spiritus agnosceretur quasi ex Deo per Filium non progressive sed efficientur . . . existeret," v, 16. Cf. vi, 23, pp. 476–7, 480–2.

[2] Pach., v, 16, 17, 21. These events took place about the close of 1273. Cf. Hefele, Hist. des Conc., vi, pt. i, p. 163, who notes that Draeseke has edited the work of Joseph in Zeitschrift fürwissensch. Theol., t. xxxiv, p. 383 ff., and that, as usual, the Latins are denounced as wholly impious, and as heretics worthy of anathema, whilst the Greeks are pure, heirs of the full inheritance of virtues, etc., etc.

[3] Pach., p. 374. Cf. ib., l. iv, c. 14.

obedient son of your Holiness." [1] Beginning by declaring
his profound pleasure in receiving a letter from one
whom he recognized as Supreme Pontiff, as well disposed
towards his Empire, and, by his words and life, as the
light of the world, Palæologus declared that, like Gregory,
he too was a lover of peace, and that though he had
in the past also worked for peace, he would now work
for it harder than ever. His reply to the Pope had
certainly been tardy, but though the differences between
the two parties were small, there was the difficulty of
getting distant bishops together to consult about them,
and there was the need of going thoroughly into everything,
lest in attempting to repair an old rent they might,
through want of care, make a new one. However, to
show the Pope what had been done, he was sending
two of his legates back to him to tell him what they
themselves knew had been accomplished. He would
keep the other two (of whom one was the future Pope,
Jerome of Ascoli) in order that they might see the end
which was close at hand, and might with the imperial
envoys return to inform the Pope about it. As for
himself, he declared that thought for the accomplishment
of the Union was with him day and night, and took
precedence over care for everything else. In conclusion,
he begged the Pope to provide safe conducts for his envoys,
and to point out the safest route for them to follow.[2]

Gregory's
reply to the
Emperor.

On November 21, 1273, Gregory, in reply, expressed
his special pleasure at the receipt of the Emperor's
letter because, as he said, many highly placed persons
had wished to make him believe that the delay which
had now been explained was caused by the wish on the

---

[1] Ep. " Multa sunt," ap. Wad., iv, 371 ff., or *Reg.*, vol. i, p. 119, n. 313.
This letter was written before Nov., 1273.

[2] *Cf.* another letter (" Qualiter et quantum ") of his regarding the
safe-conducts in which he names his chamberlain. Theodore, and the
interpreter, Godfrey, as coming with the two papal legates. Ap. Wad.,
iv, 375, or *Reg.*, *ib.*, n. 314.

part of the Greeks to do nothing but negotiate in order to prevent the Latins from attempting the recovery of Constantinople. He urged the Emperor to persevere in his good intentions, and promised the safe conducts for the imperial envoys who, he trusted, would have all the necessary powers.[1] He sent off other letters about the same time to Jerome of Ascoli and his companion in Constantinople urging them to work now harder than ever [2]; to various princes for the safe conducts,[3] and to the abbot of Monte Cassino, instructing him to meet the Emperor's envoys as soon as they should land in Sicily.[4]

Among those persons " of high condition and state " who had no faith in the sincerity of the Greeks, was no doubt Charles of Anjou [5]; and if Gregory succeeded in preventing him from attacking them without further delay,[6] it was only with great difficulty. Of this we may be assured from a confidential letter which he sent to Magister Simon de Parisius, the chancellor of the Sicilian King. In it he expressed his fear lest the differences between Charles and the Emperor might interfere with the union which was to be discussed at the forthcoming General Council. He, therefore, begged his correspondent to induce Charles to discuss the situation with the Holy See.[7]

---

[1] Ep. ap. Wad., iv, 376, or *Reg., ib.*, n. 315.

[2] Ep. ap. Wad., iv, 378. A little later, Jan.–March, 1274, he sent the Profession of Faith which the Greeks were to accept.—Potthast, n. 20810.

[3] To Philip, the son of Baldwin II., ap. Wad., iv, 377, to Charles of Anjou, *Reg., ib.*, n. 316 ; to other potentates ap. Potthast, nn. 20763–5.

[4] *Reg., ib.*, n. 317.

[5] In the *Chronicle* of Primatus (ap. *M. G. SS.*, xxvi, p. 671) we read that some believed that the Greeks had come to the Council moved by fear, and not by love of Catholic doctrine.

[6] It is the Greek Pachymeres (v, 26) who says that he did so succeed.

[7] Ep. of the end of 1273, or the beginning of 1274, ap. Potthast, n. 20778. *Cf.* ep. of Nov. 7, 1273, *ib.*, n. 20639, and nn. 20811–12.

All difficulties were, however, at last overcome, and on June 24, 1274, the ex-patriarch, Germanus, in place of the recalcitrant patriarch, Joseph, Theophanes, bishop of Nicæa, the Grand Logothete, George Acropolita, the historian, and the other Greek envoys [1] reached Lyons. Their credentials, as we know from a document edited comparatively recently,[2] had been made out for them in the month of March. Addressing the Pope in identically the same deferential manner which we have just set forth at large, the Greek Emperor begins by observing that, almost from his childhood, he had longed to see the removal of the barrier wall between the Churches, and the restitution of its ancient rights to the most holy Throne of Old Rome. His actions, he continued, had proved the earnestness of his desires, as he had often sent envoy's to Gregory's predecessors on the subject of reunion. He could scarcely say how it was that his efforts had hitherto not borne fruit. But no doubt it was by the will of God that the completion of the work had been left to the present Pope, who had sent letters and most spiritual men to him. In imitation of our Lord who came down from on high, and took the form of a servant, he begged the Pope to come down " from his spiritual altitude (a tua incorporali magnitudine) ", and to give ear to him. He confessed that the faith of the Apostolic See was orthodox, and contained

---

[1] G. Pach., v, 17.

[2] *Cf.* Ed. Delisle, *Notices et extraits des MSS. de la Bib. Nat.*, vol. xxvii, pt. ii (1879), p. 126 ff., from a Bordeaux MS. From other documents there published (p. 165) we learn that the Serbs and Bulgarians made their submission at the same time. Nicholas IV., too (1291), writing " to the archbishop of the Bulgarians " declared that the Bulgarian patriarch of the time (Joachim III.) had acknowledged his subjection to Gregory. He made profession before the emperor M. P. in the palace of Blachernæ : " oraculo vivæ vocis te Papæ Romano immediate subesse." *Cf.* Chapman, *M. P.*, p. 112.

nothing but what was in accordance with the truth.[1]
Such too is the faith of our orthodox Greek Church.
Averring that the difference between the Churches
had been caused by trifling words (verbula), he declared
that they had been cast away, and that the Greeks now
bent their necks in obedience. They acknowledged
that the Pope was the head of all the Churches, and that
to him all ecclesiastical differences must be referred.
The Emperor finally professed his determination to
strive to induce all to submit to the Pope, and told him
that he was sending to him among other most illustrious
men, his relative, master, and spiritual father (" quasi
nutritor et pædagogus meus ") the lord patriarch,
Germanus, George Acropolita,[2] almost his foster brother
(quasi conutritus imperio nostro), and others.[3]

Two triremes conveyed from Constantinople the
envoys and their suite along with the numerous presents
of sacred vestments, gilt icons, precious gums for incense,
etc., which the Emperor destined for the Pope [4] (April,
1274). Though the trireme with the presents on board
was wrecked, the principal envoys, as we have said,
reached Lyons in safety. They were met by all the prelates
present in Lyons along with their suites, by the papal
Camerarius, the vice-chancellor, the notaries, and the
whole pontifical court, and by all the households of the

Reception of
the envoys,
1274.

---

[1] " Fidei confessionem quam tenet apostolicus thronus et docet,
que at a tua magna sanctitate nobis per scripturam explanata est,
eusebam, i.e., piam et fidelem, et nos confitemur esse et per omnia
orthodoxam, et nichil est in ipsa quod non veritatem contineat." *Ib.*,
p. 156, Delisle.

[2] Both Germanus and Acropolita are highly praised by G. Metochita
also (*Hist. Dogmat.*, i, cc. 23 and 24), but it must be allowed that the
value of his testimony is lessened by the excessive praise he bestows
upon Michael Palæologus. *Ib.*, c. 21.

[3] See the letter, p. 159, for the powers given to the imperial envoys.
March, 1274, and on p. 160, a document of the same date in which,
they are accredited to the Pope to treat of various temporal affairs.

[4] G. Pach., v, 17, p. 385.

cardinals. Conducted to the papal palace, they were with great honour admitted to the kiss of peace by the Pope, who received them standing in the midst of his cardinals. They then presented the imperial letters with golden bullæ suspended from them, and the letters of the Greek prelates, and they declared that they had come to show their obedience to the Roman Church, and to acknowledge its primacy.[1] They were listened to most graciously by the Pope, who presented them with mitres, rings and the other ornaments which, says Pachymeres, are worn by bishops in the West.[2] Five days later, on the feast of Saints Peter and Paul (June 29), the Pope sang High Mass in the presence of the Greeks and all the prelates of the Council. The Epistle and Gospel were sung both in Latin and in Greek. After the gospel St. Bonaventure preached "a glorious sermon", on a text of the prophet Baruch (vv. 5 and 6).

When that was over, the *Credo* was sung in Latin. Begun by the cardinals and prelates, it was continued by the canons of the cathedral of St. John. Afterwards it was sung in Greek by the patriarch Germanus, the Greek archbishop of Calabria, V. de Morbecca, a Dominican, and John of Constantinople (J. Parastron), a Franciscan, who both knew Greek. The famous *addition* " Qui a Patre Filioque procedit " was sung three times. As soon as they had finished the *Credo*, the Greeks in their own tongue sang the solemn " laudes " in honour of the Pope.[3]

---

[1] See the acts of the Council ap. Mansi, t. xxiv, p. 64 ; Hefele, vi, pt. i, p. 173.

[2] *Ib.*, v, 21, p. 398. It was one of the trifling charges brought against the Latins by Michael Cerularius that their bishops, as though spouses of their churches, wore rings. See his letter to Peter, Patriarch of Antioch, ap. Migne, *Pat. Græc.*, t. 120, p. 794.

[3] Mansi and Hefele, *ll. cc.*, Glassberger, *Chron.*, p. 86 ; *Annales Altahenses*, an. 1274.

At length on July 6, 1274, the day dawned for which Pope Gregory had longed so earnestly. At the foot of the hill of Fourvière by the slowly flowing Saône stood and still stands the cathedral of St. John the Baptist in which one General Council under Innocent IV. had already been held. Not yet blackened by the mists and smoke of centuries, it must have towered up brightly on that July morning beneath the strong sun of southern France, and within, its walls, its pillars, and its pavement must have been bathed in the multicoloured light that streamed from its glorious stained glass.[1] Among the thousands that made their way to St. John's on July 6 for the fourth session of the Great Council, the most interesting figures after that of Gregory himself were those of the Greeks richly clad in scarlet and gold. On them were the eyes of all fixed as they took their places by the Pope. "When I entered the Church," says the royal eyewitness, James I. of Aragon, "the sight was marvellous. I saw of archbishops, bishops and abbots full five hundred or more. The Pope sat in the tribune ; the cardinals and patriarchs were on two benches in face of the Pope higher than the rest," and I was then placed on the right hand of the Pope "whose chair was not a palm higher than mine ".[2]

During the High Mass which was sung with the same ceremonies as before, and during the session the Greeks were on the right of the Pope next to the cardinals. After the sermon had been preached by Peter, the cardinal-bishop of Ostia, the Pope himself addressed the assembly. He recalled the three purposes for which the Council had been summoned, and declared what "scarcely any had believed", that the Greeks had come of their own

---

[1] There is reason to believe that the envoys of Palæologus looked on much of the very glass we can see to-day.

[2] So concludes the complacent monarch. See his *Chronicle*, vol i, p. 643. Eng. trans. by J. Forster and P. de Gayangos, London, 1883.

accord to profess the faith of the Roman Church and
to acknowledge its primacy. They were not, he said, in
search of temporal gain—about which, add the Acts of
the Council, there was much doubt. He had, he continued,
written to tell the Greek Emperor that, if he did not
wish of his own freewill to obey the Roman Church,
he might send his legates to treat of temporal affairs only.
However, he had chosen, quite of his own accord, to send
his legates to acknowledge the primacy of the Roman
Church.[1] Thereupon were read, translated into Latin,
the letters of the Emperor, his son and the Greek
prelates. At the conclusion of the reading, the grand
Logothete proclaimed in a loud voice that he had been
authorized to state that, should the Pope desire it, he
had been commissioned to take an oath on the Emperor's
behalf as to the truth of his professions. He then professed
that the Emperor and the Greeks (imperatorem et
imperium) adhered to the faith of the Roman Church,
as it had been set forth in the Council, and that, as was
declared in the form of their oath, they would never
depart from it.[2]

Michael's
profession of
faith.

In his profession of faith, Michael, after acclaiming
Gregory as "supreme pontiff and universal Pope",
set down the articles of his faith on the lines of those
in the letter of Clement IV. He believed in the Unity
and Trinity of God, in the single personality and

---

[1] " Et ipse (the Greek Emperor) Deo favente, omnibus prætermissis
spontanee, et libere fidem Romanæ Ecclesiæ et primatum ipsius
professus est, et recognovit in summa, quod prædictos nuncios ad
profitendum et recognoscendum miserat in sua præsentia, sicut in
litteris per . . . d. imperatorem sibi missis continebatur expresse."
Acts of the Council, Mansi, xxiv, p. 65.

[2] The Acts, ib., pp. 65–6. Because the Logothete could only say that
he had been authorized " viva voce " by the Emperor to take this
oath, Innocent V. later on instructed his envoys to request the Emperor
to take the oath himself—" quod illud personaliter abjuret " Ep.
Inn., n. 34, ap. Martène, Script. Vet. Coll., vii, p. 254.

dual nature of God the Son, and in the procession of the
Holy Ghost " from the Father and from the Son ".[1]
He also declared his belief in " purgatorial or cleansing
punishments " in the next life for such as depart this
life in the grace of God but without having made proper
satisfaction for their sins, whereas such as leave it pure
and free from obligations will be received straightway
into heaven.[2] He believed, further, that there are seven
sacraments as the Roman Church teaches, and that
unleavened bread is lawfully used in the Sacrament of
the Eucharist. The Roman Church, " he humbly
acknowledged," had the " full and supreme primacy
and principality over the whole Catholic Church " which
was given by the Lord to St. Peter whose successor is
the Roman Pontiff [3]; and to it all questions of faith
must be referred to be defined. To it can appeals be made,
and to it all prelates are subject. The Emperor, however,
stipulated, in conclusion, that the churches, especially
the patriarchial churches, which the Roman Church
had herself honoured, should keep their privileges, save
in all things the faith which he had just proclaimed
and which he would ever profess. He asked, however,
that the Greek Church might be permitted to continue
to recite the Creed as it always had done, and to keep
its rites which had been in use even before the schism.

This profession of faith was signed by the Emperor's

---

[1] " πιστεύομεν δὲ καὶ τὸ πνεῦμα τὸ ἅγιον . . . ἐκ πατρὸς υἱοῦ τε
ἐκπορευομενον." Cf. Wadding, iv, or Mansi, xxiv, p. 69. It was on
account of the Greek contention that the first canon of this Council
affirmed the Procession of the Holy Spirit from the Father and from
the Son.

[2] " εἰς τὸν οὐρανὸν αὐτίκα παραδέχεσθαι." Ib. It was on this
subject of the immediate reception of the just into heaven that the
theories of Pope John XXII. caused such a sensation. To make the
situation clear, the Council of Florence defined that entrance into heaven
involved the direct vision of God.

[3] The Roman Church has " ἄκρον καὶ τέλειον πρωτεῖον τὲ ἀρχὴν ἐπὶ
πᾶσαν τήν καθολικὴν ἐκκλησίαν." Ib.

own hand in the month of April in the Palace of Blachernæ.[1]

To the full profession of faith made by the Emperor the whole Greek hierarchy, as it informed the Pope, gave its complete adhesion. Proclaiming Pope Gregory as their Father, and professing their " spiritual subjection " to him, some twenty-nine metropolitans, for the most part with their suffragans, and nine Archbishops, along with all the officials of the church of Constantinople, making up, as they said, the whole ecclesiastical order, began by humbly confessing that they had broken the unity of the Church.[2] This, they continued, had the Emperor made them realize, and he had at length succeeded in inducing them to agree to acknowledge in the Apostolic See that primacy which was attributed to it by the ancients,[3] and to accept the decision of the Apostolic See as he had done. Hitherto their Patriarch had refused to act with them, but they averred that if, on their return after the completion of the union, he continued obstinate, they would elect another patriarch who would acknowledge the primacy that belonged " to your supreme Holiness ". If then " your Magnitude " will only accept the declarations of our envoys, we submit " to your Mightiness "; profess complete spiritual subjection,[4] and refuse not to you whatever our fathers before the schism offered to your predecessors.

---

[1] According to Raynaldus, *Annal.*, an. 1274, n. 14, the profession of faith sent by Andronicus, but now lost, was couched in similar terms.

[2] " Non solum nunc, sed prius . . . vestræ ecclesiæ magnam faciebamus divisionem integritatis, et ecclesiarum Christi totaliter unitatem dilacerabamus." Ep. ap. Wadding, iv, 392.

[3] " Sed a Deo coronati Imperatoris diligentia vicit in finem, et habet omnes jam concordes ad unicam hanc unionem, per quam Apostolicæ Sedi antiquæ Romæ, ab antiquissimis attributos primatus assentimus." *Ib*. *Cf*. Pachym., v. 20.

[4] " Si solum vestra magnitudo ea quæ legationis sunt admittat, . . . magnæ vestræ altitudini submittimus, et valde gratanter ea quæ

When these letters had been read and the oath of the Conclusion of the session and the Council. Logothete received, the Pope in person intoned the *Te Deum*, and afterwards preached, taking for his text the words, " With desire have I desired to eat this Pasch with you." [1] Then, when the Greeks had taken their places on high seats behind the cardinals in the nave, Gregory and the whole Council sang the Credo in Latin. They were followed by the Greeks, who, along with the Greek abbots from the Kingdom of the Two Sicilies, chanted it in Greek, singing the *Filioque* clause twice. [2]

In the sixth and last session of the Council (July 17), the Pope again spoke, and gave thanks to God for the happy close of the Greek negotiations. [3]

Gregory's deep thankfulness and joy over the Union Letters to the Emperor etc., afterwards, 1274. was manifested in the letters which he sent to Constantinople immediately after the Council (July 28). In glowing terms did he make known to the Emperor the happiness that all had felt in the return of the Greeks to the bosom of the Church. " Oh my son would that you could have seen the joy manifested by the Church during the Council at Lyons ! Would that your ears had heard the voices especially of the Prelates as, bareheaded and on bended knees, they praised and glorified God ! Would that you had beheld their eyes streaming with tears ! . . . Rejoice and be glad that . . . you have been chosen to lead the way back to the light of truth." Continue as you have begun so that no trace of schism may be left. [4]

---

sunt spiritualis subjectionis totius asserimus." *Ib.* See the version of this document ap. Delisle, *l.c.*, pp. 161–2.

[1] S. Luke, xxii.

[2] *The Acts*, p. 66. Unfortunately S. Bonaventure, who had been of the greatest use in the negotiations with the Greeks, died before the close of the Council. *Cf.* Wadding, *Annal. Min.*, iv, 397 ff.

[3] *The Acts*, p. 68.

[4] Ep. July 28, 1274, ap. Wad., iv, 406 ; or *Reg.*, i, p. 207, n. 487. Similar letters were sent to Andronicus, and to the Greek bishops. *Ib.*, p. 407, or *Reg.*, nn. 489, 490–1.

In another letter, he informed Michael that he was
sending him Bernard, abbot of Monte Cassino, who
might be able to make a truce between him and Charles
of Anjou till such times as he could dispatch a legate to
make a permanent peace.[1] At the same time he requested
the Sicilian monarch to see to the safe return of the
Greek envoys.[2]

There can be little doubt that the greatest moving
force behind all these transactions was the grim figure
of Charles of Anjou, and that, though his name was not
mentioned by the Greek envoys when they spoke to the
Pope about peace between the Greeks and their Latin
neighbours generally, he was the one that they had
particularly in view. Of the many temporal questions
besides or in connexion with peace which the Greek envoys
discussed with the Pope, we have some knowledge from
a memoir printed by Delisle.[3] In the first place, they urged
that the abbot Bernard should be named a pleni-
potentiary, so that he would be in a position to work for
peace between the Emperor and the Latins in order that
then they might safely be able to succour the Holy Land.[4]
The abbot could also arrange marriages of the Emperor's
sons and daughters in the joint interest of the Greeks
and the Apostolic See. The envoys also asked the Pope
to write to the clergy and Senate with regard to the
Reunion of the Churches ; and begged that he would not
favour any enemy of the Greek Empire, and that the
ruler of the Greeks, who was to pay due honour to the
Pope, should be the man they themselves wanted. With
regard to the Churches of Antioch, Cyprus, and Jerusalem,

[1] Ep. ap. Wad., iv, 407 ; Delisle, p. 163 ff.

[2] Potthast, nn. 20878–9.

[3] L.c., pp. 163–5.

[4] The envoys formerly declared that Michael would aid the Christians
in the Holy Land in every way, if he could arrange a peace with the
neighbouring Latins. Cf. ib., p. 162 ; and Ann. Placent. Gibel., an.
1274, p. 348, ed. H.-Bréholles.

they proposed that Latin should succeed Latin, and Greek Greek, and that the ecclesiastical revenues should be divided. They then proceeded to discuss the ecclesiastical condition of *Cagora* (Bulgaria ?) and Servia. It is well known, they said, that no ecclesiastical dignity can be constituted without the authority of the Apostolic See. Now Justinian, with the consent of Pope Vigilius, had honoured his birthplace by making Acrida a primatial see, subjecting to it *Cagora* (Bulgaria ?) and Servia. But, after the capture of Constantinople, the Bulgarians and Servians, taking advantage of the help they had given the Greeks against the Latins, had given themselves, the first a Patriarch, and the second an archbishop, both independent of any Greek prelate. They implored the Pope to put an end to that usurpation, and, moreover, to urge the Latins on the confines of the Greek Empire to be loyal to its Emperor.

During the absence of his envoys in Italy, Michael Palæologus, with the assistance of Veccus, continued to try to win over more bishops to his views. He urged, as always, principally the temporal needs of the moment. In the miserable state of the defences of Constantinople, war with the Latins must be avoided.[1] The shrinkage of old age had already begun to show itself in the imperial city. The damaged circuit of its walls was now all too large for the number of its inhabitants. Not only were there cultivated fields in the centre of the city, but many of its houses were in ruin, as we learn from travellers who visited the city between this date and that of its fall.[2] The power of the Turks too was rapidly increasing. Besides, if the reunion of the Churches were accepted, that of the Greeks would remain practically what it was before, as the union would be based on the three questions

The tenth reunion proclaimed in Constantinople, 1274.

---

[1] We are following here G. Pach., l. v. See also N. Greg., v, 2.

[2] *Cf.* J. Ebersolt, *Constantinople Byzantine*, pp. 41, 48, 59, 63, quoting the Arab geographer, Abulfeda, Clarijo, and Bertrandon de la Broquière.

of primacy, appeal, and commemoration.[1] It was not in the least likely that the Pope would come to Constantinople to exercise his primacy, or that appeals, considering the great distance, would be carried to him. But no motives of expediency, or of advantage to religion had any effect on the mass of the Greeks. Some rejected at once all three conditions, and others at least the commemoration of the Pope in their sacred diptychs.[2] Again, therefore, did the Emperor have recourse to persecution.[3] This had its usual effect in Constantinople, and at length, through fear, all the clergy signed a document setting forth their submission to the three points.[4]

At the close of the autumn (1274), the imperial envoys with those of the Pope returned to Constantinople. Soon after their arrival, Joseph was declared to be no longer patriarch (January 11, 1275), inasmuch as he had sworn that, if the reunion was effected, he would resign.[5] A few days later (January 16), in the chapel of the imperial palace, Nicholas, metropolitan of Chalcedon, sang the Mass in which the Epistle and Gospel were chanted both in Greek and in Latin, and Pope Gregory was solemnly proclaimed " supreme Pontiff of the Apostolic Church, and ecumenical Pope ".[6]

The reunion,[7] as far at least as certain of the temporal

Violent schism among the Greeks.

---

[1] " Πρωτείῳ, ἐκκλήτῳ καὶ μνημοσύνῳ." See also G. Metochita, *Hist. Dogmat.*, i, 24.

[2] Pach., 1. v, i, p. 390. *Cf.* Veccus himself writing on his deposition, i, n. 2, ap. *Pat. G.*, t. 141, p. 952 f.

[3] Among those who suffered was the rhetorician Holobolus who suddenly turned against the Emperor as he conceived he had been slighted by him. *Ib.*, pp. 392–3.

[4] Pach., v, n. 20, pp. 395–6.

[5] *Ib.*, v, 22. *Cf.* G. Metochita, *Hist. Dogmat.*, i, 28, pp. 40–1.

[6] *Ib.*, p. 399 : " ἄκρος ἀρχιερεὺς τῆς ἀποστολικῆς ἐκκλησίας καὶ οἰκουμενικος παπας."

[7] It was understood that peace between the Churches was made on the three conditions which we have already seen noted by the Emperor, viz., that the Pope along with the other four patriarchs should be com-

and spiritual authorities among the Greeks were concerned, was now completed. But the mass of the people, stirred up by the immoderate language of the greater part of the clergy, and also of not a few of the state officials who were not in favour of the negotiations,[1] now openly showed themselves bitterly hostile to the Union. Hence, says Pachymeres, many Greeks now hate their fellow Greeks more than they previously hated the Latins.[2]

That headway might be made against this state of things, the ex-patriarch Joseph was sent into exile, and the election of a new patriarch decided on. When sounded as to his successor, we are assured by the writer just cited that Joseph declared that the man to be chosen was Veccus, on account of his learning and experience. He even did not hesitate to add later on that, if he had not been troubled by the oath he had taken, he would have submitted himself.[3] However this may be, Veccus was elected (June 2, 1275) through the votes of some of the bishops, his own virtues and the influence of the Emperor who in a double election decided in his favour.[4] Veccus now threw himself into the fray, and he who, says Gregoras, had been a "two-edged sword" against the Latins, became their partisan and supported the Emperor in every way.[5]

Veccus elected Patriarch, 1275.

memorated in the diptychs; that all should have the right of appeal to Rome: "καθάπερ εἰς μεῖζον καὶ ἐντελέστερον . . . δικαστήριον"; and that the Pope should have the primacy in everything: "τοῦ προτεύειν ἐν ἅπασι." N. Gregoras, v, 2, p. 125.

[1] N. Greg., *ib.*

[2] v, 23, p. 401.

[3] G. Pach, v, 28, p. 414.

[4] *Ib.*, v, 24. The historian here enlarges on the virtues of the new Patriarch, especially on his great charity. On the high character of Veccus, see also G. Metochita, *Hist. Dog.*, i, 29, ap. Mai, *Nova Pat. Bib.*, viii.

[5] N. Greg., *l.c.*, p. 129. For the writings of Veccus, and his associates Constantine Meliteniota, the Chartophylax, and the archdeacon G. Metochita, see Migne, *Pat. Grec.*, t. 141; but, for the historical sketch

Greek
envoys sent
to Rome,
1275.

Meanwhile, Palæologus had dispatched as envoys to Rome, George, archdeacon of Constantinople, and Theodore, the great *dispensator* of the imperial court, in order to assure Pope Gregory that all that he had required for the completion of the union had been duly carried into effect. The legates were also instructed to find out what was being done by Charles of Anjou, as disquieting rumours of his activities had reached Constantinople. They were graciously received by Gregory ; but they found the redoubtable Sicilian King urging him to allow him to attack the imperial city, and " gnawing his sceptre with rage " at the Pope's refusal. Constantinople, the Pope had said to him, has but fallen again into the hands of its former owners, and, as the Greeks, he had continued, are " Christians and sons of the Church ", he could not suffer that they should be attacked by Christians, lest he should incur the anger of God.[1]

Innocent V.
begs the
Emperor's
help for the
Crusade,
1276.

Unfortunately the negotiations with the Greeks concerning the union of 1274 were, as even Palæologus noted,[2] most seriously hampered by their having to be handled by so many Popes. Further, the rapid succession of Gregory's immediate successors has, in the past, caused no little confusion among modern historians with regard to their respective relations with Con-

of the schism, from the days of Photius who began it to his own time, given by the last named writer, it is necessary to consult his *Hist. Dogmatica*, lib. i, ap. Mai, *Nova Pat. Bib.*, t. viii.

[1] This whole paragraph rests on the authority of Pachymeres, v, 26, but the names of the envoys on a letter of Innocent V.   Potthast, n. 21136.   On May 15, 1275, Gregory was able to announce that a truce of a year had been made between Palæologus and Charles of Anjou, by the efforts of his nuncio the abbot of Monte Cassino.   *Cf. Reg.*, Append. i, nn. 869–71, and Posse, *Analecta Vat.*, n. 846.

[2] In his letter to John XXI., the Emperor declared that he was much distressed " quia videbatur quoad sacrosanctam Romanam ecclesiam, proh dolor !   ex subito defectu pastorum, unitatis ecclesiarum Dei opus refrigescere ".   Ap. Wadding, v, p. 10.

stantinople.[1] However, the details published by Delisle from the Bordeaux manuscript have made the situation clear at least in this respect.

Gregory X. had died (January 10, 1276) before the imperial ambassadors could be sent back, so that his successor Innocent V.[2] made use of them to send a number of letters to Constantinople.[3] On May 23 he indited some six or seven letters relative to the Greek question. In one,[4] he urges Palæologus to make common cause with the Latins for the liberation of the Holy Land, and adds, in conclusion, that he has not interfered in the disputes between certain Latin princes and the Greek empire as he believes that they can be settled quickest without him. In pursuance of this last view, he urges the Emperor in another letter to send envoys without delay to treat with Charles of Anjou who, of course, is the chief *Prince* he had in mind.[5] He points out to Palæologus that in his various missions to the Holy See in the past concerning the reunion of the Churches, it has been his aim to induce the Roman Church to attend first to certain temporal questions, whereas, in its wisdom, the Holy See has understood that, were the Greeks once back in the bosom of the Church, it could deal with the temporal questions much more easily. For that reason, it had

---

[1] Hence three missions that belong to Innocent V., John XXI., and Nicholas III. were at one time all assigned to the first-named Pontiff.

[2] Jan. 21, 1276–June 22.

[3] *Cf.* Delisle, *l.c.*, p. 136.

[4] Potthast, n. 21136. In full, ap. Martène, *Script. Vet.*, vii, 244. No. 21145, addressed to Friar Bartholomew and assigned by Potthast to Innocent V., belongs to Nicholas III., and is dated Aug. 1, 1278. *Cf.* Delisle, " Recueils épist. de Bérard de Naples," ap. *Notices et extraits*, xxvii, p. 135.

[5] Ap. Mart., *Vet. SS.*, vii, 246. He trusts that God will unite the Greeks and Latins still closer both in spirituals and temporals. " Ipsos Latinos et Græcos non solum in spiritualibus, tua illi (God) cooperante solertia, perfectius uniet, sed et in temporalibus sua virtute reducet ad plenæ concordiæ unitatem."

attended first to the spiritual questions, so that when those more important points had been settled, the lesser ones could then be approached more satisfactorily. In this and in the next [1] letter, he begged the Emperor to receive graciously the four Franciscan nuncios, including the Minister General, Jerome of Ascoli, whom he was sending to him. Whilst he was still one of Gregory's counsellors,[2] that Pontiff had notified to the Emperor his intention to send another legate to him in order that the union which had been effected might be strengthened.[3] He was, therefore, fulfilling the intention of his predecessor, in sending this legation, and he begged the Emperor to comply with what its members should suggest as suitable to consolidate the union.

Instruction to the legates.

Two days after the legates had been given these letters along with two others to the Greek prelates and Andronicus to the same effect (May 25, 1276),[4] they were furnished with instructions as to what they were to require from the Greeks. Among other things, they were to ask that the Emperor and his son should confirm by their own personal oaths what the grand Logothete had sworn in their names relative to the Primacy of the Roman Church. They were further to request that a record of their compliance should be inscribed on durable parchment, which was to be duly signed by them, and sealed with a golden bull, and that copies of these acts should be made on papyrus and parchment. They were also to

---

[1] *Ib.*, p. 248. Guido Romanus and Angelus are described as "Ministers of provinces", and Jerome as "General": "viros utique claros veræ fidei claritate."

[2] "Et quidem nos, quem tunc de fratrum collegio existentem quasi cooperatorem hujusmodi salubre negotium contingebat, etc." *Ib.*, p. 249.

[3] "Ea quæ per te acta sunt (in the matter of the union) soliditate roboris plenioris comperimus indigere." *Ib.*

[4] The last two letters may be read, *ib.*, pp. 249 and 252. These letters, not dated in Potthast, are also of May 25, 1276.

proceed in like manner with regard to all the Greek prelates, insisting also that the Creed should be sung with the addition of the *Filioque*, as the true faith must not be concealed but made public.[1] As for the preservation of the particular religious rites of the Greeks, those could be retained which the Apostolic See should judge not to be opposed to the Catholic faith, or to the sacred canons.[2] Other documents, however, with which the legates were supplied, authorized them, if they found it necessary, not to insist on too great publicity when the oaths were taken, nor on having any large number of copies of the record of the submission of the Greeks. They were finally to suggest with great caution that the temporal affairs under discussion should be left to the arbitration of the Roman Pontiff.[3]

Unfortunately, the negotiations with Constantinople were again suspended. The pontificate of Innocent lasted only some six months, and the four Franciscans, hearing of his death when they had only got as far as Ancona on their outward journey, returned to Rome. As Hadrian V., Innocent's successor, only reigned a month (July–August, 1276), it was reserved for his successor, John XXI., to resume the negotiations. For some reason, perhaps, because he had no high opinion of the ability of the Franciscans, John replaced the four Franciscan nuncios by two bishops, James of Ferentino and Geoffrey of Turin, and by two Dominicans, Raynon, Prior of the convent at Viterbo, and Salvus, a reader at Lucca. With the documents which had been prepared for the Franciscans suitably altered, the new

The negotiations continued by John XXI.

---

[1] In insisting on this point at this early stage at least, Innocent did not show the wisdom of his predecessor.

[2] Ap. Mart., *SS. Vet.*, vii, p. 253 ff.

[3] *Ib.*, pp. 257–8. Mothon, *Vie du B. Innocent V.*, p. 155, discusses his work with the Greeks, and gives the text of his letters regarding them.

envoys were sent off to Constantinople [1] with powers to excommunicate, in the Pope's name, any who should oppose the union, and to absolve such as stood in need of absolution.[2]

Replies of
Palæologus,
etc., to the
joint
requests of
Innocent V.
and John
XXI., 1277.
John's legates reached Constantinople in the early part of the year 1277, and found the Emperor ready at least to comply with the request that he and his son should confirm by their personal oaths the formula to which the Great Logothete, Acropolita, had sworn on their behalf. Accordingly " in our sacred Palace of Blachernæ in the month of April in the fifth indiction, in the year of the world 6785 ", the Emperor, his son and the Patriarch Veccus took the required oath, and each of them duly signed and sealed copies of it.[3] These, along with letters to Pope John XXI., were sent off to him by the hands of the imperial envoys, Ypertimus, the metropolitan of Cyzicus? (*Kisicensis*), Theodore, " the exarch of the whole of the Helespont who occupied the fourth place in the Council," etc.[4]

The Greek envoys reached the papal court during the vacancy that ensued on the death of Pope John XXI., so that the documents which they brought with them were presented to Nicholas III. In his letter to Pope John, the Emperor, after declaring that every Christian was subject " to the supreme supereminence of the Apostolic Holiness ", averred once more that he had

[1] All this is clear from the Bordeaux MS. See Delisle, pp. 137–8. Possevin, in his notes to G. Pachymeres, vol. i, p. 761, states the same from Spondanus, *ex antiqu.*, 1276, n. 8.

[2] Ep. of John, ap. Mart., vii, 252, there wrongly assigned to Innocent V. as also by Potthast, 21141.

[3] *Cf.* epp. of Palæologus and Andronicus, ap. Wadding, v, p. 9 ff., or ap. *Reg. Nicolai* III, nn. 220–1, vol. i, p. 75 ff., and three professions of faith, ap. *ib.*, nn. 228–30, p. 81 ff.

[4] It is from notes at the top of these documents that we learn that the envoys reached Rome during the vacancy of the Holy See after the death of John XXI. († May, 1277), and that they were presented to his successor, Nicholas III. (Nov. 25, 1277–Aug. 22, 1280).

devoted himself wholly to securing the general acceptance of the union. He, and his son and the patriarch have in writing expressed their assent to the requirements of the papal legates.[1] Further, to the profession of faith made in his name by Acropolita, he added the following oath : " I Michael in Christ our God, Emperor and Ruler of the Romans, etc.," abjure all schism, and on oath accept the Catholic faith as taught by the Roman Church, and acknowledge its primacy. " All the above our imperial power (imperium nostrum) professes to the most holy and supreme Pontiff and venerable father of our Empire, the universal Pope, the lord John XXI. and through him to all his succesors." [2] Andronicus, as usual, followed his father's lead, and his personal oath to the same effect is also to be found in the Register of Nicholas III.[3] with the same note that its Greek text was preserved " in the treasury ".

Of greater interest is the letter of the patriarch John Veccus, for he, at least, as his subsequent history proved, was in earnest. Addressing the lord John as Universal Pope to whom he and his whole " sacred synod " offered due reverential obedience, he hailed him as his " divine and sacred head ", and declared that he was most desirous of seeing brought to a satisfactory conclusion that union which, with the help of God, that most blessed man or rather angel, Pope Gregory, had begun. The Pope can judge of this desire of his from the synodal decree which he sent to him signed by himself and the whole assembly.[4]

The letter of the patriarch Veccus.

---

[1] *Reg. N. III.*, n. 220. The letter of Andronicus, though very flowery, was to the same effect. He had been much occupied in war against the Turks (" ad reprimendum Turcorum impetum "), but he would comply with the Pope's wishes. *Ib.*, n. 221.

[2] *Reg. N. III.*, n. 228.

[3] N. 229.

[4] *Ib.*, n. 230. " Quomodo quoque nos robur præstamus et finem apponimus glorioso principio hujusmodi operis unionis poterit scire vestra a Deo magnifica sanctitas et a volumine synodicali quod sibi

He called God and His angels to witness that he abjured
the schism which to the injury of Christianity had been
evilly introduced between the Churches of Old and New
Rome, and that he freely acknowledged the Primacy of the
Roman Pontiff, and joined himself to his predecessors
who before the schism had paid canonical obedience to
the Apostolic See of Old Rome.[1] To it must questions of
the faith be referred ; to it can appeals be made, and
from it flow all prerogatives that other churches may
possess.

It would occupy too much space to give at length
the full profession of faith in harmony with that of Rome
which Veccus proceeded to give ; but it must suffice
to observe that he commenced it by affirming that the
Filioque clause had not altered the Creeds which were
said by the two Churches. A more complete expression
of obedience and of the orthodox faith no Pope could
receive from anyone.[2]

Replies of
Nicholas III.
1278.

With replies to these documents, Nicholas sent off
from Viterbo four envoys to Constantinople, Bartholomew,.
bishop of Grosseto, and three Franciscans, Bartholomew
of Siena, the minister of Syria, Philip of Perugia and Angelo
of Orvieto (October 7, 1278). The Emperor and his son
were praised for what they had done for the union, and
exhorted to make greater efforts to close the schism now

ostendetur, quod humilitas nostra cum toto sacro ipsius conventu
firmavit et roboravit subscriptionibus manualibus, que apud nos
vigorem obtinent juramenti." P. 85.

[1] Of this he gives the reason : " Quia ipsa sacrosancta Romana.
ecclesia summum et perfectum primatum et principatum super-universam
catholicam ecclesiam obtinet, quem in seipsa ab ipso Domino in b.
Petro apostolorum principe seu vertice, cujus Romanus pontifex est
successor, cum plenitudine potestatis recepisse vere ac humiliter
recognoscimus." *Ib.*, p. 85.

[2] The original Greek of John's letter may be read in *Monumenta.
spect. ad unionem Eccles.*, by Theiner and Miklosich, pp. 21–8, or in
Stapper, *P. Johannes XXI.*, p. 115 ff., John is most full and satis--
factory on the Procession of the Holy Ghost.

that the end was in sight, just as men in a race put forth
all their strength towards its finish.[1] The Greek prelates,
in the matter of abjuring the schism, were urged to comply
with the requirements of the legates [2] who were warned
by the Pope to fulfil their duties with prudence,[3] and were
given the necessary faculties [4] and instructions.[5] In
their instructions the legates were told to press for more
copies on durable parchment and not on papyrus of
the imperial profession of faith, to point out that the
Roman Church wished the Creed to be sung with the
Filioque clause both by Greeks and Latins alike,[6] and
to exact a profession of faith from all the clergy. These
professions of faith were to be duly attested, and copies
forwarded to the Pope so that they might be preserved,
" in the archivium " of the Apostolic See. Further,
the legates were to state that the Holy See was surprised
that, considering the censures the Greeks had incurred
through their schism, they had not requested that their
position should be regularized. This the Pope proposed
should be done by a cardinal-legate whom he intended to
send, but whom he wished should be asked for by the
Greeks themselves. The nuncios were to sound the
Emperor about this, and to find out how the cardinal-legate
could safely enter the Greek territory, exercise his functions,

---

[1] *Reg.*, nn. 367 and 369, or ap. Wadding, v, pp. 30 and 33.

[2] *Ib.*, n. 370, p. 126, or Wad., v, 33.

[3] *Ib.*, n. 372 ; or Wad., v, 35.

[4] *Ib.*, 371, 373–4.

[5] *Ib.*, nn. 376–7.

[6] The wisdom of thus insisting that the Greeks should also give
outward expression of their faith, and of thus compelling them to depart
from their ancient custom, may well be doubted. In this respect Nicholas
III. went further in his requirements than Gregory X. ; but
in our own time the policy of Gregory has been endorsed by both
Leo XIII. and Pius X. : and, in accordance with the decisions of these
last two Popes, the Catholics of the Greek rite recite the Creed without
the addition of the " Filioque ". *Cf. L'Unité de l'Église et Schisme
grec.* by l'abbé J. Bousquet, p. 215, Paris, 1913. *Cf.* pp. 274–5.

and receive maintenance. They were also to point out by degrees and with very modest language that the cardinal would have papal powers and should be received as the Pope himself, whose place he would take.

Here we may interrupt our analysis of the instructions of Pope Nicholas to his legates to remark that it was perhaps a pity that he did not proceed to tell them that, if the idea of a cardinal-legate should not prove to be acceptable, they should state that, as Urban II. had once intended to do,[1] he would come himself. It is obvious that the Pope must use legates, as he cannot personally go everywhere, but no little mischief has been caused in the Church from time to time by the dispatch of papal nuncios of inferior rank with extensive powers. Certainly, considering the pride of the Greeks, and the very great power and influence in the Church which the Eastern patriarchs had once possessed, it might have been well if the possible coming of the Pope himself had been insinuated.[2] At any rate, in this case, there is some historical justification for our observation. The traveller, Burchard of Mt. Sion, writing about this very time (1280) says : " I have heard one of their (the Greek) Patriarchs say in my presence : ' We would willingly live in obedience to the Church of Rome, and venerate it, but I am surprised at my being ranked below the inferior clergy, such as Archbishops and Bishops. Some Archbishops and Bishops wish to make me, a Patriarch, kiss their feet, and do them personal service, which I do not hold myself bound to do, albeit I would willingly do so for the Pope, but for no one else '." [3]

Finally, the legates were instructed, in the first place,

---

[1] *Cf.* G. Malaterra, *Hist. Sic.*, l. iv, c. 13, ap. *P. L.*, t. 149, p. 1192.

[2] *Cf. infra*, p. 448, for the opinion of a contemporary, the *General* of the Dominicans, Humbert de Romanis.

[3] *A descrip. of the Holy Land*, c. 13, Eng. trans., ap. *Palestine Pilgrim's Text Soc.*, p. 104, London, 1896.

not to use the powers given them against simply the private enemies of the Greek Emperor, but only against such as were directly attempting to prevent the religious union of the Greeks and Latins ; and, in the second place, to weigh most carefully all their words so as not to furnish any occasion for the breaking off of the negotiations.[1]

Of course, the name of Charles of Anjou was not forgotten at this time. In a special letter to the Emperor,[2] Nicholas reminded him of the efforts that Pope John XXI. had made to keep the peace between him and Charles of Anjou, in order that temporal considerations might not interfere with the union of the Churches. He was, therefore, much surprised that Michael, who was on all sides said to be a wise and prudent man, and who at one time had always pressed for the settling of the temporal difficulties first, had not replied to the suggestions of his predecessor. Accordingly he begged the Emperor to send suitable envoys to treat of peace within five months of the receipt of his letter, and to give heed to the words of his legates on the matter. Some days later, when asking Charles of Anjou to grant safe-conducts for the imperial legates,[3] he tried to impress upon him the great spiritual and temporal advantages of peace, and urged him to send envoys either to Constantinople or to the papal court, so that a permanent understanding with the Empire could be arrived at.[4]

About Charles of Anjou.

The demands of Nicholas made it clearer than ever to the Greeks that, if they were content that the union

Trouble in Constantinople, 1278-9.

---

[1] They were not to act " superficietenus " as some had done, but " eorum intima et profunda scrutemini ". The same, n. 376, p. 131. As we shall see presently, the Emperor blamed the plain speaking of certain Greeks for being the cause of these more stringent demands of Nicholas.

[2] *Ib.*, n. 368, Oct. 7, 1278 ; or Wad., v, 31.

[3] *Ib.*, nn. 379-81, Oct. 18, 1278, or Wad., v, 46.

[4] *Ib.*, n. 378, Oct. 18.

should be only a matter of words, a mere sham, the
Popes were bent on a real union, and would never be
satisfied with general professions.[1]   The consequence
was that opposition to the Emperor, to the Patriarch
Veccus and their party steadily increased on the part
of the fanatical, of such politicians as were ready to
trouble waters still more that they might the better
fish therein, of the ignorant, and of the small sincere
residue.[2]   Open rebellion broke out, and, as the rebels
ignored the excommunication pronounced against them
by the papal legates and by the Patriarch Veccus, an
army under the command of some of his ralations was
sent against the rebels by the Emperor.   But, as many of
the commanders of the imperial forces, not being in
favour of the union, would not act against the rebels,
the only result was that, while the traitorous commanders
were imprisoned, the power of the rebels increased.
They even induced John II., Prince of Trebizond,[3] to
declare himself Emperor in opposition to Michael, and
obtained the support of a number of Latins.   Further a
number of the Emperor's female relations put themselves
in active opposition to him, and had, with others, to be

---

[1] Their aim was, as Nicholas told Charles, " quod inter Latinos et
Grecos una sit fides mentium, eadem animorum idemptitas et concordia
voluntatum." This letter of the same date is also given in full, ap.
Kaltenbrunner. *Actenstücke zur Geschicte des Deutschen Reiches*
(1272–1308), n. 129.

[2] *Cf.* the declaration of Michael to the Pope through his envoys
" Marchus and Marketus ", ap. *Reg. Nich.*, n. 384. The Emperor said
that when it became clear that the Union meant obedience to the Popes
" aliqui tanquam non habentes scientiam sufficientem intelligendi
magnitudinem operationis hujusmodi unionis ecclesiarum, alii vero
propter malitiam et infidelitatem resilierunt et conturbari ceperunt ".
This *declaration* is in parts better printed in Wadding, v 65.

[2] The rulers of this Byzantine kingdom had seemingly always styled
themselves " Emperors "; but the Greeks of Nicæa-Constantinople
were in the habit of only styling them " Princes of the Lazes ".   *Cf.*
Finlay, *Hist. of Greece*, iv, p. 343 ff., ed. Tozer ; and W. Miller, *Trebizond*,
p. 28, London, 1926.

imprisoned or punished ; moreover a council, composed of a hundred monks, some abbots and eight bishops, assembled, under the protection of Nicephorus I., Despot of Epirus, about the month of December (1278), and anathematized the Pope, the Emperor, and the Patriarch, and bitterly persecuted two bishops who wished to keep their promises of obedience to Rome.[1]

All the above, at any rate, was what Ogerius, " the protonotary of the Latin interpreters " of the imperial court, instructed the imperial envoys " Marchus and Marketus " to tell the Pope when they had to explain to him how it was that Palæologus was at the moment unable to fulfil the papal requirements.

These envoys, in company with bishop Bartholomew and the other papal nuncios, left Constantinople in the beginning of the year 1279 with letters for the Pope from the Emperor and the Patriarch. After Nicholas had perused these documents,[2] which proved to contain nothing more than respectful congratulations on his accession to the papal throne, and had listened to the explanations of the imperial envoys,[3] he can scarcely have failed to realize that the Holy See was being played with. He must have had suspicions that many of Michael's troubles were political and not religious. His own nuncios too will have told him that they had heard from many of the Greeks that for most of them the union was a pretence.[4] Whatever were the feelings of Nicholas at this juncture he assuredly must have been much troubled when, not much later, a petition for help reached him from the Patriarch, John Veccus. In the month of

Veccus appeals to the Pope for protection, 1279.

---

[1] Pach., vi, 1, 24–7, *Reg.*, *l.c.*

[2] *Reg.*, nn. 382–3, or Wadding, v, 62 ff.

[3] Contained in the instructions just quoted. The envoys had received them by word of mouth from Michael, and they had been committed to writing by the notary Ogerius lest, " as is wont to happen to men," they should forget them.

[4] G. Pachym., v, 14. See below.

February (1279), Palæologus, who had been often irritated
by the patriarch's freedom of speech towards himself,
began to give heed to a number of preposterous charges
brought against him by his enemies. He may have
foolishly hoped to lessen the opposition of the schismatics
to himself and his schemes by sacrificing the Patriarch
to their ill-will. At any rate, he showed himself so hostile
to Veccus that the Patriarch offered to resign his dignity.
As the charges against him were merely vexatious or
groundless, Michael could not permit the resignation ;
but he suffered him to give up all active exercise of his
patriarchal duties, and to retire to the monastery of
Panachrantus, March, 1279.[1] Thus ungratefully treated,
Veccus, whose only fault was excessive zeal in the cause
of mercy and right, sent word to Pope Nicholas of what
had befallen him.

Nicholas
sends fresh
nuncios to
Con-
stantinople,
1279.

His messenger would appear to have reached the Pope
not long after the embassy of the Emperor. At any
rate, to help Veccus, he at once sent off nuncios who
reached Thrace in the summer.

Unfortunately, at this period, papal documents fail
us, and we have to rely solely upon the narrative of
Pachymeres which, however, seems to be trustworthy
and sufficiently accurate. According then to this narrative,
the Pope's nuncios were also commissioned to inform the
Emperor that Nicholas was not satisfied with the manner
in which the Greeks had accepted the union. They
had offered words but not deeds.[2]

Palæologus, who had met the nuncios as he was
returning from Hadrianople to the imperial city, was
filled with anxiety lest they should find complete con-

[1] G. Pach., v, 10. This monastery was probably situated near
S. Sophia. The title " Panachrantos " shows that it was dedicated
to the Immaculate Virgin. *Cf. Les Églises de Constantinople*, by
J. Ebersolt and A. Thiers, vol. iii, p. 219, Paris, 1913. It was in the
tenth region.

[2] *Ib.*, v, n. 14, pp. 455-6.

firmation of their suspicions. He, accordingly, having induced Veccus to conceal all that had been done to him, called a number of the Greek bishops together in order to speak to them privately before the nuncios should see them. He pointed out to the bishops how, in working for the union which was so necessary for the Empire, he had had to suffer in his own person by having to imprison even his own relatives, while they, by idly saying to the Latins that the union was a delusion and a snare ("χλεύην τὴν εἰρήνην . . . καὶ ἀπάτην εἶναι") had brought further demands from the Pope. However, to reassure them, he again faithfully promised that he would not suffer the smallest addition to the Creed ; but, at the same time, he required that a courteous reception should be given to the nuncios, especially as the present Pope was not so well disposed towards them as was Gregory.[1]

Thus admonished, the Greek bishops behaved with great circumspection, and the Emperor, to convince the legates how much he was in earnest, sent a bishop with them when they reached Constantinople to show them his friends and relatives in prison, because they would not adhere to the Union.[2] Furthermore, Veccus was solemnly reinstated in the patriarchal palace (August 6)[3] and a letter was drawn up with a number of signatures appended (which Pachymeres assures us were forged,[4] and which, by mistake, it is to be presumed, he says was

The reception of the nuncios, 1279.

---

[1] Pach., v, p. 458.

[2] *Ib.*, v, 16, p. 459.

[3] *Ib.*, p. 461.

[4] *Ib.*, v, 17, p. 461. It must always be borne in mind in listening to Pachymeres that he errs by omission. He never quotes one of the official documents in which the Emperor and many of the bishops accepted the faith as taught by the Roman Church, and expressly its doctrine regarding the Procession of the Holy Ghost. He evidently wished to minimize the amount of real adhesion given to the Union.

sent to Pope *Urban*) [1] in order to prove that the papal requirements had been fulfilled. Whether this fraud was perpetrated with the knowledge and consent of Veccus, Pachymeres professes not to know. At any rate, according to him, the letter avoided the use of the formula used by the Roman Church to express the Procession of the Holy Ghost, but strove, by an accumulation of texts from the Greek Fathers, to make it supposed that the faith of the writers was the same as that of the Latins.[2] In order to deceive the Pope still more, two bishops who had been condemned for opposing the Union were sent with his returning nuncios to be punished by him.[3] The fact that they were sent back by Nicholas with a request that the Emperor would receive them into favour as unduly suspected, gives occasion to Pachymeres to express his conviction that both the Pope and Palæologus were simply playing at " make believe ", with a view to prevent the complete collapse of the negotiations. However that may be, the historian himself is honest enough to blame the prejudice of his fellow countrymen who would not take the trouble to understand the Latin position in matters of faith, and who were quite ignorant that once they had been in strict union with them.[4] This caused them, he concludes, to despise the Latins, and even to go so far as to regard contact with them in sacred things as pollution.

Vain efforts of Veccus to save the Union

The life of the Union, even such as it was, could not be saved even by the zeal and learning of the Patriarch

---

[1] It has been conjectured that Pachymeres, confusing the family name (Orsini) of Pope Nicholas with Urban, who had at one time been connected with these negotiations, wrote Οὐρβάνος for Οὐραῖνος.

[2] *Ib.*, v, 17, p. 462. As this document is no longer extant, the assertions of Pachymeres cannot be checked.

[3] *Ib.*, v, 18, p. 463.

[4] *Ib.* " οἶς (certain of the Greeks) οὐδ' ἦν τὸ παράπαν εἰδέναι τὰ τῆς ἐκκλησίας τῶν Ἰταλῶν, οὔτε μὴν καὶ ἀξιοῦσι ξυνιέναι, ὡς πάλαι ποτὲ ἦσαν ἐν πρώτοις ἡνωμένοι τῶν ἄλλων πλεον."

John Veccus. When views springing from the sentiments to which we have just called attention began to be circulated in writing, Veccus applied himself vigorously to combat them. He showed that the Union was advantageous to the State, and at the same time in harmony with the principles of the Fathers. By bringing to light old books and editing new ones, he strove especially to prove that the mind of the Greek Fathers was the same as that of the Latin on the subject of the Procession of Holy Ghost. But well-nigh the only result of his labours in this direction was to arouse against himself the opposition of many who favoured the Union, because useful to the Empire, provided that its dogmatic side were kept in the background.[1]

Meanwhile, after a pontificate of less than three years Nicholas III. had died (August 22, 1280), and had been succeeded (February 22, 1281) by a man (Martin IV.) perhaps less disposed to parley with the Greeks than he had been. The new Pope, a Frenchman, is said by Pachymeres to have received with marked coldness Leo, bishop of Heraclea and Theophanes of Nicæa, whom Palæologus had sent to greet him on his accession. Some modern German historians [2] give as the reason of this that he was a weak man, and was under the influence of the ambitious Charles of Anjou. The latter proposition is accepted by many modern authors of various nationalities. The contemporary Greek historian, however, gives as the reason that the Latins had discovered that, with the exception of the Emperor, the Patriarch and a few others, the Greeks were opposed to the Union which was a sham.[3]

Palæologus is excommunicated, 1281.

[1] G. Pach., vi, 23, pp. 476-7 ; 480 ff.

[2] E.g., Bishop Hefele and Gregorovius.

[3] Pach., vi, 30, p. 505. According to some Austrian *Annals*, which would appear to be repeating the popular belief of the West, Michael was excommunicated because he was opposed " to the Christian faith " ; " as the Pope proved before the clergy and people by many arguments," especially because no Greek had come to the Roman Church for any

Latin contemporary and quasi-contemporary historians, moreover, add that the Pope had discovered that Palæologus, through the medium of the famous John of Procida, had supplied Peter, King of Aragon, with money in order that he might wrest Sicily from Charles of Anjou.[1] The strictly contemporary historian, Ptolemy of Lucca, tells us that he had himself seen the *pact* (tractatum) which Palæologus had made with John of Procida, and that with the help which Peter had received from the Greek Emperor he had at once begun to prepare a great fleet.[2] What Charles himself was to Palæologus that Peter of Aragon was to him—a thunderbolt that might fall on his head at any moment. Peter had married Constance, the daughter of King Manfred, and was being constantly urged by her to strive to recover her father's Kingdom of Sicily. No sooner then did Charles hear of the building of a fleet by Peter than, not unnaturally thinking it was being constructed to attack him, he appealed to his suzerain Pope Martin on the subject. The Pope accordingly wrote to Peter to find out whether the armament was being got ready to attack his vassal, Charles, King of Sicily. He, however, got no satisfaction from the Aragonese monarch, who "is said" to have replied that what he was doing was so much his own affair that if his tongue should betray it he would cut it out.[3] How-

cause (for advice or to have any dispute settled), proving thereby that they did not recognize the supremacy of the Pope in spirituals. *Ann. Aust. contin. Vindob.*, ap. *M. G. SS.*, ix, p. 807.

[1] *Cf.* e.g., Vincent. Ferretus, *Hist.*, i, p. 952, ed. *R. I. SS.*, p. 252, or ed. Cipolla, i, p. 29, Rome, 1908. He tells us that John of Procida went to Palæologus and told him that he knew that of himself he was unable to resist Charles of Anjou, but that if he would give him money, he could find a man who could. He obtained the wished-for gold. "Lætatus Præses (Palæologus) opulentus credidit ei, et aurea talenta dedit, quod in Carolum conjurans appetiit."

[2] *Hist. E.*, l. xxiv, c. 4, ap. *R. I. SS.*, xi, 1186. Ptolemy had been librarian of the Apostolic See.

[3] *Ib. Cf.* Villani, *Chron.*, vii, 59.

ever, it is much more likely that he told the Pope what he told the French King. He was going to wage war against the Saracens, he said ; and, for that purpose, he asked the Pope to grant him the tithes of his kingdom, and to take that kingdom under his protection.[1] Whatever may be thought of the authenticity of this communication of Pope Martin with Peter, it is now certain from the *Register* of that Pope that he was aware of the alliance against Charles between Palæologus and the Aragonese King. In his " summing up " or *processus*, against the last-named monarch (November 18, 1282), he speaks of the assistance which, according to universally accepted report, the Greek Emperor had given to him against King Charles.[2]

Undoubtedly, for many years, the Holy See had prevented Charles of Anjou from attacking the Greek Empire. Now, therefore, that it had discovered not only that many even of those Greeks who had accepted the Union had merely accepted it politically and not *dogmatically*, so to speak, but also that the Greek Emperor

---

[1] *Cf. Mem. Potest. Reg.*, ap. *R. I. SS.*, viii, p. 1155 ; Muntaner, *Cron.*, cc. 47 and 56 ; and M. Sanudo, *Istoria di Romania*, p. 133. *Cf.* Villani, *Chron.*, vii, 58, ap. *R. I. SS.*, xiii, p. 276, who gives this very year, 1281, as the date of John's taking the money of Palæologus to Peter. " Nel detto anno 1281 . . . Gianni di Procita, congli ambasciadori del Paleologo arrivati in Catalogna la seconda volta, sì richiesero lo Re Piero di Raona, ch'egli s'allegasse col Paleologo, e prendesse la signoria dell' Isola di Cicilia . . . recandoli gran quantità di monetà etc." *Cf.* also *Lu ribellamentu di Sicilia contra re Carlu*, ad. init., ad. Giovanni, Bologna, 1865, or ap. *R. I. SS.*, vol. xxxiv, new ed. Buchon, in his *Chroniques étrangères*, published a French trans. of this Sicilian Chron. Whatever may be thought of the authenticity of this quaint narrative as a whole, it is reliable enough to show the general belief that Palæologus had plotted with the King of Aragon. See also the contemporary *Les gestes des Chiprois*, n. 415, p. 213.

[2] *Reg. Mart. IV.*, n. 276, vol. i, p. 112. The Pope speaks of the " consilio auxilio et favore necnon pactis, conventionibus et confederationibus initis cum eodem (i.e., Peter of Aragon) against the Church and King Charles as " argumenta verisimilia deferunt ", and " vox prætera publica et communis continue quasi accusationis incessat ".

was supplying the sinews of war for an attack upon its vassal,[1] it was certainly, strictly speaking, justified in taking strong measures against him. Accordingly, after a delay of some months, during which apparently Pope Martin could not get any satisfaction from the Greeks, he publicly excommunicated Michael Palæologus, in the Cathedral of Orvieto, and forbade any Christian Princes to have any intercourse with him (November 18, 1281).[2] He repeated his sentence twice during the following year,[3] declaring the Greek Emperor " a supporter " of the schism and heresy of the Greeks, and commanding a copy of the form of excommunication to be affixed to the door of the Cathedral of Orvieto.

Was the excommunication wise ?

Whether, in this decisive action, Pope Martin was or was not unduly under the influence of Charles of Anjou, it would seem that in itself, as we have said, it was capable of justification. The nuncios of the Holy See who did not approve of Michael's methods of propagating

---

[1] Hence the contemporary *Memoriale Potestatum Reg.*, ap. *R. I. SS.*, viii, p. 1151, says definitely that the King of Aragon had as allies the King of Castile and Palæologus. The chronicler adds, no doubt as the excuse of the Basileus, that he was afraid that King Charles, with the support of Pope Martin, was anxious to attack Constantinople. But, he continues, the Pope was then thinking of his own affairs in the Romagna " Papa . . . prius volebat se expedire de Furlivio, quod totam Romagnolam occupatam tenebat ".

[2] *Cf.* the sentence of excommunication, ap. *Bullar. Rom.*, iv, p. 52, ed. Turin ; and Herman. Alt., *Annales*, ap. *M. G. SS.*, xvii, 409. He says that the Greeks were excommunicated because they suddenly withdrew from the promises they had made at Lyons. The continuation of the *Genoese Annals* by James Auria (ap. *M. G. SS.*, xviii, 293) gives Apr. 10, 1281, as the date of the excommunication. This, however, is certainly a mistake. The annalist adds that Pope Martin was highly favourable to King Charles. But this opinion is simply that of a Genoese whose State supported the Greeks against the Latin Empire, as we have already seen. *Cf. Reg. Martin IV.*, n. 269.

[3] At Orvieto, May 7, and at Montefiascone, Nov. 18, 1282. *Cf.* Potthast, nn. 21896 and 21948, and *Reg. M. IV.*, n. 278, vol. i, p. 115.

the Union [1] had had evidence in plenty that even of
those who had expressed their adhesion to the Union,
a large number had but given a verbal acceptance to it,
and that political considerations only had influenced
the Greek Emperor. Further, Pope Martin, as we have
also pointed out, had now proof that Michael was working
for the ruin of his vassal. Still, if these reasons of religion
and of State were sufficient in themselves to justify
Martin's action, it may be doubted whether it was wise,
or whether it would have been taken apart from the
influence of King Charles. The longer the pretence even
of union had been kept up, the more would the Greeks
have become accustomed to the idea, and by degrees
more and more of them would probably have really
embraced it. Certain it is that not a few Latins, such as
Ptolemy of Lucca,[2] believed at the time that Martin's
action was injurious to the Church. In fact, as we shall
show anon, enlightened Latins who had studied the
question—on the spot—among the Greeks themselves,
pointed out many ways in which the Latins were wanting
in their handling of this delicate question of Reunion.
However, it is curious, on the other hand, that some of the
enlightened Greeks did not find the Pope's action severe.
Pachymeres, without any adverse comment, says that
the Emperor and his party were excommunicated as
insincere (ὡς χλευαστὰς, mockers), and as employing force
instead of the arguments of truth.[3]

Whatever was the general feeling of the Greeks as to
the justice or mercy of Martin's action, Palæologus
was not unnaturally furious. Such, he exclaimed, is the
treatment I have received for all I have done, for having

Reception of
the excom-
munication
by the
Emperor,
1281-2.

---

[1] Pachymeres says that the Latins considered that the Greek Emperor
was using preposterous means (πονaîς ἀλλοκότοις) to further the
Union, vi, 30, p. 505.

[2] *H. E.*, l. 24, c. 3. " Quod quidem factum fuit dicto Carolo causa
scandali et ruinæ . . . necnon et *ipsi ecclesiæ* fuit plurimum damnosum."

[3] vi, 30, p. 505.

quarrelled with my friends and even imprisoned my relatives. He forbade the Pope's name to be mentioned in the Mass, and at first thought of publicly rescinding all that had been accomplished by the Council of Lyons. On second thoughts, however, arguing that such a measure would be to proclaim that in his work for the Union he had wasted time, and was fickle, he decided simply to let things take their course, and to allow the work to be undone by others.[1]

Andronicus disowns the Union, 1282-3.

For that, no great length of time was required. Michael himself died about a year after his excommunication (December 11, 1282), and his son, Andronicus,[2] now sole Emperor, freed from fear of Charles of Anjou by the Sicilian Vespers (March, 1282) and the events that followed it, and unmindful of his oaths, publicly disowned the Union, asked pardon for having agreed to it, exiled the patriarch Veccus,[3] recalled Joseph, degraded the bishops and punished both the clergy and laity who had agreed to the union, forced the Augusta Theodora to renounce obedience to the Pope, and required Athanasius, the Patriarch of Alexandria, to condemn all that had been done for the unity of the Churches.[4]

[1] Ib., p. 506. As a specimen of the sort of gossip which Salimbene constantly treats us to, we may note that he says (p. 510, an. 1282, ap. M. G. SS., xxxii) that letters were read before the Pope and his cardinals in consistory to the effect that Palæologus had created a Pope and cardinals.

[2] He even refused honourable burial to his father on account of his work for the Union. Cf. N. Greg., v, 7.

[3] He died in prison, March, 1298.

[4] Pach., in Andronic., i, c. 2 ff., vol. ii, p. 14, and N. Greg., vi, 1. George Phrantzes too, the fifteenth century Byzantine Chronicler, who briefly sums up the history of the Union and the new schism, confesses that under Andronicus and especially under the patriarch Athanasius, 1289-93 and 1304-10, "many regrettable things were done by the chief ecclesiastics." Chron., l. i, cc. 3 and 4, p. 21 ff., ed. Bonn. Of that Patriarch N. Gregorias (vi, 5, vol. i, p. 180) says that he was ignorant of literature and of the manners of civilized life, and that it would have been better if he had remained in his monastery. What

What were some of the immediate direct or indirect consequences of the new Schism to the Greek Church the statements of contemporary Byzantine authors enable us to judge. The first result was a continuous series of schisms of all kinds. There was a schism between the mass of the Greeks who had adhered to the original schism and those who remained true to the new Union, and there were endless schisms among the schismatics themselves, between the supporters of the various deposed patriarchs (e.g., Arsenius) and the ones that *de facto* held office.[1] There succeeded one another, also to the terrible detriment of the Greek Church, a series of incapable patriarchs. Speaking of the election of the patriarch Gerasinus (1320–2) " who had never touched Greek literature, even with the tip of his finger ", Nicephorus Gregoras had good reason to observe that the Emperors selected such ignorant and inefficient men in order that they might use them like slaves.[2] They were drawn for the most part from the monks who, in what we must call their ignorant fanaticism, had been the ones who decried the Union, and who were unfortunately henceforth to dominate the Greek Church by supplying it almost exclusively with its higher clergy. So fanatical were they in their hatred of the Latins that to Union with them they preferred to cast a Christian people beneath the heel of the Saracen. Finally Pachymeres tells us with horror how, in the midst of all these disturbances, the consecrated Bread in the cathedral of Constantinople was found corrupted (February 23, 1284),

kind of a man he was can be further discovered from the style of his biographer, who was in complete sympathy with his hero. To him the Pope is vile, the Italians are *Spirit-attacking*, and the Patriarch Beccus an *impious demoniarch*. *Cf.* cc. 10 and 14 of this anonymous biography, which has been published by Delehaye, ap. *Mélanges d'archéol. et d'hist.*, vol. xvii (1897), p. 47 ff.

[1] Pach., *ib.*, c. 28 ff.

[2] viii, 2, p. 292.

how an icon of the Blessed Virgin shed tears for days,
and one of St. George shed blood.[1] But the most serious
result of the collapse of this Union was that, as John
Cantazene (who was born soon after it, *c.* 1295) noted :
" The schism was aggravated by it, and the division
rendered more profound." [2]

Latin comments on the Schism.   Of the Latins who at this period or a little later were
acquainted with the Greeks and have left notices of them,
we will but cite two or three. The traveller, Burchard
of Mt. Sion, writing in 1280 notes that " the Greeks are
Christians, but schismatics " and then adds what has
remained true up to this day, " but a great part of them
returned to obedience to the Church at a General Council
held by our lord Gregory X." [3] In a similar work
another traveller, Ludolph von Suchem (*c.* 1350) observes
that the Greeks obey their Patriarch " in all things even
as the Latins obey the Pope, and they make no account
of the Apostolic Father, neither do they regard any of his
commands save such as please themselves ". Once,
he continues, the Greeks ruled " the whole of Asia ",
" but since they have been divided from the Church of
Rome by schism, they have almost entirely lost those
countries."[4] Of far more importance, however, than the

---

[1] In *Andron.*, i, cc. 28 and 30.

[2] *Hist.*, iv, 9, ed. Bonn, vol. iii, p. 59.

[3] *A descrip. of the Holy Land*, p. 104, trans. of the *Palestine Pilgrims
Text Soc.*, London, 1896.

[4] *Descrip. of the H. Land*, c. 2, p. 6, ap. *ib.*, London, 1895. A somewhat younger contemporary of our traveller, the author of the Chronicle
of Padua, speaks quite in the same manner, and adds much less politely
that the Greeks " merito vilissimi et abjecti a cunctis fere gentibus
reputantur ". *Chron. monach. Patav.*, ap. *R. I. SS.*, viii, 716–17.
Cf. the reflections of Brother Glassberger, writing his *Chronicle*, c. 1508.
He says that, from the time of this relapse, the Greeks so fell off in
priestly and royal power that "in our time " they have neither one
nor the other : " ab illo tempore suis demeritis tam in sacerdotio tam
in regno decrescentes, *temporibus nostris* nec unctionem habent nec
regem, Turco omnia, Græciæ regna vi detinente." P. 100, ed. Quaracchi,
1887.

casual remarks of travellers is the scientific and impartial
review of the situation which was made at the time by
the well-known fifth *General* of the Dominicans, Humbert
de Romanis, and of which a summary has been published
by Martène.[1] The work was drawn up with reference to
the Council of Lyons. Its first part, in twenty-seven
chapters, dealt with the relations of the Church towards
the Saracens, laying it down that it was the business of
the Pope to watch carefully over the interests of Christendom. The second part dealing with the Greek Schism
is that which concerns us now. Humbert begins this
portion by pointing out that the Church is one, and must
have a supreme Pontiff to represent the invisible Christ.[2]
This Pontiff is the Bishop of Rome.[3] The Greeks consequently are schismatics, (1) because the division between
the Churches took place through their fault ; (2) because
they rebel against the head and (3) because they have made
a head for themselves.[4] He then sums up the chief causes
of the schism, in the past and at the present time : (1) the
difference between the religious rites of the Greeks and
Latins,[5] (2) the vexations inflicted on the Greeks by the
Roman Church in the shape of exactions, excommunications and enactments ; and the abuse and ill-treatment
of them by the Latin Princes, and (3) the pride of the
Greeks.[6] Finally, after showing how detrimental the

---

[1] *Vet. SS. amplis. coll.*, vii, pp. 174–98 ; in full ap. Brown, *Fascic.
rer. expetend.*, ii, p. 185 ff., under the non-committal title *Opus tripar-
titum*.

[2] C. 4.

[3] C. 7.

[4] C. 10.

[5] C. 11, p. 190. Under this he includes the Greek customs of the
clergy having beards and wives : "multiplex varietas rituum in barba
nutrienda, in materia sacramenti Eucharistiæ (leavened bread), in
continentia ministrorum ecclesiæ."

[6] At the end of this chapter (11) he shows how the Greeks became
heretics as well as schismatics, and how they were led into and kept
in heresy especially by the monks "quos vocant suos calogeros". In

schism of the Greeks was to the Church of God, he lays it down that the Pope must work to bring about a reconciliation, and that he must go into Greece himself if he hoped to effect a union.[1] For this purpose, too, Greek must be studied, for, averred Humbert, " there was scarcely a single one in the Roman Curia who could read the letters that were sent to it."[2] The Pope must often send to Greece legates who must not have to look for maintenance from the people to whom they are sent. The Greeks must be received honourably when they come to the West, and must be attracted to the Church by means of marriage with Latins, etc. Especially should they not be oppressed, and every effort should be made to promote friendly relations between the influential people on both sides. Greek books too should be translated into Latin.[3] In his last chapter Humbert pleads that too much stress should not be laid by the Latins upon " the plenitude of obedience ", provided that the Greek patriarchs were confirmed by the Pope, and that the latter's legates were honourably received.[4]

this chapter and in the following (12) and in chapter 18, other causes that contributed towards the commencement or the duration of the schism are discussed, especially the Pope's transference of the Empire from the East to the West when Charlemagne was proclaimed Emperor by Leo III. He adds that many of the Greeks were in schism not because they knew anything about the matter, but simply because their fathers were ; just as in Italy, he says, many are Guelfs or Ghibellines just because their ancestors were. He also treats of such causes as language, distance, etc.

[1] C. 16.

[2] C. 17.

[3] Ib.

[4] C. 19. The work of Humbert should be studied most carefully by such as desire a deeper knowledge of the Greek Schism, and especially by such Latins as may be working for reunion between the Greek and Latin Churches. History ought to teach the Latins that the methods of Gregory X. were better than those of Martin IV., whose envoy, Gerard, cardinal-bishop of Sabina, at the council of Amalfi in 1284, insisted, under pain of suspension, that the Greek bishops of south Italy should sing the Filioque. Cf. D'Avallon, Hist. des Conciles, v, p. 209, from

Though, even from this summary of a summary, it is clear that in these negotiations with the Greeks, the Latins did not always act in the best way, the labours of the great Pontiffs of the thirteenth century were not altogether lost. A Uniat party was formed among the Greeks [1] which still exists, and the idea of Union with Rome was brought prominently before the Greek mind. Hence throughout the whole of the fourteenth century attempts were made for another reunion. Again did political motives move even Andronicus himself, John Cantacazune, and John Palæologus to turn to the Pope, and again for purely religious motives did such men as Demetrius Cydones [2] do the like. And the fifteenth century saw another Reunion, that of Florence (1439), another repudiation, and the end of the Byzantine Empire (1453). Retracing our steps to the Council of Lyons, from which we have strayed considerably, and to its fourth session (July 6), in which the union with the Greeks was consummated, we have to record that, on the following day, Gregory laid before the cardinals a draft of a new constitution which he had prepared to put an end to such disgraceful delays in the election of a Pope as had preceded his own. Gregory's scheme, based on the regulations of the Dominicians for the election of their General, was so strongly opposed by the cardinals that it became necessary for him to seek support elsewhere. [3] Having failed to come to any understanding with them, even by treating separately with each national group,

Council of Lyons, 1274: Constitution on papal elections.

Martène, *Vet. Mon.*, vii, 283. The ignorance of even distinguished Latins of the teaching of the Greeks is shown by Viller, " La question d'union," in *Rev. d'hist. écclés.*, 1921, p. 290 ff.

[1] Among the true converts would appear to have been the imperial lady Dameta Palæologus, the first abbess of Conversano (1266). See *Il chartularum del monastero di S. Benedetto di Conversano*, by D. Morea, 2 vols., Montecassino, 1892.

[2] *Cf.* his works, ap. Migne, *Pat. Græc.*, t. 154.

[3] Potthast, sub. 20857.

the Pope took council with the other members of the Council. On their side the cardinals met in consistory without the Pope, and tried hard to get support from other prelates. All their efforts were to no purpose. The Fathers of the Council supported the Pope,[1] and his constitution became law. It was published as the second canon of the Council.[2]

The Constitution "Ubi periculum".

It began by renewing previous decrees, especially that of Alexander III.,[3] on papal elections, and then proceeded with the following new regulations, suggested no doubt to the Pope by some of the incidents in his own election. When the Pope died in a city where he was residing with his Curia, the cardinals in residence had to wait ten days, but not more, for the arrival of their absent brethren. With one servant only (cleric or lay), unless real necessity compelled the presence of two, the cardinals had then to proceed to the papal palace where they had to take up their abode all together in one large open room. The door of this hall had to be so guarded that no one could go in or out. No one was permitted to see the cardinals or to speak to any of them in secret ; though, with the consent of all, an outsider might be summoned for some purpose that concerned the election. Under pain of excommunication *ipso facto*, the cardinals were forbidden to send any kind of message to anyone outside the conclave. Their food had to be passed into the hall by means of a window or drum. If, after three days, the cardinals had not made a choice, their allowance of food for the next five days was to be cut down to a single dish morning and evening. After

---

[1] See the letter of approval issued by the bishops of Germany, and of the provinces of Besançon, Lyons, etc., ap. Kaltenbrunner, *Actenstücke*, n. 52, p. 58. The bishops acknowledge the "pious intention" of the Pope, and his disinterested zeal to put an end to what is a grave danger for the Church.

[2] Ap. Hefele, *Conciles*, vi, pt. i, p. 182 ff., ed. Leclercq.

[3] See *supra*, Vol. X, p. 140.

the lapse of that period they were only to have bread, wine and water till such time as they should make an election.

As long as the Holy See was vacant, the cardinals were not to receive any revenue from any ecclesiastical source whatever. During the conclave, save in case of necessity and with the consent of all, the cardinals were not to occupy themselves with any other affair than that of the election. If a cardinal had refused to enter the conclave, or if he left it, except on account of serious illness, he was not to be afterwards received, and even if he left it on account of ill-health, the voting could take place in his absence. But he could return and resume his rights, if the voting was not finished, as could any cardinal who arrived after the initial ten days delay.

If the Pope were to die outside of his official city for the time being, the cardinals were to assemble in the city of the district wherein he died, unless it were under an interdict or in revolt, in which case they were to assemble in the nearest city.

The civil authorities, without interfering with the freedom of the election, had to see to the exact enforcing of these regulations. But the election was to be accounted null and void if it was not completely free.

During the elections the cardinals were to put aside every kind of personal considerations, pact or " understanding ",[1] and to have God's interests only before their eyes.

As soon as the death of a Pope became known, religious services must be held for him ; and, till a new one should be elected, prayers were to be offered up everywhere begging God to move the cardinals to make a prompt, unanimous and wise election.

This decree was suspended by Hadrian V., as Charles

[1] " Cujuslibet pactionis, conventionis, obligationis necessitate (deposita)."

of Anjou applied it with unnecessary severity during the election of this Pope, and was revoked altogether " with great scandal " by John XXI. in a consistory of Viterbo (October 8, 1276). The chronicler who states this [1] regards John's death soon after as a punishment, but we are assured by another author that John only annulled the decree with a view to substituting another in its place.[2] This drastic constitution, however, which, with certain modifications in the interests of the health and privacy of the cardinals remains in force to this day, was reaffirmed by Pope Celestine V., and was inserted in the Canon Law by Boniface VIII.[3]

Death of St. Bonaventure.

The drawing up and signing by the bishops of copies of this Constitution of Gregory X. for each kingdom or province caused the fifth session of the Council to be put off till July 16.[4] On the eve of that day died St. Bonaventure, " dear to God and man " says the author of the story of the Council. Gregory himself and all the Prelates in Lyons assisted at the funeral ; and a future Pope, Peter of Tarentaise, cardinal-bishop of Ostia, preached the panegyric. Taking for his text : " I grieve for thee my brother Jonathan " (2 Kings, i, 26), he

[1] *Otto Frising Cont. Sanblas.*, ap. *M. G. SS.*, xx, p. 337. John had already (Sept. 30, 1276), confirmed Hadrian's suspension of the constitution. *Cf. Bullar. Rom.*, iv, p. 38, ed. Turin.

[2] *Martin. Polon. Contin.*, ap. *M. G. SS.*, xxii, p. 443 : " Proponens eam aliter ordinare." But Nic. Trivet, *Annal.*, p. 295, attributes this intention to Hadrian V. *Cf.* Potthast, sub. 21148 (p. 1709) and 21151.

[3] *Sext. decret.*, lib. i, tit. vi, c. 3. Vol. ii, p. 946, ed. Friedberg. On the subject of conclaves generally, *cf.* Lucius Lector (Mgr. Guthlin), *Le Conclave*, Paris, 1894, with illustrations. The *Hist. des Conclaves*, in two small vols. from the time of Clement V., published in Cologne in 1703, also contains interesting illustrations. The English work *The Papal Conclaves*, by T. A. Trollope, London, 1876, must be used with caution as not too accurate.

[4] " Factæ sunt cedulæ per regna et provincias, quibus omnes Prælati sua sigilla apposuerunt." *Brevis nota de gestis Concilii*, given in all the editions of the Councils.

moved all present to tears, as " God had given Bonaventure
the grace of captivating all with whom he came in
contact ".[1] He had made himself especially esteemed by
the Greeks, and he took such a prominent part in the
work of the Council that later Popes could even speak of
his presiding over the Council.[2]

Before the arrival of the Pope to open the fifth session, Fifth and
some of the Tartar envoys were baptized by the cardinal last Session,
of Ostia, as will be narrated more circumstantially 17.
July 16 and
hereafter.[3] When the Fathers of the Council reassembled,
some fourteen constitutions were published, including
(can. 2) the important decree anent the conclave, and
others on elections. Canon twenty-one dealt with
the collation of benefices. Clement IV. (1265) had decreed
that dignities and benefices falling vacant when their
holders were " in curia Romana " could only be filled
up by the Pope. The canon in question, however,
authorized their patrons to fill them up after a month's
delay. Other canons forbade " fairs " or any non-
religious functions in Churches, and vigorously prescribed
usury and reprisals (cc. 25–28).[4]

In the sixth and last session of the Council a decree
was issued (can. 23), renewing a canon (13) of the twelfth
General Council against the foundation of new religious
orders, and suppressing all such as had been founded
in the interval without the authorization of the Holy
See. This decree was especially aimed at a number
of mendicant orders, such as those of the so-called
Apostles and of the Saccati (" sack bearers " or " Brothers

---

[1] *Ib.*

[2] *Cf.* Wadding, *Ann. Min.*, 379 f., 397 ; Glassberger, *Chron.*, 1274,
p. 85 ; and *Chronica XXIV General.*, pp. 352–3 and 356, both ed.
Quaracchi.

[3] *Cf. infra* under Nicholas IV. where the relations of the Popes of
this period with the Far East will be recounted.

[4] These reprisals already forbidden by the civil law, were much
practised in Germany. *Cf.* Hefele, *l.c.*, p. 206 n·

of the Sack ") which had sprung up after the foundation
of the Dominicans and Franciscans, and were a regular
pest to the community.[1] Complaints, as we shall see
in the *life* of Innocent V., were even raised against the
Dominicans and Franciscans themselves.

In his concluding address to the Council, Gregory
declared that two of the ends for which it had been
summoned had been fulfilled. The Greeks had been
brought into ecclesiastical unity, and good measures had
been taken for the future of the Holy Land. Unfortunately
want of time had prevented sufficient being done for the
reform of the Church. Especially did he deplore the evil
lives of many prelates. He earnestly exhorted them to
reform themselves, and so avoid the necessity of harsh
reformatory decrees. Finally he undertook to work to
provide parishes with suitable priests who would observe
the canons about residence.[2] Then, having dismissed the
Fathers of the Council, he published, a month or two
afterwards, its decrees in thirty-one chapters (November 1,
1274), but did not himself leave Lyons for Italy till
about the end of April, 1275.

[1] Salimbene speaks very strongly against them. *Cf.* his *Chron.*,
pp. 254 f., 257, 268, etc., *re* the Saccati, and pp. 279–81, etc., *re* those
" who call themselves Apostles and are not." (*Cf. Apoc.*, ii, 9.) *Cf.*
Ann. Blaendinienses, ap. *M. G. SS.*, v, p. 32, etc.

[2] " Quia ipsis correctis non erat necesse condere aliquas constitutiones super reformatione eorum, alioquin dixit se dure acturum cum
ipsis super reformatione." The *brevis nota.*

CHAPTER III.

THE EMPIRE. GREGORY'S WORK FOR A CRUSADE.

THE Chronicle of Ellenhard of Strasburg († 1304)[1] begins Gregory urges the with the statement that since the death of King Richard, election of who, however, ruled but little, " the Kingdom of the an emperor. Romans" had been vacant ; and that, for fear of a certain number of their Princes who favoured the imperial party against the Church, no German Prince was willing to take upon himself the burden of Empire. Meanwhile, continued the Chronicle, the nobles in Germany had become highway robbers, and were in the habit of committing such outrages that complaints about the state of things poured into Gregory's ears from all quarters.[2] Thereupon, after taking careful counsel, he ordered the Electors to choose a King of the Romans within a definite period, otherwise he himself, with the consent of the cardinals, would " provide for the desolation of the Empire ".[3]

The Electors accordingly met at Frankfort ; but, though they thought of every Prince in Germany, they could not agree on a candidate. At this juncture, continues our chronicler, " moved by the divine mercy ",

---

[1] It may be read ap. Böhmer, *Fontes*, ii, p. 111 ff., or ap. *M. G. SS.*, xvii.

[2] " Apud quem (Gregory) per diversos Alemanie nobiles et alios transeuntes sæpe et sæpius querimonia super tanta importunitate vertebatur." *Ib.*

[3] That it was the authority of Gregory that brought the Electors together is the assertion of all the writers of the time. *Cf.* e.g., *Ann. Halesbrun.*, ap. *M. G. SS.*, xxiv, p. 44 : " Gregorio P. mandante electoribus de eligendo rege Alemanie." Also *Notæ Weingart.*, ap. *ib.*, p. 831. The Italian authors speak in the same way as the German. See Villani, lib. vii, c. 42 ; Salimbene, pp. 450, 463, etc.

the count of Nuremburg, Frederick of Hohenzollern, went to them, and urged them to elect Rudolf, count of Hapsburg, a man to whom "a love of justice and uprightness" had given a solid character.

The Electors, with the exception of Ottocar, King of Bohemia, whose ambitious opposition ultimately cost him his Kingdom and his life, eagerly accepted the advice of the Burgrave, elected Rudolf, and commissioned the Burgrave to convey to him the news of his election (October 1). Rudolf, as much astonished at being chosen King of the Romans as Tedaldo was at being elected Bishop of Rome,[1] accepted the office for which he had been selected, and thus raised to imperial dignity a family which lost it only yesterday.

In this version of Rudolf's election, which is that of the original authorities generally, there is no mention at all of the claims of Alfonso X. of Castile. They were taken seriously by nobody but himself, except for a brief space by his brother-in-law, our King Edward I.[2] Nor is there any mention of the candidature of Siegfried of Anhalt, nor of the action of the powerful " King Primsl, who is known as the Golden or Ottocar ".[3] During the interregnum, some at least of the Electors had offered the crown to Ottocar on the death of Richard of Cornwall (April 2, 1272). Cardinal Simon de Brion too had written to him to say that he hoped he would be elected.[4] For some

---

[1] Rudolf states this to Gregory. See his letter (c. July, 1274), ap. *Mon. G. LL.*, iii, pt. i, p. 53.

[2] See a letter of Edward to Gregory in behalf of the claim of Alfonso, Rymer, ii, p. 46, May 4, 1275. *Cf.* p. 47.

[3] So speaks of him John of Marignola, in his *Chronicle* (to 1362), ap. Emler, *Fontes Rer. Bohem.*, iii, p. 571. The best account in English of this powerful monarch is given by C. E. Maurice, *Bohemia*, p. 67 ff. For the correspondence between Gregory and Ottocar, see Erben and Emler, *Regest. diplom. Bohemiæ.*, vol. or part ii, p. 340 f., Prague, 1882. The whole work in 4 vols. goes to the end of July, 1346. Prague, 1855–92.

[4] Dolliner, *Cod. Prim. Ottokari*, n. 10, Vienna, 1803.

reason, Ottocar could not or would not accept the offer.[1] Whether he thought that the offer did not proceed from a sufficient number of the electors, or that he feared opposition on the part of his own nobles who might not care to see him too strong, Ottocar affected to despise it. " It is of greater consequence to be King of Bohemia than Emperor of the Romans," he is reported to have said.[2] However, when Rudolf, who had once been in his service, was elected without his co-operation (October 1, 1273),[3] he was very indignant, and, whilst Rudolf and his supporters were writing to Gregory about his unanimous election, Ottocar wrote to him to protest against it. He began his letter by pointing out how our Lord, in returning to His Father, made " Peter and you, by consequence, his successors ",[4] so that they might so rule the world that right reason might prevail over folly, and equity over abuses. Wherefore, if the commonwealth is oppressed or injury inflicted on us, neither reason nor possibility permit us to have recourse to anyone but you. Despite the protests of our envoys, the electoral Princes of Germany elected an unsuitable (minus ydoneum) count, and proceeded to crown him despite our appeal to the Apostolic See. Do not then permit our rights to be trampled upon; nor the Empire, once respected by all, to fall into the hands of such as have no fame, power or wealth, lest justice be choked, and

---

[1] See one of the continuators of Cosmas of Prague, ap. Emler, *ib.*, ii, p. 326.

[2] Æneas Sylvius, *Hist. Bohem.*, c. 27, p. 135, ed. Hanover, 1602.

[3] He had a right to take part in the election of the King of the Romans. *Cf. Chron. de rebus.*, p. 345, and a letter of Gregory to him urging him to take prompt measures to secure the election of a King of the Romans. (Potthast, 20838.) *Cf.* on this election and Ottocar's rights, Coxe, *Hist. of the House of Austria*, i, 18–20, London, 1847, and Maurice, *Bohemia*, p. 90 ff.

[4] " Sibi (our Lord) Petrum et vos consequens fieri voluit successores." Ep. ap. *M. G. LL.*, iv, p. 19 ; or ep. 7, p. 16, ed. Dolliner, *Cod. epist. Ottoc.*

peace die. Subjecting itself to you, the Empire calls on you to have pity upon it.

Further, if any reliance could be placed on an addition, found in some manuscripts only, to the chronicle of Sifrid, parish priest of Balnhusen, Ottocar sent large sums of money to various members of the curia in the hope of obtaining the Empire for himself.[1] But Gregory, at any rate, was uninfluenced by the money, and is said in the same " addition" to have observed : " Since in Germany we have so many princes and counts, why should we choose a Slav for the Empire ? " In any case, the Pope paid no attention to any aspirations to the imperial crown in which Ottocar may have indulged[2]; but, if he would have nothing to do with French, Spanish or Bohemian candidates, it was simply on the ground that not one of those candidates had any chance of securing a substantial number of the votes of the electors. He contented himself with encouraging Ottocar's intention, real or pretended, of taking part in a Crusade,[3] and with striving to induce him to recognize Rudolf as King of the Romans, and to maintain peaceful relations with him.[4] At the same time, he gave the Bohemian King clearly to understand that he must not attempt to tamper with the rights of the Empire, and that, if he did, he must not look for support from him. " We have no thought of changing the laws of the Empire, nor of interfering with its customs. Hence it would not be right, nor would it befit my office to interdict the King from pursuing his just rights." [5] It is useless for Ottocar to talk of

---

[1] " Eo quod ipse ad imperium aspiraret." *Compend. hist.*, ap. *M. G. SS.*, xxv, p. 707. Sifrid's Universal history is a very uncritical production in any case ; but this addition, an obvious insertion in German interests, cannot even be said to have the authority of Sifrid behind it.

[2] " Reprobatis nunciis regis Hyspaniæ et regis Bohemiæ." *Ib.*

[3] Ep. of Aug., 1274, ap. Potthast, n. 20906.

[4] Ep. Apr., 1275, *ib.*, n. 20030 ; *Reg.*, n. 713.

[5] Ep. May 2, 1275, *Reg.*, n. 716.

appealing elsewhere; for to whom can he turn? There
is no appeal from one "who holding the place of the
Supreme Judge has no superior on earth".[1] Nevertheless, should that be pressed for, he is prepared later to
give a solemn decision (forum judiciale) on his claims.
But Ottocar was obstinate, and moved steadily to his
doom.

Meanwhile, immediately after his election, Rudolf
wrote to tell Gregory how "the Prince-electors, to
whom from ancient times (ab antiquo) had belonged
the choice of the King of the Romans", had elected him,
though they might have chosen many more illustrious
men. They had chosen him without any canvassing on
his part, and he had accepted the honourable burden
at their earnest request.[2] Trusting in God, he had
accepted the task in front of him for the glory of the
King of Kings, and out of reverence for holy Mother
Church, and for the support of the faith, in the hope that
the help of God and the favour of the Apostolic See
would not fail him. Finally, in order that he might the
better fulfil what was pleasing to God and profitable
(rata) to His holy Church, he begged the Pope
"graciously to bestow upon him the honour of the imperial
crown".[3]

Duly crowned King at Aix-la-Chapelle (October 28),

Rudolf writes to Gregory.

[1] Ep. July 22, 1275, ap. Raynaldus, *Ann.*, nn. 10 and 11, 1275, or
Reg., n. 645.

[2] "Nullo prorsus ambitu, teste conscientia, aspirantes, ad regimen
Imperii erexerunt, acceptione nostra nihilominus importuna instantia
postulata." Ep., p. 1, ed. Gerbert.

[3] "Placeat vestræ sanctitati nos imperialis fastigii diademate
gratiosus insignire." *Ib.* To this passage Gerbert adds a note to the
effect that it and other passages in his letters show that despite contrary
statements "even by ancient authors", Rudolf greatly desired the
golden Roman crown. Soon after the dispatch of Rudolf's letter,
Engelbert, archbishop of Cologne, sent another to the Pope to the
same effect, ap. *ib.*, p. 5. He says R. was elected "in regem Romanorum
Imperatorem futurum, una voce votoque unanimi".

we are assured by Archbishop Engelbert of Cologne, who performed the ceremony, that Rudolf was "a good Catholic (fide Catholicus), a lover of the Churches and justice, a man of counsel and piety, powerful himself, and by blood allied to many powerful people, beloved as we hope by God, and, as we can see, pleasing to the eyes of men. Strong too of body is he, and successful in war against the infidel ".[1] The archbishop concluded his eulogy by praying the Pope to grant Rudolf the imperial crown " that all men may know that God has set you as a light to the Gentiles, and that, through the wisdom of your discretion, after the time of cloud, the longed for dawn has broken over the world ".

The man on whom this eulogy was bestowed was a member of a family which from the middle of the eleventh century had been known as that of the counts of Hapsburg, from a castle built in that century about midway between Olten and Zurich, near the old Roman colony of Vendonissa (Windisch). By arms and inheritance, he had increased his paternal domains and added to them lands in Alsace by marriage. When he was elected, he was fifty-five years of age, and realizing that it would take him all his time and energy to re-establish kingly authority in Germany alone, we shall

---

[1] The letter just cited. Modern writers more or less endorse the panegyric of Engelbert. Bishop Stubbs, *Germany in the Later Middle Ages*, pp. 68–9, calls him " a good King . . . a prudent man . . . The principle that he represented, the cordial union of the imperial and papal interests, was one which had not been successfully tried before. . . . But the house of Austria . . . continued to be hand and glove with Rome ". Bishop Lightfoot (*Historical Essays*, p. 94, London, 1895) calls Rudolf " upright, wise, far-seeing ", " the founder of a long line of powerful sovereigns ". Dunham, *The Germanic Empire*, i, 257–8, says : " In him were happily combined great caution with surpassing valour, great wisdom with an unexampled spirit of enterprise . . . Limited as was the imperial power, he knew how to make the dignity respected. . . . He has truly been called the second restorer of the Empire." See also Coxe, *l.c.*, p. 20 f.

see him wisely leaving Italy to the Pope, to Charles of Anjou, and to its city-states.

Knowing that Alfonso of Castile was still pushing his candidature for the imperial crown, Rudolf not only wrote to Gregory to explain his position, but also sent envoys to him " on the business of the Empire ". [1] He promised Gregory heartily to devote himself to the honour of God and to the exaltation of the Roman Church, and he averred that he would give himself to the Crusade to which the blood of his father who had died at Ascalon called him, and that he would submit to the Pope's arbitration his differences with the count of Savoy. He also assured Gregory that all over Germany the Princes, barons and cities were submitting to his sway (February 27). [2] Delighted to have a candidate at once acceptable to the German people and well disposed towards the Holy See, Gregory thanked " the King elect " for his expressions of goodwill, urged him to remain true to them (March 25, 1274), [3] and expressed to him his satisfaction that he was in earnest about the Crusade. [4]

He also worked hard to clear away the remaining obstacle from Rudolf's path, i.e., the candidature of Alfonso. He had already tried to propitiate the Spanish King by asking his opinion about the proposed Crusade, and about the negotiations for union with the Greeks, and he had promised to fall in with the King's wishes, and have an interview with him. [5] Now he devoted himself to urging Alfonso for the sake of the common good and the cause of the Holy Land to cease aspiring to the Empire, and he offered him on condition of his giving

Gregory congratulates Rudolf, 1274.

Gregory at last succeeds in securing the withdrawal of Alfonso, 1275.

---

[1] *Cf.* epp. 16, 18–20, ap. Gerbert, p. 20 ff.
[2] Ep. 18, *ib.*
[3] Potthast, 20809 ; *Reg.*, 670.
[4] P. 20857 ; R., 569.
[5] Ep. Nov. 23, 1273. Raynaldus, 1273, n. 28.

up all claim to it, the ecclesiastical tithes of his Kingdom
for six years.[1]   After he had formally acknowledged
Rudolf, Gregory continued his expostulations with
Alfonso.   He pointed out to him that by the laws of the
Empire, the candidate for the Empire must first receive
" the crown of the kingdom of Germany " at Aix-la-
Chapelle, and, as Rudolf and not Alfonso had been given
that crown, he had acknowledged the former.[2]

Alfonso, however, foolishly continued to push his
hopeless claims, and Gregory agreed to meet him to
discuss them face to face.[3]   They met at Beaucaire
(Languedoc) in May, 1275.[4]   No good, however, seems
to have come of the meeting.   Alfonso was obstinate,
the more so as he fancied he had at least Ghibelline
Lombardy behind him.   His imagination in this direction
had possibly been helped by the verses of the troubadour,
Folquet de Lunal, who had proclaimed : " I have heard
that the Lombards, the Germans, the Brabançons, and
the Romans would have him for Emperor, and that
the people of Milan, of Pavia, and Cremona are preparing
him an honourable reception if he comes into Italy." [5]
However that may be, in the preceding November,
Alfonso had sent some five-hundred well-equipped men-at-
arms to Pavia.   They had been well received by the
Ghibellines, and in January, Pavia itself, Novara, Genoa,
Asti and other cities had sworn allegiance to Alfonso
as King of the Romans.[6]   Writing to the people of Pavia

---

[1] Epp. June, 1274, *ib.*, 1274, nn. 45–55.

[2] Ep. Dec. 19, 1274, ap. *ib.*, nn. 50–2. *Cf. Reg.*, 689–96. The Pope
in some of these letters tries to get the Queen and others to support
him against Alfonso.

[3] Apr.–May, 1275, Potthast, 21031–2, 21034, and Raynaldus, 1275,
n. 14 ; *Reg.*, nn. 710–12.

[4] *Chron. de rebus*, p. 350.

[5] Quoted by Dobson, *The Literary hist. of the Troubadors*, p. 127,
London, 1807. See also p. 219 for similar language of Will. of
Montagnogout.

[6] *Ib.*, p. 348.

on May 21, the Castilian monarch told them that the Pope had denied him simple justice, and so, trusting in God and relying on their devotion and on that of his other liegemen, he had resolved to enter Lombardy with a large force and to prosecute his claims to the Empire in every way.[1] The conference at Beaucaire, as we have said, came to nothing. Gregory had already committed himself to Rudolf, as he explained to the people of Milan when he had denounced the entry of the Spanish soldiers into Italy against his express prohibition,[2] and had called on the Milanese to resist them.[3] If, however, as Mariana notes, Alfonso for a moment allowed himself to be overcome by Gregory's eloquent appeals, and withdrew his candidature for the Empire, he showed his real mind by immediately after putting forward impossible claims to the Duchy of Suabia and the Kingdom of Naples.[4]

An incursion of the Moors caused this " most learned fool " of a King to hurry back to his own dominions, where he continued to use the imperial title and robes till the archbishop of Seville, acting under orders from the Pope, compelled him by ecclesiastical censures to desist.[5] However, Gregory did not fail to write to Rudolf, and to beg him, in the interest of the Crusade, to do justice to Alfonso in the matter of the Duchy of Suabia.[6] Rudolf

Alfonso returns to Spain, 1275.

---

[1] Ep. ap., *ib.*, pp. 350–1.

[2] Ep. Nov. 18, 1274, ap. *Reg.*, 574. *Cf. ib.*, n. 642, Apr. 11, 1275.

[3] Potthast, n. 20967.

[4] The close of bk. 13 of his *Hist. Gen. de España*, p. 216 v. of Steven's translation.

[5] *Ib.*, and especially Gregory's letters of Sept. 13 and 28, 1275, to the archbishop of Seville, nn. 342 and 343 ap. Theiner, *Cod. Diplom.*, i, p. 192 f. Alfonsus " qui super negotii Imperii nostris, sicut nosti, beneplacitis acquievit, se in suis litteris Regem Romanorum intitulat . . . affirmans in illis se a dicto Imperii negotio nec destitisse, nec velle desistere, etc." N. 343. Also ap. *Reg.*, 650–1. *Cf.* Loaisa, *Chron. des Rois de Castille*, nn. 6, 11, 18.

[6] Ep. of June 27, 1275, ap. Gerbert, p. 73, or *Reg.*, 719.

was, it appears, able to prove to the Pope's envoy that
Alfonso had no rights over the Duchy,[1] and so, unable
to help him in that direction, Gregory supported his
efforts against the Moslems.[2]

Meanwhile, as we have already stated, the claims of
the various candidates for the Empire had been examined
by the Fathers of the Council of Lyons, and the election of
Rudolf had been confirmed[3] in accordance with the
expressed wishes of the Electors and other German
Princes (June 6).[4] To maintain his cause, Rudolf had
sent on this the third legation which he had dispatched
to Gregory, his chancellor Otho, provost of St. Guy's at
Spires.[5] Otho was also empowered to renew in Rudolf's
name all the privileges and concessions which his predecessors had granted to the Holy See, and also to make
other grants which Gregory might ask for, short of
dismembering the Empire.[6] Accordingly, on June 6,
the privileges of Otho IV. and Frederick II., duly
translated into German (in Theotonico ydiomate) for
the benefit of the German nobles present, were read over
in the presence of the Pope and his cardinals, and in that
of Henry, archbishop of Trier, Engelbert of Cologne, and
other German archbishops, and before Frederick, burgrave
of Nuremberg, and Godfrey count of Bayersoien. They
were then solemnly confirmed in Rudolf's name by Otho,

---

[1] See his reply ap. *G.*, p. 76.

[2] Epp. of Sept. 3 and Oct. 14, 1275, Potthast nn. 21062, 21083,
Raynaldus, 1275, n. 16.

[3] *Cf. supra*, p. 386. See also Thos. Tuscus, *Chron.*, ap. *M. G. SS.*,
xxii, p. 528, who speaks of Rudolf as " per Gregorum X. . . . confir-
mato in imperatorem Romanum licet nondum coronato "; *Chron.
Erphes. Minor.*, p. 688, ed. Holder-Egger ; *Ann. Frisacenses*, R. elected
" favente et approbante apostolico Gregorio", ap. *M. G. SS.*, xxiv, p. 66.

[4] *Cf.* ep. of Mainhard, count of Tyrol, ap. Gerbert, p. 47.

[5] See the deed naming Otho his " procurator " ap. *M. G. LL.*,
Constit., t. iii, pt. i, p. 42. Apr. 9, 1274.

[6] *Ib.*, " Et super his omnibus patentes litteras meas dabo aurea
bulla typario regie potestatis impressa bullatas."

and the German nobility present. It was also agreed that Charles of Anjou, and the other vassals of the Holy See were not to be disturbed and that the King was not to aspire to the Senatorship of Rome, or to the Kingdom of Sicily ; and that, when Rudolf came to Rome for the imperial crown, he should renew these promises and undertakings.[1]

The expressions of goodwill which Rudolf continued to send to Gregory and the indications which he constantly gave of his readiness to pursue a conciliatory policy much impressed him. In order that truth and justice, as he wrote to the Pope, might act together in their joint persons, Rudolf submitted himself, his children, and the interests of the Empire, especially in the matter of the encroachments of Ottocar of Bohemia, to the inspired wisdom of Gregory. This he did that the needs of the Holy Land might not be neglected, and in the full confidence that the Pope would have regard to the integrity of the Empire.[2] Moreover, in order to further the Pope's desire [3] that he should live in friendly relations with the King of Sicily, he readily accepted the Pope's suggestion of a marriage between his daughter, Clemenza or Clementia, and Charles' grandson, Charles Martel, then about three years of age.[4]

Gregory's solemn confirmation of Rudolf, Sept., 1274.

---

[1] *Cf.* documents 49, 50, 51, ap. *ib.*, pp. 42–8. The promises were made " to blessed Peter, the keybearer of the Kingdom of heaven, and to you most holy Father his successor, and to your successors and to the Roman Church ".

[2] *Cf.* ep, 62 (June–July, 1274), ap. *ib.*, p. 53 f. *Cf.* epp. 63–4.

[3] Potthast, n. 20858, *cf.* nn. 20967 and 20976–7.

[4] *Ib.*, ep. 65, p. 55. He concludes his letter by saying that he would not spare his own son, if he were to act against the Pope. *Cf.* ep. of Charles to the barons of Provence, telling them of the marriage to take place between Charles the first-born of his eldest son Charles, Prince of Salerno, and Clementia, daughter of Rudolf. *Reg. Ang.*, 1274, B., n. 20, fol. 75, in C. M. Riccio, *Il regno di Carlo I. di Angiò*. Many were the intrigues around the two children till their marriage was consummated in 1287, when Charles Martel was 16 years of age. *Cf.*

Naturally much moved by all this, and by the King's expressed zeal for the cause of the Holy Land,[1] Gregory, after taking the precaution of publishing the privilege of Frederick II. which Rudolf had confirmed,[2] solemnly confirmed his election (September 26). With the counsel of his brethren, he wrote to Rudolf, " we nominate you King of the Romans," and exhorted him to hold himself ready to come promptly to him to receive the imperial crown when the time should be fixed.[3]

Negotiations about the reception of the imperial crown, 1274-5.
In the meanwhile Gregory, having duly received from Rudolf a letter of thanks for the confirmation of his election,[4] devoted himself to smoothing Rudolf's paths. He laboured to repress the imperial aspirations of Philip III. of France, and to induce him and Ottocar to maintain friendly relations with Rudolf.[5] He exhorted the Milanese to acknowledge him, and to resist the Spaniards of Alfonso,[6] and, on the other hand, he bade Rudolf send troops into Lombardy as his enemy there was never idle, and to listen favourably to the petitions of the Milanese.[7] At the same time, in order that Rudolf's position might be more secure, he urged him to begin to make preparations to come to receive the imperial crown at his hands, and, in order

M. Schipa's most valuable *Carlo Martello*, pp. 25, 59, and *passim*. Naples, 1926.

[1] Potthast, n. 20857.

[2] Aug. 18, *ib.*, n. 20901.

[3] Ep. 66, ap. *ib.*, p. 56. " Te regem Romanorum de ipsorum consilio nominamus."

[4] Ep. ap. Gerbert, p. 35, *cf.* ep., p. 46, of Electors.

[5] Nov., 1274. *Cf.* Potthast, 20957 ; *re* Ottocar, 20962–4.

[6] *Ib.*, 20967 (20969, 20974–5). Dec., 1274. Raynaldus, *Annal.*, 1274, nn. 45–53.

[7] Potthast, 20992. Feb. 15, 1275 ; in full ap. Theiner, *Cod. dip.*, i, p. 190. His rival, he says, " Non dormit in illis partibus, nec dormitat, sed ingenio conatur, et juribus ad devotionem incolarum . . . pervetendam." *Cf.* Potthast, 21035–6, of May 12, 1275, also about sending troops into Lombardy.

to facilitate negotiations between them, he begged
Rudolf to come nearer to Lyons.[1] Then, on February 15,
1275, he fixed the first of November of that year as the
date when Rudolf was to receive the imperial crown in
the basilica of St. Peter's at Rome.[2] This he did, he said,
in response to a request from Rudolf himself.[3] In the
letter in which he announced this date to the King,
Gregory discussed the relation between the Papacy
and the Empire, and began his remarks by stating that
" with good reason had learned men (sapientia civilis)
laid down that there was not much difference between
them, if they were animated by one principle ".[4] Each
has need of the support of the other, and while one has to
provide for the world's spiritual needs, the other has to
see to its temporal necessities. Both have been instituted
for the one end—the government of the world. Hence
it is bad if there is a vacancy in either the Papacy or
the Empire. A vacancy in the Papacy means that the
Empire is without its guide to salvation (rector salutis)
and a vacancy in the Empire means that the Papacy is
exposed to danger, and it is without its protector. Hence
Gregory's earnest efforts to bring the interregnum to
an end.

On the same day that Gregory sent Rudolf the notice

[1] Ep. of Dec. 1, 1274, ap. Theiner, *l.c.*, p. 187. *Cf.* n. 335, *ib.*, p. 188.

[2] Ep. ap. *ib.*, pp. 188–9. *Cf.* ep. 337, *ib.*, p. 189, or *Reg.*, n. 699–704,
to the Princes of Germany, exhorting them all personally to assist at
the ceremony of the King's " anointing, consecration, and coronation ".
Cf. epp. 338–41, and 344. The cardinals too, in writing to tell Rudolf
of the confirmation of his election, tell him that Nov. 1, 1275, was the
day fixed for his coronation. Ep. Sept. 26, 1274, ap. Gerbert, p. 37.

[3] See Rudolf's letter of Dec. 17, 1274, asking the Pope to summon
him speedily to receive the imperial diadem. Ap. *M. G. LL.*, iii, pt. i,
p. 63. *Cf. Ann. Colmar.*, for the King's embassy on the subject. Ap.
Böhmer, *Fontes*, ii, p. 8.

[4] Ep. of Feb. 15, 1275, Theiner, i, n. 336. " Sacerdotium et Imperium
non multo differre merito sapientia civilis asseruit, si quidem illa . . .
principii conjungit idemptitas (sic)."

of his coronation day, he sent him a letter requesting
him to renew himself the undertaking of his envoys
regarding the confirmation of the privileges granted by
his predecessors to the Roman Church.[1]   To this, after
duly informing his subjects that he had been confirmed
in the Empire by the Pope, and called by him to receive
the imperial crown,[2] Rudolf promptly agreed.

Gregory and
Rudolf meet
at Lausanne,
Oct. 6,
1275.

Writing from Orange, for he had left Lyons in April,
Gregory congratulated Rudolf on his showing himself
" a pacific King ", and on his readiness in agreeing to
bring about a relationship between his son Louis, duke
of Bavaria and Charles of Anjou.   He also again urged
him to send troops into Lombardy, and to hasten the
preparations for his coronation ; but at the same time
he assured him that he could not lend him money, and
that he ought not to do so even if he could.   It would
do Rudolf's cause the greatest harm if Alfonso, who was
close at hand and whom the Pope had to meet in a few
days, were to hear of the King's necessities (May 12, 1275).[3]
In conclusion, he told Rudolf that he would let him know
soon where they could meet.

After his disappointing interview with Alfonso at
Beaucaire in the latter half of May, Gregory wrote
to assure Rudolf that his delay in that city could not be
helped, that he would soon continue his journey, and that
meanwhile the King must make the most careful preparations for his journey to receive his crown.[4]   A little later,

---

[1] Theiner, *l.c.*, p. 190, or n. 70, ap. *M. G. LL.*, *ib.*

[2] N. 80, ap. *M. G. LL.*, *ib.* " Confirmatos namque in regno Romano
a SS. patre nostro vocatos nos sciatis veraciter ad recipiendum . . .
gloriosum imperii dyadema." March, 1275.

[3] *Reg.*, 708–9, or Theiner, *l.c.*, p. 191. Gregory had already given
Rudolf 12,000 marks, and yet " rubore resperso ", he asked for a *loan*
of another 5,000. See his letter, ap. Gerbert, p. 87. *Cf. Reg.*, n. 707,
for further exhortation on the part of Gregory for the sending of
troops into Lombardy to oppose the intrigues of Alfonso.

[4] Ep. June 25, ap. Theiner, *l.c.*, p. 192.

writing from Valence to the German Princes, he told them
that Alfonso had given up his claim to the Empire, and
that he had decided not to go to Germany as he had
originally intended to do, so that he might spare expense
to its people. Although it is true, he continued, that the
delay he has had to suffer has caused him to put off
the date of the King's coronation, still, if it takes place
under better conditions owing to the action of Alfonso,
it really should not be considered as having been delayed.
The Princes must, therefore, persevere in their loyalty
to Rudolf, and make ready to accompany him to Rome.[1]

While continuing his journey down the Rhone, Gregory
did not cease to keep a watchful eye on his flock, and we
find him from Vienne threatening James of Aragon with
excommunication and interdict if he did not give up
his adulterous life.[2] At length, on October 18, Gregory
and Rudolf met at Lausanne. The King came with his
wife and most of his children in great pomp, having, we
are told, spent nine hundred marks for precious robes.[3]

In the midst of the enthusiasm excited by this auspicious
meeting, Rudolf, his Queen, and most of the nobles present
took the cross [4]; and it was arranged that, of the German
clerical tenth, twelve thousand marks should be given to
the King, and that, with the Pope and King together, the
expedition should set out two months after the ensuing
feast of Candlemas day.[5] Then Rudolf's position was
solemnly discussed, and we are assured that he strove
to do " what conduced to the honour of the Roman

---

[1] *Ib.*, p. 193, ep. of Sept. 13, or ap. *Reg.*, n. 724. *Cf.* 725.

[2] Ep. of Sept. 22, ap. Raynaldus, 1275, nn. 28–31. *Cf.* n. 34. A little
before, he had been issuing a Constitution to save the church in Portugal
from the oppression of its King Alfonso III. *Ib.*, nn. 21–7, or Ripoll,
Bullar. O.P., i, 532, Sept. 4. *Cf.* Gregory's previous action in Potthast,
27742–3–5. May 28, 1273, and McMurdo, *Hist. of Portugal*, i, 466 ff.

[3] *Ann. Colmar.*, ap. Böhmer, ii, p. 9.

[4] *Ib.*

[5] *Ib.*

Curia, and to the peace of the Empire ".[1] Accordingly, when the King had agreed " not to interfere with the rights of the Roman Church, and to restore whatever had been taken from it by his predecessors ", his election was again confirmed, and it was decreed that, " when he had regulated the affairs of the Kingdom of Germany," he should come for the imperial crown.[2]

Gregory returns to Italy, 1275.

About the beginning of November Gregory, full of hope for the future, set out on his return journey to Rome to prepare for Rudolf's coronation and the Crusade. On November 22, he reached his native city of Piacenza.[3] Thence he wrote to the archbishop of Embrun saying that, whereas he had already written to the prelates " of the Kingdom of the Romans throughout Germany and Sclavonia " exhorting them in general terms to be ready to accompany Rudolf with all honour when he should set out to obtain the imperial crown, he now bade the archbishop inform them that at his meeting with Rudolf at Lausanne he had fixed next Candlemas day as the date of the coronation (November 24, 1275).[4]

[1] Thos. Tuscus, ap. *M. G. SS.*, xxii, p. 371.

[2] *Ib.* " Jussumque est ei, ut, dispositione de regno Alemanie facta, ad suscipiendam coronam imperii . . . festinaret." *Cf. Ann.*, Ebehardi, ap. Böhmer, *ib.*, p. 529. The diploma of Rudolf, dated Oct. 21, 1275, confirming the privileges and states of the Roman Church is given in Theiner, *l.c.*, p. 194 f. In view of all that Gregory had done for him, Rudolf declares it to be his wish to do even more than his predecessors for the Roman Church : " Nichil exinde (from the privileges already given) volentes diminui, sed magis augeri, ut nostra magis devotio enitescat." In the states of the Church is reckoned " terra Comitissæ Matildis ". This document sealed with a seal of wax, was to be confirmed at his imperial coronation with a golden seal. One of the lay signatories of this diploma was, of course, Rudolf's great supporter, Frederick of Hohenzollern.

[3] *Chron. de rebus*, p. 352.

[4] Ep. n. 346, ap. Theiner, *l.c.*, p. 196 : " Cum . . . ad sollempnia coronationis . . . consumanda festum purificationis B.V.M. primo venturum pro termino duxerimus prefiguendum, fraternitati tuæ, etc." The summary at the head of this letter in Theiner is most misleading. It is to the effect that the archbishop was told to admonish the prelates

All the official documents which we have quoted show that Rudolf was most anxious to receive the imperial diadem as soon as possible, and that the delay in bestowing it upon him came from the Pope, who was detained in and about Lyons by his having to wait for Alfonso, and also we are assured by " business from the Italian cities ".[1] It was obviously to Rudolf's interests to receive the crown at Gregory's hands with the least possible delay. When once he had been duly crowned the pretensions of Alfonso and Ottocar would immediately collapse.[2] Hence it is not easy to explain how it is that many modern authors have been able to write that, at this period, at least, Rudolf displayed no concern to receive the imperial crown.[3]

A few weeks before he died, Gregory had occasion to remonstrate with two of Rudolf's officials for hasty action with regard to certain matters in Romagna [4]; of Germany : " ut Rudolphum . . . ad recipiendum imperiale diadema in Urbe compellant." There is not one word in the letter about compelling Rudolf to do anything. This false summary may be the *text* which has caused so many modern authors to say that Rudolf was not in the least anxious to receive the imperial crown.

Gregory commends the Church to Rudolf, 1276.

[1] *Ann. S. Rudbert.*, ap. *M. G. SS.*, ix, p. 801.

[2] *Cf.* a letter of the Pisans (ap. Gerbert, p. 90) to Rudolf urging his prompt journey to Rome for the crown. It is, however, not certain that this letter belongs to 1275.

[3] Even Bishop Stubbs, *Germany in the later Mid. Ages*, pp. 70–1, after stating that Rudolf undertook to go to Rome to be crowned emperor, after which he was to conduct a crusade, adds : " Neither of these promises were ever fulfilled, and Gregory X., who was a sincere sort of Pope, having complained to Rudolf of his broken faith, proceeded so far as to excommunicate him ; and left him, it is said, excommunicated at his own death in 1276." No authorities are cited for these statements, and, seeing that Gregory died Jan. 10, 1276, before the dates which he had himself fixed for the fulfilment of the two promises, it is impossible to believe that he excommunicated the King for not having fulfilled them ! The way in which, especially in the story of the Popes, one writer has blindly followed another is distressing.

[4] " Super statu partium Romaniole." Ep. 348, Dec. 12, 1275, ap. Theiner, *l.c.*, 196. In connexion with the affair, as " he was desirous that the negotiations of his dearest son Rudolf, the illustrious King

and, a few days before his death, he wrote a touching letter to Rudolf himself. He told him how pleased he was to hear that all was going well with him, as he loved "the honour of the Empire", and looked on Rudolf's happiness as his own. Embracing him as his father in Christ, he tenderly exhorted him never to let human glory cause him to forget his Maker. He thanked him for inquiring about his health, and quietly added that perhaps, not without reason, had Rudolf made the inquiry, for he had no sincerer friend than himself, and he had contracted his illness in the place to which his love for Rudolf's honour had taken him. However, whether God should deliver him from his infirmity, or free him from his frail body, he trusted that Rudolf, as "a most Christian Emperor", would cherish the Church and bring it peace, so that, "whether we live or die, we may glory in your deeds in the presence of Him Whom we must serve in this world, and to Whom, should He wish to call us, we shall go with confidence, trusting in His mercy."[1]

Soon after dispatching this letter, Gregory pushed on to Arezzo in order to reach Rome in time for the coronation of Rudolf. But he never got any further south than that city. He died there on January 10, 1276, when Rudolf was on the point of setting out for Rome.[2]

---

of the Romans, should have a happy issue ", he sent to Lombardy his chaplain, Arditio, auditor of the Rota. Ep. 347, *ib.*, Dec. 11. The letters are dated from Bologna (Dec. 11), and Planorium.

[1] Lib. ii. Ep. 30, ap. Gerbert, p. 97. Writing to Charles of Anjou from Florence about Dec. 20, to tell him that he proposed to go through Arezzo, and thence to Rome, he added words which show that he was then in an unsatisfactory state of health : " prout status noster permiserit." Ep. ap. Raynaldus, *Ann.*, 1275, n. 47. From this letter of Gregory, we learn that he reached " San Croce in the diocese of Florence ", on Dec. 15, and from Villani, vii, 50, and Della Tosa, p. 146 (14th day before January) that he entered Florence Dec. 18.

[2] *Cf.* his letter to the cardinals when the news of Gregory's death reached him : " Antequam de morte . . . Patris SS. ad nos rumor

On his way to Arezzo, Gregory passed through Florence. According to Villani, he had intended to avoid it, as he had placed it under an interdict on account of its having failed to observe the peace which he had made between its Guelf and Ghibelline factions.[1] But, if we are to trust Villani, the swelling of the Arno compelled him to cross once more the Rubaconte bridge and to enter Florence. When news of his approach reached the city, the citizens were at first at a loss to know what to do, as they knew the mind of the Pope towards them only too well. However, says Leonardo Bruni, respect for his dignity, and their high opinion of his sanctity so prevailed that the whole city went forth to meet him. Touched, no doubt, by their devotion, Gregory removed the interdict when he entered the city and blessed its people ; but, as he could not prevail upon them to observe the peace, he reimposed the censure when he left their city.[2]

We must, however, in telling the story of Gregory X., Gregory's never lose sight of the fact that, as with Honorius III., one aim, a in all he did he had ever before his eyes the promoting Crusade. of a Crusade for the complete recovery of the Holy Land.[3] If he strove to make peace between Church and

pervaserat, nos et nostros . . . accinxeramus ad iter . . . Adhuc tamen in ipso procedendi proposito parati pariter et accincti . . . ipsum iter suspendimus . . . donec, etc." Ep. ap. Gerbert, p. 104.

[1] Cf. supra, pp. 365 ff. and 377.

[2] Villani, l. vii, c. 50 ; and L. Aretino. Hist. Florent., iii, p. 64, ap. R. I. SS., t. xix, pt. iii, ed. 1914. Leonardo Bruni of Arezzo (Aretino) was chancellor to the republic of Florence. His history of that city is scientific and useful. He was one of the distinguished Greek scholars of the Renaissance, and was a papal secretary under Innocent VII., Gregory XII., and John XXIII. On the abdication of John, he went with him to Florence, and became its chancellor. He died in 1444. Cf. Pastor, Hist. of the Popes, i, p. 42.

[3] He did not, however, forget the needs of Spain, and we find him praising the archbishop of Toledo for getting ready to help Alfonso X. of Castile against a fresh Moorish invasion from Africa. Potthast, n. 21062 ; and cf. 21083, where he grants Alfonso tithes.

State,[1] or between Kings, or among citizens,[2] it was largely because war in Europe prevented war in Palestine, and if he strove for union between the Church of Rome and the Greek Church, it was because he realized that their union would greatly facilitate victory over the Moslem. He was an indefatigable peacemaker because he was an ardent Crusader; and so indefatigable was he in pursuit of peace that on one occasion a chronicler notes as something extraordinary that in his native city on his return journey to Italy " he did not treat of peace ".[3]

Though nothing came of his efforts to inaugurate a Crusade, Gregory continued to labour for one throughout his whole pontificate with the same zeal which he had shown in its commencement. After the council of Lyons which, as he points out to the archbishop of York, was summoned primarily for the promotion of a Crusade, he wrote to the bishops of Christendom urging them to preach the Crusade throughout their dioceses.[4] The same commands were given by him to his legates in the different countries, and we find him bidding cardinal Simon de Brion appeal particularly to King Philip,[5] and his legate

---

[1] After a great many efforts he succeeded at last (March 21, 1275) in making peace between Philip III. of France and the church of Paris. Cf. Reg., n. 1066.

[2] Peace between Bologna and Venice, Potthast, n. 20637; between Pisa and other cities, ib., 21070; between France and the Empire, ib., 20957; between Charles of Anjou and Alfonso of Castile, ib., 21054; in Lyons (20714-15), in Florence (20,750; Reg., nn. 335774-5); in Bavaria (21085). Very naturally also he sought for peace for the States of the Church; and so he exhorts the famous warrior, Guido da Montefiltro (20806) and the city of Orvieto to cease harassing the territory or subjects of the Roman Church (20807). When striving to make peace in Genoa he asserted that he had ever been a lover of peace: " Donum pacis ab olim nostris ferventer insedit affectibus." Ep. ap. Kaltenbrunnen, Acktenstücke, n. 3, p. 4.

[3] Pot., n. 21088.

[4] Ib., n. 20920. Cf. 20925 and 20959.

[5] Ib., nn. 20884-5; and 20940, Raynaldus, an. 1274, n. 35.

in the Holy Land, Thomas, patriarch of Jerusalem, to approach Charles of Anjou.[1]

Nor did he neglect the financial side of the undertaking. At the Council of Lyons he induced the bishops to agree to a tax on their revenues of a tenth for six years,[2] and he granted tithes from the Church property in their countries to such sovereigns as agreed to take part in the proposed Crusade ; to King Edward I. of England, and to Charles of Anjou for instance.[3]

But, if the Pope freely granted church money to monarchs for the Crusade, he insisted that they must devote all that money for the purpose for which it was collected.[4] He also, as we see in the case of the bishop of Lismore, took care that others also besides Kings should be made to give up to the proper authorities the money they had collected for the Crusade.[5] He grounded his insistence on the fact that the needs of the Holy Land " required well-nigh endless sums of money ".[6] Still he would have his collectors mindful of the sick and the poor, and so he would not have the tithe levied on hospitals for the poor, nor from religious houses which were in want.[7]

Then with his eye on the details of the warlike expedition which he hoped to see sent against the Saracen, he

[1] Pot., 20534.

[2] Cf. supra, p. 384.

[3] P., n. 21086, Reg., 648, for Edward, and 21082, Reg., 636, Oct. 13, 1275, for Charles. Cf. 21004 and 21079.

[4] Ib., n. 20775. Cf. Reg., 492, and the successive letters to 568 which are mostly addressed to King Philip of France or to his legate Cardinal Simon de Brion of the title of St. Cecily. He gave the latter the most extensive powers. Cf. also Reg., 323-4.

[5] P., n. 20610. Theiner, Mon. Hib., n. 253.

[6] Ib. In England a certain Roger de Leyborne who had received 1,000 silver marks from cardinal Ottoboni for the crusade, but who had simply kept the money, was ordered to refund. Cf. Calendar of Papal Registers, i, p. 444.

[7] " De redditibus et proventibus leprosorum domorum et hospitalium pauperum . . . decima non solvatur," so he wrote to collectors in Germany. P., 20947, Raynaldus, an. 1274, n. 43.

exhorted the Genoese, the Venetians, and other maritime peoples to prepare suitable galleys for the conveying of the Crusaders to Palestine,[1] and on the other hand begged them and the people in such manufacturing centres as Montpellier not to supply the enemy with ships or any implements of war.[2]

(Claimants
to the title
of King of
Jerusalem.)
Gregory also endeavoured to allay the dispute between the claimants to the title of King of Jerusalem lest that should prove a hindrance to his projected Crusade. In 1269 the King of Cyprus, Hugh III., of Lusignan, called the Great, took the title of King of Jerusalem after the death of Conradin, the son of Frederick II., who had had that title. Hugh's claim was, however, challenged by his aunt, Mary of Antioch, granddaughter of Isabella [3] the wife successively of Henry I. and Amaury II. of Lusignan, Kings of Jerusalem. She laid her case before the Holy See.[4] Accordingly, when writing to her (April 13, 1272,) Gregory declared that the title of King of Jerusalem which had been given to Hugh in certain papal letters, was not to be taken as any recognition of his claim to the Kingdom of Jerusalem.[5] He, moreover, commissioned the bishops of Nazareth, Bethlehem, and Paneas (a suffragan of the archbishop of Tyre) to cite Hugh to present his claims before the Apostolic See within nine months.[6]

Mary's contention was that her hereditary title to the crown of Jerusalen was better founded than that of

[1] *Reg.*, n. 356 ff.

[2] P., 20594 ; *Reg.*, 351 ff.

[3] She was the daughter of Amaury I., King of Jerusalem, and her granddaughter was the child of her daughter Melisinda who married Bohemond III., prince of Antioch.

[4] *Cf. Chronique du Templier*, nn. 355, 368–9. Mary " ala outremer requerre son droit devant le pape " in 1269. *Cf.* nn. 375, 398, and 418.

[5] P., n. 20532 ; 20632. Hugh was the son of Isabella, daughter of Hugh I, King of Cyprus, and of Henry, the son of Bohemond IV., Prince of Antioch.

[6] P., n. 20632, Oct. 24, 1272.

Hugh.[1] Sentence was finally pronounced by the Pope
in her favour [2] ; but the princess found that it was one
thing to get a favourable decision and quite another to
get that decision enforced. Accordingly, she sold her
rights to one who was willing, and who at the time
thought himself capable of enforcing them, to the
ambitious Charles of Anjou. This was seemingly under
the pontificate of Innocent V.[3] It is said that this gift
was confirmed by the Pope,[4] and it is certain that in the
year (1276), Charles assumed the title of King of Jerusalem.
But it proved to be a more or less empty title, as the
Sicilian Vespers confined the attentions of Charles to his
own domains ; though, still further to strengthen his
title, he had married Margaret, a granddaughter of John
of Brienne (January 20, 1278), once King of Jerusalem.[5]

However, with all his zeal for a new Crusade, Gregory
was not prepared to sanction any hasty ill-considered
action. He was ready, indeed, to congratulate Philip
of France on his taking up the cross again after his
return from Africa [6] ; but he dissuaded him from

[1] *Chron. du T.*, she " disoit que elle estoil plus prochaine d'un degré
à aver le royaume que le roy Hugue de Chipre n'en estoit ". P. 191,
n. 369.

[2] *Ib.*, p. 198, n. 375, " Elle se douna par le pape et par sa court
coment la dite damoyssele Marie estoit plus droit heir dou royaume."

[3] Saba, *Hist.*, vi, c. 5, *Chron. du T.*, *l.c.*, Röhricht, *Reg. Hierosol.*,
n. 1411 ; *cf.* nn. 1422. The annual payment promised by Charles to
Mary was not always forthcoming ; *cf.* n. 1486.

[4] *Chron. du T.*, *ib.* " Fu confermè par le pape . . . le don que
la dite damoisele Marie avoit fait au roy Charles de son droit." *Cf.*
n. 398, p. 206, and n. 418. *Cf.* M. Camera, *Annali delle due Sicilie*,
vol. i, p. 292, 320, and 324.

[5] Even the counts of Brienne seem to have been wishful to hold
the title of King of Jerusalem, for we find Gregory urging King Charles
to prevent the count of Brienne from invading Cyprus, lest such discords
among Christians should damage the cause of the Crusades. P., 21095,
from Raynaldus, an. 1275, nn. 52–4. This letter was written within
a few weeks of his death.

[6] P., n. 20883, Aug. 1, 1274 ; Raynaldus, 1274, n. 34.

precipitate action,[1] urged the sending of experienced men to study the condition of the Holy Land,[2] and pleaded that only properly equipped soldiers should be employed.[3]

Had Gregory's pontificate been a long one, his single-hearted zeal combined with his knowledge of the state of things in Palestine and his common sense might well, at least for some time, have re-established the Latin Kingdom of Jerusalem.

[1] *Ib.*, n. 20654.
[2] *Ib.*, nn. 20754–5.
[3] *Reg.*, nn. 796, 802–3. Let inquiry be made : " quot regulares et idonei sint bellatores." N. 796.

CHAPTER IV.

THE BRITISH ISLES.

As we might have expected from our knowledge of his Conse- character, Gregory's relations with the British Isles quences of the war for the most part concerned the Crusades. But perhaps between Henry and the Barons. his first acts that regarded our country were concerned with "the Barons' War". Pope Clement IV., when cardinal-bishop of Sabina, had excommunicated Simon de Montfort, and his supporters, and had ordered the bishops to come to him.[1] Among the bishops who had incurred excommunication by not obeying the legate's order, by supporting the barons, and by celebrating the divine offices during the interdict imposed by the legate, were Henry, bishop of London and Stephen, bishop of Chichester. They had, accordingly, somewhat later, been suspended and cited to Rome by Cardinal Ottoboni. Writing to bishop Henry, Gregory stated that, in view of the fact that the bishop had "come to Rome, and shown his humility and devotion", and in view of the petition of Prince Edward, that most gentle and forgiving of men, he dispensed him from irregularity, removed the suspension, and restored him to the exercise of his office both in spirituals and temporals.[2] In treating Stephen for the same reasons in the same way, Gregory expressed a hope that he would in future be true to the King and Prince Edward.[3]

When Gregory expressed that hope, Henry III. was Kilwardby, archbishop of Canterbury. already dead († November 26, 1272) ; but, before that

[1] *Cf. supra.*

[2] Bliss, *Calendar*, i, p. 441 ; *Reg.*, n. 25. Edward "tanquam vir mansuetissimus, injuriarum dicto regi et sibi factarum oblitus ".

[3] Bliss, *ib.*, p. 443 ; *Reg.*, n. 89. Ep. Nov. 26, 1272.

event, he had had other relations with England. On July 18, 1270, had died Boniface of Savoy, archbishop of Canterbury, about whose character so many false things have so often been said, as for instance by the author of the *Annals of St. Paul* who calls him the useless minister of Canterbury.[1] Despite the efforts of Prince Edward who was anxious for the election of his chancellor, Robert Burnell, a better statesman than churchman, the monks of Canterbury elected their prior, Adam of Chillenden, to the vacant dignity. As the royal assent was refused, Adam went to Rome to state his case to the Pope. Understanding that King Henry had sworn " by the piety of God " never to receive Adam into favour, Gregory compromised. He persuaded Adam to resign ; but, instead of Robert Burnell, he himself nominated to the vacant archbishopric, Robert Kilwardby, Provincial of the Dominicans, a learned theologian and writer,[2] and also empowered him to chose his own consecrator. Accordingly, the new archbishop selected William, bishop of Bath, who, says Rishanger,[3] " was distinguished for his sanctity," and who on February 26, 1273, consecrated the first friar who had been elected to the first see in England.

---

[1] Ap. *M. G. SS.*, xxviii, p. 551. It should be noted that the archbishop had had a quarrel with the chapter of St. Paul's.

[2] B. Cotton, *Hist.*, pp. 144–6, 149 f. Adam "in præsentia papæ renunciavit juri suo ". *Cf. Annales of Osney*, and Wykes, pp. 235 f. and 252 f. Ep. Greg., Oct. 11, 1272. " In supremæ." Posse, *Analecta Vatic.*, p. 55. At the Pope's request, Robert compensated the worthy prior for the expenses he had incurred in Rome, adds Mr. Tout in the *Dictionary of National Biography*, sub voce " Kilwardby " quoting *Hist. MSS. Comm.*, 5th Rep., p. 429. The same writer notes that the new archbishop did not take much interest in political affairs, but at the Council of Lyons " upheld the papal power in its strongest forms ". The Dominican author (R. P. Mothon) of the *Vie du B. Innocent V.*, p. 62, notes that, in his regard for the Dominican Order, Gregory named no less than over twenty members of that Order bishops.

[3] *Chron.*, p. 72, *R. S.*

The nomination, however, caused trouble. The King was not pleased that his chancellor was rejected. He accordingly caused a protest against the Pope's provision to be drawn up, and read before the new archbishop and others on the Monday before the feast of St. Lucy,[1] 1272.

When the catholic churches in England, ran the protest, are vacant, they are wont to be provided for by canonical election, made principally by colleges, chapters, etc., after the King's licence has been obtained. When the election has been made, the person elected has to be presented to the King, in order to give him an opportunity of stating if he has any reasonable objection to him. Now it seems prejudicial to the King's rights and those of the Churches if the Pope should assume the power of providing for these churches when no fault has been found with the elect. Wherefore, " in order that the Roman Church shall not proceed to such provisions for the future," it is to be understood that the King is not to be bound in that case to grant the temporalities of any Cathedral Church thus provided.

However, concluded the protest, the King, in the present case, granted the temporalities to archbishop Robert " as a special favour ".[2]

From Gregory's relations with Prince Edward at Acre, one would be justified in expecting that many of his relations with England would be concerned with the Crusades. In fact, his first care, as we have already noted, was to see that Edward and his brother were reimbursed for the expenses they had incurred in the Holy Land, and so he granted them a tenth of all ecclesiastical revenues for two or three years.[3] Unfortu-

---

[1] Her feast occurs on Dec. 13.

[2] *Calendar of Close Rolls*, 1272-9, p. 39.

[3] *Cf. supra*, p. 369. Wykes says for three years, the *Flores* and *Chron. Maiorum*, p. 157, say for two, which would appear

nately, the brothers did not agree as to the amount
of their respective shares. Edward, who had, meanwhile,
become King, would appear to have wanted the lion's
share.[1] Gregory had, accordingly, to try to keep the
peace, and yet see that justice was done. He bade
Edmund talk over with reliable and prudent men what
Master John, the bearer of his letter and one of his old
clerks and friends, would suggest to him, and then
select that course of action which would be most useful,
and yet which would tend to peace. He also wrote to
the Queen-mother, and begged her to use all her influence
to prevent any breach of brotherly love between her
sons. Finally, he urged the King to grant favourable
terms to his brother, and to make it appear that the
portion which he yielded to him was the result of brotherly
love, and not merely of the claims of strict justice.[2] As
Gregory does not again allude to this subject, even when
writing to Edward about the Crusades, we may take it
as certain that his exhortations were listened to, and
that the brothers settled their differences amicably.

ii. Papal
letters to
Edward.

As Edward had had experience of war in Palestine,
Gregory was naturally especially anxious for his advice
and co-operation. He therefore begged him to arrange
his coronation so that he would not be prevented from
attending the General Council [3] ; and, through Gerard
de Roscillon (?), he exhorted him to refrain from any
military expeditions until the Council was over.[4] Then,

to be explained by the Continuator of Florence of Worcester, who
writes that Edward got the grant for one year, and Edmund for another.
Thorpe's ed. of *Florence*, p. 211.

[1] Perhaps not unnaturally as according to a document published by
W. E. Lunt, *The Norwich Valuation*, p. 483, Oxford, 1926, the grant
was made by the Pope: "propter labores et gravia honera quos
sustinuit in terra sancta crucifixi persequendo negotia."

[2] *Cf.* his letters of Nov. 30, 1273, ap. Bliss, *Calendar*, p. 446 f. *Reg.*,
n. 328 ff.

[3] Bliss, *Calendar*, i, p. 446, Dec. 1, 1273.

[4] *Ib.*, p. 620. *Reg.*, n. 816.

after the Council, he sent to the English monarch the archbishop of Tyre [1]; and, in 1275, Gerard de Grandison, formerly his chaplain, then bishop-elect of Verdun, on the business of the Holy Land generally. He was to try to induce Edward to take the cross, and to grant him tithes from England, Ireland, Wales and Scotland, if the Scottish King would agree.[2] No doubt had Gregory lived, his enthusiasm and the respect which Edward had for him would have prevailed, and our King's warlike ambitions would have been directed against the Saracen instead of against the Scot. Meanwhile, however, papal collectors, Raymund de Nogeriis, one of the Pope's chaplains, and the distinguished John of Darlington were sent into England to gather the tenth ordered for the Crusade by the Council of Lyons for six years. Their commission was dated October 21, 1274, and we find them presenting it to Walter Giffard, archbishop of York, on February 1, 1275.[3] To further Gregory's contention that all should either fight or subscribe to the best of their ability,[4] archbishop Giffard commanded, among others, the archdeacon of Cleveland "in virtue of the obedience he owed to us and to the Apostolic See" to see to it that boxes with three keys were placed in the different churches for the collection of the money for the Holy Land.[5] Some of the religions complained that this tax pressed especially hard upon them. They urged that the new collectors, Raymund and John, were not content with the Norwich valuation of their property,

---

[1] Bliss, *ib.*, p. 621 ; *Reg.*, 820, *cf.* 822.

[2] *Reg.*, nn. 842, 945. This letter which concerns the granting of the tithes is dated : " Milan, Nov. 14, 1275." *Cf.* 946, which entrusts " the word of the Cross " to Gerard and is also dated : " Milan, Nov. 17, 1275." *Cf.* nn. 960 and 962.

[3] *Cf.* the *Register of W. G.*, p. 274 ff., ed. Surtees.

[4] *Cf.* the *Contin. of Will. of Newbury*, ii, pp. 568–9, ap. *Chronicles of Stephen, etc.*, R. S.

[5] Ep. of Feb. 16, 1275, ap. *Reg. W. G.*, p. 277.

but insisted that the tax should be levied on its real value, which we are told had been ascertained by cardinal Ottoboni " with, as it were, the eyes of a lynx ".[1] The collectors, they added, also decided that all properties in the hands of religious were to be accounted as " spirituals ", so that on such of their properties as were ordinarily regarded as " temporals ", they had to pay twice over. On them they had to pay taxes to the King, and also the tenth for the crusades.[2]

Money left by Richard of Cornwall to be recovered.Master Raymond was also commissioned by Gregory to recover from his son and heir the eight thousand marks which Richard of Cornwall, King of the Romans, had left in his will for the Holy Land.[3] When they had been recovered, they were to be deposited in the New Temple at London, for, as it has already been pointed out, the Knights Templars at this period often acted as bankers.[4] He was also directed to proceed in a similar manner with regard to moneys left for the same purpose by Boniface of Savoy, the late archbishop of Canterbury, and by John Mansel, a papal chaplain.[5]

Finally, while ordering in the interest of the Crusades that usurers should desist from exacting further interest, and that the hundredth which in the case of certain churches had been remitted should be collected, he bade the bishops proceed in all cases with zeal and prudence.[6]

Scotland and the Saracen tenth.To collect the tithes in Scotland for the Crusade, Gregory appointed a canon of Asti, in Piedmont, a certain

---

[1] Cf. Chron. of Abingdon, p. 58, ed. and trans. of J. O. Halliwell. On the Norwich valuation, cf. W. E. Lunt, The Valuation of N., p. 52 ff.

[2] Cf. Lib. memorandorum de Bernewelle, p. 199.

[3] Bliss, Cal., i, p. 621.

[4] Ib. Cf. Delisle, Opera . financ. des Temp., p. 100 ; cf. pp. 112–14 ff.

[5] Bliss, ib., p. 444. In one of his letters (ib., p. 447) about the will of Boniface, Gregory tells his correspondent not to be surprised if the leaden bulla attached to his letter does not bear his name. It was sent before his consecration.

[6] Bliss, ib., p. 449.

Baiamund de Vitia, allowing him three shillings a day for his expenses. He was to employ deputy collectors who were to take an oath to collect and pay over what was due.[1] There was much dissatisfaction in Scotland also when it was announced that payment had to be made not on the old valuation, but according to the " real value " of the benefices. A council was therefore assembled at Perth (August, 1275), and it was decided that the nuncio should return to the Pope and request him to accept the existing valuation, and to spread the contributions over seven years instead of six. The old Scottish chronicler tells us that nothing except extra expense to the clergy came of the journey of Master Baiamund, for, he adds, " the procurations of legates are wont to be sumptuous." [2] On his return, he revalued the benefices, and the result of his work, known as Baiamund's Roll, served as " the guide in matters of Scottish ecclesiastical taxation until the Reformation ".[3] From a document in Theiner,[4] we learn that in two years the new valuation yielded £7,195, 6 florins and 6 pence sterling.

While looking after the money for the Crusade to be raised in the British Isles,[5] Gregory could not afford to forget the Peter's Pence that was due to him from England. He accordingly addressed a letter (April 22, 1273) to the archbishops of Canterbury and York and their suffragans in which " from the register of the Apostolic See " he sent them a list of the sums due from each diocese. The

Peter's Pence.

---

[1] Ep. Sept. 20, 1274, ap. Bliss, *ib.*, p. 449. In full in Theiner, *Mon. Hib.*, p. 104.

[2] Fordun, *Scotichronicon*, x, c. 35.

[3] Bellesheim, *Hist. of the Church of Scot.*, i, p. 368.

[4] *L.c.*, p. 109 ff. *Cf.* Dowden, *The medieval church in Scotland*, pp. 322–3. With the document in T. *cf.* the fragment in *Concilia Scotiæ*, i, p. ccciv f., ed. Bannatyne Club, 1866.

[5] In Ireland it was the bishop of Clonfert, who was appointed to collect the Holy Land tenth. Bliss, *ib.*, p. 449.

total sum works out at about £193 ; but at the end of his letter [1] the Pope gives it as £200 " di. marc." He would appear to be giving a round number, and to be making the mark equal to a pound. The amount which Master Raymund actually collected as " yearly Peter's Pence in England " and paid over to the merchant banker firm of " Perrachius de Scovaloco and Raynald de Molendinis " of Piacenza was 1,160 marks, 7s. 8d.[2]

Privilege for the abbey of Cockersand. To bring to a conclusion our notice of Gregory's dealings with England, we will quote one of his bulls cited neither by Bliss nor Potthast nor in Gregory's Register. It will serve to show the sort of questions he was called upon to decide in the course of his ordinary government of the Church in England. The Canons of the abbey of Cockersand, situated at the mouth of the Lune in Lancashire, had complained that in law suits they were often cited to places at a great distance from their home. They appealed to Gregory to put a stop to this. His reply took the form of the following bull. " Gregory, bishop, servant of the servants of God, to our beloved sons the abbot and convent of the monastery of Cockersand, of the Premonstratention Order in the diocese of York, health and apostolic benediction. Albeit we willingly show favour to those who seek it, it behoves us to bestow grace and kindness upon those who religiously renounce not only their possessions but themselves, shutting themselves up in the camps of the cloister, and crucifying their flesh with the vices and lusts thereof; so that even as the more peacefully, so the more devotedly they

---

[1] Ap. *Chronicles of Edw. I. and II.*, i, p. xliv, *R. S.* It is also inserted in the Register of Archbishop John le Romeyn, vol. ii, p. 177, Surtees Soc.

[2] Bliss, *l.c.*, p. 447. Grimaldi notes, from a book of offerings made at the confession of St. Peter's, that in 1285 the 200 " lire di sterlini " of the English Peter's Pence was worth 200 pounds of silver. See his *Brevis declaratio valoris aliquarum monetarum*, in *Cod. Barb. Lat.*, n. 2733, p. 500 ff.

may serve the Lord, and enrich themselves by the merit of a holy life and others by their example. When, therefore, as has been set forth upon your part before us, some clergy as well as laity, not so much bent on the execution of justice as to proceed injuriously against you, do maliciously cause you to be summoned from your monastery by apostolic letters, beyond the space of two or more days' journeys, whereby, wearied by travail and charges ye may be compelled either to yield or to submit to exorbitant terms.

"Desiring as far as we can by God's help, to provide for your peace, we grant you by authority of these presents, that in future you may not be dragged from your monastery into law suits by Letters obtained from the Apostolic See, beyond two days' journey upon the things contained therein, unless the said Letters shall make full and express mention of the present Indult. It shall in no wise, therefore, be permitted to any man, etc.

"Given at Lyons, on the Nones of June in the third year of our pontificate." (June 5, 1274.) [1]

While it is impossible for us to follow Gregory into all the countries into which his influence penetrated, we may follow him to Norway as in his time a controversy between the Church and State that had endured for some time reached an important stage. In 1263 there had ascended the throne of Norway Magnus VI., known by the honourable title of *Lagabeter* or Law-mender, and five years later the metropolitan see of Nidaros was filled by John *Raude*, or the Red, who had been consecrated in Rome (1268). To settle the differences between the Church and State, the King called to him at Bergen chief men of the Kingdom, while the archbishop summoned a Provincial Synod to assemble at the same place (1273).[2] At length,

Church and State in Norway.

---

[1] *The Chartulary of Cockersand Abbey*, ed. W. Farrer, i, p. 1898. Printed for the Chetham Soc., Manchester.

[2] "Magnus rex atque Johannes archiep. in conventu Frostensi

" an amicable arrangement very favourable to the claims
of the Church " [1] was arrived at, and sent to Gregory
to receive his confirmation.   This latter fact we know
from a letter of the King to the Pope dated Bergen,
August 15, 1273.   It informed the Pope that, in the
" amicable arrangement " come to between the King and
the Archbishop and sent to the Pope for his confirmation,
a clause had been omitted.   It was to the effect that
clerics who did not hold " regalia " were not to be bound
to contribute to the King's warlike expeditions or accompany him upon them unless in cases of dire necessity,
to be recognized as such by the ecclesiastical authority.
The King begs the Pope to confirm this newly dispatched clause along with the others.[2]

It has been said that, in giving his approval to the
" amicable arrangement ", Gregory added " some new
clauses which included the offering of the King's crown
on the altar at Nidaros, and the giving over to the Church
(in the case of a minority of the Crown) the government
of the country ".[3]

To clear up the mistakes involved in this statement,
we must turn to the official documents in Norway's
collection of them.   For some years, as we have said,
there had been trouble between the Church and State in
Norway.   The former, through its archbishop John, maintained that the rights of his Church were often interfered

aderant," an. 1269.   *Cf. Annales Islandici*, p. 139.   In 1271, *ib.*, p. 141,
the two had several more meetings, and from a fragment of the lost
Saga of King Magnus we learn that in 1273 " there had come to Bergen
archbishop John and all the suffragan bishops who were in the land ".
P. 380, ap. *Icelandic Sagas*, vol. iv, *R. S.*   It was only at this last
meeting that the " amicable arrangement " was finally reached.

    [1] Willson, *History of the Church and State in Norway*, p. 212.

    [2] " Supplicantes quantinus ipsum (articulum) una cum aliis in
littera vestre confirmationis nominatis, et specialiter exprimatis."
Ap. C. Lange, *Diplomatarium Norvegicum*, i, 57, Christiania, 1849,
or ap. J. Sigurdsson, *Diplom. Island.*, ii, 107.

    [3] Willson, *l.c.*, p. 212.

with by the King's officers, and the King maintained that the Church was encroaching on his royal rights. When Innocent IV. sent a legate, cardinal William of Sabina, to Norway, we saw that he did not approve of the Norwegian bishops' claim in reference to elections to the throne.[1] Despite this disapproval, archbishop John continued to press these claims. He declared that it had been decreed by a King of Norway that its Kings " ought to be elected, and that the archbishop and bishops ought to have the principal voice in the election ", and that each new King should offer his crown in the Cathedral as a sign of subjection to the see of Nidaros.[2]

After a number of conferences, a partial agreement, at least, was come to at Bergen on August 1, 1273. By it the bishops had to give up any interference with hereditary right in the matter of succession to the throne. But, if no royal heir was forthcoming, the bishops were to have the first and most weighty voice in the election of the new King.

In this convention, Magnus undertook also not to interfere with the recognized ecclesiastical privileges, and granted many favours to the archbishop. He was, for instance, to have the right to send corn to Iceland, and to get the dues of one ship coming thence to his diocese.

When the King sent this " amicable composition " to Pope Gregory, he begged him to confirm it.[3] This Gregory duly did by a bull of July 25 or 26, 1274, beginning " Cum a nobis petitur ",[4] and including the Bergen settlement.[5]

Despite this settlement, the strained relations between the Church and State in Norway were, it appears, not

The Tonsberg Concordat, 1277.

---

[1] *Supra*, vol. xiv, 85.

[2] See these contentions set forth in a document of Aug. 1 (St. Peter's chains), 1273, ap. *Diplomatarium Norveg.*, i, n. 64 *a.*, p. 52 ff.

[3] Ep. of Aug. 15, 1273, ap. *ib.*, n. 64 *b*.

[4] *Ib.*, n. 65, p. 58.

[5] Ap. Raynaldus, ann. 1273, nn. 19 and 20.

settled till 1277, when the " Tonsberg Concordat " was
accepted by both parties. This more or less reaffirmed
the " amicable arrangements ". The clergy were to be
exempt from lay jurisdiction, offences against the Canon
Law had to come before the ecclesiastical courts,
ecclesiastical elections were to be free, and the bishops
were to be allowed various civil privileges such as the
right of coining money, an armed escort, etc.[1]

Sweden. Valdemar I.

Gregory's attention was called to the sister kingdom
as well by difficulties between the Church and State,
as by the troubled condition of the country under King
Valdemar I. (1266–76). This condition was brought
about by the immoral life of Valdemar, by the ambitious
usurpations of his brothers, and by the attacks of
adjoining heathen tribes. As the difficulties between the
Church and State appear to have been merely spasmodic,
forceful usurpations by individual nobles, Gregory
addressed a letter to the leading men of Sweden (August 9,
1274) exhorting them to cease interfering with the rights
of the Church, whether such interference originated by
their own acts or by those of their subordinates.[2] Then,
to deal with pagan aggressions, at the request of Valdemar,
he exhorted Fulk whom he had appointed to the archi-
episcopal see of Upsala [3] to preach a crusade against
the Carelians and other barbarous pagans who were
harassing the country, reminding him of a similar message
of Pope Alexander IV.[4] He also forbade any Swede under
pain of excommunication supplying any kind of munitions
of war to the pagans.[5]

But it was not only pagan foes that brought trouble to

---

[1] *Cf.* Willson, *ib.*, p. 213 f., Dunham, *Hist. of Denmark, etc.*, ii, p. 290.
K. Gjerset's account of these transactions, *Hist. of the Norweg. People*,
i, pp. 458–9, is not accurate.

[2] Pot., n. 20893, citing the *Bullarium* of Celsius, n. 12.

[3] *Ib.*, 20897. *Cf.* 20899 and 20900. Aug. 1718, 1274.

[4] *Ib.*, 20898. *Cf.* 20984.

[5] *Ib.*, 20983.

Sweden. The chief cause was the loose life of its King. In 1273 there came to his court Jutta, a nun who had left her cloister, the sister of his wife Sophia. " Fair as an angel from heaven " was she said to have been,[1] and her charms proved too strong for the King's virtue. His conduct caused the greatest scandal, and brought on him the censures of the Church. He had, in pursuance of the penance imposed upon him for his crime, to present himself before the Pope ; and it is believed that it was on that occasion that he induced the Pope to intervene on his behalf against his younger brother Magnus. This Prince, a man in every way superior to Valdemar, had been named regent during the King's absence, and appears to have aimed at the throne. Gregory, accordingly, wrote to archbishop Fulk and to Henry, bishop of Linköping, to say that Valdemar had told him that " certain children of iniquity " had set up a rival to his crown, and that in consequence great troubles had arisen among his subjects. Seeing, then, that the King recognized no superior except the Roman Pontiff, and that his Kingdom is tributary to the Roman Church,[2] the Pope bade the bishops see to it that no such attempt was made again.[3] But Valdemar was a man whom it was impossible to help. Magnus ultimately seized the Kingdom, and Valdemar ended his days in exile in Denmark.[4]

Although Gregory passed a very short time in Rome, Rome. he had to occupy himself with certain questions that i. The Tiber.

[1] In the *Rhyme* or Eric's Chronicle (1229–1319) ap. *Script. rer. Suecicarum*, i, pt. 2.

[2] Each house in Sweden paid its " penny " to the Holy See. " Notandum autem quod singule domus Suetie singulos dant denarios monete ipsius terræ." *Lib. Cens.*, i, 229, ed. Fabre.

[3] Ep. Jan. 9, 1275, Pot., n. 20982.

[4] *Annal. Dano-Suecanis*, p. 140, ed. Jorgensen, Copenhagen, 1920. *Cf.* Geijer, *Hist. of the Swedes*, p. 49 f., and Martin, " L'église et l'État en Suède," ap. *Rev. des Quest. Hist.*, 1905, pp. 66–8.

concerned the city. From the first look at an inscription quoted by Gregorovius, one might suppose that he would have had to deal with the difficulties that always followed a great overflow of the Tiber. That historian's version of the inscription [1] would go to show that a flood took place on November 5, 1275. But the year 1275 was not the sixth indiction nor was the Roman See vacant at that time, as the inscription states it was. The true date was evidently November 5, 1277, which was the sixth indiction, and the Roman See was then vacant. This conclusion is made certain by the statement of various chroniclers, e.g., Geoffrey de Courlon, who tells us that, shortly before the promotion of Nicholas III.,[2] there was a great overflow of the Tiber, and that the water stood " four feet above the altar of St. Mary the Round " (the Pantheon). Besides the inscription is given correctly by Forcella, and supported by another in the Church of St. Maria Traspontina.[3]

ii. Monte Testaccio, 1274.

But if the Tiber brought up no Roman question for settlement, other parts of the city did. Gregory had to deal with the annual games on Monte Testaccio, " the hill of potsherds." On that curious accumulation of broken amphoræ and terra-cotta jars which was formed between the Aventine and the river, and about the end of the second century, ultimately rose to about the height of at least one hundred and fifty feet [4]—on and about this

---

[1] " Huc Tiber accessit set turbidus hinc cito cessit A.D. M cclxxv, Ind. vi. M. Nov. die v. Eccla vacante." He found the marble tablet bearing the above inscription " built into the wall of an arched gateway in *Banchi di S. Spirito* ". *Rome*, v, pt. i, p. 154. But the historian copied it wrongly.

[2] He was elected Nov. 25, 1277.

[3] *Cf.* Forcella, *Iscrizioni di Roma*, vol. xiii, pp. 209–10. The inscription in S. Maria T. runs : " An. D. M cclxxvii. Sede apostolica vacante Mense Novembri die V." Etc.

[4] *Cf.* Lanciani, *Ancient Rome*, p. 251 ff., and the *Ruins of Ancient Rome*, p. 532.

hill, games of a rough kind were celebrated throughout
the Middle Ages, though in 1539 they were held in the
Piazza of St. Peter's to please Pope Paul III.[1] If, at these
games, in Gregory's pontificate, took place the scenes
which occurred in 1404 and which are described by a
British eyewitness, Adam de Usk, we need not wonder
that Gregory interfered to some extent with regard to
them. Adam besides giving some description of the games
adds : " In the same games, too, the Romans run riot
like brute beasts in drunkenness (the feast of misery),
with unbridled extravagance like the sons of Belial
and Belphegor." [2] Supposing the players to have acted
in that manner in 1274, we can understand why Gregory
issued an order that the dole of bread, meat and wine
which used to be given every year in the Pope's palace
about eventide in the season of Carnival should be
given to them no more.[3] He had moreover previously
(July 22, 1272) forbidden men from Terracina, Piperno
and other places being forced to attend the said games.[4]

Gregory's attention, either by his own observation iii. St.
or by that of others, had been called to the fact that all Peter's.
was not well with the church of St. Peter's. It does not,
however, appear to be generally known to the authors
of the story of the old and new St. Peter's that our
Pope ordered a commission to inquire into the condition
of the fabric. Fortunately, however, a document has
been preserved in a manuscript of the *Liber Censuum*

---

[1] V. Forcella, *Feste sotto Paolo III.*, p. 8, Rome, 1885.

[2] *Chron.*, pp. 92 and 221 f.

[3] Pot., n. 23808.

[4] Ep. to Cantelm, the Vicar of the City, ap. Vitale, *Storia de'Senatori*,
i, p. 150. " Ut certam comitivam hominum, ad Urbem transmitterent,
causa Ludi, de Testaccio vulgariter nuncupati, qui in dicta Urbi
annis singulis exercetur." See also F. Clementi, *Il carnevale Romano*,
p. 30 ff., Rome, 1899. This author, from the *Liber Censuum*, says
p. 28, by mistake that Gregory gave the dole instead of taking it
away altogether from the *ribaldi*.

giving the report which Albert of Parma, canon of
St. Peter's, and of James Gili, citizen of Rome drew up
on the subject for Gregory. They set forth that, in
accordance with the Pope's orders, they had assembled the
master workmen and many others to discuss the repairs
that had to be made to the basilica of St. Peter's. The
master-workmen had declared, as they had already stated
in the Pope's presence, that *euscentri* (girders ?) could
be used to support the Church, but that, as they had
found that the side-walls were much out of plumb and
even cracked, it would be better to rebuild them altogether,
especially as the *euscentri* would cost as much as the new
walls.[1] The two delegates concluded their report by
saying that they had verified the accuracy of the masters'
assertions, and, as the matter is urgent and many things
necessary for the repairs had already been got together,
they begged the Pope to decide what had to be done
as soon as possible. It does not appear to be known
what decision Gregory came to on this matter. It may
be that death prevented him from coming to any conclusion with regard to it, and that the walls continued
to get more and more out of plumb and cracked till
Julius II. and his successors were compelled to demolish
the basilica entirely.[2]

Care of
ecclesiastical
property.

With his practical ability, we are not surprised to
find that Gregory contrived to find some time to devote
to the care of the States of the Church. In the first year
of his pontificate, he commissioned Guido de Zena, a
canon of Mantua to find out the fiefs and other rights of

---

[1] " Salvis expensis tecti et trabium ecclesiæ quas quasi extimabant
tantumdem." *Lib. Cens.*, i, p. 589, ed. Fabre. In 1284 we read of a
collapse of the baldachino of St. Peter's, but that perhaps had nothing
to do with the bad state of the outer walls. John de Oxnead, *Chron.*,
p. 241.

[2] Charles of Anjou also took care of St. Peter's, as he placed under
his own protection the property which that basillica possessed in his
realm. *Cf. Cod. diplom. Sulmonese*, ed. Faraglia, p. 79.

the Holy See which had been wrongfully alienated in
the March of Ancona, the Duchy of Spoleto, the county
of Campania, the city of Benevento, and the Patrimony
of St. Peter in Tuscany, and to refer the cases to the
respective Rectors of those districts.[1] Further, he
renewed (November 18, 1272) the penalties which his
predecessor had inflicted on the people of Pisa, for their
aggressions in Sardinia, and he ordered them to evacuate
the island within three months, especially the " judicatus "
of Torre, and the district of Sassari. Moreover, if they had
not made full satisfaction by the following festival
of the Purification, he threatened to deprive the city of
its bishop, and so of its rank of a city.[2] Further, in all
this connexion, he reiterated the doctrine that it required
one hundred years to establish prescription against the
rights and property of the Roman Church.[3]

But if he was watchful over the material interests of Care of
the Church, he was also watchful over the material interests the poor.
of the poor whom he benefited by its resources. He
instructed a number of clergy to distribute among the
sick and poor even of Pisa, the sum of one thousand
marks which was due to the Holy See from its citizens.[4]
He strove also to protect the poor from the oppression
of the powerful.[5] Poor professors at the Universities
also came in for a share of his protection.[6] And here
we may note that, whether he was or was not learned himself, he took an interest in learning; and he urged Charles

[1] Theiner, *Cod. Diplom.*, i, 176. *Cf.* Pot., n. 20557.

[2] Potth., n. 20642.

[3] *Ib.*, n. 20687.

[4] *Ib.*, n. 20855, or Ripoll, *Bullar. O. P.*, i, 519. The Pope's agents
were to give also to those who were ashamed to beg, and to provide
dowries to enable girls to marry: " pauperibus puellis maritandis."

[5] He asks for information regarding injury said to have been done
by the Knights Hospitallers against a widow. *Cf.* J. D. le Roulx, *Les
Archives de l'Ordre de S. J. de Jerusalem*, p. 202.

[6] Potth., nn. 20980-1 ; *Reg.*, n. 467.

of Anjou to reform the studies in his Kingdom, especially in the city of Naples " the charm of which city used to attract students from the remotest parts ".[1]

Gregory also interested himself in behalf of the Jews who, perhaps generally through their own fault, were constantly in trouble. He ordered that the letter which Innocent IV. had directed to the hierarchy of Germany in their favour, and which had now from age begun to perish, should be recopied word for word.[2] Moreover he issued an encyclical to all Christians forbidding them to baptize Jews by force or to injure their persons, or to take away their money, or to disturb them during the celebration of their religious festivals.[3]

Character of Gregory.

Unhappily for Europe, and for the Christians in Palestine especially, this wise and practical Pontiff, so careful,[4] such a lover of peace, so ardent a champion of Christendom, so charitable,[5] whose great aim was to promote the happiness and joy (jocunditas) of mankind, had but a short reign.[6]

It may be that he was anything but a learned man. Ptolemy of Lucca says that he had but a slight acquaintance with literature,[7] and Henry of Isernia, the Bohemian

---

[1] *Ib.*, n. 21096.

[2] *Ib.*, n. 20861.

[3] *Ib.*, 20915.

[4] As a further instance of the care which he bestowed on the questions which came before him, we may note how he refused to confirm without thorough examination the treaty of peace between Stephen, King of Hungary, and Ottocar, King of Bohemia. Pot., 20526. When he had had time to examine "its difficult articles", he did confirm it (May 5, 1272), *ib.*, n. 20542 ; Theiner, *Mon. Hung.*, i, nn. 529, 530, 531, and endeavoured to secure that it should be observed, Pot., n. 20612–14, 20776 ; Theiner, *ib.*, n. 534 ff.

[5] The Dominican inquisitors were ordered to exercise their office "in the charity of God ". Pot., 20720 ; Ripoll, *Bullar.*, p. 512.

[6] He worked for peace in Italy in order that the plague of war might be removed, " desiderabilis sit in eisdem terris proventura jocunditas." *Reg.*, n. 35.

[7] " Modicæ literaturæ." *Hist.*, xxiii, c. 4.

notary of Ottocar II., goes so far as to say that he was completely wanting in knowledge and culture generally.[1] But what he lacked in the knowledge of books, he more than made up for in his knowledge of men and things. This was the cause of the phenomenal success of his brief pontificate, and for this is he praised by ancient and modern authors alike. The burden of contemporary authors is that he was a man of remarkable insight in temporal affairs, and had no care for money.[2] In his knowledge of men and things we may perhaps allow with Saba Malaspina that he had somewhat too much faith in Charles of Anjou. However, we may sum up the estimates of him by his contemporaries by saying that he lived an exceptionally good and holy life, and that after his death God honoured his servant by working miracles at his tomb. But we have to wait for the days of Benedict XIV. for the assertion that it was Innocent V. who on

---

[1] "Personam tam totius expertem scientie, quam omni penitus urbanitate carentem." *Cod. epist. Ottocar.*, ed. Dolliner, n. 30. The author is no doubt guilty of some exaggeration, as his point is to contrast any of the "wise cardinals" who might have been elected with the man who was elected.

[2] "Hic P. mire experientie in secularibus, non intendebat pecuniarum lucris sed pauperum elemosinis." *Contin. Sublas.*, p. 500, ed. Pertz. *Cf. Chron. Ang. Petriburg.*, p. 149, ed. Giles ; Geof. de Courlon, *Chron.*, an. 1270 ; *Gesta abb. Trud.*, contin. iii, note that one of his fellow canons of Liège, one Henry, the son of count Gelrié, once boxed his ears, and was rewarded by receiving a paternal letter from him when Pope. Ap. *M. G. SS.*, x, p. 403. Saba, v, 8, he is most eulogistic (see his joke on the Pope's name Theobald) ; even that mordant gossip Salimbene, *Chron.*, pp. 488, 491 ff., is full of praise of Gregory ; on p. 492 f. he gives many contemporary verses in praise of him :

Patris de celis   Servus bonus atque fidelis.
Huic salvandarum.   Zelus vehemens animarum

etc. His anonymous biographer gives a detailed list of miracles worked at his tomb, and of his virtues—pointing out, for instance, how his love for the poor led him to wash the feet of some of them every day. Ap. *R. I. SS.*, iii, pt. i, pp. 603–5.

account of those miracles placed him among the beatified.[1]

It only remains to add that the praises of Gregory, unanimously sung by his contemporaries, have been equally unanimously repeated by writers of our own days.[2]

Death of
Gregory X.

It had been the intention of Gregory, as we have seen, to continue his journey towards " the country of the Patrimony ", after he had celebrated the festival of Christmas at Arezzo. But, falling ill there of a fever, he was called by God " from the valley of this present misery to the heavenly country (January 10, 1276) "; nor, continues his biographer, is it without mystery that he died in the bishop's palace which is close to the Church of St. Gregory, and in which is a chapel dedicated to the same saint.[3]

His tomb.

Speaking of the painter, sculptor, and architect, Margaritone of Arezzo, Vasari [4] says that he returned to

---

[1] De canoniz. SS., Lib. i, c. 20, n. 17, cited by P. Piacenza, Vita Greg., p. 140.

[2] We shall content ourselves with citing one. " A glorious pontific. was that of Gregory X. Italy was almost entirely pacified by his impartial spirit, at a time when the madness of civil feuds seemed to destroy all hope of repose; the interregnum of the empire was terminated by the election of a prince who covered himself with glory and who founded one of the most powerful dynasties of Europe. The Greek was reconciled to the Latin Church, and the quarrel between the Franks and the Greeks for the empire of the East was appeased by a wise and just accommodation. An œcumenical council (the second of Lyons), at which 500 bishops, 70 mitred abbots, a 1,000 theologians and representations of religious orders assisted, was presided over by this pontiff, and promulgated a code of laws useful to Christianity, and worthy of an assemblage so august." Sismondi, Hist. des Répub. Ital., t. iii, p. 422.

[3] Ap. R. I. SS., t. iii, pt. i, p. 603; Saba, vi, 5. The Church of St. Gregory no longer exists. One or two anonymous chroniclers writing at a distance from Arezzo say that Gregory died by poison. Cf. Ann. Austriæ, ap. M. G. SS., ix, p. 706; and Gilbert Chron. contin., ap. M. G. SS., xxiv, p. 140.

[4] Le Opere di G. Vasari, i, p. 363, ed. Milanesi, or in the English : The Temple Vasari, i, p. 68.

his native place " in the suite of Pope Gregory who passed through Florence on his journey from (Lyons and) Avignon to Rome (1275). Here an opportunity presented itself to make himself better known ; for the Pope died at Arezzo, after having given 30,000 scudi to the Commune wherewith to finish the building of the Cathedral (vescovado) which had been begun by Master Lapo, and had made but little progress. The Aretines therefore ordained that the chapel of St. Gregory in the Vescovado [1] should be made in memory of Gregory X., and that Margaritone should make a marble tomb for that Pope . . . He set to work upon the task, and brought it to such a successful completion, introducing the Pope's portrait from life both in marble and in painting, that it was considered to be the best work which he had ever produced ". Because it is Vasari who has ascribed the tomb of Gregory to Margaritone, some at once call the accuracy of the statement in question. But as nothing conclusive has been urged against Vasari's ascription, it is best to suppose that he knew something of the story of his native town, and that Margaritone was indeed the sculptor of the beautiful tomb of Gregory X. which is one of the glories of the cathedral at Arezzo.[2] At any rate,

[1] Margaritone afterwards placed therein a portrait of the Pope. *Ib.*

[2] Hence A. del Vita, *Il duomo d'Arezzo*, p. 26, would assign it, if not to Margaritone, at least to another local artist. " E se ci si basò forse sulla tradizione, assegnandola a Margaritone . . . non è fuor di luogo crederla di un artista locale." Balcarres, *The evolution* of *Italian Sculpture*, p. 191, regards this tomb as one of the " weak variations " of the tomb of Cardinal de Braye († 1280) at Orvieto. If, however, as some say, the tomb of Gregory was finished in 1277, another description of it relative to the tomb of de Braye would have to be found. Guglielmino degli Ubertini, bishop of Arezzo, writing on Nov. 9, 1277, and speaking of Gregory X., says : " cujus sepultura ecclesia ipsa meruit decorari." Ep. quoted by Del Vita, p. 13, from the Archivio Communale, n. 16. Certainly these words seem to imply a finished sepulchral monument. But the context would seem to show that the bishop, in urging on the completion of his cathedral, simply wished to point out that it was honoured by containing the body of the late Pope. See C. Lazzeri, *Guglielmino Ubertini*, p. 194 ff., Florence, 1920.

by whomever made, the tomb is justly admired by all,[1] though, previously perhaps to 1810 when it was moved from one part of the cathedral to another, it would appear to have been better proportioned. For it seems that at one time the canopy over the sarcophagus must have been somewhat higher,[2] as underneath it there was the fresco which showed the portrait of the Pope.[3] However that may have been, now at least, to use the description of Lord Lindsay : " the Pope slumbers on his sarcophagus, elevated on three pillars, the whole overshadowed by a Gothic arched canopy supported by two lateral columns topped with pinnacles. . . . The effigy is excellent, the drapery good, the sculptures on the sarcophagus representing (in medallions shaped like the vesica piscis), the lamb carrying the cross, between four Apostles, half figures, precisely in the style of the Greek mosaics, at once remind one of Margaritone's original Byzantine prepossessions, and show how he had emancipated himself from the rigidity and formalism of his earlier style." [4]

His tomb is not the only place in the cathedral where the figure of Gregory X. may be seen. In ruder style, standing erect, holding a book in its hands, another figure of him may be seen at the back of the old stone altar above

---

[1] Lord Lindsay, *Sketches of the hist. of Christian Art*, ii, p. 116, ed. 1847, regards it as " a work of such excellence, that remembering his (Margaritone's) productions in painting, it would be difficult to credit him with such an offspring, were not the paternity indisputable." Still, Venturi, *Storia dell' Arte*, iv, 392, assigns it to Agostino and Agnolo.

[2] Del Vita, *l.c.*, p. 24.

[3] Almost every trace of this fresco has disappeared. *Cf.* Milanesi, n. 4, *l.c.*

[4] Formerly there were to be read the following Leonine verses on Gregory's tomb :—

" Gregorius denus, virtutum luce serenus—
    Dormit in hac arca, dignus Romæ patriarca,
    Quem genuit Placentia, urbs Arretina tenet."

Cited by C. Lazzeri, *Guglielmino degli Ubertini*, p. 186, from Mariani, *Diario*, MS. Riccardiana, 3169.

which was erected the glorious marble one known as the
"arca di S. Donato". Vasari in his life of Giovanni
Pisano attributes the said *arca* to that artist; for, he
says, bishop Guglielmino Ubertini, brought Giovanni
from Siena to Arezzo in 1286. "He there executed in
marble the table of the high altar full of figures cut in
relief, of leaves and other ornaments, dividing the work
into compartments by fine mosaics and enamels on silver
plates, fixed into the marble with great care." Our Lady
is in the centre, and on her right is S. Donato, the bishop
and protector of the city, and on her left Pope Gregory,
who holds a book in his hand on which are painted
certain Gothic letters which "with a little good will"
can be deciphered to stand for "Greg. P. P. X."[1] It
would, however, seem certain from the studies of recent
critics[2] that many artists besides G. Pisano laboured
at the altar. The work of completing it dragged on
even to the year 1375. The fine half-figure of Gregory
X. was certainly not made till the fourteenth century,
as the fact that the head is crowned with a tiara with
three crowns proves conclusively. Lastly that the
Cathedral might easily be known to all as the memorial
of Gregory X.,[3] his features were displayed in the figure
of St. Gregory I. which stands in the lunette above its
side door.[4]

[1] Del Vita, *l.c.*, p. 27, n. 1, says that the letters were deciphered by
Pasqui, and "che con un po' di buona volontà vi si puo leggere, etc."

[2] *Cf.* A. Venturi, *Storia dell' Arte Ital.*, iv, 392, and especially Del
Vita on Venturi, *l.c.*, p. 26 ff.

[3] Bishop Guglielmino Ubertini decreed in 1277 that the new cathedral
was to be built "ad honorem Dei, beatæ Virginus et beati Donati
patroni, obtentuque sancte recordationis Gregorii P. X." *Archiv.
Capit.*, n. 720, ap. Lazzeri, p. 195.

[4] See the illustrations in Del Vita, figs. 57 and 59. The actual coffin
in which the body of Gregory was preserved has been renewed more
than once. It was only in 1830 that it was placed in an urn of silver.
Cf. Piacenza, pp. 141-2 n.

APPENDIX

From a Manuscript in Monte Cassino

Cod. 21, Sec. xiii, f. 163 v. Forse autografo. See p. 337.

Quinta feria xix Cal. Septembris dominus Vincentius archiepiscopus Turonensis sic proposuit in Collegio : " Dicit Apostolus prima ad Corinth. xiv, ' Volo quoque verba sensu meo loqui.' " Quod dixit Apostolus dico et ego. Non intendo vos instruere nec docere Minervam. Sapientes enim, estis et eruditione mea non indigetis. Urget me, tamen, conscientia mea ut dicam vobis pauca verba, quinque scilicet ; et certe verba amara et mala quæ dicuntur de vobis eo quod tenetis ecclesiam Romanam sine capite, et non providetis ei. Ista verba sunt ; infidelitas et scandalum, malum exemplum, damnum multiplex, rancor sive odium. Infidelitas. Ex hoc enim quod ecclesia caret pastore, hæresis et infidelitas augentur, quia non est qui contra errores se opponat. Solius enim Papæ est diffinire quid credendum, quid non credendum, et damnandum errores. Quocunque vero scandalum sit ex ista vacatione vos novistis ad plenum, quia non tantumodo minores et mediocres, sed majores scandalizantur, et verificatur quod Dominus dixit : " Væ mundo a scandalis," et scitis quod dixerit, " qui scandalizaverit unum ex pusillis istis, expedit ei ut suspendatur mola asinaria ad collum ejus, et submergatur in profundum. Si hoc dixit Dominus de illo qui scandalizat unum ex pusillis illis, quid dicturus erat de illo et de illis qui scandalizant infinita millia, et pusillorum et mediocrum, et majorum ? Tertium verbum est malum exemplum, quod præstatis aliis ecclesiis, exemplum discordiæ, exemplum negligentiæ. Jam enim habent

scutum excusandi se, si discordent in electionibus suis,
et si negligenter agant in providendo eis. Quartum
verbum dampnum quod ex hac vacatione provenit
ecclesiis viduatis, quia non habent defensores contra
illos qui occupant jura eorum, nec habent qui ministrent
spiritualia, et ideo magnum dampnum patiantur et in
temporalibus et in spiritualibus. Quintum verbum est
rancor, seu odium, quia vix potest esse quod talia
tractentur quin inde odia oriantur : Iis dictis, flexis
genibus, et cum lacrymis, dictus archiepiscopus adjuravit
cardinales, et rogavit eos humiliter et devote, ut essent
intenti et solliciti ecclesiæ providere, et quod amplius
non expectarent.

Tunc episcopus Tusculanus [1] respondet in hunc modum
pro toto collegio : " Domine archiepiscope, vos sicut
vir discretus et zelans ecclesiam Dei et salutem animarum,
proposuistis quinque verba prædicta ad instar Apostoli,
sed nos possumus assumere verba quæ immediate sub-
junguntur ab Apostolo. Postquam enim dixerat, ' volo
quinque verba sensu meo loqui,' [2] subjungit, ' ut et
alios instruam quam decem millia verborum in lingua.
Vos dixistis quinque verba quæ dicuntur contra nos
propter vacationem istam, et nos possumus vere dicere
quod non tantum quinque verba dicuntur contra nos
imo decem millia et plusquam decies centena millia
dicuntur et possunt dici contra nos, quia non providimus
ecclesiæ Dei, et non est citra Deum aliquis qui posset
enumerare quæ et qualia dicuntur contra nos, nec
possumus nos excusare. Non desperamus tamen de Dei
misericordia. Scimus enim quod verax est, et non deseret
ecclesiam suam cui promisit ' Ecce ego vobiscum sum
usque ad consummationem sæculi " (S. Mat. xxviii, 20).
Ipse providebit ecclesiæ suæ prout volunt (voluit ?)
et quando volunt (voluit ?) ; licet autem in proposito

---

[1] Otho.   [2] 1 Cor., XIV, 19.

habeamus ecclesiæ providere, verba tamen vestra ut
verba sapientis quæ sunt quasi stimuli excitabunt nos,
juxta illud, ' nil nocet amisso subdere calcar equo.' ''

Prædicta die interfectus fuit Viterbii quidam coquus
Domini Guidonis comitis Montis fortis, qui tunc erat
cum domino Simone fratre suo præsens Viterbii, et in
continenti dicti nobiles timentes ne hac occasione
familiæ suæ insurgerent (in) Viterbienses et Viterbienses
in eos vice versa, recesserunt comminantes Viterbienses,
et iverunt usque Vetrallam. Potestas autem Viterbiensis
supplicavit Collegio ut revocaret dictos nobiles et inquisitionem eis mitterent ad mitigandum corda eorum.
Inventum enim fuerat per inquisitionem quod interfectus
injuriose percusserat hominem et sine causa et
vulneraverat, nec ei parcere volebat, unde ille quasi
coactus percussit eum cultello et interfecit. Et iste vir
erat Viterbiensis, sed sequebatur curiam, et non erat de
jurisdictione Viterbiensium. Camerararius vero et
marescalcus prædictos nobiles pactaverunt, narrata eis
et veritate, et dicti nobiles propter reverentiam
cardinalium remiserunt Viterbienses, et venerunt ad
cardinales et obtulerunt se servitio ecclesiæ, et quod parati
erunt facere quidquid domini cardinales eis injungere
vellent.''

The rest of the MS. merely contains an address of
thanks for their return, delivered to the de Montforts by
cardinal Otho.

INDEX

Printed in Great Britain by Stephen Austin & Sons, Ltd., Hertford.